A History of FLORIDA

A
History of

FLORIDA

by Charlton W. Tebeau
&
William Marina

UNIVERSITY OF MIAMI PRESS
Coral Gables, Florida

Illustration credits: Mark F. Boyd Collection of Floridiana: pp. 51, 61, 67, 115, 144, 192. Mrs. Adelaide K. Bullen, for *Florida From Indian Trail to Space Age*: p. 40. Ripley K. Bullen, for *Florida From Indian Trail to Space Age*: pp. 9, 11. Governor Jeb Bush: p. 531. Central and Southern Florida Flood Control District: pp. 261, 339, 340, 342. Robert S. Chauvin for *Florida From Indian Trail to Space Age*: p. 4. Florida News Bureau: pp. 24, 29, 38, 175, 306, 316, 317, 356, 392, 412, 413, 419 (below). Senator Bob Graham: p. 440. Hillsborough County Historical Commission: p. 21. Institute for Humane Studies: p. 541. Anchor Press, from Lernoux, *In Banks We Trust*: p. 493. William Marina: pp. 527, 540, 541, 543, 544. National Park Service: p. 409. N.B.T. Roney Collection of Florida Maps: p. 78. David E. Quirk: p. 533. St. Augustine Historical Society: p. 63. Thelma Smallwood: p. 139. Smithsonian Institution: p. 143 (right and left). State of Florida, Bureau of Historic Sites and Properties, Division of Archives: p. 48. State of Florida, Department of Military Affairs: p. 350. State of Florida, Treasurer, 1970, Broward Williams: pp. 132, 164. State Photographic Archives: pp. 31, 50, 61, 71, 111, 125, 135, 147, 159, 161, 166, 179, 184, 185, 187, 196, 199, 202, 211, 214, 215, 218, 240, 245, 250, 257, 259, 263, 267, 268, 274, 278, 279, 283, 287, 288, 290, 292, 294, 295, 299, 300, 302, 303, 307, 309, 313, 320, 321, 324, 325, 326, 327, 336, 353, 354, 355, 357, 362, 363, 368, 369, 372, 375, 380, 381, 399, 400, 402, 411, 418, 419 (above), 424, 426, 428, 444, 466, 468, 478, 485, 488, 496, 502, 511, 513. University of Florida Press, from Gannon, *The Cross in the Sand*: p. 47. U.S. Army Corps of Engineers, Jacksonville District: p. 389. ©Walt Disney Productions: p. 467. T.T. Wentworth, Jr., Collection: pp. 54, 69, 87.

To Vi

Contents

Illustrations

Preface

Florida was the first of the present states of the American Union to be discovered and occupied by Europeans. Preceding that was a long period of occupation by Indians in which a culture more significant than is commonly realized developed in the region. Only since about the middle of this century has Florida begun to come into its own, to begin to realize some of its untapped potential.

This book is a synthesis of what we know about Florida's past and an effort to explain and interpret the direction and rate of changes that have occurred. The structure of the narrative is largely chronological and political, with the political aspects interpreted as reflections of underlying economic and social forces. An obvious need is for more studies of the cultural and social history of the people of Florida.

The author is indebted to far more people than can be acknowledged individually. References in the text and bibliography to the more common and useful sources give credit to some of those items and suggest further reading. The greatest contributions in recent years have come from graduate students at institutions in Florida and elsewhere who have chosen Florida topics for theses and dissertations and from those who have contributed articles to the *Florida Historical Quarterly* and other state and regional journals. The collections and interlibrary loan services of many institutions have been valuable to me, especially Duke University, Florida State University, Rollins College, Stetson University, University of Georgia, University of Florida, University of Miami, and University of North Carolina.

Special mention must be made of the assistance given me by Mr. and Mrs. Allen Morris and the staff members of the Strozier Library at Florida State University who facilitated our two-day search in the State Photographic Archives collected there under the inspiration and labor of Allen Morris. The personnel at the Florida News Bureau proved cordially and perceptively helpful in our efforts to locate other photographs of the more current developments in the state. Materials from the N. B. T. Roney Collection of Florida

Maps and the Mark F. Boyd Collection of Floridiana from the Otto
G. Richter Library of the University of Miami also deserve special
recognition.

To my own graduate students who have explored Florida sub-
jects over the past two decades I owe a personal as well as a profes-
sional debt that I wish to acknowledge by listing their names: Church
Barnard, Vera Bratz, Dianne Deutsch, Grayce Duvall, Helen
Jacobstein, Don Lester, Tony Malafronte, Lizzie Malpass, Henry
Marks, Bob McKenna, Florence Morgenroth, Elvin Pamell, Billee
Pearce, John Redding, Clay Roth, Fred Routh, Bill Schellings, David
Shubow, Marilyn Stollee, Mike Stone, Adon P. Taft, and Joe Tatol.
Professional colleagues have given generously of their knowl-
edge of special features of Florida's history and have saved the au-
thor from many of the pitfalls of error in local and state histories.
The following persons read and made contributions to one or more
chapters: Charles W. Arnade, Ripley P. Bullen, Wayne Flynt,
Durward Long, John I. McCollum, John K. Mahon, the late Rembert
W. Patrick, Samuel Proctor, John F. Reiger, William J. Schellings,
Jerrell H. Shofner, Dena Snodgrass, Julian Weinkle, and Edward
C. Williamson. And, finally. my special thanks to my co-author of
Florida From Indian Trail to Space Age, Ruby Leach Carson, who
has always been most generous with her assistance and encouragement. Mrs. Louisa Towne, head of the Southern Publishing Company of Delray Beach, generously released rights in order that we
might make use of any material we wished from the same publication.
To my wife Violet, my eternal thanks for her patience with interrupted schedules and deferred vacations, and for her constant
encouragement and helpfulness while this book was being written.

Charlton W. Tebeau

Coral Gables, Florida
January, 1971

The updating of the 1980 edition was funded by a grant to the
University of Miami Press by Mr. John B. Amos of Columbus, Georgia. The Indian portion of chapter one has been rewritten, spot
changes have been made throughout the text, a chapter on the seventies added, the bibliography expanded, and the index reworked.
The author wishes also to acknowledge with sincere thanks the professional assistance of Professors David R. Colburn, James W.
Covington, Harry W. Kersey, Jr., and Jerald T. Milanich, also Mr.
Allen Morris and Miss Dena Snodgrass.

Charlton W. Tebeau

September, 1980

Preface to the Third Edition

Given developments in the history of Florida during the last
decade and a half, it became evident that a new edition should dis-

cuss in detail many of the changes which have occurred during these years. The original author asked his student of many years ago at the University of Miami, Professor William Marina of Florida Atlantic University, to serve as coauthor of this new edition. We hope that new readers, as well as old ones, will find these revisions and additions useful.

The original Preface noted that "[o]nly since about the middle of this century has Florida begun to come into its own, to begin to realize some of its untapped potential." With that in mind we have extensively revised and added to the chapters covering the last fifty years since the end of World War II through early 1997, thus greatly extending the coverage of the twentieth century.

The original Preface also observed that "[a]n obvious need is for more studies of the cultural and social history of the people of Florida." In expanding the coverage of the last half century we have added considerable cultural, social and economic history, placing these within the political matrix developed in the original volume.

Florida's recorded history began with its emergence as a kind of "cockpit" in the mercantilist struggle to control the trade and resources of the Caribbean area, hence from the very beginning there was always an international dimension to its development. That is still true almost five hundred years later. Revolutions and social turmoil in the Caribbean, Central and South America have resulted in the emigration of hundreds of thousands of political refugees to Florida from Cuba, Nicaragua and Haiti, to name several countries, which has changed enormously the demography of the state. From blacks to Hispanics to Haitians, among others, Florida has become one of the centers of multicultural diversity within the United States.

This internationalization of Florida's population has caused problems of assimilation and political representation. One aspect, for example, of the growth of international trade and banking has been the smuggling of drugs and the laundering of funds derived from the sale of such commodities. This informal economy has become so great as to throw doubt on some of the official trade data compiled by governments.

In addition, the influx of millions of Americans from northern states has helped to make Florida the fourth largest state in population within the United States. This growth in population has in turn raised problems related to rapid development and economic growth.

One result of this explosive growth has been that "public policy" studies have themselves become a growth industry both in academia and the interwoven governmental bureaucracies in Tallahassee which formulate policies for politicians in the Legislature, the Governorship and Cabinet in areas ranging from education, health, international trade and the environment, to growth management. In keeping with the statement in the Preface of the first edition about Florida's "untapped potential," we have sought in the final chapter of the book to discuss the alternative public policy options facing future generations of Floridians in the hope this information will be useful in formulating policies of public choice.

In tracing the remarkable continuity of this debate over economic growth and the proper political economy throughout Florida's history, what emerges is an awareness that the present debate, especially since the 1970's, is very much a part of an on-going discussion about how best to create an environment conducive to the growth of a "good" society. The discussions of the last several decades reflect many aspects of the debates both before and after the Civil War as well as into the late nineteenth and early twentieth centuries.

We especially thank Professor Donald W. Curl of F.A.U. for his insightful comments on all but the final chapter on public policy as well as David E. Quirk, now a doctoral candidate at F.A.U., for scanning into the computer the contents of the second edition for revision, reading over all the chapters, helping design the web pages and for the photograph of the headquarters of the Seminole Tribe, Inc. Leigh Johnson and Lorraine Kalfayan Marina also helped with editing the manuscript. Robert Fuerst, the Director of the University of Miami Press, provided on-going support throughout the project. Any errors of fact, interpretation or in the typescript, are the responsibility of the junior coauthor, who laid out the text for the printer in PageMaker™ on a Macintosh computer.

We welcome comments all by readers, especially those teachers who use the book in classes on Florida history. We have prepared a *Teacher's Guide* as well as a bank of examination questions for use with the book. Instructors using the book in their classes can secure downloads of these by contacting Professor Marina at marina@fau.edu/.

As indicated in the introductory comments to the Selected Bibliography at the rear of the book, readers will find an extended Bibliography, updated on an on-going basis, as well as other materials on Florida history, including other "Links," at www.wmarina.com/ and www.floridareport.com/.We hope you will visit these web sites and send us suggestions about how to improve these materials for exploring the history of the Sunshine State.

Charlton W. Tebeau
William Marina

November 7, 1999

A History of FLORIDA

1.

Natural Endowment and First Inhabitants

The writing of Florida's history frequently begins with the coming of the first Europeans to its shores around the year 1500. This practice overlooks two topics essential to an understanding of the white man's experience. First, the natural environment conditioned when it did not determine what man's life in Florida would be. Secondly, the first true Floridians were the Indians who "encountered" Florida and began to occupy it at least ten, some say twenty, thousand years ago. By the beginning of the Christian era, Indians had occupied the entire peninsula and the Florida Keys and by 1500 had reached a population estimated at 100,000 persons.

Perhaps nowhere in North America has climate been such a factor in the lives of people from the first comers to the present inhabitants. Major contemporary sources of livelihood such as tourism, the growing of citrus fruits and winter vegetables, and some aspects of the aviation industry depend upon the climate. And in spite of the marvels of modern technology and science which allow us to control the climate in the home, office and factory, the warm, wet, and humid summers slow down human activities considerably and create problems of control of insect pests and plant diseases. But climate is only one feature of the natural endowment of land, water, plants, birds, and fishes that help to explain man's life in the peninsular state.

Natural Features

Florida lies between 24° and 31°30' north latitude and between 79°48' and 87°38' west longitude. This is farther south than the southern tip of California and farther west than Pittsburgh, Pennsylvania. Jacksonville, Florida, is at the same latitude as Cairo in Egypt, Shanghai in China, and Houston in Texas. Thus Florida lies wholly in the temperate zone. Yet its climate, particularly in the lower peninsula, is subtropical, with wet, humid summers and relatively dry and cool winters. The influence of the waters of the Gulf of Mexico on the west and the Atlantic Ocean on the east tends

to moderate extremes of heat and cold. The warming influence of
the north-flowing Gulf Stream and the prevailing winds from the
southeast make for a higher temperature in winter than is characteristic of an inland climate in the same latitude. The average temperature in the state for January is 58°F., but the average minimum in the lower peninsula is 50 degrees. Rainfall fluctuates widely
from year to year and is less seasonal in the north. The average is
53 inches but in one year may be twice as much as in another.

The total area of Florida is 58,560 square miles, of which 4,298
are water. Though it is twenty-second among the fifty states in
area, its shape is such that no point is more than sixty miles from
sea water. Yet it is a state of great distances. From the Georgia
border to the tip of the peninsula on the eastern side is 392 miles,
and to the southernmost key 444 miles. Miami is 150 miles from

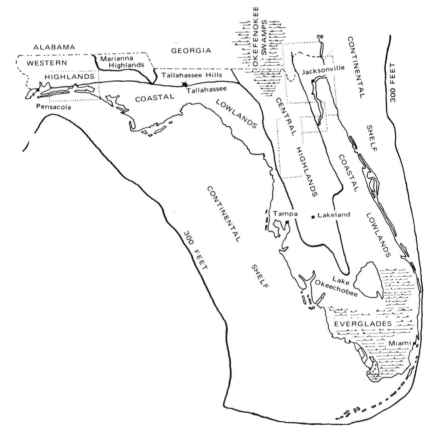

Natural Regions of Florida

Key West, 350 from Jacksonville, 500 from Tallahassee, and 700 from Pensacola. Florida's shape also accounts for its long coastline, second only to that of Alaska, 472 miles on the Atlantic and 674 on the Gulf of Mexico.

Geologically, Florida is probably the youngest part of the United States, the last to emerge from the ocean. The land area is the highest portion of a submerged plateau that rises above the sea to form the state. The area of the continental shelf, 500 feet or less below the sea, most of which is in the Gulf of Mexico, is equal to that of the land area. This has had great commercial importance for fishing and for gathering sponges and may have potential importance for oil production.

Six physical or natural regions are commonly identified in the state. The Coastal Lowlands form the entire coastline and reach inland as much as sixty miles at some points and include the Florida Keys. The soils are principally sands of low fertility except in the Everglades and the Big Cypress where organic deposits overlie them. All of the large commercial, industrial, and resort areas are in the Coastal Lowlands along the east and west coasts. The West Uplands includes most of the panhandle between the Perdido and the Apalachicola rivers between the Coastal Lowlands and the Alabama line. It is a plateau, sloping southward, hilly in the northern part, and trenched by narrow, steep-walled stream valleys. The highest measured elevation in the state, 345 feet, is south of Lakewood in northeast Walton County, and many of the hills rise to 300 feet. The area is covered with pine woods and has only a thin rural population.

The Marianna Lowlands, west of the Apalachicola in Jackson, Washington, and Holmes counties, is a low, rolling, hill and sinkhole region, with numerous small lakes, partly enclosed by the Western Upland region. It is a thickly populated rural area where cotton has been the principal crop. The Tallahassee Hills region reaches north of that city to the Georgia border and to the Coastal Lowlands from twenty-five to thirty-five miles south, and from the Apalachicola River to the Withlacoochee. Approximately twenty-five by 100 miles in extent, its rolling hills and gentle slopes form a level plain 300 feet high around Mount Pleasant.

The Central Ridge and Lakes region reaches from the Tallahassee Hills and the Okefenokee Swamp in the north to Lake Okeechobee in the south. Most of the peninsular part of the state, that part lying south of Ocala, here consists of rolling hills dotted by thousands of lakes, some spring-fed, some sinks or solution holes. The Everglades and the Okefenokee Swamp are the two great swamp areas that constitute the sixth region. The Everglades is a broad depression, 1,200 square miles in extent, south of Lake Okeechobee, while the Okefenokee lies mostly in Georgia.

The Gulf coast has the easily recognizable appearance of a "drowned coastline" that is sinking into the sea, while the east coast is somewhat less obviously rising from the ocean. The plateau has tipped on an axis that runs obliquely up the peninsula from Key

West to a point south of Fernandina, lifting some six feet at Miami but dipping as much as thirty feet at Pensacola. Consequently, there are better harbors on the Gulf coast, and Indian living sites have been found there that are now below the surface of the water.

Within the boundaries of the state are an estimated 30,000 lakes, ranging in size from mere ponds to Lake Okeechobee, the second largest freshwater lake wholly within the limits of the United States. Most of the smaller lakes are sinkholes formed when water dissolves the limestone under the surface, which then caves in to form the holes that later become lakes.

The state has the country's largest number (seventeen of a total of seventy-five) of first magnitude springs, which discharge 100 cubic feet or more of water per second, and fifty second magnitude springs discharging from ten to 100 cubic feet of water per second.

Florida's rivers have been less important in its history than might have been expected. The Saint Johns, the largest and most important, lies wholly within the state, and exits to the sea at Jacksonville. The Saint Marys River, which rises in Okefenokee Swamp, and flows southwesterly to the Gulf once had some local commercial importance but is best known as the boundary between Georgia and Florida. The Suwannee whose importance has been romantic rather than utilitarian, also rises in the Okefenokee Swamp and flows southwesterly into the Gulf near Cedar Keys. The Apalachicola, formed by the confluence of the Flint and the Chattahoochee, was by far the most important historically before the days of the railroad because of the long reach of these streams into Alabama and Georgia. East-west flowing streams are lacking, which explains efforts to link the Atlantic to the Gulf by canals.

The Florida Everglades is a natural phenomenon so complex in all of its relationships that a century of increasingly intensive and expensive effort has failed to comprehend it in terms of controlling and using it effectively. It is part of a large drainage basin that originally began with the Kissimmee and lesser streams that flowed into Lake Okeechobee, through it, and southward about 100 miles in what Marjory Stoneman Douglas called a "River of Grass" some thirty miles wide. This broad, shallow, slow-moving stream is separated from the Atlantic by a coastal ridge and is bounded on the west by the slightly higher Big Cypress country. The Everglades is covered over by saw grass and at the lower end is dotted with small hammocks or Everglades keys, only a few of which are large and high enough to once be inhabited and cultivated. The Everglades drains into the Gulf of Mexico in a series of short rivers, of which Lostman's and Shark are the best known. Before the water table was lowered by drainage, the volume of fresh water discharged by these streams was so large as to produce speculation as to where such a large amount of fresh water could come from, and gave rise to the notion that there must be large lakes in the interior. In the lower peninsula the Everglades constituted an effective barrier between the west and east coasts except for canoe and small boat travel until roads (actually causeways) crossed it in this century.

Natural Resources

The mineral resources of the state are chiefly nonmetallic. The most important are phosphate, limestone, kaolin, fuller's earth, titanium concentrates (zircon, ilmenite, rutile, and monazite), peat, petroleum, cement, sand, and gravel. Florida leads all of the states in the production of phosphate rock, rutile, and zircon, is second in ilmenite, and third in fuller's earth. In the Southeast, only Tennessee and Alabama have more mineral products. Titanium, the only metallic ore, is recovered from sand deposits along the eastern coast from Jacksonville south and in the northwest area from Panama City to the Alabama border.

Phosphate production began in 1888, and by 1895 Florida superseded South Carolina as the leading producer. Most of it is of land pebble variety and comes from the limestone ridge in the counties of eastern Hillsborough, Manatee, the northeast corner of Sarasota, northwest DeSoto, all of Hardee, and a large K-shaped region in western Polk. Soft phosphate occurs north of the land pebble area but contributes only a small portion of the total. Uranium recovered from land pebble phosphate yields from three to seven ounces per ton.

Limestone deposits formed under water constitute a major portion of the underground strata of the Florida plateau. It is widely used in road construction and as a concrete aggregate in the lime and cement industries. Kaolin is also widely used in cement industries, in refractories, in ceramics, and as fillers in other products such as textiles, crayons, soap, and matches. Putnam County is the largest kaolin producer. Fuller's earth was used originally to absorb fats and greases from woolen cloth, and is still important in absorbing grease spills.

More than 500 test wells, some in every county in the state, have been sunk in the search for oil. The earliest discovery of commercial importance was the Sunniland Field in northern Collier County in 1942. The oil was found in the porous limestone of the Lower Cretaceous period of the Mesozoic era some 11,500 feet below the surface. The next discovery came in 1964 in the nearby Felda Field in Hendry County. Continued drilling in the area has expanded the field into adjacent areas. Since the 1970s, despite the concern of environmentalists, the search for new oil fields continues.

Florida's Prehistoric Indians

Florida's first Indians were part of the great migration from northeastern Asia that began as early as 35,000 BC. Those people apparently came across the land bridge from Siberia to Alaska during the Pleistocene or Ice Age, when the oceans were considerably lower than at the present time, and spread themselves over the Western Hemisphere.

The earliest human migrations into northern Florida occurred at least ten to twelve thousand years ago when many animals now extinct still lived here. These first Indians were hunters and gatherers who used flesh for food, skins for clothing, and bones and sinews for tools and ornaments. Wild plant foods and nuts were also eaten. They had wooden thrusting spears or javelins tipped with distinctive, lanceolate points called Suwanee points which were similar to those used by other Paleo-Indians elsewhere in the United States. Such points are found from Fort Myers and Vero Beach northward.

The hunting and gathering lifestyle of the Florida Indians seems to have undergone few changes until about 5000 BC, although there were changes in the types of stone points used to hunt. Projectile points became smaller, side notched, and frequently beveled and were propelled by atlatls or spear throwers. Recent work by paleontologists has demonstrated that some of the Pleistocene animals were present in Florida until about the same time. They include the ground sloth, dire wolf, North American spectacled boar, saber-toothed tiger, American mastodon, Pleistocene horse and peccary. Although there is no concrete evidence, it is possible that their extinction was due at least partially to human hunting activities and/or to the changes in Indian subsistence that occurred at that time.

Around 5000 BC the first suggestions of villages, or at least semi-permanent settlements, begin to appear. The Indians began increasingly to depend for their food upon freshwater shellfish, snails, and mollusks, supplemented by nuts and edible roots. Piles of shells along the Saint Johns and Withlacoochee rivers mark sites where Indians settled, and the shell heaps became their dwelling places. The typical tool was a fairly large stemmed spear point, the most common chipped artifact of Florida. The Indians still used spear throwers and imported stone balance weights of steatite, a non-Florida rock. They also secured beads made of jasper. Their tools included a great variety of stone knives, scrapers, and drills. In this period they also developed gouges and celts, probably for constructing dugout canoes. In every case these were made of saltwater shells, the heavy *Busycon* from the Atlantic coast or the *Strombus* from extreme southeastern Florida.

The very early interstate and intrastate migration of people and trade goods is significant. Early settlements were largely limited to large river valleys, but later small villages sprang up along small tributaries. Only two Preceramic middens made of marine shells are known to Florida; one is on Amelia Island near the Atlantic Ocean and the other is in Osprey on the Gulf of Mexico. Apparently some additional settlements of this period also existed some distance out in what is now the Gulf of Mexico. The new way of life supported more people than did the previous hunting cultures, but there was still much seasonal movement of sites, presumably to permit shellfish to replenish themselves and to take advantage of better hunting opportunities. Many such hunting camps are found in northern Florida.

At about 2000 BC, late in Archaic times, the seemingly independent invention of pottery-making occurred in Florida and Georgia,

Projectile points and other stone tools

earlier by some 800 years than the occurrence of pottery in any
other part of the continental United States. This fiber-tempered
pottery in Georgia had decoration different from that in Florida,
but a few trade shards as well as radiocarbon dates prove their
contemporaneity. The vessels were flat-bottomed and basin shaped
or rectangular like a box. Fibrous materials such as shredded palmetto fibers, Spanish moss, and native grasses were used as temper. The earliest known incised examples bear concentric diamonds
suggestive of a basketry motif based upon previously existing bas-
kets.

Late in the Orange period, around 1400 BC, the importation of
carved stone vessels made of steatite commenced. The nearest source
of this heavy material was the hills of north Alabama and north-
western Georgia, from which area steatite was transported for many

years in large quantities, presumably over most of the distance in dugout canoes.

More profound changes started about 1000 BC in the Transitional period. New ideas and new tools brought by new people changed Florida from a hunting, fishing, and collecting economy to one which produced some of its food by horticulture. Among the results were a semi-sedentary way of life, a greatly increased population, the abandonment of Archaic sites, and the expansion of settlement into hitherto unoccupied areas. The first evidence of Transitional culture in Florida is the presence of thick, flat-bottomed cooking vessels with incised sides, copies of Orange period utensils but made of a soft temperless paste referred to as chalky or Saint Johns paste. These containers, apparently developed in the Saint Johns region, were dispersed all over Florida from the Chattahoochee River to Fort Myers and Miami.

In late Deptford times, about the beginning of the Christian era, burial mounds began to be introduced into Florida, the practice coming direct from Mexico or indirectly through the Adena-Hopewell cultures of present-day Ohio and Illinois. In some of the burial mounds, copper panpipes, copper ear spools, platform smoking pipes, and cut mica ornaments typical of Adena-Hopewell are found, while shell beads, shell pendants, and conch shell dippers are found in both the Florida and the Ohio-Illinois mounds. The large number of conch shells in the northern mounds indicates extensive trade between that region and Florida.

By 500 BC the practice of adding vegetable fiber to clay used to make pottery vessels had totally disappeared; sand, limestone, and grit had become popular as tempering agents throughout nearly all of Florida except in the east and central portions of the state where the St. Johns chalky ware still predominated. Many different types of pottery were manufactured and many different forms of surface decoration were used. Because the pottery manufactured by a specific culture was different from the pottery of other groups, archeologists are able to define separate prehistoric Indian cultures and to study their development from 500 BC into the period of European exploration and conquest.

Along the St. Johns River, its tributaries, and the many lakes of Central Florida, lived the St. Johns people. They hunted, gathered wild foods, fished, and collected shellfish. They also grew corn and probably squash. During a portion of the year some of them moved to the Atlantic coastal lagoon to live off marine products. Corn, relatively insignificant in the early St. Johns peoples' diets, became much more important after AD 800, as it did elsewhere in northern Florida. The St. Johns culture lasted into the historic period. Many of the Timucuan tribes were descendants of the St. Johns peoples.

After 500 BC the Gulf Coast of Florida from just below Tampa Bay all the way to Alabama was occupied by the Deptford culture which is characterized archeologically by pottery stamped with wooden paddles carved with checks or grooves. Shell middens, some quite large, are found along the coast adjacent to salt marshes and

Vessels of Fort Walton, Safety Harbor, and Weeden Island periods

estuaries. Smaller camps, perhaps for seasonal hunting and gathering, are found inland in North and Northwest Florida. Although
the Deptford peoples grew corn, it probably constituted only a small
portion of their total diet.

Most likely, mound burial was reserved for religious or political
leaders and perhaps members of their families. The importance of
these individuals is reflected in the objects placed with them in the
mounds. Copper beads from the Great Lakes region, stone ornaments from the piedmont in Georgia and Alabama, pots, and other
valued items obtained through trade accompanied the burials and

may have been possessions of the individuals while they were alive. Such exotic goods flowed through a trading network that encompassed most of the eastern United States and resulted in many shared beliefs and practices.

The influx of new ideas was at least partially responsible for the evolution of the Deptford culture into several new and regional cultures after AD 200. In the western panhandle it was the Santa Rosa culture which had ties to the cultures in the lower Mississippi River Valley. In the eastern panhandle the Swift Creek culture appeared with its characteristic pottery stamped with paddles carved in complicated geometric designs.

In the peninsula, excepting East Florida, Deptford developed into several related Weeden Island cultures which inhabited the Gulf Coast north of Charlotte Harbor and inland locations north of Ocala. The early Weeden Island cultures apparently were separate political units, each with a "capitol town" which consisted of a village area and several mounds. The mounds were originally built as platforms for houses of important individuals. At the death of the leader, the individual was buried within the house and the structure was burned. A layer of earth was placed over the entire platform and house and left as a monument to the departed leader.

By AD 500 the Weeden Island culture spread into Northwest Florida replacing the Santa Rosa and Swift Creek cultures. There is some evidence that after that date much of the northern half of Florida as well as portions of southwestern Georgia and southeastern Alabama were united into one or more Weeden Island political units. Chiefs and their families became more important and often many goods were placed within or around their burial tombs. Special pottery vessels in the shape of animal effigies were manufactured for the leaders. Possibly they were symbols of the leader's great importance, since they frequently were placed in their tombs. Also buried in the mounds were people who had been sacrificed to accompany the leader to the after-life. At the height of Weeden Island such effigy vessels were probably manufactured at craft centers and traded over many hundreds of miles. The influence of Weeden Island reached into East and Central Florida as well as southern parts of the state.

But the Weeden Island way of life was not to endure. After about AD 800 a group of people from the coastal plain of eastern Georgia who made new types of tools and pottery, moved into Alachua County and ousted the population of Weeden Island-related culture inhabiting the region. They brought with them better knowledge and perhaps better varieties of maize. Hundreds of years later their descendants, the Potano Indians (a Timucuan group), witnessed the passage of the DeSoto entrada.

The end of Weeden Island in Northwest Florida began shortly after AD 1000 in the Apalachicola River Valley. There, new ideas, perhaps brought southward from the Alabama and Georgia piedmonts and coupled with new agricultural techniques, resulted in the appearance of the Ft. Walton culture. Ft. Walton villages had extensive village areas and very large mounds on which temples and the residences of chiefs were built. Ft. Walton bears many affinities to similar cultures in the Southeast, all of which are often referred to by archeologists as Mississippian cultures.

The organization of Ft. Walton society into rigid classes which included warriors, gave the chiefs the military clout to extend their domination. Within several centuries, the Ft. Walton culture had spread throughout Northwest Florida and adjacent areas of Georgia and Alabama. Populations were very dense and some towns may have housed hundreds of people. When the Spanish arrived in Florida, Ft. Walton peoples had begun to make inroads into North Florida. Wars between the Ft. Walton peoples and the Utina, a Timucuan group in North Florida, were observed by early Spanish and French explorers.

The influence of the Ft. Walton culture reached down to Tampa Bay where the Safety Harbor culture developed after about AD 1400. In the historic period the Safety Harbor peoples were called the Tocobaga Indians.

The Indians of the southern portion of Florida, south of Tampa Bay and Cape Canaveral, developed somewhat apart from the northern cultures. After 500 BC or slightly before, the South Florida peoples were divided into three major geographical regions. These Indians shared many cultural traits but remained separate ethnic groups into the historic period. All of the South Florida Indians relied heavily on marine products and a large variety of aquatic and land animals for the meat portion of their diets.

One South Florida group, the predecessors of the Tequesta Indians, lived along the coasts from Broward County around to about Cape Sable, establishing small villages at the mouths of estuaries and camps on small hammocks at the edge of or within the Everglades. The second group inhabited the coast and offshore barrier islands from Charlotte Harbor down to Cape Sable. They lived adjacent to the Gulf in compact villages, some of which featured mounds (constructed of shell) as much as thirty feet tall that served as platforms for civic and religious ceremonies. These people were the prehistoric ancestors of the Calusa Indians.

The Calusahatchee River provided a canoe highway for contact between the southwest coast and the third region, the Lake Okeechobee Basin. There, by 450 BC, the Indians grew corn in villages placed along or close to the shore of the lake. Later, a series of remarkable, large, ceremonial centers developed, each composed of many mounds and earthworks connected by roads and canals, and arranged in a complicated manner.

At the beginning of the historical period at the opening of the sixteenth century the Florida Indians numbered about 100,000 people. They had developed relatively complex economic, social, and political institutions. They had developed governing, religious, and warrior classes. They planned and executed large construction projects that required the labor of large numbers of people over long periods of time. Some of them lived in large communities and traded at greater distances than seems likely for a primitive people. Much as elsewhere in the Americas they were sometimes friendly and helpful and sometimes hostile to the coming of the white man; the hostility was more than likely engendered by the attitudes and activities of the newcomers.

The Indians found in Florida by the white man have been divided variously into six or more major groups with numerous subgroups. Principal among them were the Timucuans with 40,000 persons; the Tocobaga with 7,000; the Calusa, including the Indians of the Lake Okeechobee Basin region, 20,000; the Apalachee and related tribes of the western panhandle, 25,000; the Tequesta, 5,000; and the Ais and Jeaga, 2,000. The population figures, especially for the agricultural tribes of northern Florida, may be too low; the agricultural soils of Florida were capable of supporting much larger populations. The Seminoles did not enter Florida until early in the eighteenth century.

The Timucuans, like other North Florida Indians, were hunters and gatherers who also practiced agriculture. Maize (Indian corn), beans, and squash were grown for food while tobacco was cultivated for smoking and other uses. Archival and archeological data indicate that the Timucuans were actually fourteen or fifteen separate tribes who shared many aspects of social and political organization and religion but who made different types of pottery and other tools.

The Tocobaga Indians living around Tampa Bay were composed of a number of separate towns, each with its own village area and mounds on which temples and the chiefs houses were erected. Like the Timucuans, they were agriculturists but they supplemented their diet with the abundant marine foods that were taken from the Bay. The DeSoto and Narváez expeditions landed among the Tocobaga in the sixteenth century.

The Apalachee occupied the area from the Aucilla to the Ocklockoneo and its tributaries in the west and north into Georgia. Their center was at present-day Tallahassee in a fertile country that supported a concentrated population. They lived principally on corn, beans, pumpkins, fruits, birds, venison, and fish. The Ais occupied the coastal and Indian River region from Cape Canaveral to the Saint Lucie River and inland twenty to thirty miles. They were described by Jonathan Dickinson in 1696 as nonagricultural, eating principally fish, palm berries, coco plums, and sea grapes. By that time they had added Spanish knives and hatchets to their basic bow and arrow technology. The Jeaga, "cousins" of the Ais and usually included with them, occupied only three villages.

The Tequesta held possession of the region from modern Pompano Beach in Broward County to Cape Sable where they merged with the more powerful Calusa from the west coast. They were separated from the main body of the Calusa by the Everglades, in which Indians lived only on a few of the larger and higher keys and then only temporarily. The Tequesta lived near the mouths of streams, on inlets, coastal beaches, and offshore islands. Their food seems to have been palmetto berries, coco plums, sea grapes, palm nuts, pigeon plums, prickly pears, perhaps wild figs, and a nutritious flour made from the coontie root. They practiced no agriculture but were great fishermen. They were especially fond of sea cows or manatees, sometimes called the pork of the sea. Inland they ate terrapins and other land turtles and a great deal of venison.

The Calusa occupied the region from Tampa Bay or Charlotte Harbor south to Cape Sable, and they most certainly exercised control over Lake Mayaimi, now known as Okeechobee. They may also at times have exercised political control over the culturally related Tequesta. Usually considered nonagricultural, as all others in the lower peninsula, they lived principally on shellfish, which abounded in the nearby shallow waters of the Ten Thousand Islands region. They used bows and arrows as well as spears and atlatls, both with stone projectile points, and made many tools and ornaments of bone and shell. Though not the only ones to use wood, an outstanding aspect of their culture was the use of wood for practical and ceremonial implements ranging from bowls and masks to boxes and boats, some of which were painted. They had an unusually high level social structure for a nonagricultural people.

The continuing role of the Indian as the white man began to move into Florida will be traced throughout this history. In two and a half centuries after Ponce de León's visit most of these aboriginal Indians were gone. They fell victims to European-introduced diseases, to warfare among themselves and with the white man, and to slave catchers; in addition, some of them migrated out of the area. The last of the Indians numbered less than 200. Most left Florida with the Spanish in 1763 and did not return with them in 1783, although a few did stay to be absorbed later by the Seminoles.

To occupy the very attractive land left by the departing aboriginal Indians and to escape the pressure from whites in Georgia and Alabama, Indians who came to be known as Seminoles began to move into Florida early in the eighteenth century. Their migrations were not completed until about a century later on the eve of the acquisition of the territory by the United States. The Seminoles survived a number of unique cultural shocks as they moved into Florida and settled first across the northern part of the state. Subsequently they were engaged in wars of removal that pushed them into the southern part of the peninsula and resulted in all but some two hundred being forced to move to Oklahoma. Never more than 5,000 in number, strong elements of their culture nevertheless survive in Florida today.

2.

Discovery and Exploration

The discovery of Florida by the white man was one of the results of the expansion of Europe that led to the search for new trade routes and the discovery of the New World at the end of the fifteenth century. Indeed, explorers of Florida continued to search for a water passage westward to India. After the voyage of Christopher Columbus to Hispaniola in October 1492, the Spaniards extended their explorations and added to their knowledge of the region. As the radius of their expanding circle of discovery lengthened, they reached Florida. Other nations of western Europe had their interests in the New World increased by the reports of Spanish findings. Though there are evidences of prior discovery, the official credit for finding Florida goes to Juan Ponce de León because his voyage in 1513 was made under official Spanish auspices, recorded, and recognized.

John and Sebastian Cabot may have visited the lower Atlantic coast in 1497 and 1498, perhaps sailing as far south as Cuban latitudes. Three maps that are representations of the Florida coast appeared before 1513. The Alberto Cantino map of 1502 may very well have been based upon reports of the Cabot voyages; the two other maps appeared in 1508 and 1511. It is certain that slave hunters came to Florida from Spanish settlements. It is difficult otherwise to account for the hostility Ponce de León and his successors met when they landed. There were also reports of Indians who shouted Spanish words.

Three more voyages by Columbus and five by former companions of his within a decade revealed the coastline from Honduras to Mexico; voyagers had discovered every large island in the West Indies except Barbados. By another decade there were seventeen towns on Hispaniola. Anton de Esquival had made a settlement in Jamaica and Diego Velasquez in Cuba. Ponce de León himself had planted a settlement in Puerto Rico. Mining, the growing of grain, cotton, and sugarcane, and a thriving trade in slaves as well as the products of the new lands were all well established. Juan Ponce de León was typical of the great number of men of noble birth trained in arms who were released from active duty at the end of the Moorish wars by the fall of Granada in 1492. They welcomed the opportunity to carve out kingdoms for themselves in the New World. However, he could not compete with Francisco Pizarro, Hernán Cortés, Hernando de Soto, or Juan Vásquez de Coronado for public acclaim, and his not inconsiderable achievements tended to be forgotten. Puerto Rico became neither basis for fortune nor base for further conquest. Florida was a disappointment to the Spanish and did not begin to come into its own until more than four centuries had passed. In consequence, amazingly little is known about the details of Ponce's life. The date of his birth, if not indeed the place, and his parentage are somewhat in doubt.

It is generally agreed, however, that Ponce de León was a native of San Servos in the province of Campos in the Kingdom of León. Certainly his family lineage was ancient and honorable, and he had a host of influential friends. He had come to Hispaniola with Columbus on the second voyage in 1493 to plant the first permanent colony in Spanish America. He found employment for his skill at arms in putting down a native insurrection and won a place in the colonial establishment, but he soon desired to launch an enterprise of his own.

In 1508 Ponce journeyed to Puerto Rico in a small caravel to investigate rumors of gold there. When his benefactor Nicholas Ovando was displaced as governor of Hispaniola by Diego Columbus, son of the discoverer, he returned to Spain and reported Ponce's exploits. The king made Ponce governor of Puerto Rico, whereupon he proceeded to build a town, establish his authority, and distribute among his followers as slaves those Indians who refused to submit. Ponce lost the governorship because Don Diego Columbus had prior rights; he retained his property and the favor of his sovereign, but he needed a new scene for his activities.

His king came to the rescue with a patent dated February 2, 1512, to discover and govern the island of Bimini and its people. Ponce undoubtedly knew of the fountain fables so common in that day, and the near legendary search for the fountain of youth was neither unique nor vitally important in his thinking. Spanish experience in the New World provided ample motivation for the investment of his fortune and talents. Precious metals, though not yet in fabulous amounts; native populations for trade, labor, and missionary enterprise; and new lands yet to be discovered, settled, governed, and exploited provided challenge and opportunity enough. The terms of Ponce's contract reveal the powerful motives that inspired him and his associates. Within three years, at his own expense and with persons recruited from Spain and the New World, he could establish a claim to Bimini and other lands he might discover. He was to have the ownership of all the houses and estates that he would establish with his own funds. He was to assume the executive and judicial functions in the new territory, but the construction and direction of forts was to be a royal prerogative and responsibility. He would receive a share of all the revenues and profits except from royal properties. Gold and other precious metals and other valuable commodities were to be the property of Ponce and his men except the share reserved for the crown. The king would distribute the Indians to the Spanish lords, with priority to those who had participated in Ponce's expedition. Finally, Ponce was to receive the titles of adelantado and governor of Bimini and the other lands.

In Puerto Rico, where Ponce had been assigned the command of the fort, he prepared at his own expense three ships for an exploring expedition. On Tuesday, March 3, 1513 he set forth and after twenty-five days of sailing among the Bahamas in search of Bimini, on March 27 sighted land and on April 2 reached the Florida coast. At some time during the next week he went ashore, probably between Saint Augustine and the Saint Johns River, and took possession in the name of the king, naming the land Florida after *Pascua florida,* the Feast of Flowers at Easter time. He then sailed northward at least as far as the mouth of the Saint Johns and then turned southward, stopping at Cape Canaveral and quite possibly at Biscayne Bay. Passing on down the line of the Florida Keys, which he called Los Martires, and the Tortugas, he turned northward and proceded up the coast, certainly as far as Charlotte Harbor and some say Pensacola Bay, after which he returned to Puerto Rico in September. He had not found Bimini, but he sent Anton de Alaminos with one vessel to search further for it. Ponce had discovered the Bahama Channel, the seaway for the Spanish fleet to move from the Caribbean into the Atlantic on the homeward journey. He had discovered Florida and given it a name. And he had found the natives uniformly hostile.

The king then granted Ponce the promised patent to conquer, govern, and colonize the lands he had discovered. He was also to take along priests to try to convert the Indians, who, after they had three times been summoned to embrace the Christian faith and refused, might be enslaved. Before Ponce could realize this purpose, his sovereign sent him on a mission to subdue the Carib Indians in the Lower Antilles, and it was 1521 before he could return to Florida.

Meanwhile, other expeditions explored the Gulf and Atlantic coasts of Florida. In 1519 Francisco de Garay commanded four caravels for Alonzo de Pineda, agent of the governor of Jamaica, on an expedition to search in the Gulf of Mexico for the western strait or water passage to the east. He mapped the Gulf coast as far west as present-day Texas. Lucas Vasquez de Ayllón sent Francisco Gordillo on a cruise among the Bahama Islands. He joined a slavecatcher, and the two journeyed to the Cape Fear River on the North Carolina coast in June 1521, landing at what they called Chicora. They repaid the hospitality of the natives by carrying away 150 of them. They sold them as slaves in Santo Domingo, but Governor Diego Columbus ordered that they be released; their fate apparently was not recorded. Ayllón secured a patent to the newly explored region and sent a small body of men to occupy it in 1525. The next year Ayllón himself led an expedition from Hispaniola consisting of six vessels, 520 men, women, and slaves, eighty-nine horses, and much equipment to establish a colony. They landed at the mouth of the Cape Fear River but soon moved to San Miguel de Guadalupe where they disembarked on September 29, 1526. Authorities disagree as to where this effort to settle was made. It was probably as far north as Chesapeake Bay, but it may have been southward to the Pedee or the Savannah River. The cold winter, a dwindling supply of provisions, and the death of Ayllón led to the abandonment of the enterprise. Florida was not an island. It was part of a great land mass that revealed no passage by water to the east. "La Florida" embraced the continent from the Rio Grande northward.

For the second voyage to Florida, Ponce de León sailed from Puerto Rico in February of 1521 to plant a colony. He had two ships, 200 colonists, fifty horses, livestock, and farm implements. The expedition reached the west coast probably at Charlotte Harbor, went ashore, and started the construction of houses and shelters. In a fierce attack, the Indians killed several Spaniards and wounded Ponce with an arrow. The expedition's members boarded their ships and sailed to Cuba, where the wounded leader died. Ponce's body was shipped to Puerto Rico and was buried there. His heirs showed no disposition to claim his rights or to sponsor other efforts to settle in Florida.

Pánfilo de Narvaez, the next major explorer of Florida, first appears in the Spanish conquest of Cuba. In 1520, he was sent to arrest a disobedient Cortés in Mexico, lost an eye in the effort, was taken prisoner, and finally became an associate of Cortés. When he returned to Spain in 1526 after a quarter of a century of service in the New World, his grateful emperor Charles V rewarded him with a patent to settle Florida. Inspired by the exploits and wealth of Cortés, he sailed from Spain on June 17, 1527, with 600 colonists and soldiers. One-fourth of the colonists deserted in Santo Domingo and the two ships Narvaez sent to Trinidad were wrecked, so he set out for Florida in 1528 with only 400 men. They reached Tampa Bay on Good Friday, April 4. The Indians at first fled, but then were induced to return. They spoke of Apalachee and gold. Narvaez decided on a march inland and sent the ships up the coast for a rendezvous. On June 24, the party reached Apalachee in the present-day Tallahassee region, exhausted and hungry. They found forty clay huts occupied by Indian women and children but no gold or rich land. Nine days later they reached the coast but found no ships waiting.

Their plight was desperate, and they decided upon heroic measures. Thinking that Mexico was nearby, they set to work without tools, iron, forges, rigging, sails, or caulking and constructed five crude boats for the journey. All of the frail crafts were lost in a storm on the Texas coast, and Narvaez and all but eighty of the 242 men lost their lives. Alvar Núñez Cabeza de Vaca, the treasurer of the ill-fated expedition, and three other survivors finally reached Mexico City on June 24, 1536, eight years after they had hopefully sailed for Florida and long after being given up for dead. De Vaca related a fantastic story of hardships at the hands of Indians and the journey with his three companions southward and westward into Mexico.

Hernando de Soto at thirty-six years of age was already a wealthy and famous man as a result of his association with Pizarro in the conquest of Peru. He was looking for new worlds to conquer when he received the titles of adelantado of Florida and governor of Cuba. In Spain, as he prepared for the expedition to the New World, he was swamped with volunteers ready to risk their lives and fortunes in the gamble for wealth in Florida. This army of knights and gentlemen was perhaps the most resplendent that had been brought to Spanish America. It resembled a medieval crusade.

Exploration of the Tampa Bay area continued into the 18th century.

The expedition left San Lucar in April 1538 for Santiago de Cuba and thence to Havana. A year later, on May 18, 1539, the fortune hunters sailed for Florida and landed in Tampa Bay on the thirtieth. There they found Juan Ortiz, the sole survivor of a small expedition that the wife of Narváez had sent to search for her husband. Ortiz had survived through the intercession of the wife and daughter of the chief and proved invaluable as an interpreter. Thus Florida had its "Pocahontas" story some seventy years before that of John Smith in Virginia. Ortiz reported hearing of a rich country thirty leagues inland, a fatal lure that had led some Spaniards to fortunes, others like Narváez to death. On the first day of August an imposing force of 550 armed men, 200 horses, and some priests and Dominican friars set out. On the way to Apalachee they seized chiefs as hostages and forced them to provide Indian guides and slaves. In October the marchers reached Apalachee, where they found a goodly supply of grain, beans, and pumpkins gathered by the Indians for the winter. A side expedition discovered Pensacola Bay, and de Soto sent the officer Diego Maldonado to Cuba for supplies. He was to meet de Soto at Pensacola late in 1540.

In early March of the same year the eager searchers set out northeastward across Georgia to about present-day Augusta, where they found only freshwater pearls to appease their appetite for treasure. They moved on to Swain County, North Carolina, and crossed the Great Smoky Mountains into Tennessee. De Soto then led the march back into Georgia and westward to Coosa in Talladega County, Alabama, on July 23; there they found an abundance of food. On October 15, they reached Mavilla, a large town near Choctaw Bluff on the Alabama River, where in a desperate fight with Indians, de Soto was wounded and the Spaniards lost all their baggage.

The time had arrived to meet Maldonado at Pensacola, but de Soto elected rather to continue the march. He had lost 102 men but remained undaunted. The party wintered in present-day Mississippi and came to the river of that name in May 1541 at Chickasaw Bluffs; there the men made boats in which the entire party crossed the river and then dismantled the boats to save the metal. They then moved through present-day Arkansas and Missouri, possibly as far as Kansas, before they turned back to Oklahoma, where they spent the winter of 1541. In March they broke camp. Now reduced to 300 effective men and forty horses, they made their way to the mouth of the Arkansas River where de Soto died and was buried. Luis de Moscoso succeeded to the command and, after starting out on an overland march to Panuco, turned back to the river and built boats. On July 3, 1543, 330 Spaniards and 100 Indian slaves set sail; 310 of them successfully completed the return journey. Moscoso gave an optimistic account of what he had seen but declined any opportunity to return to the scene.

Indian hostility had been at least partly responsible for the failure of three major expeditions. Already in other parts of Spanish America, churchmen, frustrated in their efforts to win the Indians, had concluded that soldiers and armaments served only to alienate Indians. Bishop Bartholomé de las Casas supported the view and by his writing created the "Black Legend" that Spanish civil and military officers were abusing the native population and working many of them to death. Father Luís Cancer de Barbastro, a priest of the Dominican order who had notable success at winning over hitherto hostile Indians in Guatemala without the support of armies, seemed to prove the point. Father Cancer became interested in the Florida Indians in Mexico in 1546 and, supported by las Casas, received authority from the king to try an experiment. He asked only that he be landed where Spaniards had not yet had any dealings with the Indians. His pilot, Juan de Arano, by accident or design ignored that wish and landed them on the shores of Tampa Bay in May 1549, where Narváez and de Soto had already aroused the hostility of the natives. In the first contact with the Indians they met no overt acts of hostility, but four persons left alone at the first landing place disappeared. Cancer learned that two of them, a priest and a lay brother, had been murdered; the third, a sailor, had been enslaved, and Magdalena, an Indian interpreter, had deserted to the Indians. On June 26, Father Cancer went ashore to treat with the Indians and learn the fate of his companions. The now openly hostile Indians clubbed him to death in the water before he reached the shore.

Interest in Florida declined sharply after the failure of the de Soto expedition. The area had been robbed of any hope that there was either the possibility of great wealth in precious metal or a thriving Indian society. Seventeen years passed before another major effort to colonize the forbidding land was made. Meanwhile, interest in the region increased for new reasons. In spite of the failure of the Cancer expedition, zealous churchmen continued to be interested in the conquest of the souls of the natives. In 1555 the bishop of Cuba urged immediate settlement. Native Florida women, he urged, could replenish the decreasing native population in Cuba. Continued shipwrecks on the lower east coast cried out for rescue stations to save victims from starvation and Indian attack. There was, finally, the threat that one of the European powers envious of Spain's New World wealth might establish a base in Florida from which to prey upon it. Spaniards were fully aware of the importance of the Florida peninsula, which lay alongside the route of the homebound convoys of treasure ships and other valuables from the New World. Their real interest was in the Atlantic coast, but the enterprise that was designed to settle there foundered in a preliminary effort on the Gulf coast.

By 1558, decisions to occupy the region had been reached both in America and in Spain. Spaniards knew the Bay of Ochuse, or Pensacola, on the Gulf coast, though they sometimes confused it with Mobile Bay. A second bay, Santa Elena (now Port Royal) on the Atlantic coast had also captured their imagination. A royal cedula dated December 29, 1557, inaugurated the settlement of these two places, with greater emphasis upon Santa Elena. Responsibility and authority rested in the viceroy of Mexico, Luís de Velasco, who had long supported the occupation of Florida to defend the richer lands to the south. On October 30, 1558, the viceroy named Tristan de Luna y Arellano to head an expedition to Florida.

De Luna, a wealthy Spanish nobleman, had been an associate of de Soto and had joined the Coronado expedition to the American southwest in search of the fabled seven cities of Cibola. He had the status, the experience, and the wealth that the projected settlement demanded. The viceroy gave encouragement and assistance in the preparations. By mid-April the army of 200 cavalry and 300 infantry was ready for the march to the coast. Many of the soldiers had one or two servants. Farmers, artisans, Indians, Negroes, women, and children rounded out the well planned but oversized, unbalanced, and sometimes unruly lot. Velasco visited the marching colony early in May and noted too many disreputable people among the civilians, too many servants and dubious women. There would be too many mouths to feed and too few productive workers.

The 500 soldiers and 1,000 civilians embarked on thirteen ships and set sail for Florida on June 11. On board also were 240 horses, food, tools, weapons, seed, and breeding stock to equip and maintain the colonies. The plan was to plant a settlement on Ochuse

Bay and from that base to move overland to Santa Elena, thought
to be some 250 miles distant. De Luna was also to visit Coosa, the
only rich Indian settlement de Soto had found.

Delayed by storms, the expedition lost 100 horses and stopped
at Mobile Bay to land the remainder of the horses to complete the
journey overland. The rest of the party sailed into Ochuse on August 14. De Luna planned to settle some eighty persons on the bay
and lead the remainder inland, where it was hoped there would be
a greater supply of native food. Troubles began almost immediately.
Two scouting parties failed to find food or any large Indian villages
and found themselves without food. On September 19 a tropical
storm blew for twenty-four hours and scattered the ships, many of
them not yet unloaded, with great loss of seamen, passengers, cargo,
and ships. One of the few ships that survived the storm's fury sailed
to Mexico immediately to report the disaster and seek relief. De
Luna sent a larger expedition into the interior in an urgent search
for food. Neither of them produced adequate returns.

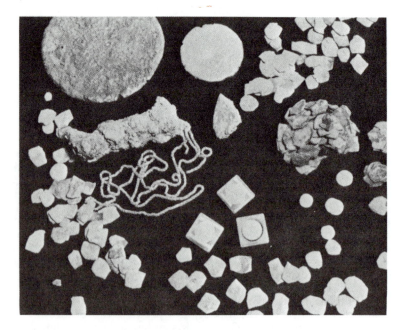

Spanish ships sailing northward along the coast were often
wrecked; this treasure was recovered off Vero Beach in 1964.

By February 1560, a council called by de Luna decided to move inland to Nanicapana on the Alabama River, where the largest amount of Indian food had been found. The expedition to Coosa returned to report that any wealth that might once have been there was now nowhere in evidence. Nanicapana proved to be another disaster. Beset with ill health and dissension, and with his leadership seriously questioned, de Luna led the famished colonists back to Pensacola Bay, where he found not reinforcements but a royal order to occupy Santa Elena at once. Accordingly, on August 10, 1560, the governor dispatched two frigates and a small bark with men to claim and occupy the site. Stripped and damaged in a storm, the small ships made their way to Mexico. The settlement at Santa Elena had to await new pressures to occupy that coast. Travelers from Pensacola went to Cuba and to Mexico to complain of de Luna's leadership. By September of 1560 he had lost control of his unhappy charges, who refused to follow his order to go inland again to the fabled Coosa. In April 1561, Angel de Villafañe, who had been appointed on January 31 to replace de Luna, arrived at Pensacola. The frustrated and defeated de Luna returned to Spain by way of Havana to defend his regime in Florida.

Villafañe was also a man of courage and experience, but he proved unable to cope with the problems he inherited from his predecessor. He was to evacuate the colonists to Cuba except for a small contingent that was to hold Pensacola and to organize an expedition to Santa Elena. Some 200 persons embarked for Havana on three ships. Once safely there, many of them deserted the enterprise, and only about seventy-five men accompanied Villafañe to Santa Elena. They arrived safely but on June 14, while seeking a better harbor, a tropical storm inflicted such heavy damage that Villafane could only return to New Spain in defeat. Pensacola would be forgotten for 125 years.

Spanish efforts to occupy and settle Florida seemed doomed to defeat. Ponce de León, Narváez, de Soto, de Luna, and Villafañe had tried in vain only to lose fortunes and reputations. Perhaps 2,000 lives, and more ships and property than New Spain could well afford, had been lost. Possibly nobody could establish a base there. If King Philip II of Spain did not, as is sometimes suggested, reach that conclusion and order the expenditure of no more life and treasure, he might very reasonably have done so. His worst fears, however, were about to be realized. An interloper was already on his way from Europe to Florida.

3.

Florida's First Permanent Settlement

French rather than Spanish initiative inspired the first permanent Spanish settlement in Florida. Even as Philip II and his advisers were deciding to abandon the coasts of Florida, a French expedition was on its way to the Saint Johns River. Shortly after
Columbus discovered America, Pope Alexander VI had issued a series of decrees dividing the New World between Spain and Portu-
gal, with Spain being allotted all but Brazil. La Florida had not all
been explored, much less occupied. For a time no European power
dared to attack the Spanish monopoly, but as France and England
grew in national ambition and strength in the sixteenth century,
they looked with greater envy upon the wealth Spain was deriving
from these possessions, and they gradually lost their fear of Spanish power.

The sponsor of the French expedition was the admiral of France,
Gaspard de Coligny. Behind the voyage lay a mixture of motives:
national, religious, and economic. Coligny was a patriotic Frenchman and an ardent Huguenot, two loyalties that frequently involved
him in difficulty with his Catholic sovereign. He was seeking to
serve his country and his religion and enrich himself and his followers, all at the expense of Spain, in the New World. It was not too
difficult to convince his sovereign that colonies would enrich the
mother country and add to her national prestige. Spain and Portu-
gal had been demonstrating this for half a century. He no doubt
also pointed out that France would be relieved of some unwanted
Protestants. When an effort to plant a colony in Brazil in 1555
failed miserably, Coligny turned his attention to Florida, certainly
a better base for preying upon Spanish commerce.

Three French ships carrying two smaller boats arrived at the
Saint Johns River on April 30, 1562, with 150 persons aboard. In
command was Jean Ribault, also an ardent Calvinist. The visitors
found the Indians curious and friendly, a sharp contrast to the Spanish experience on the southwest coast. Ribault named the stream
River of May, and planted a stone pillar on the bank near its mouth
with the arms of France, the date, and his name graven on it; a

replica of it now stands on Saint Johns Bluff. After two days of friendly trading with the Indians, the visitors sailed northward to Port Royal. There Ribault left a small garrison of twenty-eight men to build a fort (named Charles Fort) and to hold the land in the name of the king of France. He also left eight pieces of artillery and provisions for several months at the fort, and promised to return within six months with reinforcements and supplies. Then everything seemed to go wrong. Fire destroyed much of the food and supplies, and the Indians resisted efforts of the white men to acquire food from their slender winter stores. Mutiny broke out among the men in protest against the arbitrary rule of "Captain Albert," who hanged the drummer boy Guemache without sufficient cause and exiled another member of the garrison to a nearby island where he would certainly have died of starvation. Feeling that they could not survive until Ribault's return, the desperate men constructed a small boat and took to sea, without compass or navigator, to return to France. Halfway across the Atlantic the boat was becalmed for several weeks, and the starving Frenchmen were almost reduced to cannibalism. They had chosen by lot one of their number to be sacrificed to their dire need when an English ship came upon them and returned them to France. The Spaniards meanwhile had learned of the French visit, and the governor of Cuba sent a force under the command of Don Hernando de Manrique de Rojas to drive the intruders out. The Spaniards found the abandoned fort, completed its destruction, and took away with them a French youth who had preferred to take his chances of survival by remaining with the Indians rather than fleeing by boat.

Ribault had not fared much better. Upon his return to France in July he found the country locked in civil war and Coligny out of favor at the court. When the city of Dieppe fell to the forces of the Catholic sovereign in October, Ribault escaped to England where he published an account of his voyage to Florida.

The Peace of Amboise in March 1563, in the meantime, ended the war in France and made it possible for Coligny to return to royal favor and to his American adventure. He chose René Goulaine de Laudonnière to replace the absent Ribault as leader. On April 22, 1564, the new commander sailed for Florida in three ships with 300 men and four women; they arrived on June 22. The Indians welcomed the returning French and remained friendly and helpful for a time. On June 25, Laudonnière selected a site for the colony on a broad flat knoll about five miles from the mouth of the Saint Johns and named it Fort Caroline.

The history of Fort Caroline was destined to be troubled and brief, but it left more than the record of a short life with a bloody ending. Among the colonists was the artist Jacques Le Moyne, who had been commissioned by the government to prepare an account of what he saw in the New World. His *Narrative of Le Moyne surnamed DeMorgues* included with the text forty-two drawings of aborigines with fifteen pages of description. After the author's death, his widow sold them to Theodore de Bry, who etched and published

Restored upper portion of Fort Caroline

them in England in 1591; unfortunately, the originals were lost. The narratives of Laudonnière and Le Moyne are the earliest and best accounts of the land and the natives in northeast Florida.

Fort Caroline consisted of several palm-thatched buildings surrounded by a triangular-shaped wall of earth and logs. The Timucua Indians, whose chief Saturiba was friendly and helpful, aided also in the building of other homes outside the protecting walls of the fort. The colonists scarcely deserved the name. They were for the most part far more interested in adventure and the prospect of quick wealth at the expense of Spanish shipping in the nearby waters. Food became scarce, and though the Indians supplied what they could, Laudonnière found it advisable to reduce rations of food and drink. Restless members of the group staged a mutiny, stole two small sailing vessels, and set out to sea in search of quick wealth. After some early successes, which alerted the Spanish to their presence, one ship was captured; the crew of the second sailed back to Fort Caroline to accept their fate as deserters.

Laudonnière's health began to fail and his leadership to be questioned. By the summer of 1565 the discouraged Frenchmen had decided to return to France. In the midst of their preparations, which included the building of one small ship, the Englishman Sir John Hawkins, on the way home from a successful slave trading expedition in Spanish waters, stopped at the Saint Johns for fresh water. He offered passage to Europe to the Frenchmen, but they refused, fearing that they might find themselves prisoners of war before they reached home. They did exchange guns and ammunition for one of the Hawkins ships, and when the Englishmen departed two days later they hastened their own plans for departure. They were waiting for favorable tide and wind when Ribault returned just in time to prevent their departure. He brought seven ships with 500 soldiers and artisans and seventy women. He also brought orders to supersede Laudonnière in command. Knowing that they might soon expect attack by Spaniards bent on driving them away, he set the men to work immediately to strengthen the defenses of Fort Caroline.

He did not have long to wait. Spanish authorities knew about the settlement and had hoped to break it up before Ribault could arrive with reinforcements. For the task Philip chose one of Spain's ablest and most trusted public servants in the person of Pedro Menéndez de Avilés, who knew from experience the necessity to protect the trade route between Spain and the New World. He also knew the geography of the area in which he was to operate.

His was to be no mere naval and military expedition to drive out the French interlopers. If Philip II had meant to abandon the effort to settle the Florida coast, he had quickly reversed himself and ordered an all-out effort to colonize and hold it. Menéndez, when he had ousted the French, was to plant Spanish settlements in strategic places and to Christianize the natives partly for the purpose of making allies of them. In spite of the failures of his predecessors, he undertook to invest his private fortune in the venture. His patent was not unlike those of the others, from Ponce de León to Tristán de Luna. He and his heirs would have the title of marquis of those territories. In time he acquired other titles, captain general of the fleet he commanded, governor of Florida with the right to appoint a lieutenant governor to act during his absence, and adelantado with the right to transmit the title to his heirs. Valuable trading privileges included a certain number of ships to sail duty free in the Indies trade.

Menéndez gathered together in Spain the largest armada of ships and colonists that had yet come to Florida. On June 20, 1565, he sailed from Cádiz leading nineteen ships with 1,000 persons on board; others were soon to follow. Forced by storms to return to port, repair, and re-form, when he set out again the number of persons was swelled to 1,504. Among them, in addition to sailors and soldiers, were locksmiths, millers, silversmiths, tanners, sheepshearers, and farmers, some of them with wives and children. After the fleet passed the Canary Islands, a storm scattered the ships, so only five continued together to San Juan, where they found four others that had preceded them.

The expedition was thus considerably diminished in size, but the urgency to intercept the French did not permit delay to wait for others to follow. On August 15, Menéndez left for Florida with five ships carrying 500 soldiers, 200 sailors, and 100 noncombatants referred to as "useless peoples." This was primarily a military venture. The ships reached the Florida coast at about Cape Canaveral

LaLeche Shrine commemorates the first mass said at Saint Augustine, September 8, 1565.

on June 28 and sailed northward to the French-named River of Dolphins, which Menéndez renamed Saint Augustine because he had reached Florida on the day of the festival of San Augustine. He did not yet know that Ribault had won the race to the Saint Johns. There followed next an incredible series of coincidences that gave Menéndez a smashing victory over a superior enemy, a victory that must have convinced him of the righteousness of his cause and the favor of God.

On September 4, Menéndez sailed up to the mouth of the Saint Johns to assess the situation of the French. He found four of Ribault's ships that were too large to cross the bar anchored outside. Some of his officers, seeing other French ships on the river, urged caution and would have waited for the arrival of others in the expedition. Menéndez chose to challenge the French, who cut their chains and sailed away. It was not expedient to attack Fort Caroline, and he hastened to Saint Augustine to prepare for the attack sure to come. He had little time to seek a better base. Saint Augustine offered a safe anchorage for his ships and a defensible position. If some of the larger Spanish vessels could not cross the bar, the same would be true for an enemy. By September 8, all of the personnel were ashore and every effort was being made to unload two ships that had to remain outside the harbor. On that day in 1565, Saint Augustine was officially born and the land claimed in the name of the king of Spain. Meanwhile, two ships had been sent to Havana to report the situation and ask for reinforcements.

The expected attack materialized a few days later. Ribault sailed from the Saint Johns on September 10, taking some of Laudonnière's men as well as his own for a total of 200 sailors and 400 soldiers, leaving only 240 persons at Fort Caroline, half of them too ill to fight in their own defense. The next day the attackers almost caught Menéndez crossing the bar at Saint Augustine in a small boat but found they could not pursue him into the harbor. While they waited for a favorable tide and wind, a storm drove the ships southward along the coast and wrecked them. Menéndez marched overland to attack Fort Caroline. He set out on the morning of September 16 and after four days of marching through brush and swamp, 400 of the men reached their objective late in the day, attacked at daybreak on September 20, taking the French completely by surprise. Some sixty of the French escaped in two ships including Jacques Ribault, the son of the French leader, Laudonniére, and Le Moyne.

Menéndez renamed the fort San Mateo, left 300 men to hold it, and hurried back to his anxious compatriots at Saint Augustine, arriving on September 24. Four days later Indians brought word of a body of Frenchmen on the shore below the mouth of the Matanzas Inlet, which they were unable to cross in their attempted march along the shore. Menéndez with fifty men marched down to the river, parleyed with the destitute and shipwrecked men, and ferried them across the river and executed all but ten who were Catholic. On October 10, word came that Ribault and the remainder of his men had also arrived at the mouth of the Matanzas. After a parley, Ribault and 150 of his men (which was all but 170 of his party who refused to trust themselves to the mercy of the Spaniards), were ferried across as the first group. Only sixteen were spared, four of them professed Catholics and a dozen fifers, drummers, and trumpeters.

The 170 who had refused "rescue" made their way southward to about Cape Canaveral where the ship *Trinity* had been driven ashore by the storm. They used the ship's timber and stores and worked at the construction of a fort to defend themselves and at building a boat large enough to effect their escape. When Menéndez learned of their whereabouts he set out by land and by sea to capture them. On November 26, the Spaniards reached the French and induced all but twenty to surrender without a fight, promising them that they would be sent back to Europe as prisoners, a promise that was kept. Menéndez himself escorted half of them to Havana. The fate of the other twenty is unknown.

The massacre of the two groups of helpless Frenchmen appropriately enough gave the name Matanzas, "Place of Slaughter," to the site where it had occurred. It also has brought condemnation upon Menéndez, although arguments designed to justify his conduct persist until this day.

Menéndez carried out the first and most pressing purpose of his Florida assignments with complete and final success and at surprisingly small cost in Spanish life and resources. In fact, French property captured at Fort Caroline far outvalued that which Spain lost.

Dominique de Gorgues came from France on a punitive expedition in June of 1567, but with no purpose to remain, only to raid. He found Saturiba and his people still loyal to the French cause and together they raided and destroyed San Mateo, hanging in retaliation any Spaniards they captured. The French attempted no other settlement in Spanish Florida until late in the next century on the Gulf coast, but they did not lose interest in the region. Much of this interest was shown by privateers and pirates. The French established the French West Indies Company in 1664 and acquired island possessions in the Caribbean.

Meanwhile Menéndez met with no success in his other objectives in Florida. The conqueror of the French set out energetically to secure Florida for Spain and for himself the fame and fortune that success would bring. He had the favor and support of his sovereign, some of it in the tangible form of ships and men and salary, but he also had an assignment to protect the trade route between New Spain and the mother country. This meant ridding the New World of the growing numbers of corsairs from the nations of western Europe who were preying upon Spanish ports and shipping ever more boldly each passing year. This was to prove a task beyond the resources of Menéndez and his sovereign. This dual assignment provided him with some of the means for the closely related Florida venture, but it divided his time and attention, and he was absent from Florida more than present after the first two years.

The adelantado's grand design for Florida included at least seven settlements on the Atlantic and Gulf coasts. Saint Augustine and San Mateo originated as military ports, and only the former ever became much more than that. A blockhouse at Matanzas Inlet to guard the southern approach to Saint Augustine became a permanent part of the fort's design in 1569. At Santa Elena, Menéndez had a greater measure of success than his predecessor but failed in the end to achieve a permanent settlement. Twenty farmers settled there under the protection of Fort San Felipe and its garrison, but they did not prosper. Indian hostilities pushed back the settlement in 1576, and it was reestablished only to be finally abandoned in 1587. At Santa Lucia the Ais Indians remained relentless in their hostility and forced abandonment of the site. At what is now Miami on Biscayne Bay a Jesuit mission presided over by Brother Francisco Villareal and supported by a small garrison of Spanish soldiers enjoyed some success for a brief time, but a clash between the military force and the Indians terminated the effort.

On the west coast at Charlotte Harbor, Menéndez made a special effort to win the favor of the powerful Calusa chief Carlos. Carlos gave him his sister Antonia for a wife and tolerated for a time the mission presided over by Father Juan Rogel, but when Menéndez departed Carlos became so hostile that the soldiers killed him and elevated Don Felipe to the caciquedom. Then Don Felipe also became relentlessly hostile when the Spaniards threatened to interfere with any of his prerogatives. Finally the Spaniards put to death the recalcitrant and treacherous cacique and fourteen of his followers, whereupon the Indians burned their village and fled to the forest, leaving the Spaniards no choice but to abandon the settlement. A small garrison at Tocabaga (now Tampa) met similar hostility and withdrew.

A final Menéndez project deserves some attention. He had been interested in Charlotte Harbor and Tampa Bay in the belief that the source of the Saint Johns River might be there. He was even more interested in Chesapeake Bay, about which he knew less, for he thought it might prove to be the elusive northwest passage to the Pacific coast and the Far East. In 1570 he approved the project of Father Juan Bautista de Segura and eleven companions to separate themselves from all military power and found a mission near the Rappahannock River. This attempt ended in 1571 with the assassination of all the company except a small boy. Menéndez went in search of the courageous party of Jesuits and found the boy but no trace of the others or of those responsible for the murders. Menéndez could only hang eight Indians he found in the vicinity. In 1573 he requested his nephew, Pedro Menéndez Marqués, to explore the region further in search of the northwest passage. In 1572 the Jesuits abandoned Florida for other fields more suited to their talents. In the following year, on February 23, Philip II authorized six Franciscan friars to take up the missionary work to the Florida Indians and thus inaugurated a movement destined to give a special character to the seventeenth century. By 1597 a dozen Franciscans were working with the Indians from Saint Augustine to Santa Elena. Two years later a revolt in Guale (in southeastern Georgia) ended the lives of five of the missionaries and halted but did not end the work they had begun.

When Menéndez wrote his will he left his debts to Philip II, who had promised him payment for some of his expenditures in behalf of the crown in the New World. For his years in Florida, Menéndez left only the enduring settlement at Saint Augustine and a garrison at San Mateo, for the struggling settlement at Santa Elena would not long survive him. He had demonstrated that private resources were inadequate to meet the requirements of the Florida problem. The region would not yield the profits in farms, slaves, mines, and trade that had enriched conquistadors in other parts of Spanish America. This did not mean that Florida must not be occupied and held at all costs, but thereafter it would be a charge against the revenues of New Spain for the protection of which the frontier military outpost would be maintained.

Menéndez's nephew Pedro Menéndez Marqués had acted as lieutenant governor, resident in Saint Augustine during the absence of his uncle. He continued in office until a successor to Menéndez, Hernando de Miranda, was appointed in 1575 and served two years, after which Marqués served as interim governor until he became governor in 1578, serving until 1589. From an annual subsidy, the *situado*, payable each year in New Spain, the cost of the civil, military, and religious establishment in Florida was supported after 1574. Based upon the number of persons to be paid and the needs of the colony, the amount was set each year after a process of accounting and negotiation. The sum might be paid in money, supplies, or equipment. Most of the money would be spent in Mexico or Cuba, the source of most purchases. A representative of the Florida governor usually journeyed to Mexico by way of Havana. By the second century of colonization, Florida depended more and more upon Havana for most goods and services. The bishop of Cuba was the spiritual head of the church in Florida, but the material and spiritual support was never satisfactory. Paid reluctantly and sometimes not until after interminable delays, civil and military servants waiting for their pay had to secure credit at heavy charges and remained perpetually in debt. These early Floridians also found great difficulty in making purchases of good quality at reasonable prices. On the way home they ran the grave risk of being robbed by pirates who lay in wait for them, for their ships were one of the richest prizes to be captured in these waters.

By 1585, the twenty year-old outpost at Saint Augustine had a council house, a church, several stores and other buildings, and houses for its almost 300 men, women, and children. In the next year Sir Francis Drake paid the tiny village a visit. It was a minor incident in a voyage of great proportions but a disaster for Spanish Florida. Drake had left England in the summer of 1585 at the head of a fleet that carried 2,300 men aboard two men of war, nineteen merchant ships, and an assortment of lesser vessels. A joint stock company financed the venture to raid and trade on the Spanish main. Illness among the men nearly wrecked the enterprise, and Drake had to stop short of his major objectives, one of which was the capture of Havana. After calling at Santo Domingo and Cartagena, where he exacted heavy ransom by threatening to destroy the captured cities block by block until the money was paid, he decided to return to England. If he had plans to stop in Florida he apparently had Santa Elena in mind. His men may have discovered Saint Augustine by chance when they saw a lookout tower at the south entrance to Matanzas Inlet and went to investigate.

Governor Menéndez Marqués had been warned of the possibility of such an attack and had made what plans he could to evacuate civilians and hold a fort, which was hastily erected by fifty slaves.

When Drake approached, leading twenty-three heavy warships, nineteen auxiliary vessels, and 2,000 men, there were only eighty armed men to man the defenses. The Spanish fort, the third on the site, was constructed of pine timbers. The defenders fired from their flimsy fort on the mainland but eventually fled, leaving behind a dozen or more brass cannons and the king's treasure chest containing some two thousand pounds sterling, probably for the pay of the garrison. Before he departed Drake for some reason ordered the complete destruction of the settlement, including some orange groves and crops of corn, squash, and melons. The burning of the town may have been due to the killing of some twenty of Drake's men, including one of his close friends. Drake did not proceed up the coast, so Santa Elena was spared a visit because the approaches were not deep enough to accommodate Drake's ships. The Spanish at Santa Elena and San Mateo rushed food and supplies to Saint

View of Saint Augustine at the time of the Drake raid.

Augustine, but the rebuilding process was a slow one.

The Drake raid spread consternation throughout Spanish America. Forts had to be made of stronger materials, be provided with heavier guns, and garrisons increased. Inevitably the advisability of maintaining military outposts in Florida began to be questioned. A series of events at the end of the century strengthened the doubts and the voices of protest by those who felt a more suitable site for the settlement could and should be found. In 1597 the Guale revolt resulted in the death of five of the nine Franciscan missionaries and raised doubts about what had seemed a most promising development. Finally, on September 22, 1599, a hurricane flooded the presidio and the town at Saint Augustine and sharpened the criticisms of the site for a colony. The protest from lay and clerical sources reached such proportions that the king, in a cedula dated November 5, 1600, ordered the governor of Cuba to hold a formal hearing at Saint Augustine to determine its fitness for the purposes for which it was being maintained.

The criticisms leveled against the location were serious. Drake's raid had proved that the harbor could not be defended. Only smaller ships could get across the bar at the entrance. Hurricanes flooded the fort and the town. There was not land enough for the presidio and the settlers. There was no land for agricultural purposes. There was no easy access to the interior. It was far removed from the trade route it was to protect and from the victims of shipwreck on the Florida reef that it was supposed to save from starvation or Indian attack when they reached shore. It was too far removed from the centers of Indian population to please the Franciscan missionaries, who favored a location farther to the north. The Franciscans were as unhappy with the new governor, Gonzalez Méndez de Canzo, as they were with the governors before and after him. They felt they received too small a share of the *situado* and that the governors did not give them sufficient support in their dealing with Indians. They were, in short, attacking the administration as well as the location of the capital.

The testimony at the hearings provides some unflattering descriptions of Saint Augustine at the end of the sixteenth century. In 1598, there were more than 120 houses, but they were mainly huts made of palmetto. There were 225 soldiers and 400 other persons, including Indians and blacks. In 1602, royal officials reported thirty-six old black slaves and twenty new ones. Another source reported fifty-seven married men and 107 children. Governor Canzo complained of animals that roamed the streets, concluding that every family owned four to ten cows. The streets were of mud, more often water than dirt. The main church was made partly of palmetto and straw. A disastrous fire in 1599 burned the Franciscan friary and many other thatched roof buildings. Canzo had added a six-bed hospital with a black female as nurse, but his successor called it a miserable hole. Canzo had also constructed a plaza where people could barter their produce and a horse-powered mill to relieve the residents of grinding corn by hand. A great variety of fruits and

Fort Matanzas on Rattlesnake Island guarded the southern approach to Saint Augustine by way of the Matanzas River

vegetables grew there, but none in sufficient quantity to feed the population.

Whatever the weaknesses and criticisms may have been, Saint Augustine had its defenders. The critics failed to note that Menéndez had chosen well for a defense post if not for a colony, that Spanish forces at Havana and Saint Augustine could together protect the vital trade route along the Florida coast. And, unlike posts at river mouths, it was relatively safe from Indian forays from the interior. There was no harbor any nearer to the shipping lanes. Nor was there a bay to the north that could accommodate so large a number of ships of the Spanish navy. If they did not occupy this best of harbors, someone else would. Saint Augustine probably survived partly because it was there and partly because there was not enough initiative or money to relocate the defenses of Spanish America. Its defenders said it needed only men and money to make it effective. It never received enough of either, but it remained Spain's only foothold on the Atlantic shore of North America, and it survived more than two centuries against formidable obstacles.

4.

Christianizing the Indians

In the hearings of 1602 Saint Augustine had been found wanting in some respects, but it was not to be abandoned. It was, in fact, largely to remain Spanish Florida for the next century. It was already becoming clear that the province would be little more than a military outpost, dependent upon the *situado* for its economic existence; that it would not attract white settlers and become a populous and self-supporting colony as its sponsors had hoped. There remained, however, the possibility that the considerable Indian populations in Timucua, Guale, and Apalachee might help to provide some of the security that a resident Spanish population would have guaranteed. In the middle decades of the century it appeared that Franciscan missions might bring about that happy state of affairs in which the Indians would be Christianized, "civilized," and Hispanized to become effective allies of Spain.

To properly understand the role of missions it is useful to consider them as a multipurpose frontier institution, in Florida different from other Spanish American colonies only as the difference in the Indian cultures and in the natural environment made them so. Throughout the first three-quarters of the seventeenth century in Florida, the leading role was played by the missionary. The closely related encomienda system had been designed to convert, "civilize," and exploit the Indians by distributing the land and the people among Spaniards who would hold them in trust. The encomienda made it possible, in keeping the Indians in a fixed place of residence, to guide and control them. It worked very well among those docile and semi-civilized natives who had fixed abodes and were accustomed to labor. Abuses discredited the system, however, for it became too easy to use it exclusively for exploitation. It was not suited to the Florida frontier, where the roving tribes were unaccustomed to labor. The mission there took over the same functions with primary emphasis upon conversion but with other motives also important. The abuses associated with the encomienda had already given rise to the Black Legend that the influence of Spanish settlers, soldiers, and administrators hindered rather than helped the missionaries in their efforts to win the souls and the allegiance of the natives. The encomienda never became a part of the Florida

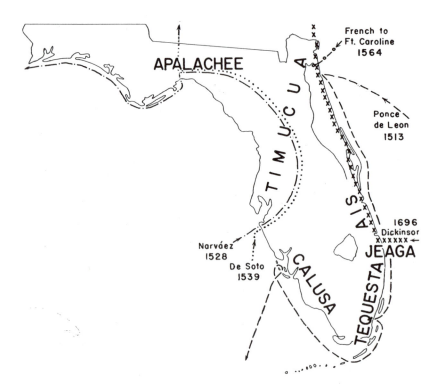

APALACHEE

TIMUCUA

French to
Ft. Caroline
1564

Ponce
de Leon
1513

AIS

1696
Dickinson
XXXXXX ←

Narváez
1528

De Soto
1539

CALUSA

JEAGA

TEQUESTA

Principal Indian tribes in Florida in the year 1500

experience, but missionaries made the same complaints about civil
and military interference.

The missions were agencies of the state as well as of the church.
In Florida the state provided for their financial needs partly because there was no other source of support in the province but also
because they served purposes of the state that were economic and
political as well as religious. Since the *situado* supported the civil,
the military, and the religious establishments there was always competition among them for a larger share. The number of religious
supported by the state in the seventeenth century is a measure of
the high relative importance attached to their work.

It is always a mistake, of course, to try to separate the influences of church and state in early modern Spanish or Spanish American history. Nationalism and religious orthodoxy had been developed to a high degree in religious wars, first with the Moors and
then with Protestant heretics. Nor does this imply the subordina-
tion of church or churchmen to purposes of the state. They were

twin representatives of the same ideals and objectives. If the functions of the missions were more than religious, they were first of all to convert the Indians to Christianity. The king and the Council of the Indies made the more important decisions and plans for the missionaries in Florida, and the House of Trade provided funds for their travel and subsistence on the trip from Spain. The bishop of Cuba, who had confirmatory powers for the mainland, also had a primary responsibility for the Florida missions. In 1612 the bishop created the Province of Santa Elena, which included present-day Florida, Georgia, and South Carolina, with headquarters on Saint Catherines Island. In Florida the governor assigned the missionaries to their posts, provided them with the basic equipment for their tasks, and paid them monthly stipends from the *situado*. The role of the governor was all-important. He sometimes went along with a missionary to his new assignment, taking along other civil and military personnel to impress the natives with the importance of the new official stationed in their midst. The missionary might otherwise have lacked the status to be effective. Governors also stood ready to send military forces to deal with recalcitrant and rebellious Indians. They differed considerably in the amount of support given to the missions, but neither king nor governor ever abandoned support for an active program in the seventeenth century.

Missionaries differed widely on the subject of the desirability of Spanish soldiers and settlers around the missions. In the early part of the century many of them wanted no soldiers around, believing that they hindered the work. Nor was it possible to garrison each of the missions adequately. A too small force might easily be too weak to be effective but large enough to be an irritant. In other situations the missions could survive only with the presence of or the threat of effective military support. Missionaries also recognized the importance of teaching the Indians useful occupational skills, particularly the development of agricultural communities around the missions, tasks for which they were often ill-suited. On the other hand, they too often found that farmers and planters rode roughshod over Indian property rights, exacted labor and produce from them, and alienated them from anything or anyone Spanish. Had it been at all possible, the missionaries would have preferred to work alone with their charges, but in addition to an occasional violent uprising against the discipline imposed by their mentors, the Indians began to come under non-Spanish influences in the last quarter of the century that threatened the tenuous hold that the zealous Franciscans had established and finally brought ruin to the missions. No help that Spanish colonial authorities could give to the missions could save them or hold the frontier they were designed to maintain.

In the sixteenth-century the first efforts were largely those of Jesuits. Duke Francisco de Borja, proprietor general of the order, was a friend of Pedro Menéndez. He could at first supply only three of the twenty-four priests asked for, and their experiences were prophetic of what was to characterize missionary efforts in the province. Father Pedro Martínez, who led the trio, went ashore on Cumberland Island with six Flemish seamen and two Spanish soldiers to seek food and water. During a storm, they were attacked by hostile Indians and the only survivors were Father Juan Rogel and Brother Francisco Villareal, who later made futile efforts to establish missions on Biscayne Bay and Charlotte Harbor.

In the spring of 1568, Menéndez brought eleven Jesuits to Havana to establish a school for Indian boys and in 1569, he brought settlers to the Fort at Santa Elena. Unfortunately, the Indians rebelled and the Jesuits left for Virginia. This ended the role of the Jesuits in Florida and enabled the ascendance of the Franciscans in 1572. The next 100 years saw the establishment of Franciscan missions throughout Florida, some successful and others not.

The Florida assignment was not a popular one. It was not only that the Indians were at times hostile, rebellious, and violent. Everything about the Florida province was poor. The priest often lacked the means to carry on his work. He no longer could enjoy the social, intellectual, and spiritual companionship of the religious community from which he came. He had to undergo personal discomforts and learn the Indian ways of life and thought. Some of the Indian practices, particularly nakedness and polygamy, he found repulsive. He had to learn the language and work very gradually with the untutored savages, whose languages often lacked words to express the sophisticated Christian ideas. Only a few of the missionaries, like Francisco Pareja and Baltasar López, spoke Timucuan well, and though Indians appear to have learned Spanish rather easily, working through interpreters was frustrating. It is not surprising that thoughtful people suggested teaching Spanish to all of the Indians.

In 1656, in the midst of the most successful period of mission activity, Chief San Martín de Ayococuto and eleven other chiefs in Timucua and Apalachee rose in revolt against the combination of pressure and persuasion being applied by the Franciscan fathers and killed three of them. They began by killing some people in charge of several cattle ranches; the treasurer, Francisco Menéndez, in West Timucua; and the soldiers stationed there. Governor Diego de Rebolledo went to the rescue and punished the rebels severely, garroting eleven of them one by one to cow and also to infuriate their fellow tribesmen, and condemning twenty-six to forced labor on the fortifications in Saint Augustine. The Apalachees, who had been little involved, were let off easily, but twelve soldiers and a captain were stationed at San Luis to guarantee their good behavior. A small fort was later erected there when a new threat to Spanish security in that area appeared.

This golden age of mission activity reached its high water mark in 1674 with the visit to Florida of Bishop Don Gabriel Díaz Vara Calderón, the first since that of Bishop Altimarano in 1606. By this latter visit an effort was being made to reach the Indians as far west as the Apalachicola River region, spurred to renewed energy by the penetration of English traders to that area. The bishop arrived in August and remained until the following June. He visited every mission and every settlement in which a Spaniard was located and left in his report the most complete list of missions and their locations that has come down to us. He mentions thirteen in Apalachee, concentrated mostly around present-day Tallahassee, eleven in Timucua, and eight in Guale. He counted 13,152 Christian Indians.

The bishop described the Indian weapons as the bow and arrow and the hatchet, called *macana*. The Spaniards had not allowed firearms to the Indians, a practice which may have made them easier to manage but left them relatively defenseless against whites and Indians who came later with such weapons. The men still went half-naked, with the skin of some animal worn from the waist down and sometimes a coat of serge or a blanket. Many of the women wore a sort of tunic made of Spanish moss, though not all, since the bishop reported that he requested that 4,081 women naked from the waist up should be clothed in the moss.

The diet of the Indians consisted of corn, pumpkins, beans, game, and fish. They drank only *cazina* (sometimes *cassina)*, which was medicinal rather than intoxicating. They slept on the ground in warm weather and in winter in homes made of a frame covered by bearskins, with a fire set in the center. In the center of each village was a council house made of wood and covered with straw, round in shape, with a large opening at the top. The bishop thought most council houses large enough to accommodate 2,000 to 3,000 persons.

When twenty-nine friars appeared in Saint Augustine in 1612 and 1613, the governor became somewhat alarmed at the prospect of maintaining more and more friars, but they continued to come. Losses by transfer were large, but twenty-four arrived in 1676, perhaps as a result of the bishop's report of successes and needs in the field. They were clearly in high favor at the time, and a very considerable proportion of the annual government subsidy went for their support.

The number of missionaries increased from forty in 1676 to fifty-two in 1680. In 1679 a group of secular priests at Saint Augustine, led by pastor Sebastian Perez de la Cerda, proposed to revive the effort to missionize the Calusa Indians where a Franciscan effort to plant a mission the previous year had failed. The project received royal approval but was never implemented with personnel and funds. Partly because of the extent of the activity, partly because Cuba wished to be free of the responsibility, there was also a move to create a separate diocese for Florida. Governor Rebolledo had urged this in 1655 and Juan Marques Cabrera in 1683, but nothing had ever come of it.

Already the missions were being caught up in the international struggle among Spain, France, and England to control North America, a struggle which came to Florida late in the seventeenth century with disastrous consequences. The settlement of Charleston in 1670 meant trouble for the Spanish-Indian frontier. In 1680 a band of Indians directed by the English raided the mission on Jekyll Island but were driven off. Shortly thereafter Captain Francisco Fuentes, with five Spanish musketeers and sixteen Indians he had armed with guns, drove off attackers at Santa Catalina. Governor Cabrera sought to withdraw to more defensible positions at Santa Maria, San Juan, and Santa Cruz farther south but failed to induce most of the converted Indians to make the move. In 1684 the Indians of northern Guale went over to the English in great numbers. They were attracted by the trade goods, the prices paid for skins and furs, the sale of guns and ammunition (and on occasion whiskey), the noninterference with their Indian ways, and in great measure by the obviously superior military power of the English.

In 1685 some of the same Indians raided the Santa Catalina mission in Timucua, burned the pueblo, killed some Indians, and carried others away as slaves. A series of pirate raids on the missions on Sapelo and Jekyll islands added to the confusion and insecurity of the undermanned Spanish government. In 1686 the few Indians still loyal to Spain retreated to stations south of the Saint Marys River; these stations constituted the Spanish-English border.

Students of these missions suggest that the Franciscans may have contributed to their own downfall. Fuentes, who may have been paying back the friars in their own coin, reported that friars were demanding stipends from the Indians and forcing them to perform menial services without pay. They exacted heavy penalties for disobedience, and some Indians were reported fleeing from the whips of priests. Lending support to this theory is the conclusion that the order had lost some of its zeal and that the friars had settled down to routine performance of duties.

There is probably a measure of truth in all of the charges made against friars, soldiers, civilians, and other Spaniards who dealt directly with the Indians, but this does not account for the failure of the mission system to play the hoped-for role in the defense of the frontier. Their hold on the Indians was never strong enough to withstand the blandishments and the power of the English. The real tests came in 1702 and 1704. The English and their Indian allies, led by Governor James Moore of Carolina, sought to take Saint Augustine in 1702 and in the process destroyed the missions north of that city. They failed to take the great stone fort but returned in 1704 to lay waste the missions in Apalachee, rightly judging them to be an integral part of the Spanish frontier defense system. At only one mission, La Concepción de Ayubale, did they meet any opposition, but there it was in vain. Nor could the small garrison at Fort San Luis near the mission aided by Indians loyal to Spain drive away the intruders. Governor Moore had destroyed eight of the fourteen missions in Apalachee. In 1706 and 1708 others raided the remaining Timucua Indian villages. After 1708 there were no Florida missions outside Saint Augustine. The Spanish

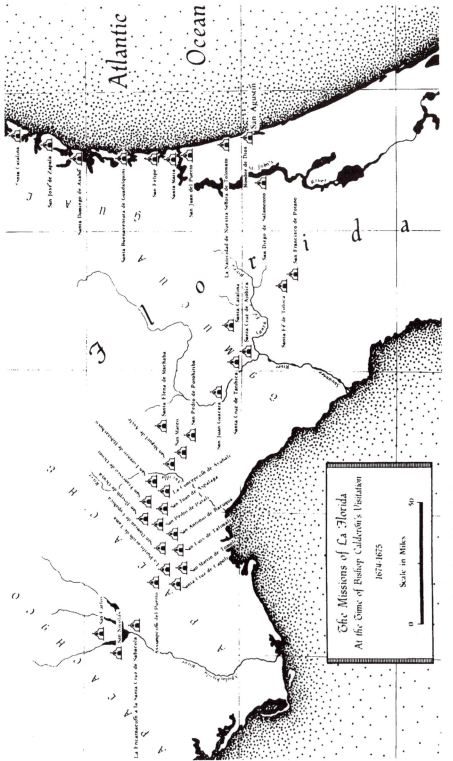

Location of Florida missions at the time of Bishop Calderón's visit visit, 1674

governor estimated that as many as ten or twelve thousand Indians had been carried away as slaves, probably too high an estimate, as many of the Indians went willingly if not gladly. The Spanish defense perimeter and the missions associated with it had shrunk to the region that could be defended at the Castillo de San Marcos.

The English invaders left stark ruin in their wake. On the first day of the invasion they had burned the library of the friars; they now burned the parish church so that the city was without a church for the first time in its history. They also burned the hermitage of Nuestra Senora de la Leche and the convent and chapel of the Franciscans. They also attacked the mission stations of San Jose and San Francisco, killed many of the Indians, and took away five hundred prisoners.

The Spanish rebuilt the hermitage at the mission of Nombre Dios as a place of worship for the few Indians who remained there. In March of 1728, Colonel John Palmer with a force of Carolina Indians raided and burned the hermitage chapel and carried off the altar furnishings. Governor Antonio de Benavides broke up the remaining stones of the mission to destroy any shelter they might provide for attackers and built a new chapel and a new hermitage inside the outer defenses of the city.

In the midst of all these difficulties Florida's first resident bishop arrived. He had been authorized in 1703 but did not arrive until June 23, 1709. With the hospital chapel the only church building, no episcopal residence, and no Indians to be presented for confirmation, he left after three weeks. In 1723 the see in Cuba agreed to underwrite another auxiliary bishopric. In 1731 Francisco de San Buenaventura y Trejada, a professor of theology and guardian of a Franciscan convent in Seville, received the appointment and arrived at Saint Augustine in July 1735. The able and energetic leader infused new life into the religious establishment, putting a new roof on the church, reinforcing the plank walls, and building a stone sacristy alongside. He gathered the children together three times a week for instruction and opened a classical school for young boys, the first school since the English invasion. By April 1736 he had confirmed 630 Spanish and 143 slaves and free blacks. He rallied the morale of the populace during the thirty-seven day siege by the forces of General James Edward Oglethorpe from the new English colony of Georgia. In 1745 he left for a new assignment in Yucatan. His successor did not arrive until nine years later and then remained only ten months.

The bishop of Santiago de Cuba himself, Pedro Augustín Morell, paid Florida an unplanned visit in November 1762. When the British captured Havana they sent Morell as a prisoner to Charleston, making him the first bishop to enter one of the original thirteen colonies. In early December he was sent to Saint Augustine, where he made a formal visitation of the parish and the few remaining towns of Christian Indians. Between December 29 and April 11 he confirmed 693 persons, after which he returned to Cuba.

An opportunity arose in 1715 to restore some of the missions, but the Spanish in Florida were too weak to rise to the challenge. Caciques from fifty villages speaking for some 15,000 Yamassees, Lower Creeks, and Apalachees, when their alliance with the English collapsed, came to Saint Augustine seeking friendship and protection. Within four years only nine new friars came out, and ten more in 1722, but all but two soon left for Cuba. By 1724 there were Franciscans in only eleven of the 161 Indian villages ready to receive them. In 1738 there were twenty-five priests serving in Florida, and in 1759 only ten. More and more of the scanty funds available went to strengthen military defenses.

Most of the Franciscans who remained in Florida were Creoles, creating a situation unique in Spanish America. Normally the colonial born and trained friars had played only a secondary role in the missions, as was true of the colonials in the government. In 1707 when nine new Spanish friars arrived, three of them complained to the king that Spaniards were being discriminated against by being assigned to unimportant and undesirable posts. Two years later the king and the Franciscan commissary general sent ten more members of that order to Florida, but only two of them remained by 1776. The Florida field was going to the Creoles by default. Governor Antonio de Benavides, himself a Spaniard, supported the Creoles, but King Philip V considered this a potentially anti-Spanish political situation and ordered the governor and the Creoles to accept the lead of the priests from Spain. In 1732, when nine Spanish friars arrived, the colonials defiantly assigned them to difficult situations without preparation in the language or briefing them in the ways of the Indians. In 1735 seven of the Spaniards accused Governor Francisco del Moral Sánchez of collusion with the Creoles to persecute the friars. The crisis came in September when the Creoles named one of their number head of the order in Florida and the Spaniards withdrew to name a rival superior. Only the timely arrival of auxiliary Bishop Francisco de San Buenaventura y Tejada prevented the governor from seizing the Spaniards.

When the bishop of Cuba and a Franciscan officer from New Spain favored the Creoles, King Philip objected; he removed the governor in 1737. The new governor, Manuel de Montiano succeeded in inducing the Creoles and the Spaniards to work together. He proposed to consolidate the Indians loyal to Spain and to teach them Spanish as there were too many Indian dialects to learn. The bishop approved, but royal authority forbade it.

The Franciscans became involved in another feud in which they did not come out so well. There had always been some friction between them and the secular priests who ministered to the spiritual needs of Spaniards and other Catholics in Saint Augustine and other white settlements. When the Indians withdrew to the vicinity of Saint Augustine and the mission field shrank to little more than the environs of that city, the missionaries declined in number and importance. In 1746 the crown awarded jurisdiction over all Christians residing in Saint Augustine to the pastor and assistant pastor of the parish church. By 1759 only ten Franciscans remained. One of their last and lasting achievements was the construction of a new monastery begun in 1724 and occupied first in 1739. It was a coquina rock structure 168 feet by eighteen feet, and eighteen feet high, located at the south end of town overlooking the Matanzas River. It had twenty-five cells, more than enough at the time, but by 1763 it ceased to have any religious role in the city.

There are practically no remains of Florida's missions today. Only in this generation have serious efforts been made to locate the sites and to learn something of their history. Constructed entirely of wood, the structures rotted away when they did not burn. The walls were built of upright posts set in the ground and interlaced with horizontal poles or wattles. When filled with a heavy coating of red clay, they became substantial and could be plastered with white lime. From this came the "wattle and daub" name given to this technique, widely used in construction of Indian buildings. The roofs were framed with heavy timbers nailed together with hand-wrought spikes. The palm or palmetto thatched roofs made the structures very vulnerable to fire. The packed red clay floors were often well preserved where they had been fire-baked during the burning of the structure. More substantial structures have often been assumed to be mission buildings, but there had been neither money nor building materials on the Florida frontier for anything more substantial and permanent.

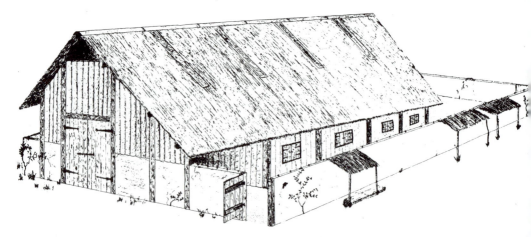

Conjectural reconstruction of the mission building
San Juan de Aspalaga in 17th century Apalachee

5.

International Rivalry in Florida, 1670-1763

The Spaniards had great difficulty holding their frontier posts in Florida when they had only the natural environment and the Indians to contend with. The appearance of English settlements on the south Atlantic coast and French settlements in the lower Mississippi River valley in the latter part of the seventeenth century brought new pressures that ultimately made the position of the Spaniards untenable. The English attempts at settlement on Roanoke Island in 1585 and 1587 had worried the Spaniards. The planting of a colony at Jamestown early in the century frightened them, but other than sending reconnaissance expeditions in 1609 and 1611 they made no move to stop it, perhaps hoping that it too might fail. The founding of Charleston (first known as Charles Town) in 1670 portended disaster. In a very short time English traders had pushed westward to the Apalachicola River country and soon to the Mississippi River to lure away the Indians, whose allegiance the Spaniards had so carefully cultivated. English raiders by land and pirates by sea soon drove the Spanish mission frontier on the Atlantic coast down to the present-day northern boundary of Florida and posed a serious threat to those in Timucua and Apalachee.

Two years before the English established a base at Charleston, Robert Searles, alias Davis, made a spectacular raid on Saint Augustine. On May 9, he used two Spanish ships and crews that he had captured to lull the suspicions of the harbor patrol and dropped anchor off the bar. Then under the cover of night when the tide was high he slipped into the harbor and attacked the sleeping town, killing sixty people and plundering the buildings. Since he had brought no artillery he made no effort to take the fort, but the garrison was too small to drive him from the town. The raider had killed nearly a fourth of the resident population and proved once more the inadequacy of the Spanish defenses.

The Searles attack revived again proposals to construct a powerful stone fort and provide arms and men to defend Saint Augustine, which was in effect Spanish Florida. If the resolution to do something about defenses required any reinforcement, it came with

Restoration of the wall and moat, the
Castillo de San Marcos, Saint Augustine

the settlement at Charleston. Ground-breaking ceremonies on October 2, 1672, inaugurated construction. Though several decades were required to complete the fortress and all of its supporting works, the basic structure was complete in fifteen years, and it was in a state of sufficient readiness in the early 1700s to enable the defenders to repel formidable invaders.

There had been nine wooden forts at Saint Augustine, six of them on approximately the site chosen for the stone fort. The new structure practically surrounded the old–the last of the wooden forts—which remained for another three years before being torn down. Standing on the west bank of the Matanzas River opposite the north end of Anastasia Island, the fort dominated the northern entrance to the harbor as well as the only feasible approach by land-from the north. The general features of the design are obvious to an observer today. The rectangular parade ground is made of solid masonry walls on every side with a four-sided bastion at each corner, each with a name: San Augustin on the southeast overlooking the town and the harbor; San Carlos, the northeast; San Pablo, the northwest; and San Pedro on the southwest. A wide moat filled with sea water surrounded the fort. Two doorways, one facing north and the main entrance south toward the town, with a drawbridge where an ordinary wooden bridge now stands, provided access. The main entrance was protected by a triangular outer fortification on the banks of the moat, which was also of masonry construction. The entire population, some 1,500 civilians and soldiers, could find refuge behind its twelve-foot thick walls. A deep well in one corner provided drinking water, and a latrine flushed by the ebb and flow of the tide made it relatively self-sufficient when a supply of non perishable food was on hand.

Work on the project, a mammoth undertaking for the time and

Coquina quarry, Anastasia Island

circumstances, did not proceed evenly or smoothly. Labor, skilled and unskilled, was scarce. Skilled stone masons came mostly from Havana. For unskilled labor, large numbers of Indians were requisitioned from as far away as Apalachee. Black slaves proved the more useful as many of them became skilled in cutting and laying the stone. Food supply for such a large number of workers, storms, irregularity of the payment of the yearly subsidy of 10,000 ducats to carry on the work, and quarrels over matters of policy and procedure often delayed the work. Coquina stone was the principal building material, but substantial amounts of rough-hewn timber and lumber went into the structure too. The stone came from a quarry on Anastasia Island about a mile away, where it was sawed into blocks of the proper size and shape. From the quarry it had to be carried to barges for crossing the river, then loaded onto carts and hauled to the building site; all this required tremendous effort by a large number of workers.

The Spaniards did not neglect diplomatic efforts to stay the southward advance of the English. In 1670 they accepted a line running due east from a point in Port Royal Sound near the site of old Santa Elena and at the same time recognized British ownership of Jamaica. The English, in disregard of the line, placed the southern limit of the Carolina grant at 29° north latitude, or about at Saint Augustine. The Spanish were not disposed to yield but could do little about it. They did establish a garrison on Saint Catherines Island in an effort to hold Indian support and stay the English advance. In 1686 Tomás de León led an attack that destroyed Port Royal and sacked plantations en route, but a hurricane crippled his fleet before he reached his real objective at Charleston. Guale could not be held and the Saint Marys River was tacitly accepted as the boundary.

While the Spaniards at Saint Augustine were bringing all of their resources to bear to meet the English threat on the Atlantic coast, a new challenge was shaping up on the Gulf coast. The French, who had been working their way slowly up the Saint Lawrence, through the Great Lakes, and down the Mississippi toward the Gulf of Mexico, reached the mouth of the Arkansas River in 1673. In 1682 Robert Cavelier Sieur de La Salle finally made his way to the mouth of the Mississippi and claimed the valley for France. He proposed to his sovereign that the land be colonized, that the Indians be used to halt the northward thrust of the Spanish, and perhaps held out the prospect of moving into Mexico. Three years later he came back with 300 colonists but missed the mouth of the big river with its confusion of channels and ended up at Matagorda Bay on the coast of Texas, where he built Fort Saint Louis. Two years later he died at the hands of an assassin, and Indians wiped out the entire colony.

The Spanish knew the French were in the vicinity but they knew not where. Between 1685 and 1690 they sent out no less than eleven expeditions to search for them and in the process rediscovered Pensacola Bay and proposed that a settlement be established there. The fourth in the series of searching parties, a naval expedition from Vera Cruz, scoured the region from Tampico to Pensacola but missed the site of the French settlement when they ignored the significance of a stranded French vessel in Matagorda Bay. When they were almost ready to write off the suspected settlement as a bad dream, relics turned up in the hands of Indians. This led to renewed efforts to locate it and pointed the way up a creek about five miles from the bay, where the site was discovered in 1689. Induced by the belief that the Indians on the Texas coast might be Christianized, the Spaniards founded the mission of San Francisco de Texas, which they soon abandoned when the natives proved less tractable than was hoped.

Finding the remains and discovering the fate of the La Salle colony did not remove the French threat to the Spanish lands. In 1689 Captain Andrés de Pez, the leader of three of the search voyages, urged the viceroy of New Spain to fortify and hold Pensacola, pronounced by Juan Jordan de Reina, a well-known pilot, in 1686 to be "the best bay I have ever seen in my life." The viceroy sent Pez to Spain to present his ideas and recommended that the defenses at Saint Augustine be made unusable by sinking ships in the channels. The king ordered the viceroy Conde de Galve to make a thorough investigation before he made a final decision. Galve sent two vessels from Vera Cruz, commanded by Pez, now an admiral, in April 1693. Dr. Carlos de Sigüenza y Gongora, a well known mathematician and geographer of New Spain, accompanied Pez and joined his voice to those urging the settlement.

The king responded on June 13, 1694, with an order to the viceroy to begin the occupation of Pensacola Bay, but when Galve died in 1696 before he could get the expedition under way, there was no one sufficiently interested to keep the project alive. Again the French provided the necessary spur to action when early in 1698 they were reported fitting out four ships for an expedition to the Gulf of Mexico. The ordinarily procrastinating Spaniards then literally sprang into action. The new viceroy, the Count of Montezuma, received a cedula dated April 19, 1698, ordering him to dispatch a Spanish expedition to occupy the bay immediately. At the same time, Martín de Arranguren Zavala, sent out from Cádiz to Havana to check on some overdue treasure ships, received orders to proceed from Havana to Vera Cruz to join and strengthen the expedition originating there. Another order directed Juan Jordan to go with Zavala to Havana, where he was to requisition men, weapons, and supplies, hurry to Pensacola, and hold it until Zavala should arrive.

Dr. Sigüenza and Andrés Arriola planned the expedition at Vera Cruz, gathering three ships and 357 men, some of them convicts and others pressed into service from the streets. Jordan reached Havana on October 13, acquired two small vessels, and recruited fifty men. Arriola departed from Vera Cruz on October 15 before Zavala arrived. Jordan left Havana on November 6 and reached Pensacola Bay on the seventeenth, four days ahead of the Vera Cruz expedition. With the latter came Jaime Franck, the best known military engineer in the Spanish New World, to lay out Fort San Carlos de Austria while the men busied themselves putting up palm-thatched huts and other buildings.

The Spaniards had moved barely in time. On January 26, 1699, the French expedition under Pierre le Moyne d'Iberville, which had been underway since October 24, arrived, and five ships carrying 200 men dropped anchor off Pensacola Bay. When Arriola refused them permission to enter the bay they sailed eastward a short distance before–to the great relief of the Spaniards–they sailed westward and on February 27, 1699, settled at Biloxi. They found the bay too shallow, however, and abandoned the site in 1702 to found Mobile on a bluff twenty-seven miles up the Mobile River. A flood swept away the fort and the town in 1711, and Mobile was relocated where the city stands today. The French, however, did not immediately give up their interest in a settlement on the east Gulf and never lost sight of the fact that Pensacola was the best site for it.

The Spanish position at Pensacola was more precarious than at Saint Augustine during its early days. Since volunteers for service and labor could not be found, convicts were often recruited as soldiers and laborers, a practice soon abandoned. The large number of convicts posed serious problems of discipline that required all of the energies of the regular troops to control. Anglophile Indians had burned all buildings outside the fort in 1707. The fort was reported rotting before it was finished. The location was considered bad by the governor of Pensacola, Gregorio de Salinas Varona, not to be confused with the governor of Florida, who proposed in 1712 that it be moved to Santa Rosa Island.

Fortunately for the isolated garrison, relations with the French at Mobile remained friendly for two decades. Supplies for the post usually came from New Spain, but uncertainties and delays frequently forced the Pensacolians to go to Mobile for food and other immediate needs, a service they were occasionally able also to render to the residents at Mobile. Efforts to produce food at the new settlement generally failed. The soil was too light and dry. There were some references to sheep in the earlier years and to cattle later, but not in significant numbers. In 1761 the local governor, Don Miguel Román de Castilla, reported three plantations in the area, each with fifteen or more cattle, but Indians destroyed all three plantations that year. Indians, in fact, remained hostile much of the time and cut the Spaniards off from the interior. The only export from Pensacola consisted of ship masts cut from the yellow pine forests. There were 220 places in the garrison, but in 1702 it consisted of 150 infantrymen, twenty artillerymen, and fifty convicts for labor. A year later the roster fell to 193, and in 1708 to

A view of Pensacola engraved for the Universal Magazine, *1747*

only a little over a hundred. In 1703 three Franciscan chaplains are reported but ten years later only one, a Frenchman whose knowledge of Spanish was limited. Since it was largely a military establishment, women were scarce; only about a hundred resided there in 1760.

When Louis XIV of France claimed the throne of Spain for his Bourbon grandson, the prospect of a close family alliance between France and Spain in America frightened the English settlers, particularly those in Carolina. English America would be facing the family alliance on three sides, and Carolinians would bear the brunt of the pressure on the southern frontier. Indeed, the governor of French Louisiana had a plan for an allied offensive with Saint Augustine as a base from which to push the English out of Carolina if not off the continent. He expected as a reward for French assistance that Pensacola would become French.

The Carolinians overestimated the French threat, perhaps because England had been unable to drive them out of North America in King William's War in 1689. They looked upon the Spanish as the immediate problem, though they felt that Spain would ultimately lose in North America unless something like the much feared French alliance strengthened her. James Moore, who became governor of Carolina in September 1700, understood the danger. He felt that England must destroy Saint Augustine before it could become an allied base. When the War of Spanish Succession (Queen Anne's War in America) broke out in 1702, the legislature authorized an expedition and placed the governor in charge, with Colonel Robert Daniel second in command. The two leaders assembled a force at Port Royal and set out in fourteen boats mostly commandeered from private sources. Colonel Daniel was to sail up the Saint Johns to a point opposite the city and march overland to the attack, while Governor Moore led the attack from the sea.

The Carolinians had made the mistake of underestimating the Spanish capacity for defense. They knew that Spain had abandoned Santa Elena almost a century before the English arrived. The missions north of Amelia Island had been abandoned recently. The Spanish garrisons on Amelia, Saint George, and Cumberland islands were known to be too small to be of any consequence in a military contest. Englishmen from Drake to Searles had overrun Saint Augustine almost at will. Only the new stone fort had not yet been tested. Otherwise the town was not much changed.

A Chatot Indian woman who learned of the projected raid from some Apalachicola Indians brought the information to Governor Joseph de Zuñiga y Cerda at Saint Augustine, but that official doubted that he could count upon the Indians to fight off the invasion. He suspected rather that many of them would join the English.

The governor accordingly decided that the entire population-Indian, white, Negro, civilian, and military-should take refuge in the fort when the enemy arrived. The English met no opposition as they approached. Colonel Daniel marched into the city on November 6, and Governor Moore arrived by sea two days later. Neither Daniel nor Moore had guns heavy enough to reduce the fort, but Zuñiga lacked the force to drive off the invaders, who laid siege to the fortress. Meanwhile Moore sent to Jamaica for heavier cannons, and the Spaniards had already sent urgent pleas to Havana for assistance. When four Spanish warships appeared late in December and blocked Moore's escape by sea, he burned some of his small fleet, abandoned the remainder, burned what remained of Saint Augustine, marched overland to the mouth of the Saint Johns, embarked for Carolina, and was gone by December 30.

The invaders burned 118 homes, later appraised at 47,140 pesos, and lost only two men but had failed to achieve their objective. Instead of the estimated 2,000 pounds, the expedition had cost nearly 8,500. Actually it seems to have been assumed that captured property would pay the costs. The discredited Moore resigned the governorship.

Two years later, lured by the prospect of plunder and slaves he might secure, and by the opportunity to neutralize at least a portion of Florida and redeem his reputation, Moore set out to destroy the missions in Apalachee. This time, as described in the previous chapter, he was completely successful. His own estimate of the importance of his achievement is instructive. "Apalatchee," he reported, "is now reduced to that feeble and low condition that it can neither supply Saint Augustine with provisions nor disturb, damage, or frighten our Indians living between us and Apalatchee, and the French. In short, we have made Carolina as safe as the conquest of Apalatchee can make it."

Late in 1703 Moore set out with only fifty Carolina volunteers and some 1,500 Indians, mostly Yamassees, bent upon plunder and revenge. The invaders focused their attention on the concentration of Indian settlements in present-day Leon County where they failed only in taking San Luis de Talamali, which was protected by Fort San Luis and a small Spanish garrison. They met resistance only at La Concepción de Ayubale on January 25, 1704, where Father Angel de Miranda remained with the Indians to direct their efforts. Moore probably could not even if he wished to restrain the attacking Indians, who massacred Miranda and his Indian associates.

Captain Juan Ruíz Mexía came from San Luis with thirty Spanish soldiers and 400 Indians to drive Moore away, only to meet defeat and withdraw to the fort. Moore withdrew without attacking San Luis, but "Apalatchee" was indeed in ruins. In the next two years other raids by English-led Indians completed the ruin of the mission chain.

The Spanish did not abandon Apalachee. In fact, in 1716 the *Junta de Guerra de Indias* advocated the removal of the Florida capital to that area where the land was fertile, food plentiful, and harbors broad and deep. Two years later they rebuilt San Marcos de Apalachee six miles up the Saint Marks River on a narrow headland where the junction with the Wakulla River makes a good harbor. Pirates had begun to make it a place of call to careen their ships and trade with the Indians. Governor Pablo de Hita Salazar had been so concerned for the safety of Apalachee that he had on his own authority constructed an inadequate fort there. The governor failed to get the hoped for authority and financial support. All effort was being concentrated on the fort at Saint Augustine at the time. Pirates captured it easily on March 22, 1682, carried away everything movable and useful, and burned it. The restored structure stood to the transfer of flags in 1763, and Governor Manuel de Montiano had earlier endeavored to win the allegiance of the Indians by transforming the fort into a well-stocked trading post. Nor were Spanish settlers interested in proposals to restore the granary of Saint Augustine by settling there.

Shifting international alliances altered circumstances at Pensacola in 1719 when Austria, Holland, France, and England went to war against Spain in the War of the Quadruple Alliance (1719-1721). On April 13, the French learned that war had been declared the previous December. Jean Baptiste Le Moyne and Sieur Bienville, a brother of de Bienville, who had founded New Orleans in 1718 about 100 miles up the Mississippi River, and was now its governor, quickly organized an expedition which took Pensacola authorities by surprise and compelled them to surrender on May 14. Terms of capitulation provided that the French transport the Spaniards to Havana. The governor of Cuba ordered the vessels seized and the Frenchmen arrested as prisoners of war, and hastily made preparations to recover the captured city. Using the two French ships as decoys, the Spanish achieved unsuspected entrance to Pensacola Bay on August 6, and the French surrendered two days later. The restored governor of Pensacola, Don Juan Pedro Metamoras, erected a battery on Point Sigüenza on the western end of Santa Rosa Island to command the entrance from the sea, and a small stockade to guard Fort San Carlos from the land side where attackers had used the sand dunes for cover.

On September 18, a French fleet under Commodore de Champmeslin arrived at Mobile and Bienville seized the opportunity to retake Pensacola on September 18. This time Bienville sent the captive Spaniards to Havana to exchange for the Frenchmen taken there in August; among the prisoners was his brother Chateaugue. Champmeslin burned all except three buildings, which he saved for a guard he was leaving there. He also destroyed Fort San Carlos and the battery at Point Siguenza, sparing only the powder magazine a half mile away. Peace came the next year, but the final disposition of Pensacola was delayed. The French authorities still hoped to acquire the excellent harbor, but Bienville had already decided that the importance of the site was exaggerated and that France's future lay not in the Gulf of Mexico but in the Mississippi valley, to which the east channel of the Mississippi River was also proving to be a usable entrance from the Gulf. The Spanish negotiators clung tenaciously to their determination to retain the base. The contending powers signed a treaty on March 27, 1721, that provided for the return of Pensacola to Spain, but the French garrison did not retire until late 1722.

During the hostilities Bienville had been dismayed by orders to occupy Saint Josephs Bay, for he realized that it was useless for the defense of Louisiana and sure to stir the Spanish to hostile action. Fort Crevecoeur was a stockade with four bastions and a garrison of fifty men. The French had hardly completed the structure when they abandoned it. A Spanish force then moved into the fort, but after the peace treaty they dismantled the buildings and used the timber to help rebuild Pensacola.

Don Alejandro Wauchopee took possession of Pensacola and set about rebuilding the town and the fort. He abandoned the site of Fort San Carlos, which had been undercut by water and was dominated by sand dunes, and constructed a new fortification at Point Sigüenza for 150 men and a new town on Santa Rosa Island. When a hurricane destroyed the settlement in 1752, the soldiers and the settlers moved back to the mainland where early in 1757, a new governor, Don Miguel Román de Castilla y Lugo, reported the Santa Rosa garrison now on the mainland was without a stockade and that an Indian attack was reported as coming. Present were 150 troops and twenty-five civilians. The Indian attack did not materialize, however, and there were three years of comparative peace that came to an end with a surprise attack on the nearby town of Punta Rosa in 1761. A disastrous hurricane had seriously damaged the place on August 12, 1760. When Pensacola's new governor, Don Diego Ortiz Parilla, arrived on October 21, 1761, he reported that Punta Rosa was a shambles, with Indians forcing the residents to remain under the protection of the guns. Small wonder that the British were not much impressed with what they found there when they took over in 1763.

The settlement of Georgia by the English in the "debatable land" between Florida and Carolina in 1733 posed a new threat on the Atlantic coast. The interlopers had earlier built Fort King George, a wooden blockhouse on the bank of the Altamaha River near Darien. King Philip V and the Council of the Indies protested and ordered Cuba and New Spain to prepare for war. The blockhouse burned in 1725 and the garrison withdrew to Port Royal. The English rebuilt, then abandoned, the fort in the fall of 1727, but it was no more than a temporary reprieve for the hard-pressed Spaniards. On March 9 of the same year Colonel John Palmer, who had been a member of Governor Moore's expedition in 1702, marched into Florida and dealt the Yamassee Indians at Nombre Dios a smashing defeat almost under the guns of the fortress at Saint Augustine. When Governor Benavides would not come out and fight, Palmer marched back to Carolina. The Indians found it difficult to understand that the governor could not muster a sufficient force to take the offensive. The Yamassees had gone away with the English early in the century but had rebelled in 1715 and threatened Charleston before they were stopped. When the English no longer needed them as allies they had abandoned their efforts to cultivate their friendship and exhibited instead the disregard of Indian rights and sensibilities more commonly found on the English frontier. The Yamassees returned to Florida in great numbers; it seems possible that the Spaniards might have won their active allegiance but they lacked the resources to capitalize on the situation.

Governor Benavides rightly viewed Georgia as primarily a military project aimed at Saint Augustine and possibly after that at New Spain. His successor, Moral Sánchez, observing that Oglethorpe had won over the Indians by a return to previous English methods of dealing with them, abandoned all hope of help in that area. Instead he proposed that Spain settle Canary Islanders in Apalachee to hold Florida. In 1734, to avoid other attacks like that of Colonel Daniel in 1702, he constructed Fort San Francisco de Pupa and Fort Picolata on opposite banks of the Saint Johns where the trail to Apalachee crossed the river. When the governor protested the weaknesses of the defenses to his superiors, the Council of the Indies sent Cuban engineer Antonio de Arredondo to survey the establishment. He found only 297 soldiers, of whom eighty were too old or too sick to be active. In his alarm at what he discovered, he secured the transfer of 100 Cuban Grenadiers to Saint Augustine. He also recommended eighty small boats and 400 seamen to operate in the waters around the capital. He thought the garrison should be increased to 800 men and that a determined effort should be made to cultivate the favor of the Indians with rum, muskets, tobacco, and cloth. For an attack on Georgia he judged that 1,500 regulars would be needed. Such an expedition was actually being prepared in Cuba in 1738, only to be abandoned when almost ready to embark. Instead, Governor Güemes of Cuba sent 400 troops and eighty-two laborers to Saint Augustine to strengthen its defenses. Among the men were two military engineers, a master bricklayer, and six Negro stonemasons. Twelve new iron cannons and 6,000 pesos to build six new barracks and four patrol boats completed the list of additions.

General James Edward Oglethorpe wasted little time before he moved against Florida. Once again an international conflict with only a remote connection with Florida provided the provocation. In 1739 the English precipitated the War of Jenkins' Ear in the doubtful defense of a smuggler by that name who claimed his ear had been cut off by Spaniards when his vessel was overhauled on the Florida coast some nine years earlier. It soon became a part of the European war of Austrian succession (King George's War in America), which lasted until 1748 with no important changes in the position of the powers in the New World. The Georgia governor courted and egged on the Indians and prepared Fort Fredericka on Saint Simons Island. In January 1740 he sailed up the Saint Johns and took the small forts Pupa and Picolata. Oglethorpe, in planning to attack Saint Augustine, also gained control of the sea and by May 1 had 1,600 men on seven warships carrying forty dugouts for landing operations. On May 12, the invaders took Fort San Diego eighteen miles north of Saint Augustine on the coast. Four days later they reached Moosa, a fortified black village one mile north of the city, where they seized thirty horses in the deserted settlement. Discouraged by incessant rains and dysentery, the Georgians withdrew to recover and regroup, but were back at San Diego by the end of May and prepared to encircle the city on June 6. A week later the siege of the fortress began in earnest. Again the English guns proved to be too light for the task of reducing the fort. The Spanish defenders were better prepared than at any previous time. There were 613 men in Saint Augustine and another eighty in Apalachee. They could not match Oglethorpe in manpower, but at midnight on June 25 a Spanish force of 300 moved out of the fort and surprised their old enemy, Colonel John Palmer, who was camped at Moosa, and killed eighty-seven whites and thirty-five Indians. In July when seven heavily armed Spanish warships appeared, Oglethorpe abandoned the siege and returned to Savannah.

For a time the Spanish went on the offensive. Their privateers plied the coast and brought thirty English prizes to Saint Augustine in 1741, and plundered plantations on the Georgia and Carolina coast. In the next year they staged an abortive effort to capture Fredericka, hoping to go on to Savannah and Charleston. Governor Montiano led a formidable armada of fifty vessels with 1,800 soldiers and 1,000 seamen. They reached Saint Simons in early July and lost the Battle of Bloody Marsh, defeated more by the difficulty of negotiating the maze of channels and inlets on the coast than by the enemy. Then the Spanish, surprisingly, since they clearly outnumbered the Georgians, withdrew to Saint Augustine, moved, no doubt, by fear that the superior British naval force might trap them there by cutting their communications with Saint Augustine and Havana.

Oglethorpe returned to Saint Augustine in September 1742 with a dozen warships. The Spanish drove him off repeatedly on September 8, and two days later he moved down to Matanzas Inlet for a try at entering there. On the following day a storm scattered his fleet, and he again abandoned the effort to take the city.

For the next twenty years Saint Augustine was quiet and secure. Montiano and his successors strengthened the defenses. They were at their strongest in 1763, getting a garrison of regular troops on two-year tours of duty instead of retirees and exiles. Faith in the defensive power of the Castillo de San Marcos had proved well founded. Ironically, however, the fate of Spanish Florida was not to be determined by what happened at Saint Augustine.

In other respects, too, the Spaniards seemed to be making progress in the last generation of the first Spanish period. There was always a distinctly military atmosphere in Saint Augustine, but it was more than an armed camp. Soldiers brought their families and became permanent residents, and other civilian residents helped to create a normal domestic and commercial life. Though women were relatively few in number, there were enough families from Spanish provinces to give a distinctive character to the population and society, and mixed marriages with Indians were also less

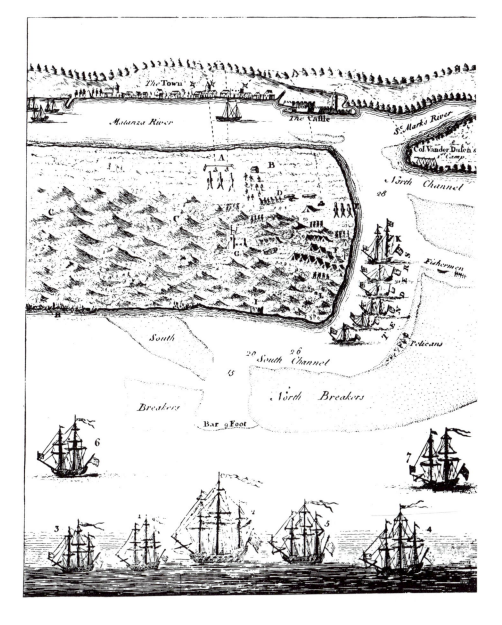

"A View of the Town and Castle of St. Augustine and the English Camp Before it." Engraved by Thomas Silver, June 20, 1740.

frequent than might be expected. The Creole population was becoming increasingly important in all aspects of the local life. They could aspire to any office except the governorship and frequently made careers for themselves in the military and civil service, commercial pursuits, and ranching, which gained considerable importance.

The first buildings had been made of wood with sharp-pitched roofs thatched with palm fronds in the Indian fashion. Then thick clay or tabby walls and finally coquina became the principal building material. Though coquina had been known for at least a century, it was not much used until the construction of the Castillo de San Marcos. Coquina was soft and porous until quarried, after which it became hard and strong. The principal difficulty was the quarrying and transportation, but by 1763 the walls of most public and private buildings were of the very durable stone. Buildings stood close together with doors opening directly onto the street. They had shuttered windows and balconies, really covered extensions of the second floor, over front doorways and windows. In the rear of the buildings were usually patios or gardens surrounded by coquina rock walls with arched openings onto the street. Solemn religious ceremonies with long processions and marching armed and uniformed soldiers provided the principal public spectacles.

Though never really successful there was always some effort to make the colony self-sufficient in food production. Plans to develop cochineal and indigo never were implemented, nor did farming, fruit growing, fishing, or silkmaking fare much better. The Indians in Apalachee provided an uncertain supply of corn and beans. There was a promising development of naval stores production of tar, pitch, resin, and turpentine, but it all ended in 1763. It was left to the English to demonstrate the possibilities of marketing forest products.

The Spanish had begun to alter their Indian policy to meet the English competition but may be said to have had no greater success than with the missions in the previous century. The governor never had the means to sustain the gift giving it required. There were not enough soldiers, missionaries, or traders for effective relations with the natives. Spanish trade goods could not compete with those of the French and English, both of whom were increasingly active and successful in the Indian trade which also meant Indian alliance. Governor Montiano had urged that a large trading post in Apalachee could be self-supporting, but the means to establish it were not forthcoming. The sphere of Spanish Indian influence shrank gradually from close to a thousand seeking Spanish aid and protection in 1726 to fewer than 400 in 1739; by 1743 the villages around Saint Augustine shrank from nine to four.

In 1763 after two centuries of settlement, Spanish Florida consisted of Saint Augustine, the garrison at Saint Marks, and the struggling settlement at Pensacola. Beyond the reach of the protecting forts at these centers, there was a no-man's-land inhabited largely by Seminole Indians, with English and French traders exercising

Governor's house at Saint Augustine in East Florida, November 1764

more influence than did the Spanish.

The Seven Years' War, the final phase of the century-long, worldwide, Anglo-French struggle for colonial and commercial supremacy, broke out two years earlier in 1754 in America as the French and Indian War. Florida figured scarcely at all in the war itself, but became a pawn in the game of international politics when the time came to make the peace. In the Treaty of Paris (1763) England took over Canada from the French, and Spain received France's trans-Mississippi lands (Louisiana). Spain also exchanged Florida, which now extended westward to the Mississippi River, for Havana, which had been captured by the English. England had emerged victorious over France in the New World, and the stage was set for what was to prove a brief rule in Florida.

6.

The British Floridas

The English, although they may not have been the first Europeans to visit Florida, were increasingly interested in the region from the time of its discovery. They finally achieved by diplomacy in 1763 what they had failed to gain by the efforts at conquest by Colonel James Moore and General James Edward Oglethorpe earlier in the same century.

Mercantilist England had previously preferred the sugar-producing West Indies islands, but now seized the opportunity to round out her possessions on the continent, adding Canada on the north and Florida on the south. The Floridas, and particularly the eastern portion, were soon on the way to becoming integral parts of English America. They were in most respects extensions of that imperial system in America, and, given more time for development, they might well have become the fourteenth and fifteenth colonies in the American Revolution and we might be referring to the "original fifteen colonies." As it was, England introduced changes in government and administration, land disposal, Indian relations, and economic activity that after two decades the returning Spaniards found inexpedient if not impossible to undo.

Lieutenant John Hedges received Saint Augustine from the Spanish, but soon turned the authority over to Major Francis Ogilvie, who governed the region until the civil governor arrived a year later. Lieutenant Augustin Prevost assumed British authority at Pensacola on August 6, 1763, and Major Robert Farmar took over for the British at Mobile and governed West Florida for a year.

The Spanish, who had abandoned San Marcos de Apalachee late in the French and Indian War, sent a small garrison there on August 3, 1763, to make the formal transfer to England. Captain Don Bentura Díaz did not complete his mission until February 20, 1764. Captain John Harries and a company of English troops arrived on November 8, 1763, but sailed away a week later. Meanwhile, the Spanish, not having planned a long stay, were barely able to subsist. Harries called attention to the geographical isolation of the post, which he felt should always have three or four months supplies on hand, and observed that the soldiers would be at the mercy of some 500 hostile Indians. The English accepted this assessment and abandoned the fort.

The Spaniards departed from Florida almost to a man. Dependent as they were upon the financial support of the government, perhaps they could see little other chance of economic survival. With them also went the small remnant of the aboriginal Indians. The Seminoles had not yet arrived in full force. The British may be said to have had a more free hand to develop Florida than the Spaniards had found two and a half centuries earlier.

The smallness of the Spanish achievement in Florida is difficult to realize. In 1763 a Spanish census at Saint Augustine showed 3,046 persons. The settlement, less than a mile long and a quarter of a mile deep, was a mere beachhead restricted to a narrow strip of habitable land with perhaps 300 houses. Conspicuously absent were the activities of the Franciscans that a century earlier had been so much a part of the scene at Saint Augustine. The old Indian church near the city became a military hospital after 1770. The Spanish hospital became a courthouse and jail. The bishop's home and the Franciscan convent also became public buildings.

At Pensacola were about 100 huts and the fort, and the only cultivated land a few neglected gardens. There were no cattle but an abundance of game and fish. The total population was under 800, of whom only slightly more than 100 were civilians, another hundred convicts, and a similar number of Indians. At Mobile were 350 Frenchmen who, unlike the Spaniards at Pensacola and Saint Augustine, elected to remain there after the exchange of flags. The few residents at Biloxi did not constitute a settlement.

While Major Ogilvie was still in command of East Florida affairs at Saint Augustine, Don Juan Elixio de la Puente, probably the wealthiest Spaniard in the city, returned as agent of the king to dispose of all Spanish goods and properties remaining in Florida. He also brought along proxies to sell properties for former Spanish residents who had not been able to find buyers before their departure. Puente became involved in two important controversies. When he found that the treaty ceding Florida to the British did not make clear the status of the Florida Keys, he maintained that they had always been considered a part of Cuba. He urged his superiors to support his claims, pointing out the strategic importance of the chain of islands, but the British claim was never contested.

The departing Spaniards had been given eighteen months in which to dispose of their property, but buyers were few. The soldiers in the English garrison lacked the money, and others expected land grants to be free to settlers. The only other Britishers present were agents of trading companies and a few merchants. Puente succeeded in disposing of 110 properties for merchandise, slaves, and money, and transferred another 185 to Jesse Fish just before the time limit expired. Fish, an agent of the Walton Exporting Company of New York, made no down payment but entered into an agreement to sell the properties when the market improved and turn the proceeds over to the original owners. Consequently, English officials, including Governor James Grant, were frustrated to find Fish

*General James Grant of Ballindalloch,
Governor of East Florida. Engraving
by I. Kay, 1798.*

claiming all the properties they sought to use. The British government failed to approve all the transactions, but Fish was still in possession of much of the property when the Spanish returned in 1784, nor did he then lose any of it.

The British reorganized their American possessions in a proclamation dated October 7, 1763, that, among other things, created East Florida and West Florida. That portion of the new province from the Gulf of Mexico northward to the 31° latitude between the Mississippi River and the Chattahoochee River and down the Chattahoochee and the Apalachicola to the Gulf became West Florida. A year later the northern line was pushed up to the mouth of the Yazoo River and eastward to the Chattahoochee, or to about 32°28'. The northern boundary of East Florida was set at a line directly eastward from the confluence of the Chattahoochee and the Flint to the headwaters of the Saint Marys River and down that stream to the Atlantic Ocean.

James Grant, a leading citizen of South Carolina with wide experience in Indian and military affairs, came to his assignment as governor of East Florida at the end of August 1764, but postponed his inauguration until the end of October. He immediately constituted the Royal Council and thereby started the colony on its way toward a new experience in representative government. Grant was able to attract men of considerable reputation and some wealth, for he could offer land and offices. Prominent among the new officials were Chief Justice James Moultrie, who had been attorney general in South Carolina, and his brother John, a man of considerable wealth destined to become the colony's best known planter and as lieutenant governor to preside over the government for three years after Governor Grant's departure. John Stuart, also of Charleston, was the superintendent for Indian affairs and surveyor of customs for the southern district. James Box, the attorney general, had been a lawyer in Savannah. Robert Catherwood, a physician, was also surgeon general of the military hospital at Saint

Augustine.   John Ainslie and John Holmes were also Charlesto-
nians.   Grant proved to be an able and relatively popular governor
and remained at the head of the administration until the summer
of 1771 when he inherited the family estate and went home to preside over it.

Governor Grant gave immediate attention to Indian afairs, well
aware from experience that the Indians might hold the balance of
power among the contenders for dominion in the region.   He favored conferences to settle differences and the distribution of gifts
to court their favor.   Saint Augustine seldom had less than fifty
Indians to entertain.   Grant did not oppose the sale of guns and
ammunition, and on occasion rum, but he attempted to control the
practices of traders by licensing them. The policy kept the Indians
loyal during the American Revolution and the returning Spaniards
in 1784 found it necessary to adopt and continue it.   In November
1765 the govemor and superintendent John Stuart met the Indians
in a conference at Picolata on the Saint Johns, where they agreed
that whites might settle east of that river and up to the Saint Marys,
the interior being left to the Indians.

West Florida was less fortunate in its first political leadership.
Governor George Johnstone arrived at Pensacola, the capital, on
October 31, 1764, bringing a reputation for controversy, quarrel-
ing, and dueling.   He found there little more than a military establishment and a few people who made a business of serving and supplying it.   His chief quarrel was that he was denied the control of
the military command.   When orders for his recall, dated February
19, 1767, arrived in Pensacola, he had already departed on a six-
month leave of absence. Johnstone also attempted to deal with the
Indian problem.   In spite of his reputation for discord and the small
population in West Florida, Johnstone had called an assembly to
meet on November 3, 1766, with Campbell Town and Mobile sending representatives to the Pensacola sessions. The assembly failed
in its short life to develop the independence exhibited at Saint Augustine or to offer any such opposition to the royal government as it
did in the older English colonies in America.

Lieutenant Governor Montfort Browne took over at Pensacola
when Johnstone departed.   When Governor John Eliot arrived on
April 2, 1769, he found Browne under attack, charged with supplying his family and slaves from stores set aside for the Indians. Eliot
instituted an investigation of his accounts, but on May 2, before it
was completed, the governor committed suicide and Browne resumed
the governorship and purged the administration of his enemies. Elias
Dumford, who Browne considered a friend and ally, sailed to England with an official account of the events.   To Browne's consternation his friend returned with a commission to replace him as lieutenant governor, with orders for recall and a further examination of
his administration. The confusion ended on August 10, 1770, when
Governor Peter Chester arrived to take the office which he held
until the end of the British period.

The British Floridas were in one important respect much like

Spanish Florida had been. Funds for use in treating with the Indi-ans, like those to pay for the civil and military establishment, came from an annual subsidy provided by the mother country. Only Geor-gia of the other English American colonies had enjoyed such sup-port. Like Georgia, the Floridas were military outposts, bases from which to watch for French or Spanish efforts to recover lost terri-tory. In 1764 the East Florida subsidy was £5,700, of which £2,700 was for salaries, £1,500 for the Indian trade, £1000 for unforeseen contingencies, and £500 to encourage the culture of silks, wines, and other tropical products. The subsidy for West Florida was the same but allocated somewhat differently; Georgia still received aid in the sum of £4,031/8/8. The appropriation for each of the Floridas provided for a schoolmaster and a clergyman.

The Anglican Church never became an important part of the English establishment in the Floridas. The bishop of London, in cooperation with the Society for the Propagation of the Gospel in Foreign Parts, licensed only nine clergymen for work in the two provinces. Other unlicensed ministers and schoolmasters at times conducted Anglican church services. The Reverend John Forbes arrived at Saint Augustine on May 5, 1764, and served throughout the two decades of British occupation. He also became a member of the Governor's Council. Mobile and Pensacola never had a church building. The Reverend Samuel Hart left Mobile for Charleston after a year, the Reverend William Dawson left Pensacola for Colleton, South Carolina, and Michael Smith Clark, assigned to the

View of Pensacola and the Bay, 1781

garrison at San Marcos de Apalachee, settled in Jamaica instead and never saw Florida. Replacements at Pensacola and Mobile were irregular and unsatisfactory. Teachers were assigned to Pensacola and Apalachee but none to Mobile.

British authorities at home and in the colonies were anxious to attract settlers to occupy, defend, and eventually sustain the governments of the newly established provinces. Two types of land grants became available. The Privy Council in England made grants up to 20,000 acres to be settled at the owner's expense with white Protestant families, at least one person to each one hundred acres. The governor and council in the colonies granted family or head rights, one hundred acres for the head of the family and fifty acres for each additional person, white or black, and an option to buy up to one thousand additional acres at five shillings for each five acres. Claimants must clear three acres in fifty and pay a small quit rent. The Privy Council between 1764 and 1774 issued 242 grants in East Florida, only half of which were actually presented in Saint Augustine, and 1,440,000 acres were deeded to 114 persons. Holders of the large grants discouraged settlement by preempting large tracts and holding them for speculation rather than settling them with colonists.

Other obstacles made development slow if somewhat more self-sufficient than in the Spanish era. The Floridas had to compete with more favored areas for settlers. Immigrants came to East Florida by way of Charleston and Savannah, both of which were also relatively undeveloped and seeking settlers. In West Florida the lands along the Mississippi River were more attractive and the isolated Pensacola area was largely neglected. Governor Johnstone hoped to attract Frenchmen who might not like Spanish rule and also unsuccessfuly wooed German and Swiss settlers from the New Orleans area. Settlements on the British side of the Mississippi River could scarcely be considered a part of the colony. Overland travel to the capital at Pensacola was next to impossible, and the long way around by water was through Spanish New Orleans.

The necessity for making personal applications for grants at the capital both for survey and for completing the process of land acquisition discouraged many. Bernard A. Romans, an assistant surveyor who left a valuable account of his Florida experience, warned that fees were excessive. He insisted also that certain basic capital was necessary to start an enterprise in the wilderness. He thought settlers might need from $400 to $2,500 in capital. Ignorant land agents of absentee proprietors defrauded unwary immigrants. Lack of roads limited settlement to areas accessible by water.

The council for West Florida took a step most unusual in a frontier community at its first meeting at Pensacola in November 1764 by planning for the orderly settlement of towns in the colony. They began by declaring void all titles purchased from the departing Spaniards and ordered surveyor Elias Dumford to present a plan for a town. After setting aside sections for public buildings, he proposed

Old Spanish Cathedral, Saint Augustine, prior to the fire of 1883

to divide the remainder into town building lots 80 feet by 160 feet and assign each a garden bordering on a small stream flowing by the north side of the settlement. Towns were also planned in similar fashion at Mobile, Campbell Town at the mouth of the Escambia River near Pensacola, and Manchac on the north bank of the Iberville River where it flows into the Mississippi.

Settlers did come to the Floridas, some on their own initiative, some as a result of larger projects. Though it was a frontier province, something like a hundred landed estates or plantations were established in East Florida between the Saint Marys River and New Smyrna and east of the Saint Johns River. Officials like Grant, the

Moultries, Turnbull, and Tonyn engaged in planting. Lieutenant Governor John Moultrie had twelve tracts totaling 14,300 acres, and he lived in the grand manner at "Bella Vista" on the Matanzas River near the capital. He also developed "Rosetta" on the Tomoka near present-day Daytona and in 1773 was cultivating several hundred acres with 180 slaves. He was undoubtedly the most active and versatile of the planters. Among his properties are mentioned rice barns, rice cleaning machines, dams for flooding 200 acres for rice, 150 acres cleared for indigo, some 25,000 trees boxed for turpentine on Woodcutter's Creek, a lime kiln, an orange grove, and equipment for sugar making and for experimenting with the making of wine and rum. Francis Philip Fatio, a Swiss from Berne who acquired land first in 1772, called his plantation up the Saint Johns "New Switzerland."

Denys Rolle attempted to establish an estate near present-day Palatka in 1764 with indentured laborers. When that effort failed he returned to England and brought to Florida forty-nine vagrants, beggars, and debtors from London. He returned to England in 1767 and sent several other shiploads of unfortunates to his estate, which he visited briefly on two other occasions. Only when he turned to slave labor was he at all successful, and then a dishonest agent stole all of the profits. By 1772, he claimed 80,000 acres on which he had spent £23,000. The East Florida Claims Commission awarded him £6,597 for the £19,886 he claimed as losses when the British departed.

A group of well placed British officials, including Dr. Andrew Turnbull, a London physician, as resident manager acquired adjoining 20,000 acre grants on which to establish a colony in East Florida. They expected to invest up to £9,000 and divide the property at the end of ten years. They hoped to realize the English dream of producing Mediterranean products in the New World. With the aid of Governor Grant and his administration they selected a site at Mosquito Inlet, to which they gave the name New Smyrna in honor of Turnbull's wife, a native of Smyrna in Greece. The Lords of Trade in England also encouraged the project to produce tropical products by providing a sloop of war to transport colonists and a bounty of £4,500 on hemp, cotton, and indigo that might be produced.

The proprietors sought colonists in the Mediterranean already familiar with the production of the desired crops. Turnbull, who had spent some time in Greece, believed that some Greeks might migrate to escape Turkish rule, but he could get permission to bring away only 200 described as wild tribesmen still in revolt against their overlords. He received permission to recruit colonists in southern Italy but could bring away no silk manufacturers. He found 110 persons willing to accompany him. He was still short of the desired number of indentured servants when he learned of a three-year crop failure at British Minorca that had left many farmers destitute. He undertook to transport to America some 1,100 of these Spanish-speaking, Roman Catholic people, bringing along a priest and a monk to provide spiritual guidance for them. The introduction of Catholics into the colony was a breach of English law and had in it the seeds of trouble for the colony in America, but the Catholic Minorcans became a permanent part of the Florida population.

In June 1768 some 1,500 persons on board eight ships reached New Smyrna after a voyage of four months. Governor Grant had prepared for their arrival by placing provisions for four months at the site, erecting some large shelters for temporary living quarters, and by conditioning the Indians to receive them without protest. The colonists lived cooperatively until separate family homes could be erected. All did not go well with the oversized and unwieldy enterprise. The indentures resented the overseers, who were accustomed to working slaves. Foreign languages did not help. Greeks and Italians became mutinous but the Minorcans remained quiet.

By the spring of 1769 the colonists had cleared seven miles along present-day North Indian River and were growing—in addition to vegetables for their own use—corn, cotton, sugar cane, rice, and indigo. They could not immediately produce marketable products in sufficient quantity to satisfy the demands of the proprietors for returns on their investment, a story reminiscent of the beginnings of the Virginia Colony. Govemor Grant was giving as much aid as his authority and resources permitted but it was not enough, and neither the proprietors nor the London government proved willing to invest any more. Bernard Romans, a hostile critic, blamed Turnbull's management for the difficulties. The authorities discovered in 1774 that the Minorcans had been secretly in communication with Havana for several years. They meted out harsh punishments for what was interpreted as treason. Actually it seems to have been no more than a desperate attempt to maintain a purely religious contact with the bishop of Cuba. When Turnbull became involved in political controversy after Governor Grant's departure and lost the support of the administration at Saint Augustine, the fate of the New Smyrna enterprise was sealed.

The political factionalism that broke out in Lieutenant Governor John Moultrie's three-year administration had been brewing for some time. It took the form of a demand for an elected assembly which the popular Governor Grant had successfully resisted. When Colonel Patrick Tonyn arrived in March 1774 to take over the governorship, the explosive situation required tact and judgment which he did not possess. Though the factionalism appears to have been limited pretty much to the political leadership, it served to confirm Tonyn's suspicion of disloyalty, for which he had been instructed to be alert. He feuded with Chief Justice William Drayton until that official was recalled and returned to England. He placed Turnbull under arrest, accused him of plotting to defraud his partners at New Smyrna, and took up the cause of the Minorcans by releasing them from their indenture and inviting them to Saint Augustine. When the governor released him, Turnbull migrated to Charleston in 1781 to practice medicine. He received less than 1,000 pounds for his personal losses in Florida. He contributed services as manager rather than property to the New Smyrna project, and his partners received £12,144 for the £28,900 estate of 101,400 acres they claimed.

Saint Augustine was the economic as well as the political capital of East Florida in the British interlude as in the Spanish era. The small volume of trade showed a three-to-one balance of imports over exports as was normal in a new and developing area. In 1771 the Floridas imported goods from England in the value of £66,647, whereas three years later exports were valued at only £22,335.

Charleston was really the center of the East Florida trade. Ships in the trade were usually about thirty tons, but might be as little as ten or twelve, and were engaged only in the coastwise trade. Only an occasional larger vessel came directly from England. Charleston merchants acted as brokers for English and Florida interests. A summary of shipments from East Florida in the years 1766-1768 lists principally products of field and forest. Among them were pine boards and timber, oak staves, mahogany, shingles, tar, turpentine, indigo, rice, deerskins, tanned leather, raw hides, calfskins, and also, interestingly enough, 65,000 oranges and two casks of orange juice.

There are no comparable records for the West Florida trade. The greater part of it was at Manchac on the Mississippi, and was irregular if not illegal, as there was no customs house there. Fewer farm products and more hides and furs than in East Florida appear in such records as exist. Names of traders that appear prominently were Panton Leslie and Company, which operated throughout the Floridas but had headquarters at Pensacola; Swanson and McGillivray at Mobile; and Swanson and Company at Manchac. The Indian trade probably accounted for the greater part of the volume of all three.

In February 1781, Governor Tonyn saw fit to issue a writ for the election of an assembly, which met on March 27 and sat until November 12. By that time the opposition leaders had been discredited, the number of loyalist refugees in the colony had increased, Charleston and Savannah were in British hands, and there was no immediate threat of invasion. In fact, all but six of the nineteen persons elected had come to Florida since the beginning of the Revolution. The assembly met again the following year, but everything else was so overshadowed by the American War for Independence that it never played the customary role of that representative body in an English colony.

Governor Tonyn need never have feared that the Floridas might join their sister colonies to the north in the struggle for independence. They were too new, too small and undeveloped, and too dependent upon the mother country. Differences over trade and taxes had not developed. There was little trade, and England was paying the costs of the government. Though West Florida fell to Spanish invaders, East Florida was at no time an important theater of war. Governor Tonyn had other reasons to be apprehensive. Both colonies had to face the possibility that Spain or the United States might try to liberate them. Florida's supplies of all kinds often came from New York by way of Charleston and Savannah. Tonyn thought it might be necessary to attack the two colonies immediately to the north in order to make Florida secure and keep open the supply line. He also carefully cultivated the favor of the Indians and made it clear that loyalist refugees would find a welcome at Saint Augustine.

If Governor Tonyn felt secure from revolutionary influences and attack in East Florida, the same could not be said for the governor at Pensacola. A few loyalist refugees arrived from the very beginning of the conflict but not enough to provide much defense from attack. The threat came first from the north. In 1778, James Willing, a brother of the Robert Morris partner, Thomas Willing, and who had once operated a mercantile establishment at Natchez, led a band of marauders from Pittsburgh down the Mississippi River, plundering as he came. He found a welcome in Spanish New Orleans, but Spain showed no disposition to support the Americans in their fight for independence, and the British soon reoccupied Manchac, Baton Rouge, and Natchez. Spain did make preparations to take advantage of England's involvement in that conflict.

On January 1, 1777, the able and youthful Bernardo de Gálvez became governor of Louisiana. His father was viceroy of New Spain and an uncle was a minister of the Indies. Gálvez brought vigor and purpose to an administration not previously noted for those qualities. He sought the allegiance of the Indians with gifts, a not too difficult undertaking as the British had neglected Indian relations on the Mississippi. He courted the favor of the revolutionary Americans by offering them trade and refuge in his province. Meanwhile he worked at strengthening the military garrison by recruiting and training militia.

When Spain declared war on England on June 21, 1779, Gálvez, having been alerted that it was coming, was ready to move before the British in West Florida received the news. When he captured Natchez on October 5, he had taken all British settlements on the river and had made New Orleans more secure from any attack, British or American, that might come by way of the river. When Governor Chester built Fort George at Pensacola there were rumors that Brigadier General John Campbell, who had brought reinforcements in January 1779, was preparing a joint attack on New Orleans from Canada and Florida. It appears more likely that the British abandoned hope of holding the small settlements on the river and concentrated their efforts on the Gulf at Mobile and Pensacola.

Gálvez then turned his attention to the two principal British settlements. Largely by taking matters in his own hands, for the Captain General of Cuba had disagreed with him, he set out on January 28, 1780, with eleven ships and 745 men for an attack on Mobile. Slowed by a storm, the expedition did not reach its objective until February 10. He was able to move into the bay and land troops and cannons for a siege. Ten days later reinforcements, 567 strong, came from Cuba. Captain Elias Dumford, lieutenant governor of the province, was in command of the defenses. He had only 300 men, some black laborers and little food. After a brief fight the fort fell on March 14th.

Attacking Pensacola was a more serious matter. General Campbell had as many soldiers as Gálvez, many Indian allies, and a strong defensive position. With the prestige of the earlier success behind him, Gálvez was able to get more cooperation and assistance. He went to Havana and prepared an expedition of sixty-four warships and transports that carried 4,000 troops and their equipment and supplies. He sent 500 men to reinforce Mobile. The final plan of battle called for a concerted attack on Pensacola from New Orleans, Mobile, and Havana. The invading fleet began to move into Pensacola Bay on March 8, 1781, and to land troops on Santa Rosa Island. Ten days later the last of the fleet moved in, in another three days men arrived overland from Mobile, and on March 23, 1,400 troops arrived from Havana.

Campbell refused to surrender. He was in a position to give a good account of himself, although he had only about 2,000 men, not counting Indians. How long he might have held out and who might first have been reinforced or run out of supplies and food is speculation. On May 8, a shot fired the powder magazine at the advanced redoubt, killed some eighty-five men, and breached the walls of the fort. Campbell had little choice but to surrender Fort George, which he did. This ended the British regime in West Florida, a fact that must have weighed heavily in determining the fate of East Florida in the peace negotiations.

Meanwhile, the British in East Florida appeared relatively secure with little premonition of the fate that awaited them. No serious fighting occurred there. Raids back and forth across the border in 1776 and 1777 principally to drive off cattle could have developed into real invasions but failed to do so. The governor authorized Thomas Browne and Daniel McGirt to raise bodies of rangers for local defense. In August 1776 the inhabitants of Amelia Island fled to the mainland when three small vessels from Georgia came to the Saint Marys River. In the next three years three abortive campaigns against Florida originated in Georgia. The first stopped at Sunbury because of sickness among the troops. On a retaliatory raid in early 1778 Lieutenant Colonel Lewis V. Fuse with 500 regulars, 100 rangers, and some 400 Creek Indians took Fort Barrington on the Altamaha River, burned it, and returned to Saint Augustine with 2,000 head of cattle. Early in April 1778 Colonel Samuel Elbert led a contingent of continentals to Sunbury, moving some overland and some by ship. By the end of May the expedition broke up when the two wings could not be brought together and because of the opposition posed by Browne and 300 of his rangers. A third and larger expedition composed of 1,100 continentals and a number of militia under Brigadier General Robert Howe landed at Amelia Narrows in late June for an advance on Saint Augustine. After taking Fort Tonyn, which had been constructed by Floridians the previous year on the Saint Marys, they retired, defeated by disagreement and disease rather than by the defenders of East Florida.

The only role of the big stone fort at Saint Augustine was as a prison, first for French, Spanish, and American seamen from captured prizes. In the fall of 1780 British authorities sent sixty-three more important individuals with some of their servants as hostages for parole violations, many of whom were permitted to live out in town. Among them were three signers of the Declaration of Independence, Arthur Middleton, Edward Rutledge, and Thomas Heyward, Jr. In August 1781 they were moved to Philadelphia and exchanged.

By early 1778 the problem of refugees reaching East Florida was becoming acute. Nearly 700 came that year fleeing the hostility of people and governments in Georgia and South Carolina. When the British captured Savannah late in 1778 and Charleston in May 1780, the pressure was released and any threat of invasion disappeared. Then in March 1782, when the British government decided to abandon the effort to hold the unwilling colonies and ordered the evacuation of the port cities even before the negotiations were complete, a new and overwhelming flood of refugees came to East Florida. A census of newcomers early in 1783 counted some 5,000 whites and 8,300 blacks. Added to the resident population of 2,000 whites and 3,000 blacks, it was clear there would be serious problems of housing, food supply, and employment.

The loyalists who came to Florida were doomed to disappointment, and they felt betrayed when late in February 1783 the order came to settle their affairs and be prepared to abandon Florida. East Florida was again a pawn in the game of international politics and West Florida had been conquered by the Spaniards. In June of 1784 the new Spanish governor, Manuel de Zéspedes, arrived. The British evacuation proceeded slowly and reluctantly, the last ship departing from the Saint Marys on November 19, 1785. There was a lingering hope that a rumored exchange of Florida for some other territory might be arranged. The British government did acknowledge some obligation to its subjects. An East Florida claims commission set up in London processed 372 claims for £647,405/6/9 and awarded damages of £170,351/11/10. Florida was no longer British nor would it ever be exclusively Spanish again. The British impact was brief and limited but it proved permanent. Other new forces too would operate to frustrate the Spanish effort to reclaim Florida. Some loyalists returned to the states from which they had fled or went to other parts of the new nation. Some went to other British provinces while a considerable number, notably the Minorcans, remained in Florida. A period of disorder ensued during the change of flags. Robbery and plundering were common. Planters from Georgia and South Carolina were hunting slaves they alleged had run away or had been stolen. Some of the volunteer militia organizations, somewhat irregular at best, easily turned into bands of marauders bent upon plundering and looting. Too much of this was to characterize the entire second Spanish occupation and became an argument for acquisition of the troubled land by the United States.

7.

The Second Spanish Era 1784-1821

At the conclusion of the American Revolution, the Treaty of Paris in 1783 returned Florida to Spain, but the second Spanish occupation (1784-1821) was only nominally Spanish. Spain was weaker than when Florida had been lost to the English two decades earlier, whereas the opposing forces were much more formidable. The English interest and influence could not be removed. Land-hungry citizens of the United States, assisted covertly if not openly by their government, moved into Florida with the confident expectation that it would become a part of that country. Unruly Indians, runaway slaves mostly from nearby Georgia, and renegade whites proved unmanageable. Unrest and revolution in other Spanish American colonies absorbed the energies of the mother country and turned loose upon Florida a number of professional revolutionaries and freebooters who hoped to make capital of Spanish weakness.

Vincente Manuel de Zéspedes, who became governor of East Florida at the age of sixty-four, had been in the royal service in the New World since 1741 when he had come to Cuba. He was a close friend of Bernardo de Gálvez, the youthful and well connected governor of Louisiana who had achieved the conquest of West Florida in 1781. As a reward, Gálvez became captain general of Louisiana and West Florida, with East Florida added when it again became Spanish, and in rapid succession captain general of Cuba and viceroy of New Spain before his death in 1786. Arturo O'Neill, who had remained at Pensacola as military commander in 1781, then became the governor. Estevan Miro, who also had served under Gálvez, was governor of Louisiana, a situation that promised friendly relations among Florida's new administrative leaders.

The Floridas and Louisiana together gave Spain more territory in North America than she had ever before actually occupied. That Spain's future in North America might not be promising was not immediately apparent. The French and English rivalries appeared to be eliminated. The immediate course and future of the new American nation was not yet revealed. The treaty of cession left unanswered two questions that were to interfere with peaceful relations between American frontiersmen and Spain for some time. It set Florida's northern boundary at 32°30' if it remained English, but at 31° north latitude if it became Spanish, a provision that the Spanish would not at first accept. The English guaranteed navigation of the Mississippi River, but the Spaniards controlled the lower reaches of that river and the vital right of deposit at New Orleans, and they were less generous in their attitude toward the Americans.

When Zéspedes left Havana on June 19, 1784, for his new assignment at Saint Augustine, he led a fleet of fifteen vessels carrying 500 troops, ammunition and supplies, and members of the military and civil staffs and their families, making altogether several hundred others dependent upon the government. When his government was fully established, Zéspedes had from 1,500 to 1,800 people for whom he had to provide a basic diet of flour and salt meat. Scarcity of money and uncertainties of payment forced a partial subsistence economy on the Saint Augustine garrison and the civil population. Many persons raised vegetables on plots of ground on the edge of town. Some plantings continued on the nearby English plantation lands. James Hume's "Oak Forest" became the king's woodcutting preserve to furnish firewood for the barracks, bake ovens, and cookhouses.

Gálvez, recognizing that the Indians were the most effective allies that the English had in Florida, had instructed O'Neill to cultivate their friendship. In September 1783, O'Neill had recommended that the English firm handling the Indian trade at the time of the transfer of flags be allowed to continue to operate as the only alternative to having the trade fall into the hands of Americans. At stake was the allegiance as well as the trade of some 45,000 Indians, mostly Creeks, living as far north as the Tennessee River. A letter from Alexander McGillivray, a half-breed Creek chief, sought Spanish aid and protection and also urged that the English traders be kept in business. Gálvez learned also that some Englishmen violently resented the recession of Florida to Spain, hoped that it might somehow be averted, and were reluctant to depart. As a result of the close association with the English, there was potentially if not actually a strong anti-Spanish feeling among some of the Indians.

The city of Saint Augustine to which Zéspedes came was not much changed by twenty years of English occupation. Less than three hundred houses, about one-half of them of masonry or shell construction, stood on the three main streets paralleling the Matanzas River. The English had converted the monastery into barracks, a use which the Spanish continued. One effort was made to restore the monastery and the missions formerly associated with it, but Zéspedes protested that the buildings had been converted to other purposes and could not be returned. The English had also added some wooden barracks nearby, but these had been burned and only the chimneys were left standing.

The state of the Catholic religious properties was generally shocking. The sole place of worship the returnees found was a chapel fitted out by Father Pedro Campos on the ground floor of a residence near the city gate. The hospital-church of La Soledad was still standing but was pronounced a useless pile of masonry. Only the bishop's house, which had been kept up and used by the English, was habitable, and Father Thomas Hassett decided to use the upper floor for his parish church. A new church was finally started in 1793 and was finished four years later. The weakness, poverty, and decline of the second Spanish dominion were all reflected in the state of this church building.

The greatest changes wrought by the English had been on plantations outside the city; they were described as a tiny local representation of fashionable eighteenth century English society. Especially impressive was John Moultrie's "Bella Vista" four miles south of the city where Woodcutter's Creek entered the Matanzas. There was a 52 feet by 44 feet house surrounded by ten acres of formal gardens, fruit trees, fish ponds, and pens for geese. Some 300 of the 1,000 acres were cleared and fenced to grow corn, beans, potatoes, and rice. Chief Justice James Hume at Oak Forest had a young orange grove, rice land, and dairy cattle. On Anastasia Island, Jesse Fish had taken over an old Spanish estate of 10,000 acres where he experimented in raising dates and olives, exemplifying the dream of English mercantilists that they might produce tropical products in American colonies. Fish expected to remain in Florida, but many others of the several thousand English loyalists had already vacated farms and estates in various stages of development, leaving behind an air of abandonment and desolation.

Several hundred of the 1,500 Englishmen yet to be evacuated were in Saint Augustine. Prominent among them were Governor Patrick Tonyn, Brigadier General Archibald MacArthur, Indian Superintendent Thomas Brown, and Moultrie. William Panton and his partner John Leslie, who managed their business in Saint Augustine, were also a part of the social set, but they were planning to remain in the province. They helped to make a place for themselves in the new regime by providing Zéspedes with the trade items essential for good Indian relations. The returning Spaniards found the society of the English planters agreeable, and there was a succession of dinners and balls. The new governor hoped that many of these people might remain in Florida.

Then began a troubled coexistence that lasted more than a year. Under the terms of the treaty of cession, the English had until March 19, 1785, to depart; the deadline was extended to July 19, but Tonyn and a few others did not get away until mid-November. Meanwhile, Tonyn had some responsibility and some authority to look after the interests of the departing English. Not surprisingly, he frequently differed with Zéspedes on matters of policy, particularly those items affecting the disorderly activities of banditti and of blacks whose status was in doubt.

The years of the American Revolution had spawned much violence along the Georgia-Florida frontier, which made it difficult at times to distinguish between lawful and lawless elements in the population. Many no longer respected the authority of Tonyn; the authority of Zéspedes had not been established outside the capital city and indeed would never fully be so. During the festivities on the evening of July 14, bold thieves stole eight slaves from the Saint Augustine residence of Samuel Farley, a well known friend of Tonyn. Among the troublemakers were loyalists from South Carolina and Georgia who resented the transfer of the province to Spain. Both English and Spanish authorities feared rebellion on their part, but when they realized the hoplessness of their cause and began to leave, the movement collapsed. One of their leaders who did not plan to leave was Daniel McGirt, a Carolina patriot turned Tory, who had come to Florida to combine planting with highway robbery, specializing in the stealing and selling of cattle and slaves, continuing that which had so flourished during the war years. Before Zéspedes arrived Tonyn had McGirt and some of his associates arrested and locked up in the Castillo, but McGirt had bribed his way out.

Zéspedes had reasonably hoped that the English would hasten their departure and remove such problems. To make it easier for them, he offered anyone accused by the English of misconduct a passport to leave Florida. Others might register their intention to become Spanish subjects. At the same time, Tonyn's light horse troops authorized to guard plantations on the Saint Johns River were actively trying to apprehend McGirt and others. Some of their number accepted the offer, and McGirt went through the formality but took advantage of the situation to continue his marauding practices. Though his brother James and his family settled peacefully in Saint Augustine, the governors continued to feud over Daniel.

In the period of transition and disorder, property owners frequently did what seemed expedient to protect their holdings. Tonyn distrusted men like Francisco Sanchez, the only Spaniard of large property who had remained in the English period. In 1782 Sanchez had befriended some Spanish soldiers shipwrecked near Saint Augustine in a storm. In 1783 when he learned of the recession to Spain, he had presented himself to Zéspedes in Cuba, attested his loyalty, and proposed to sell him beef for the garrison. While he was absent, some 700 persons–white, Indian, and black–had camped on his property and disposed of 400 cattle. Without protection from Tonyn he felt forced to come to terms with McGirt. Zéspedes, unlike his English counterpart, refused to consider Sanchez one of the banditti.

The black population was a constant source of difficulty. Being the most valuable and marketable property that could be removed, raids across the border during the Revolution often had no more worthy motive than to steal blacks. There were in Saint Augustine free blacks and slaves from the English era and refugees, slave and free, from the United States. None of them were personally secure, for they might be picked up and carried away to the West Indies by the departing English to be sold, and planters from Georgia came frequently to reclaim blacks they alleged had been stolen or had run away. Zéspedes raised a storm of protest on July 26 when he sought to establish the status of blacks. All persons having blacks of undetermined ownership were required to declare them in eight days, or twenty days if they resided outside the city. Vagrant blacks without papers to prove their free status had to register with Carlos Howard within twenty days and secure permits to work. Those failing to do so were liable to become slaves of the king. No passenger, white or black, might embark on a ship without a license from the governor. Anyone, English or Spanish, who participated in the escape of a slave was declared subject to Spanish law. The English protested the legality and the reasonableness of the orders, and though relaxed in case of the English, they helped to settle many cases of identity and ownership and to relieve pressure on other legal processes for establishing personal and property rights.

Zéspedes in his first proclamation had created a board of arbitration, presided over by Francis Philip Fatio and John Leslie, to settle disputes involving property of British subjects. Most of these involved slave ownership. Frequently the judges knew the contending parties, but since they both planned to remain in Florida, Tonyn suspected them of favoring the Spaniards. Fatio owned three plantations on the Saint Johns, including New Switzerland, and a store and a home on the bayfront in Saint Augustine. Leslie hoped to remain active in the Indian trade. Results of some cases were ruinous to the principals.

Tonyn was further incensed when Zéspedes received two revolutionary leaders from Georgia, General Nathaniel Greene and Colonel Benjamin Hawkins. The visitors complained that English loggers from Florida were still cutting valuable timber on the general's property on Cumberland Island. Green also hoped that he could induce English evacuees to settle on his property. Saint Marys harbor was the center of evacuation activity, and logging continued beyond March 19, the last date of legal English right of residence. In May, transports took 387 persons to Nassau, and on June 3 Tonyn and his staff left Saint Augustine for Saint Marys. Zéspedes had been in no position to hurry the English too much, for many of them waited to collect money for goods sold to the Spanish. The *situado* was as usual long overdue and did not arrive until August 30. Tonyn and the last of the English departed on November 13, 1785.

The problem of the English evacuees departed with them, and that of refugee blacks became less pressing but continued to plague the government. More far-reaching in its consequences was the matter of Indian relations. The Americans would most likely be able to succeed the English in the Indian trade unless steps could be taken to prevent it. Indian leaders, fearful of the threat to their lands, hoped to resist the advance of the Americans, but they knew that the Indian rank and file would trade where they found the most attractive bargains. They hoped that the Spaniards might adopt English trade goods and English methods to hold the Indian trade. English traders sought their own private advantage, and if they favored any nation it was England. Circumstances dictated

that the Indians, the Spanish, and the English, in spite of any conflicts of interest among themselves and however uneasy the alliance at times might prove to be, should cooperate against the Americans.

Spanish governors at Pensacola and Saint Augustine were
agreed that the English trading firm of Panton Leslie and Company should continue a monopoly of trade. They alone had the trade
goods, the capital, and the experience that the trade required.
Alexander McGillivray, spokesman for the Indians, had also thrown
his support to the English. In a congress at the end of September
1784, the Indians asked for trading posts on the Saint Johns River,
at Saint Marks, and at Pensacola.

The principals in the intensified struggle to control the Indian
trade both for the profits and for the alliance with the Indians had
reestablished themselves in Florida during the years of English control. McGillivray was only twenty-five years old in 1784 and was
already in failing health, but by means of diplomacy and fair dealings he held the loyalty and the trade of the estimated 45,000 Creeks,
Chickasaws, Choctaws, Cherokees, and Seminoles, which he organized into a loose confederation. McGillivray was educated by his
Scottish father Lachlan's relatives and friends in Savannah and
Charleston to prepare him to manage the family's considerable property and its trading enterprises. The father, a loyalist, forfeited
$100,000 worth of property in Georgia and returned to Scotland at
the outbreak of the Revolution. The son returned to the Creek nation to assume the role of chief (inherited through his mother) and
established his great power and influence by the exercise of his talents as a leader. The English had made him commissary to the
Creeks, to handle the distribution of all presents and arms, and a
colonel in the army. He lived near present-day Montgomery, Alabama, and dealt directly with thousands of Indians in west Georgia
and in Alabama.

At a Pensacola meeting in 1784, McGillivray signed a treaty
accepting Spanish protection and the promise of arms and ammunition with which to resist the American advance. Four years later
the Spaniards withdrew the promise of military support and urged
the Creeks instead to make peace with the Americans. However,
when McGillivray and a band of lesser leaders, after negotiating
with agents of the United States government, went to New York in
the summer of 1790 to discuss the settlement of outstanding differences, his Florida allies became alarmed—and more so two years
later when he showed a disposition to listen to the schemes of William Augustus Bowles, who hoped to break into the Panton Leslie
Company monopoly and challenge the Spanish government. The
governor of Louisiana planted a Spanish agent to watch McGillivray
and undercut his influence. After the death of the Indian leader,
Spaniards acted as Indian agents, but as long as he lived,
McGillivray was the key man in Indian relations. It was not difficult to believe that he had held commissions in the Spanish and in
the United States armies as well as with the English.

Modern view of an old Saint Augustine street

Young McGillivray had known William Panton in Charleston. Panton held land in Savannah and Charleston, and as early as 1770 he had had some dealings with his Scotch relative, James Spalding, a trader on Saint Simons Island who operated posts at Palatka and Lake George on the Saint Johns River in Florida. Panton entered business with John Leslie at Fredericka, Georgia, and Thomas Forbes handled the firm's interests in London. At the outbreak of the Revolution, Panton and Leslie came to Saint Augustine and by 1783 had a monopoly of the Indian trade in East Florida. They superseded Spalding, who moved to Georgia, and retained his chief trader, Charles McLatchey. Panton, Leslie, and Forbes distributed military supplies and presents to the Indians for the English late in the war and set up a trading post at Saint Marks in 1783. The Spanish re-garrisoned this post in 1787.

At the end of the war Panton went ahead as if the future of the enterprise was not affected by the change of flags. He kept McLatchey at Lake George, maintained the store at Saint Marks, and later established headquarters at Pensacola, where McGillivray became a member of the firm as the price of his continuing support. A Mobile conference assigned trade there to Mather and Strother of

New Orleans, but that firm failed in 1789 and Panton, Leslie and Company enjoyed a complete monopoly in West Florida, which became several times as important as Saint Augustine in the volume of trade. The substantial, three-story brick building, the only non-wooden building there, that housed the business also served as residence, office, and hospitality center for the Indians.

In 1793 McGillivray died, and with him went his largely personal hold on the Indians. In 1795 the Treaty of San Lorenzo set the boundary between the United States and Florida at the 31° of north latitude, putting the Indians north of that line beyond reach. At the time those Indians owed some $60,000 at Saint Augustine and $140,000 at Pensacola. Panton offered to sell the business to the Spanish government for the total debt of $400,000 (the Spanish government itself owed another $200,000 to repay loans) and to train a Spaniard to operate it. In the same years, 1793-1795, the war that pitted England and Spain against France opened the ocean-borne trade to raids by French warships and privateers.

On February 26, 1801, Panton died at sea, and the firm became John Forbes and Company. In 1817, Forbes retired and left the control to the Inneraritys. Meanwhile, the Indians had been induced to cede 1,200,000 acres of land, known as the Forbes Grant, on the lower Apalachicola River in payment of their debts. Approved by Governor Juan Vicente Folch in 1806, it was confirmed by the United States Supreme Court in 1835.

Other ambitious and restless Englishmen who found little outlet for their energies and talents in the Bahamas looked with envy on the Panton Leslie Company's monopoly of the Indian trade in Spanish Florida. Among them was William Augustus Bowles, who apparently also acted as agent for others. He had arrived in Florida at the age of fifteen, an ensign in a Maryland loyalist regiment defending Pensacola. Thereafter he went to live among the Indians, learned their language and customs, and married the daughter of Chief Perryman. By 1785 he was in the Bahama Islands plotting a return to Florida. Three years later, merchants who resented the Panton Leslie warehouse in New Providence sponsored Bowles' return (with the secret support of Lord Dunmore, the last royal governor of Virginia, and then governor of the Bahama Islands). It is doubtful that Bowles' backers knew all of his designs, if indeed he himself did.

Bowles met McGillivray and explained that he and English friends wished to supply the Creek Indians with arms and ammunition for a war against the further advance of Georgia frontiersmen. McGillivray fondly hoped that he could stay the expansion of the Georgians, but hesitated to resort to war. Georgians knew of his hostility and courted him with an offer to restore the property confiscated from his father if he would join forces with them and divert the trade their way. Bowles was also promising to bring presents and ammunition to Apalachee in the fall. In the spring he had been reported at Indian River Inlet where Bahamians came to hunt turtles, cut wood and gather salvage from ships wrecked on the Florida reef. A small expedition sent by Zéspedes failed to find him, but word of the proposed expedition came to the Spanish authorities from several sources with an added promise of presents on the Saint Marys.

In October, Bowles did return to Indian River Inlet with thirty followers, most of whom soon deserted and made their way to Saint Augustine and reported his purpose to attack the store at Lake George. By November 19, Zéspedes had twenty-six deserters in the fort, and Bowles had bypassed the store to go to the Alachua villages. In 1792 when he attacked the store at Saint Marks, he was captured and imprisoned in turn at Havana, Madrid, and Manila. Five years later, en route to Spain, he escaped at the British colony port of Sierra Leone, returned to England, and found new support for his Florida ventures. He returned to Florida, where he was again arrested in 1803. He died a prisoner in Morro Castle in Havana three years later.

Preoccupation with Indian affairs and the disturbing influence of English and American adventurers and settlers obscured almost all other concerns in the Florida capitals. Zéspedes hoped to restrict residence in East Florida to Spanish and non-Spanish Catholics. He could not deny the property rights of the Englishmen who elected to remain, but he hoped that they might be converted and that he could restrict inheritance by non-Catholics. He proposed to create new parishes on the Saint Johns, on Amelia Island, and on North River just above Saint Augustine and to provide Catholic services there. Failing that, and realizing that the Americans could not be kept out of the province, he and his successors for a time sought to win them by an offer of land and private Protestant worship if they would take a modified oath of allegiance to Spain. When this failed to control the flow of immigrants, Spanish authorities attempted to close the border in 1804. Meanwhile, a number of English planters from the Bahama Islands, some of whom had left with the English in 1784, returned to accept Spanish land grants on which they established sugar plantations that flourished until the Seminole war led to their destruction in 1836.

In West Florida the offer of land failed to attract settlers to the Pensacola region. New-

The old Spanish jail, Pensacola

comers continued to find the lands in the Mississippi valley more attractive, and when the free navigation of that river was secured for Americans in 1795 and Louisiana was purchased in 1803, settlement flowed that way.

Pensacola remained small and isolated. Mobile and Saint Marks, accessible by sea or by poorly marked and seldom used overland trails, were the nearest settlements. Other than the garrison of 795—reduced to 460 after 1783 and almost never up to strength—there were less than 300 persons, mostly Canary Islanders and French Creoles. All plantations from the English period were abandoned, and a trade of perhaps half a million dollars a year in lumber, naval stores, skins and indigo had all but ceased. Fort George became Fort San Miguel, and other defenses received Spanish names. Panton's was still the only non-wooden house when Vicente Folch became governor. Pensacola, which had been subordinate to New Orleans, became the center of Spanish interest in West Florida after 1803. Louisiana had never really been Spanish, and Spaniards were apparently willing to sell it at any time after they pulled back to the thirty-first parallel in 1795 and opened the traffic on the river to Americans. They had welcomed the transfer to France in 1800 but were dismayed by the cession to the United States twenty days after France took formal possession. In 1810, the number of Pensacola residents had reached 1,000. New signs of enterprise were two sawmills on a branch of the Escambia River, which sent lumber to New Orleans and Vera Cruz, and a brickyard which produced bricks and plaza tiles. There was still no church except for the old warehouse, and there was no school.

At Saint Augustine, Indian relations were only somewhat less important. Governor Zéspedes placed the able Luciano Herrera, a Spaniard who had remained in the British period, in charge until his death in 1788. He received the Indian leaders who came from villages fifty or more miles beyond the Saint Johns. He dealt with the Indian leaders and kept records of the arrivals and departures of groups and of trade items and gifts from the Panton Leslie warehouse. He also supervised the withdrawal of supplies and provisions from the king's storehouse. To avoid unpleasant incidents, he attempted to keep the Indians from taverns and to prevent tavern-keepers from serving them illegally, and he returned drunks to their companions or had them cared for during the night.

Historians are indebted to two priests who came to Saint Augustine in 1784 after a long series of delays for a census of the East Florida population in 1786 and 1787. Father Pedro Campos, who ministered to the spiritual needs of the Minorcans, had asked to be relieved in 1776 after his assistant had been deported and before the colony left New Smyrna. Two secular priests, Thomas Hackett and Miguel O'Reilly, volunteered in 1778 to go to the English colony, but the American Revolution prevented their making the trip. Ordered to Florida again in 1784, Father Hackett arrived after surviving a shipwreck. The aging Father Campos, however, did not yet receive the hoped-for relief, for neither of the newcomers spoke the Minorcan dialect. When Zespedes received a request for a census of the East Florida population, he asked Father Hackett to prepare it for Saint Augustine. Father O'Reilly accompanied the governor on a four week inspection tour of the outlying settlements in 1787 and made a similar count. Father Hackett counted 460 survivors of the New Smyrna colony; others had gone away with the English. These refugees from New Smyrna brought their skill and industry to the capital city. In 1777 they began to raise vegetables on the outskirts of the city, and by 1784 had proved themselves to be highly skilled in agriculture, fishing, and general craftsmanship. They had vineyards, groves of fruit, and dairy cattle, and their small ships had developed an active coastal trade. Foreigners, principally former English subjects, numbered eighty-six, with 127 Negro servants. Thirty Spanish families, fourteen of whom had lived there before 1763, five recent arrivals from the Canary Islands, and eleven from peninsular Spain totaled fifty whites and ten more blacks. This may be contrasted with 343 families who left in 1764 and the much greater English exodus in 1784-1785. A few residents like Francisco Sanchez had never left Florida. He and his black wife had seven baptized children in the city and thirty-nine slaves with fourteen children at a ranch. In 1788 he married the seventeen-year old daughter of a North Carolina planter and developed a new plantation on the Saint Johns.

A few miles up the coast on the North River were thirteen English and Minorcan families numbering forty-six people, who held fifty-six slaves. At San Vicente Ferrer (Saint Johns Bluff), twelve miles up the Saint Johns River, was a military post to which Zéspedes sent fifteen soldiers in 1784 to guard the approach from the sea. At the post were five separate buildings of pine boards on cedar post foundations. In 1782 the English evacuees had some 300 temporary homes there; these they had dismantled to take the lumber to use for their new homes. On Talbot Island were five American families of twenty-eight people with twenty-two slaves, and one family of six lived on Fort George Island. Twenty-five soldiers occupied the fort on Amelia Island, and along the south side of the Saint Marys River lived twenty-two English loyalist families of 123 persons and twenty-six blacks.

Moving up the Saint Johns, the inspecting party found another 126 persons in twenty-eight families, plus 240 slaves, on plantations near Cow Ford, present-day Jacksonville. The largest number of slaves was on the plantations of Francis Philip Fatio. Near Picolata, the travelers reported Job Wiggens, son of a free black, with a wife and four children; they cultivated several hundred acres and had seventeen slaves. Wiggens, a former Indian trader and interpreter, also operated a ferry principally for Indians on their way to and from Saint Augustine.

The governor and his party completed their tour with a visit to the upper Saint Johns store near present-day Astor on Lake George. Here Charles McLatchey had been in charge when William Bartram had visited there in April and May of 1774. McLatchey and Wiggens had guided Bartram and must be credited with supplying much of the local data reported by Bartram. The establishment the governor visited was presided over by the Hamblys, who had four children. The establishment was considerably larger; in addition to the store there was a packing house for hides, a farm and a cattle ranch with several hundred cattle, and fifty or more slaves to perform the labor, which included collecting bark with which to tan leather. Eight well-armed soldiers guarded the post. Outside of the city there were then 283 whites and 388 blacks for a total civilian population of 1,390. In 1764 the grand total had been 3,096, contrasted to 3,190 in 1787.

Fray Cyril de Barcelona, auxiliary bishop in charge of parish visits to new provinces, sent by the bishop of Cuba, visited East Florida from July 1788 to June 1789. He reported 400 soldiers, mostly unmarried, and fifty-five unmarried women between sixteen and forty years of age. No salaries had been paid to anyone since 1786, he reported. He found a primary school of creditable quality there but none in West Florida or Louisiana. Father Hackett had founded the school for boys, black and mulatto as well as white, to Hispanize the polyglot population. Father Campos was delighted that the visiting cleric also spoke the Minorcan dialect. Fray Cyril did not visit Pensacola until 1791, where he reported 571 persons besides the garrison; 292 of them were whites, 114 were black Catholics, 161 were Protestant, and four were unidentified.

There were stirrings of new economic enterprises in East Florida, but more often the names associated with them were not Spanish. Governor Zéspedes heard again in 1787 the urgings of Francis Philip Fatio to encourage the naval stores industry. He insisted that he had previously exported tar, pitch and turpentine as well as lumber from his three plantations but was at the time exporting only cured lumber and cypress shingles. In fact, Fatio had addressed a memorial on the subject directly to Madrid. As a result, Lieutenant José del Rio Cosa came on orders of the Spanish government to inspect East Florida resources of lumber and naval stores. He gave enthusiastic support to Fatio's urgings and pointed out that Spain might easily rid itself of dependence upon the Baltic countries for these products. In later years, Florida governors made twenty sawmill grants for a total of 312 acres and cowpen or cattle ranch grants in the amount of 129,000 acres.

Governor José Coppinger, who succeeded to the office in 1816, perhaps realizing that the province was about to be lost to Spain, made some large grants that had previously been contrary to Spanish policy. These included the Delespine grant of 42,000 acres; to George Fleming, a son-in-law of Fatio, 20,000 acres on the San Sebastian River near Saint Augustine; to Fatio, 20,000 acres on the Nassau River; and the Clark's grant, 16,000 acres on the Saint Johns near Palatka. Other spectacularly large grants were made by the Spaniards on the eve of the cession to the United States.

In spite of policy and orders to the contrary, the trade of East Florida went more and more to Americans. Their markets were more accessible and they offered a greater variety of goods at better prices. Of forty-two ships in Saint Augustine in 1806, only five came from Havana and the other thirty-seven from ports of the United States. The best known planter and trader was Zephaniah Kingsley, who arrived in 1803 and lived successively in Saint Augustine, on the Saint Johns near Orange Park, and finally on Fort George Island. This now legendary individualist imported slaves directly from Africa to cultivate his plantations and allegedly bred the blacks for special physical qualities. After he had trained and conditioned them, they brought prices fifty percent above the going market. He defended slavery as a patriarchal system superior to free labor for blacks, married a slave, and recognized his children from this union as well as some not legitimized by marriage.

In addition to cattle raising, the planters produced sea island cotton, rice and sugarcane as well as food crops. Fernandina on Amelia Island was a better representative than Saint Augustine of the new economic order. It derived its importance from a combination of factors. It was a free port on the boundary between Florida and the United States, largely unpoliced by either country. The Jefferson embargo in 1807 made it the base of a vast smuggling trade, and the prohibition by the United States of the international slave trade in 1808 made it the logical center for that activity. In 1811, Governor Enrique White ordered the surveyor general, George Clarke, to bring order out of the helter-skelter collection of buildings that had been put up by squatters, blacks, businessmen, and planters by planning a town. Many planters had homes outside of the town on their lands, but others resided in the settlement. Fernandina had larger relative importance in the latter part of the second Spanish dominion than it would ever have again. It also served as an important springboard for Americans and others eager to establish themselves in Spanish Florida.[1]

8.

American Intrigues and Acquisition

Quite early in the second occupation it became clear that Spain could not people, develop, and govern Florida effectively. It was equally obvious that it would fall to the United States unless some great power, possibly England, should intervene to prevent it. The struggle to control the destiny of Florida was far more than a local affair. The wars of the French Revolution and Napoleon kept the major powers of western Europe in turmoil and strife from 1789 to 1814 and eventually involved the United States in the War of 1812. The struggles for independence of Spain's American colonies absorbed that country's energies and left little resources with which to protect Florida. Spanish power continued to decline in Europe and in America. The United States, on the other hand, was growing ever more rapidly in population, resources, and self-assurance.

The Treaty of San Lorenzo in 1795 was the first step in Spanish withdrawal in the face of growing pressure from the United States. Spain agreed to accept the thirty-first parallel as the northern boundary of Florida, to open the navigation of the Mississippi River, and to permit the right of deposit at New Orleans for the transfer of cargo to oceangoing vessels. Spaniards on the scene were not always happy at the necessity to pull back. Not until March of the following year did the Spanish actually pull back their frontier force. Surveys began the next month and reached the Apalachicola in October 1799, at which point the hostility of Indians along the boundary line led Ellicott to withdraw and survey the Saint Marys River to its source, leaving the line from there to the Apalachicola to be settled at a later date.

Spain probably welcomed the transfer of Louisiana to France in 1800 for it relieved her of the intolerable burden of maintaining Spanish government against growing odds. The sale of Louisiana to the United States in 1803 then ended all hope of the Spanish that they could hold Florida. The wonder is that so much time was required to bring about its addition to the United States.

The election to Congress in 1810 of some sixty young "War Hawks" from the South and the West prepared the way for aggressive action to solve America's problems on the high seas, where impressment of seamen and violation of neutral rights roused the anger of Americans. Border troubles with Indians and Spaniards aided and abetted by Englishmen on the Florida boundary demanded attention. The acquisition of Canada and Florida in the process of avenging insult on the high seas would solve all of the problems and satisfy American land hunger at the same time.

The popular clamor in the United States to acquire the Floridas first bore fruit in that narrow strip below the thirty-first parallel between the Perdido and the Mississippi rivers where Spanish power was weakest and where there was a growing number of Americans. Encouraged by the prospect of annexation to the United States and urged on by agents of that country, sixteen delegates from the four districts west of the Pearl River on July 25, 1810, met in convention, with John Rhea as chairman, on Saint Johns Plains near Baton Rouge to organize themselves into a government. Two months later, early on the morning of September 23, some eighty men on horseback and on foot attacked and easily captured Baton Rouge. The Americans then in classical fashion stated their grievances against their Spanish governors and declared West Florida free and independent. Shortly thereafter, Chairman Rhea sought annexation to the United States, requesting at the same time a loan of $100,000 and the reservation of the public land of the province for those who had planned and carried out the West Florida Rebellion or Revolution.

The United States government had other plans for the acquisition of West Florida. President James Madison ignored the revolution and failed to recognize the independence of the province. Instead, in a proclamation on October 27, 1810, he claimed Florida from the Perdido to the Mississippi as part of the Louisiana Purchase, stating that the United States had not hitherto seen fit to occupy it pending an amicable settlement with Spain. On the same date the secretary of state, James Monroe, instructed Governor William C. C. Claiborne to occupy the area and govern it as a part of the Orleans Territory. He also alerted Governor David Holmes of the Mississippi Territory, who had earlier reported a state of anarchy on his southern frontier, to stand by for any eventuality. American forces soon occupied the territory to the Perdido except for Mobile and the region around it and completed the acquisition by taking over Mobile on April 15, 1813. When Louisiana became a state in 1812 the eastern boundary was fixed at the Iberville River. In that same year Governor Holmes organized the region between the Iberville and the Perdido as a county of the Mississippi Territory. Though still referred to as East and West Florida and having separate governments, the boundaries of the once extensive Spanish La Florida had now been reduced to the limits of present-day Florida.

The acquisition of so much of West Florida had perhaps been too easy. It suggested the possibility that Spanish authority in the rest of Florida might be yielded in the same way. If not, there was always the possibility of an East Florida revolution that would achieve independence of Spanish authority and provide the opportunity for the United States to annex it. The approach of the War of 1812 raised new apprehensions that England might seize the occasion to occupy Saint Augustine and Pensacola as bases from which to attack the American frontiers.

Governor Juan Vicente Folch of West Florida had seemed to be ready to acquiesce in American occupation there. He had, in fact, on December 2, 1810, in a letter to Indian Agent John McKee signified his readiness to deliver his province to the United States unless support reached him before January 1, 1811. McKee hastened to Washington to show the letter to President Madison whose administration moved immediately to take advantage of the opportunity.

The Congress of the United States acted secretly on January 15, 1811, authorizing the president to occupy the Floridas peaceably if delivered by local authorities or forcibly if necessary to prevent seizure by a foreign power. He might use the army and the navy and up to one hundred thousand dollars in the effort. The special agent to conduct negotiations with Folch was seventy-two year old General George Mathews of Georgia, who had made frequent trips along the Florida boundary and knew the country from experience in Mississippi and New Orleans. He had a legendary war record, had been governor of Georgia in 1787, one of Georgia's representatives in the first Congress of the United States, and governor again in 1793, only to be ruined politically by signing the Yazoo Land Grant Act. Mathews and McKee received official instructions on January 26, 1811, to carry into effect the act of Congress providing for the occupation of the remainder of Florida.

Mathews and his aides journeyed to Fort Stoddert on the Mobile River fifty miles above the city of Mobile, arriving on March 21. Ralph Issacs, secretary to Mathews, had arrived earlier, on February 25, with a letter to Governor Folch at Pensacola, offering to accept Florida in the name of the United States. The United States would assume local debts of the Spaniards, pay the cost of moving out Spanish troops, confirm land titles, grant religious toleration, and continue local officials in their jobs. Should the governor refuse, he was told the United States would occupy Florida in the face of any threat by a foreign power to move in. Folch, however, proved adamant in his refusal to carry out the promise of his December 2 letter. Conditions were different, he pointed out, and he now had orders from his government and the promise of financial and military assistance. Mathews himself went to Pensacola, where he was received cordially by Folch, but with no yielding on the matter of ceding the territory. Mathews had failed in West Florida but he had seen the eagerness of Madison and his secretary of state, James Monroe, to secure the rest of Florida, and he had learned the possibility of revolution as a prelude to annexation. He was ready for a move into East Florida.

Mathews and Issacs reached Saint Marys on June 9, 1811, to try dealing with the new governor at Saint Augustine. In the fall of

1810 Mathews had been dissuaded from calling on Governor Enrique White by the insistence of his friends that he would only suffer imprisonment for his impertinence. Juan de Estrada, who became governor on March 13, 1811, shortly before White died, was proving equally opposed to the cession of Florida. Realizing this, Mathews made no effort to see him and instead planned the East Florida Rebellion.

In Saint Marys, General Mathews shared the summer cottage of Major Jacint Laval near the United States military post of Point Petre on the Georgia side of the Saint Marys River. Laval had joined the American struggle for independence and was still serving in the army. General Mathews received visitors in his room then visited settlers north and south of the river, sounding out their attitudes toward his purpose. He found Saint Marys, the fifth Georgia city in size with its 585 inhabitants, most suitable as a base from which to launch his coup. Like Fernandina it had its lawless elements, but it was the stable property owners that Mathews sought to enlist in his cause. Slave runners and smugglers favored the weaker Spanish government. At Fernandina, men grown wealthy under the Spanish flag hesitated to expose themselves to the disorders and risks of revolution.

Mathews required for his plans a well-placed resident of Spanish Florida, preferably one with money and military experience. He found his man in John Houston McIntosh (not to be confused with the more famous General John McIntosh, who arrived later on April 17, 1812, to lead the Patriots), a well-known Georgian who had purchased the Florida lands of John McQueen in 1803 and could qualify as a subject of Spain. Their plan was simple. They would create a local authority for the purpose of transferring the territory to the United States and Mathews would act for the United States in accepting it. He believed that he had the promise that the United States army and naval forces on the border would support him. The general openly recruited men, offering them land in amounts appropriate to their status and offering some of them offices in the territorial government. To Spaniards who would join he guaranteed their property, their religious freedom, payment of any claims against Spain, and equivalent positions in the civil and military service of the territory.

The original plan of campaign to liberate East Florida was to cross the international boundary at Saint Marys, bypass Fernandina on Amelia Island at the mouth of the Saint Marys River, and attack the Castillo de San Marcos at Saint Augustine on March 16, relying upon the United States naval force on the Saint Marys to keep the supply lines open. On March 13 a force of some seventy Georgians and nine Floridians moved into Florida. They issued a manifesto citing their grievances, raised the Patriot flag, and invited all who loved liberty to join the move for independence from Spain. Plans went awry when Major Laval, temporarily in command at Point Petre, and Commodore Hugh Campbell, in charge of the United States naval force, refused the hoped-for support. Mathews and

McIntosh then moved instead to occupy Fernandina, supported by five gunboats that Campbell somehow felt justified in ordering to their support, perhaps because of the location on the international boundary.

Mathews then moved on toward Saint Augustine and demanded its surrender, claiming that he had the support previously denied to him of the army and navy. Governor Estrada refused to confer with him. The Patriot force, encamped at Moosa Old Fort about two miles west of the city, was joined there by the troops of Lieutenant Colonel Thomas Adam Smith, who had returned and replaced Laval and had decided to support Mathews. English warships did bring supplies to Saint Augustine but did not participate in any military action. Some Americans, eager to involve the United States in the conflict, hoped that the Seminoles might join the Spanish cause and afford an excuse for intervention.

By May only help from Washington could save the Mathews scheme, and it was not forthcoming. Congress refused to support the president, and he had no choice but to repudiate Mathews. On April 4 he revoked Mathews' powers as special agent. Actually, the president had not given up hope of success in Florida. He named Governor David Mitchell of Georgia special agent to provide for the orderly evacuation of Americans from Florida since they had been led to expect United States protection, and thereby at least for a time left the way open for his new appointee to remain in Florida. Both sides built up their forces, and on May 16, Spaniards drove the Americans from Moosa Old Fort. On June 11, a new governor, Sebastian Kindelan, arrived at Saint Augustine with nearly one hundred trained black colonials, refused to deal with Colonel Smith, and demanded his withdrawal from Florida.

On June 18, 1812, the United States Congress declared war on England but refused to support the occupation of Florida. On July 6, the administration advised Mitchell to withdraw his troops though he might later be called upon to act under the law of 1811. A regular government in East Florida that could be recognized was still desirable, particularly after the repudiation of Mathews. On July 10, 1812, the Patriots elected delegates to write a constitution for "The Territory of East Florida," held elections on July 25, and on July 27 chose John Houston McIntosh to be director of the Territory. On August 30, Mathews died and matters seemed to go from bad to worse.

Governor Kindelan turned to the Indians for help and offered a thousand dollars for the scalp of McIntosh and ten dollars each for others. Blacks who feared American success also proved able allies and together with the Indians forced Smith to retire from Saint Augustine. Colonel Daniel Newman had come to the assistance of the Patriots with a contingent of Georgia militia, but he too met defeat at the hands of Kindelan's allies. The president of the United States again found it necessary to repudiate his agent, this time Governor Mitchell, and Major General Thomas Pinckney succeeded to the unenviable post of special agent for the president, convinced that he was meant to hold onto Florida. In early February 1813, Tennessee volunteers crossed the Saint Marys to aid the Patriot cause and raided down to the Alachua country, venting their wrath on Indian property and persons where they could be found. Again in that month the United States Senate refused to support Madison and Monroe in Florida, where they had kept army and navy units since March of the previous year without authorization.

On March 7, 1813, Pinckney was ordered to withdraw if Kindelan would grant complete amnesty. This was prompted by the threat of English assistance to the Spanish if the Americans persisted in their efforts to remain there. Pinckney agreed to evacuate the Saint Johns on April 29 and Fernandina a week later. He left behind a ravaged and despoiled land, ruined Patriots, and frustrated hopes. Yet one more abortive effort to occupy East Florida was to be made. Buckner Harris, with the approval of Governor Mitchell, proposed to lead a colony of Georgians to the Alachua country and establish a settlement that would hold back the Indians and destroy the haven there for fugitive slaves. He was naive enough to expect Indian acquiescence in his plans. He and 160 followers founded Fort Mitchell in January of 1814 and formally declared themselves a district of the to be repudiated Territory of East Florida. The new governor of Georgia, Thomas Pinckney, and the president withheld support. Benjamin Hawkins expressed the fear that a general Indian uprising might be set off. Avenging Indians and blacks killed Harris and drove his followers back to the Saint Marys.

The Florida affair was about to take still another turn. Napoleon was finally defeated, and England could turn her attention to the American question. The worst fears of the president and his secretary of state were about to be realized. England would use Florida as a base from which to attack, but the occasion could not be used to acquire the territory for the United States.

In May a squadron of English warships equipped with invasion barges appeared off the mouth of the Saint Marys River. English sympathizers welcomed the British on Amelia Island, where they immediately set to work to organize Indian support elsewhere in the province. On July 1, Vice-Admiral Alexander Cochrane sent Colonel Edward Nicholls to treat with the Indians of West Florida. Indians were to encourage blacks to flee the plantations, promising to feed, clothe, supply, and arm them. Captain George Woodbine assisted Colonel Nicholls in the work of bringing Indians into the alliance.

The activities of the English alarmed Kindelan, who suspected that they meant no help to his cause. He feared that Americans might hold him responsible, but the English could ignore his protests. On January 11, 1815, the British occupied Cumberland Island, from which they moved two days later to take Point Petre and sack Saint Marys, where nobody was harmed but a few prisoners taken. When the British commander sent a force of 250 men up the river to destroy Clark's mills, the men on the barges were literally cut to pieces by sharpshooters on both banks of the river and were lucky to get back at all. Meanwhile, peace had been declared on December 24, but not before other stirring events had transpired in West Florida.

On April 15, 1813, General James Wilkinson had marched into Mobile without a fight and strengthened its defenses, completing the occupation of the region west of the Perdido. Indians, responding to the blandishments of the English, went on the warpath. In alarm, some 500 Americans gathered at Fort Mims near the confluence of the Alabama and Tombigbee rivers for protection. On August 30, Indians killed several hundred Americans in a surprise attack. This set off the Creek War, which ended when General Andrew Jackson defeated the Indians at Horseshoe Bend on March 27, 1814, and forced them to cede two-thirds of their lands in Georgia and Alabama. Some of the chiefs refused to go farther west and joined other Seminoles who were already in Florida.

In August two English warships anchored at Pensacola and landed Nicholls, Woodbine, and 200 marines with field artillery, guns, and swords. They occupied Fort San Miguel and other Spanish defense installations without protest from the Spaniards, who allowed Woodbine to drill Indians and blacks in the streets. Andrew Jackson, now a major general in command of the seventh military district, reached Mobile on August 22 and further strengthened the defenses erected by Wilkinson in time to enable the defenders to repel an English attack on September 12 and for them to return to Pensacola.

Jackson, finally tired of waiting for authority to drive the English from Pensacola and trounce the Indians who had taken refuge there, marched toward the city on November 3 on his own authority, reaching Pensacola on the sixth. When the Spaniards fired on his note bearer, who carried a message that he meant no war against them but that the English must go, he stormed the town on the next day and the English sailed away. On November 9, the Americans, having achieved their objective, marched away to Mobile and on to fight the historic Battle of New Orleans, which ended with an American victory on January 8, 1815, two weeks after the war was officially ended.

When Nicholls, Woodbine, and the marines left Pensacola they repaired to the Apalachicola River, taking along a number of blacks many of whom had belonged to Spaniards. On the east bank of the river at Prospect Bluff, fifteen miles upstream from the Gulf of Mexico, they erected a fort and supplied it with artillery, powder, and shot; Nicholls remained at the fort until the summer of 1815 and distributed arms and ammunition to Indians and blacks. When the English finally withdrew they left the well-armed fort in the possession of the Indians and blacks and it became known to Americans as Negro Fort. The Indians moved away to the eastward, and some 300 blacks, mostly runaway slaves, established a refuge for any others who chose to join them, settling up and down the river from the fort. The banditti caused much alarm on the Georgia frontier and made travel on the river hazardous. General Edmund P.

Gaines offered friendly Indians fifty dollars for each captive black if they would reduce the fort. In April 1816, Jackson wrote the Spanish governor at Pensacola demanding the breaking up of the base and warning that the Americans would act if he did not. The Spanish reply was unsatisfactory, and Jackson ordered the fort destroyed and the blacks returned to their owners.

In July the Americans were busy constructing Fort Scott on the Apalachicola just above the Florida line. Stores came by way of the river. On July 10, a boat crew from a vessel at the mouth of the river awaiting instructions was ambushed while seeking fresh water. Gaines then moved to destroy the fort, and sent Colonel Duncan L. Clinch by armed boat on the mission. Firing at the fort from the river was difficult because of the elevation. While firing to get the range, hot shot were used. One fell into the powder magazine, and the resulting explosion blew up the fort, killing 270 of 344 occupants and leaving only three unhurt. The incident removed any immediate danger to users of the river and also strengthened the American demand that the Spanish either police Florida's unruly inhabitants or cede the territory to the United States.

In the years 1816 to 1817 another type of adventurer sought to capitalize upon American desire for Florida and Spanish weakness there to promote revolutionary movements by setting up temporary government in exile. In September 1816, Jose Alvarez de Toledo accompanied by Pedro Gaul visited Secretary of State Monroe in Washington to explain their need for a port on the Gulf of Mexico and suggesting that they might take and use Pensacola and Fernandina as bases for expeditions against Mexico. Pensacolans did what they could to strengthen their defenses and remained on the alert, but the expected attack never came. In December a Mexican privateersman brought rumors to Pensacola of an impending attack by General Xavier Mira and pirates from Galveston that caused many citizens to flee the city. A storm had disrupted plans for a joint attack by Toledo and Mira, and the latter went away to join another pirate, Luis Aury, at Galveston. Aury would turn up later at Amelia Island. One authority suggests that the Spanish crown may have instigated some of these rumors of raid to precipitate a war with the United States and bring England into the conflict on the side of Spain.

Perhaps related to these schemes was the appearance at Fernandina on June 29, 1817, of Gregor McGregor, who landed in the name of the Republics of Venezuela, New Granada, Mexico, and Rio de la Plata. McGregor, an English veteran of the Napoleonic Wars in Europe, fought with Miranda and Bolivar to free Venezuela. He tried settling there but feared loss of identity among foreigners. He visited Americans in Baltimore and Philadelphia and secured promises of aid from other revolutionaries. He was able, by promises of land, to get pledges for supplies at Charleston and Savannah and to raise an armed invasion force from among discharged veterans of the War of 1812. He assembled his recruits at the mouth of the Altamaha River and moved on Fernandina with such fanfare and advance notice that the Spanish garrison surrendered without a shot when McGregor arrived on June 29, 1817. McGregor then raised another of the many flags that have flown over Florida, this one the Green Cross of Florida, a St. George Cross in green on a white field.

McGregor clearly expected aid from persons he had visited in Baltimore and Philadelphia, but it never materialized. On August 28, Ruggles Hubbard, high sheriff of New York City and a former Congressman, arrived on the brig *Morgiana*. The reports brought by Hubbard apparently encouraged McGregor, for he declared the coast of Florida blockaded from Amelia Island to the Perdido River as if to give new life to his projects. Between September 4 and 13 a Spanish attack from Saint Augustine that might well have ended the tragic farce failed because of bad management. McGregor might have felt encouraged by this, but instead he placed the affair at Fernandina in the hands of Hubbard and Jared Irwin and sailed away. Two days later a new adventurer, the pirate Luis Aury, arrived and on September 21 raised the flag of the "Republic of Mexico." There was little pretense of legality about the regime. Privateers and pirates brought their cargoes there to be sold. The now illegal slave trade flourished, and an estimated one thousand of the unfortunates were moved up the Saint Marys River and smuggled into Georgia during his short stay.

Aury could scarcely have expected to be tolerated very long by the United States. He had fled from an imminent attack in force on his headquarters in Galveston Bay. The United States government received many protests of disorder on the Florida frontier. On December 23, 1817, a naval squadron of the United States sailed into Amelia River and protected the landing of 200 troops. Aury hauled down his flag and departed without a shot. United States troops held the island in protective custody to the end of the Spanish period, offering to turn it over to the Spaniards when they could police and govern it.

McGregor sailed from Florida in the company of Colonel Woodbine, the associate of Colonel Nicholls in an earlier venture in West Florida. Perhaps they plotted another invasion of Florida, for McGregor commissioned a former British officer, Robert Chrystie Ambrister, to proceed to Tampa Bay and prepare the Indians to receive the new deliverers. Ambrister gathered Indians and raided stores operated by Alexander Arbuthnot, a British trader, with goods from New Providence. He then gave the loot to the Indians and blacks who followed him. The British agents may have represented only themselves, but they were not restrained by the Spanish government, and fear grew that they would foment a general uprising of Indians on the frontier.

Late in the summer of 1817, Indians were reported gathering near Tallahassee. On November 20, General Gaines sent a detail to bring in some of the chiefs for a talk. The Indians fired on three men, whereupon Gaines attacked and destroyed the village. The Indians retaliated on November 30 with an ambuscade on the

The Suwannee River

Apalachicola River, attacking a supply boat and killing thirty-seven soldiers, seven soldiers' wives and four children. Gaines dispersed the Indians, but they returned for a second attack on the convoy, killing or wounding fifty-nine persons.

Secretary of War John C. Calhoun on December 6 instructed Gaines to proceed against the Seminoles, marching into Florida to get at them if they did not take Spanish refuge. Meanwhile, Jackson was on the way to Florida to take personal charge of the campaign. On January 6, 1818, when he received a copy of the December 16 order to Gaines, he wrote President Monroe the letter that created one of the most heated controversies in Amercan history. "Let it be signified to me through any channel (say Mr. J. Rhea) that the possession of the Floridas would be desirable to the United States, and in sixty days it will be accomplished." On January 12, Jackson wrote to the secretary of war acknowledging his own orders. On the same date Senator John Rhea of Tennessee wrote the letter that Jackson later used to prove that the president of the United States approved his proposal for the invasion of the Floridas, but it was never possible to prove that President Monroe had authorized the "Rhea Letter."

Jackson arrived at Fort Scott on March 9 and relieved Gaines. He had in his command 800 regulars, 900 Georgia militia, and 300 Indians in what he thought was an effort to wrest the Floridas from Spain. Jackson crossed the boundary on the next day to march down the river to meet supply boats at the mouth of the Apalachicola. On March 16 he camped at and built Fort Gadsden on Prospect Bluff. On the twenty-sixth he set out for Saint Marks, ordering the supply ships to meet him there. On April 6, he reached Saint Marks and took it over from the Spaniards on the grounds of controlling Indians; it was held until late 1818. Here he captured Arbuthnot by a ruse, displaying English colors to catch him and a number of Indian chiefs. He marched eastward to the Suwannee and found only a few Indians, but on the night of April 17 Ambrister and some companions stumbled into camp. Jackson had bagged two Britishers he was sure were responsible for inciting the Indians to border warfare. On April 29, after a court martial found them guilty, Ambrister was shot and Arbuthnot hanged. On the same day Jackson left Saint Marks for Fort Gadsden. The war seemed to be over until he learned that hostile Indians were gathering at Pensacola and that the Spanish governor there was interfering with the transportation on the Escambia River of army property bound for the border Fort Crawford. When Spanish officers continued to refuse free passage after Jackson's protest, he set out on May 7 with 1,200 men to march the 275 miles to Pensacola. He arrived on May 22. Two days later his men occupied the city, and after three more days the Spaniards surrendered Fort Barrancas. Jackson signed for all property he took over, offered to transport the Spaniards wherever they wished to go, and promised to hold the city until the two governments should decide what disposition to make of it. The general then wrote a full account of his actions and returned to Tennessee, thus concluding the military phases of the First Seminole War.

The British government found it inexpedient to defend the activities of Arbuthnot and Ambrister in spite of press demands for an official United States apology. The Spanish protested loudly and set off a great debate. Public opinion in the United States clearly approved of Jackson's conduct, but many public officials felt deeply embarrassed. In twenty-seven days of debate in Congress, the House refused four times to vote censure, and the matter never came to a vote in the Senate. In the cabinet only Secretary of State John Quincy Adams supported Jackson. Adams continued to argue the American claim to Florida with his colleagues and in his dispatches to Spanish authorities, urging that Spain must either demonstrate power to govern and police the unruly population or turn the Floridas over to the United States. The President returned the forts and at the same time managed to avoid a showdown with Jackson.

Meanwhile, negotiations were underway that resulted in a treaty of cession signed at Washington on February 22, 1819, in which the United States received the Floridas but accepted a southwestern boundary at the Sabine River, thereby surrendering any claim to Texas as a part of the Louisiana Purchase. The United States did, however, receive whatever claim Spain had to the Oregon country. The United States assumed Spanish debts to United States citizens whose claims totaled some five million dollars. On February 24, the United State Senate ratified the treaty, but the Spaniards delayed until October 25 to restrain the United States from recognizing the revolutionary Spanish Republics. A second ratification by the Senate on February 22, 1821, set the stage for the transfer of flags later that year, and the same Congress made provision for establishing diplomatic offices in the capitals of the former Spanish colonies.

The Spanish era in Florida was finally concluded. President Thomas Jefferson had foreseen the end when Americans were permitted to settle in Spanish Florida, predicting that they would secure the domain for the United States without a war. Claims against Spain had mounted steadily. Spain owed citizens of the United States some five million dollars to satisfy spoliation claims dating back to the closure of the Mississippi River to their traffic late in the eighteenth century. The mortgage must now be foreclosed. Florida had become a refuge for runaway slaves, renegade whites and Indians, and foreign adventurers and pirates who could not be policed by the Spaniards. Travel on international rivers necessary to the welfare of the United States was no longer secure. Finally, Spain could not prevent powers hostile to the United States from using the provinces as a base from which to attack the United States. The only answer under the circumstances that would satisfy Americans was annexation.

9.

Territorial Politics and State-Making

President James Monroe proclaimed the Adams-Onis treaty ceding Florida to the United States on February 22, 1821. By this action he set the stage for General Andrew Jackson to make a third entry into the province. The president had offered the governorship of Florida to the general as early as 1819, but he had rejected it. He did accept when the offer was made again in a letter of January 24, 1821. Secretary of State John Quincy Adams on March 12 issued to Jackson three commissions: to receive, possess, and occupy the ceded lands; to govern the Floridas; and to establish territorial government. There may well have been reservations about the wisdom of the appointment, but this time there was no doubt of his authority to enter the province. The general was about to lose his position in a reduction of the size of the army that would eliminate the command that the major general held. The new position acknowledged the important role that he had already played there and could be interpreted as vindication for what his critics called unauthorized and unjustifiable invasion of Spanish territory. In making the appointment, the chief executive wrote flatteringly, "I have full confidence that your appointment will be immediately and most beneficially felt. Smugglers and slave traders will hide their heads; pirates will disappear, and Seminoles cease to give trouble."

Jackson and his family traveled from Nashville, Tennessee, to Florida by way of New Orleans, where they arrived on April 22. They proceeded to Blakely on Mobile Bay and then to Montpelier, Alabama, to await the readiness of Spanish officials to turn over the province, for Jackson refused to enter Pensacola until he could go in as governor. Meanwhile, he fretted over delays which he insisted could only be deliberate. Colonel James Grant Forbes, who delivered the royal Spanish order to the governor-general of Cuba for the transfer of the provinces and their forts, had reached Havana aboard the *Hornet* on April 22, but waited until May 26 for the orders to the Spanish governors at Saint Augustine and Pensacola to turn their authority over to officials of the United States.

Forbes was able to secure the land records and archives for East Florida, but was not so successful with those relating to the Pensacola area. Fortunately, most of the land claims were in East Florida. In West Florida, missing records left land claims in dispute much longer than should have been necessary. Some years later, when Jackson was president of the United States, he sent Richard Keith Call to Havana in 1829 as special agent to secure from Spanish authorities the archives relating to West Florida. Call was well received and royally entertained but like others who made similar attempts, he brought away with him no significant records.

Finally, on June 9, Forbes arrived at Pensacola with papers authorizing the transfer of West Florida. Five days later Jackson moved to a Spanish home north of the city, where he remained until July 17 when the formal transfer took place. A twenty-one gun salute on board the U.S.S. *Hornet* was the signal for the raising of the United States flag and the lowering of the Spanish flag. West Florida was finally a part of the United States, but there was yet time for a series of embarrassing incidents before the Spanish governor departed.

Colonel Robert Butler, adjutant general for the southern district, acted for Jackson to accept the transfer of East Florida. On May 24 Butler presented himself and his credentials at St. Augustine, and final arrangements were completed on June 6. On the morning of July 10 the American troops formed lines near the fort, the Spanish flag came down, the Spanish troops marched out, and the American troops marched in. A third exchange took place at Fort Saint Marks without undue formality. In late June three companies of United States artillery garrisoned the fort, and the Spanish troops sailed for Pensacola where they arrived on July 19, having been delayed by unfavorable winds.

Jackson was never happy at Pensacola. He disliked dealing with the Spaniards, who had six months to wind up their affairs. He had discovered that President Monroe had appointed the most important officials for the Territory without consulting him. It was summer and the weather was at times uncomfortably hot and humid. His personal quarters, a large two story house, very comfortably furnished, led Mrs. Jackson to pronounce Pensacola the most healthful place she had ever seen. The new governor, on the other hand, found some of the public buildings unusable.

One of the governor's first acts was to organize the Floridas as a single territory with two counties, Escambia, from the Perdido to the Suwannee, and Saint Johns, the area east of the Suwannee. The designation of East Florida and West Florida did not disappear, and Middle Florida appeared in 1824 when the Territorial Council provided for a third court to sit in the region between the Apalachicola and the Suwannee rivers. Jackson then issued executive orders setting up a civil government, providing for administrative and judicial offices with appropriate regulations for their guidance. Each county was to have at least ten justices of the peace, of which five would make up the County Court. Pensacola and Saint

Augustine continued under the Spanish system of mayor and aldermen. Henry M. Brackenridge became mayor of Pensacola and the lesser patronage went to Jackson's political followers. James C. Bronaugh, Jackson's physician and confidant, was named resident physician at Pensacola.

President Monroe drew men from widely separated places to fill the ten most important offices. Eligius Fromentin, judge for West Florida, came from Louisiana, and William P. Duval for East Florida from Kentucky. The two United States attorneys were Alexander Anderson of Tennessee and John G. Bird from Georgia; the United States marshall, James G. Forbes, was from New York. George Walton of Georgia, whose father had been one of the signers of the Declaration of Independence, was secretary for West Florida and William G. D. Worthington of Maryland for East Florida. Others came from North Carolina, South Carolina, Virginia, Indiana, and the District of Columbia.

Jackson's relations with the few Spanish civil and military officials who remained in the city were far from cordial, but many of his own officials joined the genial company that gathered around ex-Governor José Callava, who had stayed on in his capacity as the king's commissioner for the transfer. Jackson particularly resented this on the part of Judge Fromentin and John Innerarity of Forbes and Company, who had long been associated with Spaniards in New Orleans and Pensacola. The new American governor was ready to seize any opportunity to exhibit his dislike for Callava and his associates. In August Mayor Brackenridge brought him the story of Mercedes Vidal, a free octoroon, the natural daughter of Nicholas Maria Vidal, a Spanish official who had died in 1806, leaving considerable holdings of land in Louisiana and other property in Pensacola to his half-caste children. Forbes and Company, charged as executors of the will with responsibility for settling the estate, had failed to do so. The Vidals had appealed to the courts for an accounting, but John Innerarity, head of the company, had refused orders to deliver records of the case to the court. A directive from the governor had been ignored without visible effect upon his close personal relations with Innerarity. Mercedes Vidal secured copies of enough documents to substantiate her case and also reported that the documents had been removed from the municipal archives to the residence of Lieutenant Domingo Sousa, one of Callava's clerks, in preparation for their removal to Cuba.

When Jackson demanded the papers, Sousa refused to deliver them without orders from his superior. When Colonel Robert Butler went to bring in Sousa and the papers, he found that they had been sent to the Callava residence. The governor next sent Brackenridge, Butler, and Bronaugh to request the papers of Callava, and, if they failed to secure them, to jail Sousa. They found Callava at the house of Colonel Brooke of the Fourth Infantry, and Innerarity and Judge Fromentin were also there. When Brackenridge delivered the request, Callava claimed immunity as royal commissioner and would neither surrender the papers nor return to his house. His host refused to allow service of papers on his premises.

On the next visit Jackson's emissaries found Callava and Innerarity at the commissioner's house, and they renewed the request. Callava agreed to surrender the papers if a list were presented but, apparently supported by his American allies, declined to do so when a list was provided. Jackson rose to this challenge by sending an officer and twenty men to back up the request of his agents. When Callava refused to respond to repeated knocks, the men entered the house and found him in bed fully clothed except for his military jacket. When he again refused to turn over the papers, the invaders led him before Jackson sitting as chief justice of the Floridas. When the commissioner refused to acknowledge Jackson's authority (Jackson insisted that Callava had only the rights of a private citizen in this case) he ordered Callava to jail. A search produced the papers, and Callava and Sousa were released from prison. In the meantime, Judge Fromentin, not knowing of the release, issued a writ of habeas corpus, demanding that the governor release the Spaniards. Jackson's response was to demand of him his authority to challenge the authority of the governor. Callava went to Washington to lodge a protest with the Spanish ambassador, and the *National Gazette,* Nov. 3, 1821, published his long account of the affair. John Quincy Adams, the secretary of state, continued to defend Jackson, and most Americans probably approved his actions, but he was again embarrassing the administration by his abrupt methods. When some of Callava's officers still at Pensacola published a protest of Jackson's treatment of their superior, Jackson replied with an order for all Spaniards to depart within four days—when the time allowed them to settle their affairs would elapse.

The general's liking for Florida did not improve, and on October 5, he notified Monroe that he considered his mission accomplished and that he was departing, but stated he would return if the public good required it. The occasion for the return never came, but he had brought to the Territory a number of men destined to play prominent roles, including Richard Keith Call and James Gadsden.

Captain John R. Bell exercised authority in East Florida until Secretary Worthington arrived in Saint Augustine in August. On August 22, Worthington read the ordinances of the governor to the mayor and council of Saint Augustine. Only one councilman could take the oath of allegiance, so Worthington appointed Colonel Forbes who served as mayor until Edmund Law, the new appointee, arrived. Jackson had hoped to appoint local people to office but found only one who could or would serve.

On March 30, 1822, the Congress created a territorial government for Florida that followed the pattern set in the Northwest Ordinance of 1787 by providing orderly political steps toward greater self government and eventual statehood as population increased. In the first stage the act provided for a governor, a secretary, a thirteen-man legislative council, judges appointed by the president, and a delegate to the Congress to represent the interest of the Territory in that body but with no voting power. The appropriate laws of other states were applied until the territorial legislature began to function.

Certain political issues appeared from the very first that were to persist throughout the early years of the territorial era. The legislatures of Alabama and Georgia indicated willingness to annex appropriate parts of the newly acquired land. West Florida gave some support to annexation to Alabama, but East Florida opposed any such move. East Florida preferred to continue the two territories and eventually make two states, a proposal unacceptable to Middle Florida because it postponed statehood. Others, aware that two more slave states could only arouse the issues that had been laid to rest temporarily in the Missouri Compromise of 1820, also opposed the two-state idea.

William Pope Duval, judge of East Florida, became the first territorial governor and served four three-year terms. John H. Eaton, a Jackson favorite who had been United States Senator from Tennessee and Jackson's secretary of war, served two years from 1834 to 1836. Richard Keith Call, another Jackson protégé, had a three-year term to 1839, and Robert Raymond Reid a brief stay in 1840 and 1841, after which Call came back for another three years. Finally, John Branch, who had been governor and United States Senator in North Carolina and Jackson's secretary of navy, served from 1844 to 1845. The legislative council, made up of the governor and thirteen others appointed annually by the president, exercised the legislative power until 1826 when the council became elective, one member being chosen from each of thirteen counties. In 1838 the Congress provided for a two-house legislature of eleven senators and twenty-six house members. Representation in the house was based on counties, but senators were chosen from the judicial districts, three from West, four from Middle, three from East, and one from sparsely settled southern Florida. Many names appeared in the membership of the first council which were destined to play prominent roles in Florida's development

In spite of the designation as a single territory for purposes of government, there were two Floridas geographically and administratively, one at Pensacola and the other at Saint Augustine, with almost four hundred miles of unoccupied wilderness between them. To meet this circumstance, the first session of the territorial council met at Pensacola and the second at Saint Augustine. Called to the first meeting on June 10, 1822, a quorum was not present until July 22. The council sent Joseph M. Hernandez of Saint Augustine to Washington as territorial delegate, but provided for the election of the delegate annually thereafter. The council also divided the Territory into four counties, adding Duval in the East and Jackson in the West.

Recognizing the impracticability of meeting in alternate years at the western and eastern extremes of settlement, first the council requested the president of the United States to have the army engineers about to survey Tampa Bay to explore the interior of the Territory, report to the govemor a likely place for a more centrally located capital, and lay out roads to it from Pensacola and Saint Augustine. The usual trip from Pensacola to Saint Augustine was twenty days, but in 1823 Call, Fry, and Walton made it in fifteen days. At that time the president had not responded to the request, and the council authorized the governor to appoint two commissioners to locate a site for a capital between the Suwannee and the Ocklockonee rivers. Governor Duval selected John Lee Williams of Pensacola and Dr. William H. Simmons of Saint Augustine to determine the location. In October of the same year they selected Tallahassee, which had been an Indian settlement but had no whites at the time. The governor formally proclaimed it the capital on March 4, 1824, and the third session of the territorial council was convened there in November in a temporary log building.

The cornerstone of the first "permanent" capitol building was laid in 1826. This was a 24 feet by 30 feet two-story brick structure, the upper floor designed for use by the council and the lower for executive and judicial offices. In 1839 it gave way to a more adequate building, which forms the central unit of the restored old capitol building. Tallahassee soon became the economic and social as well as the political center of the Territory. Within two decades Middle Florida was overtaking the older settlements in population and wealth, being advertised and helped somewhat by the location of the capital there.

The territorial delegate was the most important elective official in the Territory, where so much depended upon the willingness of the national government to assist in its development. Three main problems absorbed the major attention of the delegate: land disposal, internal improvements, and Indian affairs. Richard Keith Call won the first election over three opponents and served until 1825 when he resigned to become receiver of the public land office in Florida. Joseph M. White then held the office until 1838, followed by Charles Downing for two years and thereafter, David Levy of East Florida, to the end of the territorial period.

The establishment of private claims and locating them when the land had not been surveyed hampered orderly settlement, particularly in East Florida where such claims were more numerous. The treaty of cession provided that titles to land granted or conveyed to private ownership before January 24, 1818, were to be confirmed by the United States. This proved to be a gigantic task. Records were often nonexistent and usually were in Spanish when available. Some claims originated in the British period, were confirmed in the second Spanish era and recorded in that language, and another translation of the document might render it somewhat different from the original. The United States dealt reasonably with claimants, many of whose documents were fraudulent as to origin, location, and extent, a circumstance not unusual in the United States where land was so plentiful and claimants so few. Congress in 1822 created a board of three commissioners to sit alternately in Pensacola

Florida's first capitol was a crude log cabin, which was replaced by this two-story structure in 1826.

and Saint Augustine to examine claims. Sessions began on July 15, but the pressure of business was such that the Congress created a separate board for East Florida and extended the terms to 1825. In 1824 the boards began also to examine the claims of renters, squatters, and purchasers of land with doubtful titles that had accumulated as a result of delays in opening public land for sale. After 1826 the Register and Receiver of the Land Office for East Florida handled claims and reported 135 claims still pending in the courts ten years later.

Several large Spanish land grants were in litigation for years. The Forbes Grant, one and a quarter million acres, was not confirmed until 1835, at which time many settlers on the tract pulled up stakes and moved to the town of Saint Joseph rather than buy the land from the company. In Alachua County the Arredondo Grant of 289,647 5/7 acres, made in 1817 for services to the King of Spain, was confirmed in 1832. Richard S. Hackley purchased the claim of the Duke of Alagon on May 29, 1819. The grant, covering some eleven million acres, had been made on February 6, 1818, some two weeks after the January 24 deadline after which grants were no longer valid. Hackley maintained that since he made the purchase prior to the ratification of the treaty of cession it was legal. He sold the claim to Colonel George W. Murray and Associates in New York, who with their heirs and successors kept the case in the courts until January 3, 1905, when the United States Supreme Court finally ruled the grant invalid under the terms of the treaty.

In 1824 Colonel Robert Butler, surveyor-general for Florida, began surveys by establishing base and meridian lines at Tallahassee, from which the rectangular system of surveys established in 1785 by the Continental Congress was extended over the public lands. Land selling began at Tallahassee in 1825, Saint Augustine in 1826, and Newnansville in 1843. The pattern of growth in the Territory up to the year of statehood in 1845 can be measured by land sales at these offices. At Tallahassee, where most new development occurred, 796,891.81 acres; Saint Augustine, around which most of the land was already in private hands, 70,155 acres; and in the recently opened Newnansville office on the expanding frontier only 5,448.78 acres.

Initiating the surveys did not immediately make land available everywhere that people desired to settle. As early as 1826 delegate White supported a federal bill to grant settlers the right of preemption on the purchase of public land on which a pioneer had established a home before it was surveyed and offered for sale. The act covering certain lands in the states of Alabama and Mississippi and the Territory of Florida passed that year permitted such settlers to acquire the land at the minimum price of $1.25 an acre, which the buyer usually paid at the time the land would normally be offered for sale at public auction, to the highest bidder. Otherwise the pioneer might be forced to buy the improvements he himself had made. A series of these relief measures preceded the general law of 1842 providing for preemption on any public lands in the nation.

The ultimate objective of citizens in a Territory is statehood, but Floridians remained so divided over the desirability that it is remarkable that the national Congress saw fit to grant it. Divisionists who wanted to wait until there were enough residents to make two states and thereby strengthen the position of the South in the United States Senate were concentrated in East Florida. Others in the same section opposed statehood in principle and supported division to postpone it. Yet two of the strongest individual supporters of statehood were in East Florida. They were David Levy, who perhaps best deserved the title, architect of statehood, and Robert Raymond Reid, who became the chairman of the constitutional convention and was later territorial governor. The Second Seminole War (1835-1842) was fought principally in East and Middle Florida, and people there looked to the national government for protection and security. The strongest sentiment for statehood was in the Middle Florida plantation belt, while West Florida was about evenly divided between statehood and division, with proposals for annexation to Alabama commanding some support. The panic of 1837 and its aftermath also dampened enthusiasm for statehood.

Home rule was perhaps the strongest argument for statehood. Floridians complained that territories were too likely to be looked upon as the patrimony of the decayed or neglected politicians of other states. Persons from non-slave states sometimes held public offices. It was charged early in Governor Duval's career that he was going to Kentucky without attending to some pressing Indian problems, and that he would sometimes be gone for as much as six months. The strongest argument against statehood was the necessity for the state to pay the costs of administration and government. The advocates of early action argued that the sixteenth section of public land in each township set aside for education, two whole townships for support for higher education, and the prospect of a 500,000 acre grant from the national government for internal improvements offset the economic disadvantages. In 1837 the vote for statehood revealed the divided minds and sectional attitudes of Floridians. In Middle Florida were 1,152 votes for and 226 against; in West Florida 732 for and 324 against, while East Florida had 614 against and 255 in favor. In 1839, voters approved a constitution by the close vote of 2,065 to 1,961.

Middle Florida grew most rapidly. The capital was there and good cotton land free of disputed claims. The removal of Seminole Indians under the Treaty of 1823 promoted rapid settlement. The region soon accounted for almost half of the population and wealth in the Territory, but sectional jealousy was such that it could not dominate the constitutional convention but had to make heavy concessions to the other sections to win support for statehood. East Florida was allotted twenty delegates and West Florida sixteen, while Middle Florida had only twenty. West Florida was to have the site of the convention and East Florida the chairman. Robert Raymond Reid of Saint Augustine became the presiding officer and, in spite of all the logic of the selection of Tallahassee for the convention, Saint Joseph won the prize largely through the efforts of the promoters of that boom town.

Though it is commonly referred to as the Constitution of 1838, the convention sat from December 3 of that year until January 4, 1839. The fifty-six members came from twenty-six states of the Union. Four were foreign born, and only three were Florida born. Lawyers and planters were most numerous. Over one-third of the delegates had legislative experience, eighteen of them in the legislative council of the Territory. They included Florida's most distinguished citizens. William P. Duval had been governor for twelve years, and Reid would later have a term in that office. Three others would represent the state in the United States Senate, two would become governors, five would serve in the state supreme court, and five would participate in the secession convention.

The work of the convention was accomplished by eighteen committees, on each of which there was one or more persons with experience in that area of government. Constitution making was actually a rather simple process. The constitutions of other southern frontier states, especially Alabama, provided models, and only on the subject of banking did Floridians depart from the usual pattern. That question involved sectional, class, and political antagonisms that were more than local issues. Anti-bank sentiment was a phenomenon of national politics following the panic of 1837. Banks and bankers as usual inherited a full share of the blame for the collapse of prices and credit. In the nation at large, Whigs gained at the expense of Jacksonian Democrats, whose loose banking policies had helped to bring on the inflation and collapse. Whigs had dominated the Florida legislative council at the time when banks were chartered and continued to be their principal supporters. As a result they lost favor with voters. Generally speaking, the planters and their business allies were Whigs and pro-bank, while the farmers and small business interests were Democrats and looked upon banks in the Territory as primarily for the benefit of the plantation and slaveholding interests.

When political parties did emerge they produced some surprises. The first three civil governors of the Territory were personal friends of Andrew Jackson and were at the time Democrats. In 1840, however, William P. Duval, Richard Keith Call, and John H. Eaton all supported the Whig candidates for president and vice-president, William Henry Harrison and John Tyler. Tyler was a Virginian whose views on sectional issues Floridians and other southerners could trust. The rank and file who made up the Florida Whigs were largely persons turned conservative as they grew older and more successful in their economic endeavors. The exceptions to any generalizations about party membership are too numerous to make it possible to draw clear lines. They divided in Florida principally on the issues of statehood, faith bonds, and banking, with the Middle Florida Whigs opposed to division, favoring statehood, and defending banks. On the sectional issues developing around the growing controversy over slavery they differed scarcely at all. This meant that when northern Whigs showed anti-slavery tendencies, southern Whigs could rather easily go into the Democratic party.

Only the framing and adoption of the section of the constitution on banking produced any considerable debates. James D. Westcott, Jr., David Levy, and Richard H. Long represented anti-bank Democrats, and Samuel C. Bellamy, Walker Anderson, and Thomas Brown represented the Whig defenders. But Anderson defected to the opposition and the committee was four to two in its anti-bank attitude. The committee recommended and the convention approved such stringent rules on banking that a state-chartered financial institution did not begin to function until ten years after the constitution went into effect in 1845. Bank charters were for a maximum of twenty years and could not be renewed. They could engage only in the business of exchange, deposit, and discount, being specifically forbidden to deal in real estate, corporate stocks, or merchandise or to become involved in manufacturing, commerce, or the insurance business. These prohibitions were the areas of banking activity that it was assumed had led to disaster in the panic of 1837, but they were also precisely the areas where a developing commu-

Geographical, Statistical, and Historical Map of Florida, 1822.
From the Martk F. Boyd Collection of Floridana

nity desperately needed money and credit. All liabilities of state-chartered banks were made payable in specie, and stockholders were liable for their share of the bank's debts if it failed. Nor could the state pledge its faith and credit to support any corporation. A minimum capital stock of $100,000 made it unlikely that any group would meet the requirement.

The Declaration of Rights in Article 1 of the constitution included twenty-seven items. The governor was to have a four-year term but was ineligible for reelection to a successive term. The president of the senate and the speaker of the house in that order succeeded to the governor's office when it became vacant. House members were to be chosen for one-year terms on the first Monday in October and senators for a two-year term, one-half being elected each year. No president, director, cashier, or other officer of any banking company in the state could be elected to the governorship or to either house of the legislature until one year after he left this position. Sentiment for separation of church and state was reflected in the disqualification of preachers of the gospel for any of the same offices.

Each county was to have one representative and the more populous counties were to receive additional representation on the basis of a formula to be set by the General Assembly. The population of a county could not be reduced by division below the number set by the legislature for representation in the house. House membership was limited to sixty and the senate to one-fourth to one-half of that number. Senators were to be elected from districts as nearly equal as possible, but counties in a district must be contiguous and a county could not be divided. A state census to serve as a basis for apportioning representation was to be made in 1845 and every ten years thereafter. An indication of the distribution of population was the rule that until the census the numbers in the lower house were set at one each for Dade, Hamilton, Hillsborough, Madison, Monroe, Mosquito, Nassau, Walton, and Washington counties; two each for Alachua, Calhoun, Columbia, Duval, and Franklin; three each for Escambia, Jackson, Jefferson, and Saint Johns; four for Gadsden; and six for Leon. Sixteen senatorial districts elected one each, with two for Leon, the seventeenth.

Strong pro-slave sentiment was evident in the convention. The legislature could not pass any law to prevent an owner from bringing his slave property into the Territory except for such reasons as having committed a crime. Nor could that body enact any law to emancipate slaves or permit free blacks to move into the state. The laws of the Territory had revealed the same deep concern for the security of slave property. An 1828 statute provided the death penalty for a master to conceal on shipboard and carry away a slave owned by a Floridian. At the next session, a law set the death penalty for slave stealing, and another forbade manumission except by judicial process and a guarantee that the freed black would leave the Territory within thirty days. Blacks could possess firearms only under the most rigid regulations that made the owner responsible for them. Patrols made up largely of owners or their agents kept a close watch on the goings and comings of slaves, and woe unto a black discovered unable to account for himself, particularly at night.

Rumor or report of slave uprisings or organized attempts to escape led to increased vigilance by the patrols. Actually, the controls were probably not as strictly enforced as the rules suggest.

Certainly blacks on the plantations frequently used guns for hunting. Running away was relatively futile after the removal of the Seminole Indians. The Underground Railway did not extend southward to this remote frontier. The only way out was by boat and that was never notably successful. Only one delegate, Richard Fitzpatrick of Dade County, voted against the finished documents on January 11, though only forty-one of the delegates were actually present to sign. The convention provided for a vote on ratification in May when the territorial delegate would be chosen and for the election of state officers in October. The constitution makers also created a committee made up of Walker Anderson, Robert R. Reid, and James D. Westcott, Jr., to present their work to the Congress. The committee prepared a "Memorial to the Congress of the People of the Territory of Florida" and sent a copy of the constitution along with a petition for admission to the Union, together with a statement of the arguments for statehood.

It sometimes appeared during the convention that sentiment for statehood was growing, but the reception of the constitution by Florida voters was less than enthusiastic. Statehood was the principal issue in the election of the territorial delegate. Charles Downing, the incumbent, a leading Whig, dropped his opposition to division and in East Florida expressed dislike for some of the new document's provisions, though in Middle Florida he did not oppose statehood. Baltzell, speaking for the Democrats, campaigned for the constitution and for statehood. Downing won with strong support from East and West Florida. In the vote on ratification, however, strong support in Middle Florida overcame the opposition in East and West by only one hundred votes, some of them questioned. Anti-bank Democrats won a majority of the seats in the lower house in 1839 and 1841, and they also replaced Downing with Democrat David Levy, a strong advocate of statehood, in 1841. Annexationists and divisionists continued to petition the Congress and must have left considerable doubt in that body that Floridians knew what they wanted. It must be conceded that Florida was not yet ready for statehood. The population and taxable wealth were too small to support a state government under the best of circumstances, and depression and the Indian war rendered the existing economic and financial situation anything but good.

There was little disposition to levy taxes or to pay the limited dues already on the statute books. East and West Florida largely ignored the revenue act of 1839, and the legislative council suspended taxes on land and slaves in 1840 and 1841, leaving the treasury only the tax on auction sales. With some $13,000 in auditor's warrants already issued and less than $500 on hand, the council suspended the assessment for taxes in 1841. A poor cotton crop in 1840 and 1841 added to the economic woes of Floridians and further discouraged talk of statehood.

Hopeful Floridians thought that Georgia might be willing to cede a southern tier of counties to help them to statehood, but the interest of Georgians had ceased with a resolution to annex East

Florida some years earlier. For that matter, the boundary line between the two had never been settled, and the right to 1,507,200 acres was at stake. It will be remembered that a boundary commission had surveyed the line from the Mississippi River to the Chattahoochee along the thirty-first parallel and down that river to the mouth of the Flint, but hostile Indians prevented the survey to the headwaters of the Saint Marys. Operating from the Atlantic side, the same surveyors built up a mound of earth, Elliott's Mound, and designated it the source of the Saint Marys but left the remainder of the boundary undetermined. In 1822 Elliott's Mound was questioned as the proper source of the Saint Marys. A dispute arose that, in spite of efforts by the states and the national government to reach an agreement, was not settled until 1866. In 1872 the Congress approved the action of the states that accepted the Elliott's Mound line, giving most of the disputed land to Florida. Fifteen years later a court action settled questions of land title arising from the dispute.

In 1843 David Levy, staunch supporter of statehood, won election as territorial delegate and continued to labor to that end. To those who argued that Floridians could not pay the cost, he replied that it need not cost anything. Public lands would pay for it all and more. The half a million acres of public land the state would receive for internal improvements would build a railroad across the state that would produce enough operating profit to pay all the costs of state government. The sixteenth section of school land in every township of public land would provide more than enough to pay for schools. In 1843, Levy may well have believed that the state could and should build and operate such a railroad, but a dozen years later he was proposing that private investors build it with aid from state and national governments, and he headed the company that eventually built the Florida Railroad from Fernandina to Cedar Key.

The voters returned a legislative council in October 1844 favorable to statehood. The cessation of Indian hostilities in 1842 and the signs of recovery from the panic of 1837 created a more optimistic outlook. Some divisionists perhaps began to despair of getting two states, and Iowa, a matching free state, was also ready to be admitted. Other divisionists presented a petition to Congress as late as January 1845, but John Branch, who became governor in 1844, supported statehood, as did the council, though it left open the door for Florida someday to become two states.

A bill to admit Florida as a state passed the national House of Representatives on February 13 and the U.S. Senate on March 1, and the president signed it two days later, making March 3, 1845, the date of Florida's entry into the Union. The news reached Tallahassee five days later, and Governor Branch finally received an official copy of the act ten days later. In Tallahassee there was much rejoicing with the ringing of bells, firing of cannons, bonfires, and a gala reception at Live Oak, the home of the governor, who gave full support to the move that would see the executive leadership pass to others. The people of the twenty-seventh state moved rapidly to establish their new status. The legislative council met on March 11 and set elections for May 26. Voters would at that time choose a governor, a member of the national House of Representatives, seventeen state senators, and forty-one house members. June 23 was set for the meeting of the first General Assembly.

10.

Territorial Florida—
A Frontier Society

At the end of two and a half centuries of Spanish occupation Florida was still little more than a frontier military outpost dependent upon an annual subsidy for survival. Military garrisons at Saint Augustine, Saint Marks, and Pensacola maintained Spanish authority that reached scarcely beyond the walls of the forts. The twenty-five thousand aboriginal Indians were gone almost to a man. Some five thousand Seminoles had moved into the land left unoccupied by their departure. A few settlers remained from the British interlude, many of them Minorcans. The brief British occupation had left almost as much impression upon the provinces as the long Spanish tenure. A few runaway slaves from Alabama and Georgia and a slightly larger number of whites, some of them with slaves, had moved into the northeastern section of Florida. A larger band of runaways had gathered in the Apalachicola River area. These, with a small number of Spaniards who elected to remain, made up the population in 1821. Florida had fewer inhabitants than at any time since discovery in 1513 and there were few alien dwellers in the newly acquired territory.

In Pensacola a Spanish census in 1820 counted 713 inhabitants, but more important for the future of the region were 380 white Americans with seventy-three black slaves living along the Escambia River only a few miles from the town. The Spanish governor, José Callava, looked upon them with mixed feelings because they did not acknowledge his authority. But they did not pose any immediate threat to his position. They grew rice, corn, beans, tobacco, and cotton and raised cattle and hogs, which provided food for Pensacola's inhabitants, much of which would otherwise have had to be imported. The Spanish garrison except for thirty-six officers left on the day following the transfer of sovereignty. A large number of adventurers and prospectors probably arrived soon after the change of flags and as quickly drifted away when they discovered the limited opportunity for official patronage and speculative profits in real estate. The departure of General Andrew Jackson and a severe epidemic of yellow fever in 1822 reduced the appeal of the locality.

Only about one thousand persons were counted in the United States census in 1830 and only 2,300 ten years later.

The first territorial census in 1825 was incomplete and unreliable, but estimates based upon it and other data put the number of persons west of the Apalachicola at 5,780; between that river and the Suwannee at 2,370; east of the Suwannee at 5,077; and only 317 in South Florida. The rapid growth of Middle Florida is clear five years later in the federal census in which West Florida had 9,478; Middle, 15,779; East, 8,956; and South, 517 inhabitants. In 1840 Middle Florida had reached 34,000; West, possibly because of a shift in district lines, had dropped to 5,500; and East counted 15,000. In the state census of 1845 Middle Florida had forty-seven percent of the population, and four counties there with black majorities (Jackson 52.9%, Gadsden 53% Jefferson 64.3%, and Leon 68.9%) were producing eighty percent of the cotton in the new state. Only Nassau County in the extreme northeast also had as much as fifty percent blacks in the population. Rice was a more important crop than the sea island cotton that was also grown there.

A contemporary description of Pensacola is unflattering. Though there were a few brick sidewalks at the end of the Spanish period the streets were principally deep white sand. The government house that Jackson had found unfit for use in 1821 was a frame building propped up with logs. The barracks had been built during the British period and were largely without windows or roofs. Port facilities had never been constructed, and most ships were unloaded by lighters until the United States government provided a one thousand foot wharf.

No description of Saint Augustine at the time of the transfer is available, but Achille Murat reached the town in the spring of 1824 and recorded his impressions. To him it looked more like a small Italian market town than an American village. There were in fact a few Greeks and Italians in Saint Augustine in the 1820s. The society was half American and half Spanish (Minorcan), each of the two nationalities living in its own way. Murat had a low opinion of the local citizens, particularly the squatters, whose poverty he attributed to idle and drunken habits. The Indians, "the noble savages" so much romanticized in his own country at the time, disappointed him. They had lost their simplicity and had become dependent upon the white trader and his merchandise, thereby losing the manly independence of their primitive and self-sufficient life in the American forests. After a year, Murat moved to Tallahassee, where he found the society of the pioneer planters from Georgia, the Carolinas, and Virginia far more to his liking. Another observer of the times, Ralph Waldo Emerson, in 1826 wondered why people who had cellars elsewhere felt compelled to dig them in Saint Augustine where they only filled with water. He thought the people lazy and the housekeeping bad. He found it incongruous that the Bible Society was meeting inside the government house while a slave auction was going on outside. Tallahassee, which he apparently did not visit, he nonetheless reported as being settled by office holders, those

seeking office or political favors, land speculators, and desperadoes.
Doctor William H. Simmons and John Lee Williams, who made
a visit to the region in 1823 to locate a site for the capital, gave the
best contemporary accounts of the interior. In 1827 the Reverend
Michael Portier journeyed overland from Pensacola to Saint Augustine. On a twelve-day journey to Tallahassee he found ferrymen
and the few scattered settlers eager for news of the outside world.
Tallahassee was located in beautiful country and, though not yet
four years old, had over a hundred neat well-ordered buildings. After
a three day stay Portier resumed the journey to Saint Augustine,
arriving on July 5. En route he learned of trouble with Indians and
predicted that the Seminoles would suffer the same fate as the
Creeks.

The Comte Francis de Castelnau spent four months in Middle
Florida in late 1837 and early 1838. He thought cotton the most
important crop but must have been in error when he placed sugarcane second. Cuban tobacco grew well there and a few cigars were
being made at Quincy. Governor William P. Duval had introduced
the seeds of Cuban tobacco in 1828, but John Smith brought from
Virginia a broader leaf that was more popular. Castelnau reported
horses costing fifty to one hundred dollars but mules were much
preferred as work animals. Long-horned open range cattle sold at
four to six dollars per head. Sheep did not do well, but all farmers
had hogs. He wondered that all men carried arms, at the amount of
lawlessness, drinking, and gambling, and speculated that the absolute authority exercised over slaves was the cause. He was wit-
nessing the characteristic behavior of frontiersmen all over America.
He thought stealers of horses and slaves were usually lynched.
Charles Hutchinson, a well-educated New Englander who was a
tutor in the James B. Gamble home from 1839 to 1843, also thought
Tallahassee politics full of turbulence and violence. In November
1843 when he returned after a brief absence he found Port Leon in
ruins as a result of a hurricane. Tallahassee had had a fire that
spring which destroyed eighty-nine houses and buildings.

The Lafayette land grant did much to advertise Middle Florida.
The American people never forgot the generous support, including
some $200,000 of his private fortune, that they received from the
Marquis de Lafayette in the American Revolution. In 1796 the Congress appropriated $24,424, the amount of the pay he had not col-
lected as a major general in the Continental Army. In the first
Jefferson administration Congress granted Lafayette 11,520 acres
of land. Again in 1824, the grateful government of the United States
granted him $200,000 and a township of land, which he selected
near Tallahassee because of his friendship with Richard Keith Call.
Hopes that the illustrious Frenchman might come to Florida and
that he might himself develop the land never materialized, and he
eventually sold it to Florida speculators. In 1850 two of his grand-
sons visited Florida and received a welcome that would have pleased
their famous ancestor.

In 1835 Marcus Cicero Stephens of Newbern, South Carolina,

came to establish a home near Quincy for his wife and eight children. He reported that flour brought eleven dollars a barrel, lard fifteen cents a pound, butter twenty-five cents, pork sixteen to eighteen dollars a barrel, and bacon thirteen and a half to fifteen cents per pound. Only beef was cheap, a good sized steer costing only from seven to twelve dollars.

A romantic but historically important settler who left a valuable account of his life in Florida was Prince Achille Murat, exiled son of the late king of Naples, who had married a distant relative of George Washington, and lived in Jefferson County, twenty miles from Tallahassee, on the thousand acre plantation, "Lipona." Murat described the arrival of planters with possessions in wagons, slaves on foot, and families in coaches, and how they camped at night, opened up roads, and even built bridges on the way. First the newcomers put up temporary wooden huts and cabins for family and slaves, and then they cleared land to plant the first crops. The Frenchman described these people as citizens of substance "come with the resolution of founding a new country." Log houses soon gave way to more substantial structures, most of them modest but some in stately colonial style. The planters were addicted to the gentlemanly sports of horse racing and ring tournaments, denounced only by those who considered themselves guardians of the morals of the community. Only the hard times following the panic of 1837 seem to have ended jockey clubs and horse racing.

A large number of families long prominent in Florida history settled in and around Tallahassee to make it the social and cultural as well as political center of the state. In 1933 Annie Randolph Dozier listed more than 150 family names in the city whose history went back to the antebellum period.

One of antebellum Florida's most illustrious professional men was Dr. John Gorrie, who came to Apalachicola in 1833 from Charleston. He practiced medicine and became socially and politically prominent, serving as postmaster, city councilman, city treasurer, mayor, president of the Apalachicola branch of the Bank of Pensacola, Episcopal vestry man, and treasurer of his Masonic Lodge. His chief professional interest was the treatment of malaria and yellow fever, in which he experimented with air cooling devices in the care of patients. In 1848 he demonstrated a machine to make ice, but a British patent was recorded on August 22, 1850, and a United States patent the next year preceded his. He lived until 1855 a defeated if not broken man. If he had not actually been the first man to manufacture ice, he had arrived independently at a method at much the same time it was being done in England.

East Florida development might also have been rapid and prosperous in the territorial period except that it suffered from two serious drawbacks. Much of the land was involved in disputed land claims, and by the time the claims began to be cleared up, the Seminole war intervened to destroy much that had been done and to bring a stop to any further advance. Indigo lost its importance as a plantation staple, but rice and sea island cotton grew well in the coastal regions in Nassau County. British planters who had withdrawn in 1783 returned at the end of the century to establish flourishing plantations to grow sugarcane and to manufacture sugar, only to fall in some of the first raids of the Seminole war. A severe freeze in 1835 killed a promising development of citrus growing that dated back at least to the British period. The only redeeming features of the Indian war were payrolls and markets at military installations; employment for teams, wagons, boats, and civilians; and the laying out of some roads.

The Gorrie ice machine

By the 1850s Florida was leading Georgia and South Carolina in the production of the black-seeded, long staple cotton. The Eli Whitney saw gin could not be used for the sea island variety, but it was relatively easy to separate seed from the lint by hand, and a small roller type gin came into general use in the early 1840s. Fones McCarthy, a native of Georgia, patented it in Demopolis, Alabama, but shortly moved the business to Florida, where the gin accounted for extensive production. The Levy holdings in East Florida illustrate the potential there. Moses Elias Levy began to acquire land late in the Spanish period and arrived in Saint Augustine at the time of change of sovereignty. Born in Morocco, where his father was a public official who thereafter migrated to Gibraltar, Moses Elias grew up on the island of Saint Thomas, where in partnership with Philip Benjamin, father of Judah P. Benjamin, he became a prosperous merchant. He divorced his wife in 1815 and moved to Havana, where he served as a supplier of military goods to the Spanish government and where he made plans to move to Florida. He received 36,000 acres in Middle Florida near the F. M. Arrendondo and Son grant and was required to validate the claim by moving in families to populate it. He purchased an additional 52,900 acres and went to Europe in 1816 to raise more capital and find settlers for his land. When the Arrendondo grant was ordered sold at auction in 1849 to clear the title, the elder Levy was entitled to 34,175 acres, to which he had established his claim, but he bid in 49,692, paying $17,145.83 for the balance. Levy's son, David, destined to play an important role in Florida history, was due 6,069 acres but bid in only 2,778. Moses Levy died in 1854, leaving his sons David and Elias $100 each and the remainder of his estate to two daughters and a sister, but the will was apparently broken and the children received equal shares. David had come home from Harvard College, managed the plantation lands in Alachua and Marion counties, and studied law in the office of Robert Raymond Reid of Saint Augustine. He was admitted to the bar in 1832 and entered politics, being elected to the legislative council in 1837 and 1838. He played the already described role in the constitutional convention and the new state.

George Fleming also came to Florida late in the second Spanish period and settled on Fleming Island, north of Black Creek on the west side of the Saint Johns River across the river from the plantation of his father-in-law, Francis Philip Fatio at New Switzerland. The Flemings received thirty-two slaves as a wedding gift and proceeded, frontier fashion, to begin the clearing of the wilderness and the planting of crops. Two sons, Lewis and George, Jr., spent their lives on the island as planters, Lewis inheriting "Hibernia," the family plantation, and adding to its tillable acres.

The Bulow plantation of 4,675 acres about eleven miles north of present-day Ormond produced a tragically romantic story. Charles W. Bulow came from South Carolina to settle in Florida in 1821 and died two years later, leaving his estate to a son, Joachim, who became one of Florida's most prosperous planters. Three hundred slaves cultivated 1,000 acres in sugarcane, 1,200 acres of cotton, and some food and fodder crops. In 1831 Bulow installed a sugar mill in some stone buildings. The ruins of these were sometimes, years later, mistaken for mission buildings. Actually, no mission buildings were as well constructed as the brick and stone structures that housed sugar mills in East Florida at about that time.

Major Benjamin A. Putnam, charged with the defense of the region between Saint Augustine and New Smyrna, made the Bulow plantation his headquarters from December 28, 1835, to January 23, 1836, in the early days of the Seminole war. Over the protests of the owner, Putnam launched from this base the ill-fated Dunlawton expedition on January 18, which turned out so badly that the officer abandoned the plantation and returned to Saint Augustine, using Bulow's teams, wagons and boats to transport government property and personnel. Soon after Putnam's departure, Indians overran, looted, and burned much of the property. Bulow died on May 7 of the same year without direct heirs. His estate passed to his sister, whose heirs tried without success to collect damages of $82,000 from the United States government.

General Duncan L. Clinch's "Auld Lang Syne" plantation ten miles below Micanopy was primarily a sugar-making establishment, but there were also corn cribs, storage bins for a small cotton crop, a blacksmith shop and other buildings. The slave quarters are described as huts with mud floors, reed thatched roofs and no windows except openings between logs. The overseer's house was a decaying, small cabin with four rooms, each with one open window –no glass, no shutters. The sugar works consisted of a mill, a molasses warehouse, and a rum distillery. Cane was brought to the mill on bullock carts and moved down an incline to be put into the rollers. Juice flowed into a reservoir until ready to be poured into vats for boiling. The dirty juice and skimmings from the boiling liquid went by a trough to the distillery. An Englishman from Jamaica came for three months each winter to supervise the sugar and rum making.

Any considerable development in South Florida lay far in the future, but there was some interest by white settlers as early as the British period. Five other land grants made by the Spanish in the second period were in the Miami area, and the Arrambide grant at present-day Fort Lauderdale in 1813 was at the mouth of the New River. Perhaps because of the hostility of Indians there, the attempt at settlement was made nearer to Miami. The United States courts ruled the claim invalid because it was not properly located or validated. The other five made between 1790 and 1815 proved valid and became the source of title to some 2,695 acres in modern Miami. Richard Fitzpatrick acquired four of the claims and established a cotton plantation on the Miami River where some of the buildings became part of Fort Dallas in the Seminole war. Fitzpatrick represented Monroe County in the legislative councils of 1832, 1833, 1835, and 1836. In the constitutional convention he represented Dade County, which he helped to create in 1836 when he was president of the council. The new county reached from the west end of Bahia Honda Key to Lake Okeechobee. Indian Key, the most important settlement, was the county seat. This small key, about halfway between Miami and Key West, was a convenient location for the business of marine salvage or wrecking on the Florida Reef. Jacob Housman, with a reputation for operating outside the law, preferred Indian Key to the more orderly capital of the wrecking business at Key West and was largely the architect of its fortunes. The customs inspector reported 637 ship arrivals at Indian Key in 1834 and 703 the following year. The United States Navy maintained a depot there for a brief time in the Seminole war, during which the Chekika raid in 1840 destroyed much of the Housman property and ended the key's importance. Miami became the county seat in 1844 but did not soon gain the importance that Housman had given to Indian Key.

No territorial problem was more important than the development of adequate transportation into the interior, which was not reached by navigable streams. Residents looked to the national government for roads to connect the principal settlements. The Congress on February 28, 1824, authorized a public road from Pensacola to Saint Augustine, specifying that the old Spanish road from Fort San Luis near Tallahassee to Saint Augustine that crossed the Saint Johns River at Picolata should be followed as closely as possible. The law provided that the road commence at Deer Point on Pensacola Bay and run from there to Cow Ford on the Choctawhatchee, thence to natural bridge on the Econfina, and on to Ochese Bluff, the only place on the Apalachicola with high banks on both sides of the river, and from there directly to Fort San Luis. The road, obviously little more than a blazed trail, was to be plainly marked. It was planned to be twenty-five feet wide, but was actually only wide enough for wagons to pass when any grading was required. Captain Daniel E. Burch of the Quartermaster Corps, United States Army, who directed the entire project, estimated that only 240 of the 642 mile distance was new road. Normally the road would have been constructed by the army, but when John Bellamy proposed that he be given the contract for the Saint Augustine-Tallahassee portion, Captain Burch concluded that the planter, using his own slave labor, wagons, and teams, could probably do the work less expensively. So it was agreed, and the road became known as the Bellamy Road. Since only $20,000 was appropriated for construction, there was obviously going to be only a limited amount of work done to improve the roadway. Some causeways and bridges did materialize, but ferries provided crossing of all major streams. Causeways washed out with the first freshet, stumps were left too high for some wheeled vehicles, bridges were crude and dangerous, and ferry service was uncertain. Citizens living nearby were required to work twelve days a year on the road or pay a sum of money equivalent to keep it in usable condition, but their numbers were never sufficient. Most travel was on horseback or on foot. The King's Road from New Smyrna to the Saint Marys River by way of Jacksonville was reopened in 1828 and 1829 but was little used.

The greatest contribution to road making in the territorial period came from the armed forces in the Seminole war. As they pushed the Indians farther southward down the peninsula, they opened trails almost anywhere that teams drawing wagons could penetrate. A military map of the region south of the Caloosahatchee, for example, shows a network of roads connecting the forts and temporary depots there. Their bridges and causeways were inadequate and impermanent, but they had shown the way to the interior, and when the Indians were gone, the white man found his way there by following them.

Floridians clamored for canals and river improvement where possible rather than for highways. The national government responded with limited appropriations for the improvement of navigation on the principal streams such as the Apalachicola, the Saint Marks, and the Saint Johns and its principal tributaries. This usually meant no more than removal of snags, logs, and sandbars. Steamboating on Florida streams enjoyed a brief heyday until the railroad came to offer more adequate transportation. The American clipper ship, constructed of wood and powered by sail, held its own in transoceanic travel well into the eighteen fifties, but the steamboat appeared earlier on rivers where it offered the only really feasible means of travel upstream.

Steamboat service began on the Apalachicola in 1827 and grew rather rapidly as the owners and operators reached well up into Georgia and Alabama for freight and passengers. Castelnau reported some thirty boats operating on the Apalachicola in 1838. Steamers were beginning to operate on the Suwannee by the end of the territorial period. The *George Washington* initiated steamboat service in East Florida when it arrived at Jacksonville from Savannah after a thirty-four hour run in 1831. A great handicap was the shifting sandbar at the mouth of the Saint Johns River, which limited passage at low tide to ships drawing only six or eight feet. Coastwise traffic was usually in small wood burning sidewheelers that carried passengers and freight to Savannah and sometimes to Charleston for transfer to larger ocean vessels. In April 1834 the steam packet *Florida* began running once a week between Savannah and Picolata, stopping at intervening points. A stage carried passengers the eighteen miles from Picolata to Saint Augustine. The ancient city began to enjoy direct travel by water when the Saint Augustine Wharf Company was chartered in 1834. The Seminole war gave a healthy boost to steamboating in Florida. In addition to operating its own boats, the government chartered forty steamboats in 1838 to carry troops and equipment, stores, horses, and mules.

Another center of boat traffic was in Key West, where the ships of the navy as well as those serving the needs of the station and the resident population made it a thriving port. A small fleet of boats engaged in the salvage business, the town's most lucrative occupation. In the year 1845 wreckers brought into the city twenty-six ships that had come to grief on the Florida Reef and the next year the number totaled fifty-five.

In the first years of territorial government canals seemed to offer the only solution to the problems of inland transportation, and every session of the council took some action on the subject. As early as 1822, Secretary of War John C. Calhoun ordered army engineers to explore the possibility of connecting the Saint Marys and the Suwannee by a canal, with a view to inland communication between the Atlantic and the Gulf. The Congress authorized a survey in March 1826. Brigadier General Simon Bernard, once Napoleon's principal military engineer, was in charge of the canal survey, and he made the report three years later. The engineers reported the proposal unsound because of lack of a deep water harbor on the Gulf coast anywhere between Tampa Bay and Apalachee Bay. Nor was there enough water on the 150-foot high ridge for locks on the canal. They suggested instead a route from the Saint Johns by way of Black Creek to the Santa Fe, crossing the Suwannee at the natural bridge and thence to Saint Marks, where water was eight feet deep at high tide. Practically every name prominent in planting, politics, and business may be found on the boards of directors of companies seeking charters for canal properties, but they produced nothing of importance. Congress in 1830 appropriated $10,400 to complete a survey; a lock and barge report was submitted in 1832, but it did not comment on practicability, cost or economic advantages.

The railroad offered the best solution to Florida's transportation problem, and officials in the Territory recognized it immediately. Territorial and state governments together chartered at least twenty corporations to build railroads between 1830 and 1860. Much of this was premature but pointed surely to the future. In 1831 six Tallahassee men secured a charter for the Leon Railway Company to construct a road from the capital city to Saint Marks. The distance was short, only thirty miles, but the terrain was sand which merged into swamp as one neared the Saint Marks River, which was navigable only a few miles from its mouth. Reorganized in 1832, it became the Tallahassee Railroad Company in 1834 with a land grant of 500,000 acres. Construction was completed to Port Leon, twenty-two miles away, in 1836. The roadbed was a primitive and flimsy affair on which mules pulled small wooden cars over iron strips laid on longitudinal wooden stringers. The passenger coach was a box with two benches to seat eight people, but Saint Marks shipped as much as 50,000 bales of cotton a year, most of which came by rail. The town's population never exceeded 500, but the long row of cotton sheds on the river bank attested the importance of the trade. In the fall of 1843 a devastating hurricane struck Port Leon, and a tidal wave destroyed the town and tore up the railroad to a point above the Saint Marks River bridge. Thereafter Port Leon was abandoned; the road terminated at the river with cotton storage provided at Tallahassee. It was the only railroad in operation in 1845 when Florida became a state. In 1855 mules were still providing the motive power, but the next year the owners rebuilt the road and brought in two Baldwin locomotives, named the "H. L. Rutger" and the "General Bailey."

In 1834 the legislative council chartered the Florida, Alabama and Georgia Railroad to build northward from Pensacola. Reorganized a year later, it failed to survive the depression beginning in 1837. Thanks to the financial assistance provided by the Bank of Pensacola, some right-of-way was graded but no track laid. When the Louisville and Nashville Railroad later provided Pensacola with its principal connection to the north it did not even follow the same route.

The promoters of Saint Joseph produced two efforts at railroad building. In 1835 the council chartered the Lake Wimico and St. Joseph Canal and Railroad Company to construct a canal or a railroad to connect the Apalachicola River with Saint Josephs Bay by way of Lake Wimico. In 1836 a steam engine pulled a train of twelve cars carrying more than 300 passengers the nine miles from Saint Joseph to the lake in twenty-five minutes. The lake proved too shallow to accommodate the river steamers that the builders hoped to divert from Apalachicola, and the road was abandoned. The second effort was a thirty-mile line from Saint Joseph to Iola on the west bank of the Apalachicola a little north of the junction with the Chipola, which involved a long bridge over the Chipola and the adjacent swamp. This too was abandoned when the effort to divert river traffic failed, and Saint Joseph went into a rapid decline after so promising a start.

Frontier communities always need but always lack adequate capital, credit, and banking facilities. Governor Jackson forwarded a petition of some Pensacola citizens to establish a branch of the United States Bank there in 1821, but trading establishments usually provided these services as Panton Leslie and Company and its successors had. An effort to charter a bank at the second session of the territorial council failed, and in 1824 the city of Saint Augustine issued bills up to five hundred dollars signed by the mayor and the treasurer. In 1825 the governor vetoed measures to charter banks and, though pressure of demand for banks grew, proposals could not be passed over his opposition until 1828 when the council chartered the Bank of Florida at Tallahassee. A year later the council reduced the minimum of paid-in capital required to open a bank from forty to twenty-five thousand dollars and limited liability of stockholders to three times the amount of capital paid in. In 1832 the council chartered the Central Bank of Florida at Tallahassee; it absorbed the Bank of Florida with its capital of $100,000 and note circulation of half that amount.

The council chartered eighteen banks between 1828 and 1839, but only three achieved any importance. At least six of these never opened their doors, and others, if they opened at all, were absorbed by rivals or failed to contribute significantly to the financial needs of the community. The approaching end of the Bank of the United States in 1836 spawned a wave of new state bank charters, but the Congress required charters in territories to be approved by that body and acted to limit their number. The Bank of Pensacola, the Union Bank of Florida at Tallahassee, and the Southern Life Insurance and Trust Company at Saint Augustine grew to major importance, but they could not attract enough capital to provide for the financial needs of the growing communities.

An attempt by the council in 1831 to get a branch of the United States Bank failed, and the promoters turned to the council itself for the solution. That body responded by authorizing the banks to sell bonds guaranteed by the territorial government. By 1843 the three favored institutions had sold $3,900,000 of these "faith" bonds. The Bank of Pensacola invested heavily in the Alabama, Florida and Georgia Railroad, but $259,000 failed to produce more than ten miles of railroad and the bank went down with the badly managed transportation facility. Governor Duval approved the bill to charter the Union Bank with a capital of one million dollars which might be increased to three. John G. Gamble, a Virginian who became the president of the new bank, is usually credited with originating the idea of this real estate mortgage bank designed to aid planters. A planter might subscribe for $3,000 worth of the stock, giving a mortgage on his land and slaves, and then mortgage the stock to the same bank and receive $2,000 as a twenty-year loan, leaving the $1,000 in the bank for its routine operations. When the planters redeemed the twenty-year notes the bank could retire the territorial bonds. This scheme was not unlike many others in the United States at the same time, and it produced charges of too high appraisals of property and pledging of the same slaves several times. The territorial council brought the bank operation to an end in 1843.

The Saint Augustine Bank, which reached its end at the same time, was owned largely by northerners who used it to sell insurance, make loans, engage in the export and import business and develop land and timber projects. With branches at Jacksonville, Tallahassee, Apalachicola and Saint Joseph, it became known as the cotton bank because of its extensive trade in that staple.

The Florida economy in the territorial period was almost exclusively agricultural and extractive, primarily products of field and forest. Business was limited pretty much to providing the limited commercial services of an undeveloped community. Seats of county government had an essential if limited role to play, and the Seminole war gave at least temporary importance to other towns. To Pensacola, the only town on the Gulf coast in 1821, were added Apalachicola, Saint Joseph, Port Leon, Magnolia, Newport and Tampa. Pensacola's large and excellent harbor brought no comparable growth to the town, which lacked contact with the interior by river or rail. Apalachicola thrived on cotton from Alabama and Georgia brought to market there by way of the Flint and the

A faith bond of the territorial period. Note the identification with the United States of America.

Chattahoochee and the Apalachicola waterway. Pine timber and lumber were also important exports. Saint Marks won over Magnolia as a port of entry and remained the most important of the river ports. After a severe hurricane in 1843 most of the inhabitants of Port Leon moved upriver to the safer Newport. Tampa had its origin when Fort Brooke was established on Tampa Bay in 1824 to keep watch on the Seminole Indians on their reservation in central Florida and prevent their receiving arms and ammunition from Cuba or other foreign sources. By 1830 when the establishment was complete there were 256 square miles of the military reservation with a guardhouse, barracks, storehouses, powder magazine, wharf, and stables. Soon civilians began to move in, and in 1828 William G. Saunders of Mobile established a general store. There were enough residents to create Hillsborough County in 1834, at which time Tampa and Fort Brooke were for all practical purposes the same. Saint Augustine, lacking access to the interior, failed to hold the same relative importance it had previously enjoyed. With 1,708 inhabitants in 1839, it grew to about 3,000 in 1840, due largely to the stimulus of the Seminole war. Jacksonville originated early in the American period and showed some signs of the importance it later achieved. Indians and travelers found there a convenient place to cross the Saint Johns. Robert Pritchard became the first settler with a Spanish land grant dated 1791; he established a farm and a home but lived there only a few years. Lewis Z. Hogans and his wife Maria, who moved into a log cabin at Cow Ford late in 1816, are usually considered the first permanent settlers. In 1821 Mrs. Sarah Waterman with four daughters and two sons came up from Saint Johns Town at the bluff to manage the first inn. In the summer of 1822 D. S. H. Miller, a civil engineer, laid out the city and John Brady, who had kept a tavern since 1818, established a ferry. Jacksonville's population in 1830 was only 100, but Duval County had a total of 1,970 inhabitants living largely on farms. Isaac Hart, considered the father of Jacksonville, built the first hotel in 1830 and the town received its charter two years later. It suffered a series of setbacks in the thirties, hit in succession by the freeze in 1835, the outbreak of the Seminole war later in the same year, followed by the panic of 1837, but counted nearly 600 residents in 1840.

Fernandina lost its importance and scarcely a ship a year used its fine harbor. Only the establishment of the Atlantic terminus of the Florida Railroad there on the eve of the Civil War started it growing again. Palatka, an important crossing on the Saint Johns directly west of Saint Augustine, was depopulated of whites by the Indian war but then gained some importance during the war. It was only a small village when it was incorporated in 1853.

Key West, which oddly enough had no permanent residents in 1821, had already gained considerable importance by the end of the territorial period. It had earlier been used as a base by fishermen, spongers, and pirates. Its great assets were the deep channels which provided protected anchorage, its strategic location for a naval base, a coaling station for coastwide steamers and the business of marine salvage on the nearby Florida Reef. Juan P. Salas acquired Key West as a grant in 1815 and sold it on December 20, 1821, for two thousand dollars to John W. Simonton of Mobile. Simonton took possession on January 19, 1822, and started it on its way to becoming for a time Florida's largest city.

On February 7, 1822, Lieutenant Matthew C. Perry was ordered to take possession of Key West for the United States and to leave two men to hold it until further orders. They were to make a preliminary survey of the island and the adjacent waters. On March 25, the American flag was formally raised over the island. In September 1821, a squadron of the United States Navy had received orders to cruise in the waters of the West Indies and in the Gulf of Mexico to discourage the widespread piracy rampant there. By the end of 1822, the squadron had grown to twenty-one vessels, and on November 8, Lieutenant William H. Allen of the schooner *Alligator* was killed in a fight with pirates. President James Monroe responded on December 20 with a request for a special force to operate against the pirates. Congress approved and Commodore David Porter, a veteran of fighting Barbary pirates and the War of 1812, left the Navy Board to take command of the new force. He added eight small schooners to work in shallow waters where the pirates took refuge from seagoing ships and the first steam powered vessel to fight in the navy. The second-hand ferry the *Sea Gull* was used to tow five rowing barges, each manned by twenty men and mounting a small cannon for even closer action. On February 1, 1823, Porter proceeded to Key West which he called Thompson's Island and the harbor Port Rodgers to establish a naval base and build barracks for marines who were to protect the base and the stores. Captain Alfred Grayson commanded the marine contingent and exercised both civil and military authority. Then in July came the first encounter with Key West's worst enemy in the nineteenth century, yellow fever. Twenty of the 188 marines died and Porter lost forty-eight. As a result Key West was declared unfit for occupation from July to October.

Porter lost command of the squadron early in 1825. On October 24, 1824, Lieutenant Platt of the *Beagle* heard that stolen goods were hidden at Foxardo in Puerto Rico. When he landed to investigate he was jailed for a short time. When the news came to Porter he sailed into Foxardo harbor in force and demanded an apology for the treatment of Platt. Key Westers who resented the military control of the island joined other protesters. Porter's trial before a court martial began on July 7, 1825. For conduct unbecoming an officer and for exceeding his authority, he was suspended for six months. He resigned and accepted a commission as General of Marine in the Mexican Navy, with control over all naval affairs. He sometimes used Key West as a base to prey upon Spanish commerce and occasionally kept prisoners there. When a Spanish squadron threatened to blockade the harbor in 1827, Porter sailed away and did not return for several years.

An early view of Key West

In 1826 the naval base was moved from Key West to Pensacola and only a coal and supply depot remained on the island. There was limited activity at Key West in the Seminole war, but the base remained at Pensacola for the time being. In 1825 a lighthouse was completed at Garden Key in the Dry Tortugas. Four years later President Andrew Jackson ordered a survey of the Tortugas as a military base. In 1845 the war department announced that forts would be constructed at Key West and Garden Key. These subsequently became Forts Taylor and Jefferson.

Meanwhile, Key West received a charter in 1828, and William Adee Whitehead surveyed the town the following year. It had not yet become Florida's first city. The population was estimated at about 300 in 1831 and two estimates for 1835 were 600 and 582.

The establishment of Tallahassee as the state capital in 1824 and something of its growth have been related earlier. Most of the people who gave it importance lived on plantations outside the city. In 1940 for the first time, half of Leon County's population, 16,240 of 31,646, lived in Tallahassee, its only urban center. In 1900 there were 2,981 persons in the city, while there were almost 20,000 in the county. Quincy in Gadsden County became known as the tobacco growers capital with a society only less important than that around Tallahassee. Monticello, the county seat of Jefferson County, also derived its importance from planters residing nearby. If the Seminole war retarded settlement in some places it stimulated it in others. In 1840 Senator Thomas Hart Benton of Missouri, well known for his interest in frontier settlement, proposed an armed occupation act to plant settlers on the frontier as a barrier against Indian raids. Benton thought the government should provide them with food and arms as well as land. President John Tyler opened the question again on May 10, 1842, when he announced the end of hostilities in Florida. Delegate David Levy was less sanguine about the pacification of Indians and felt that settlers might need military support. A law approved on August 4 made available 200,000 acres outside the already developed regions of Florida south of Gainesville as far as the Peace River, barring coastal lands and those in a radius of two miles around forts. Any head of family or single man over eighteen years of age able to bear arms could earn title to 160 acres by erecting a habitable dwelling, cultivating at least five acres of land, and living on it for five years. Migrants selected their sites and in nine months filed 947 claims at Newnansville and 370 at Saint Augustine. The land office finally issued 1,184 permits for 189,440 acres.

When a new county was created in the area covered by the Armed Occupation Act it received the name Levy in recognition of the delegate's part in securing the legislation, and Hernando County adopted the name Benton in 1844 only to revert to the original name in 1850 when the Senator showed anti-southern sentiment. The number of settlements that may be attributed solely to the act is doubtful. Those who went were usually unarmed and had no occasion to use such weapons as they did possess. Perhaps their most useful service was to dispel notions of danger from Indians.

Claims to land were often without legal basis, and much abuse accompanied the taking up of land in all ways that it might be acquired. Most attractive were the lands with stands of live oak, which grew in hammocks all over east Florida but particularly near the coast and along navigable streams. This timber on public land was reserved for the United States Navy, but it was too easy to remove and practically impossible to police the cutting. Since it was impossible to distinguish between private and public land, timber thieves blandly claimed ownership. John James Audubon reported their activities in 1831-1832. They came mostly from the shipbuilding East and worked mostly from December to March, after which they usually returned home for the summer, though more and more of them remained the year around as time went on.

By the end of the territorial period in 1845 the pattern of Florida development for the immediate future was fairly clear. The economy was an extension of that of nearby southeastern states, based on the plantation system with slaves growing cotton, tobacco, rice, and some sugarcane as cash crops. The vast majority of the inhabitants were yeomen farmers dependent largely on the labor of the family, but they accepted the leadership of the larger landholders and outdid them in their support of the institution of slavery. The beginnings of urban life and nonagricultural pursuits were discernible, particularly at sea and river ports, but the center of gravity was already moving to the interior, a trend to be greatly accelerated with the coming of the railroad.

11.

The Wars of Indian Removal

The British and the Spanish during their tenure in Florida had left the Indians in undisturbed possession of most of the interior. The Americans, on the other hand, could hardly tolerate their presence. The Indians had produced problems before the territory became a part of the United States, which was one of the principal reasons for acquiring it. Indians had raided across the international boundary and then fled to the comparative security of Spanish Florida, where they were scarcely policed. Black slaves running away from plantations on the southern frontier of Georgia and Alabama found easy refuge among the Indians. These circumstances had precipitated General Andrew Jackson's invasion of Spanish Florida in 1818, which later was appropriately called the First Seminole War. Acquisition of Florida by the United States made the Indian problem more acute. As planters came into the new region with their slaves, the nearness of the Indian refuges increased the lure of freedom and the temptation to escape. Unlike their white predecessors in the territory, the Americans desired to settle on the fertile lands of north central Florida where the Indians had been in undisputed possession. Finally, the national government was receptive to demands for Indian removal because of the possibility of recovering by land sales the money paid out in the acquisition.

The Seminoles were themselves comparative newcomers to Florida; they had moved into the area after the aboriginal inhabitants were almost all gone. The first of the Seminoles probably came at the invitation of the Spanish government after Queen Anne's War (1701-1713) had depopulated much of north central Florida. After Colonel James Moore's raid from Carolina into Apalachee in 1804 and others that followed, practically all of the Apalachees and Timucuas went away as allies or prisoners, leaving the area almost without Indian population. The Spanish governor sent Diego Peña on three expeditions to try to induce some Lower Creek bands to settle in Apalachee west of the Aucilla River, and a few did move in. The settlement of Georgia in 1733 opened the way to further migration into Florida. Lower Creeks came as allies of General James Edward Oglethorpe and ranged over north central Florida while he attacked Saint Augustine. Some of the bands then settled in Florida, one of the most important of them the Oconee. This tribe had lived on the Oconee River in Georgia but had migrated to the lower Chattahoochee River as a result of the Yamassee war and was well established by 1750 in the Alachua region of Florida. At much the same time other Lower Creeks were moving into the Apalachee region, and yet others occupied other north Florida areas. During the British period these groups became known as the Mikasuki, and by 1835 they were the most militantly determined to remain in Florida.

In 1767 the first band of Upper Creeks settled northeast of Tampa Bay in what is now Hernando County. Whereas all of the Creeks who came earlier spoke some variation of Hitchiti, the Upper Creek migrants spoke Muskogee, derived from a common root but different enough to be mutually unintelligible. The last major movement of Indians into Florida came after the Creek War in Alabama Territory in 1813-1814, which started as a war between Upper and Lower Creeks. When the Indian war led to the massacre of a number of whites who had taken refuge at Fort Mims, General Andrew Jackson took the field against them and crushed the Red Stick faction of the Upper Creeks who led the fighting, killing some 800 of their warriors at the Battle of Tohopeka or Horseshoe Bend on the Tallapoosa River on March 27, 1814. When the treaty of August 9, 1814, ceded two-thirds of the Creek lands, numbers of the Red Stick remnant migrated southward into Florida. They brought with them a hatred of the Lower Creeks who had aided Jackson to bring about their defeat. This arrival of some 1,000 warriors and their families doubled the Florida Indian population, which reached about 5,000 who lived in twenty to twenty-five villages.

These Indian newcomers had arrived in small bands at widely separated intervals over a period of a hundred years until the larger migration of Red Sticks in 1814. Some of the earlier bands were pro-British, some pro-Spanish; some spoke Hitchiti, some Muskogee; some were Lower Creeks, some were rival Upper Creeks. Their only common bond was the Creek culture. In the British period they began to be called Seminolies or Seminoles, a name later applied to all Florida Indians. This identified them as seceders or runaways from the Creek Federation, with which they did not finally break until 1814. Each band lived in a separate village and governed itself almost without any central authority to coordinate their various activities, a condition that has prevailed among the Seminoles almost to the present day. In spite of the fragmentation and the bitter hatreds between Upper and Lower Creeks, they lived in comparative harmony in Florida. Since they had moved into an area that once supported several times their numbers, there was little rivalry for living space. Deer were plentiful, and there were considerable numbers of wild cattle that had come from the abandoned Spanish ranches. A wide variety of berries, fruits, and nuts, and land well suited to their agricultural needs, provided an abundance of food.

There was general agreement among white Americans that the Indians must go, but when and where remained to be determined.

Early twentieth-century Seminoles

Andrew Jackson seems to have suggested the Apalachicola Valley, but he could scarcely have considered it more than a temporary solution. Sentiment for removal to the trans-Mississippi West had not yet developed, and the most likely answer seemed to be a reservation farther south in the Florida peninsula. Meanwhile, uncertainty ruled, and the apprehensive Seminoles had a genuine fear of what might happen, for they knew the land hunger of the Americans–they had felt it before. Some of them, accepting the inevitable, had migrated westward when that land became a part of the United States.

Negotiations began uncertainly when a conference was called at Saint Marks on November 20, 1822. Few on either side seem to have been ready for talks. Only a few chiefs came, and Gad Humphreys, the Indian agent for the United States, failed to appear. Governor Duval had gone to Kentucky in late September and was to be gone until March. A year later, as if to make amends for a bad start, white officials made careful plans for a conference at Moultrie Creek five miles south of Saint Augustine. James Gadsden, Bernardo Segui, and Governor Duval, negotiating for the United

States, meant business and asked for a show of military force to give a hard tone to their talks. Gadsden and an interpreter helped to secure a representative group of Indians by personally conducting the travel of some 350 Indians over the 250-mile distance from West Florida to the treaty site. About 425 Indians attended the seventeen-day conference. Seventy chiefs and warriors took part in the deliberations, and thirty-two chiefs signed the resulting document, which was ratified by the United States Senate on December 23, 1823.

The Indians had stopped about a mile and a half from the treaty site to choose a spokesman for the group. They selected Neamathla, who was the recognized leader of the Mikasukis and the only chief likely to be able to exercise any authority over the heterogeneous bands. The next year territorial Governor William P. Duval boldly deposed Neamathla in a confrontation near present-day Tallahassee when he appeared to be about to lead the resistance to the terms of the treaty negotiated at Moultrie Creek the previous year. The governor installed Tuckose Emathla, known to the whites as John Hicks, a man equally able but more willing to work with whites and to migrate farther southward, and Neamathla dropped out of the front rank of leadership. In spite of the circumstances of his elevation to the high post, John Hicks was installed as chief of all the Seminoles in July 1826 after a close election that had been brought about by Indian agent Gad Humphreys in the effort to bring about some sort of centralized organization through which the government could deal with all of the Seminoles. The plan fell far short of the hopes of Humphreys, as each tribe continued to insist upon the right to speak for itself.

The Moultrie Creek gathering was the most representative Seminole group ever brought together in Florida, and, in spite of the unequal bargaining power of the two participants, the terms of the treaty were negotiated rather than imposed. The agreement as finally signed set aside four million acres north of Charlotte Harbor and south of Ocala for the exclusive use of the Seminoles. To prevent contact with foreign sources of aid and trade, none of the reservation land was within twenty miles of the coast. The Indians were to receive $6,000 worth of farm tools and livestock, $5,000 a year for twenty years, and meat, corn, and salt for one year. To compensate for property other than lands that they had abandoned, they were to receive up to $4,500, another $2,000 for transportation, $1,000 a year for a school and a like sum for a blacksmith and a gunsmith. The government agreed to maintain on the reservation an agent, a sub-agent and an interpreter. The Indians on their part agreed to prevent the reservation from becoming a haven of refuge for runaway slaves. Interestingly enough, six chiefs who resided near the Apalachicola River and were reluctant to move down into the peninsula received small reservations of two to eight square miles and remained where they had settled.

The Treaty of Moultrie Creek never satisfied either the Indians or the whites. Neither knew very much about the potentialities of the country, but the Indians had misgivings from the first. Neamathla expressed them well at the conference when he said: "We rely on your justice and humanity; we hope you will not send us south to a country where neither the hickory nut, the acorn nor the persimmon grows; we depend much on those productions of the forest for food; in the south they are not found." If it asked too much of the Indians, it was not enough to satisfy the whites. Charges of bad faith and fraud on the part of the white negotiators began to be heard. The three commissioners certainly favored removal from the Territory as the only completely satisfactory policy. Gadsden conceded six years later that placing the Indians on a reservation was but a first step toward their removal to the West at a later date. Not all public officials looked upon the reservation as temporary. The secretary of war in 1825 made the mistake, too frequent in dealings with Indians, of assuming that whites would not for a long time have any interest in the reservation lands.

Almost before the treaty went into effect the United States government was moving toward a policy of general Indian removal. President James Monroe made it the subject of a special message on January 27, 1825, and though it did not become law for another five years, the prospect gave aid and comfort to advocates of Indian removal from Florida and bred dissatisfaction with the local reservation as a solution.

The Treaty of Moultrie Creek set no specific date for the Indians to move southward. They moved reluctantly and almost immediately began to complain that the reservation was too small to support them, whereupon the governor investigated, agreed, and took steps to increase the size of the area allotted to them. When drought in 1825 added to Indian unhappiness, they went beyond the reservation limits to seek food where they could find it. Whites continued to visit the reservation lands seeking blacks they alleged were runaway slaves. The legislative council in 1827 took note of the problem and enacted laws to keep the Indians on and the whites off the reservation, but these laws had little effect.

As the demand for Indian removal in Florida grew in volume, the United States government sent Joseph M. White to propose to the Indians that they move to more attractive lands west of the Mississippi River. The Indians rejected the suggestion at a conference on May 20, 1827. On October 19 of the next year, agent Humphreys called a conference with the chiefs at McKenzie's Pond and urged, or perhaps warned, the Indians to cease their hostile attitudes and actions or prepare to move to the West. The chiefs agreed to send a deputation to look over the new land the next spring. The agent was to accompany them and the government would pay the cost, but there would be no obligation on the part of the Indians to move. What might have happened if the Indians had seen the new land was never to be known. Whatever opportunity there existed for peaceable removal was lost when the government ignored the proposal of its agent. When Andrew Jackson became president in 1829, proposals for general removal of all Indians to the West got new official support. In his first annual message he asked for land in the West to which Indians could elect to move or to come under the jurisdiction of the states where they lived. Congress responded by enacting the legislation on May 28, 1830, and the fate of the Florida Seminoles was sealed. The inadequacy of the Florida reservation and the desperate situation of the Seminoles living there, plus the mounting demand of the whites for their removal, soon produced action. In 1832, James Gadsden, who had negotiated the earlier treaty, called a meeting at Payne's Landing on the Oklawaha River, a site well known to all of the Indians, to persuade them to go West. The agent apparently convinced them that further resistance was useless, possibly that the government would no longer feed them, and certainly that they would live under the laws of Florida if they elected to remain in the Territory. Some Indians later charged that they had been coerced; others said that Abraham, the influential black interpreter, had been bribed to mislead them; and yet others denied that they had signed the agreement. Significantly, only seven chiefs and eight subchiefs signed the document in contrast to the thirty-two signers at Moultrie Creek.

The Indians in the small reservations along the Apalachicola who were separated from the treaty site by white settlements did not participate in the negotiations at Payne's Landing. They probably also had developed separate interests, but their position too was becoming untenable. They charged that whites violated the reservation boundaries, and the whites in turn charged the Indians with harboring runaway slaves. Their leaders proved more tractable than the main body of Seminoles, and Governor Duval was able to negotiate an agreement with three of them on October 11, 1832, to migrate on the first of November a year later in return for the payment of $13,000. On June 18, 1833, Colonel Gadsden made a smiliar agreement with the remaining three groups after reminding them that they must live under the laws of Florida without the protection of the United States government if they elected to remain there. The last of them did not leave until early 1836.

The Treaty of Payne's Landing provided that before the agreement to migrate became binding, a delegation of seven chiefs must inspect the new lands and approve them. The Indians would then leave in three shifts within three years after the ratification of the treaties. The delegation of chiefs visited the land offered them, a separate part of the Creek reservation in Indian Territory, and on March 28, 1833, signed the "Treaty of Fort Gibson" approving and accepting it for their fellow tribesmen. This, however, did not end the matter. Two of the chiefs, wishing to repudiate their action., claimed that they had not signed, and another said that he had agreed knowing that members of the delegation could not bind the other Seminoles by their signing. Others back in Florida insisted that they were not bound by the acts of the signers of either treaty and would not in any case leave before the twenty-year period covered by the Treaty of Moultrie Creek had expired. The United States government, on the other hand, ratified the documents on April 8,

Micanopy, Seminole chief, during his captivity at Fort Moultrie, South Carolina, in 1838 (left). Seminole women, a captive at Fort Moultrie, South Carolina (right). Paintings by George Catlin, 1838.

1834, providing for removal within three years. Indian agent General Wiley Thompson started talks with the Indians in October of the same year but soon concluded that only force could induce them to move. General Duncan L. Clinch, in charge of the United States troops in Florida and who had been negotiating with the Indian leaders for a year, warned them to go peacefully or face the prospect of removal by force. Other council sessions the following December and April served only to reveal the determination of the Indians to resist removal by force of arms if necessary. Thompson finally set January 1, 1836, as the date for migration.

As the year 1835 progressed, signs of increasing Indian unrest, resentment, and tendency to violence multiplied. A skirmish between militia and Indians occurred at Hickory Sink near Gainesville in June. In August, Indians killed an army courier, Private Kinsley

H. Dalton, near the Hillsborough River on the trail from Fort Brooke on Tampa Bay to Fort King near present-day Ocala. Younger and more daring Indians were seizing leadership among the Indians. John Hicks, who had already lost much of his moderating influence, died in 1833, and his successor opposed emigration. Osceola, who lacked the status of a chief, emerged as the leader and symbol

Osceola, sketched in May, 1837, while he was on parole at Lake Monroe, Florida, by F.R. Vinton, U.S. Army.

of the opposition and became the nearest thing to providing common leadership that the Seminoles ever achieved. Many descriptions, several original sketches and paintings, and numerous engravings that have come down to us tell a great deal about this unusual man. The reports and likenesses are so colored by prejudice, romantic notions, and artistic inventions that there is little agreement on which could have best described the real Osceola.[1]

Osceola is generally described as somewhat delicate and European looking in appearance and with a distinctive and pleasing personality. The facial features in the portraits may have arisen from the tendency of artists of the day to give European features to Indian subjects, from the fact that many eastern Indians were actually somewhat European in appearance, or to the possibility of mixed Indian and white ancestry. Osceola, often referred to as Billy Powell, was assumed to be the son of a Creek woman and an English trader of that name in Georgia. There is general agreement about his mother but not about his father, some arguing that Powell was only his stepfather, while others insist that his father was a half-breed son of a Creek woman by a Scotsman. One scholar concluded that he was a purebred Indian, relying strongly upon the statements of George Catlin, the famous painter of Indians, who knew Osceola well. Catlin judged this both by what Osceola told him and by his own knowledge of the physical features of Indians.[2] Osceola certainly was not of the original Seminole stock, that is of the early Creek migration to Florida. He belonged to the Red Stick faction of Upper Creeks who were primarily responsible for the decision to resist removal by force. Their aggressive leadership induced and possibly forced other Indians to join them in that policy.

General Thompson set December 1, 1835, for a sale at which Indians about to emigrate might bring and sell their cattle. Charley Emathla, one of the more important chiefs, brought his cattle and was ambushed and killed on his way home. Osceola and a band of Mikasukis received credit for the outrage, as they would in the future be suspected of all acts of violence not otherwise easily explained. Fourteen other chiefs committed to removal fled with 500 of their people to Fort Brooke for protection. When it was reported that Indian warriors were sending their women and children away for safety, whites also began to abandon outlying settlements and to gather at strategic points to protect themselves. On December 17, Indians attacked the plantations of Captain Simmons at Micanopy south of Gainesville and of Captain Priest of Wacahonta in the same area, damaging property and stealing cattle but not harming any whites. The first pitched battle occurred the next day at a point six miles southwest of Micanopy in which eight whites lost their lives and six were wounded. Two days later, Florida militia marched to the scene and recovered some of the property that had not been destroyed, but the elusive Indians had disappeared.

Rich sugar plantations in the Matanzas, Tomoka, and Mosquito areas became the next targets of the raiders. As early as October, General Joseph M. Hernandez, commanding the militia in East

Florida, warned the governor that these properties with their valuable cattle and slaves that might easily be driven away might require protection. On December 17, militia units took up stations in three places but proved to be inadequate to defend them. On Christmas Day of 1835, Seminoles raided a number of them, burning all of the buildings at New Smyrna. Within sixty days even the owners of undestroyed plantations had abandoned them, fleeing to safety with such property as they could carry away. Not one of the plantations was ever again restored to sugar production. Two of the sugar mills are under the custodianship of the Florida Board of Parks and Historic Memorials, and other ruins are in private hands.

Meanwhile events were moving even more rapidly in other areas to hasten the coming of all-out war. On the afternoon of December 28, 1835, Indians shot General Thompson and Lieutenant Constantine Smith from ambush within three hundred yards of the stockade walls at Fort King as they strolled outside after dinner. They also killed the sutler, Erastus Rogers, and several others working with him to move the stock of goods into the fort for safety from Indian raid. On the same day Major Francis Langhorne Dade, in command of two companies of soldiers marching from Fort Brooke to Fort King, walked into an ambush about five miles from the Wahoo Swamp near Bushnell in Sumter County in which 108 men lost their lives and only three escaped. Major Dade was killed by the first shot, and the command fell to an artillery officer whose tactics were ill-suited to fighting Indians.

Another series of events leading to a major encounter between Indians and whites not far away was working toward a climax. President Andrew Jackson had ordered General Duncan L. Clinch to move with his regular troops against a concentration of Seminoles reportedly gathering on the Withlacoochee River at a point some thirty-five miles south of Fort Drane where he had concentrated his forces. At Clinch's request, territorial secretary and acting Governor George K. Walker (Governor John H. Eaton was frequently absent for long periods) ordered general of militia Richard Keith Call to raise Florida volunteers to join the regulars for one campaign against the Indians. Five hundred mounted men supplying their own horses and arms joined half that number of regulars at Fort Drane on Clinch's plantation ten miles south of Micanopy for the single campaign they believed would convince the Seminoles of the folly of resistance. The short term enlistments of the volunteers were to expire in four more days when Clinch marched to the attack, leaving Fort Drane on December 29 and moving to within three miles of the river on the next day. On the last day of the month the guides led the marching men to what was supposed to be a wide shallow crossing of the Withlacoochee where horses and men could wade across the stream. Instead they came to a deep and swift moving point on the stream about 150 feet wide, with only one small canoe available to put men and equipment across. In a sense this was a fortunate circumstance, for the Indians were lying in wait for them at the crossing miles upstream where they might expected to cross. As it was, Clinch had a half day in which to put the regulars and twenty-seven of the volunteers across the stream before the Indians attacked the divided force, killing four and wounding fifty-nine of them and losing three killed and four wounded of their own number. The great body of the militiamen unable or unwilling to attempt the crossing merely looked on and contented themselves with covering the retreat of their hard pressed comrades at arms. The few volunteers who did participate in the fight held the left flank and gave a good account of themselves, seven being wounded, but the event renewed the time honored conflict between the professional and the volunteer soldier which was to continue throughout the seven years of the conflict.

General Clinch had underestimated the possibility of Indian resistance, but now that the conflict had begun in earnest the United States government moved quickly to strengthen the armed forces

Dade Memorial Park, near Bushnell, Florida, the battlefield where Major Francis L. Dade and his officers and men were ambushed and massacred.

in Florida. General Call, meanwhile, was urging his friend President Jackson to put him in command of the 2,500 to 3,000 men he considered necessary to defeat and round up the Indians for the journey to the West. In January 1836 the President ordered General Winfield Scott to take command in Florida and the war department sent fourteen companies of regulars to join Clinch's command. Commodore Alexander J. Dallas, in command of the navy in Florida waters, received orders to prevent any trade in arms between the Seminoles and traders from Cuba and the West Indies.

Sporadic violence broke out all over the territory where whites lived on the frontier. In isolated and thinly populated South Florida on January 6 Indians killed the family of William Colee on New River. Other frightened settlers in the locality fled to Key Biscayne and found refuge with the keeper of the lighthouse until they could be taken to Key West. The lighthouse fell to the Indian attack on July 23. Shortly thereafter, the navy established Fort Dallas on Key Biscayne, a post which the army was later to move to the north bank of the Miami River.

When General Edmund P. Gaines, commander of the western military district in which the Dade massacre occurred, learned of the incident he proceeded immediately to the scene of the disaster, unaware that Scott had been ordered to Florida. Gaines arrived at Tampa Bay early in February with 1,100 regulars and volunteers and marched to Fort King along the route followed by Dade's unfortunate men. He stopped en route to bury the victims of the massacre and reached Fort King on the tenth. When Scott reached Palatka on the Saint Johns on July 26 and discovered that Gaines was already on the scene, it set off a furious feud between the two that made direct communication impossible.

General Call succeeded John H. Eaton as governor of the Territory on March 16, and used his new position to energetically push the effort to remove the Seminoles. When he learned that General Scott was about to cease campaigning in the summer months he protested vigorously and demanded that he be allowed to conduct a summer campaign to prevent the Indians from using the time to produce crops and prepare to renew the conflict in the fall. The administration finally yielded, and on May 18, 1836, placed Call in command of all troops in Florida to serve until General Thomas S. Jesup should arrive in the fall to take over the command. However sound his notion of summer campaigning may have been, the general-governor was doomed to failure before he started. Regular army and navy personnel resented him as a militia officer. Too many regular officers had already been given long summer leaves of absence. The task required talents of a high order. Call had neither the training nor the experience it demanded. Services of supply broke down, the movements of some Tennessee volueners were poorly coordinated and the first effort to go on the offensive resulted in little more than some futile marching. Before a letter dated November 4 relieving him of command could reach him, he had reorganized his forces for a second effort, in which he attacked the Indians along the Withlacoochee on November 17, 18 and 21 and drove them away but was unable to engage them in battle and inflict any real damage. He was embittered by the necessity to turn the command over to Jesup, but he was only one of several military men including his successor to achieve little more than frustration in the Florida campaign against the Seminoles. General Scott had already produced a list of formidable obstacles to successful campaigning in Florida. Among them were the short terms of service of so may of the volunteers, insufficient services of transport and supply, the hot climate, the rainy season, inadequate roads and bridges, scarcity of grazing and forage for horses and lack of guides and information about the country in which he was to operate.

General Jesup took over from Call with some 4,000 men under his command for a campaign along the Withlacoochee through the winter 1836-1837. When he had brought what he hoped was convincing pressure upon them, he turned to treating with the Indians to induce them to move peaceably. A considerable number agreed to depart if the government would buy their cattle, hogs and ponies and allow them to take along their blacks. Jesup urged whites to accept the terms and not to interfere with their departure. By the month of June 1837 some 700 Indians had gathered at Fort Brooke to await transportation to the West. There seemed to be no hurry, but delay proved disastrous. On the night of June 7, without warning, almost all of the Indians vanished into the woods. Slave hunting whites may have arrived to arouse new fears among them that their blacks would not be allowed to go. A soldier may have shot a young squaw fleeing his attention. An outbreak of measles may have been thought to be the dreaded small pox. Perhaps it had merely been possible for dissenters to work upon Indian fears and doubts. At any rate, all of the work of force and persuasion had to be done over again, a mistake Jesup never made again.

Active campaigning ceased during the summer months of 1837 to be resumed in the fall. Early in September four blacks who came in to surrender to General Joseph M. Hernandez of the territorial militia commanding east of the Saint Johns reported a body of Indians in the region of Mosquito Inlet making coontie starch. Hernandez moved immediately and on the ninth surprised and captured King Philip and his band without a shot being fired. On the next day he accomplished the same with Yuchi Billy and his followers with the loss of only one white man and one Indian. The general confined his captives in the big stone fort at Saint Augustine, then called Fort Marion. Philip secured permission to send Tomoko John, one of the captives, to bring his family in to share his captivity. In a few days his son Coacoochee, or Wildcat, and three others came in. Coacoochee proved friendly and cooperative and was allowed to return to the woods upon his promise to use his efforts to bring in people, stolen cattle, and blacks. To the surprise of Hernandez he did return on October 17 with Philip's brother and his own younger brother, and reported that Osceola with several other chiefs and about a hundred Indians were about a day's march distant on their way in for a conference. Osceola did come in, and at about the same time General Jesup arrived and ordered that the assembled Indians not be allowed to escape under any circumstances.

General Hernandez met Osceola standing under a flag of truce, surrounded the Indians with troops, and captured them without any effort at resistance on their part. When the new prisoners were added to those already in the fort, the noise they made and the uneasy fear that they might escape frightened the citizens of Saint Augustine. On November 19, Coacoochee and nineteen others did escape, in time for the young warrior to rally Indian forces and lead them in the Battle of Okeechobee, the last pitched battle of the war. In late December, authorities moved Osceola, five other chiefs and 116 warriors, and 82 women and children to Fort Moultrie at Charleston, South Carolina. There, Osceola, already in poor health because of chronic malaria, sickened and died of quinsy aggravated by malaria on January 30, 1838. Frequent if sometimes half-hearted efforts to return his remains to Florida have failed. Had he not been captured under a flag of truce and sent away to die in prison, he might have died as ignominiously as many of his brethren. As it is his place as the most romantic if not the most heroic figure in the annals of the war seems secure.

Twenty years after the incident so great was the criticism that Jesup found himself compelled to offer an explanation for his actions. He argued that Indians knew he would treat with them only on terms of surrender and migration, that Osceola had only a safe conduct through the lines, that on Osceola's part the white flag was only a ruse to get near enough to the camp to attack it, but to his surprise he found it reinforced by Jesup's arrival, that Osceola had not hesitated to violate truces, and, finally, that capture was more humane than letting the Indians go back into the woods to be hunted down again.

General Jesup had a fully developed plan of campaigning for the winter of 1837-1838 that would push the Seminoles farther southward into the peninsula and leave the north Florida frontier relatively free of Indian danger. General Persifor Smith was to operate from the Caloosahatchee River to Cape Sable. Colonel Zachary Taylor was responsible for the region from that river northward to the Withlacoochee and eastward across the peninsula north of Lake Okeechobee. Others who were to play less conspicuous roles guarded Middle Florida. Major William Lauderdale east of the Saint Johns operated from Picolata to Lake Monroe and General Hernandez on the upper Saint Johns. The navy in the person of Lieutenant Levin M. Powell, who sailed southward from Fort Pierce as far as Jupiter Inlet, cooperated by providing reconnaissance and supply services. In the midst of these preparations for a forward movement on all fronts, Colonel Shelburne appeared with five chiefs to try again to negotiate for the peaceable withdrawal of the remaining Seminoles.

Meanwhile Colonel Taylor had moved out from Tampa at the

end of November with 800 regulars, 180 Missouri volunteers, some Florida volunteers, and seventy Delaware and a few Shawnee Indians. They reached the Kissimmee River, bridged it, and constructed Fort Gardiner. Having scouted the river and the northern shore of the lake they moved against a concentration of Indians reported to be gathering northeast of the lake.

On Christmas Day, Taylor found some 400 Indians awaiting attack in a carefully prepared position. They were in a hammock with about a half mile of swamp in front of them. The saw grass was five feet high and the mud and water three feet deep. The Indians had cut the grass near the hammock to make firing more accurate and had notched the trees to rest and steady their rifles. Coacoochee, who had escaped from the fort at Saint Augustine only the previous month, held the left with eighty of his followers. Taylor had about twice as many men who were already tired from the day's march, but he decided to charge through the swamp directly at the enemy. The Indians inflicted relatively heavy damage but could not withstand the pressure of the heavier force. The Seminoles lost 11 killed and 14 wounded and killed 20 whites and wounded 112 in a fight that lasted from about a half hour past noon to three o'clock. If the Battle of Withlacoochee two years earlier had convinced the Indians that they could stop any force the whites sent against them, this largest of all battles of the war must have changed their minds completely, for there was never again in the more than four years of fighting yet to be done a pitched battle involving any considerable number of combatants. Zachary Taylor emerged as the only commander who had defeated the Seminoles in a major engagement.

On January 18, 1838, General Jesup moved from the headquarters of the Saint Johns toward Jupiter Inlet, which he reached the next day after encountering some resistance as he was crossing the Loxahatchee River. He erected Fort Jupiter, little more than a stockade, and waited until February 5 for supplies to come by water. Before he was ready to take to the field again, Brigadier General Abram Eustis, apparently supported by other senior officers, came forward with a proposal to end the war by allowing the Indians to remain on a small reservation in the southern peninsula. Jesup reluctantly consented to give it a try but said he must have the approval of Washington for such a plan.

While a Seminole black went out to invite the Indian chiefs in for the parley, a messenger carried the proposal to Washington. The Indians began to come in, saying they too were tired of the struggle, and gathered near the army at Fort Jupiter to await the return of the messenger. When a negative decision arrived on the seventeenth, Jesup found himself unable to communicate it to the Indians and see them return to the forests where he would be compelled to continue to hunt them down. Accordingly he ordered General Twiggs to surround and capture them, thereby taking at one time 513 Indians, of which 151 were warriors. The severity of the blow to the Indians in the region was such that another 360 were induced to come in and join the move to the West. The storm of protest over the violation of the flag of truce was louder than the previous year, but Jesup stuck to his insistence that it was more humane than fighting.

A dwindling number of Indians continued to hold out against pressure to move. Major Lauderdale with a company of the Third Artillery and 200 Tennessee Volunteers explored the country southward and established Fort Lauderdale on New River. On April 24, Colonel William S. Hamey found a group of Indians some twenty miles below Biscayne Bay who fled into the Everglades after a brief skirmish. On the west coast, Surgeon General Thomas Lawson with 248 men probed the coast from the Caloosahatchee to Cape Sable, seeking to break up any contact Indians might have with foreign sources of aid. He found no Indians but established Fort Poinsett at East Cape to continue the watch.

In April 1839, General Alexander Macomb, commanding general of the army, came to Florida to take personal charge of the military operations, hoping to end the war and restore the prestige of the service. General Jesup had already warned that Florida was no place to make a military reputation, and he defended himself against his critics by pointing out that during his stay nearly 2,400 Indians had been captured, killed, or persuaded to migrate to the West. He concluded: "I and my predecessors in command have not only been required to fight and beat the enemy but to go into an unexplored wilderness and capture them. Neither Wayne, Harrison nor Jackson was required to do this . . . ." Jesup's tenure in Florida was longer than any other. He did not bring the war to a conclusion, but during that year and a half many of the principal chiefs and their followers were captured or persuaded to come in and give themselves up, and hostilities on the same scale would never occur again.

General Macomb began by inviting the chiefs to come to Fort King for a conference to discuss ways to end the war. He offered a reservation south of the Peace River which turned out to be a temporary solution. He sought to remove the Indians from any contact with whites by establishing a trading post on the Caloosahatchee. James Baxter Dahlam and four civilian employees to set up the store, and Lieutenant Colonel Hamey with twenty-eight dragoons and three civilians to guard it, worked at their task on one side of the river while a large body of apparently peaceable Indians gathered on the other side. Early on the morning of July 23, 1839, the fourth day of their stay, a force of about 160 Indians led by Chekika, chief of the "Spanish Indians," attacked the camp. The raiders killed Dahlam and one of his clerks, captured three civilians and a sergeant named Simmons, and killed thirteen soldiers and three other civilians, while fourteen soldiers including Harney escaped by way of the river, as the Indians stopped to loot the camp. Harney blamed Secretary of War, Joel R. Poinsett, who had somehow allowed the Indians to learn that they were not to be allowed to remain in Florida but had not notified him.

This was the first appearance in the war of the isolated Spanish Indians, but they continued active. On August 7, 1840, Chekika led seventeen canoe loads of Indians in a raid on Indian Key in which they killed Dr. Henry Perrine and six others and looted and burned the store of Jacob Housman and other buildings. The Indians had moved southward through the Everglades from an island just below present-day Forty Mile Bend on the Tamiami Trail west of Miami. Colonel Harney, then stationed at Fort Dallas, willingly accepted the assignment to seek out and eliminate Chekika and his band. On December 4, 1840, ninety men in sixteen canoes left the fort and made their way across the Everglades, surprised Chekika on his island hideout and killed him. Harney had developed a technique that made it possible to follow the Indians to their most remote hiding places. This raid produced one of the first accounts of a trip across the southern Everglades. Instead of returning to Fort Dallas by way of the Everglades and the Miami River, he moved southwest toward the Gulf of Mexico by way of what has since been known as Harney River, where larger craft picked up the members of the expedition and brought them back to Fort Dallas.

General Macomb retired from the field and left the leadership to General Taylor, who suffered a severe attack of fever late in 1839 and left Florida on May 11, 1840. Taylor, an old hand at the Florida war, achieved notoriety by importing bloodhounds from Cuba to track down Seminoles. The thirty-three dogs and five handlers cost several thousand dollars and trailed no Seminoles in the watery wilderness but did bring upon the general a nationwide protest against the inhumanity of using dogs to catch Indians. Taylor shared the professional soldiers' dislike of militia and made himself unpopular by charging that Floridians wanted only to prolong the war and "partake of the government expenditures."

General Walker K. Armistead, who succeeded Taylor, found 5,000 soldiers in his command who continued to catch an occasional Indian and bring pressure enough upon others to induce them to give up the fight. His year of command netted about 450 Indians. The center of the conflict had moved steadily southward, but a spectacular Indian raid occurred in north Florida in 1840. On May 23 they fired on a company of actors en route to Saint Augustine on the road from Picolata on the Saint Johns, killed four of them, and stole all of their finery. The August 7 raid at Indian Key in South Florida also demonstrated a considerable capability to deliver a hard blow. At the end of March in 1841 all citizen soldiers were discharged, and the war was assumed to be drawing to a close. On August 31 Colonel William J. Worth relieved Armistead. In November Coacoochee, for several years the most aggressive of the Indian leaders, gave up the fight and brought in some 300 of his followers. A year later, on August 14, Worth announced that the war had come to an end. In conferences at Fort Brooke and Cedar Key he had reached an agreement with the remaining Seminoles to occupy a temporary reservation from the mouth of the Peace River to the fork of its southern branch, to the head of Lake Istokpoga, down the Kissimmee to Lake Okeechobee, and through the Everglades to Shark River. Since the most of the Seminoles were already there, this was but an agreement to accept the status quo.

The six and a half years of fighting had been costly. The number of servicemen on duty in Florida ranged from a high of 8,866 in 1837 to 3,801 in 1841. There were 1,466 deaths, including 215 officers; 328 men were killed in action. Deaths in the navy were 69; battle deaths among the citizen soldiers were 55 with an indeterminate number of deaths from wounds and disease. In addition to the costs of the regular army, the usually accepted estimate is twenty million dollars, or about the same amount as it cost the army. Other costs were also high. Plantations, homes, slaves, livestock, and other forms of property were destroyed or stolen. Settlers abandoned the frontier and gathered at towns and forts for security. The conflict helped to weaken territorial banks, deepened the depression, and delayed statehood.

In January 1844 a report to the secretary of war listed 3,824 Indians removed, 212 of them in the previous year after the close of hostilities. There were other items on the credit side which are too often overlooked. For the first time the interior was explored and mapped. The army laid out many trails and roads. An amazing number of forts became the nuclei of settlements that survive in place names today. Federal payrolls, employment of civilians, rent of teams and wagons and boats, the purchase of food and forage, and relief supplied to refugees repeatedly brought the charge that maybe Floridians would like to prolong the war. The Armed Occupation Act of 1842 provided homesteads for a goodly number of settlers who might not otherwise have moved to Florida. Florida was no longer a remote and unknown part of the country.

The military lessons of the war, some of them learned over again, were considerable and may be said to have relevance today in such conflicts as the Vietnamese war. The subtropical climate and the watery wilderness terrain with the sea on three sides made it different from other wars and gave the navy its largest role in any Indian war. Cooperation between the services was remarkable. Sailors and marines did duty as foot soldiers, and the two arms of the service joined forces in amphibious operations. While the army was developing guerrilla or partisan style warfare, naval officers were developing small boat search and assault tactics which enabled them and the cooperating army to carry the war to the nerve centers of the enemy in hitherto inaccessible areas. The naval flotilla was small and was never designated a squadron. It served for at least half of the time under the command of the secretary of war. When it was dissolved on August 3, 1842, it consisted of seven vessels, fifty officers, 385 enlisted men, of whom 100 were marines, and was using 140 dugout canoes.

When Colonel Worth declared the war at an end in 1842, the informal arrangement was hardly more than a truce, for whites would not tolerate a permanent settlement that left Seminoles in possession of any considerable land in the state. Worth and others had underestimated the number of Seminoles left, fixing the number as low as 300. The Indians did stay within the reservation lines and few whites ventured that far south. Perhaps the prospect that swamp and overflowed lands would be turned over to the state in which they were located helps to account for the renewed and insistent demand that the few Indians still there also be removed. The United States government responded with efforts designed to induce them to migrate. In 1851 Luther Blake, appointed by the Commissioner of Indian Affairs, accompanied Billy Bowlegs and other Seminoles to New York and Washington in a futile effort to induce them to emigrate. Blake finally, at a cost of more than $20,000, induced thirty-six Indians to go West. John Casey again became the Indian agent and brought pressure on the Indians to make them fight if they wished to remain. Military patrols scouted the region. Surveyors laid out trails and roads into the "reservation." In 1850 Fort Harvie was reactivated and renamed Fort Myers. Four years later troops reactivated Forts Denaud, Thompson, and Center on the Caloosahatchee. They also reopened roads and forts and constructed new ones southeastward from Fort Myers.

Lieutenant George L. Hartsuff, a topographical engineer, directed much of the surveying and reported on the land he observed. He called it fit only for Indian habitation and practically impregnable in case of renewal of the war. After a summer lay-off, Hartsuff returned to the Big Cypress country in early December of 1855 with six mounted men, two footsoldiers and two wagons drawn by mules, largely on a reconnaissance mission. They saw two Indians on the third day out, found Fort Drum burned on the fourth, as also was Fort Shackleford on the edge of the Everglades. After examining the situation in all directions the party was ready to return to Fort Myers when, without warning, some thirty-five Indians attacked the camp early in the morning on the twentieth, killed two men and wounded four, including Hartsuff, who did not make his way to safety until the third day. The Seminole war was underway again.

The first raiders struck on Sarasota Bay, at the Braden plantation and two other places on the Manatee, attacked a wagon train in Hillsborough County and killed three men, and attacked the home of Willoughby Tillis near Fort Meade. In the biggest battle of the renewed conflict, a force under Captain Francis Durrance killed fifteen Seminoles near present-day Bowling Green. The center of the action, however, was in the Big Cypress, and Fort Myers was the principal base of operations. Fort Cross was added at Middle Cape and Fort Poinsett at East Cape was reactivated. Fort Dallas and Fort Lauderdale again became scenes of military activity. The tactical lessons learned in the second war were applied with good effect. Constant patrols pushed the Seminoles into a more and more limited area, found and destroyed homes and fields, but caught few Indians. Spurred by the offer of $500 for males, $250 to $500 for women, and $100 for children as rewards for live Seminoles, boat companies pushed the search deeper and deeper into the swamps and accounted for forty-one captives. In November 1857 Captain

John Parkhill's company of 110 men with Captain Richard Turner as guide ascended the Chokoloskee, now Turner River, to its head, landed, and marched in a north and westerly direction. On the fourth day they found the last hiding place of the Indians. Parkhill died in an ambush, but the backbone of Indian resistance was broken when Colonel George Rogers followed with a force of 300 men and moved through the heart of the Indian country. Billy Bowlegs, the chief who gave the name "Bowlegs' War" to this phase of the conflict, was ready to give up the fight. When the steamer *Grey Cloud* left Egmont Key on May 7, 1858, on board were thirty-eight warriors and eighty-five women and children who had surrendered with him, plus the forty-one captives and Polly, a Seminole woman guide. Bowlegs had accepted $5,000 for himself and $2,500 for cattle he alleged had been stolen. Each warrior received $1,000 and each woman and child $100; the government bought any movable property the Indians claimed.

The war was over, but not all of the Seminoles were yet gone. Another seventy migrated the next year, but the remainder disappeared into the Everglades and the Big Cypress, their number estimated at one to three hundred. Floridians abandoned the demand that they be moved. The federal Indian Service, however, continued efforts to induce them to join their kinsmen in Indian Territory, but they showed no disposition to give up the land which they had struggled so long to keep. When Floridians rediscovered the Seminole in the twentieth century, he had become an asset.

12.

A Maturing Frontier Society, 1845-1861

Economic and social development in the first decade and a half of statehood followed very much the pattern of experience in the preceding territorial period. The economy remained predominantly agricultural, with a substantial extractive industry chiefly in the form of forest products and local service industries for agricultural communities. The only major new developments were in railroad building and the acquisition by the state of millions of acres of swamp and overflowed land. These were to be of closely related and almost incalculable importance in Florida's growth, but their full impact was not felt until after the American Civil War. This impending conflict cast scarcely a shadow on the life of the average Floridian until the war actually came. It was reflected most noticeably in growing fear of slave insurrection and more careful regulation of the lives of free blacks as well as slaves.

With Indian removal accomplished except for a few hundred Seminoles hidden in the wilds of the lower west coast, and with the panic of 1837 and its depressing aftermath but an unpleasant memory, Floridians were in a position to enjoy the prosperity that was general except for the minor economic and financial setback in 1857, which affected the South much less than the remainder of the country. Population growth was steady if not spectacular, from about 70,000 in 1845 to 87,445 in 1850 and 140,424 in 1860. Slaves continued to make up more than forty percent of the population. In 1845 there were 35,500 whites, 33,950 slaves, and 560 free blacks. Fifteen years later whites numbered 77,746, slaves 61,745, and free blacks 932, with less than 7,000 slaves living in towns. The value of real and personal property as reported by the United States census nearly quadrupled, from $28,862,270 in 1850 to $82,592,641 ten years later.

Middle Florida and adjacent parts of East Florida continued to experience rapid expansion of cotton growing. The extreme eastern and western sections that had been the scenes of most activity in the Spanish and the British periods failed to keep pace with the interior, which had been almost completely untouched by white settlement two decades earlier. A significant feature of the agricultural expansion was the prominence on the frontier of the plantation system with slave labor. The yeoman farmer and the single family farm are popularly associated with the opening up of new land to settlement, but on the Florida frontier slaves were clearing land for growing cotton on a large scale side by side with small farmers. In fact, this was clearly one section in which plantation operations frequently pushed the small farmer into less desirable land.

The center of cotton planting and the concentration of slaves was in the region between the Apalachicola and the Suwannee rivers in Gadsden, Jefferson, Leon, and Madison counties. In 1845 only Jackson County in West Florida belonged in this group of counties, which produced eighty percent of the cotton and where slaves outnumbered whites. Only Nassau in East Florida where rice, sea island cotton, and some sugarcane were grown had a comparable proportion of slaves in the population. After 1845, cotton growing expanded into nearby counties in East Florida, and Alachua and Marion became known as plantation counties. Population growth was significantly more rapid in the newly developing areas. Alachua and Marion counties reported only 1,262 bales of cotton in 1850, but ten years later 3,294 whites and 5,314 slaves produced 7,713 bales. West Florida increased twenty-three percent in population from 1850 to 1855, Middle Florida thirty-four percent, East Florida seventy-three percent, and South Florida appears for the first time as a separate section. In 1860, growth for the five year period was 21.6% for West, 6.5% for Middle, 63.6% for East, and 27.1% for South. This trend of growth eastward and southward thereafter came at an accelerated rate.

A special case of planter migration was that to Manatee County, which slave holders helped to open up in this period. Early in 1840 Josiah Gates, an innkeeper from Alachua County, followed the Seminole war troops to Fort Brooke and established a hotel on Tampa Bay. In January 1842 when the war was drawing to a close he settled with his family on the bank of the Manatee River. Henry Clark, a former New York merchant, set up the first store there. Other settlers took up Armed Occupation Act grants on both sides of the river.

At much the same time, 1842, Major Robert Gamble and Dr. Joseph Braden, prominent planters from Leon County who had lost much of their property in the depression of 1837 came to the new frontier in an attempt to restore their fortunes. Braden and his brother Hector acquired by grant and purchase 1,000 acres and put up the first buildings on the site of present-day Bradenton. Major Gamble acquired some 3,000 acres on the north side of the river. Other refugees from the financial debacle in the depression soon joined them, among whom were the Wyatts, Wares, Ledwitts, Reeds, Snells, and the Craig brothers. Together Gamble and Braden brought in 180 slaves.

By 1845 sugarcane was growing on a dozen plantations, and sugar was being sent to the New Orleans market. Gamble's mill, housed in three brick buildings with an aggregate length of 340

The Gamble Mansion, Bradenton.

feet, was the largest. The sugar planters prospered for a time. Dr. Braden built Braden Castle of native limestone. Gamble Mansion had thick tabby walls with huge columns on three sides. Judah P. Benjamin found refuge there in the summer of 1865 on his flight to England after the collapse of the Confederacy. These planters proved again, as did others in various parts of Florida, that sugar could be produced successfully in Florida, but if the panic of 1837 ruined the Manatee group as cotton planters, the panic of 1857 ended their careers as sugar planters, and many like Gamble abandoned the effort and returned to Tallahassee.

The number of planters in Florida as in other southern states was relatively small, but in their day by any measure of importance they dominated the life of the state. The best measure of a planter's wealth was the number of slaves rather than the acres of land he owned. Any owner of twenty or more slaves probably devoted all of his time or that of an overseer to the direction of their labor and was designated a planter. Owners of smaller numbers of slaves usually worked along with them. In 1860 there only two persons in Florida who owned more than 200 blacks, 808 who owned 20 or more and 4,344 owners who held fewer than twenty and 863 of them only one.

Planters accounted largely for the fact that nearly half of the population and wealth was in Middle Florida in 1845, and almost two-thirds of the cash value of farms in 1850 was in five plantation counties. In 1860 the cash value of farms in seven cotton counties was $11,662,243 out of a total for the state of $16,435,727. Every ante-bellum governor was from the seven-county plantation belt, and all but one were planters. William D. Moseley was from Jefferson County and Thomas Brown had been a Leon planter. James E. Broome migrated from South Carolina, owned a farm, and practiced law in Leon. Madison Starke Perry was an Alachua planter, and John Milton, wartime governor, had been a planter and lawyer in Jackson County. In a reapportionment of representation in the General Assembly in 1846 the five plantation counties in Middle Florida had sixteen of the thirty-nine members of the lower house and five of the nineteen in the senate. East and West Florida complained that in view of their 31,102 people and the 22,567 whites in Middle Florida, the counting of three-fifths of the slave population for purposes of representation gave too much power to the plantation belt.

The frontier offered opportunity for the industrious and able individual to rise rapidly in the economic if not always in the social and political aristocracy. Frederick Law Olmstead, after three journeys into the South on the eve of the Civil War, was greatly impressed by the number of instances where he observed this phenomenon which, after all, is the typical American success story. He reported of plantations with as many as 100 slaves, where the owners could scarcely read or write. Living in crude buildings, it might be another generation before some of the more entrepreneurial families would become more educated and live in the grand manner associated with the planter class. Often overlooked in the romantic story of Scarlett O'Hara in *Gone With the Wind* is the fact that her father was an Irish immigrant who started his career from "scratch" by the accumulation of land and slaves. The setting for the initial phase of the process of creating the planter class might as well have been the Florida frontier. It was happening all over the cotton South in the last pre-Civil War generation.

Nor should plantations be thought of as devoted exclusively to the production of staple crops of cotton, tobacco, rice, or sugar, as the case may be. In a new country the landowner might resemble the classic frontier type as much as the planter. Along with cotton he might easily be raising cattle, hogs, horses, and sheep on the open range. Well-established planters aimed to make their operations as nearly self-sufficient as possible. Particularly they sought to produce as much of their food needs as possible. Since corn, meat (usually pork), and sweet potatoes were the most important items they required, this was relatively easy. Planters did frequently buy corn and bacon from the Mississippi valley region and horses and mules from Tennessee and Kentucky.

In other respects also planters managed to produce their needs. The coarse cloth for the clothing of slaves might be made by slave

"Plantation sur le lac Jackson," Tallahassee, late 1830s

women in seasons when their labor was not required in the fields. Slaves became craftsmen—carpenters, blacksmiths, wheelwrights, and masons—and were often hired out by their masters to do this kind of labor. Plantations usually had their own gristmills and would sometimes grind the corn of their neighbors.

Far more characteristic of the Florida frontier were farmers with few if any slaves who, with the assistance of their families, lived a much more nearly self-sufficient life. They wore homespun made by their wives and daughters from their own cotton and wool. They were likely to live in a double pen log cabin with a passage through the middle and with sheds attached. Huge chimneys and fireplaces, sometimes made of sticks and clay, were common. Heavy shutters closed the window openings. Other common features were cane- and hide-bottom chairs, water pail and gourd, tin basin and roller towel, split pine bedsteads, and mattresses filled with straw, Spanish moss, cotton, or occasionally wool. When increasing prosperity made possible a frame house, it was likely to be modeled somewhat after the log cabin, with a hallway down the middle, rooms on either side, and with porches on as many as three sides. Anyone with a nostalgia for the rural Florida of a century ago can find many survivals of these buildings and furnishings in the state today.

The slave population had grown as rapidly as the white. The total also includes the natural increase of Florida-born children of slaves, nowhere near enough to expand the old plantations and man new ones. The sources of additional slaves were threefold. Probably the greatest number was brought in by owners who migrated from Georgia and other southern states. The next largest group came from the domestic slave trade, of which a Savannah, Georgia, merchant had practically a monopoly of the Florida business. Not clearly distinguished from these was an undetermined number, perhaps greater than we would guess, smuggled in from abroad in spite of state and federal laws prohibiting the importation of slaves. One historian set the figure of 270,000 as the number of illegal immigrations into the United States from 1808 to 1860. It is known that such a cargo came into the state as late as 1862.

The lot of Florida slaves differed very little from that described in the territorial period. As the institution of slavery came more and more under attack by abolitionists at home and abroad, owners became increasingly concerned for the safety of their property and feared more and more the possibility of servile insurrection. The result was more careful enforcement of laws and practices that restricted any freedom of movement or any gatherings of slaves not in the presence of whites. Any new legislation was likely to be directed at free blacks.

In a sense it may be argued that the less than one thousand free blacks in Florida in 1860, of whom about two-thirds were mulattos, were the object of more concern and the subject of more legislation than all other persons combined. They represented the exception to the commonly held assumption that blacks could live successfully only in some subordinate status, and they were looked upon as a bad example to slaves and a potential incitement to servile insurrection. Free blacks in the older Spanish settlements had a special status inherited from the more lenient Spanish law and practice. They could own property; the census of 1860 listed property of free blacks valued at $97,985. In Pensacola where their freedom dated back to the Spanish period they were called Creoles, meaning mixed bloods. They owned property and businesses and served on juries with whites. In Pensacola and Saint Augustine they could carry firearms without a license. In a newer city like Key West, on the other hand, there was protest as early as 1834 that the anti-immigration laws were not being enforced. Most of the free blacks worked at unskilled labor, but there were a few exceptions where they worked at one or another of the skilled trades.

Legislation aimed first of all to exclude free persons of color. Few new laws were necessary in this field after 1845. Laws in the territorial period made a free Negro guilty of a second entry, subject to being sold at public auction for five years, and owners were forbidden to free slaves unless they also provided for their leaving the state. In 1846 a ship's captain bringing a free black into Key West became subject to a $100 fine for each except in case of shipwreck. At all seaports the free black crew members had to remain aboard ship, even in the case of disabled vessels, and have no contact with persons on shore or be subject to arrest.

A law enacted in 1842, repealed, and then re-passed in 1848 required all free blacks and mulattos over twelve years of age to have a white guardian. In 1856 all of them who had not secured guardians became subject to a ten dollar fine and imprisonment until the fine and costs were paid. The same law forbade any buying or selling of free blacks or mulattos without consent of guardian. As a result of this law at least thirty-five free blacks from Pensacola declined the offers of friendly whites to become their guardians and migrated to Tampico, Mexico, in 1857. Some of them returned to the city after the Civil War, but others remained expatriates. A statute of 1858 permitted free persons of African descent to elect their own masters and become slaves. The records of the Escambia County Circuit Court show two mulattos accepted this course in 1861. In another instance the orphan children of free blacks were apprenticed to whites for ninety-nine years to learn a trade.

There had been four railroad building projects in the territorial period that got beyond the paper stage, but the only railroad in operation in 1845 was the twenty-three mile line from Tallahassee to Saint Marks, completed in 1836. Since it did not relieve planters from continued dependence on water transportation, they wanted a railroad connection from Middle Florida to Savannah and Charleston and thence to northern cities. The stakes in this new form of transportation that would accelerate Florida development were increasingly high, and Floridians were alert to the possibilities for investment. David L. Yulee had promoted statehood with the proposal that the state build an Atlantic to Gulf railroad, using the 500,000 acres of land the state would receive from the national government. He urged that the profits of operating the state-owned railroad would pay the costs of state government.

But projects were slow to get under way. Capital outlays were beyond the resources of the promoters. Experience with earlier attempts was not encouraging. Efforts to provide capital by using the credit of the state government had been pretty well discredited by the faith bond fiasco of the recent territorial period. Equally important, other states had withdrawn from the business of providing internal improvements after the severe losses they suffered as a result of the panic of 1837 and its aftermath. But the railroad age had definitely arrived, and ambitious Floridians meant to have their region participate in its benefits. And the state was about to be put into a position where tangible assistance could be given.

The General Assembly chartered the Florida, Atlantic and Gulf Central Railroad in 1851 to build a line west from Jacksonville to Alligator (later named Lake City). Two years later that body chartered the Pensacola and Georgia Railroad to build from Pensacola

A state-endorsed railroad bond, 1860

eastward, and the Florida Railroad to build a trans-state line from a port on the Atlantic to another on the Gulf of Mexico, and the Florida and Alabama was to build a road from Pensacola to Montgomery, Alabama. The only other lines projected before the Civil War interrupted building operations were the Perdido and Junction at Pensacola and the St. Johns Railroad Company to operate a line from Saint Augustine to the Saint Johns River.

Chartering a company did not provide the means to construct and operate a railroad, but help was at hand. Under an act of Congress in 1850, swamp and overflowed lands were turned over to the states in which they lay for purposes of drainage and reclamation. Under this law Florida was to receive an estimated ten million acres of land loosely defined as swamp and overflowed. Some of it obviously could not be reclaimed. Much of it was already usable. All that remained was for the state to put this tremendously valuable asset at the disposal of railroad builders.

The General Assembly in 1851 created the Internal Improvement Board to manage the swamp and overflowed lands and the 500,000 acres of public land transferred from federal to state ownership when Florida entered the Union. In 1854 the Internal Improvement Board reported the need for a system of railroads to connect Jacksonville to Pensacola, Fernandina to Tampa, and a Saint Johns-Indian River Canal. This report recommended that the state lands be used to assist private corporations to construct the needed internal improvements. To achieve these ends, they proposed that the Board of Internal Improvements be reorganized with the governor and other state officials as ex-officio members. Significantly, there were two railroad presidents on the board at the time–David L. Yulee of the Florida Railroad and Dr. Abel Seymour Baldwin of the Florida Atlantic and Gulf Central.

The General Assembly in 1855, acting upon the recommendation, created the Internal Improvement Fund to be supervised by the governor and four other state officials–the comptroller, the treasurer, the secretary of agriculture, and the registrar of state lands– as trustees. Railroad and canal projects that met the approval of the trustees might receive state assistance. The approved companies would receive a 200-foot right-of-way through state lands and alternate sections of land six miles deep on both sides of the railroad. When the grade had been constructed and the crossties laid, the trustees might issue bonds up to $10,000 a mile for the purchase of rails and rolling stock. Bonds were also authorized for the construction of bridges and trestles. The bonds were a lien on the railroads and their equipment.

These bonds carried a far more tangible guarantee of payment than was the case in the faith bonds where only the promise to pay of the territorial government was involved. The bonds, thirty-five years at seven percent, were endorsed by the state, and state lands were pledged in promise of payment if the railroad companies failed to pay the principal and interest. A rather elaborate provision was also made to create a sinking fund from railroad receipts to guarantee payment of bonds, but it never became operative, for the Civil War intervened before the roads became profitable enterprises, and eventually the payment for the bonds became an obligation of the trustees of the Internal Improvement Fund. Meanwhile, Yulee, elected to the United States Senate in 1854, had secured for the Florida Railroad the right-of-way through national lands and alternate sections six miles deep as in the case of state lands. Specified recipients were to be builders from Fernandina to Tampa with a branch line to Cedar Key, from Jacksonville to Pensacola, and from Pensacola to Montgomery.

The way was now open to proceed with the construction of the approved new lines and the improvement of the one existing railroad in operation. The Tallahassee-St. Marks Company immediately moved to improve the track and replace mule power with steam engines. By the end of the year 1855, the Florida Atlantic and Gulf Central had surveyed the sixty miles from Jacksonville to Alligator. The Pensacola and Georgia was proceeding at the same rate from Alligator to Tallahassee. Meanwhile the Florida Railroad officers had determined the Atlantic terminus at Fernandina and the Gulf at Cedar Key.

By far the most ambitious of these projects was the Florida Railroad. Its purpose was more than to serve residents and businesses along the line. It was designed to pick up passengers, freight, and mail from oceangoing vessels at either terminus and move them across the state, thus saving the long sea journey around the peninsula, a railroad idea that remained operative into the twentieth century. Yulee also hoped that the railway line could be owned by Floridians. Stockholders could purchase an interest by paying only ten percent down, but they obligated themselves to pay in the remainder as it was needed to finance the building operations. Financial resources in Florida proved inadequate, and as in the case of many other such enterprises Yulee and associates found they must go to sources of capital from the East for financial assistance. They sold a controlling interest to E. M. Dickerson and Associates of Boston, who provided the means to push the road to completion.

The first train reached Cedar Key on March 1, 1861. Yulee meanwhile had secured the extension of telegraph services to Fernandina and along the route of the Florida Railroad to Cedar Key and a mail route from Cedar Key to Havana. The Jacksonville-Alligator line opened traffic operations in June 1860, and Alligator became Lake City by an act of the General Assembly.

Oldest bank building in Florida, Adams Street, Tallahassee

The railway system was designed to develop the interior of the state rather than make connections with railroads to the north and to keep the trade of Florida in Florida ports. The only railroad connection with other states in 1860 was west of the Chattahoochee River, which was of little service to the interior of the state. Over the Florida and Alabama, traffic and freight moved northward from Pensacola to Alabama, where connections were made to Mobile and other points. This lack of overland transport northward became a handicap, particularly during the Civil War, for it left Florida isolated from the Confederacy in the matter of railroad connections, and the federal embargo rendered water traffic difficult if not impossible. But until invaders interrupted service, travelers could go from Fernandina to Jacksonville, Tallahassee, and Cedar Key.

There was not a single state-chartered bank in Florida in 1845. Indeed another ten years passed before the Bank of the State of Florida opened at Tallahassee. Meanwhile, private banks and branches of financial institutions in Savannah, Charleston, and New York provided some banking services. The board of trustees of the Internal Improvement Fund used the Tallahassee agency of the South Western Railroad Bank of Charleston. The state borrowed more than $200,000 from Savannah and Charleston institutions to help finance the final phase of the Seminole war, 1855-1859.

The state collected an annual tax of $150, later $165, for each branch of an out-of-state bank, but there was a growing resentment that Floridians should be forced to pay for banking services and to use currency from other states over which they had no control. The anti-bank sentiment, typical of the American frontier, that had led to placing in the state constitution so many limits on banks continued to be strong. Banks could engage only in deposit, exchange, and transfer operations. The real need of business in the state for credit and currency was not being met by any Florida-chartered institution. In fact the only effort to launch a bank under the constitutional restrictions was the chartering of the State Bank of Florida at Tallahassee in 1851, but it never got beyond the paper stage. Nor did a general banking law of 1853 prove any help. Under this act persons wishing to engage in banking business might deposit with the state comptroller specified types of bonds. The comptroller then would provide the banks with notes of five to twenty dollar denominations equal to the value of the bonds deposited. At first the bonds required were those of the United States or of individual states. Three years later bonds of county, city, town, and certain railroads were approved for deposit.

By a special act of the General Assembly in 1855 Florida got its first state-chartered bank, the Bank of the State of Florida at Tallahassee, following rather closely the general law of 1853. Chartered for twenty years with a capital stock of $500,000, it was strictly limited to holding of property and trading in produce only when received in payment of debts. Its bills and notes had to be redeemed in gold and silver when presented at the bank. It could establish branches at Lake City, Newnansville, Tampa, and three other locations in Middle and West Florida. The bank was a success from the beginning. Within three years after the subscription books were opened in March 1856, $130,000 in specie had been paid in. The presence among its officers and directors of members of the "ragocracy" of the old Union Bank of Tallahassee, among whom were William Bailey, B. W. Bellamy, Robert H. Gamble, Joseph Chaires, and George T. Ward, must have caused mixed feelings among those accustomed to blame these men for the bank failures of the territorial period.

The legislature continued to charter banks, some of which never opened their doors. In 1860, besides five state banks from Fernandina to Pensacola, thirteen private banks operated on a largely local basis, and eight agencies for out-of-state banks were operating in Florida. The great bulk of the population, particularly those living at a distance from the larger towns, continued as they had from the beginning to depend upon barter with local merchants or with their neighbors to satisfy their needs. Such transfers of funds as may have been necessary were more than likely provided by the merchants with whom they dealt.

A combination of economic and political considerations promoted an interest in cotton mills all over the South that had a small influence in Florida. As southerners considered the low profits from cotton growing, they concluded that they paid too much for brokerage and transportation and too much for products manufactured of cotton. The obvious remedy was to keep the cotton at home and make it into yarn and cloth, all of which would also rid the section of the much talked about dependence upon the North, where an increasingly large number of people were critical of the South and its institutions. The region had the raw material, the labor was at hand, as were waterpower and the small amounts of capital required, and the slave owners purchased large quantities of coarse and cheap cotton cloth to clothe their chattel. All that was lacking was a little initiative, ran the argument.

Florida produced enough of all these requisites to start three cotton mills in the pre-Civil War years. The legislature chartered the Escambia Manufacturing Company in 1835, but it apparently did not get under way until ten years later, opening operations in April 1846 at Arcadia, near Milton in West Florida, as the Arcadia Manufacturing Company. It used water power and had a capacity of 1,000 yards of heavy cotton cloth a day, later 1,300 yards a day. Three white managers supervised the labor of 100 slaves brought from Virginia to tend the machines. There is no record of its operation after 1851.

Captain N. P. Willard established a mill at Madison at a reported cost of $30,000, with 1,000 spindles that had a capacity of 1,000 pounds of twist yarn a day. Thirty white boys and girls from ten to eighteen years of age earned from eight to fifteen dollars a month as workers. Most of the yarn was sold locally and woven into cloth by slaves or housewives. The mill burned on February 5, 1857, was uninsured at the time, and was never replaced.

A more successful enterprise was established by the Southern Rights Manufacturing Association near Monticello. The only stockholders of record are John Finlayson and General William Bailey, and the latter was clearly the prime mover. Aware of the danger of fire, the more so because he used a wood-burning thirty-five horsepower steam engine, Bailey made the buildings as fireproof as possible. Completed in December of 1853 with 1,500 spindles and fifty looms, it had a capacity for making 400,000 pounds of cotton into 60,000 yards of osnaburg (a coarse cotton fabric) and 100,000 pounds of yarn a year. In 1856 machines to use wool were added.

But Bailey found it hard to keep the project going. Merchants, he said, could buy the cloth cheaper in New York and preferred to send their cotton to the broker who handled their other business. Though the mill was employing forty men and twenty-five women who made $400,000 worth of cloth, it was on the verge of bankruptcy when the Civil War came along to give it a new lease on life. Bailey refused to profiteer during the inflated price era of the war but kept his mill going and placed the yarn and cloth where it was most needed in the state. In the summer of 1864 he and Governor Milton managed to prevent the Confederate government from impressing the mill and its products to help clothe the army. But this worthy project probably failed with the collapse of the government at the end of the war, for there is no record of its operation thereafter. Florida was not and would not be a textile manufacturing area.

Otherwise manufacturing was but an expansion of that described for the previous period. According to the 1850 census the state had 103 manufacturing establishments representing a capital value of $547,060, employing 991 wage earners who were paid wages totaling $199,452, using raw material valued at $220,611 and turning out products valued at $668,333. Between 1850 and 1860 the number of mechanics rose from 26 to 206, blacksmiths from 120 to 169, machinists from 11 to 70, millers from 42 to 71, gunsmiths from 6 to 12, and shingle makers from 3 to 40. In 1850 the first circular saw was brought into East Florida. Three years later there were fourteen sawmills around Jacksonville and six at Fernandina. Three hundred ships were taking on lumber in Jacksonville per year, and the railroads soon began to play a role in the timber business, making it possible to reach stands of timber at greater distances from the watercourses by which timber had previously been marketed. By 1860 Pensacola, Jacksonville, Cedar Key, and Fernandina were exporting two million dollars worth of lumber each year. North Carolinians had begun to establish the turpentine industry along the line of the Florida Railroad, an industry which, along with sawmilling, was destined to play the leading role in the exploitation of the state's pine forests for nearly a century until the use of pine for making paper began to rival them in importance.

The end of the Seminole war and the removal of the Indians from the prairies north and west of Lake Okeechobee resulted in the rapid expansion of the open range cattle industry into that area.

Cattle raising was no new enterprise in Florida, but this was new cattle country. Cattlemen from North Florida and from other states moved their herds to the upper Saint Johns, the Kissimmee prairie, and the Peace and Caloosahatchee valleys. Tampa soon became a shipping point for 250 head of cattle each week, and Jacob Summerlin emerged as Florida's first cattle king with cows ranging from Fort Meade to Fort Myers.

As the state gained population and wealth, educational needs began to receive more attention. The Florida Educational Society to promote education was formed in 1831, but not until 1839 did the territorial legislature act to use the sixteenth section in every township of public land for the support of schools. At that time residents were authorized to elect three trustees in each township to apply the income from the school lands to the support of public schools. A law of 1849 added to the school funds five percent of the sales return from all public lands, escheated property, or property along the coasts. The registrar of public lands became the ex-officio Superintendent of Common Schools, a position held by David S. Walker for many years. Tallahassee had a free school supported by a city tax, and a few counties supported public schools usually for three months in the year. Secondary education remained largely a private matter reserved for those who could pay for it. Planters commonly employed tutors to instruct their children. The federal census reported sixty-nine schools in 1850 with 4,746 enrollments and ninety-seven schools in 1860 with 8,494 pupils. In 1860, 138 private academies enrolled 4,486 students.

The Legislative Council on March 3, 1823, set aside for sale one township each in East and West Florida to support a seminary. In 1836 Governor Richard Keith Call named a fourteen-man board of trustees to plan a University of Florida. When Florida became a state, the land grants were reconfirmed, and 92,120 acres were set aside for a system of public schools. But not until January 1851 when the General Assembly authorized two seminaries for teacher training did higher education actually get under way. The curriculum was to include anatomy, astronomy, chemistry and other sciences, literature, history, moral philosophy and language, mechanical arts, animal husbandry, agricultural chemistry, and instruction in the fundamental laws and rights and duties of citizens for both male and female. After twenty weeks of study students could be certified to teach if they passed an examination by the principal and the Board of Education. At Ocala in 1853 the East Florida Seminary opened its doors, and from it the University of Florida claims direct descent. The West Florida Seminary opened at Tallahassee in 1856 and in time became the Florida State University.

Frontier communities, as soon as they could, established those institutions familiar to them in the more settled communities from which they came, none sooner than the church. Pioneers frequently brought their church affiliations with them and organized congregations. The first Baptist congregation in Florida was established as early as 1821 by the Reverend Fleming Bates and Elder Isom

Peacock in the Pigeon Creek Community of present-day Nassau County and became a member of the Piedmont Baptist Association in Georgia. The Baptist's congregational form of church government made it easy to form congregations, choose lay preachers, and use the services of itinerant ministers until the churches could afford one of their own. By 1835 there were eight Baptist churches in Florida. They organized the Suwannee Association, which ten years later split off the Florida Baptist Association in a fight over support for foreign missions.

The Methodist church grew almost as rapidly as the Baptist. Methodists were a part of the Patriot group who staged the abortive East Florida Rebellion in the late Spanish period. The first regularly assigned Methodist minister to preach in Florida was sent by the South Carolina Conference to Saint Marys and Amelia Island in 1822. In the same year the Mississippi Conference sent Alexander Talley to Pensacola. By the fall of 1849 six circuits were established, and circuit riders brought, along with the gospel, mail and news of the outside world. The congregations organized the Florida Conference of Methodist Churches.

Presbyterians organized a congregation at Saint Augustine in 1824, and a Presbyterian minister was the chaplain for the 1826 session of the Legislative Council in Tallahassee. They organized a church in Tallahassee in 1823 and completed a brick church in 1838 that was still standing 125 years later.

Episcopalians were active from the first and established Trinity Church in Saint Augustine in 1825. In Tallahassee Reverend Williston founded an Episcopal church that was to become the largest in Florida and produced the first bishop of the Florida diocese, Francis Huger Rutledge. This denomination organized a congregation in Key West in 1847.

Roman Catholicism lost most of its communicants in Florida (except the Minorcans at Saint Augustine) when the Spaniards departed in 1821, and the two parishes in the state, Saint Augustine and Pensacola, had no priest for a time. In 1830 Alabama and Florida were joined in a diocese. By 1835 there were eleven priests in the diocese and another eight by 1841. Most of the 11,000 Catholics in 1845 were in Mobile, Pensacola, and Saint Augustine. By 1858 a parish in Jacksonville was added and there were mission chapels at Middleburg, Mayport, Mandarin, Fernandina, Palatka, Tallahassee, and Key West, but no school, convent, or educational facility. Augustin Verot became the first bishop of Saint Augustine in April 1858 and the church began to show new life. The following year the bishop went to Europe and brought back six priests, four brothers, and two nuns, all French. Later in the year he brought five sisters of the Order of Mercy and three Christian Brothers to start a girls' academy and a boys' day school. On January 4, 1861, Florida's bishop earned the title "rebel bishop" when he recognized the rights of slave owners but called for the humane treatment of slaves. On the same day in St. John's Episcopal Church in Tallahassee the Reverend William J. Ellis preached strongly in favor of secession. On July 22, 1861, Verot also became bishop of Savannah and divided his time between Saint Augustine and that city. When East Florida suffered invasion early in the war, church activities were seriously disrupted. The Sisters of Mercy closed St. Mary's Academy, and the bishop sent seven of the eleven sisters to Columbus, Georgia. Invaders broke into the church at Fernandina and stole the vestments and sacred vessels, and in March 1863 burned the parish house and the church in Jacksonville. During the conflict Verot visited the Confederate prison at Andersonville and shortly after the war also paid a visit to Fort Jefferson where Dr. Samuel A. Mudd assisted him in a mass.

From the first, blacks were part of the membership in almost all Florida congregations. Churches in areas of large slave population frequently had more slave than white members. In 1856 the Sunday School at St. John's Episcopal Church in Jacksonville reported 140 in attendance, of whom ninety were blacks. By 1860, forty-two percent (8,110) of all Methodists in Florida were black. They usually sat in reserved sections or balconies set aside for them. The slavery controversy affected Florida congregations very little. Clergymen usually reflected the sentiments of their flocks and supported slavery and secession.

While there were a few Jews living in Saint Augustine and Pensacola as early as the British period, organized synagogues did not come into being until after the Civil War. Abraham Mordecai was an Indian trader who operated in West Florida during the 1780s. He married an Indian woman and became a member of the Creek tribe. Moses Elias Levy, Senator David Levy Yulee's father, was an Orthodox Jew, and on his land in Alachua County he established a Jewish agricultural colony. The oldest organized Jewish congregation was in Pensacola, and the oldest Jewish cemetery was established in Jacksonville in 1854. By the end of the Civil War there were enough Jews living in Jacksonville and Pensacola that they began to meet for religious services in private homes.

13.

Florida Enters and Leaves the Union, 1845-1861

Admission to the Union ushered in a new era in Florida history. The obstacles and differences that had slowed development and postponed statehood were largely gone. The panic of 1837 and the associated bank failures and economic depression were but a fading memory. The nightmare of Indian warfare gave way to prospects for a more peaceful and orderly future. Annexationists, divisionists, and doubters accepted statehood without further protest. The only cloud on the horizon, the sectional controversy that would lead to secession and civil war, was too small and too distant to cause any alarm.

Home rule in local affairs and full participation in the national government had been principal appeals of statehood. Floridians would now choose all of their state officials and manage and finance their own government. Two senators and one member of the House of Representatives, instead of the nonvoting territorial delegate, gave new pride of status to Floridians and new strength to the South in national affairs. May 26, 1845, two months after the proclamation of statehood, was the date to elect a governor, a member of Congress, seventeen state senators, and forty-one house members from the twenty counties in the state. All free white males twenty-one years of age, citizens of the United States, residents of Florida, and identified with a district could vote if they were enrolled in the militia or had a legal exemption from that duty.

Since the Democrats were in the stronger position they rejected the Whig move to make it a nonpartisan election. William Bailey, a prominent Jefferson County planter, had rejected a tentative Whig nomination unless he could also be nominated by the Democrats. The Democrats met at Madison Courthouse on April 14-15 with forty-seven voting delegates present. On the second ballot Bailey received thirteen votes and William D. Moseley, another Jefferson County planter, thirty-three, with only one for Robert Butler of Leon County. David Levy became the nominee for the congressional seat. The Whigs elected to run Richard Keith Call for governor and Major Benjamin A. Putnam for Congress.

The only difference between the platforms was economy in government against economy and low salaries in government. The election became a bitter contest of personalities and a dirty campaign indeed. Call and Levy bore the brunt of the attacks. Call, it was charged, had deserted the Democrats to improve his political and financial fortunes, had pocketed public money, had been a corporation man, and had belonged to the Union Bank of Tallahassee. His judgment and his leadership, not his bravery, had been challenged in the Seminole war; now he was charged with having called the people of Florida cowards in that conflict. Levy, on the other hand, had not participated in the war but charged with speculating in Indian war claims; as well as the beneficiary of a corrupt bargain, for he was really known to be expecting to be named one of Florida's first United States Senators. Finally, his opponents alleged that he was an unnaturalized alien, ineligible for the office. Actually his father, who entered Florida just at the time of the change of flags, had made a careful point of establishing the United States citizenship of his children.

None of this changed very many votes. Other factors favored the Democrats. They were the party of statehood. The Whigs had opposed the constitution, had voted to postpone the application for statehood in 1843 and 1845, and had voted for division in 1844. The record of the Whigs on the banking issue cost them heavily. Major Putnam had never recovered from the defeat at Dunlawton in the Seminole war and the charge of ineptitude associated with it. Moseley had been associated with none of the controversial issues. He won over Call by 3,392 to 2,679 and Levy over Putnam by 3,614 to 2,395. The General Assembly, which was to be convened on June 23, was overwhelmingly Democratic. James A. Berthelot became president of the senate and Hugh Archer, also from Leon County, speaker of the house.

When the new governor took the oath of office on June 9 he delivered a strong state's rights inaugural address. He argued the rights of nullification and interposition in defense of what he termed federal encroachment upon rights of citizens in the state. On July 1 the assembly elected James D. Westcott, Jr., and David Levy to the United States Senate by a vote of 41-16, Levy winning the long term by lot. The assembly also authorized Levy to change his name to Yulee. He took his seat in the United States Senate as David Levy Yulee, the first Jew in the country's history to be selected to sit in that body.

At the inaugural ceremony the committee on arrangements presented a new United States flag with a star added for Florida and a state flag of five horizontal stripes-blue, orange, red, white, and green with the words "let us alone" on the second stripe. Though the words probably represented the sentiments of most Floridians, the flag never appeared again. The Constitution of 1868 first provided for an official state flag with the state seal on a white background. The great seal of the state as we know it today was adopted at the same time, but the flag was changed by an amendment in

*Florida's present capitol, built on the highest point of land in Tallahas-
see. The original portion of this building was completed in 1845 just
prior to statehood. The dome, which replaced a small cupola, was
built in 1891. Wings on the north and south sides were added in 1901-
1902, and the east and west wings in 1921-1922. In 1940 an additional wing was added on the north side, and in 1947 an addition to the
south wing was completed.*

1900 that added the diagonal red bars and provided that the proportions should be depth three-fourths of fly, the seal of diameter
one-third of fly, and the red bars one-eighth of the fly in width.
Other state symbols are of more recent origin. In 1909 the orange
blossom became the official state flower, and in 1927 the mocking-
bird the state bird. In 1935 Stephen Foster's "Old Folks at Home"
with its tribute to the Suwannee River became the state song. In
1953, the Sabal Palm, already on the great seal and the most widely
distributed and used of the palms, became the state tree.

The first General Assembly proceeded to the organization of
the executive and judicial branches of government for the state.
The legislators created the offices of secretary of state, attorney general, comptroller, and treasurer, and provided for the governor's
staff. The system of courts included circuit, supreme, probate, and
county levels and justices of the peace. The law fixed the governor's

salary at $1,500, the comptroller and the treasurer each $800, the secretary of state $600, the attorney general $500, the secretary to the governor $300, and circuit judges $2,000 for a total salary budget of $13,500. The governor received no rent allowance until 1851 when $500 was added to the pay, presumably for that purpose. Not until 1906 did the governor reside in the mansion provided by the state for that purpose.

The first budget totaled $41,500, a sum easier to determine than to raise. The lawmakers lacked the statistical data on which to levy a tax. The citizens of the Territory had a notoriously bad reputation for paying the limited levies of that period. The same law provided for tax assessors and a census of the population, and the county sheriff became the tax collector. Items selected for taxation were land, slaves at thirty-seven and one-half cents per head, free men of color between twenty-one and sixty years of age three dollars per year, inventory, taverns, restaurants, hawkers, peddlers, sales at auction, money at interest, bonds and stocks, banks, insurance companies, carriages, cattle, and an income tax of sorts on professional income of doctors and lawyers. When the assembly next convened it raised the land tax, added a poll tax of fifty cents on all white males over twenty-one years of age, taxed values of sawmills, gold and silver watches, twenty cents per $100 on incomes of weighers of cotton, inspectors, and pilots, and taxed all agencies of foreign insurance companies $25 a year. The promise of economy in costs of government was well kept. From July 26, 1845, to October 31, 1846, expenditures of public money totaled $56,009.65, and at the end of ten years, in 1855, state government was only costing $76,420.01 for an average year.

Yulee, probably the most popular man in Florida, suffered little if any loss of political popularity when, as had been charged he would, he was appointed to the Senate. He added nothing to his support by favoring the annexation of Cuba to the United States, a proposal quite popular among southern expansionists generally but less so in Florida, where Cuba was looked upon as a competitor best left outside the American Union. The Whigs chose Edward Carrington Cabell, a newcomer not associated with earlier Whig liabilities, as their candidate to fill the vacancy created by the Yulee election to the Senate. Cabell appeared to have won the election, but the Democratic contender, William H. Brockenbaugh, contested his election in the House of Representatives and unseated him. Cabell won by the small margin of 3,000 to 2,887 over Democrat William A. Kain in 1846. In that year the Whigs also gained one senator and seven representatives in the General Assembly and went on in 1847 to win control of both houses. Zachary Taylor, the Whig candidate for president in 1848, commanded considerable support in Florida. He was a southerner and a slaveholder, and had served creditably in the Seminole and the Mexican wars, all of which strengthened the Whigs in the state. They nominated Cabell for Congress and Thomas Brown, a Tallahassee businessman and planter with some previous political experience, for governor. The Democrats nominated

William Bailey for governor and William P. Duval, four-term territorial governor, for Congress. Because Florida Whigs differed from
Democrats only in degree if at all on the sectional issue of slavery
expansion, Whig support of the Wilmot Proviso to exclude slavery
from any territory received as a result of the Mexican War did not
hurt the party locally as much as might be expected.

Thomas Brown became Florida's second governor after statehood by a vote of 4,145 to 3,646, and Cabell won over Duval by
4,382 to 3,805. Whig electors outran their Democratic rivals by 4,539
to 3,238 and gave the state's three electoral votes to Taylor. Jackson Morton of Pensacola became Florida's only Whig senator but
more often than not voted with Democratic Senator Yulee. This
same tendency was common in the General Assembly, as for example when in January 1849 the majority favored a resolution
against any law which prohibited slavery in the territories. Whigs
remained more unionist in their sympathies and sought by compromise to avoid disunion. In the votes on the Compromise of 1850,
the entire delegation voted against the admission of California as a
free state and against abolishing the slave trade in the District of
Columbia. They all favored organizing territorial government in
New Mexico and Utah and leaving the question of slavery there to
be decided by the residents. They also supported the strengthening
of the fugitive slave law, though Yulee rightly thought it a poor
gain for the South. Yulee, a strong supporter of John C. Calhoun,
was strongest in opposition to the compromise. James C. Broome,
later to become governor of the state, came from South Carolina to
attend a meeting in Marion County to discuss a union of all parties
in the South to protect southern rights, while Governor Brown led
the fight for moderation and compromise.

Florida's congressional delegation favored the Nashville Convention called for June 1850 to organize opposition to the compromise measures, but Governor Brown refused to participate, arguing that it would only bring out southern differences. Floridians
made the compromise measures the principal issue in the 1850 elections. Cabell defeated the Democratic challenger, Major John Beard,
who advocated extending the Missouri Compromise line to the Pacific and barring the admission of California. Democrats came out
with a majority of one in the house and two in the senate of the
General Assembly. When the assembly met the members voted
down several efforts to keep the compromise differences alive. The
assembly sent Stephen R. Mallory of Key West to the United States
Senate to replace David Yulee, but not because of his opposition to
the Compromise of 1850. Yulee faced the opposition of other railroad promoters in his own party. None of his proposals offered any
advantage to South Florida and in fact might have diverted traffic
and trade from Key West. It required only a few Democrats to join
the Whigs and select Mallory. In the spring of 1852 James E.
Broome, now a Leon County planter who had dropped his opposition to the compromise, became the Democratic candidate for governor, and August E. Maxwell for Congress. They defeated by a

narrow margin the Whigs, George T. Ward for governor and Cabell for Congress. The fight over the Kansas-Nebraska bill in 1854 completed the ruin of the Whigs in Florida as in the nation. Northern Whigs lined up against the measure, and some of them joined the new Republican Party, which among other things opposed any further extension of slavery. Florida Democrats renominated Congressman Maxwell and supported the bill. The Whigs nominated former Governor Thomas Brown, who had been a compromiser in 1850, and he lost by 4,564 to 5,633. Moderation was not dead, but it thereafter lacked a great national party to support it. Floridians were already moving toward the one party system. In the ensuing struggle for Kansas pro-slave newspapers urged emigration from Florida to the territory, and one went so far as to propose a public fund to aid migrants but met with little or no response. Florida had few people to spare for any cause.

Some Florida Whigs joined the American or "Know-Nothing" Party, but it scarcely expressed their views. Opposition to foreigners and Catholics was not an issue in Florida. They could support only its Unionism. Richard Keith Call was their spokesman and attended the national convention that nominated Millard Fillmore and Andrew Jackson Donelson in 1856. Call presided over a state convention, which nominated David S. Walker, a cousin, for governor, and James M. Baker for congressman, and stumped the state for the nominees. Both nominees were trustees of the Internal Improvement Fund, which administered millions of acres of swamp and overflowed land that came to the state under the provisions of a law of 1850. Democrats charged that Walker speculated in these lands and worked to keep the price low. Democrats nominated Madison Starke Perry for governor and George S. Hawkins for congressman. The Democrats won the state and national contests. The American Party made a respectable showing but did not reappear in Florida politics. The Republican Party, which was offering a platform and a candidate for the first time, had no Florida organization and received no votes. The political ascendancy of the Democrats was no longer challenged. In 1858 Democratic candidates easily won election to the General Assembly. Governor Perry charged afterward that Republicans had inspired John Brown's raid on the federal arsenal at Harper's Ferry in 1859. He urged the assembly to strengthen the state militia, which they did on paper at least, and also authorized the governor to cooperate with other states and to call a special session of the legislature if the sectional crisis worsened.

By the time of the national election in November 1860 the course that Florida would follow was already clear. Supporters of radical action in defense of southern and state rights had been gaining ground steadily. The conservative and unionist Whig position was becoming untenable. A biographer of Richard Keith Call, the best known of the Unionists, said of him, "His personal tragedy was that of all the staunch national minded southerners who could not give up or compromise with slavery or the Union."

The Knott house in Tallahassee was built in the 1830s.

The Constitutional Union Party agreed that the South had grievances but urged rational and judicial approaches to solution. Delegates from twenty-seven counties met at Quincy on June 27, 1860. They endorsed John Bell of Tennessee and Edward Everett of Massachusetts as their national standard bearers and approved the national platform: "The Constitution of the Country, the Union of the States, and the enforcement of the laws." For governor they nominated Edward A. Hopkins of Duval County and Benjamin F. Allen, editor of the *Tallahassee Sentinel,* for Congress.

The Democrats held their state convention to choose delegates to their national convention on April 9, and approved Negro slavery as an unalterable domestic institution of the states which Congress must protect in the territories. A second convention at Quincy on June 4 declared for secession and nominated John Milton, a Jackson County planter, for governor (but only after twenty-three ballots) and R. B. Hilton of Leon for Congress.

The secessionist Democrats controlled the political machinery of the state. Governor Madison Starke Perry and most of the members of the state legislature were radicals on the subject. Sixteen of the state's newspapers, all of the largest ones, supported them. Only five supported the Constitutional Unionists. Men like Richard Keith Call were called submissionists and "Union Shriekers," and lesser people were beaten and driven from the state, at least one being shot and seriously wounded.

Yet Constitutional Unionists ran surprisingly well. In fact, John Reiger, one student of the election, suggests the possibility that in a less emotional campaign they might have won. They drew stature from such well known men as Call, George T. Ward, Columbus F. Drew, David S. Walker, Edward Hopkins, and Thomas Brown, two of whom would become governors of the state after the war. Milton defeated Hopkins by 6,994 to 5,248. Bell and Everett received 5,437 to Breckinridge and Lane 8,543. Douglas and Johnson, who represented compromise, had the support of only one newspaper and received only 367 votes. Stephen A. Douglas probably lost any Florida strength he may have had by his doctrine that despite the Dred Scott opinion by the U.S. Supreme Court, the people of a territory could exclude slavery by simply refusing to enact a slave code. The name of the Republican candidate was not on the Florida ballot.

The General Assembly met in regular session on November 26, 1860, and Governor Perry, who would serve until the following October, urged immediate secession. Two days later a bill introduced simultaneously in both houses to call a secession convention to meet in Tallahassee on January 3, 1861, passed unanimously. A motion to table the measure failed in the senate, as did a proviso that the action of the convention be submitted to popular vote. The governor signed the measure on November 30, and set December 22 for the election.

Early in December Richard Keith Call issued a pamphlet condemning the legislators for their action. Secession, which he saw as the next likely step, he called treason. He would not yield on the right of secession but offered as a substitute the right of revolution. On the appointed day the voters chose sixty-nine members for the convention, of whom about one-third were said to be cooperationists who would wait to act in concert with other states rather than go it alone.

When the convention met, temporary chairman John C. Pelot of Alachua County sounded the keynote of the deliberations when he described Abraham Lincoln as a wily abolitionist whose election had destroyed all hope of continued union between the North and the South. Prominent men from other secessionist states appeared to urge Floridians to act immediately. On January 5, John C. McGehee, an ardent secessionist planter from Madison County, became the permanent chairman of the convention, and McQueen McIntosh of Apalachicola introduced a resolution avowing the right of secession and agreed that the convention had the right to proclaim secession. Two days later, by a vote of 62 to 5, the resolution was adopted and a committee of thirteen, eight of whom were immediatists, set to work to prepare an ordinance that would take the state out of the Union.

On the following day when the ordinance was introduced two Whigs, George T. Ward of Leon County and Jackson Morton of Santa Rosa, moved unsuccessfully to defer action until Alabama and Georgia decided what course to follow. The delegates continued the debate on the ninth and deferred the vote to the next day. In the final session, after two more hours of discussion, the delegates voted 62 to 7 to adopt the ordinance, and Florida became third (after South Carolina and Mississippi) to abandon the Union. The action evoked enthusiastic response throughout the state. The great majority of Floridians accepted the right of secession, and perhaps also the inevitability, and differed only as to when the step should be taken.

An exploration of the background and interests of the members of the convention suggests a group of conservative men intent upon protecting their slave property engaging in revolution, a most unlikely step for men of their temperament to take. Fifty-eight of them (84%) owned slaves or held them in trust for others. Nineteen of them owned ten or less slaves, while eighteen owned more than forty. Thirty-three gave farming as their principal occupation, and twenty others made it secondary. Thirteen were merchants; eight, lawyers; six, physicians; two, mill owners; one was a judge of the United States District Court; one a judge of a probate court; one a clerk of a circuit court; two were ministers, one a cotton agent, and one a carpenter. Forty-nine (71%) of them owned estates in excess of $10,000, and only ten claimed less than $5,000 value, while thirty-one were worth more than $30,000. Only nine were under thirty years of age and forty-three were over forty. Of the seven delegates who voted against the ordinance, six were farmers, one a merchant-farmer; five of them owned slaves (one of these 112), and five had property in excess of $7,000.[1]

Floridians may be said then for a brief period of time to have enjoyed the sovereign status that John C. Calhoun claimed for the people in a state. Floridians, though, had no purpose to pursue an independent course thereafter and were in fact in no position to do so. When the delegates of six southern states gathered at Montgomery, Alabama, to form the Confederate States of America, three delegates appointed by the governor represented Florida. James Patton Anderson, a Tennessee-born lawyer who had served in the Mexican war, a term in the Mississippi legislature, and as United States Marshal for the Territory of Washington, and congressman from Washington, came to Florida in 1859 to manage "Casa Bianca," the plantation of a deceased aunt. Jackson Morton, a Virginian, had settled the plantation "Mortonia" near Pensacola and engaged in the lumber business. Formerly a Whig, he was one of those who sought to delay secession. He helped to frame the permanent constitution at Montgomery. James Bryan Owens, a South Carolinian, had acquired a cotton plantation in Marion County in 1859 and represented that county in the secession convention. The three were college graduates; two of them had served in the national Congress and they played more important roles at Montgomery than might have been expected or permitted so new and undeveloped a state.

Only Texas, like Florida, had no native-born delegate. Anderson resigned and was succeeded in turn by George T. Ward and John P. Sanderson in the Provisional Congress. Owens and Morton served out one-year terms. August E. Maxwell and James M. Baker served in the four sessions of the First Congress and two sessions of the Second, all in Richmond. Robert B. Hilton served as Representative in both congresses, while James B. Dawkins and John M. Martin divided the terms of the second representative in the First Congress and St. George Rogers was Hilton's colleague in the Second. Anderson, Morton, Ward, and Martin later served in the Confederate Army.

14.

The Civil War in Florida

Although a sizable percentage of Floridians opposed secession, once the decision was made they committed themselves to a war they were ill prepared to fight. With only about 140,000 people, nearly half of them black slaves, not many men were available to defend the state and the Confederacy, even recognizing the fact that blacks made an important manpower contribution by performing labor that freed white men for military service.

With an undeveloped and one-sided economy, Floridians were hard put to supply their own needs. There was literally no commercial manufacturing, a lack that was made up to some degree by domestic production in homes and on plantations. There was cotton to be exported in exchange for manufactures, but the Union blockade reduced that activity to a mere fraction of what it might have been. The only other items produced in quantities sufficient for more than local consumption were cattle and salt. The state's railroad system, only just over 400 miles, had no connections with railway lines of nearby states, and the rolling stock was inadequate in both quantity and quality. Finally, there was a long coastline to defend.

Clearly Florida had to cooperate closely with the Confederate government in the hope that it could provide economic and military assistance. Floridians were as individualistic and as devoted to local and state institutions as any other southerners, but they could not afford the luxury of the independent course pursued by the more self-sufficient states like Georgia and North Carolina. Early in the war it looked as if Florida's loyalty to the Confederate government might be rewarded by the defense of key points in the state. It soon became clear, however, that southern independence would be won or lost in fighting far removed from the state, and that Florida's soldiers would fight mostly outside its borders.

Warlike preparations commenced before the national elections in November 1860, and warlike actions began before the process of secession was formally completed. As early as January of that year, military companies were organized at Fernandina and Tallahassee. On November 12, eighty-three men responded to the election of Lincoln and the Republicans by forming a company at Madison

Fort Clinch, Fernandina, photographed in 1954

courthouse. A week later, Governor Madison Starke Perry, an ardent secessionist, accepted the first organization of minutemen for the defense of the state. On the same day he recommended to the General Assembly that the state militia be reorganized and proposed an appropriation of $100,000 for the purchase of arms. Thereafter as the march of events moved the state closer to secession and the possibility of war, the recruiting, equipping, and training of men grew apace.

Florida's United States Senators Stephen R. Mallory and David L. Yulee watched the course of events from the national capital and gave what aid they could to the state's independent course of action. On December 21, Yulee asked and received from Secretary of War John B. Floyd the names and rank of all officers from Florida in the United States Army. On January 2, 1861, the war department refused the request of the two senators for an inventory of munitions and equipment in federal forts and arsenals in Florida. Secession of the state on January 10 ended the official duties of the senators, but they did not formally withdraw from the Senate until January 21. Mallory returned to Florida two days later, but Yulee remained until early February to watch developments and advise his state government.

Fort Marion (Castillo de San Marcos), Saint Augustine, scene of limited action in the Civil War, taken by a Union photographer.

Early in January, Florida officials learned that Washington had authorized the reinforcement of the Pensacola forts and the destruction of the Chattahoochee arsenal lest the state secede and seize them. This spurred the Florida government to action. On January 5, the Quincy Guards took over the arsenal from an ordnance sergeant and three men. The 500,000 rounds of musket cartridges and 50,000 pounds of gunpowder made a valuable addition to the state's almost nonexistent stock of munitions. Two days later the single federal soldier guarding Fort Marion (the Castillo de San Marcos) at Saint Augustine surrendered the historic fortress with its valuable guns and ammunition to a local company of volunteers. On January 8, Governor Albert B. Moore of Alabama revealed that Governor Perry had sought his aid to seize the federal installations at Pensacola. On the same day, Governor Perry appointed Colonel William Chase, a retired United States Army officer at Pensacola, to the command of Florida's troops and authorized him to take possession of the forts there if he felt sure of success. Florida troops also took over Fort Clinch on Amelia Island. There the successful take-over of federal military establishments in Florida ended, and the real prizes had eluded the state's grasp. At Key West and Pensacola, where the stakes were higher, the strategic forts remained in Union hands. As early as November 10, 1860, Captain Montgomery C. Meigs of the United States Army Engineers had urged reinforcements so that Key West, Pensacola, and Fort Jefferson would not be lost. Federal policy at the time did not permit the sending of the reinforcements lest the action precipitate a sectional crisis, but enterprising and resourceful officers and their small complements of men frustrated the efforts of the state and saved them for the Union. On the night before the secession convention voted to take Florida out of the Union, Lieutenant Adam J. Slemmer, in command of Fort Barrancas at Pensacola, received orders to take the necessary steps to prevent seizure by the secession forces. At the time five companies of Alabama troops were moving from Montgomery to Pensacola to join forces with Florida troops assembling there. Only a sergeant and his wife lived at Fort McRee as custodians. Lieutenant Slemmer was at Fort Barrancas with forty-six artillerymen. Fort Pickens on Santa Rosa Island had never been completed and was not occupied, but it commanded the entrance to the bay and could easily be reinforced and supplied from the sea. The Pensacola Navy Yard at Warrington on the outskirts of the city was fully active. It consisted of a million dollar dry dock, workshops, warehouses, barracks, a marine hospital, and cannons and shells valued at half a million dollars. Its commander, Commodore James Armstrong, a veteran of fifty-years of service, and his subordinate officers appear to have been mostly Confederate sympathizers.

Lieutenant Slemmer used his authority to move his forty-six men and thirty-five ordinary seamen to the more strategically located Fort Pickens, which had a capacity for 1,260 men and was beyond the reach of the shore batteries. Commodore Armstrong, moved by caution and indecision or possibly sympathy for the southern cause, gave Slemmer only limited assistance. A boat crew from the U.S.S. *Supply* appeared at Fort McRee, and when the wife of the absent sergeant denied them the keys, they broke into the fort, spiked its guns, and dumped the powder into the water. The reinforcements from Alabama arrived and on the twelfth some 500 Alabama and Florida troops accompanied by a large crowd of citizens demanded the surrender of the navy yard. Commodore Armstrong, who had but fifty men, yielded the valuable property with scarcely more than a word of protest. State troops then occupied Forts McRee and Barrancas, but Slemmer and his small force, who watched helplessly the taking over of the other forts, refused to give up Pickens and were left in undisputed possession for the moment.

At Key West, Captain James M. Brannan found himself in a dilemma. He realized that he lacked authority to do anything about it, but he was determined that he would not surrender control of the island's defenses. His small force of forty-four men was quartered in barracks on the northeastern shore of the island. Fort Taylor, where he might hope successfully to resist attack, was across the island on the west shore. He hesitated to move his men through the city whose population was largely southern in sympathy. He therefore decided to move secretly by night. After attending public worship in the city on Sunday evening, he repaired to the barracks, divided his men into small units, and sent them through the sleeping city to the fort without incident. He worked rapidly to improve the living quarters and mount the defenses of the unfinished fort. His position was never seriously challenged, and reinforcements soon made the fort and with it the city of Key West secure in Union hands for the duration of the conflict. Actually the state made only one move to take over the city and that was peaceful. All federal officials resigned except District Court Judge William Marvin and Collector of Customs, Charles Howe. Governor Perry sent McQueen McIntosh, an ardent Confederate, to take over Marvin's office. The judge refused to yield it but used his influence to prevent McQueen's arrest and permit him to return to the mainland.

Federal troops also occupied Fort Jefferson. Like Forts Pickens and Taylor, this fort became obsolete before it was completed and was never been garrisoned. It was to be the scene of no military or

Rebel battery, 1863, Warrington, entrance to Pensacola Bay

naval action but served a dramatic role as a military prison during and after the conflict. State forces had not been inactive. They removed the lenses from the lighthouses at Saint Augustine and Jupiter, effectively putting them out of action for the duration of the war and hampering any naval operations on the coast at night. Lieutenant Slemmer's refusal to surrender Fort Pickens left Florida's civil and military authorities in a deep quandary. An assault on the fort might start a war. Not to make the effort might mean its permanent loss to the southern cause. On January 28, Yulee reported from Washington to Pensacola that President Buchanan, feeling perhaps that the military buildup there justified it, had decided to reinforce Pickens. Governor Perry, like his counterpart in South Carolina where a similar situation existed at Fort Sumter, found the flying of the United States flag in the bay an irritating challenge to the sovereignty which the state claimed, but he hesitated to answer it by any military action. He and General Chase took their problem to Senators Mallory and Yulee, who proposed that three prominent southerners still in Washington, John Slidell, R. M. T. Hunter, and Governor William Bigler of Pennsylvania, be asked to call upon the president and induce him to reconsider his action or face the prospect of war. Buchanan shared the wish of the Floridians to avoid a showdown that would commit his successor to any course of action and possibly earn for himself the blame for starting a civil conflict. He assured his visitors that the status quo would be maintained at the forts so long as they were not attacked and so advised his secretaries of war and navy. Thus was born the Fort Pickens truce.

Both sides honored the truce until the Fort Sumter crisis of April 12 broke the tension and precipitated action all along the line. Both sides meanwhile continued preparations for a struggle. Pickens was not actually reinforced, but federal warships stood by to put men ashore if occasion should arise. On February 6, Captain Israel Vogdes arrived aboard the *Brooklyn* and went ashore to take command of Pickens. He found the small garrison exhausted. In fact, the thirty-five seamen there had become insubordinate and could not be depended upon. Only fifty-four cannons were in position, fifty-seven embrasures had no guns at all, being protected only by wooden shutters, and there was no ammunition for some of the guns. On the same date there were about a thousand Alabama, Florida, and Mississippi troops encamped on the bay, busy with preparations aimed at taking over the fort when a propitious time arrived.

Meanwhile the Confederate government organized in February began to take over some of the responsibility hitherto exercised by the states. On March 6, the Confederate Congress formally created an army. On the following day General Braxton Bragg, a West Point graduate with a good record in the Mexican War, assumed the command of all troops in the Pensacola area. He had once been stationed at Pensacola and knew something of the region. On March 9, the Confederate War Department asked the governors for a total of 11,700 troops, 5,000 of which were to go to Pensacola. Georgia,

Louisiana, and Alabama were each to send 1,000 troops to Pensacola. Mississippi was to provide 1,500 and Florida 500. On April 5, the Florida contingent met at the Chattahoochee arsenal to be mustered into the Confederate service. There were two companies from Leon County, two from Alachua, and one each from Franklin, Jackson, Madison, Gadsden, Jefferson, and Escambia. As was the practice at the time, the men of the companies had elected their officers and now elected their regimental officers. James Patton Anderson of the Jefferson County Volunteers became the colonel, William K. Beard of the Leon County Artillery the lieutenant colonel, and Thaddeus A. McDonnell the major. Before the end of the year requisitions for Florida troops would total 5,000 with more to come.

The inauguration of Abraham Lincoln on March 4, 1861, in time meant a change of policy, but at first the new president played a game of watchful waiting. Like James Buchanan, his predecessor, he did not wish to precipitate an armed conflict. He hoped that the secession movement might collapse if it could be limited to the seven states of the lower South that had left the Union to form the Confederate States of America. Lincoln did state in his inaugural address that he did not accept the right of secession and that he would hold and possess the territory and property of the United States, thereby showing little disposition to yield Fort Sumter and Fort Pickens. The status quo could not be maintained indefinitely at the forts. Sumter had become the symbol of federal authority not only in South Carolina but in the whole of the Confederate states. Lincoln was loathe to yield it unless some compensating advantage could be gained elsewhere. For a time at least Lincoln and some of his advisers looked with favor on a proposal to surrender Sumter but hold on to Pickens, where the situation was less explosive, as the symbol of federal authority in the South. Indeed, the relief expedition to Sumter was weakened by detaching the battleship *Powhatan* and sending it instead to Pensacola. If the president ever was committed to the plan, he abandoned it, but the commander of the *Powhatan* refused to acknowledge an order he received at sea to rejoin the Sumter expedition. Though it represented powerful support, it is difficult to see that it could have made any difference in the outcome.

Confused communications may have accounted for the misunderstandings about the role of the *Powhatan* as they did in other cases. On March 12, General Winfield S. Scott, Commanding General of the United States Army, sent orders to Captain Vogdes to land his men and strengthen Fort Pickens. When the order reached him on April 1, Vogdes asked Captain Henry A. Adams, the senior naval officer, for boats to land his men. The captain refused to believe that the Pickens truce was to be terminated and requested orders from Secretary of Navy Gideon Welles. This delay created a near crisis. Lincoln was about to send relief to Fort Sumter, and he meant to secure Fort Pickens before the Confederates could move on it. To meet the crisis, Welles on the same afternoon sent Lieutenant John L. Worden, U.S.N., with orders for Captain Adams to assist in reinforcing Pickens. Traveling overland, Worden reached Pensacola on April 11 and after an interview with the unsuspecting General Bragg received a pass to visit the Union fleet to deliver a verbal communication to Captain Adams. He communicated the new orders, and that night Captain Vogdes moved an artillery company of eighty-six men and a detachment of 115 marines into Fort Pickens. The firing on Fort Sumter began at 4:30 on the morning of April 12, and the war had begun. On April 1, Colonel Harvey Brown had been appointed to the command at Fort Pickens with orders to strengthen the defenses. He arrived on April 17, and by the end of June there were 2,088 men and officers on the island.

On the same day that Brown arrived at Pickens, General Bragg placed Pensacola under martial law and announced that he had 5,000 men on hand with another two thousand on the way to join him. Two days later a small flotilla of some twenty-five steam tugs, schooners, and large launches filled with Confederate soldiers approached the *Powhatan* and the *Atlantic,* which were anchored on the Gulf side of Santa Rosa Island, but a shell from an eleven-inch Dahlgren on the *Powhatan* induced them to put back to Pensacola. The weeks passed and the expected Confederate attack on the fort did not materialize. Both camps suffered from disease and lack of proper food. Federal supplies came by ship, and the Confederates brought overland in wagons what they could not purchase locally.

The delay may well have been due to inadequacies in the highly publicized Confederate fortifications and fire power at Pensacola. Actually Bragg had only fourteen batteries that described an arc of about 135 degrees for three miles around the island fortress, which was about one and one-third miles distant. The quality of the ammunition was inferior and there wasn't enough of it. The armament of Forts McRee and Barrancas and the batteries totaled only fifty effective pieces of light artillery and twenty-five ten-inch columbiads. The armament in and around Pickens consisted of seven batteries mounting twenty-two guns, including four ten-inch columbiads, two forty-two pounders, eight ten-inch seacoast mortars, one twelve-inch and one thirteen-inch mortar, plus the firepower of the battleships.

Early in May a series of actions pointed the way to the inevitable clash. The Confederates sought to block the principal passes from the Gulf by sinking four old vessels in the channel between Barrancas and Pickens. Since the huge drydock was useless as long as federals controlled not only the entrance to the bay but also the sea outside, the Confederates planned to sink it in the channel between Barrancas and McRee. Colonel Brown, perhaps aware of these plans, sent out a boat with a dozen carefully picked men on the night of September 2; they met no resistance, fired the drydock, and withdrew without a shot being fired. To add insult to injury, two weeks later a launch and three cutters from the federal warship Colorado with a hundred men on board slipped into the bay in the early morning and reached the armed Confederate ship *Judah* as she lay at the docks under the guns of the navy-yard batteries.

The *Judah* had been a blockade runner and was recently returned from Saint John, New Brunswick, and was being outfitted at the time of the attack. The surprised Confederates were driven from the vessel before they could rally their forces. The raiders cut the *Judah*'s lines, fired the ship, and retreated into the darkness. The burning vessel floated to a point opposite Fort Barrancas, where she sank. In the raid the federals lost three dead and eight wounded, the first bloodshed of the war in Florida. If there were Confederate losses, they are not recorded in the official accounts of the engagement.

In response to the two daring challenges, General Bragg retaliated with a raid on Santa Rosa Island. General Richard H. Anderson led an expedition of just over a thousand men to a point four miles east of Fort Pickens at two o'clock on the morning of October 9. The invaders made their way along the shore for the three mile distance to the camp of Billy Wilson's Zouaves, the Sixth New York Volunteer Infantry. The surprise they hoped for was lost when alert federal pickets fired upon them and set off a general alarm. Anderson's men attacked from the front and both flanks and entered the camp on the first rush. They set fire to tents, storehouses, and sheds as the New Yorkers fled to the protection of the fort's guns. The raid ended short of the objective to destroy the batteries being erected in the rear of the fort. After a sharp skirmish with two companies of United States regulars, the Confederates withdrew to their boats. They had destroyed large stores of provisions, clothing, camp equipment, guns, and ammunition; possibly they had salvaged their pride, but the fortunes of war at Pensacola had not been altered. The raiders had lost eighteen killed, thirty-nine wounded, and thirty prisoners; the federals suffered fourteen killed, twenty-nine wounded, and twenty captured, among them Major Israel Vogdes.

The guns of Fort Pickens and its outlying batteries and those of the battleships *Niagara* and *Richmond* finally opened the long-awaited bombardment on November 22 at ten o'clock in the morning. The Confederates replied in an artillery duel that lasted until nightfall. Federal fire was concentrated at Fort McRee, and at the end of the day much of its armament was disabled and its powder magazine dangerously exposed to shells falling all around. The Confederates made emergency repairs during the night and held the fort during another day of bombardment, which continued until nightfall with a few shots throughout the night until four in the morning.

The whole affair proved to be much ado about nothing. Some 5,000 cannon shots had been fired, but only eight lives were lost. The federals lost one killed and six wounded on the first day, and the Confederates one killed by gunfire, twenty-one wounded, and six smothered when a magazine caved in. On the second day the federals directed their fire at installations on the shoreline, which damaged or destroyed a great deal of property without loss of life. The villages of Warrington and Wolsey went up in flames, which

[CIRCULAR.]

HEAD-QUARTERS.

Army of Pensacola, March 31st 1862.

FOR THE INFORMATION OF ALL CONCERNED!

THERE are certain lounging worthless people, white as well as black, who frequent the neighborhood of Pensacola, and have no observable occupation, their intention may be honest, but the Colonel Commanding does not believe the fact, and as he has no use for their presence, they are warned to leave, or the consequences rest on their own heads—the gallows is erected in Pensacola and will be in constant use after the 3d day of April, 1862—the town is under complete MARTIAL LAW.

By order of
COLONEL JONES.

J. H. BUTT.
A. A. A. Genl.

Proclamation of martial law, Pensacola, Civil War

spread to the navy yard but only one important building was destroyed. It was clear that neither side was prepared to do conclusive damage to the other. On the afternoon of January 1, 1862, in a sort of New Years celebration, a four-hour artillery duel was opened when guns of Fort Pickens fired on a small ship at the navy yard without visible damage to anything. The fate of Pensacola was being determined elsewhere.

Not all attention was focused on Pensacola. On June 1, Governor Perry expressed to the Confederate Secretary of War, Leroy P. Walker, a fear that Floridians were more and more to feel. Could they rely upon the Richmond government to act in their behalf? As if to underscore their concern, the Union blockade of Fernandina began on that day. On October 18, Governor John Milton, who had succeeded to the office on the fifth, wrote President Davis of the deplorable state of Florida's defenses. Too many Floridians, he complained, were enlisting in the cavalry. Everyone with a pony was joining up and expecting the government to outfit him. Soon there would be no horses for farming operations. Fear grew that Fernandina with its good harbor and the terminus of the Florida Railroad would become an early object of attack. When the invaders took Port Royal, South Carolina, on November 9 and established a base there, the fear grew into certainty. Meanwhile General Bragg's force at Pensacola was being reduced. On December 1, he had four regiments with about 3,000 men. He had recently sent a company of marines to Virginia, the third such draft made upon him for troops. That this was increasingly to be Florida's fate was not yet apparent.

Early in 1862, Floridians began to feel the brunt of the growing federal power. On January 6, sailors and marines from the U.S.S. *Hatteras* out of Key West landed at Cedar Key where they destroyed the railroad wharf and depot, several boxcars of military supplies, the telegraph office, and a turpentine storehouse. In the harbor they captured four schooners, three sloops, one ferryboat, a sailboat, and a launch. Only a lieutenant and twenty-two men were there to protect the railway terminus. Two companies of troops had recently been transferred to the other end of the railroad to meet the anticipated attack on Fernandina.

Yet when the invaders reached Amelia Island on March 3, they found the last of the Confederates leaving. A shot hit the last car, but the train escaped without other damage. They easily took possession of Fort Clinch, Saint Marys, and Cumberland Island, capturing in the process a small steamer loaded with refugees and supplies. In spite of all the talk and effort, Fernandina had remained without adequate defenses. Only thirty-two guns had been mounted in the fort and elsewhere on the island, and they were said to be outmoded and incorrectly mounted. The story was much the same elsewhere. The defenses at Saint Augustine had been for all practical purposes dismantled. Four of the cannons went to Fernandina, four to Saint Johns Bluff, and others outside the state, leaving only five cannons in the water battery to defend the city. The artillerymen had gone with the guns, leaving the defenses to two companies of the Third Florida Infantry. On February 8, Bragg received an urgent request to send at least four regiments to Knoxville. Pressure on the Confederate forces in Tennessee made reinforcements there imperative. On February 15 Bragg urged that New Orleans, Mobile, and Pensacola be garrisoned strongly enough to hold them, but three days later he received orders to withdraw all army units from Mobile and Pensacola. On February 27 he reported that he was abandoning Pensacola after destroying everything useful that he could not carry away.

The worst fears of Floridians now began to be realized. Most of the state's military men were being called to fight for the life of the Confederacy in faraway places, and those at home must be prepared to defend themselves as best they could. The coastal communities would be raided and occupied at will by Union forces. Fortunately there were no military objectives in the interior to draw attention, and no invasion occurred until 1864.

Jacksonville suffered most, being invaded and abandoned four times before the war ended. On March 11, 1862, federals occupied Saint Augustine and on the next day another force moved up the Saint Johns and the Fourth New Hampshire occupied Jacksonville. A few days later it was reported that they planned to fortify and hold that city as well as Fernandina and Saint Augustine, but on April 8 they began to pull out of Jacksonville, though they did hold the other two throughout the war. The city suffered from friend and foe alike. When the Confederates left ahead of the first invasion, they burned eight sawmills and over four million board feet of lumber. In the city they destroyed an iron foundry, a nearby ironworks, and a boat under construction. As they moved westward toward Baldwin they tore up several miles of railroad tracks. The famous racing yacht *America,* which had been purchased by the Confederacy, was at Jacksonville to be fitted out as a cruiser. To avoid capture by the raiding federals, they took it upriver and scuttled it in the mouth of a creek. The federals found and raised her, and she later became a part of the South Atlantic Blockading Squadron. When irregular groups of Confederate troops came through from Fernandina they attacked the homes and property of some known Union sympathizers and killed three men. The Judson House, a large tourist hotel on Bay Steeet, was razed. Only a heavy rain prevented further damage. Small wonder the residents were ready to believe that the incoming federals might burn the property of Confederates. Actually the retiring Union forces agreed that Confederate troops should come into the city after the Unionists went on board their transports in the river but before they sailed away.

At Pensacola the evacuation proceeded slowly. The necessity to haul everything overland slowed the operation. The removal of supplies and equipment had been under way for some two months directed by General Samuel Jones, who had succeeded Bragg. They removed all of the heavy guns and most of the smaller ones, as well as the powder and most of the larger shot and shells. The official West Florida papers that remained in Pensacola were sent to Greenville, Alabama, for safekeeping, but many were lost en route and others irreparably damaged because of carelessness. They stripped the navy yard of its valuable machinery and saved all of its commissary stores. Their last act was to fire Forts Barrancas and McRee, the navy yard, the marine hospital, barracks, and two small steamers. The federals on Santa Rosa Island merely waited until the Confederates departed beginning on May 7, completing the withdrawal two nights later. On May 10, the federals received the surrender of the city by the few citizens who remained. Pensacola remained a veritable ghost town. Perhaps ninety percent of the population had left with the departing Confederate forces. Since the city had no military importance as long as they occupied Fort

Pickens, the federals evacuated it in March of 1863 and reported only ten men, thirty women, and thirty children still living there. By the beginning of the second year of the war, Florida was surrounded by federal forces except on the north. The same forces that maintained an even tighter blockade of the coast could move in and out almost at will. General Robert E. Lee, who served as adviser to President Jefferson Davis before he assumed the command of the army of Northern Virginia in April 1862, visited Florida (Fernandina) twice–in November 1861 and January 1862. He suggested that Confederate strength be concentrated in the interior of the state, ready to move to any area that was menaced by federals. When the need for troops on the western front became imperative, he further suggested that only troops enough be left in Florida to defend the Apalachicola River, the cotton port for West Florida, southeast Alabama, and southwest Georgia and a pathway for the invasion of the interior of Georgia and Alabama. Lee knew something of Florida's defense problems. He was one of a detail of officers and men charged with making a detailed examination of the Florida coastline from Pensacola to Jacksonville in 1849. The Confederate policy seemed reasonable since federals made no move to invade the interior, but Floridians resented it and turned their wrath upon Brigadier General James H. Trapier, commander in East Florida, with such vehemence that he was replaced by General Joseph Finegan on April 8. But the policy did not change. Finegan had orders to defend the Apalachicola and the Saint Johns rivers and protect any supplies that came in through the blockade. His command of 6,368 men shrank by two-thirds by the end of the summer and remained at about that strength throughout the year 1863.

Ships of the federal blockading squadron continued to raid coastal settlements almost at will. In early 1864 these raids were the principal military action in Florida. In spite of the talk of defending Apalachicola it fared no better than the others. When state troops there were disbanded, the city was left defenseless, and most of the population fled ninety miles up river to Ricco's Bluff. The people that remained at Apalachicola were reported surviving on fish and oysters. The channel entrances to the river were already under blockade and on April 2, federals entered the city but did not occupy it permanently, for the blockade had effectively neutralized it. On March 22, the federals sent a gunboat to New Smyrna to capture a blockade runner and its crew and cargo. The defenders prepared an ambush in which forty-two of the Union men who came ashore were killed. Union retaliation was devastating. On July 26, four vessels of the United States navy entered the inlet and fired over a hundred shells into the settlement, after which a landing party fired homes that had been missed. Raids continued, at Saint Marks on June 1 and again on October 16. On the second raid a landing party moved up the river and burned a small ship there. As the men were wading back to their boats a Confederate cavalry unit charged into the shallow waters killing 3, wounding 12,and taking 3 prisoners while losing 6 killed and 12 captured.

Union signal tower, December 12, 1864, Public Square (now Hemming Park), Jacksonville. These towers enabled federal units to communicate with each other and with offshore fleets, and were reinforced to protect the signalmen against Confederate snipers.

In what was to prove to be a futile effort to defend the Saint Johns River, General Finegan erected batteries below Jacksonville at Yellow Bluff and Saint Johns Bluff. On September 30, a federal force of 1,573 men supported by six gunboats left Hilton Head, South Carolina, for an assault on the new defenses. Colonel Charles F. Hopkins had only about 500 men to hold Saint Johns Bluff and prudently decided to retire. The powder trail meant to blow up the magazine and destroy the arms and ammunition failed to burn, and the raiders captured the batteries intact. The retiring Confederates also evacuated Yellow Bluff, and the way to Jacksonville was open. On October 5, the invaders occupied Jacksonville, only to return to Hilton Head four days later, but gunboats continued to control the river.

The third federal occupation, on March 10, 1863, had a variety of objectives. The invaders were seeking black recruits for the army and any cotton they might find. They also came partly in response to the appeal of Union men in Jacksonville to create a loyal government for the state. Unionists there insisted that a show of force would bring forth a large enough number to make it feasible. Apparently the results of the occupation were disappointing, and on March 29 the troops began to move out. It is not clear from the records which side started the fire, but a third of the city burned. Had not General Finegan and the Confederates been nearby to move in quickly to put it out, the whole city might have been destroyed.

When hostilities broke out again, the most important battle of the war in Florida occurred near Olustee on February 20, 1864. A combination of military and political objectives inspired the invasion. In addition to recruiting blacks and picking up cotton, lumber, and turpentine that might be confiscated, Union forces planned to move into the interior and cut the supply route of cattle and pork to the Confederate army. Although the promoters of the invasion emphasized the military objective, it seems unlikely that it would have been undertaken without the underlying political objects. It was an election year and a loyal government there might play an important role in the outcome.

Most Florida Unionists resided in East Florida. They had hesitated to declare themselves. Confederates suspected the loyalty of some. Jacksonville and Saint Augustine editors suggested that they ought to be made to take an oath of allegiance to the Confederate Constitution. The Sequestration Act of August 30, 1861, authorized the seizure of the property of enemy aliens, but no action had been taken. To support an abortive attempt to establish Union authority would prove disastrous. Their experience in early occupation was not reassuring. Many of those who had welcomed the raiders had found it expedient to depart with them to escape the wrath of the returning Confederates. Unionists received the greatest encouragement early in 1864. Both President Lincoln and his secretary of the treasury and political rival Salmon Portland Chase were interested in the possibility that Florida might be restored for their campaign purposes. Chase men had been in East Florida since October 1862 as federal tax commissioners in occupied areas. Leaders of the move were Lyman D. Stickney, a tax commissioner, Harrison Reed, a Wisconsin editor, and John Sammis, who had moved to Jacksonville before the war, had married a daughter of Zepheriah Kingsley, and had become a tax commissioner.

President Lincoln sent his personal secretary, John Hay, to Beaufort, South Carolina, with a major's commission to oversee the move to construct a loyal government for Florida. General Quincy A. Gilmore promised his support. Hay was ready to enroll voters in the areas already occupied and to follow the army into the interior for the same purpose. Stickney reported these moves to his champion and assured him that any political advantage would surely accrue to his cause. Hay, who had been busy registering voters in Jacksonville in the initial stages of the invasion, was equally optimistic. When the invasion was turned back at the Battle of Olustee he realized that he would never get the ten percent of the electorate required to initiate the Lincoln plan and refused to support action with anything less. Stickney was not displeased by the failure of his rival, but his own cause was not going well either, for his candidate was proving to be no serious rival of Lincoln for the Republican nomination. On May 17, a convention of Union men met in Jacksonville to choose delegates to the Republican National Convention in Baltimore on June 7. Delegates from Fernandina and Saint Augustine came by steamboat under Union protection.

The convention proved hostile to Stickney and Chase and chose Calvin Robinson to head a delegation that included Buckingham

Smith, John W. Price, John S. Sammis, Philip Fraser, and Paran Moody, all Lincoln supporters. The Stickney faction also sent a delegation, but the convention seated the Robinson group, though without voting rights. When the convention made Robinson a member of the Republican Union National Committee, the defeat of the Chase faction was complete. There had never been a large enough number of Unionists in Florida to justify a loyal government, but it took the Union failure at Olustee, the collapse of the Chase boom, and the renomination of Lincoln to bring this to final realization.

The invasion that had set the stage for all of this political activity had begun on the morning of February 7 when Union transports brought troops to Jacksonville a fourth time. The invaders moved on westward and two days later were in Baldwin, the junction point of three railway lines nineteen miles west of the city. The next day they reached Sanderson fourteen miles farther west. The Confederates withdrew ahead of the federal advance and, without stopping to give battle, did slow it up until General Finegan could gather a force large enough to meet this first major threat to the interior of the state. This strategy of retreat so alarmed Governor Milton that he asked for Finegan's removal, but it was too late, the crisis was at hand. Since the line of advance seemed to be along the railroad to Lake City, Finegan concentrated there to await the attack. General Truman A. Seymour, the Union commander, had been compelled to weaken his forces somewhat by leaving men along his supply and communications line to Jacksonville, but the two armies had about the same number of men.

General Finegan selected Olustee, thirteen miles from Lake City, as providing the greatest natural advantage to him. His men took up positions on a line about a mile and a half long running between Ocean Pond on the north and a large cypress swamp on the south. The fighting began soon after noon on Saturday, February 20, and by mid-afternoon the main bodies of both armies were engaged. By a little after six in the evening the battle was over, and the federals began an orderly retreat, made easier by some reinforcements that came up too late for the battle. Although the Confederates failed to follow up their victory, it was decisive. The supply lines in the interior were secure. The two sides had been about evenly matched, each with about 5,000 men. The defenders had the advantage of position. The federals went into battle after several hours of marching and did not succeed in bringing all of their force to bear in a coordinated fashion. Losses were comparatively heavy. Finegan lost 93 killed, 847 wounded, and six missing for a total of 946 casualties. The invaders lost 203 killed, 1,152 wounded, and 506 missing for a total of 1,861. The Confederates also captured some much needed equipment: nine cannons, 1,600 small arms, 400 accoutrements, and 130,000 rounds of small arms ammunition.

Seymour retreated to Jacksonville, where he prepared to make a stand. The Confederates fortified a position above McGirt's Creek twelve miles west of Jacksonvllle, where by March 1 the new commander for Florida, Major General James Patton Anderson, had over 8,000 troops. The expected renewal of the fighting never occurred. On April 8, the federals began to retire, leaving a small garrison that proved large enough to make raids out toward Gainesville and up the Saint Johns. The Confederate troops also withdrew to fight farther north with the hard pressed armies there.

The Florida strategy remained the same. Landings in coastal areas could not be prevented, but any enemy advance inland must be met with all resources that could be mustered. All supplies, railroads, and bridges in the path of the invaders were to be destroyed to gain time to mount another defense such as that at Olustee.

Military and naval activity on the west coast in 1864 was more extensive and more destructive of property if not of lives. It had little military significance and probably no effect on the outcome of the war except possibly to increase the growing defeatism in the population. Although most of the raids continued to originate in the blockading squadron in the Gulf of Mexico, some of the larger operations had their inception in the forts at Pensacola, one of them extensive enough to be designated the Battle of Marianna. On September 18, General Alexander Asboth moved out from Fort Barrancas with 700 mounted men and raided as far as Marianna. His objective was to capture scattered rebel forces in Washington and

Battle of Olustee, Februarty 20, 1864

Jefferson counties, to liberate any federal prisoners held there, to secure recruits for the Union forces, and to secure horses and mules. Four days out the raiders reached present-day De Funiak Springs and on the next day surprised the village of Eucheeana, where they rested for a day and visited local plantations. At noon on September 27 the cavalry force reached Marianna, a trading center for Jackson County with some 500 inhabitants. The townsmen had put together what defense they could. About 150 youths and old men in a home guard organization dubbed the "Cradle and Grave Company" were armed with such privately-owned arms as they could scrape up. There was also a group of home guards and a handful of Confederate regulars home on sick leave. They constructed a barricade of logs and old wagons, behind which they attempted to halt the federal advance. They could not protect their flanks and when fired upon from the rear had no choice but to surrender. Five of their number died, sixteen were wounded, and fifty-four taken prisoners. The Confederates tore up the planking on the bridge crossing the Chipola River and the Episcopal church was burned, probably as an accident in the fighting. The invaders lost fifteen killed and forty wounded, among the latter General Asboth. The raiders looted the town thoroughly, but did not burn it, and carried away, among other things, 200 horses and mules and 400 cattle.

Governor Milton, alarmed by the continuing raids and the inadequacy of the Confederate force to meet them, on July 30, 1864, called upon all Florida citizens capable of bearing arms to organize into militia companies for the defense of the state. By the month of November forty-one companies totaling over 3,000 men had been organized. The Confederate government supplied arms for half of them but could offer no other support. When the legislature met in November it approved the governor's action and made every able-bodied man between fifteen and fifty-five not in the Confederate service a member of the state militia. There was no occasion to use the newly organized troops except for purely local defense until late in the war. Instead there were raids and counter-raids, much destruction of property, and some loss of life, all of which had no possible military importance to either side.

A long feared attack on Saint Marks and Tallahassee, which resulted in the Battle of Natural Bridge, finally came in March 1865. The stakes seemed high enough but if it had been successful it would have been of no military signiflcance, for the war was about to be concluded. After the fall of Fort Fisher on January 15, 1865, closed Wilmington, North Carolina, to blockade runners, federals feared that some of the operations might be transferred to Saint Marks. Equally important was the closely related capital at Tallahassee, which was also the center of the most productive agricultural region in the state with the added lure of cotton and blacks to be carried away. On the morning of March 4, fourteen Union vessels landed about one thousand troops near Saint Marks for the march on the capital. Brigadier General William Miller, commanding the reserve forces in the state, moved in that direction also with the local militia and a company of cadets from the West Florida Seminary. Tallahassee residents began the construction of Fort Houston on the outskirts of the city. On March 5, the federals started inland and reached Newport but remained on the left bank of the Saint Marks River. Delay in negotiating the narrow channel into the bay and the slow move up the river had given the defenders time to burn the railroad bridge, and the invaders were moving on toward Natural Bridge to cross the river there. The Confederates got the advantage of position at the bridge and repulsed two assaults. When reinforcements for the defenders arrived, the invaders retreated to their ships. They had lost twenty-one killed, eighty-nine wounded, and thirty-eight missing. The defenders counted three killed and twenty-two wounded, none of them seminary cadets.

Coordinated with the raid on Saint Marks was a campaign through Levy County by Major Edmund C. Weeks of the Federal Second Florida Cavalry stationed at Cedar Key. With 400 men, one-half of them foot soldiers of the Second U.S. Colored Infantry, Weeks set out on February 8, moving eastward along the Florida Railroad. At Levyville the invaders were met by a squad of cavalry from Captain John J. Dickison's command. Dickison's irregular troops constituted the most effective defense Florida could mount against such a raid. This highly mobile unit had just returned to its base at Camp Baker near Waldo from an expedition east of the Saint Johns. Dickison had only ninety officers and men and one twelve-pound howitzer, and the men had not recovered from ten days in the saddle on their recent expedition to the east coast, but they could slow up the federal advance until reinforcements could arrive. After an inconclusive engagement at Station Four, both Weeks and Dickison, not having men or ammunition enough to risk a general engagement, withdrew. Weeks listed five killed, eighteen wounded, and three captured. Dickison reported only six severely wounded, and he sent the raiders back to Cedar Key minus the cattle, horses, and wagons they had captured earlier.

The war was all but over in Florida and in the nation. The ultimate outcome was already clear. The interior of Florida had been saved from invasion at Olustee and Natural Bridge. It brought little comfort to Governor Milton that his was the only Confederate capital east of the Mississippi not captured. On April 1 he committed suicide, perhaps defeated by the failure of his best efforts to defend the state. On May 20, the Stars and Stripes once again flew over Tallahassee. The fighting was over, but many questions remained unanswered and a long period of reconstruction lay ahead.

Florida's contribution to the war is difficult to assess. Statistics do not tell the whole story, and what data we have are not entirely reliable. Some 14,000 to 15,000 men entered the Confederate service. Some 1,200 white Floridians and nearly as many blacks served in the Union army. At least a third of the Confederates lost their lives in battle or from disease. Blacks entered the army largely toward the end of the conflict. Florida men fought in all the theaters of war, east and west, and were at Gettysburg.

Three outstanding contributions to Confederate leadership were made by Florida men—Stephen Russell Mallory, who became secretary of navy in the Davis cabinet, and two professional soldiers, William Wing Loring and Edmund Kirby Smith. Mallory, born on the island of Trinidad, moved about 1850 to Key West, where his father soon died. His widowed mother kept a boarding house for seamen and managed to give her son a fairly good education for the day. He served as a naval volunteer in two campaigns of the Seminole war. Mallory studied law in the office of Judge William Marvin and like his mentor became a well-known marine lawyer. In 1851 he replaced David L. Yulee in the United States Senate, where he continued the interest in naval affairs that was to lead to a place in the Davis cabinet. He became chairman of the Naval Affairs Committee in 1855, where he championed several unpopular causes aimed at increasing the efficiency of the navy, but remained strong enough in Florida to be returned to the Senate for a second term. When he gave strong support to the Ostend Manifesto, aimed at the acquisition of Cuba by the United States, he established him-

Jacksonville river front, apparently Bay Street, during Union occupation. The lone Union sentry silhouetted against the sky guards the army wagons, probably loading from a federal transport in the Saint Johns River.

self as one of ardent southern expansionists but made enemies among the anti-slavery men. He was suspected of being only luke-warm in his support of secession and southern nationalism, and a majority of the Florida delegation opposed his appointment to the cabinet post. His experience in Key West and Washington made him a logical choice for the post. He brought a body of knowledge and experience to the Confederacy that was unequalled, and it is generally conceded that he did remarkably well with the limita-tions and handicaps under which he labored. Mallory was ahead of Lincoln's Secretary of Navy Gideon Welles in his recognition that fundamental changes were taking place in naval warfare, notably steam powered ships, shell guns, screw propellers, torpedoes, rifled guns, and armored ships. All of this expert knowledge availed him little when his government lacked the means to put it to effective use. The slender resources of the Confederate government went mostly for military purposes. Lacking conventional ships and weap-ons, Mallory resorted to novel methods of naval war, particularly mines, underwater explosives, and a crude submarine. He could claim the sinking of the blockader *Housatonic* outside Charleston harbor by the Confederate submarine *H. A. Hunley* in February 1864, the first such sinking in history. His failures to achieve the impossible earned for him sharp criticism, but he weathered the political storms to the end of the conflict. He accompanied Davis and other members of the official family on the flight southward after Appomattox and was arrested soon after the party broke up in Georgia. He remained in prison ten months, after which he re-turned to Pensacola where he practiced law until his death seven years later.

William Wing Loring, born in 1818 in Wilmington, North Caro-lina, came to Saint Augustine with his family at an early age in 1824. His father, Reuben Loring, came down to settle land. He was a builder and helped construct Trinity Church in Saint Augustine. Loring served in a local militia unit during the Second Seminole War, holding the rank of second lieutenant. After this he served a term in the state legislature. He entered the regular army in 1846 and served as a major in a regiment of mounted riflemen in the Mexican War, losing his left arm in the final battle for Mexico City as he was going through the Belen Gate. On December 30, 1855, he was promoted to colonel. He resigned his commission to become a brigadier general in the Confederate army on May 13, 1861, and became a major general the following year. When he surrendered with General Joseph E. Johnston in April 1865 he was the senior major general in active field duty in the Confederate service. He continued the life of a professional soldier after the American con-flict by entering the service in 1869 as inspector general of the Khedive of Egypt, where he was twice decorated. He returned to the United States in 1879, died in New York City on December 31, 1886, and was buried in Saint Augustine.

The much more colorful and better known Edmund Kirby Smith was born at Saint Augustine on May 16, 1824, of New England parents. At West Point where he graduated in 1845 he was known as "Seminole." After distinguished service in the Mexican War he taught mathematics at West Point from 1849 to 1852, after which he served principally in Texas until he resigned on March 3, 1861, to enter the Confederate service as a lieutenant colonel. He served in the Shenandoah Valley as adjutant to General Joseph E. Johnston and suffered a severe wound at First Manassas in July. In October he was assigned to the Middle and East Florida command, but his orders went astray, and before they could catch up with him the military situation changed and he became a division commander in the Department of Northern Virginia. In February 1862 he became commander of the Department of East Tennessee, and a year later he assumed the command of the Confederate forces west of the Mississippi River. He was almost the last Confederate general in the field when he surrendered to General E. R. S. Canby on May 26, 1865.

Kirby Smith did not return to his native state to live. He was for a time the president of an accident insurance company in Nashville, Tennessee. After two years as president of the Pacific and Atlantic Telegraph Company he opened a school in New Castle, Kentucky, and later became president of the University of Nashville. From 1875 until his death March 28, 1893, the last survivor of the full generals of the Confederacy, he was a professor of mathematics at the University of the South.

15.

Floridians at War 1861-1865

The people of Florida experienced all of the hardships commonly associated with a major armed conflict of four years duration. They found themselves called upon to solve undreamed of administrative, financial, and political problems at state and local levels, to make extraordinary sacrifices, to perform unusual services, to suffer great direct and indirect property losses (though most of the interior was spared invasion), to experience deprivation and want because of scarcities, inflation, and absence of breadwinners, to lose a relatively large part of their manpower, and, finally, to suffer the psychological shock of defeat.

Political leaders bore heavy responsibility for taking the state out of the Union, which made more burdensome the obligation to protect the sovereignty and independence they claimed for the state and for the South. Governor Madison Starke Perry, who governed until October 1861 although his successor John Milton had been elected before the war began, was a strong advocate of secession. He seemed at times to be heedless of the consequences of radical action but at other times to be more aware than some of his fellow citizens of what might be involved. He recognized that secession would not likely be peaceable and urged the legislature to strengthen the militia and prepare to defend the state. Floridians generally did not catch the martial spirit until secession and the organization of the southern confederacy had been accomplished. During the conflict, the best efforts of the governor, the legislature and the people proved inadequate to defend the state.

Considering the troubled times and difficult problems facing the state government, there was less political controversy during the war than might have been expected. Some confusion arose from differences between the governor and the governor-elect. Perry had the support of the General Assembly and was in a position to appoint his friends and supporters to key positions and set the course the state was to follow. He wished to have the Confederate government assume full responsibility for all military matters and to allow the state forces to be absorbed by the Confederate Army. He realized that the undeveloped state could not pay the cost of a large armed force and could not provide for its own defense. Milton, on the other hand, believed in a strong state militia that had many of the characteristics of a state army and was to be controlled by the governor and be employed largely in the defense of the state. Had Perry perceived that the Confederate government would use Florida troops elsewhere and leave Florida relatively undefended, he might have been more sympathetic toward Milton's view.

The governor's position was made more difficult by the continued exercise of constituent power by the secession convention, which went so far on occasion as to override the executive and the legislature. The convention met on February 26, 1861, to approve the provisional Constitution of the Confederate States of America and on April 13 to ratify it in its final form, after which it adjourned *sine die* on April 27 unless convened by the president on or before December 25. Since the convention generally approved Perry's actions it made no move to interfere with his administration, but when Milton took over the executive leadership in October and moved to reverse some policies of his predecessor, it came to life again. President John C. McGehee issued a call on December 13 for the convention to meet January 14, 1862, at Tallahassee. On February 10 it forestalled Governor Milton's purpose to strengthen the state militia by ordering that it be abolished on March 10. The new governor would have lost this battle in any case, for the Confederate Conscription Act in April 1862 left little if any place for a state army of the sort Milton favored. The governor continued to be torn between a desire to protect the state by reserving its small manpower and slender resources and the realization on the other hand that Florida's future lay wholly in the hands of the central government. He generally found it expedient to cooperate with Richmond authorities and content himself with trying to temper Confederate demands upon the state and maintain some sort of home guard.

Milton challenged the convention's constitutional authority, but the attorney general refused to support him. The members of the convention argued that the extraordinary powers of a wartime executive should not be placed in the hands of one man, and they appointed an executive council of four men to share the authority. To forestall the governor's opposition and failure to convene the council, it was to meet on February 28 if not called by the governor. James A. Wiggins of Marion County, Mariano D. Papy of Leon, W. D. Barnes of Jackson and Smith Simkins of Jefferson made up the council. Only Papy, who had been attorney general from 1853 to 1860 and would appear in state government again after the war, had any political status. The convention did grant to the governor and the council the powers to meet the crisis of war. These included declaring martial law, arresting disloyal persons, appropriating private property for public use, bringing any of the population into public service, securing or making arms and ammunition, creating new state agencies and appointing military officers.

The hopes of the creators of the council were never realized.

The quartet met five times for two or three days at a time between February 28 and May 1, 1862, when it adjourned never to meet again. Generally they approved Milton's policies. When the central government failed to provide for the defense of key points in the state, the council ordered state troops to remain at Apalachicola. Confederates failed to occupy the post and gave some support to rebuilding the state militia, which the convention had been disposed to disband. Any opposition to Milton soon subsided. In October 1862 the voters chose a General Assembly favorable to him, which repealed the action by which the convention had created the executive council and ended in controversy. The more pressing questions of economic scarcities, inflation and defense absorbed all of the attention of Democrats and Whigs alike.

Preparations to defend the state became the first order of business for the General Assembly. On February 14, 1861, the lawmakers created Florida's Civil War militia, which had the characteristics of a state army until the Confederate army took over some of its functions. The statute authorized the chief executive to raise for the immediate defense of the state two regiments of infantry and one of cavalry. Included were elaborate rules for enrolling men, organizing them into appropriate units, and for choosing their own officers. The mobilization of the Confederate Army got under way at much the same time. Formal organization began in early March, and by the end of June the Confederate authorities began raising troops in the state rather than receiving them through the governor.

The first call for Florida troops by the Confederacy came on March 9. The first regiment, appropriately called the First Florida Infantry, came mostly from West Florida. Mustered into Confederate service at Chattahoochee on April 5, it arrived for duty at Pensacola a week later. On April 8, the Confederacy asked for 1,500 men and on April 16 for another 2,000. On the last day of the same month the state was asked for 1,000 men for the Confederate Reserve Corps. The men were to report for instruction to camps under control of the Confederate War Department, and the president could at his discretion muster them into the Confederate service. Before the end of 1861, five thousand Florida troops had been called up. They were organized into four regiments of infantry, one of cavalry, and nine unattached companies of infantry, four of artillery, and three of cavalry. The unattached units came mostly from the state militia, which counted only 762 men in its ranks by the end of the year.

Florida found the outfitting of so many men on such short notice to be a major problem. Nor was the Confederate government in a position to make up the deficiency. Florida had to make all purchases outside of the state, where every other state and the national government were all bidding for arms, ammunition, clothing and equipment. The rapidly inflated prices put a severe strain on the state's slender financial resources. An original appropriation of $100,000 left many troops not yet provided with basic equipment, a condition which produced some discontent and grumbling and a decided loss of morale on the part of the men. Some of the southern states were charged with holding back arms and ammunition from the Confederacy and thereby crippling the war effort in the early months of the war when recruits were coming forward more rapidly than they could be equipped. No such charge could be made against Florida; there were none to hold back. Milton cooperated very closely with the Confederate government, unlike Governor Joseph E. Brown of Georgia, who became an obstructionist. In May 1862, General Joseph Finegan, commanding the Department of East Florida, appealed successfully to the people of the state to give their private weapons to equip one or two of Florida's regiments already in camps for instruction. He asked for single and double-barreled shotguns, rifles, and muskets. In September 1863, the state quartermaster-general reported less than fifty rifles and pistols on hand. Blockade runners helped to bring in arms, but in October 1861 when the steamer *Salvor,* owned by James McKay of Tampa, was captured, the state lost 21,000 stands of rifles, 150 boxes of revolvers, six rifled cannons, and large quantities of ammunition.

The first volunteers often came in resplendent uniforms, but soon many of those enlisting could not supply them. Soldiers' aid societies early came into existence to make up the deficiency in military clothing. Among the earliest was the Pensacola Committee of Relief, an organization of leading citizens financed by voluntary contributions to purchase the items needed to outfit volunteers. The citizens of Alachua County on July 1861 decided to assess each taxpayer an amount equal to thirty percent of his state taxes to provide funds for the purchase of clothing and supplies for the county's troops. When not all men received the same treatment, unhappiness resulted, and many citizens resented the extralegal levy. The result was what amounted to failure for that approach to the problem.

The people of the state continued to be called upon to help clothe Florida men in the Confederate service. On December 17, 1861, the legislature appropriated $10,000 to purchase cloth for the Ladies Military Aid to make into uniforms. On September 20, 1862, Governor Milton announced that the state had purchased a quantity of good homespun and invited the ladies' organization to apply for as much as they could use to make into shirts and drawers for Florida's soldiers. A month later the committee set up in Tallahassee to receive donations of money and clothing for Florida men in Virginia was asking for old flannel garments not yet completely worn out to be made into shirts much needed in the "bleak climate of Virginia." On October 28, Captain Edward M. L'Engle was reported coming home to Florida on behalf of the Florida forces in Virginia to make an appeal for shoes, blankets and clothing. In the late summer of 1863 the governor's representatives inspecting camps and hospitals in the West where Florida men were located asked also that food and clothing be collected for them.

The care of sick and wounded men posed special problems for

the Confederate and state governments throughout the war. There were never enough hospitals, doctors, nurses, and attendants. Medicines and equipment became more scarce as the blockade tightened, and it was often impossible to supply a proper diet. Florida like some other states set up a hospital in Richmond in an effort to provide better care for its men fighting on the Virginia front. Mrs. Mary Martha Reid, widow of a territorial governor, along with Dr. Thomas M. Palmer of Monticello and others, backed by the governor's promise that he would secure a legislative appropriation, converted a large Richmond house into a 150-bed hospital which opened its doors on September 26, 1862. Later Florida wards in Howard's Grove Hospital replaced the separate state unit, but Mrs. Reid served as matron throughout the war. In 1866 the Florida legislature provided a six hundred dollar annuity in recognition of her services. She became a schoolteacher at Fernandina, where she died June 24,1894, at the age of eighty-two. Appropriately, the first Florida chapter of the United Daughters of the Confederacy is named for Mary Martha Reid.

A report on the Florida hospital at the end of a year of operation reveals some of the health problems encountered. There had been 1,076 patients, of whom only fifty-three had died. Approximately one-third, 360, had suffered gunshot wounds; typhoid fever afflicted 111, catarrhal fever 103, chronic and acute rheumatism forty-eight, pneumonia eighty-six, diarrhea seventy-one, erysipelas thirty, neuralgia twelve, inflammation of the brain thirteen, hernia three, hemorrhoids three, ulcers three, syphilis two and asthma one. Most deaths occurred in December, January, and February when winter weather was most severe.

The Confederate government maintained six hospitals in Florida with a total of 515 beds—150 at Lake City, 126 at Quincy, 100 at Tallahassee, seventy-five at Madison, fifty at Marianna and fourteen at Camp Log near Madison. Contributions for the support of the hospital came from many sources. Colonel F. L. Dancy's plantation "Buena Vista" in Saint Johns County sent grapefruit, limes and oranges. Individuals and organizations sent sums of money ranging up to nearly two thousand dollars. In December 1862 the state legislature provided $30,000. Fund raising was usually spearheaded by ladies who put on numerous money-raising events to support hospitals and a host of other activities.

Providing relief for families of men in the army and for refugees from the invaded coastal areas taxed the private and public resources of the state. On December 13, 1861, the governor approved a bill authorizing county commissioners to levy a special tax for the relief of soldiers' families. About a year later the state provided $20,000 for the aid of needy families and thereafter made such provision as were made, getting no help from the central government and but little from local governments. In 1862-1863 aid to 11,744 persons in 3,431 families totaled $186,639, and in the following year $291,443 to 13,248 persons in 3,633 families. Aid more often came from private sources, much of it unorganized. Tallahassee citizens met on

February 11, 1863, to secure aid for refugees from Saint Augustine. In June ladies from Jefferson, Madison, and Leon counties presented theatrical productions for the benefit of soldiers' families. They played to full houses three nights in the capitol building in Tallahassee and raised a thousand dollars for their cause. Stories of heroic devotion and service on the home front could be repeated many times as men and women struggled against scarcities and inflation to provide help for the needy at home as well as in the army.

Nothing in Florida's financial history prepared the state for the burdens imposed by the war. There were only three state chartered banks (at Tallahassee, Fernandina, and Jacksonville) with a total paid-in capital of $350,000. The resources of a dozen or more private banks operating at the time are unknown. The taxable wealth of the state was small, and Florida citizens were not yet conditioned to paying more than the most limited amounts in taxes. The credit of the state had been extended severely to meet the costs of the final phase of the Seminole war that erupted late in 1855. The strict legal limitations imposed upon banks in the St. Joseph Constitution had not been relaxed to any great degree. The Bank of St. Johns in Jacksonville suspended specie payment on December 12, 1860, and the others followed suit, but not until December 13, 1862, did the legislature legalize the action. Bills in February 1861 approving the creation of other banks and authorizing increased bank note issue in existing banks failed to expand the money and credit facilities in the state. Bank notes ceased to exist by the end of 1862, and state and Confederate treasury notes became the principal circulating medium. Municipalities and business houses also issued currency, particularly in small denominations, to facilitate exchange.

State budgets, which had never exceeded $50,000 per annum, averaged at least $500,000 during the war. Taxes were at no time increased, collections were at times suspended, and payment was irregular, particularly in the invaded areas. Borrowing made up the difference. On February 14, 1861, the legislature authorized the issue of $500,000 in treasury notes and $500,000 in eight percent twenty-year bonds. The bonds could not be sold at less than par and failed to find a ready market. The state government used them to pay creditors willing to receive them, but not more than $370,000 of them were actually issued. Altogether the state issued during the war $2,236,640.38 worth of treasury notes and redeemed only $397,370.36, leaving in circulation at the end of the war $1,817,269.99. Add this to the bonded debt, and the total obligation representing most of the cost of the war was about two and one-quarter million dollars.

Efforts of the Confederate government to raise financial support in the state probably produced more resentment than tangible return. The levying of a direct tax apportioned among the states according to population caused no serious problem. The state legislature issued enough treasury notes to pay it but made no effort to collect it from citizens. Floridians suffered more from the efforts of agents of the United States treasury department to collect the direct tax in the state. Property of citizens in occupied areas was subject to the seizure in payment of the $77,000 levied on Florida.

Civil War era money, state and private

In some instances property abandoned by owners in places like Saint Augustine and Fernandina was actually sold, often to the tax agent or his associates. The Confederate Impressment Act of March 26, 1863, did reach Floridians directly. This law was designed to enable the hard-pressed government to get what it needed at a price fixed by an impressment board rather than in the market, and it was sometimes arbitrary in procedure if not confiscatory in effect. Food was the principal item collected in Florida. Corn, beef, pork, rice, potatoes, peas, molasses, sugar and forage were impressed and sent out of the state or placed in commissary warehouse depots at Milton, Marianna, Quincy, Tallahassee, Monticello, Baldwin, Starke, Gainesville and Tampa.

With one exception the comprehensive Confederate tax of April 24, 1863, had little consequence in Florida. The act included an 8% levy on the value of agricultural products, a license of $50 to $500 on occupations, trades, and professions, an income tax of from one to 15%, a sales tax of 10% on profits from sales of certain commodities, and a tax in kind of 10% on all agricultural products. Only the last was seriously enforced. Farmers felt discriminated against but, like the impressment law, it secured much needed food for the Confederate government. If adequate transportation had been available, it is possible that the nonperishable food needs of the army might have been supplied from government warehouses throughout the South.

Governor Milton disliked impressment but sought to regulate rather than to forbid it in Florida. There were abuses in the system. Unscrupulous individuals sometimes posed as agents of the government and swindled people out of their property. Two dramatic instances of private resistance to impressment occurred. When the Confederate government impressed the iron rails and spikes of the Florida Railroad on the wrecked portion between Baldwin and Fernandina, railroad president David Yulee and his associates secured a court order to prohibit the seizure, but the army officer in charge ignored the injunction and proceeded taking up the rails—but only those needed for the specific project. In another instance Yulee had sold 50,000 pounds of sugar at a dollar a pound to the city of Savannah. Confederate officials impressed it en route, and when Yulee protested the forty-five cent price offered by the impressment board and took his case to court, he was awarded seventy-five cents per pound; coming as it did at the end of the war, however, he probably collected nothing.

Disloyalty to the southern cause posed problems of growing seriousness toward the end of the war. Florida had its share of "layouts" and deserters from the beginning but there was no general opposition until late in the war when war weariness and defeatism began to affect morale. Nor was there an excessive number of exemptions from the draft. A report in 1865 listing 750 exemptions showed 237 for physical reasons, 173 overseers, 152 railway employees, 120 public officials and twenty preachers. Floridians like many others North and South considered the draft unconstitutional, unnecessary, and an affront to their patriotism, but there was little organized and violent opposition. It has commonly been stated that probably five percent of the population was Unionist at the outset of the war and that the number was doubled by 1865. More recent scholarship suggests considerably larger numbers of anti-war if not always pro-Union Floridians. They were often persons of foreign or northern birth whose personal convictions made them supporters of the Union. They were sometimes poor frontiersmen who had no association with the slavery question and preferred not to be involved. These last usually refused state or Confederate service but were not likely either to go into the Union Army. They often felt they could not leave their families. The unoccupied wilderness frontier was hard to police, and the long and much indented coastline became the gathering place of deserters and draft evaders from other sections and even from other states. By contrast, the Union men of Jacksonville, Saint Augustine, Fernandina and Key West were active supporters of the Union when circumstances permitted it.

The Confederate government never succeeded in dealing effectively with the problem of the disloyal and deserter bands. Nor was the Union government any more successful in making any effective use of them. They usually cooperated with the federals only enough to get some arms and supplies and to have a refuge from pursuing Confederates. Federal military and naval authorities encouraged them, but when they sought to enroll them in the army they could not locate them in their hiding places. The refugees preferred to carry on irregular guerrilla raids principally as a means of replenishing their supplies. They did prove a serious menace to anyone living near them. They ambushed patrols, raided plantations, stole blacks, stole and slaughtered cattle in a fashion to threaten the Confederate supply, and sometimes diverted the beef to Fort Myers and thence to Key West. They on occasion also informed blockaders of any troop movements they observed.

A campaign in the spring of 1864 made an all-out effort to stop the stealing of Confederate supplies and mail. Irregular cavalry units led by men like John J. Dickison and Charles J. Munnerlyn carried on a sort of guerrilla warfare on deserters and outlaw bands and summarily lynched those they caught. But the hunted men retired to the coast to the protection of blockaders, destroying bridges, trestles, and telegraph lines wherever they operated. In March, Lieutenant Colonel Henry D. Capers was assigned to drive them from Lafayette and Taylor County swamps where they seemed to be most numerous, aggressive and dangerous. Colonel Capers found their camp in the Aucilla River swamps deserted and concluded that they spent most of their time in their nearby homes with their families. His men systematically destroyed the homes on the east and west banks of the Econfina and Fenholloway rivers and sent the families to Camp Smith, literally a concentration camp, six miles south of Tallahassee where nine houses had been constructed to receive them. This proved too drastic for Floridians to accept. Governor Milton protested making war on women and children. Friends and relatives of the imprisoned families were in the Florida and the Confederate service. The plan was abandoned. Thereafter the authorities offered pardon to those who would come in and treated severely those they caught. In 1865, for example, they captured and executed William W. Strickland, a guerrilla leader, and a federal soldier trying to burn a railroad bridge.

The effectiveness of the Union blockade of the southern coast and the importance of the role of blockade running in Florida and in the Confederacy are still subjects of disagreement. The blockade was effective. The Confederacy was deprived of many items that might otherwise have been brought into the South; and there was plenty of cotton, which commanded a high price in European or even northern markets to exchange for the imports if it could be shipped out. Much that has been written argues that the blockade need not have been effective, that the state and Confederate governments should have gone much earlier into the business of blockade running or should have regulated private operations to secure a higher proportion of cargo for war purposes. This second view presupposes that a large supply of nonmilitary goods was always available, a point of view obviously false. The blockade made everything scarce that was not being produced at home.

Statistics on blockade running are often misleading. If the number of ships and the number of trips they made are counted, the resulting total is impressive. If the size of ships and the weight of cargo they carried is the measuring stick, the result is more realistic and less impressive. Only small, shallow-draft, fast boats that carried small cargoes were successful in getting through with any regularity. In Florida this was particularly true. The blockade closed all rivers and harbors that could accommodate larger ships and left only those that would take small craft.

The South Atlantic Blockading Squadron was assigned to watch the coast down to Cape Canaveral, though in practice the boundary was the Indian River. The East Gulf Blockading Squadron patrolled the area from that point around to Saint Andrews Bay, leaving the remainder to the West Gulf Squadron. Promise of profit as well as patriotic duty spurred the vigilance of the blockaders. Captured ships and cargo were prizes of war, adjudicated in admiralty court at Key West and usually sold. The officers and crew in the blockaders shared in the proceeds. They often destroyed all cargo except cotton, tobacco, and naval stores. The United States District Court

New Fernandina and Cedar Keys Railway under occupation, 1862

at Key West handled 299 cases during the war. The top price for a capture was $173,955.77 for the steamer *Magnolia* with a cargo of cotton. The open ports usually provided no access to the interior, and in almost all cases the cargo had to be hauled to river or railroad by wagons. In March 1862 a ship brought arms to New Smyrna and unloaded them on the beach to be hauled away. A favorite entry was to a point on the Indian River by boat, a short haul across land to the Saint Johns River and shipment downstream to a railroad or wagon train contact. When a blockade runner unloaded a cargo on Saint Andrews Bay, Governor Milton rounded up 200 wagons in a radius of eighty miles to haul away the munitions. Runners were caught more often on the outgoing trip and ships were frequently deserted by their crews.

Though the blockade runner was a vital source of much needed arms, ammunition and medicine, operators turned more and more to consumer goods, which commanded higher prices. The effect was demoralizing. State and Confederate officials invested. Government officials found that they had to bid against the dealers in non-essential items for the services of wagon and team owners. Samuel A. Swann, a Fernandina man associated with the Florida Railroad, and his associates became blockade brokers. The combine, located at Gainesville and acting for the Confederate government, organized three adventures to Cuba in 1863. David L. Yulee received a return of $3,939.99 in two months for an investment of $1,433.

Governor Milton was bitter in his opposition to blockade running. He charged that Floridians were helping the North by buying goods from New York and Boston that came in by way of Havana and Nassau. The Confederate government generally encouraged the trade and toward the end of the war attempted to reserve space for government cargo in all runners. Early in the business there had been some legal formalities observed and some regulations. Boats cleared from Confederate customs officials or military officers and in return for permits to export cotton, tobacco and naval stores gave bond to assure imports for the government, but regulations tended to break down and many boats were so small as to require no papers. Nor did blockade runners take serious financial risks. They often sold for Confederate money, but they used it to buy cotton, which commanded a high price in gold once beyond the reach of the blockaders.

Florida was an important source of two items much needed during the war—cattle and salt. Cattle went to market live and, after being slaughtered, salt was vital to preserve as well as to season

View of Fernandina in 1862 after capture by Union forces

the meat. Cattle growing in the valleys of the upper Saint Johns, the Kissimmee and the Caloosahatchee boomed after the removal of the Seminoles and became a chief source of beef for the Confederate Army. As early as October 1863, a commissary agent received an urgent appeal to purchase more Florida beef, being told that General Braxton Bragg's army was entirely dependent upon Florida sources for it. In the same month Georgia and South Carolina sources were reported used up. In 1864 the Confederacy hoped for 25,000 cattle, 10,000 hogs, 100,000 gallons of syrup and 20,000,000 pounds of fish from Florida.

In the first years of the war, Jacob Summerlin, already well established as a cattle baron, was a principal supplier, handling the cattle of other ranchers as well as his own. It is calculated that from 1861 to 1863 Summerlin provided 25,000 head of cattle at an average price of eight dollars. Thereafter the Confederate government sent Major Pleasanton W. White as commissary agent to Florida to make purchases of food and supplies. Captain James McKay of Tampa headed the South Florida district and directed the cattle drives. Cattle were driven north from the prairies at the rate of six hundred a week from April to August. The drive required about forty-five days. A 700-pound animal lost about 150 pounds in the process — which did nothing to improve the quality of the beef. The drives ended in late August when summer rains made too much high water, and could not be resumed until spring when grass was again green on the northern end of the trail, for the cattle subsisted entirely on grass on the open range.

Easily overlooked is the importance of the cattle business in South Florida to the Union. A considerable number of cattlemen in the Caloosahatchee valley apparently were Union men. Their detractors said it was because they could sell their cattle at Fort Myers for United States money or gold to supply the federal garrison there for shipment to Key West. Fort Myers had been abandoned at the conclusion of Indian hostilities in 1858 but was reoccupied by the federals in December 1863. Five companies of regular troops and Florida Rangers occupied the fort. The buildings were still in excellent condition. They added a breastwork of earth and logs fifteen feet wide and seven feet high. They also reopened the Colonel Persifor F. Smith Trail to Punta Rassa and built barracks and a long wharf there for cattle shipping. They held Fort Myers until May 1865. From that base they made forays into the interior to gather cattle for themselves as well as to deprive the Confederates of the source of meat. Some of the raids may have been, in reality, sales. Owners, it was said, allowed their cattle to be taken, knowing that they would be paid for them but by this ruse escaped the wrath of Confederate sympathizer neighbors. Francis A. Hendry, a Confederate cattleman in that area, estimated that by the end of the war they probably took 4,500 head of cattle, some from as far away as Fort Meade. The Confederates responded by occupying Fort Brooke on Tampa Bay and using it to protect and promote their interest in the cattle of the area. Late in 1864, Captain McKay sponsored the organization of a cow-guard battalion, known familiarly as the "Cow Cavalry," made up mostly of Confederate ranchers and cowboys who were exempt from other military service. On May 6, 1864, two days after the garrison had gone on a cattle drive, the Union ship *Adele* came into Tampa Bay, captured Fort Brooke, spiked the large cannons, took away the smaller ones and destroyed the machine shop. The Confederates returned only to depart six days later. After three days the federals occupied it in sufficient force to hold it but sailed away after a month. On February 21, 1865, Major William Footman, leading 275 members of the Cow Cavalry, approached Fort Myers but found it too strongly defended and withdrew. Though the Confederacy and the Union may have protected a small portion of their meat supply, the principal beneficiaries must have been the cattlemen, who could sell to either side or could send their cattle to Havana for even better prices.

Salt making had some local importance in Florida before the Civil War but never any great commercial significance. The blockade cut off the imports on which Floridians depended at a time when the need for salt was greatly increased by the war-created demand. In addition to the ordinary daily uses it was now required in great quantity by the army to help preserve its fresh meats and to prepare hides for tanning in the leather making process. Both dire necessity and high prices stimulated the industry. The Confederate government went extensively into the business, as did private adventurers. Florida had the best natural conditions for extracting salt from seawater. Commercial operations during the war centered on the Gulf coast from Manatee to Pensacola but concentrated most on the shores of Taylor County and Saint Andrews Bay. In the marshes along the bay there had been a three-year period of dry weather, which left the water there practically saturated with salt. There was an abundant supply of wood nearby and the area could be reached by land or water.

Salt sold for as much as a dollar a pound, and the industry employed as many as 5,000 men. Salt makers and salt making were peculiarly exposed to raids by ships in the blockading squadron on the Gulf coast. As the blockade increased in effectiveness and the salt industry grew in extent and importance, the question of military protection arose. But unless the industry was more concentrated, protection was virtually impossible. Every operation would require a guard to be stationed to meet the attack of ships moving at will up and down the coast. Early in 1862, in response to a popular demand for protection, General Joseph Finegan stationed three companies of soldiers in the Saint Andrews Bay area. Then the salt makers lost popular favor. The Confederate conscription law was interpreted to exempt salt workers from the draft, and speculators moved in to control the best salt-making locations and to manipulate the price of salt to their advantage.

The General Assembly in the fall of 1862 refused to come to their defense. The government provided that they might enroll in military companies with officers appointed by the governor. Though

Destruction of Confederate salt works on Saint Josephs Bay, by the crew of the U.S. bark Kingfisher. *From* Harper's Weekly, *1862.*

they were not true military units, the state would provide arms and ammunition. The result was never satisfactory, for there were not enough arms, and the untrained and undisciplined salt workers showed no disposition to use the few available.

Raids were frequent on the Gulf coast, the most important beginning in September 1862. Some of the early raiders walked into ambush as they left boats and moved in to destroy the salt works. Thereafter the standard procedure was to shell the site from the ship to drive off the defenders and then send in a landing party to complete the job. Thereafter raiders seldom met opposition and sometimes did their work with operators and workers looking on from a safe distance.

After a lull during the winter, the federals destroyed four large establishments on Alligator Bay on June 14, 1863. In December they returned in earnest again and inflicted heavy losses. On Lake Ocala they destroyed six steamboat boilers converted to saltwater evaporators, two flatboats, six oxcarts and various and sundry other equipment. On December 10 and 18 on Saint Andrews Bay they destroyed some 500 salt works including thirty-three wagons, twelve flatboats, two sloops, six oxcarts, 4,000 bushels of salt, 700 buildings and 1,000 kettles and iron boilers. The retiring Confederates had also done some destruction. The combined works had a capacity of nearly 16,000 bushels a day and reportedly represented an investment of six million dollars of private and government funds.

The Confederate government and some of the private operators immediately started rebuilding on Saint Andrews Bay and were going full blast in another two months. But on February 17, 1864, the federals returned to destroy works producing some 2,400 bushels of salt per day for the government. The final raid on salt works in the bay came in February 1865. In spite of the risks involved, salt making had been profitable to some and important enough to the Confederate government to justify the investment of millions of its very scarce dollars.

Florida's four hundred miles of recently constructed and not yet fully equipped railroads suffered grievously during the war years. As related elsewhere, the Florida Railroad lost both the Atlantic and the Gulf termini early in 1862, and the retreating Confederates tore up several miles of track west of Jacksonville. When federals took over Jacksonville and Baldwin, the railroads lost more equipment. The first wartime legislative session chartered four railroads and at least two later, but only in vital military areas was any building done. The rails from twenty-four miles of the east end of the Florida Railroad were removed to build a line from Lake City to DuPont on the Georgia line. It was the impressment of these rails that Yulee had resisted.

Railroads were in trouble from the beginning. Before the end of 1861 the Tallahassee Railroad and the Pensacola and Georgia considered asking the state to take them over. Instead the governor provided some financial assistance. Most of the traffic was in East Florida, and before the end of 1864 the Florida Railroad abandoned the track west of Gainesville but kept its operation going in the interior around Gainesville, Lake City and Baldwin. What was left of the railroad properties at the end of the conflict was in a sad state of deterioration when not actually worn out.

Agriculture continued to be the mainstay of the economy. The cotton growing counties were never invaded, and the labor supply was not seriously affected until the end of the war, but marketing the crop through the blockade was difficult, and the state and the Confederate government discouraged planting cotton in favor of food crops. Since cotton was nonperishable and commanded a good price when it could be gotten to market, it continued to be produced in considerable quantities. White sugar became scarce, but the unrefined brown sugar and syrup made from sugarcane made up some of the shortage. Corn to feed man and beast continued to be produced but not in quantities for export. To protect the corn supply, state law prohibited the distilling of corn whiskey except for those distilleries under contract with the Confederate government, which had to post $20,000 bond with the state to limit production to the government orders. Other important farm products were peas, sweet potatoes, pork and beef. The loss of manpower to the army and the disruption of production in the invaded coastal areas sharply reduced the total output of the farmers.

Substitutes for the scarce items usually imported came into general use. Coffee made from parched wheat, rye, sweet potatoes or corn, and tea made from sassafras or blackberry leaves made acceptable drinks. Finely ground cornmeal made a usable flour. Soap was made from ashes and fats, and dyes from herbs. Neighborhood gristmills received more grain, backyard tanneries reappeared and blacksmiths and crude foundries mended worn out hardware and metal tools. Farm families and slaves had long been accustomed to make much of what they used. More spinning and weaving than usual was done. Shoes were made from cow, deer and alligator hides. For many families all of these handicrafts had long been familiar, and the reversion to such a degree of self-sufficiency was not so difficult as it seems a century later.

The behavior of slaves during the conflict has been the subject of never-ending comment. They could have disrupted the economy and could have ended the war by engaging in civil insurrection, which would have brought the soldiers home from the Confederate armies. Until federal forces of some sort appeared, they usually remained peaceably at work, often directed by women or by one of their own number acting as overseer. This need not be interpreted as satisfaction with their lot. They were illiterate and superstitious. They feared the unknown and clung to the limited certainties of the only world they had ever known. It was also due to the long conditioning to obedience, the lack of initiative and leadership and sometimes in the case of family servants, an attachment to families. Almost to a man, however, they abandoned the plantations when Union forces approached.

The status of the liberated slave became a matter of increasing concern to the Union army and government. Should they be confiscated as property, returned to their owners, or set free? Union army commanders often felt they should be set free and resented returning them to owners. The confiscation acts in 1862 declared slaves of disloyal owners free, and Lincoln's Emancipation Proclamation late in 1862 did essentially the same and certainly portended the end of slavery when the Union won the war. General Rufus Saxton, the Union commander of the Department of the South, toward the end of the war used refugee blacks as guides and received permission to enroll them as soldiers, but fewer than 1,000 Florida blacks entered the Union army, mostly at the end of the conflict.

In December 1862 the General Assembly authorized the impressment of slave labor for state defense workers. They were employed in the spring of 1863 on the Apalachicola River defenses, and a year later 700 slaves were working in the vain effort to prevent another federal raid on Jacksonville. On February 17, 1864, the Confederate government provided for the impressment of black labor, slave or free, and fixed the Florida quota at 500. Officials conscripted free blacks first but soon were taking slaves as well.

Near the end of the war the Confederate Congress authorized freeing blacks and taking them into the army, but it was too late and the idea was not popular. As Howell Cobb of Georgia put it, the whole southern argument about the place of blacks in society is nullified if they become soldiers.

Aside from the production of salt, the only increase in manufacturing was in domestic production generally for consumption rather than for market, though some of it was for the army. Sawmilling except for purely local purposes ceased when lumber could not be shipped to market. Sawmills around the principal ports were early victims of raiders. General Bailey's cotton mill continued to produce yarn, which was distributed to Floridians to be made into cloth. Bailey's workers were not exempted from military service, but the Confederate government did assign several soldiers to work in the mill, and soon the working force was made up of persons not eligible for any duty. In 1864 the Confederacy threatened to take over the mill to process tax-in-kind cotton, but the governor argued successfully that Bailey was using the property largely for public purposes, was not profiteering and should be allowed to continue. In 1862 when the legislature provided $20,000 to purchase cotton and wool cards for distribution to families, the governor elected to use the money to start the Florida Card Manufacturing Company by purchasing in advance 2,500 cotton and 500 wool cards. But the project was not a success. Labor and materials of the right kinds were scarce and the product inferior, with the result that users preferred the much higher priced imports that came through the blockade. The leather factory and the shoe factory at Madison, employing twenty-six slaves, produced 11,000 pairs of shoes annually as well as wagon and buggy harnesses and other leather goods for the Confederate government. But what Florida could produce was a mere trickle in a vast river of items needed by the people of the state and the Confederacy.

Women undoubtedly felt the effects of the war more deeply than men, and they suffered more in the defeat when it came. The life of the frontier woman on a single family farm was, of course, less changed than that of the plantation mistress. Farm women had always contributed substantially to the nearly self-sufficient life the family lived. During the war they worked more, taking over much of the heavy labor formerly done by the man of the house. They suffered greater privation and were forced more than ever to subsist on what they could produce. They experienced loneliness because of the absence if not the death of the man of the family on some faraway battlefield. They often lacked even the consolation of an exchange of letters.

Women who lived on plantations and depended upon a staff of servants also found their way of life greatly altered, especially where the routines of that existence were disrupted by military invasion. Ellen Call Long, who lived in the very heart of Florida's plantation area at Tallahassee and knew planter society at its best, wrote of wartime life in *Florida Breezes*. She paid a tribute to the faithfulness of the blacks on the plantations where only the mistress remained to direct their efforts, pointing out that the commissary would not be so well supplied without their labor. She reported also that blacks probably would leave when opportunity presented itself, for that had been the experience of owners living on the Saint Johns River where it soon became impossible to keep blacks. Deprived of their slaves, plantation women took up unaccustomed tasks, "knitting, weaving, and experimenting in improvisation of food, medicine and clothing...." Susan Bradford Eppes reported in *Through Some Eventful Years* how half-forgotten skills were revived. Old blacks dragged out discarded looms and taught the others, including whites, to weave the needed cloth. She also described how the Bradford family ran a hospital and made bandages, blankets, socks, salve and the like.

Nor was life reduced to a dreary round of work and worry. Mrs. Eppes insists that a powerful effort was made, with parties, balls and concerts, to keep up morale. When General Trapier and others made their headquarters in Tallahassee, there was much gaiety and socializing, but it never obscured the grim facts of scarcity, inflation and deprivation they suffered, and many of the balls and concerts were for the benefit of one kind of relief or another. Only southerners in the United States have known what it is to be invaded and defeated. The experience left its mark on them for years to come, as it did on the many former slaves whose lives were changed forever by emancipation.

16.

Political Reconstruction, 1865-1877

Floridians like their fellow secessionists, having suffered defeat at arms, then had to undergo the equally unique American experience of Reconstruction under the authority of the victors. That this had been a civil conflict did not make the process less difficult. It involved for a time the presence of a small army of occupation, which frequently included blacks freed from slavery as a result of the war, and control of an outside if not strictly alien authority. This experience was not made easier by uncertainty and divided opinion among the victors as to who should make Reconstruction policy and what should be required as conditions of readmission to the Union. Nor were southerners always ready to accept the consequences of their unsuccessful effort to leave the Union.

At the close of hostilities it seemed that the restoration of the lately rebellious states to their former place in the nation might be a relatively simple matter. President Lincoln had assumed that Reconstruction was an executive function, that the states had never really been out of the Union, that they had only been in the hands of disloyal persons, and that when loyal persons again governed them, they might proceed much as before the effort to withdraw. When ten percent of the electorate of 1860 could take an oath of allegiance and form a constitution that repealed the ordinance of secession, abolished slavery, and repudiated the war debt, the state could resume its place in the national government. The terms of surrender imposed upon Lee and Johnston by Grant and Sherman seemed to bear out this promise of leniency. Overlooked was the fact that Grant's terms covered only military matters and that when Sherman would have included equally easy nonmilitary conditions he was overruled. Economic, political, and social rearrangements were left to the future with no clear indications of what they were to be.

Such limited conditions for readmission to the Union were too easy for defeated southerners to hope for under any circumstances, but the assassination of President Lincoln at the end of the war made it infinitely easier for those favoring other requirements to have their ways. Nor had those who accepted Lincoln's plan of Reconstruction as final taken sufficiently into account the possibility that the attitudes of Congress might have to be reckoned with. The legislative branch of the national government resented the extraordinary powers exercised by the chief executive during the war and planned to recover lost ground and readjust the balance between the two. Further, there were individuals and groups in the Congress that had always felt that war aims should extend beyond restoration of the Union and the abolition of slavery to include a guarantee of full civil and political rights to black citizens. To these may be added those who felt that the ex-Confederates should pay heavy penalties for their effort to disrupt the Union, perhaps the confiscation of property and loss of political rights for at least a period of probation. Others saw it desirable to keep the South in a subordinate status or make it politically solid for Republicans in order to extend their control of the national government, possibly also to make the region easier prey to economic exploitation by the North. Yet others felt that the opportunity to reform southern society should not be lost, and particularly that the lot of poor whites and blacks should be improved. Time and circumstances, with southerners themselves giving an assist, played into the hands of the radicals, and after two years of indecision and uncertainty, the more lenient presidential Reconstruction gave way to a decade of more drastic congressional control, after which Reconstruction was largely turned over to native white Floridians again. With nearly a century of perspective there is still wide disagreement among students as to the motives, the legality, the justification, and the value of much that was done.

There is little connection between the efforts to organize loyal governments in Florida during the war and policy and practice as it finally developed. Upon the death of Governor John Milton by suicide, the executive responsibility fell upon the president of the senate, Abraham K. Allison, who succeeded to the governorship. When the Confederate armies had surrendered he assumed that he might initiate steps to bring about resumption of normal relations with the national government. He went ahead without consulting Brigadier General Edward M. McCook, who reached Tallahassee on May 10 to receive the surrender of any Confederate forces remaining in Florida. Allison did notify McCook three days later that he had appointed five commissioners to go to Washington to confer with authorities there regarding the restoration of normal relations between Florida and the Washington government. The governor also summoned the General Assembly to convene on June 5 and set the election of a governor for two days thereafter.

These moves surprised and shocked Union men in Florida, who reasonably assumed that they would have a part in any new political arrangements. General McCook was unprepared to meet such a situation and wired Washington to learn how he should proceed. President Johnson was as well disposed toward the people of the secessionist states as Lincoln had been, but he could not approve

Allison's actions. Orders came for McCook to recognize no local, state, or Confederate authority, and on May 22, the general placed the state under martial law. Thus the brief Allison regime ended abruptly, and he found himself, along with Stephen R. Mallory and David L. Yulee, under arrest, in prison, and likely to be charged with treason. The others were soon let out of prison; Yulee did not secure his release until the spring of 1866 and there were no indictments.

Military occupation of all principal places soon followed. This was fortunate, for in the confusion and absence of authority that followed the collapse of the Confederacy a considerable amount of lawlessness prevailed. This was not continued resistance to the Union but a breakdown of law and order at the local level, accompanied by some pillage and robbery. Five companies of federal troops were stationed at Tallahassee and at Gainesville, two at Tampa, and one each at Lake City, Madison, Monticello, and Palatka. After several changes in personnel and organization, Major General John S. Foster became the commander of the Department of Florida. Blacks made up a part of the occupation force. Floridians resented this deeply and assumed, as did historian William Watson Davis, that it was done to impress Floridians with the thoroughness of the changes being introduced. In view of the generally conciliatory attitude toward the South at the time this view is hardly tenable. It is more likely that war-weary white veterans were being mustered out of the service, leaving a proportionately larger number of recently enrolled blacks to be used in the occupation force. The military regime certainly was not harsh though it was by no means popular. It represented an alien authority, but it did maintain order and security and took some steps toward the restoration of orderly labor relations. General McCook antagonized the people of Tallahassee when he threatened to close the Episcopal church because the minister omitted the prayer for the president of the United States. Floridians provided other reasons for irritation and resentment if not for action on the part of the occupation forces. Residents resented their presence and felt no necessity to conceal their feelings.

Steps leading toward the restoration of civil government began on July 23 when President Johnson appointed William Marvin of Key West as provisional governor. Marvin was a moderate Unionist, well known in the state and generally acceptable in the role. He had come from New York to Key West in 1835 as United States district attorney for the Southern District. He had been defeated by a secessionist in the voting for delegates to the secession convention. His sympathies were definitely southern, but he could not accept secession. Some of his political and legal friends in the state had condemned him for his stand, but few harbored any lasting resentment.

The new governor's first step was to prepare for the election of delegates to a constitutional convention, which he set for October 10, and the meeting of the convention for October 25. He worked closely with General Foster, with whom he shared authority, for the state was still until martial law. Since all other forms of communication and transportation had been seriously disrupted, military couriers distributed the election notices and poll books. Government transports had orders to pick up delegates in coastal cities and deliver them to a port adjacent to Tallahassee. All white males twenty-one years of age who could and would take the oath of allegiance and those who had received presidential pardons were eligible to register and vote. Marvin went about the state urging moderation on the whites and speaking to the freedmen on the responsibilities involved in their new status. He acted to restore the property of Union men confiscated by the Confederacy and to stop sales of property of Floridians confiscated for taxes by the United States Treasury.

In an uneventful election only 6,707 voters cast ballots. There was no contest to arouse the interest of voters and many of them had not troubled to take the oath and register. President Johnson had grudgingly conceded that qualified blacks might well be given the right to vote. The suggestion went unheeded and there was no readiness yet at the national level to require it as a condition of the restoration of the states, for seventeen of the twenty-five northern states still barred blacks from the ballot. It was not surprising under these circumstances that the old pre-war and wartime leadership won the places in the convention. Their reappearances in places of political power and influence also logically enough were cause for some concern in the North, and people there who were apprehensive about the intentions of southerners watched the work of the convention with great interest.

The delegates to the convention accepted without much protest the requirement that the ordinance of secession be repealed (though they used the word "annulled") and that slavery be abolished. They ratified the Thirteenth Amendment on December 29, "with the understanding that it does not confer on Congress the power to legislate on the status of freedmen in the state." When it came to the repudiation of the war debt they were reluctant, and only the urging by Governor Marvin that it was an unconditional requirement induced them to abandon plans to scale it down and pay it or leave it to the voters to decide. When they turned their attention to the place of the freedmen in the new order, the delegates were under no specific requirements and were less certain what it might be necessary or expedient to do. Mostly former owners of slaves, they were ill-prepared to concede any status approaching equality to blacks, whom they considered incapable of self-direction and self-government. Since nothing in the experience of slavery had prepared the blacks for freedom, it was urged that they could function successfully only under continuing white tutelage.

Laws respecting free blacks had become increasingly harsh in the three decades before the war when there were less than a thousand free blacks in the state. Race relations had been institutionalized by a code of practices as well as by statute. It is small wonder that Floridians and other southerners faced with a great increase in the number of freedmen felt the need of special laws to restrain them and induce them to work. They could also feel that the new laws actually meant a softening of the prewar codes, but it seemed more appropriate to treat them as free blacks had been before the war rather than as free men. Provisional Governor Marvin sympathized with these southern views, saying that neither whites nor blacks were ready for black suffrage, but he saw political risks in doing nothing about it. He made what proved to be a very prophetic statement when he expressed the fear that Congress might refuse to seat senators and representatives from the former Confederate states if black rights were not recognized and they were not allowed to vote. Florida's constitution makers and the legislators who undertook to complete the work of reorganizing state government failed to heed Marvin's advice or to learn from the experience of other states also engaged in working out adjustments to the new order. In Mississippi and South Carolina, harshly discriminatory legislation produced alarm and criticism in the North, and military authorities countermanded some of the regulations and punishments. The result was a growing impression in the North that black rights must be brought under federal protection.

Since the Florida legislature did not tackle the problem until early 1866 there was less justification for their action than there had been at the end of 1865. Some blacks had shown a disposition to leave the plantations and congregate near the towns or wander about the countryside, giving the impression that they would not return to work unless compelled to do so. United States army officers and agents of the Freedmen's Bureau seem to have shared this view, and while they acted to protect the freedom of blacks they used their offices to encourage them to make contracts and return to work on the plantations, almost the only occupation available to them. The rumor that each former slave would receive forty acres of land and a mule at Christmas in 1865 added to the uncertainty about the future. Probably the number of black vagrants in town or country was never as large as many whites thought. Quite likely the sight of any blacks "exercising their freedom" was so novel as to be alarming. All doubts and fears concerning the freedmen proved groundless. They never proved vindictive toward whites, and by the middle of January 1866 when it was time to get the year's crop planting under way they were returning to the farms and plantations to work.

Floridians, by enacting a series of laws that applied only to blacks, made their contributions to the "Black Codes" that proved to be the most effective political boomerang ever conceived by lawmakers. A first impression was that they did not mean to give up slavery if it could be maintained in some other form. A logical corollary was that black rights could not be left to southern state governments. The extension of the Freedmen's Bureau, the Civil Rights Act of 1866, the Fourteenth Amendment to the Constitution, the eventual overthrow of the moderate, almost pro-Southern, presidential Reconstruction, and the inauguration of radical Republican congressional Reconstruction owe much to the codes, which went a long way to bring about the very things they were designed to prevent.

The constitutional convention contented itself with laying down some general principles and recommending to the governor that he appoint an interim committee to draft legislation to be considered by the General Assembly when it met. The fundamental law provided that all inhabitants should enjoy the rights of person and property without distinction of color and that blacks could testify in all cases affecting the rights and remedies of black persons but not sit on juries. In contrast, it provided that persons leading an idle, profligate, or immoral life should be punished by fine or imprisonment or sold to service for a term not exceeding twelve months.

The convention set November 29 to vote on the constitution and to elect state and local officials. Many candidates were unopposed, and only about 4,000 votes were cast. David S. Walker, who had been a slaveholder and a Whig, had served in both houses of the General Assembly and on the state supreme court was elected Governor. In his inaugural address on December 20, 1866, he acknowledged the need to enact some statutes relating to freedmen's affairs, but refused to grant them suffrage. When outgoing Governor Marvin finally received orders to turn the office over to Walker on January 18, he warned that Congress would surely intervene unless "we accept fully the freedom of the negro and give him the same security and protection we give to the white man."

Governor Marvin had appointed to the interim committee on freedmen's affairs three North Florida ex-slaveholders, C. H. Dupont, A. J. Peeler, and M. D. Papy. They prefaced their report to the General Assembly with a characterization of slavery as a benevolent institution, and the happiest and best ever designed for a laboring population. The only evil they saw was inadequately regulated sex and marital life. They frankly favored preserving as much as possible of the "good" features of slavery.

The General Assembly chose to follow the lead of the committee, and when a small group of senators proposed to soften the most harsh features of the proposed code, that body responded by making the statutes even more comprehensive and obviously discriminatory. Assuming that there would be a great increase in crime to deal with, much of it consisting of offenses that would have been taken care of by slave masters under the old regime, they created a system of county criminal courts. In cases where the laws of the state made a crime punishable by fine and imprisonment, a judge might substitute a public whipping up to thirty-nine lashes or standing in the pillory for as much as an hour. Almost immediately, military authorities prohibited the use of whip and pillory and recommended sentencing to hard labor instead. The new code also provided the death penalty for assault with intent to rape a white woman, for being accessory thereto, or for inciting to insurrection. Damages to private or public property carried penalties up to $1,000 fine and imprisonment up to six months. Ownership of knives, dirks, swords, or firearms was strictly regulated, and when the attorney general pointed out that such a law was unconstitutional and the governor recommended its repeal, the General Assembly defiantly refused.

Particularly objectionable were laws regarding vagrancy; these were so broadly defined as to cover idleness of any kind. A convicted vagrant could post bond in an amount that would satisfy the judge as a guarantee of good behavior and industry for one year. In the very likely event that he could not post bond he might be placed in the pillory, whipped, imprisoned, or hired out for as much as one year. Anyone unable to pay a fine imposed in a county court could be hired out at public outcry to the person offering the highest amount for the shortest period of labor. Also added to the constitutional provision that blacks could give testimony in court was the prohibition of sworn depositions by them as evidence. The law provided for black schools but at no expense to the state, the cost to be paid by a tax of one dollar on black men plus tuition fees.

The effect of the Black Codes was not as harsh as their language suggests. Local officials did in fact enforce the contract, vagrancy, and marriage provisions and collect the capitation tax, but the threat of military intervention certainly acted as a deterrent. When the legislature passed a law prohibiting blacks from bearing arms, General Foster raised the question of its constitutionality, whereupon the attorney general agreed and Governor Walker directed that the law not be enforced. When the worst fears of whites regarding the behavior of freedmen were never realized, the enforcement of other measures tended to be relaxed. Critics of the codes made no distinction among them as to severity or the degree of enforcement. To them they added up to discrimination and peonage at best.

Presidential Reconstruction faced the final test when representatives and senators from the southern states presented themselves for seats in the national Congress. The Florida voters chose Ferdinand McLeod for the state's one seat in the House, but he could not take the required oath and made no effort to take the seat. The General Assembly selected William Marvin for the short term and Wilkinson Call, a nephew of Richard Keith Call, for the six-year term in the Senate. Marvin presented his credentials on January 19, 1866, only to have no action on them taken. If Marvin, a loyal Union man throughout the war, could not be seated, an ardent Confederate like Call could hardly hope for recognition. Marvin as an individual probably was acceptable, though his moderation might have been displeasing to the radical Republicans who had spearheaded the movement to deny seats to claimants from all of the states of the former Confederacy. Senator-elect Call soon joined Marvin, and the two remained in Washington to work with President Johnson to do what they could for Florida, but they never gained their Senate seats.

In Washington the struggle between the president and the Congress for the control of Reconstruction reached an impasse, but Congress held the stronger hand as long as members from the southern states were denied their seats. For the time being a sort of probationary home rule continued in the state, with units of the United States army and agents of the Freedmen's Bureau standing by ready to intervene if occasion arose.

In the year 1866 the Congress expressed its attitude on the southern question with two laws and an amendment to the Constitution. In a direct response to the Black Codes, the civil rights bill defined citizenship to include blacks and brought certain rights of all citizens under federal protection. When President Johnson vetoed the measure, the Congress overrode the veto, but questions of constitutionality that he raised troubled supporters of the legislation. The Congress then enacted the Fourteenth Amendment, which incorporated essentially the intent of the civil rights act. Johnson could not veto an amendment, but he could and did advise the southern states to refuse to ratify it. Only Tennessee approved the amendment. The Florida legislators probably did not need the president's advice or the urgings of Governor Walker to reject it unanimously. It would sweep away the Black Codes that they so strongly supported and place in federal hands powers which states claimed and which they had left the Union to preserve for themselves. They counted on President Johnson to save the day for them, and he with equal lack of foresight assumed that the congressional elections in November of that year would return a Congress favorable to his point of view. It is probably not true that ratification of the amendment would have ended political Reconstruction as is sometimes suggested. Tennessee's representatives did get their seats, but the Congress refused to say that the same would be true for the others.

The second of the laws would extend for two years the life of the Freedmen's Bureau, which had been created on March 3, 1865, to operate until one year after the end of the war. Johnson vetoed the measure as an unjustifiable and unconstitutional extension of military power into the postwar era. The veto was sustained, but the bill became law in another effort later in the year.

Johnson and the southerners badly misjudged the temper of the northern electorate in 1866, and both contributed to the growing radicalism. Johnson's political ineptitude, particularly in dealing with Congress, his veto of the civil rights act, and the Freedmen's Bureau bill gradually alienated moderate Republicans, and radical aggressiveness made the most of these matters. The election of ex-Confederates to state and local offices, the enactment of Black Codes in most southern states, the defiant attitudes of some southern leaders and sections of the press, and, finally, enough acts of racial violence all together convinced a majority of northerners that southerners could not yet be trusted to control the state governments nor to respect the rights of the freedmen.

In the newly elected Congress, radical Republicans had enough votes to override a Johnson veto and in March 1867 began by sweeping away all of the previous steps toward Reconstruction, returned the ex-Confederate states except Tennessee to military rule, and set up machinery to create new state governments that would be acceptable to Congress. Military authorities began by registering all white men not disqualified by participation in the rebellion and all eligible blacks.

This second military occupation of Florida began on April 1, 1867. Colonel John T. Sprague, the commander for the District of Florida, established headquarters at Tallahassee and proclaimed martial law on April 8. Local government continued to function in a provisional fashion, subject always to intervention by the military authorities. Since they had known the presence of troops since 1865, Floridians accepted the new order without too much protest, and its brief regime in the state was never harsh.

The new political order revived the possibility of a Republican party in the state. Efforts during the war had failed because the number of Unionists was too small, but opposition to the Walker administration had kept alive hopes. Newcomers to the state, principally federal appointees, added to the potentially Republican ranks but introduced a rivalry between them and residents for control. There was from the beginning and throughout the Reconstruction era so much personal and factional rivalry among Florida Republicans that it is remarkable they were able to win and hold political control of the state for a decade. There were four rather clearly defined political groups in the state. The majority of resident whites supported the Florida Democrats, sometimes called Conservatives. Another smaller group had always been Unionist in their sympathies, moderate in the views, and Republican in their politics. Usually dubbed "Scalawags," they were often looked upon by their white neighbors as traitors to their own section and people. They deserved a better fate, for they had been consistent in their Unionism and usually had been Whigs in prewar days. There were then two factions of Carpetbaggers who followed rival leaders but otherwise differed relatively little. In the bid for the votes of the newly enfranchised blacks the Carpetbaggers won the political allegiance of the greater part of them for the Republican party and the control of the state government.

The Freedmen's Bureau agents became a powerful factor in the Republican party because of their close association with the blacks in other respects. To native white Floridians whatever good the Bureau had done was obscured by the fact that it represented an alien power in the state, that it existed to protect the rights of freedmen, and that its agents became a potent factor in Republican politics. Other leadership could be found among postal employees, treasury agents, army personnel, and in private business. Assistant commissioner of the Freedmen's Bureau, Thomas W. Osborn, took the lead in organizing the Lincoln Brotherhood, in which secrecy and ritual played a large part. In the spring of 1867 three other Carpetbaggers organized the rival Loyal League of America. William U. Saunders was a mulatto ex-barber from Baltimore, Maryland. Daniel Richards came to Florida in 1865 as a treasury agent and with Saunders worked as representative of the Republican National Committee to organize the blacks for their first voting experience. Liberty Billings was an ex-Unitarian minister who had joined the army as a chaplain and later commanded a black regiment and settled in Fernandina at the end of the war. By making more radical promises than Osborn and his associates, talking of confiscating and dividing property of ex-Confederates, and encouraging more defiant attitudes toward the white man's law, they won adherents very quickly and claimed 15,000 members by April of 1868.

The third or Scalawag faction was led by Colonel Ossian B. Hart, whose family had been prominent in the founding of Jacksonville early in the century. He had organized the moderately pro-black Republican Club of Jacksonville, which included in its membership most of the whites who had been Unionist during the war.

The Conservatives proved to be curiously apathetic as registration of voters to choose delegates for a constitutional convention proceeded. Some of this was perhaps due to a feeling of futility, a conclusion that all was lost, some to reluctance to appear before registrars and take the required oath, or sympathy for ex-Confederates disqualified. On the other hand, it should not be forgotten that some of the former slaveholders hoped to be able to control the black vote. Newly created districts replaced counties as the units for representation. The pairing with counties that had large black majorities sometimes minimized the influence of those with white majorities. Only 11,148 whites registered while the black total was 15,434. On November 14, 15, and 16, 1867, the vote in favor of the convention was 14,300 of the total of only 14,503 votes cast. At the same time the voters chose forty-six delegates, of which forty-three were Republicans but only eighteen of them blacks, whereas the blacks made up nearly fifty percent of the state's population.

When January 20, the date for the opening of the convention, arrived, the Richards-Saunders-Billings faction was organized to seize control. On the opening day they could claim twenty-two of the twenty-eight delegates present and proceeded over the protests of Osborn and his followers who worked for postponement. C. H. "Bishop" Pearce, head of the African Methodist Church in Leon County, became temporary chairman and David Richards the president. When it became clear that the Radicals would control the convention, fourteen of the moderates absented themselves on February 4, leaving less than a quorum, and the local military commander refused to compel their attendance. The remaining members went ahead with the business of constitution making. On January 21, they acted to forbid the sale of property for debt, suspended the collection of all taxes, and released from custody all persons held to labor for non-payment of fines. They also voted themselves ten dollars a day in pay and forty cents a mile for travel, and set the pay to begin on December 28 when the call for the convention was issued. Since only forty-one members had ever presented credentials, this faction concluded they had a quorum, resolved themselves into a nominating convention on February 7, and selected Billings to run for governor, Saunders for lieutenant governor, and Samuel Walker for Congress. They then waited for General George C. Meade, military commander for the Third District, to arrive from Atlanta to approve their work.

The seceders had not been idle, and they pulled a coup that won for them control of the convention. Just before midnight on February 10 they returned from Monticello where they had been meeting and seized the convention hall in Tallahassee. They brought in the two members who had not yet claimed seats, four to replace Radicals they charged were disqualified, and two blacks from the Radical camp for a total of twenty-four. With that majority they organized the convention by deposing Richards and placing Horatio Jenkins in the chair. Their committee on privileges and elections ousted Billings, Saunders, Richards, and Pearce and replaced them with J. W. Butler, J. E. Davison, Marcellus L. Stearns, R. Will, and Ossian B. Hart. The rival organizations continued to meet for five days. On February 16 Richards asked the governor to arrest Jenkins and other leaders, but he refused to intervene and there the matter rested until General Meade arrived on the next day. Interestingly enough, the military authorities had refused to remove Governor Walker. On the morning of February 18 General Meade, after he failed to reconcile the two factions, ruled in favor of the seceders, and it was they who wrote the constitution of 1868.

There were not very many differences between what the two factions proposed. The Radicals made county offices elective while the Monticello group created more offices and made them appointive. The Radicals would have apportioned representation according to population, giving Leon County seven members while four counties with small populations—Orange, Volusia, Brevard, and Dade—shared one. The moderates provided for each county to elect one representative and not more than four to any one. This served to reduce the relative importance of the populous counties with a large number of black voters, and Democrats found it quite satisfactory when they returned to power at the end of Reconstruction.

The enfranchisement of blacks was by far the most important new departure. In other sections the governor was to have a four-year term, be ineligible for reelection, and appoint the cabinet with the consent of the senate. The governor also appointed all county officers, a device to put Republicans into office in the counties which were predominantly white and Democratic, a measure the Democrats found equally useful when they came into power. Taxes were required to be uniform on all citizens, and a capitation tax could not exceed one dollar a year. The state could not grant its credit to any company chartered by the General Assembly. A system of public schools with some state tax support and institutions for the insane, blind, and deaf and a state prison meant a considerable expansion of state services and expenditures. A homestead exemption of 160 acres of land or a half acre of city property, or $1,000 of personal property from forced sale under process of law, protected debtors

from being sold out completely. Salaries set for state officials were
by Florida standards high, $5;000 for governor, $2,500 for lieutenant governor, $4,500 for the chief justice, and $4,000 for associate
justices of the state supreme court, $3,000 each for cabinet officers,
$12,000 for twelve senators, and $26,950 for fifty-three representatives.

For governor the victorious faction nominated Harrison Reed,
with William H. Gleason for lieutenant governor and Charles H.
Hamilton for the national Congress. Reed had come to Florida from
Wisconsin as a treasury agent but had moved into a position in the
post office. Gleason, also from Wisconsin, unlike many other Carpetbaggers remained in Florida after Reconstruction, spending seventeen years in Miami before moving to Eau Gallie, an area with
which he and his family continued to be associated. Hamilton, a
lawyer from Pennsylvania, came to Florida with the army in 1865
and elected to remain. He practiced law in Marianna, became an
agent of the Freedmen's Bureau, and after serving the term in the
Congress became postmaster in Jacksonville and later collector of
customs at Key West before he resigned in 1873 to return to Pennsylvania.

The conservatives nominated Colonel George W. Scott, a Florida
resident since 1850 and a Confederate army officer, Thomas W.
White, a southern unionist from Jackson County, and Jackson
Friend, a northerner who threw in his lot with Floridians and lived
in Fernandina. Saunders supported Reed and the constitution while
Billings and Richards, who had announced their intention to run as
independents, withdrew from the race before election time. When
the votes were counted, the constitution won ratification by 14,520
to 9,491, Reed won the governorship by 14,170 to Scott's 7,852, and
Hamilton won the congressional seat. The newly elected state senate had sixteen Republicans and eight Democrats, and the lower
house thirty-seven Republicans and fifteen Democrats. Among the
fifty-three Republicans were thirteen Carpetbaggers, twenty-one
Scalawags, and nineteen blacks.

The new administration was inaugurated on June 8, 1868, and
on the next day the General Assembly as required by the Reconstruction Acts ratified the Fourteenth Amendment to the United
States Constitution. At the same session the legislators elected
Adonijah S. Welch and Thomas Osborn to the United States Senate, with Abijah Gilbert to succeed Welch when the short term expired in March of the following year. Welch was a far cry from the
common notion of a Carpetbagger. Formerly the head of Michigan
State Normal School, he had come to Florida in 1865 as an army
officer. When his senate term ended he left Florida to become the
president of Iowa State College. On July 4, civil government was
resumed in Florida, and on July 25, Congress declared Florida again
in the Union.

Florida government in the four years of the Reed administration was far from tranquil. Reed survived four efforts at impeachment and was saved from removal in the last only by the possibility

that a Democrat contesting the lieutenant governor's office might win and succeed him. He seemed to favor the conservatives and their planter leadership and to make only enough concession to blacks and whites in his own party to win their votes. Unhappily for him, the conservatives would not cooperate. No matter how efficient, economical, fair, and honest the Republican administration might be, the native whites would not support it. Instead, they stood ready to defeat good and approve bad legislation if it would discredit Reed or any other of his party. The appointment of Robert H. Gamble as state comptroller and James D. Westcott, Jr., as attorney general and later associate justice of the State Supreme Court failed to win any significant support from conservatives but was frustrating to both wings of the Republican Party. No blacks were named to the first cabinet, though Reed later appointed Jonathan Gibbs secretary of state when he needed some black support. Reed had begun by vetoing a bill to give equal rights to all persons in hotel and railroad accommodations. The governor quarreled with Senator Osborn over patronage, and Gleason broke with him and allied himself with the senator.

Reed's trouble was partly financial. The General Assembly was willing to appropriate money but not to levy taxes. The state then resorted to treasury warrants to be redeemed later and to the sale of bonds to pay up debts and to defray current expenses. In January 1869 the governor pointed out that the state debt was $578,045.08 and another $200,000 was needed for operations that year. Schools were not yet provided for, nor had the state's immigration program been started. The Internal Improvement Fund was in trouble and railroad building was languishing.

By 1870 the conservative Democrats had concluded that they could oust the Republicans by a campaign of terror and violence in a dozen North Florida counties, where their strength lay in large black populations. Violence had been the order of the day since the return to civil government on July 4, 1868. From that time to mid-November some fifteen murders were reported. In early 1869 at least ten more occurred in Jackson, Hamilton, Duval, Hernando, Alachua, Columbia, and Madison counties, and in the fall there were seven in Jackson alone before soldiers restored order. In the summer of 1870 armed men besieged Congressmen Charles Hamilton and William Purman in the home of the sheriff at Marianna for a week. During the summer and fall, parties of armed men came regularly into Lake City, where they finally forced the sheriff to resign. On November 2 on the eve of the election they attacked and wounded the Madison County sheriff. The governor promised to request troops for the 1870 election in Columbia, Jackson, and Hamilton counties.

In the balloting on November 8, Republicans put up for congress Josiah T. Walls, a black from Pennsylvania residing in Alachua County, and Samuel T. Day, a native southerner, for lieutenant governor. The revitalized Democrats offered Silas Niblack, an ex-Whig, for the congressional seat and William D. Bloxham, a young

Leon County planter, for lieutenant governor. Violence on the part of Democrats and fraud by Republicans characterized the election, but the canvassing board was controlled by the Republicans. The canvassers rejected the votes of nine counties and three districts in Duval, charging irregularities, and declared the Republicans winners, but if the rejected votes had been counted the Democrats would have won by 209 for Niblack and forty-seven for Bloxham. Both Democrats contested the election, demanding that the canvassers count all of the votes. Niblack unseated Walls on January 29, 1873, a fate he was to suffer again in later elections. He was reelected in November 1872 and again in 1874, only to be unseated by J. J. Finley on April 19, 1876. On June 1, 1872, the Florida court ruled in favor of Bloxham; Day had resigned on May 27 and Bloxham took office on June 3, but as the term ended on January 3, 1873, he never presided over the senate. In the 1872 election Ossian B. Hart defeated Bloxham for governor, but only because some Democrats withdrew support from their candidate. Bloxham had sought to win black votes by concessions and persuasion. On his plantation he had set up a school for blacks and installed a teacher who became active in politics, but other planters refused to go along. In the new General Assembly were thirteen Republicans and eleven Democrats in the senate and twenty-eight Republicans and twenty-four Democrats in the house. In 1873 Florida sent Simon B. Conover, a Republican, to the United States Senate with Democratic support. Two years later the two parties were evenly divided in the upper house and the Democrats controlled the lower twenty-eight to twenty-five; a Democrat, Charles W. Jones, went to the United States Senate.

There was less strife after 1870-1871. Native white Democrats were restrained somewhat by the enforcement of Ku Klux Klan Acts. In December 1871 fourteen cases were on the docket in Florida courts, and by 1875 trial of thirty-eight cases had brought six convictions, enough to discourage the use of violence. The rather even balance in the state legislature made it possible for Democrats to make trouble for Republicans by encouraging dissident factions and urging blacks to demand more offices as well as supporting efforts to impeach Governor Reed. The next governor, Ossian B. Hart, who died in March 1874, was a moderate, as was Marcellus L. Stearns, who succeeded him. Stearns was a Carpetbagger from Maine who came to Florida as a Freedmen's Bureau agent and settled in Gadsden County. Stearns made his pitch to conservatives of both parties and was more effective than Reed had been at controlling a working majority in the legislature, but he always had to contend with the rivalry of Conover. Also such black leaders as Josiah Walls, John Wallace, and H. S. Harmon always opposed him. Democrats had in effect already regained a measure of power in this coalition with the Republican governor.

The combination of conservatives and moderate Republicans began by bringing order into state finances. By 1876 except for railroad bonds, which were assumed to be supported by railroad properties, the state debt of about $1,400,000 was mostly funded. Amendments were introduced to change from annual to biennial sessions of the legislature, to abolish county courts and turn their functions over to circuit courts, and to forbid the lending of the state's credit to individuals or corporations. To encourage business a bill to provide tax exemption for a limited time to new manufacturing enterprises was offered.

When the elections in 1876 came around the Democrats knew they had an excellent chance to win control of the state. When they met at Quincy on June 21, they nominated the principal candidates by unanimous votes. For governor they offered George F. Drew of Ellaville, who had come from New Hampshire to Georgia and then to Florida. Known as a Unionist during the war, he was willing to sell salt and timber to the Confederates. He had been a Whig and nearly all whites could support him.

By contrast factionalism broke out again among the Republicans, and three rival candidates for governor threatened to destroy each other's chance. Congressman W. J. Purman and Senator Conover opposed the renomination of Stearns but could not join forces. When the convention nominated Stearns, a portion of the members seceded and nominated Conover, but on September 5 Conover withdrew. Democrats needed only to repeat what Republicans were saying about each other.

On the national scene both major political parties nominated reform candidates. The reaction against the corrupt alliance of business and politics at municipal, state, and national levels and weariness with Reconstruction required new faces. The Democrats chose Samuel J. Tilden, who as governor of New York had been in the fight to clean up the Tweed Ring. Republicans chose Rutherford B. Hayes, who had a good war record and a fair score as a reform governor but had not been a part of the liberal Republican bolt in 1872.

The campaign was heated, but there was little national interest in Florida until the election was over. The first returns indicated a Tilden victory, but late on election night it became clear that the votes of Florida, Louisiana, and South Carolina could save the election for Hayes. Both parties were claiming the three states and the Republicans controlled the election machinery. Visiting dignitaries from both parties appeared on the scene and practically took charge of party affairs in the state. Democrats and Republicans began to collect evidence, each expecting the other to cheat, and charges of fraud began to appear. The canvassing board met on November 27 and counted 24,337 votes for Hayes and 24,294 for Tilden, but results were contested in fourteen counties. When claims and counterclaims were considered, the board reported 23,843 for Hayes and 22,919 for Tilden and certified the election of Hayes. Democratic electors met on the same day and certified to the President of the United States the election of Tilden.

In the state election the Democrats sued in the state supreme court for a recount of the votes without going behind the returns in the disputed counties and won a court order which gave the state offices to Democrats. Stearns declared he would not surrender the office, but armed supporters of Drew outnumbered his, and Drew took the oath of office without incident on the second day of January 1877. The General Assembly on January 18 directed that a new canvass of the votes for president and vice-president be made. Two days later a committee of three Democrats reported a Tilden victory and Florida sent a third certificate of election to Washington.

When Congress met on December 4, the Senate was Republican and the House Democratic. There was nothing in law or precedent to guide them in a disputed election. The two bodies finally agreed upon an electoral commission of five senators, five representatives, and five supreme court justices to make a final decision. The best hope for the Democrats was in Florida, and when the commission decided eight to seven in favor of Hayes, their chances seemed gone unless they acted to prevent the count, but cooler heads prevailed. Southerners decided to accept Hayes in return for home rule and the withdrawal of troops from the three states where the election had been in doubt. Other considerations affecting the compromise were the promises of more southern representation in the new administration and the greater likelihood of Republican support for much needed internal improvements.

Who really won the election of 1876 in Florida? Since there is no way to discover how many voters were kept away from the polls by intimidation and violence or how much fraud was committed, the question has produced endless conjecture. One conclusion seems to be justified. Split-ticket voting in 1876 caused the Republican state ticket to trail the Hayes ballot count by several hundred votes. This suggests the possibility at least that the Democrats carried the state while Republicans actually won the electoral vote. Perhaps the compromise was made in Florida by the voters before it was made by party leaders meeting subsequently in the Wormley Hotel in the national capital. Reconstruction, contrary to the way the story is usually written, did not end with the return of Democrats to power. It was the southerners who finally worked out the economic, social, and political future of the state. It prevailed until a "New Reconstruction" began in the middle of the twentieth century and raised again the unsolved problems growing out of the Civil War and its consequences.

17.

New Directions in Economics and Society, 1865-1880

The war completely disrupted many of the economic and social arrangements that Floridians had seceded to defend and perpetuate. New approaches to economic and social stability and progress then had to be worked out in the midst of the economic ruin left in the wake of the conflict, the bitter taste of failure and defeat, and the uncertainties of political Reconstruction. In time new directions became evident in agriculture, commerce, and industry, in race and labor relations, and in the relative importance of social classes that in the long run outweighed in importance the more dramatic events of political Reconstruction. Cotton growers had had their day, and Floridians moved in new economic directions that set them apart from the people of the other states of the lower South. The black was no longer a slave, but he was principally a laborer without property and his future was uncertain. The landed gentry, already reduced in material circumstances, gradually sank in relative importance as new men with business interests made their way into the economy, politics, and society of the state.

Florida was still largely an undeveloped frontier offering welcome and opportunity to new settlers. Blacks as well as whites continued to move into the state, with an increase in the proportion of blacks in the total up from 44 1/2% to about 47%. The federal census in 1870 counted 187,748 people, an increase of 33.7% over 1860; and in 1880, 269,493, a 43.5% increase for that decade. These statistics of population growth do not reveal the whole story, for they reflect nothing of the effects of the war. Cotton production dropped from 65,153 bales in 1860 to 39,789 in 1870 and 54,997 in 1880. The fleecy staple was never to recover its prewar importance. After rising to 57,298 bales in 1890, acreage began to decline, and in 1900 production fell to 53,994 bales. The value of farms, $16,435,727 in 1860, dropped to $9,947,920 in 1870 and rose to $20,291,835 in 1880. The percentage decline in property values was greater in Florida than in Virginia where so much of the fighting occurred and was exceeded only in frontier Arkansas of all the Confederate states. The numbers of livestock had been so depleted that

Cotton picking, late nineteenth century

breeding animals were reduced below requirements for immediate restocking. Interestingly enough, the value of livestock reported in the census for the three periods remained almost constant, $5,553,356 in 1860; $5,212,157 in 1870, and $5,358,980 in 1880, due perhaps to declining prices as numbers increased.

As much of the interior had suffered nothing at the hands of the invaders, much of the decline in property value was due to wear and neglect when repairs and replacement were impossible. An even greater loss in the Middle Florida counties arose from loss of the labor supply occasioned by emancipation of slaves. Single family farmers who depended upon the labor of the family were in a much better position to carry on or restore production, but in many instances the head of the family had been killed or wounded.

The experiences of some persons whose careers in antebellum days we have described may profitably be followed through the war and its aftermath. The widow of Achille Murat found herself impoverished and driven to ask for commissary stores and medicines

Waiting their turn at the cotton gin, 1879

from the local military commander. She sold her jewels to provide for her own needs and encouraged ex-slaves to produce at least enough for their own subsistence. When the blacks offered her a gift of flour and other food at Christmas in 1866 she graciously declined. Two years after the war when Francis Fleming returned to Hibernia, he found deserters from the Union army in possession of his house and the whole place growing up in weeds and pine seedlings. Clearing the fields again was necessary before planting could be resumed. Francis Eppes, a grandson of Thomas Jefferson who had come to Leon County in 1827 and established himself successfully, moved away to Orange County in 1867 to occupy a rude cabin in an orange grove.

On El Destino and Chemonie plantations change came more

slowly. The blacks were excited and exuberant over the news of the end of the war and of their emancipation but they did not leave. Black foremen had replaced white overseers during the war. They had been producing more foodstuffs, tanning leather, and doing more millwork. Continuity was thus easier to maintain. Mrs. David L. Yulee, who also had a black overseer, wrote from the family plantation at Homasassa to her husband in prison on June 20, 1865: "The Negroes are not doing very well, but I will be patient, for I want to do them good. They will take some time to settle in their new condition."

In the summer of 1865 Whitelaw Reid, a New York newspaperman, accompanied Chief Justice Salmon P. Chase of the United States Supreme Court on an official tour of inspection in East Florida. In Fernandina he said rebels were returning and trying to recover their property that had been sold by treasury agents for taxes. In Jacksonville, principally a few brick warehouses and stores on a street facing the water, he reported blacks in uniform about the street and living in a neatly policed camp on a city square. General Israel Vogdes, the local Union military commander, still occupied the best home in town and his staff used the library and the billiard room. Black troops in Saint Augustine were on dress parade for Chase's visit. Not many rebels had yet returned. The region was producing little more than a bare subsistence. The wife of one absent ex-Confederate was doing a lively business in objects made of palmetto fibers. He felt there was not yet much change in planter-freedman relations. At Key West, Reid observed that this largest town in Florida had grown during the war but was still full of southern sympathizers, some of whom thought blacks ought to be put under state control. He observed many tropical plants and alien voices and had to remind himself that this was an American city.

The less developed parts of the state felt the effects of the war less and recovered more quickly. Late in 1865 Colonel Thomas W. Osborn, head of the Freedmen's Bureau in the state, sent out five teams to report on economic and social conditions. Only the report that covered South Florida has ever been found, but it covers a region about which relatively little is known. Colonel George T. Thompson, accompanied by William H. Gleason, a special agent of the Bureau, visited Hillsborough, Polk, Manatee, Monroe, Dade, Brevard, Orange, and Volusia counties. They traveled by rail to Tampa. There they conferred with civil and military officials and concluded that blacks were faring very well and northern men not being as badly treated as had been reported. They abandoned a plan to cross the peninsula on horseback and continued the journey southward on the Gulf coast to Charlotte Harbor, Peace Creek, the Manatee River, Fort Myers, and Estero Bay. They met many cattlemen in the employ of Jacob Summerlin. They found them living mostly in rude log houses that lacked windows. The visitors disliked their diet of fried pork, boiled potatoes, and hominy. The cattle they tended were being shipped mostly to Cuba but some to Savan-

nah and Charleston. On the coastal islands they discovered fishermen from Connecticut salting and drying fish, an occupation previously belonging almost exclusively to Cubans. At Key West they
found two schools for whites and one for blacks with a total of 160
pupils, whereas Tampa had two schools and half as many pupils.
Also at Key West were four churches for whites and one for blacks,
in contrast to three churches at Tampa, which had somewhat irregular services.

In Dade County they found only three blacks in need of Bureau
assistance. They estimated two hundred whites, living mostly on
the Keys, who exhibited a passion for wrecking and liquor. The
report mentions 600 Indians, but they had no contact with any of
them. The Seminoles were not so numerous and had no role whatever in the Civil War. The inspectors remained in Miami two weeks,
and Gleason later came back to be a resident for seventeen years.
They saw hides of deer, bear, panther, and other animals being
brought in and much coontie starch making. Others were engaged
in wrecking, fishing, turtling, and sponging. Oranges, lemons, limes,
bananas, coconuts, and grapes were growing. They observed a need
to drain the Everglades and Lake Okeechobee.

The matter of greatest concern everywhere in 1865 was the condition of the freedman so recently released from slavery. Emancipation left many blacks without any guidance or sense of direction.
They knew only that they did not wish to return to the conditions of
life and labor that they had known. Since slavery had imposed
strict limitations on their movements, freedom of travel became the
real test of their new status. They visited the previously forbidden
villages and towns or wandered about aimlessly, enjoying for the
moment freedom from restraint. The very young and the very old
were too often left to shift for themselves. But some of the harsh
realities of freedom were soon pressing. They had to work. Resort
to petty thievery could not long support them. Nor could they hope
to continue for long to be fed by the United States army or the
Freedmen's Bureau. In fact, both organizations used their influence to get them back to work on the plantations by helping them to
make contracts with landowners, almost the only employment open
to them. Public assistance under federal auspices saved many blacks
and whites from near starvation, but such help was never designed
to be more than temporary.

Caution should always be practiced in reading and assessing
accounts of black conduct during the war and Reconstruction. Early
in the conflict Governor Milton compared the loyalty and sense of
duty of slaves favorably to that of many whites. Every slaveholding
family reported loyal care by family servants during the war and
even after. That the slaves remained peaceably at work during the
war, which they must have known would determine their futures,
was a matter of frequent comment. It was too often interpreted as
acceptance and approval of the status of slavery. Such a conclusion
ignores the fact that they usually escaped the plantations when
Union armies came near during the war. Freedmen's Bureau agents

reported larger numbers of freedmen remaining on the plantations in the interior that had not been disturbed by the invading armies.

Inertia seems to have kept Florida blacks at work on the plantations during the conflict when civil insurrection on their part could have ended the war at any time. The explanation of their conduct probably lies in the fact that the institution of slavery had seemingly bred all of the initiative out of them and that the illiterate and superstitious people preferred the known with all of its hardships to the uncertainties of the unknown, however alluring it might sometimes appear. The same inertia plus kindly and reasonable treatment kept them on the plantations after the conflict had set them free.

Few white Floridians sought to escape the consequences of participation in the rebellion by leaving the country. Stephen R. Mallory, the only Floridian in the group fleeing with Jefferson Davis and his cabinet, was captured at La Grange, Georgia, before he reached his home state. Paroled in March 1866, he was the last of the Confederate cabinet to be released, apparently being held responsibile for the activities of privateersmen and commerce raiders in the Confederate service. When it seemed likely that fleeing Confederate leaders might try to escape by way of Florida, an aide of General William T. Sherman arrived at Key West on May 1 to organize the search for fugitives. He dispatched one vessel up the west coast to alert all officials and another to Key Biscayne to stand guard. Others cruised along the reef and among the keys on the lower Atlantic coast. A detachment of soldiers took a position at Cape Sable to watch for any effort to sail around the peninsula.

Federal pursuers captured Davis and postmaster Reagan at Irwinville, Georgia, on May 10, but missed Davis' papers and the fabled Confederate treasure, which had been sent ahead to David L. Yulee's "Cotton Wood" plantation near Gainesville. The pursuers later found remnants of the papers in several trunks and boxes at Baldwin, but the only money left was Confederate paper. On August 17, Lieutenant Hollis at Cape Sable captured seven persons, but none of them prominent. Meanwhile John C. Breckinridge and Judah P. Benjamin had made their ways separately into Middle Florida and later left by separate routes. Breckinridge appeared near Madison on May 15, made his way to Jupiter Inlet by June 3, and moved southward along the coast by boat, reaching Havana on June 12. Benjamin made his way to Bradenton disguised as a French farmer hunting land and engaged the services of Captain Frederick Tresca, a local boatsman who knew the coastal waters from long experience, to travel to Knight's Key (present-day Marathon); from there Benjamin took a heavier boat to Nassau and eventually made his way to England. Had Lieutenant Hollis remained a little longer at Cape Sable he might have bagged the cabinet member. George Davis, the last man to hold the post of attorney general in the Confederate cabinet, reached the home of a cousin south of Lake City on June 3 and hid out in north-central Florida for several months. He then made his way to Key West on October 18, but hearing that

Shade-grown tobacco grew in importance as cotton growing declined and cigar making increased

others like himself had already been released, he surrendered to the authorities there, only to be arrested and held prisoner until the end of the year.

The Freedmen's Bureau, whose role in political Reconstruction has already been related, came into being near the close of the war to meet the economic and social problems created by the large number of blacks who came into the Union army lines as they moved into the South. The Bureau continued during Reconstruction to assist in relief of the destitute, the establishment of new labor relations, and the organization of education and other services for the freedmen. The army personnel in the state exercised that function until September 1865 when Colonel Thomas W. Osborn, a former Union army officer, became assistant commissioner for the agency's affairs in Florida. Since he was rarely accused by white Floridians of favoring the freedmen, it is perhaps a reasonable conclusion that he used his office to induce the ex-slaves to make contracts and continue their labor on the farms.

First the army and then the Bureau agents distributed food to destitute freedmen and whites. Between June and December 1865 almost 80,000 rations were distributed. Between September 1866 and 1867 the Bureau reported dispensing 58,036 rations; 1,500 Floridians, a third of them whites, were still dependent upon the Bureau for half of the year. A poor cotton crop in 1867 raised the number of rations in the year 1868 to September to 59,216. Each ration included pork, bacon, beef, flour, corn meal, beans, peas, hominy, pepper, sugar, vinegar, candles, and soap. Not all Bureau agents were competent and honest, nor was the administration of policy uniform. Some agents took the side of freedmen, but more of them appear to have worked with white employers except in the matter of politics. They did not allow the agency to be used to support people who could be gainfully employed. The most severe critic of the Bureau was a black, John Wallace, who had been a slave in North Carolina until 1862, after which he served two and a half years in the Union army, was discharged at Key West, and made his way to Tallahasse. He served two terms in the lower house of the legislature and two in the senate. He had learned to write and was employed as a teacher by William D. Bloxham for the blacks on his plantation. In a book *Carpetbag Rule in Florida,* which Bloxham helped him to write, Wallace charged that army officers and Bureau agents treated blacks worse than local whites until they learned that the blacks could vote.

In addition to providing relief to the destitute and supervising the making and execution of contracts, the Bureau provided other services to the freedmen. The breaking up of customary relations with owners left freedmen without medical services. Late in 1865 the Bureau attempted to set up facilities for the freedmen in the larger towns and cities. Blacks rarely availed themselves of the medical aid, as they usually went to work in rural areas remote from urban centers and looked to their employers for assistance much as they had the slaveowners.

The educational efforts of the Bureau met with an enthusiastic reception by the freedmen and all persons interested in their education. As early as 1862 when the Union army occupied Fernandina, the Freedmen's Aid Society established a school there, but the significant growth came after the war ended. Funds and teachers at first came largely from northern philanthropic and religious groups, with some aid from tax sources later. The role of the Bureau was largely to coordinate the activity of the various groups and provide buildings to house the schools.

Public education was little developed in Florida before the war and what there was had largely disappeared during the conflict. An act of the legislature in 1866 authorized the state superintendent to draw the interest on the state school fund and send it to the county superintendents for the education of indigent white children. Black schools were to be supported by a tax of one dollar on all black men between the ages of twenty-one and forty-five, and a fee of fifty cents per pupil per month. Teachers had to be licensed by the state, and failure to do so made one liable to a $500 fine. The military authorities refused to allow this to be enforced in schools sponsored by the Freedmen's Bureau and supported by churches and philanthropic groups. The Constitution of 1868 authorized a uniform system of common schools, but it could not be financed and developed in so short a time. Nor was there any general demand for it. Not until January 30, 1869, did the legislature provide for a comprehensive school law. In 1870 Governor Reed reported that more than 200 schools had been established and 7,000 pupils enrolled. Eighty-seven school buildings had been provided by the Freedmen's Bureau. In 1876 the state was spending $158,846.36 on 28,444 pupils in 676 public schools. In 1872 Reed called for the establishment of a college of agriculture under the Morrill Land Grant Act of 1862, but failed to find sufficient support to initiate such an undertaking.

In 1866 and 1868 the legislature requested the governor to acquire from the United States government the buildings of the old military arsenal at Chattahoochee to be used as a state prison. In 1868 Governor Reed secured the use of the property on a loan basis, and started the remodeling to accommodate an estimated three hundred prisoners. In the same year the legislature authorized the commissioner of public institutions to lease prisoners at his discretion. In 1870 Governor Reed urged that more prisoners be leased to relieve crowding at the unfinished facility. In 1872 the Congress approved the transfer of the prison to the state, but financing its operations required more money than the state was willing to provide. In 1874 a law set aside a section of the prison as an asylum for the insane committed by the courts.

Other social problems received equally grudging attention. A law of 1866 required children to care for their aged parents. On January 1, 1869, when the Freedmen's Bureau referred twenty old and destitute blacks to the governor's office for help, he sent them to the Chattahoochee prison. The legislature in 1872 charged the county commissioners with the responsibility to provide for the poor and indigent in their counties. The legislature in 1866 appropriated $5,000 to purchase artificial limbs for crippled veterans and empowered county commissioners to levy a tax to support disabled veterans, widows, and orphans, but the act was not renewed the next year. A public accommodations law in 1873 antedated by two years the Civil Rights Act of 1875, which would have done the same thing at the national level, but nothing tangible came of either law in Florida.

Freedmen's Savings Banks chartered by Congress in March 1865 to receive and hold in trust the savings of ex-slaves were not a part of the Bureau, but Colonel Osborn advertised them and paid the rent on buildings used for that purpose. A branch opened in Jacksonville in March 1866 and another in Tallahassee in August of the next year. In 1874 they both failed, partly due to poor management but more because they were caught in the depression which followed the panic of 1873. The 766 depositors lost $30,610.35 in Tallahassee and 1,608 lost $39,400 in Jacksonville. The greatest loss may well have been in the habits of saving and thrift the sponsors aimed to develop among the freedmen.

The Bureau also assisted freedmen to take up land under the Homestead Act of 1866. This law ended all cash sales in five public land states of the South and reserved the land for homesteaders until January 1, 1867. Since ex-Confederates were ineligible, only the freedmen and loyal white immigrants could receive the eighty-acre farms. Bureau agents helped to locate suitable tracts and provided transportation and subsistence for as much as one month. The land office opened in Florida in August 1866 and in two years over 3,000 blacks had filed claims. By October 1876 when the law was repealed they held only 2,012 homesteads for a total of 160,960 acres. The lands available were relatively poor and the cost of moving and establishing farms was prohibitive. White people, fearing black domination of the state, resenting the closing of the lands to themselves, and actively opposing black ownership of property, often intimidated them with the result that they abandoned the homesteads or sold them to whites.

The existence in Florida of large bodies of federal and state lands gave rise to other projects that involved blacks. On January 1, 1866, General Osborn proposed to General Oliver O. Howard, the national head of the Freedmen's Bureau, a plan to colonize freedmen in Florida. He suggested that the United States acquire from Florida the land, mostly characterized as swamp and overflowed, south of the twenty-eighth parallel, in the counties of Hillsborough, Brevard, Manatee, Monroe, Dade, and Polk and give it territorial organization and government. In the tropical climate he envisioned the production of tropical fruits, cattle raising supplemented with fishing, and forest industries carried on by owners of eighty-acre homesteads. This would provide a home for the surplus freed people in all of the states. There they could learn the responsibilities of property holders and self-government.

An earlier scheme proposed during the war was attributed to Eli Thayer of Massachusetts, who had supported the work of the New England Emigrant Aid Society in its effort to plant anti-slave settlers in Kansas in the decade preceding the war. He proposed to confiscate the lands of the disloyal, give the homesteads to loyal men, and apprentice slaves to them. He wanted to send 50,000 white volunteer soldiers to win the state for the Union and set up a loyal government. The discharged northern soldiers would then create an ideal Yankee community with "forges, factories and schoolhouses." One supporter thought it at least as justifiable as the Armed Occupation Act of 1842 designed to win the land from the Seminole Indians.

W. H. Hunt, a Virginian, proposed that the Bureau build some mills in Florida on government land. He would operate the mills for the Bureau, he said, and provide income to a thousand freedmen and their families provided they were placed on lands of his selection under the homestead law. Another Virginian, Orlando

Brown, proposed to General Howard a plan to invite up to 50,000 Virginia blacks to Florida and other public land states. It was this proposal that prompted Howard to order the survey of public lands in Florida conducted by Thompson and Gleason at the end of 1866.

Timber was the real prize at stake in many land deals during the Reconstruction era. The beneficiaries were not homesteaders, black or white, but influential men of all parties in the corrupt state government. Indeed, if the state lands had not been pledged as security for bonds sold by the Florida Railroad on the eve of the war, much of them might have been disposed of fraudulently. In March 1870 the trustees of the Internal Improvement Fund, the managers of state lands, conveyed to the New York and Florida Lumber Company 1,000,000 acres of land at ten cents an acre paid largely with depreciated scrip, whereupon the holders of the now defaulted railroad bonds, to protect their interest in state lands, secured an injunction against such sales. In February 1871, in defiance of the court order, the trustees planned to transfer another 1,360,000 acres to the Southern Inland Navigation Company, of which the governor and other public officials were directors. Justice William B. Woods from an Alabama district, sitting in place of Philip Fraser of the Federal District Court of North Florida, who was frequently absent from the bench because of illness, voided the transaction and put the Internal Improvement Fund in the hands of a receiver to protect the interests of the railroad bondholders and, incidentally, the people of Florida.

Some new device was needed to bring land and labor together to produce crops, but it was not to come from any government agency's action. Neither the white man nor the freedman understood the workings of a wage labor system even if there had been money with which to pay the wages. Some attempts to use black overseers worked very well but did not solve the problem of scarce capital. Nor did a wage system work well for northern men who had the capital but were unfamiliar with the management of black labor and cotton growing. In time the native white landlords and the propertyless workers, black or white, worked out in experience a new labor system known as "sharecropping," which, though not unique in the country, had a special meaning in the cotton South. The landlord had land worthless without cultivators. The freedmen and some whites had only their labor and that of their families. Landlords and workers entered into agreements to produce crops and share the proceeds. These contracts also became the basis for credit needed to finance the farming operations. Crop liens made it possible to borrow money on the unplanted crops. The sharecrop system and the abuses to which it was so easily open have rightly been condemned, but it is difficult to see what else could have been done at the time without the intervention of government with large amounts of capital and credit. The tragedy is that the system remained unchanged for two generations, in spite of the fact that it not only impoverished the tenants but made neither the landlord nor the region prosperous. It is at least arguable that the sharecropper enjoyed a greater measure of security than his successor, the migrant laborer. A personal relationship and a paternalism on the part of some landlords that was feudal rather than modern was associated with it. Fortunately, Florida escaped the worst effects of dependence upon cotton produced by sharecroppers but was to have a large share of the migrant labor problem in fruit and vegetable growing.

In sharp contrast to political fortune hunters were the economic carpetbaggers who came seeking homes and investments. They were sought out, encouraged, and welcomed as long as they stayed out of the political war. Some of them were Union soldiers who had seen opportunity while campaigning in Florida; others reasoned that men with capital might do better with the new labor system.

Ambrose Hart came from Duchess County, New York, in 1866 looking for a promising investment and reported on the local scene

The Oklawaha River, now well known as one of the last great wilderness waterways, was the scene of logging operations in the 1880s.

in letters to his father. He saw a great future in winter farming for the New York market. The soil "beat anything for sand" but seemed to produce good crops. Orange fever in the Saint Johns area was highly prevalent and speculatively contagious. Jacksonville was full of Union men, and former soldiers were settling on homesteads along the railroads. Hart joined forces with S. B. Thompson, a local man, in the logging business. They, like others, purchased land on a creek tributary to a navigable stream at $1.25 an acre. They cut the felled trees into logs and hauled them by high-wheeled carts to the water's edge; there they were formed into rafts to be floated downstream to sawmills owned mostly by Yankees. The partners turned to cotton growing in 1868. Hart thought the lack of banking facilities, the high price of supplies, and the unreliability of labor were holding back business.

Banking was largely private for at least a decade after the war. Some of those engaged in private banking later organized groups to charter state or national banks. There were four private banks in Jacksonville, two at Pensacola, and one each in Apalachicola, Fernandina, Key West, and Gainesville. The first bank south of Jacksonville on the mainland was started at Palatka in 1881. National banks could be established in cities of not less than 6,000 with a minimum capital stock of $50,000. In 1874 James M. Schumacher of Mohawk, New York, who later became treasurer of the United States, two of his sons-in-law, and a number of other New Yorkers opened the first national bank in Florida at Jacksonville. In 1880 it had deposits of $157,023 and loans of $128,556. When economic recovery was speeded up after 1880 banking services became more adequate.

Railroad history in the first fifteen years after the war reflects both the slowness of economic recovery and the level of politics at the time. The manipulation of railroad stocks and bonds by Carpetbag and Scalawag politicians with some participation by conservatives as well resulted in little new building, only about sixteen miles being added, and little improvement of the existing roads and their services.

The story of the Florida railroads was not different from that in most other states. Late in 1868 and early in 1869 the state sold three railroads that had defaulted on state-endorsed bonds. The Florida Atlantic and Gulf Central Railroad from Lake City to Tallahassee went for $110,000 and was reorganized as the Florida Central. The Pennsylvania and Georgia from Lake City to Quincy and the Tallahassee from that city to Saint Marks brought $1,415,000. The first two were then organized in June 1869 as the Jacksonville, Pensacola and Mobile; its capital stock of $6,000,000 was held by George Swepson and Milton S. Littlefield. They had fled North Carolina, where they sold bonds ostensibly to expand the Western North Carolina Railroad, but took some of the money instead to buy into Florida railroads. They bought the bonds of the bankrupt lines at about a third of their value and used them to pay the purchase price, and when they still lacked cash to make full payment they gave a bad check for $472,065. The General Assembly in January 1870 authorized the exchange of thirty-year state bonds for railroad bonds in the amount of $16,000 a mile to complete, equip, and maintain the company's lines. Littlefield, who had bought out his partner's interest, received $4,000,000 in bonds, which he sold in Europe at an average of seventy cents on the dollar. He spent only $308,938 on the roads, another $350,000 to make his peace with North Carolina authorities, and distributed much of the remainder to Florida supporters. Governor Reed, who had been director in one of the companies, was alleged to have been among those paid off. It should also be noted that voting on the railroad question was usually bipartisan in both houses during the two sessions of the legislature. The state later seized the railroads when the debt was declared unconstitutional and sold them for the benefit of Dutch stockholders, the Pensacola and Georgia for $305,000 and the Tallahassee for $50,000.

On the Florida Railroad, the terminal facilities at Cedar Key and Fernandina had been destroyed in 1862, and much damage occurred at Baldwin when the federals passed through on the way to Olustee in early 1864. From Baldwin eastward the rails had been taken up to build the connecting line from Live Oak to Dupont, Georgia; at the close of the war the road had only five engines, three of which were unusable. Nine boxcars, twelve flat cars, and two dilapidated coaches made up the rolling stock. A blacksmith shop at Gainesville served as a repair shop. Except on the mileage between Baldwin and Gainesville, bridges and trestles, some of them extensive near the coast, when they had not been burned were too rotten to be usable and needed to be replaced. Crossties were also rotted and the soft rails bent because of lack of support. The soft metal in the rails also resulted in "snake heads" when the ends bent upward with obvious results if the heads were raised too high. The remedy was to heat the rails and straighten them by pounding with hammers.

Barely enough work was done in the first decade to keep the trains running. By mid-April 1866, work trains on the Florida Railroad were running as far west as Gainesville. One difficulty was the uncertain financial status. In October 1866 the trustees of the Internal Improvement Fund sold the road for $323,400 to Isaac K. Roberts, acting for Edward N. Dickerson and Associates, who had financed its building in the late fifties. Reorganized and named the Atlantic, Gulf and West Indian Transit Company, the new owners added two locomotives, but not until the years between 1876 and 1881 was the line rebuilt in an effective fashion. The next decade would witness a railroad building boom.

Some of the political support for railroad financing that turned sour was due to the belief in the importance of the services to general economic recovery. *The Gainesville Bee* of December 9, 1881, reported on the situation at that date. At Baldwin, lines from Lake City, Fernandina, Jacksonville, and Cedar Key intersected. Several side tracks led to sawmills, warehouses, and turpentine stills.

Fuel for the engines was piled on wood racks. As the trains moved across the state the passengers hardly ever lost sight of stacks of lumber and piles of sawdust along the right-of-way. At Waldo was a junction with the Peninsular Railroad, operating trains from Jacksonville to Wildwood; Waldo at the time had 500 inhabitants, several stores, a boardinghouse, and a neat little park and bandstand near the depot. At Gainesville, the county seat of Alachua, were some three thousand people, numerous stores, a cottonseed mill, two depots, and the East Florida Seminary. Six miles beyond Gainesville was Arredondo, described as the "boss vegetable station," and Archer, the next stop, had five or six stores.

Another obvious sign of recovery as the war years receded farther into the past was the revival of tourism. Whitelaw Reid had predicted that Florida might again be used as a "grand national sanitarium." The number of hotels increased and people with large houses began to cater to visitors. At "Hibernia," Margaret Fleming offered rooms at the plantation house and cottage which could accommodate thirty-five persons at $2.50 a day or $15.00 a week. Daniel G. Brinton described it in 1869, and William D. Kelly in 1875 mentioned it as a place he visited. Ledyard Bill in 1869 thought the spirit of the people excellent. They were busy making a living, he said, and welcomed newcomers who came with other than political motives. But Kelly thought Floridians needed an infusion of northern energy and spirit. It was he who provided the oft-quoted reply to his inquiry as to how Floridians made a living: "We live on sweet potatoes and consumptive Yankees," and "we sell atmosphere."

William Cullen Bryant, who had been in Florida in 1843, returned thirty years later and reported on the local scene to the *New York Evening Post.* Palatka, he wrote, was still largely a forest. Jacksonville was thriving, with four thousand people and two new hotels, both full. Saint Augustine had some new homes and two new hotels, with orange trees growing everywhere. The northern invasion was under way! Invalids and idlers came by tramroad from Tocoi, south of Picolata, in carriages drawn by mules. He predicted that in time only the old fort would remain to remind one of the past. He visited Green Cove Springs and went up the Oklawaha to Silver Springs and Ocala. Two hotels at Silver Springs, one at Magnolia, and two at Palatka were full, and though the accommodations at Saint Augustine had been doubled over the previous year, they were also full. He predicted a rosy future for the sunshine state.

General Robert E. Lee made his third visit to Florida in 1870. The final visit was part of an extended tour in search of health. He visited Cumberland Island, where his father had died on the way home from the British West Indies and was buried. The party ascended the Saint Johns nearly to Palatka to visit the home of Colonel Robert G. Cole, after which they turned northward. Beyond favorable comments on the climate, the fish, the oranges, and the beautiful estates on the river front, he gave little impression of what he saw.

A more significant type of visitor was beginning to come to Florida. In 1876, Henry A. DeLand, a manufacturer from New York, toured the upper Saint Johns area, bought land, and founded the community that bears his name. Another northern manufacturer later came to DeLand to found the school that bears his name, the John B. Stetson University. General Henry S. Sanford, a former minister to Belgium, acquired a large tract on the southern shore of Lake Monroe near old Fort Mellon, planted groves, invited settlers, and gave his name to the town. The era of the developers was about to begin.

Fort Jefferson, remote from the more populated parts of Florida, was the scene of activities not too closely related to the state. During the war it became a prison and one prisoner, Dr. Samuel A. Mudd, gave it a dramatic touch. Born in 1833 into a Maryland plantation and slaveholding family, he became a physician practicing in Charles County, a short distance from Washington, D.C. On the night that John Wilkes Booth shot President Lincoln, Booth fled southward in the night and appeared in disguise at Dr. Mudd's residence to have the leg set that he had broken when he jumped from the box onto the stage of the theater. After military trials conducted in less than a month, four persons implicated were condemned to death. Dr. Mudd, though he came forward at once with what information he could provide, and three others were sentenced to life imprisonment, and the doctor was sent to Fort Jefferson.

The first contingent of prisoners had arrived in 1861 and there were at times as many as 1,400 men in the fort and on the adjacent islands, nearly half of them prisoners. Dr. Mudd arrived on July 24, 1865, and soon became a nurse and acting steward in the post hospital. When he attempted to escape he was put under heavy guard and no longer worked in the hospital. Then on August 18, the dread scourge of yellow fever struck the prison fortress, spreading terror among the inmates, 270 of whom contracted it. Fifty-eight died, among them the fort's surgeon, leaving the post without a doctor. Dr. Mudd resumed the role of physician and worked day and night for the relief of the ill. Dr. Daniel W. Whitehurst came from Key West to take over the responsibility for medical care, but Mudd continued to work with him. By the summer of 1867 not more.than fifty prisoners remained, but Mudd was not released until March 11, 1869, made a free man by the pardon from President Andrew Johnson. He returned to Maryland, where he died on January 10, 1885.

18.

The Bourbon Era

The results of the election of 1876 meant the end of radical Republican congressional Reconstruction and the return of political control in state and local affairs to native white Democrats in Florida, Louisiana, and South Carolina, the last of the Confederate states to be "redeemed" from Carpetbag-Scalawag-black government. This meant a return in some respects to the white leadership that had led the state into secession and war and guided its destinies in the brief period of presidential Reconstruction, but there were also new elements in it. This leadership in the post Civil War South is commonly called Bourbon. If in the French Bourbon tradition this meant that they had forgotten nothing and had learned nothing, it is a serious misnomer. The Florida leadership shared in the romantic if not the realistic devotion to the lost cause and everything associated with it, but the men who exercised the political power had learned a great deal. They had felt the power of the national government in war and Reconstruction. They did not lose sight of the fact that they might again bring it down upon themselves. They acknowledged that slavery could not be restored. It is doubtful that any considerable number wished that it might, but few of them had changed their minds about the black and the subordinate role he should play in the society. They now, however, had to have more regard for the federal constitution and world opinion. As individuals they had little fear of economic or social equality of the races. From a secure social position and as the only employers of black labor they confidently expected to control the political future of the state, even to use the black to that end. The effort to reclaim the state from Republican control had drawn all whites into an unnatural political alliance that forced any dissenting whites to accept their leadership for another quarter of a century.

The Bourbons had learned another lesson of far-reaching importance. The agrarian society they deemed superior had proved itself inadequate for purposes of war when pitted against a society in the early stages of industrial development. That the future lay in new economic directions was already becoming clear, and by the end of the congressional phase of Reconstruction the leaders of the ex-Confederate states were committed to outdoing the Yankees at their own game of industrial development. Progress in the future meant railroads and factories and cities, not immediately in Florida, but as rapidly as political encouragement could bring in the capital and people needed to develop them. Every governor's administration since the Civil War has made increased efforts and promised more in this direction. Florida was on the way to becoming a typical southern cotton state in 1860, but changed that course before it was fully realized and became less a southern prototype as time went on.

The transition from Republican to Democratic political control was not as sharp as it has commonly been described. Republican control was never absolute and never meant black control. Sharp factionalism among the Republicans weakened them. Moderate Republican leadership in cooperation with Democrats controlled the state government from 1870 to 1877 and it was Republican in name only. There had been some extravagance in appropriations for internal improvements financed by bond issues, but Democrats had supported it, and before 1877 most of the state's debt was funded. Since the excess was repudiated it had never cost Floridians a great deal. There were fewer Republicans in state government after Reconstruction than there had been Democrats in the Republican era, but there was relatively little policy change. In fact many of the leaders like Governor Drew were ex-Whigs who but for the Civil War issues might easily have become Republican. In some states the coalition of whites called themselves Conservatives rather than Democrats.

Republicans had started organized efforts to attract capital and settlers, had brought order into state finances, had encouraged large scale development, and had even proposed to lease state convicts to private employers. Nor had the constitutional and statutory provision for education and other public services ever been implemented; nor yet was there any protest from those allegedly deprived of educational opportunity. The day of tax supported public education lay at least a generation in the future.

The Bourbon blueprint for state development was fairly simple. Government activity and costs had to be kept at a minimum and taxes correspondingly low with no incubus of state debt. Government encouragement but never restraint was offered to those who would invest their money and look for their futures in the state. Bourbons maintained an image of economy and honesty in contrast to the previous regime and could be accused of extravagance only in the wanton fashion in which they offered the state's natural resources for development and exploitation. They gave lip service rather than substance to their endorsement of public education, but in so doing they reflected the attitude of most of the people of the state. The Florida Agriculture College, to be located at Eau Gallie, for political reasons was never finished and never opened there. It was later located at Lake City.

Their critics differed from the Bourbons largely in the means rather than the objectives they sought. Principally the critics ob-

Steamboats were bringing visitors to Silver Springs by the 1880s

jected to granting the state's land resources to developers and railroad builders rather than to individuals and to the total absence of regulation of railroads and other public utilities. They complained of machine politics but were unwilling to pursue a more representative form of government at the cost of black participation. In short, Bourbonism had its constructive features, and its critics differed only in means and degrees. Florida had to be developed, any differences were in the means used to do so A casual review of economic and political developments for the next quarter century, aptly called "the era of the developers," reflects clearly the effort to convert the blueprint into a reality.

In his message to the legislature on January 10, 1877, Governor Drew proved himself a true Bourbon when he said: "That government will be most highly esteemed that gives the greatest protection to individual and industrial enterprises at the least expense to the tax payer . . . the simple truths that have been the basis of nearly all personal success in business can be equally well applied to state finances. Spend nothing unless absolutely necessary and pay all bills when made, or at the earliest point thereafter."

Drew and the conservative Democrats set themselves to work at the task of reducing the costs of state government. They found the salaries of the top executive and judicial offices fixed in the constitution at a total of $44,500 a year. A self-denying amendment in 1879 reduced the salary of the governor from $5,000 to $3,500, the chief justice of the state supreme court from $4,500 to $3,000, and others proportionately. Other budget items had averaged $236,755 annually for several years, and $220,000 had been appropriated in 1876. Drew recommended that the pruning knife be used with "a fearless and impartial hand." He again called attention to the $40,000 yearly cost of the state penitentiary and urged that the convicts be leased to private employers who would feed, clothe, and work them and pay an annual fee to the state. A law authorizing such leases reduced costs to the state to $4,600 in 1878, but left unanswered many questions about prisons as correctional institutions.

In the matters of debt management and tax reduction, Drew and his associates overdid the economizing. By 1879 the governor could report that the floating debt was reduced from $250,000 to $65,000 and the bonded debt to $1,284,000. In another two years the bonded debt was down by another $50,000 and the floating debt was only $30,000. Current operating expenses fell from $212,530.31 in 1877 to $133,970.36 in 1878. When the legislature in 1877 failed to reduce the 12 1/2 mill ad valorem tax on property, the governor by executive order reduced it to ten and in August 1878 to nine. When he asked the legislature in 1879 to approve the reduction, the lawmakers outdid him and lowered the rate to seven mills and dropped the bond retirement tax enacted first in the Republican Stearns' administration. As a result the Drew administration wound up some $100,000 in the red, and in his last message Drew warned the legislature against unrealistic tax policy.

Now that normal relations with the national government were restored, the governor revived the state's claim on the national government for reimbursement of Seminole War expenditures amounting to about $250,000 and accumulated interest in the final phase of that struggle in 1855 to 1859. That issue dragged along until 1903 when the state received $700,000 in settlement.

In other than debt and tax reduction the legislators tended to ignore the governor's recommendations, which included statewide uniformity in assessment and taxation, reform of election laws, and a state board of health. Drew, though a newcomer to the state, had been everything Bourbons could desire, but they refused to renominate him. This was not repudiation of his leadership but recognition of the expediency that led to his nomination four years earlier. They no longer needed him. The leader of the Florida Democrats was William D. Bloxham, who had finally been declared the winner to the contested election for lieutenant governor in 1870. Drew, an ex-Whig, had been selected as a compromise candidate who could

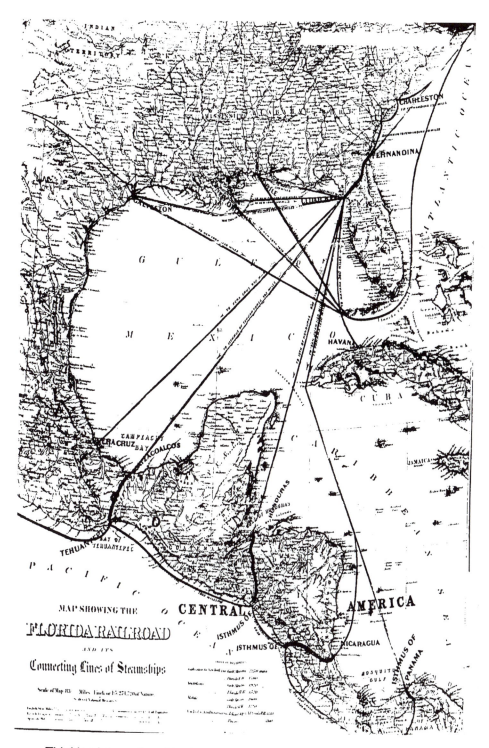

Thinking international in the 1870s! Railroad lines from Fernandina to Cedar Key and steamship lines from that port and Key West

win the support of all factions of whites in 1876. The names of Samuel Pasco and General Edward A. Perry were also placed in nomination at the Democratic convention in Gainesville on July 10, but Bloxham won the required majority of votes on the third ballot.

Republicanism was by no means dead in Florida. In 1878 Horatio Bisbee of Jacksonville and Senator Simon B. Conover conducted a spirited campaign for the state's two congressional seats. Conover received the support of northern settlers interested in politics and of some wealthy northern Republicans. R. H. M. Davidson easily defeated Conover, but Bisbee won over Lieutenant Governor Noble Hull in a contested election settled in the national House of Representatives in January 1881. Democrat Wilkinson Call won over conservative Bourbon General Robert Bullock in the election to the United States Senate seat vacated by Conover. In 1880 Republicans selected Conover to run for governor. He had withdrawn in favor of Stearns in 1876, but he meant to lead Florida back into the Republican ranks this time. Bloxham carried thirty-three of thirty-nine counties and won by 28,378 to 23,297. Davidson returned to the House, but Bisbee won again in a contested election that gained the seat for him over General Jesse J. Finley on June 1, 1882.

In his inaugural address Bloxham abandoned the retrenchment and reform theme and stressed the need for immigrants, transportation, and education to achieve growth and prosperity for the state. His administration was marked by recovery from the economic doldrums resulting from the uncertainties of political Reconstruction and the panic of 1873. To correct the inadequacies of the revenue policy of the previous administration, the legislature in 1881 increased the millage to eight and provided for higher assessment of property. Improved economic conditions permitted a reduction to seven mills a year later and to five in 1883 and four in 1884. The assessed value of property rose from $31,500,000 in 1881 to $70,677,000 four years later, and the bonded debt was reduced to $524,000, all held in several state trust funds, and Bloxham left a balance of $50,000 in the state treasury. Much of the flnancial success arose from adding to the tax roll $3,700,000 of railroad property that had been enjoying exemption under the interpretation of an act of 1855. General Edward A. Perry took the state's case to the United States Supreme Court before the exemption was voided.

Bloxham faced a severe financial crisis involving title to public lands that constituted the state's most valuable asset. The trustees of the Internal Improvement Fund had pledged these lands to underwrite railroad bonds on the eve of the Civil War. When the railroads failed, their property reverted to the state, but when sold the sum realized fell short by almost one million dollars of the amount necessary to pay principal and accumulated interest on the debt, and the lands remained mortgaged. In spite of the best efforts of Governors Stearns and Drew, both of whom had sent agents to Europe in an effort to make large scale land sales, the debt continued to grow by about $70,000 a year of interest due.

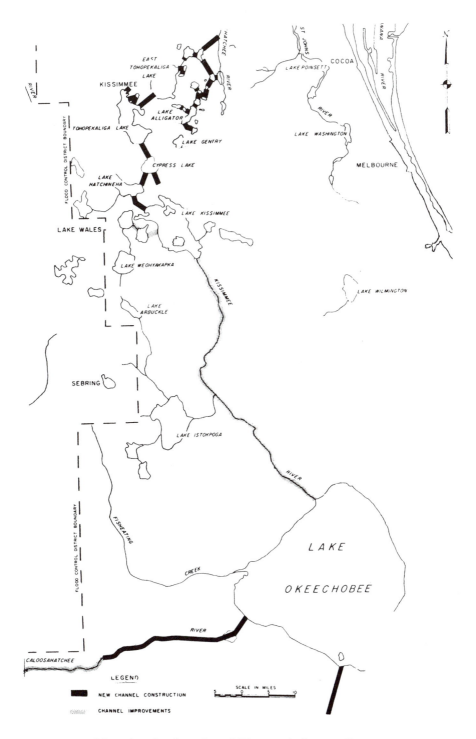

RIVER

ST. JOHNS

INDIAN

COCOA

LAKE POINSETT

RIVER

HATCHEE

RIVER

EAST
TOHOPEKALIGA
LAKE

KISSIMMEE

LAKE WASHINGTON

LAKE
ALLIGATOR

TOHOPEKALIGA LAKE

LAKE GENTRY

MELBOURNE

FLOOD CONTROL DISTRICT BOUNDARY

CYPRESS LAKE

LAKE
HATCHINEHA

LAKE KISSIMMEE

LAKE WALES

LAKE WEOHYAKAPKA

LAKE WILMINGTON

KISSIMMEE

LAKE
ARBUCKLE

SEBRING

LAKE ISTOKPOGA

RIVER

FISHEATING

FLOOD CONTROL DISTRICT BOUNDARY

LAKE

CREEK

OKEECHOBEE

RIVER

CALOOSAHATCHEE

LEGEND

NEW CHANNEL CONSTRUCTION

SCALE IN MILES

CHANNEL IMPROVEMENTS

Map showing location of Disston drainage efforts

Bondholders had become alarmed during the years of Republican government when the trustees began disposing of state lands at ridiculously low prices paid partly in depreciated scrip. Associated with the sales were commitments to do reclamation and bring in settlers, none of which was being accomplished. The real interest of the purchasers was the virgin timber, which they proceeded immediately to cut. In 1870 Francis Vose, an original investor in bonds of the Florida Railroad, which he accepted in payment for railroad iron, secured a court order forbidding payment for land in anything but United States money. When land sales continued without any payments to creditors, Vose and his associates had the lands placed in receivership, after which sales could be made only with consent of bondholders. Vose bought up other claims and threatened to take over the lands or to force a public sale.

Florida's good fairy in this crisis proved to be Hamilton Disston of the Philadelphia tool-making family, who had visited Florida primarily to fish with his good friend Henry S. Sanford. In 1881 Disston contracted with the trustees to drain land in return for one-half of the acreage he could reclaim. When it became apparent that Vose and the court would not approve transfer of land under the contract, Governor Bloxham induced Disston to purchase 4,000,000 acres of land at twenty-five cents an acre to provide funds to pay the bondholders and clear the title to state lands.

Governor Bloxham never doubted the wisdom of the sale, but it earned him much criticism. The price was too low, and the rights of squatters and homesteaders were not recognized. Disston had been allowed to select much land that wasn't actually swampy or overflowed. Finally, big interests were again being favored. Actually squatters had two years in which to acquire the land on which they were living at $1.25 an acre, the price fixed for preempted land by the state and the national governments, a not inconsiderable sum for a Florida squatter. The alternatives to the sale if the state's interest in the land was to be protected were to raise an impossibly large sum by taxation or to have the state authorized to sell new bonds to raise the money, neither of which was ever seriously suggested. Otherwise, even if the bondholders did not seize or sell the lands, they would remain encumbered and unavailable to subsidize canal, railroad, and reclamation projects whose promoters were clamoring for state aid.

Disston sold half of his purchased land to Sir Edward J. Reed, M.P., famous for engineering and construction projects for the Japanese and Russian governments. Reed had become interested in Florida through Jacobus Wertheim, attorney for Dutch bondholders in the Florida Railroad, and through efforts of Florida's agents to sell him a large acreage at about the time of the Disston sale. Reed soon withdrew from this interest in Florida and left the field to American developers.

To execute the drainage contract, Disston assembled a dredge at Kissimmee, then only a cow camp on Lake Tohopekaliga, and dredged canals to Cypress, Hatchineha, and Kissimmee lakes to the headwaters of the Kissimmee River. Another canal from Lake Tohopekaliga to East Tohopekaliga to expedite the flow of water into Lake Okeechobee made possible settlements at Saint Cloud, Runnymeade, and Ashton. The dredge men then straightened and deepened the Kissimmee River, which meandered in an almost impossible fashion in the marshy swamp. Another dredge working on the upper Caloosahatchee was being used to make easier the flow of water from the big lake to the Gulf of Mexico. The workers cleared the river to Fort Thompson, where they blasted and dug out the falls there that held back a ten-foot head of water in Lake Flirt. Digging on through Lettuce, Bonnet, and Hicpochee lakes, the channel tapped Lake Okeechobee at Moore Haven. Only then did the Caloosahatchee have its origin by way of a canal in the big lake.

For his drainage efforts Disston eventually received 1,652,711 acres for his half of land reclaimed. A legislative investigation in 1885 concluded that he had permanently drained no more than 50,000 acres. Disston defended himself by pointing out that between 1881 and 1885 he had made forty miles of canal and river improvement at a cost of $250,000 and had actually drained more land than he claimed. At any rate he had demonstrated that the water level could be lowered and that when the water was removed the land would produce crops. He had also demonstrated the enormously complex nature of the drainage problem and the likelihood that it could not be accomplished by private capital.

First passenger train, St. Johns and Halifax Railway, into Daytona Beach, 1886.

Steamboat trafffc was now possible from Kissimmee to Lake Okeechobee and out to the Gulf of Mexico by way of the Caloosahatchee. Disston was aware of the importance of a cross-state waterway and had dreams if not actual plans for a connection with the upper Saint Johns that would open the way to realizing the dream. He was also aware of the importance of the railroad, which did not reach Kissimmee until 1911 where it made the town a flourishing port. He had plans for a railroad to the Gulf.

His principal interest in the streams and lakes was drainage of his extensive lands. To further expedite the flow of water from Lake Okeechobee, which was really a shallow depression in a huge natural drainage system, he planned a canal southward from the lake to the headwaters of Shark River, a distance of some seventy miles. In the face of two surveys that raised questions about the feasibility of the project, a dredge started from present-day Lake Harbor and dug southward a dozen miles, following the streambed of the small Ritta River, where it encountered hard rock that the dredge could not handle. Here as in the other instances his vision exceeded his capability for accomplishment. It is interesting to speculate on what a difference it would have made if the excess lake water had been carried away by way of the canal to the present Everglades National Park, a means now being sought to provide water for the Park.

Disston moved in many ways to develop his property and attract settlers. He persuaded the United States Department of Agriculture to establish an experiment station near Saint Cloud, where by 1891 some thirty varieties of sugarcane were introduced. Experiments under his direction also included the production of rice, potatoes, peaches, grapes, pineapples, vegetables, and cattle. He planned settlement of families as well as land sales. On Lake Constance near Orlando he designed a settlement for some 250 families, to whom he sold twenty to eighty acres at $1.25 to $5.00 an acre. He hoped to achieve success and permanence for the venture by requiring that they each have a thousand dollars of capital with which to get started, and gave them every possible assistance in selecting suitable crops and nursery stock. In partnership with R. E. Rose, who brought knowledge of sugar making from Louisiana, he established a huge sugar mill and made extensive plantings of sugarcane. What the future may have held under Disston's vigorous direction was never to be known. The panic of 1893 brought the enterprise to a temporary halt, and his untimely death in his fifty-second year precluded their continuance. His family had never favored the project and sold the property for a fraction of its potential worth for someone else to reap the profits of development.

Railroads were the principal beneficiaries of state assistance during the benevolent rule of the Bourbons. By the end of the Bloxham administration the state had received from the federal government 15,686,243 acres of land. Including the Disston lands, over 10,300,000 acres had been disposed of, leaving about half that amount. The grants made by his and succeeding legislatures in ninety-two acts between 1879 and 1899 amounted to considerably more acreage than the state ever possessed. Fortunately, perhaps, many of the projects for which grants-in-aid were made never got beyond the paper stage of qualifying. Florida railroads also received 2,200,000 acres from the United States before the end of the century. Originally state grants were limited to alternate sections on both sides of the road six miles deep, but beginning in 1879 the legislature approved grants beyond the six-mile limit. Ultimately many grants were made in areas remote from the area served directly by the railroads.

Whatever may be said of the cost, the policies of Drew and Bloxham did promote settlement and development. The same policies generated opposition directed at the Disston sale, the Disston drainage contract, developers of railroads and other corporations, and the Bourbon leadership. Bloxham conceded nothing to his detractors and pointed proudly to the 776 miles of railroad built and put into operation, which, added to the 537 miles in operation in 1881, gave the state 1,313 miles of railroad in operation and another 224 miles graded and ready for crossties and rails.

The Disston land sale and the freeing of the public lands from the claims of earlier railroad building opened the way to a quarter of a century of railroad building that extended well beyond the Bourbon control of state government. In the Drew administration new construction was limited to three short lines that totaled only ninety miles, but in the Bloxham era the state legislature chartered new lines rapidly, most of them relatively short. They were, however, by the end of the era consolidated into five main systems that formed the pattern of railway ownership and operations since that time.

In 1877 the Louisville & Nashville Company acquired several lines in southern Alabama, including the Pensacola Railroad, successor to the Florida and Alabama, which was rebuilt to Flomaton, Alabama. William D. Chipley, a native of Georgia, became "Mr. Railroad of West Florida" in his position as manager of the L & N properties in that region. He secured a new charter for the Pensacola and Atlantic in 1881 to build from Pensacola eastward to the Apalachicola River. The company was to receive alternate sections of land six miles deep on both sides of the 160 miles and a further special grant of 10,000 acres for each mile. The state delivered 2,214,014 acres of this 3,860,619 acre commitment. This railroad, constructed largely through unoccupied country, reached the Apalachicola late in 1883 and crossed the river on a bridge at River Junction to join railroads into Georgia and East Florida. Under Chipley's leadership the L & N invested heavily in Pensacola, appropriating a quarter of a million dollars in 1895 to build warehouses and wharves, a grain elevator, and a coaling station. Thereafter Pensacola became the thriving Gulf port that its fine harbor had always promised when transportation to the interior became available.

Another railroad developer, Henry B. Plant, paved the way for the Atlantic Coast Line to enter Florida. This native of Connecticut first visited Florida in 1853 and returned later as manager of an express company in Atlanta. After the Civil War, starting from his base as president, general manager, and principal owner of the Southern Express Company, he purchased several bankrupt short-line railroads in Georgia and South Carolina and organized them into the Savannah, Florida and Western. In 1888 he secured charters for the Waycross and Florida and the East Florida, and early in 1881 completed the "Waycross Short Line" into Jacksonville for through trains to Savannah. Attracted by the liberal land subsidy offered in Florida, he secured control of the South Florida, from Sanford to Kissimmee, and bought an undeveloped charter to extend the line to Tampa in 1884. In quick succession he added sixteen small railroads in Florida and seven others in Georgia and South Carolina and organized all of his railroad properties as the Plant Investment Company in 1892. The absorption of six other Florida roads in the next ten years brought the mileage in the state to six hundred out of the total of 1,665 miles in the system. He contemplated a line from Fort Myers to Miami and went so far as to send James E. Ingraham and a party of twenty-one others on an exploring expedition across the Everglades to Miami in 1892.

In 1899 Plant died at eighty years of age. In 1902 the Plant system merged with the Atlantic Coast Line, which was operating 1,676 miles, making a network of some 2,250 miles from Richmond to Tampa. The Plant Company had maintained an agriculture and immigration bureau and a large land sales organization, all to attract settlers and provide traffic for the railroad. The same company built the Tampa Bay Hotel and developed Port Tampa on the bay some ten miles from the city proper to accommodate the Plant Line steamers that plied the waters of the Gulf and the Caribbean. Other Plant hotels at Punta Gorda, Fort Myers, Clearwater, Winter Park, Ocala, and Kissimmee catered to tourists who came to the state by way of the Plant railroads.

John Shelton Williams, a Virginian, was never so closely associated with Florida as were Chipley, Plant, and Henry M. Flagler, but he played a prominent role in bringing the Seaboard Air Line Railroad into the state. By 1900 he had acquired and organized a number of mostly bankrupt short lines into a system that operated trains from Richmond to Tampa. The first unit, the Florida Central and Peninsular, included the lines of the Yulee-built Florida Railroad, the Jacksonville, Pensacola and Mobile from Jacksonville to the Apalachicola River, the Fernandina and Jacksonville from Jacksonville to Yulee, and short lines connecting Ocala to Tampa, Wildwood to Orlando, and others. In 1893 new construction from Yulee to Savannah and from Starke to the Suwannee River gave a total of 600 miles in Florida in 1890, and by 1893, by leasing a line with access to Columbia, South Carolina, it reached 941 miles. A stock transfer in 1900 placed the roads in the hands of the Seaboard for operation, and merger was completed in 1903.

The Southern Railway with its extensive southern mileage entered Florida over the lines of the Georgia Southern and Florida

Tampa in 1882 still had less than 1,000 residents

from Macon, Georgia, to Lake City and later Palatka. The Southern achieved direct access to Jacksonville by the acquisition of the Atlantic, Valdosta and Western, from Valdosta to Jacksonville.

Henry M. Flagler and his Florida East Coast Railroad are far more closely associated with Florida history. It was an all Florida enterprise, and he was sole owner and architect of its design and fortunes. Henry Morrison Flagler had risen from comparative obscurity in a Connecticut family to amass a fortune as a John D. Rockefeller partner in the Standard Oil Company. His Florida ventures constituted a second major business enterprise at a time when he might reasonably have been expected to retire.

Flagler visited Florida first in 1878 on a trip for his wife's health, going only as far as Jacksonville. The first Mrs. Flagler died in 1881. Flagler remarried in June 1883 and spent the winter months of December and January in the Jacksonville-Saint Augustine area. During this visit he apparently decided upon Saint Augustine as a place to settle and launch a new career. In 1885 he returned to the ancient city to complete plans for the Ponce de Leon Hotel, to cost a quarter of a million dollars and accommodate 450 guests. This first of the Flagler hotels opened for the 1888 season and continued to be opened annually until 1967, long after it had ceased to have significant commercial importance. In Saint Augustine he also opened the less pretentious Alcazar in 1888 and the following year purchased and completed the Casa Monica, which later became the Cordova.

Cigar making in Tampa at the turn of the century

So inseparably linked in Flagler's plans were hotels and railroads that it is not possible to determine which was the more significant. In 1885 he also began to improve railroad service to Saint Augustine by buying the thirty-six mile Jacksonville, St. Augustine and Halifax River Railroad and rebuilding it. In 1888 he added the St. Augustine and Palataka and the St. Johns and Halifax, making possible continuous service from south Jacksonville to Daytona. In the next two years Flagler bridges spanned the Saint Johns at Jacksonville and Palatka.

Thereafter Flagler built his own railway lines down the hitherto untouched lower east coast. In 1893 he secured a charter to build toward Miami with a land grant of 8,000 acres per mile for construction south of Daytona. Land owners along the way gladly contributed rights-of-way through their holdings and some gave more to secure the benefits promised by a railroad to hitherto inacessible areas.

No city in Florida illustrated better than Tampa the dynamic influence of transportation developments in the last two decades of the nineteenth century. Chartered in 1834, Tampa did not escape the limitations imposed by isolation and lack of inland transportation until after 1880, when it counted only 720 inhabitants.

Hillsborough and Polk counties to the north and west began to fill up rapidly with settlers who added their trade to that of cattlemen who traded in Tampa. In 1883 Henry Bradley Plant started construction on the South Florida Railroad to connect the Gulf coast community with lines leading to Jacksonville. In the same year the War Department deactivated the Fort Brooke military reservation and its sixteen square miles on Tampa Bay became available for private development. In 1883 also the discovery of vast deposits of phosphate started one of the area's greatest industries. Two years later the cigar industry began operations, induced by the Tampa Board of Trade's offer of assistance in getting land and buildings. Thousands of workers followed the new industries. The Plant Railway system extended its lines ten miles to Port Tampa and developed docking, shipping, and storage facilities there in 1888. In the previous year Tampa had become a port of entry and received a United States Customs House.

Urged on by the Board of Trade, Tampa had two telegraph lines by 1884 and a street railway system a year later. The Tampa Electric Company began to operate in 1887. By the end of the decade a water company was providing water to citizens and business houses. In 1889 the board sponsored a bond issue to raise $65,000 for sewers and $35,000 for street paving. In 1890 the Southern Bell Telegraph Company brought telephone service and the Florida Central and Peninsular Railroad reached the city.

The population of Tampa reached nearly 6,000 in 1890. Another bond issue of $100,000 in 1891 provided more streets and sewers to be constructed, but raw sewage was still being dumped into Tampa Bay. Outside capital began to play a larger role when Stone and Webster took over the Tampa Electric Company. The American Tobacco Company became interested in cigar making in 1901, and Plant's railway system became part of the Atlantic Coast Line Railway Company in 1902.

In 1891 the Tampa Bay Hotel opened its doors. The War for Cuban Independence followed and brought a short period of feverish economic activity in 1898, a story to be related more fully in a later chapter. In 1899 the United States Congress approved further harbor development, and new appropriations in 1905 and 1910 transformed Tampa into a modern port. In the next two decades Tampa grew 186 and 138 percent while the state as a whole grew thirty-five and forty-two percent. A large population of foreign born, mostly Spanish-speaking Cubans, and a smaller number of southern Italians who came to work in the cigar industry gave a special character to the life and culture of the city, particularly in Ybor City where the cigar industry was concentrated.

The importance of the railroad in the development of towns along the coast is also illustrated at West Palm Beach and Miami. By November 1894 when the line reached West Palm Beach the community had 1,000 people and was unincorporated. Flagler apparently meant to make that area the center of his activities. He built the Royal Poinciana Hotel on Lake Worth to accommodate 1,200 guests, with a dining room to seat 1,600, one of the largest wooden structures of its kind in the country. He added the Breakers in 1896 and built Whitehall in Palm Beach as a private residence. He bridged Lake Worth and extended a railroad spur to the hotels. Meanwhile he was building branch lines from New Smyrna to Orange City Junction, from Enterprise to Titusville, and from Jacksonville to Pablo Beach. On the way southward from Daytona he drove out of business only one local railroad, the eight mile Jupiter and Lake Worth, dubbed the "Celestial Railroad" because of its four stations, Jupiter, Mars, Venus, and Juno, which transferred freight and passengers between Indian River and Lake Worth.

Miamians were at first fearful that the southern terminus might remain at the Palm Beaches. The two principal Miami land owners, Mrs. Julia D. Tuttle and William B. Brickell, offered Flagler half of their considerable land holdings to extend the railroad to the small settlement. The severe freeze in the winter 1894-1895, which killed most of the citrus in all except Dade County, is credited with convincing Flagler that he should push the line farther down the coast. In April 1896 the first trains reached Miami. On May 15, the *Miami Metropolis,* the first newspaper, appeared, and on July 28, 343 voters decided to incorporate the city. In mid-January 1897 Flagler's only Miami hotel, the Royal Palm, opened its doors on the north bank at the mouth of the Miami River. In 1903 the Flagler line was extended to Homestead and in 1912 to Key West. These facilities meanwhile had much to do with the ensuing development of Miami Beach in the second decade of the twentieth century.

The acquisition and building of hotels had continued apace with railroad building, so that by 1908 Flagler hotels could accommodate 40,000 guests, and the separate Florida East Coast Hotel Corporation was created to manage them. The Model Land Company managed the considerable landholdings of the Flagler interests. In 1890 Flagler had acquired one of the better known of the smaller hotels, the seventy-room Hotel Ormond at Ormond, which became famous for the millionaires it attracted. These included John D. Rockefeller, who spent his last twenty winters there, most of them in a house which he built. In 1898 he added the Royal Victoria at Nassau in the Bahamas. Flagler, like Plant, had expected to expand this travel facility into the Caribbean area, but Key West remained pretty much the end of the line for Flagler, who died in 1913 at the age of eighty-three.

Critics of Governor Bloxham and his immediate successors decried the grants to railroads, which sold the land to nonresident speculators. They had argued for a homestead price of twenty-five cents an acre. The people reacted strongly against the rates and services of the carriers, the litigation over tax-paying, and the killing of livestock by railroad trains. An internal political feud between Drew and Bloxham for control of the party also threatened to wreck the Democratic chances at the polls. The stage seemed set for a new gubernatorial candidate in 1884. When the Democratic State Convention met at Pensacola on June 25 the delegates passed over the warring pair and selected General Edward Alsworth Perry on the sixth ballot. A native of Massachusetts, Perry had come from Alabama to Pensacola in 1856; he practiced law until 1861 when he entered the Confederate army. He was disabled in 1864 in the Wilderness campaign. He again practiced law after the war and won popular support when he represented the state in the tax case against railroads.

Democratic unity behind a compromise candidate had been stimulated by the action of some dissidents in the party who launched an independent movement to capitalize on the factional strife. On June 18, a hundred delegates from twenty counties gathered at Live Oak in a state convention and named Frank Pope of Madison for governor and for lieutenant governor, Jonathan C. Greeley, a Jacksonville Republican and banker, who represented the business people who wanted a two-party system in the state. The Independent Democrats agreed to give the Republicans second place on the ticket. Some Republicans feared the Independents would take over second party activities in Florida. The platform stressed aid to public education, free elections, railroad regulation, and local option on liquor selling. The Republicans, some of whom had supported the Independent movement from the beginning, proved so badly divided that they could not agree on a candidate after two conventions several months apart. They finally adopted the suggestion of Josiah T. Walls that the party endorse, but not nominate, the Independent candidates.

The campaign was full of bitterness. The Independents lost largely because success would have meant alliance with the largely black Republican organization in the state, a price deemed too high so soon after the Reconstruction experience. Both Perry and Pope solicited the black vote, and the Bourbons perhaps found it easier to do than did the Independents. At that, Pope won forty-six percent of the vote and carried nine black belt counties, losing by 27,845 to 32,087. Regular Democrats also elected the lieutenant governor, the two Congressmen, twenty of thirty-two members of the senate, and sixty-five of eighty-eight members of the lower house.

The Independent movement may have been premature, but it showed widespread dissatisfaction with Bourbonism. The Independents went back into the two major parties, but the issues reappeared in the Farmers' Alliance and the Populist movements soon thereafter. The discontent was one reason for the rather strong support for a new state constitution in the 1884 voting. Emotionally, the Carpetbag constitution of 1868 was a wrong to be righted. Practically, the strongest appeal was for home rule in the counties where the appointment of all county officials deprived white dissidents as well as blacks of any effective voice in the government. It was not so much that these criticisms of the Bourbons were based on a demand for radical reforms, for they were conservative in thought and action. For example, they wanted economical government; one proposal was to abolish the state school superintendent and let the attorney general run the free schools. They no longer feared Republican success if they differed with the Bourbon leadership. Most of the Carpetbag leadership had given up the unequal contest after 1876 and the blacks, without that leadership, under the pressure of their white employers and on occasion including fraud and intimidation, had largely surrendered the right to vote. Republicans were beginning to look more and more to a "lily white" party that had little place in it for blacks. Marion County in the black belt named a Republican to the convention, and Leon County sent Conover and William F. Thompson, a black. Duval, Nassau, and Hamilton counties also sent Republicans, as did eight others, none of whom were Carpetbaggers or Scalawags.

Thirty-four of 108 delegates were natives of Florida, and sixteen others came from southern states. Seven of the twenty Republicans were blacks. Eighty were Democrats and the remainder Independents. Thirty-nine were Confederate veterans. At least forty-two had some college education if not earned degrees. Thirty-five were lawyers, twenty-eight farmers, ten merchants, six doctors, six teachers, and two ministers. The control was conservative; only one non-Bourbon headed a major committee. Vote was by majority of the whole number of delegates, and Democrats used the party caucus to maintain unity. At the opening session on June 9 the delegates chose Samuel Pasco of Jefferson County to preside. The convention remained in session until August 3, a total of forty-five working days.

The legislative article remained relatively unchanged. In the executive article, the residence requirement for governor was increased and he was forbidden a second consecutive term. The office of lieutenant governor was abolished in favor of succession by the president of the senate and the speaker of the house in that order should the governor's office become vacant. To further limit the governor's power, the six-man cabinet became elective, a unique constitutional device in the United States. The new document also reduced the salaries and allowances of all legislative, judicial, and executive offices of the state. Annual sessions of the legislature had been abandoned by amendment ten years earlier, and biennial sessions remained in the basic law.

The new constitution made possible the first steps toward the elimination by law of blacks from participation in the election process when it provided that the legislature might make the payment of the poll tax a prerequisite for voting, the revenues from which were to become part of the school funds. The legislature in 1889 passed the necessary legislation and went on to revive the multiple ballot law that required separate ballots and separate ballot boxes for each of the principal offices and separate polling places for national and state officers. There was some opposition to these measures on the ground that they would eliminate the poorer and illiterate whites as well as most blacks. The results in the election in 1890 showed the effectiveness of the restrictions. In 1888 the Republican candidate for governor polled 26,485 votes. Two years later, a Republican candidate for comptroller, a statewide office, received less than five thousand votes. The Australian ballot replaced the multiple ballot in 1895, but the poll tax remained until 1937.

Reapportionment in the state legislature provided for thirty-two senatorial districts and one from each county in the house, not more than three in any one county, for a total of sixty-two. Decennial reapportionment became mandatory. Except for county commissioners, who remained appointive until 1900, local officers became elective. A forward-looking item was the formal provision for tax support of schools, beginning with a state levy of one mill, a county school tax of at least three mills but not more than five, and a school district tax of not more than three mills. Two normal schools to be created by the legislature were also authorized. The most debated issues were the elective versus appointive local office and the poll tax prerequisite for voting. The ratification question on the November 1886 ballot won approval by 31,803 to 21,243.

Although the making of the new constitution overshadowed all other accomplishments in the years of the Perry administration other significant steps were also taken. In 1887 the creation of six new counties, to bring Florida's total to forty-five, indicated the areas of population growth. Osceola was formed from Brevard and Orange; Lee from Monroe; DeSoto from Manatee; Lake from Sumter and Orange; and Pasco and Citrus from Hernando. The land grant policy of the Bloxham era continued and excited growing protest. A response to the increased opposition to railroad practices was the creation of a railroad commission in 1887, which proved ineffective in the short run but led ultimately to more effective action.

The year 1886 experienced a cold wave, with temperatures the lowest since 1835. An earthquake, a rarity in the state, did some damage in the summer. Fires damaged large sections of Key West and DeLand in 1886 and Saint Augustine in 1882. In 1887, yellow fever in epidemic proportions appeared in Key West, Manatee, Tampa, and Plant City. In the late summer of 1888 an epidemic of 4,656 cases and 427 deaths occurred in Jacksonville. Hundreds of residents fled the stricken city, and the Jacksonville Sanitary Association spent $350,000 raised from contributions to aid the victims and fight the disease. The near total ignorance of the cause of the disease was demonstrated by the efforts made to drive it away. Huge fires of pine and tar were used to "purify the air." Fifty rounds of heavy ammunition were fired to test a concussion theory. Lime and disinfectant were applied to tree trunks, posts, and curbs, and streets were sprayed with a solution of bichloride of mercury. Yellow flags marked infected houses, and the city was quarantined and transients were held for ten days. The population of the city fell to 13,757, from 17,201 in 1890.

A significant outcome of the yellow fever epidemic was the calling of a special session of the legislature in February 1889 by the newly elected governor, Francis P. Fleming, to create and staff a state medical board. The Florida Medical Association had been organized in 1874 in the home of Dr. A. S. Baldwin, its first president, who had been actively promoting the creation of the agency. The

Bay Street, Jacksonville, 1888; fires were set to "destroy" yellow fever germs. Drawing from Florida Times-Union.

Constitution of 1885 had provided for a state board and any county boards deemed necessary to meet health problems, particularly the dreaded yellow jack, which did so much direct and indirect damage. The law created the State Board of Health with adequate authority and funds. Governor Fleming appointed Dr. Richard P. Daniel, a prominent Jacksonville physician, the chairman and William B. Henderson of Tampa and W. K. Hyer of Pensacola the other members. Dr. Joseph Y. Porter of Key West, already well-known as a student of the then little understood disease, became the first state health officer, a post he held until 1917 when he retired. He died at his home in Key West in 1927.

Florida's 269,500 people in 1880, of whom about 127,020 were blacks, were still largely rural and concentrated across the northern part of the state. The leading ten counties in order were Leon with 19,662 persons; then Columbia, Duval, Alachua, Jefferson, Jackson, Marion, and Escambia, to Gadsden with 12,169 inhabitants. The only cities were Key West with 9,890, Jacksonville with 7,650, and Pensacola with 6,845 inhabitants. The white population grew relatively more rapidly after 1880, numbering 190,000 to 147,000 blacks in the state census in 1885, a trend that continued until 1960 when blacks made up only seventeen percent of the population.

The more rapid increase in population was due in part at least to the beginning of organized efforts by the state to attract settlers. The Constitution of 1868 established a commissioner of immigration in the cabinet. An act of the legislature in 1879 provided for the establishment of the Bureau of Immigration to promote the movement of people into the state. J. S. Adams, the first commissioner, directed the first of an unending series of publications designed to advertise the state far and wide. A constitutional amendment in 1871 created a Commissioner of Lands and Immigration, an assignment that combined the offices of surveyor general and commissioner of immigration. The Bourbons who took over control of the state's affairs in 1877 pledged themselves to continue the efforts to attract people to live in Florida. In 1879 the trustees of the Internal Improvement Fund, in their frantic effort to promote land sales, also began to send out literature.

The Constitution of 1885 created the State Department of Agriculture; this included the Bureau of Lands and Immigration, and the Commissioner of Agriculture divided the bureau under an act of 1889. The bureau remained in the Department of Agriculture until 1925, and promotion of land sales and settlement by the state centered in that agency.

Railroad companies and other promoters and developers like Disston and Flagler began to send out an increasing volume of printed matter designed to sell land to prospective settlers. Other items appeared under private auspices. In 1882 George M. Barbour, a correspondent of the *Chicago Times,* wrote the book *Florida for Tourists, Invalids and Settlers,* using information and impressions he had gathered in 1879 while accompanying General U. S. Grant on a tour of the state. Sidney Lanier wrote for the Atlantic Coast Line Railway Company a guide book called *Florida, Its Scenery, Climate and History* after he visited the state in 1875. Ledyard Bill, in *A Winter in Florida,* described a trip up the Saint Johns to Sanford and from Picolata on the river to Saint Augustine. Interest in Florida was widespread enough to produce dozens of descriptive articles in magazines of national circulation such as *Scribners* and *Harpers.*

19.

The Politics of Protest and Reform, 1884-1896

The political combination put together by the leaders of Florida's whites of all persuasions to recapture control of the state's political machinery in 1876 was never an entirely happy one. Too many differences on too wide a spectrum of issues made the one-party system unrealistic except to gain home rule and maintain white supremacy. There is no one date at which the Bourbon ascendancy ended and the more popular faction of the Democratic party took over the lead. It was rather by a series of steps that the dissenters won a place in state government. In fact, the Bourbons never lost influence entirely, and what emerged at the end of the century was in many respects Bourbonism tempered by more concern for the wishes and welfare of their rivals, who had become known as Populists.

The revolt of the Independents under Frank Pope in 1884 failed because of the threat to white control of state politics, but it revealed the underlying unrest. Restrictions on voting that followed shortly after the adoption of the Constitution of 1885 eliminated the black as a factor in elections, and with his departure went any chance that the Republicans could offer any threat to control by the Democrats. White Democrats could safely disagree more freely among themselves. An increasing number of Republicans began to think in terms of an appeal to white rather than black voters and earned the title "Lily Whites."

Made up largely of farmers and small businessmen who felt that the Bourbons had overlooked their interests, the Populists focused their attack on all forms of monopoly and privilege. One of their favorite targets was land monopolizers. Feeling that their only chance for a successful future lay in continuing access to new land at low prices, they saw the end of that frontier of opportunity rapidly approaching. Federal and state governments were disposing of the public domain in large tracts to favored customers, or granting it in ever larger amounts to subsidize railroad building and reclamation projects. Between 1866 and 1876 public lands in Florida and the other four public land states of the Confederacy

Steamboats stopped at wood stations along the route to pick up fuel.

were reserved for loyal homesteaders, meaning freedmen and immigrants from the North. Thereafter for a dozen years the same lands were opened to unrestricted sale. In that brief time six northerners bought 64,243 acres and a dozen southerners 125,172 acres. The prodigal gifts and sales of state lands in the same period were related in the previous chapter. Farmers and their political allies felt that the land should be reserved for actual settlers, and that transportation and land companies should not be allowed to hold it for speculative purposes. They overlooked the fact that railroads frequently sold land at reasonable prices to attract settlers and create traffic along the lines. They also failed to realize that the day of the frontier homestead as the road to realization of the American dream of economic independence if not affluence was being brought to an end by forces other than the end of the public domain. Machinery, science, and power would soon swing the balance too strongly in favor of larger enterprises in agriculture as well as in industry.

These people so dependent upon railroads for transportation

had joined the chorus of approval when the building began. When the hoped-for benefits failed to materialize they turned critics, but even then they hesitated to go too far for fear that the building that had gone on so furiously (519 to 2,326 miles between 1880 and 1888) might be halted. The railroad companies charged high and discriminatory rates and paid rebates to favored customers. Their services were irregular and undependable. Railroad owners and officials had too much influence in state politics and received too liberal treatment by the state legislature, some said. Floridians were but repeating the experiences of their counterparts in other states where railroad building had occurred earlier. By 1886 twenty-five states had railroad regulatory commissions, and the legislatures of five others attempted to regulate rates and practices without resorting to special administrative agencies. In 1887, the Interstate Commerce Act and the creation of the Interstate Commerce Commission put the national government in the business of railroad regulation.

The halting steps by which Florida moved in the same direction reveal the confused balance of economic interests in the legislature and the desire of people at large to have more railroad mileage and service, but somehow to have it regulated in the public interest. As early as 1866 the Florida legislature in a statement of principles forbade railroad discrimination against rival companies or favoring

Ferries rather than bridges were common on the larger waterways; this shows Irvine's Ferry on the Suwannee River at Luraville.

Mail moved by steamboats on the larger streams; this scene was on the Oklawaha River

customers of one community over those of another. In 1879, with more mileage and experience, the lawmakers sought to limit passenger fares to three cents a mile; this was raised to five cents two years later in an effort to help the operating companies to remain solvent. Continuing problems persuaded an increasing number of people that the remedy lay in more effective controls by the state. Although they secured the passage of eighteen measures affecting railroads in 1883, a move to create a regulatory agency to administer policy failed.

In 1884, a Republican with gubernatorial ambition, himself a railroad man, endorsed the idea of a regulatory commission. Frank Pope, the Independent, campaigned vigorously for regulation. Only Edward A. Perry, the Democratic nominee who was to win the office and who had gained prominence by handling the state's case against some earlier railroads, remained noncommittal on the subject. Nor were advocates of a regulatory authority able to get a provision into the new state constitution. Significantly, it did empower the legislature to enact laws to prevent discrimination and exclusive charges. Another section provided penalties for giving or accepting passes for any member of the state government. Governor Perry recommended in 1887 that effective regulations be instituted to protect the people and the railroads. The acceptance of the proposal by the carriers disturbed some of the critics. Actually some of the less powerful lines welcomed the regulatory commission as an escape from the conditions of competition in which they found themselves.

The legislature responded by creating a three-man commission, to be appointed by the governor, authorized to establish passenger and freight rates, to set regulations, and to investigate, institute suits, subpoena witnesses, and require railroads to adopt uniform classifications of freight. The railroad companies were also forbidden to cut rates for the delegates to a political convention. They had to fence their tracks or pay for livestock killed by their trains.

The promise of effective regulation was not realized. A suitable ratemaking basis could not be agreed upon. The carriers never did accept the authority of the commission. William D. Chipley of the Pensacola and Atlantic defied it from the first. The state body could not regulate interstate shipments. Shippers were reluctant to enter complaints. The yellow fever epidemic in 1888 was a serious blow to the railroads, which had to raise rates to compensate for loss of traffic. Regulations became the principal issue in the senatorial election of 1891 that pitted Wilkinson Call, the eventual winner, against William D. Chipley of Pensacola. Call had fought the riilroads for years, particularly the land grants. Chipley had courted the favor of the Farmer's Alliance by granting free passes to the delegates to the organization's national convention in Ocala in December 1890, and reduced rates to those traveling to the Alliance Exposition held in conjunction with the convention. The Call victory proved fruitless for his Alliance supporters in the state legislature. Call's floor leader, Frank Clark of Polk County, introduced a bill in the same legislative session to abolish the commission. This came about when the governor was reported about to appoint his secretary, a well-known supporter of railroads, to a post on the commission. When they could not succeed in an effort to make membership on the commission elective, they killed it. A contributing factor also was the charge that the commission cost too much. Economy-minded Alliance men considered the $27,275.33 three-year cost to be excessive. Reform came at too high a cost for their taste, a not infrequent problem faced by Populists in their efforts to come to grips with the powerful forces with which they sought to cope.

The political manifestations of farmer discontent in the post Civil War era found expresssion in a series of economic, social, and political organizations that received support in Florida. One of the first of these and the first large scale organizations of farmers in the state was the National Grange of the Patrons of Husbandry, better known simply as the Grange or the Granger Movement. Founded in 1867 to bring farmers together in social and educational organizations that would rescue them from the loneliness of rural isolation and help them to improve their lot by cooperative efforts, it reached Florida in 1873. By October of that year there were fourteen Granges across the northern part of the state, and on November 26 nineteen representatives met to organize the Florida State Grange with Colonel Benjamin F. Wardlaw of Madison as state master. Like many other leaders of the movement, he was a man of considerable property and local prominence. He attended the annual meeting of the National Grange in 1874 and played an important role in its deliberations. The Florida organization published the *Florida Agriculturist,* with Charles Codrington as editor, to promote the programs of the order. By early 1875 there were 148 Granges with a total of 5,000 members.

The Grange was opposed in principle and practice to political acitivity, but some of its critics feared it might even become a political party. The declared objectives of the Florida Grange were to protect the rights of property, to replace cotton with diversified crops, to eliminate the middleman in the buying and selling done by farmers, and to promote the movement of settlers into the state. In 1874 the organized farmers attacked the long standing evils of stealing farm produce and livestock, resorting in some cases to vigilante activities. Cotton in the seed was stolen and sold at night. The state legislature responded to the protests of farmers in a bill signed by the governor on March 2, 1877, which forbade the selling of cotton between sundown and sunrise. The effort to stop the thievery of cattle, hogs, and even horses took the form of local organizations to seek out and punish offenders, sometimes in the summary fashion usually attributed to frontier justice.

Efforts to eliminate the middleman resulted in enough instances of mismanagement and financial abuses that the movement itself was discredited. In 1875 the Florida Cooperative Stock Company, based on the Rochdale Plan of paying patronage dividends, opened the way to the establishment of ten cooperative stores. The average capital value of $1,500 suggests that the cooperative store never became very popular.

Women participated in the Grange activities on equal terms with men, a policy to which many Floridians were opposed. Many Granges supported the temperance movement then just getting underway in Florida. By 1876 dissent and disinterest began to weaken the organization. The admission of nonfarmers to membership threatened the integrity of its goals, and some members wished to expel them. Local Granges sought autonomy to escape any limitations of policy or practice by the parent organization. Decline in interest and membership was rapid after 1877, and incorporation with a charter from the state legislature in 1879 failed to achieve more than temporary revival. The National Grange did not die, but an effort to revive it in Florida in the depression thirties of this century failed. An effort in 1961 was more promising, and by 1967 thirty-three locals had a membership of 1,635. The 102nd annual session of the National Grange met in Daytona Beach in November 1969.

The Farmers Alliance, organized in Texas in 1876, found many Floridians ready to join a protest movement. Two organizers came from Texas in 1887. Membership grew with considerable rapidity, particularly in the northern part of the state. On October 4, 1887, at Marianna the publication of the *Florida Farmers Alliance* began. In the peninsular region, which was only in process of development, the movement found less favor. Also, fruit and vegetable and cattle growers proved to have little in common with the more traditional cotton, corn, and tobacco farmers of the northern counties who produced mostly nonperishable crops. In 1890 the Alliance had not yet appeared in Dade, Lee, and Monroe counties.

The Farmers Alliance began as an economic rather than a political movement. The organization sought a remedy for the ills of its members in cooperative buying and selling. It opened a Florida exchange in May 1888 in Jacksonville and subsequently added a

Restoration of grist mill, near Falco, Escambia county

dozen branches in as many counties. Ten years later the Alliance abandoned the exchange project without having achieved its objectives. The organization had not been able to raise sufficient capital, could not or would not compete with private business for skilled management, and could not discipline its own members in the face of private and corporate enterprise that engaged them in price wars; all of which had much to do with the collapse of the Farmers Alliance.

Divisions among the farmers in the Democratic party were evident in 1887 when the overwhelmingly Democratic legislature balloted from April 5 to May 19 before deciding to send Samuel Pasco to the United States Senate. Similarly, the Democratic state convention in Saint Augustine in May 1888 required forty ballots to nominate for governor Francis P. Fleming, descendant of two Florida families of the British period, the Fatios and the Flemings. Fleming won easily over his Republican opponent V. J. Shipman; the Labor party polled 704 votes and the Prohibition party 417.

Alliance men had not been active in the gubernatorial contest in 1888, and the platform of the Democrats did not mention the farmers' problems. Two years later the farmers had moved from economic to political action. The Democratic state convention found Alliance men in control. More than three-fifths of the state legislature elected in November had Alliance connections or leanings. It remained to be seen how well they would stand together in the legislative session.

Meanwhile, the national convention of the Farmers Alliance met at Ocala in December 1890 to provide the high point of Alliance activity in the state. For Florida it was primarily an opportunity to advertise its invitation to settlers and investors. At the conclusion of the convention the delegates set out on a two-week tour of the state, visiting Tampa, Orlando, Titusville, Saint Augustine, Tallahassee, and Jacksonville, after which they went home with boxes of oranges and lemons. The "Ocala Demands," a reiteration of the organization's previous stand on the issues of the day, serve to place the movement in national perspective. They called for the abolition of national banks, which served few of the farmers' needs; the creation of a sub-treasury to issue currency on nonperishable products stored in warehouses; the raising of the circulating medium from the existing thirty-four dollars per capita to at least fifty; the free and unlimited coinage of silver at the ratio of sixteen to one of gold; the prevention of dealing in futures in farm products; the recovery from railroads and alien owners of any land held for speculation; no tariffs on necessities; a graduated income tax; control and supervision of transportation and communication; the direct election of United States Senators; and keeping the costs of government down.

It is rather remarkable that the Alliance met in Florida for its national convention. Not only was the state small and unimportant politically, but also the loyalty of Floridians to Alliance principles and techniques for political action was highly doubtful. Alliance men controlled the legislature in eight southern states, but the results in Florida have little resemblance to the comprehensive list of demands adopted at Ocala. The platform served to divide rather than unite the victors. Many southern Alliance men remained conservatives. The decision to remain in the Democratic party and unseat the Bourbons separated them from their more radical western wing, which favored the formation of a third party.

When the 1891 session of the Florida legislature abolished the railroad commission instead of strengthening it, the Alliance movement collapsed in the state. Their candidate for governor in 1892 carried only five North Florida counties and polled but 8,309 votes to 32,600 for his Democratic opponent. Measures to create a new railroad commission in 1893 and 1895 failed by narrow margins. Alliance men also refused to support the re-election of Senator Call, a well established anti-corporation and anti-railroad man, whose only sin apparently was support for national banks. William D. Chipley, "Mr. Railroad of West Florida," led the fight against Call. On the eighty-fifth ballot the Democratic caucus failed to agree, and on May 26 the anti-Call majority in the Senate absented themselves and allowed fifty-one votes to be cast for Call and one for Danitte H. Mays. Governor Fleming concluded that he was not bound by the peculiar voting procedure and appointed R. H. M. Davidson to the post, but when Call contested the appointment the United States Senate seated him in February 1892. The 1891 legislature also revised the tax laws to provide more adequately for state administration and services. Costs had increased under the new constitution, but taxes had remained unchanged and the tax base had not grown fast enough. The governor had found it necessary to borrow $100,000 for the year 1889 and a like sum the following year. The Old Confederate Soldiers' and Sailors' Home received a hundred acres of land as a site for a home and a grant of 50,000 acres to provide funds for maintenance.

The Alliance influence appeared to some degree in the Democratic state convention in 1892. Clarence B. Collins, a former state official in the organization, became the nominee for state treasurer and William N. Sheats of Alachua for Superintendent for Public Instruction. The Alliance also gave support to the choice of Judge Henry L. Mitchell to run for governor but later broke away to offer their own ticket. The Alliance made no headway running as a third party, polling only about a fourth as many votes as Mitchell.

Mitchell was a native of Alabama who came to Florida in 1846 and was admitted to the bar in Tampa three years later. He spent the greater part of his professional life as a lawyer, judge, or other court official and had one term on the state supreme court. He served in the Confederate army, of which he might have made quite a lot politically but did not. In Tampa he worked hard to get a railroad for the small port city and saw his dream realized when the Plant system reached Tampa in 1884.

Mitchell's platform for the governorship in 1892 seems to have been written by Populists but fell so far short of the Ocala demands of 1890 that some more ardent supporters of that agrarian party's platform refused to accept it; however, it was liberal enough to make Mitchell, whose attitude on such questions was little known, acceptable to Democrats. The Democratic platform denounced the McKinley Tariff, outlawed dealing in futures of agricultural and mechanical products, favored unlimited coinage of silver, the abolition of national banks, the substitution of legal tender treasury notes for national bank notes, and the increase of circulating medium enough to provide fifty dollars per capita. Among other items supported were graduated income tax, government control of railroads, and economical state and national government. Mitchell mentioned few of these items in his campaign talk but did add support for the public school system.

Mitchell's was a hard times administration that began with the panic of 1893 and continued through the ensuing depression. He showed no disposition to support any reform or regulatory legislation. He proposed to avoid a budget deficit by saving money rather than by new taxes. A freeze in the winter 1894-1895 induced him to postpone tax payments for 1894, and the 1895 legislature extended the time to November of that year but refused tax relief to hard-hit citrus growers. Like the administration of Grover Cleveland at the national level, Mitchell's government did not feel that it was a function of the state to do anything about such matters. He failed to mention schools, which lacked facilities in 1895. Teacher training was poor, salaries low, and illiteracy was too common, but neither Populist nor Bourbon lawmakers were yet ready to make

education a state responsibility and least of all in a depression year.
A legislative effort to recreate the railroad commission failed.
Mitchell himself definitely favored the railroads, but the depression was sharpening the attack on them, and with a third of the
mileage in receivership the way was open for the return of the reform and control issues in the election of 1896.

In 1896 a hurricane came ashore at Cedar Key and blew northward across the state to Nassau County. The 135-mile-an-hour
winds completely destroyed Cedar Key. Governor Mitchell called
the Southern States Harbor Defense Commissioners to Tampa for
a meeting on January 20, 1899, and later added the northern and
western states to the invitation list. By the time it met Mitchell
was out of office, but it brought representatives from the United
States government and from twenty states, including Minnesota,
Nebraska, and North Dakota, and such notables as Henry M. Flagler
and Henry Bradley Plant. By that date Mitchell had returned to
his judicial interests, this time as clerk for the sixth judicial circuit.
He was a modest man and saw no reason why a former state supreme court justice should not run for the lesser office while governor. In fact, he signed his own commission for the title. He became
county treasurer in 1902 and died on October 14, 1903.

In 1896 the Democrats turned to William D. Bloxham, governor from 1881 to 1885, to unite the several factions in the party. It
is significant that they turned to this Bourbon, for it serves again to
show the strength of conservatism even among the Populists. Actually, the overriding issue in national politics in 1896 was the proposal for unlimited coinage of silver at the ratio of sixteen units of
silver for one of gold, an issue which also found Floridians badly
divided. At their state convention in Ocala the Democrats supported
the proposal, advocated tariff for revenue only and antitrust legislation. They expressed sympathy for the Cuban rebels in their fight
for independence and urged President Grover Cleveland to extend
to them belligerent rights. The convention chose Bloxham by accla-
mation and then proceeded to neutralize the Florida delegation to
the national convention on the money question by choosing four
silver and four gold delegates. When the Republicans selected William McKinley on a gold platform and the Democrats came out with
Bryan and free silver, Bloxham declared for bimetallism. Florida
Republicans, sensing the possibility of dissension in Democratic
ranks, chose Edward R. Gunby of Tampa to run for governor, and
the Populists nominated William A. Weeks. The gold Democrats
nominated a different national ticket, John M. Palmer of Illinois
and Simon B. Buckner of Kentucky. The results in the general
election in November ran true to long established form. Bloxham
received 21,172 votes to 8,290 for Gunby and 5,270 for Weeks. The
regular Democratic presidential electors received nearly twice as
many votes as for the other four party tickets together.

In the 1897 session of the state legislature the forces of Popu-
lism scored some positive gains. They also suffered a black eye
when one of their number, C. B. Collins, resigned as state trea-

Digging for phosphate in 1890 near Dunnellon

surer, charged with bad management of state funds that he had deposited in weak banks. The last of the long drawn out contests to choose a United States Senator before popular nomination determined the election occurred when Wilkinson Call's term expired on March 4, 1897. Governor Bloxham showed his true political leanings when he appointed his close friend John A. Henderson, vice president of the Florida Central and Pacific Railroad, to serve in the special session called for March 15, 1897. When Call and Chipley fought to a draw for the office in the legislative session, that body turned to Stephen R. Mallory of Pensacola for the appointment. He was the son of the first Stephen R. Mallory who had served as Florida's United States Senator on the eve of the Civil War and then as Confederate Secretary of Navy. The compromise on Mallory would have eliminated Chipley from the race in 1898 when Samuel Pasco's seat became vacant, but Chipley died on December 1, 1897, and the Pasco seat went to James P. Taliaferro, Jr., of Jacksonville, heir to the Chipley role as spokesman for conservatism. Call received six votes, Frank Clark, one, and Taliaferro fifty-nine.

The same session established Florida's second and what proved to be permanent railroad commission. The act on which the Democrats and Populists joined forces became law without Bloxham's signature. *The Florida Times Union* urged him to veto it, charging that further railroad development would be halted. Significantly, the new commission had support from segments of the business community seeking to equalize the conditions of competition. Phosphate mine operators charged that over a seven-year period the Central and Peninsula Railroad had paid the C. B. Rogers Company an average of $36,000 per annum in freight rebates.

*Modern phosphate mining, highly mechanized, is one of
Florida's largest enterprises.*

The law also sought to prevent misuse of railroad passes and
financial abuses. Corporations were forbidden to contribute in any
way to a party organization, committee, or individual for political
purpose or seek to promote or defeat any candidate for nomination
or office. A bill to require railroads to post lists of cattle killed and
pay for the carcasses failed, but two years later the lawmakers gave
the railroads two years to fence rights-of-way or be liable for full
value of cattle killed, and they were to start fence building in sixty
days.

A final victory for Populist principles was the establishment in
1897 of the direct primary to nominate local officials and two years
later for all state offices as well. United States Senators were thereafter nominated by voters and elected by the state legislature until
the seventeenth amendment to the United States Constitution provided for direct election.

The second railroad commission made progress slowly but
surely. The commissioners learned to be wary of the courts. Governors did not give them strong support. Businessmen were reluctant to give testimony. But the climate of progressivism in the early
years of the new century favored their cause. A series of United
States and state supreme court decisions also helped. One compelled the Jacksonville Terminal Company to admit the Atlanta,
Valdosta and Western Railway trains to its Union Station and other
facilities as ordered by the commission. Another freed the commission from an injunction that suspended all rate regulations on the

ground that the railroad company could not pay its bonds if it accepted the rates. Finally, in 1911, all consolidations, leasing, or purchasing of railway lines were required to have commission approval.

The last two decades of the nineteenth century saw the railroads built and then effectively regulated by a commission, and the election process democratized for whites in the Democratic primary at the cost of eliminating black participation. These decades also saw the real beginnings of the present-day system of education in the state in public elementary and secondary schools and public and private institutions of higher education. Faint beginnings before 1860 were snuffed out by the War Between the States, and recovery was delayed during the period of Reconstruction and recovery that followed. It was late in the 1880s before any progress could be reported.

In 1889 the legislature made statutory provisions for the return of school management to county and local boards in contrast to the highly centralized administration under the Constitution of 1868. Albert J. Russell, who was State Superintendent of Public Instruction until 1893, aimed to have at least one high school in each county and inaugurated a few schools for vocational education projects for white and black children. In 1892 William N. Sheats, who had drafted the education section in the state constitution, was elected State Superintendent and assumed the office in January of 1893. He took the extraordinary step of revoking all teachers' licenses and holding reexaminations to establish proficiency. He encouraged the consolidation of smaller schools and tried to prevent the establishment of new schools within a radius of three miles of existing ones. School enrollment grew from 62,327 in 1885 to 119,539 in 1902. By 1898 as many as seventy-one percent of children of school age were in school, but whereas the average number of days of attendance per year in the nation was sixty-seven, in Florida it was only fifty. The Florida school year was only 104 days in contrast to 140 for the nation. Nor was Sheats without opposition, particularly in regard to the taxes involved.

State-supported higher education for white students began in a law of 1851 to provide for seminaries in East and West Florida. The East Florida school began at Gainesville in 1853 and the West Florida one at Tallahassee three years later. In 1870 the Florida Agricultural College opened its doors at Lake City. In 1887 the state established a normal school at De Funiak Springs and in 1895 the South Florida Educational and Military Institute at Bartow. The six institutions, none of them adequately supported, competed for students and what money was available. As early as 1891 Governor Fleming suggested the possibility of giving all of the support to one state university or at least creating a Board of Regents to coordinate the work of the existing ones; both of these recommendations were in a measure at least accomplished in 1905.

Several of Florida's oldest private schools originated late in the nineteenth century and shared with state-supported schools a

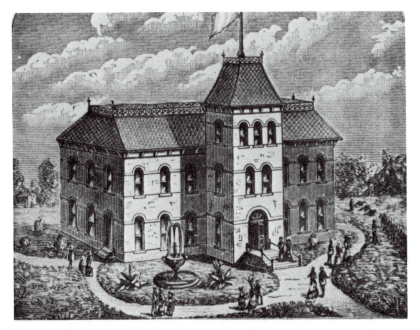

The East Florida Seminary at Gainesville, once located at present-day 1st Street and 5th Avenue. Engraving from Eden of the South, *by Carl W. Webber, 1883.*

struggle for existence. Florida Southern College, now at Lakeland, in the forty years before 1925 used four different names in five locations. The Florida Conference of the Methodist Church, which included South Georgia, established its first school at Thomasville, Georgia, and in 1852 the East Florida Seminary began to function at Micanopy but did not survive the Civil War. Its modern beginnings date from 1893 with the establishment of the South Florida Seminary at Orlando, changed to Wesleyan Institute in 1885, moved to Leesburg in 1886 as Florida Conference College, moved again in 1902 to Sutherland near Clearwater under the name Florida Seminary, changed to Southern College four years later, and moved to Lakeland in 1923 where it received its present name in 1935.

Rollins College originated at Winter Park in 1885 when the Florida Congregational Association, representing thirteen churches, met at Orange City and sent out a committee to seek money and a site for a new school. Winter Park provided both. Alonzo W. Rollins of Chicago provided $50,000 and his name for a college on a site of equivalent value provided by supporters in the city.

Stetson University originated in 1883 with thirteen students meeting in a lecture hall in a Baptist church in DeLand. Called DeLand Academy after Henry A. DeLand, who founded the settlement and the school, it had its own building a year later. It became DeLand Academy and College in 1885 when DeLand deeded the property to a self-perpetuating board of trustees to be administered under the supervision of the Florida Baptist Convention. John B. Stetson, the hat manufacturer, was its benefactor from 1886 until his death in 1906, although the school did not take his name until 1899. In 1900 Stetson University opened the first law school in Florida.

Benedictine monks began to operate a school at St. Leo Abbey at San Antonio, Florida, as early as 1889, though it did not become St. Leo College until 1959.

State-supported higher education for blacks began in 1883 when, on the urging of Governor Bloxham, the legislature appropriated $4,000 annually for teachers' institutes and normal schools for both races. The first normal schools for blacks began in July and August of 1884 in Tallahassee and Gainesville. In three years of operation the two schools reported a total of 331 students for the two-month term. This pointed to the need for a full-year institution to train teachers for black schools. The Constitution of 1885 provided for two normal schools, and two years later the schools were established. Significantly, the two schools began in a separate but equal framework. The State Normal School for Negroes began in Tallahassee on Monday, October 3, 1887, with fifteen students enrolled. Thereafter the story of that school is the story of state-supported higher education for blacks until 1949. In 1890 the State Board of Education divided the Morrill Land Grant funds between the Tallahassee school and the Florida Agricultural College for whites at Lake City; the latter school was moved to Gainesville fifteen years later. The Tallahassee school became a four year college in 1909 (Florida Agricultural and Mechanical College) and Florida A & M University in 1953. In 1949 two developments opened up new opportunities for Florida's blacks. Under the auspices of the Southern Regional Education Board, Florida participated in a plan to provide professional education in medicine, dentistry, and veterinary science in schools outside the state. Up to 1964 the state had paid out slightly over a half million dollars for this purpose, but the quotas allowed Florida blacks were never filled. This was not to be the answer. Also in 1949 the first junior college for blacks was established at Pensacola. Eight years later a second was established at Saint Petersburg; this was followed rapidly by others, but beginning in 1962, they began to be integrated with what had been white junior colleges. Professional schools in the state also began to admit black students.

Inadequate state appropriations and differences in philosophy for black education impeded any significant growth in the institution. The first president of Florida A & M, Thomas DeSaille Tucker, a native of Sherbro, Sierra Leone, Africa, and a graduate of Oberlin College, held that a sound liberal arts foundation should be provided for all students. Superintendent Sheats would have limited instruction to practical agricultural and other vocational training in the manner advocated by black educator Booker T. Washington. As a result, Tucker lost his position in 1901. During his thirteen

Dr. Mary MeLeod Bethune, 1943

years of leadership, the college grew from one building to eight and from fifteen students to 159 taught by fourteen professors. Nathan B. Young, another Oberlin graduate, became president in 1901 and supported emphasis upon teacher training and agricultural and mechanical arts.

Under private and church auspices, other black colleges began to function at much the same time. The Reverend D. B. S. Darnell founded Cookman Institute in Jacksonville in 1872. Mary McLeod Bethune in 1904 started the Daytona Normal and Industrial Institute for Girls. In 1923 Cookman and Bethune merged to form what became Bethune-Cookman College. Edward Waters College was also early if uncertainly in operation. The Reverend Charles H. Pierce, the first presiding elder of the African Methodist Church in Florida, started raising money for a school as early as 1866; he received a charter for Brown Theological Seminary in 1872 and Brown University two years later. The school suspended operations shortly thereafter but reopened in 1883 in Jacksonville and began to offer college level courses in 1892 as Edward Waters College. Florida Memorial College, with a background under Baptist auspices in Live Oak, Jacksonville, and Saint Augustine, moved to Miami in 1968.

20.

Florida and the War for Cuban Independence

Floridians have always been peculiarly sensitive to events in Cuba. This derives from more than just the accident of geography that places them so near each other and from more than fear of invasion or economic rivalry. Added to these must be the long pull of historical association. In the more than two centuries of Spanish control, Havana was the principal source of all things Spanish– government and administration, money, goods and services, religious authority and guidance and defense. Indeed, Spanish Florida was little more than a military outpost of Havana. A few Spanish families remained in Florida to add to the flavor left by Spanish architecture and place names. Cuba was long an important market for Florida cattle and salted fish. Some 6,000 Cuban cigar makers migrated to Key West and Tampa after 1868 to make cigars, for which much of the tobacco was imported from Cuba. Only New York received more Cuban tobacco. Political refugees from Cuba in the last decades of the nineteenth century operated principally in Key West, Tampa and New York.

The earlier effort of the Cubans to achieve their independence from Spain in the Ten Years' War, 1868-1878, stirred little response in Florida. Cuban revolutionaries had organized their junta in New York to coordinate the activities of social and political clubs in Florida and elsewhere, but only the small Cuban population reacted positively. Floridians were still too deeply involved in the Reconstruction period following the American Civil War to give the Cuban patriots more than their sympathy. Nor could the United States government be stirred to action. The case of the *Virginius* in 1873 might easily have precipitated a crisis such as did the *Maine* a quarter of a century later. The Virginius, flying the flag of the United States, was carrying arms to the Cuban rebels. A Spanish gunboat captured her on the high seas, and the captain summarily ordered the execution of fifty-three of her seamen, including eight Americans, for piracy. The ship had no right to fly the flag of the United States. Spain disowned the harsh treatment, paid an indemnity, and the crisis passed.

In 1898 the temper of many Americans had changed. The wounds of civil strife were healed. The country was growing rapidly in wealth, population and industrial strength. Florida's population had doubled in the last two decades. Influenced by imperialist tendencies among the great powers of Europe as well as by her own growing sense of power, many influential Americans felt that their country should play a larger role in world affairs. They often thought in terms of big navy, overseas trade and even overseas territory. The economic stake of the United States in Cuba had increased enormously. An estimated fifty million dollars was invested in Cuban enterprises, and the annual trade was reckoned at twice that value. Cuban tobacco and raw sugar were closely tied to the United States market.

Some Americans and the Cuban revolutionaries stood ready to exploit these sentiments. Newspapers using new techniques and sensational methods made the most of the latent martial spirit of nationalism. The best, or the worst if you will, example was to be found in the circulation war being waged between Joseph Pulitzer's *New York World* and William Randolph Hearst's *New York Journal,* which raised yellow journalism to its greatest extremes of sen-

Primitive carts and small boats called coast traders were common along Florida's coast; this scene, Key West, 1900.

Sponge markets at Key West, 1898

sationalism. The atrocity stories coming out of Cuba depicting Spain's ruthless efforts to suppress the rebellion were made to order for the purposes of these papers.

In 1891 Cuban patriots José Marti and Tomás Estrada Palma reorganized the junta in New York City to arouse sympathy and seek aid in the United States for the new strike for freedom they planned. Of some 200 political clubs they founded, seventy-six were in Florida; sixty-one among Key West's three thousand Cubans and fifteen larger units in Tampa where some 3,500 Cubans resided. Martí frequently visited Tampa, where he always received a tumultuous welcome. The junta provided much of the sensational news out of Cuba, for there was no dearth of "firsthand" accounts after American correspondents were expelled. The junta collected and spent considerable sums of money in Florida. Cigar workers reportedly contributed ten percent of their earnings. The money went largely to purchase arms in Florida for shipment to Cuba. This involved the connivance of Florida firms to acquire the arms for resale and of local officials to permit the illicit traffic to go under their noses at such places as Jacksonville, Fernandina, Cedar Key, Key West and Tampa. In 1896 alone seventy-one filibustering expeditions were counted. The risks must have been great, for only thirty-two of these were known to have been successful. Florida's best known filibusters were Captain "Dynamite" Johnny O'Brien with the *Dauntless* and Napoleon Bonaparte Broward and his ship *The Three Friends*. These exploits helped to make Broward governor of Florida a few years later.

President William McKinley came into office in March 1897, committed by his party's platform to support Cuba's independence but in no sense committed to active intervention. Like President Grover Cleveland before him, he sought to maintain strict neutrality. His proffer of the good offices of his administration to settle the dispute and restore peace and order in Cuba was rejected but may have induced the Spanish government to offer a program of reform, including home rule for Cubans. It is now clear that McKinley's restraint and diplomacy might have brought about a satisfactory settlement of Cuban and Spanish differences if events beyond the control of his administration had not forced his hand.

The Cuban rebels no longer were interested in anything less than independence. They feared the success of McKinley's efforts to bring about a conciliatory settlement. Events played into their hands, perhaps not without an assist from them. On February 9, 1898, the *New York Journal* printed a letter of the Spanish minister to the United States, Enrique Dupuy de Lôme, to a friend in Cuba. It had been stolen from the mail in Havana. The minister wrote disparagingly of the American president as a weak politician who would yield to the growing clamor for intervention. De Lôme's immediate resignation hushed somewhat the clamor for punitive action, but more was to come.

Meanwhile the American consul general in Havana, Fitzhugh Lee, was growing more and more alarmed for the safety of American citizens and property and requested that a warship be dispatched to the scene to stand by to evacuate the citizens if crises should arise. The battleship *Maine* sailed quietly into Havana Harbor and dropped anchor for what was to prove the last time. On February 15 the ship blew up, for causes unknown to this day, with the loss of 260 lives. Americans, not stopping to consider how little Spain had to gain by such an act and how much the insurgents might benefit generally, assumed that it was the work of the Spanish.

The already emotionally aroused Americans were ready to react violently, and they supported the demands of the national press for war. Florida newspapers, on the other hand, had taken a conservative line from the first. As early as December 15 the Jacksonville *Times Union and Citizen* wished the Cubans well in their effort to achieve independence but let it be known they must do the job themselves. There was no sensational coverage of the *Maine* disaster. As in the case of the de Lôme letter, Floridians refused to consider that the sinking made war inevitable. The *Tampa Tribune,* which might have been expected to reflect the attitude of Cuban patriots there, pointed out logically enough that if it were not an accident, insurgents must have been responsible.

This conservatism grew out of the realization that a war might have serious consequences, both immediate and long range, for Florida. The winter tourist season was not yet ended. A naval war, which all assumed it would be, in nearby waters would find the coast undefended and would drive visitors away. While Floridians played down the possibility of war, they began to demand coast defenses. On April 5, the War Department announced batteries for the east coast cities of Jacksonville, Fernandina, Saint Augustine and Miami. Home guard units functioned at Pensacola, Miami, Palatka, Lake Worth, Palm Beach, Coconut Grove and other places. There was special concern for the Plant system's freight yards and docks at Port Tampa and the shops of the Florida East Coast Railway at Saint Augustine. Not until May 25 did the Secretary of War direct the Chief of Engineers to prepare plans for the defense of Tampa Bay, relying no doubt upon the possibility of defense by naval vessels stationed there.

Floridians also feared that Cuba might become a part of the United States, a prospect they viewed with grave misgivings. Cuba was in many respects a competitor better left outside the Union. Important areas of rivalry were in fruits, vegetables, tobacco, cigars, sugar and tourism. Florida might easily become only a way station for tourists en route to Havana. Until the declaration of war actually came on April 25 with the Teller Amendment forswearing any purpose to annex Cuba, newspaper editors in the state continued to warn of the dangers to Florida if a conflict should result in annexation of the island. By mid-March, however, the press had begun to accept war as probably inevitable.

Another group of Floridians from the first began to see advantages for Florida if a war should come. J. P. Beckwith, passenger agent for the Florida East Coast Railroad, offered to the War Department 367 miles of railroad from Jacksonville to Miami and 235 miles of steamship service from Miami to Key West, which was expected to be the center of warlike activity. The *Times Union and Citizen* noted trainloads of ammunition and equipment moving through the city en route to Tampa and from there by Plant Line steamers to Key West. Also at Key West civilian, army, and navy activity increased before the declaration of war actually came, but only a few people moved away. At any distance from the railroad centers people were little affected by the precautionary steps being taken.

In mid-March the War Department announced that military camps would be located somewhere in the southeast. New Orleans, Mobile and Savannah seemed to be the most likely sites. Although they assumed that Key West would be the principal base for American forces in a naval war, Tampans began to call attention to its advantage as a supply base. Tampa was only 223 miles from Ha-

vana, whereas Mobile was 440 and New Orleans 660 miles distant.
On April 15, Adjutant General H. C. Corbin ordered seven regiments of infantry to proceed to Tampa. If training camps were to
be located in Florida, other cities began to demand that they also be
considered. Jacksonville newspapers urged Miami as a likely embarkation point on the east coast if Saint Augustine, Fernandina
and Jacksonville were too far distant from the scene of the anticipated conflict. Jacksonville, it was urged, could send troops to east
or west coasts as circumstances dictated.

The impending movement of troops to Tampa stirred considerable excitement and not a little apprehension in the state. Some of
the one thousand Spaniards residing mostly in Key West and Tampa
moved to New York, but only 153 of them accepted the opportunity
to return to Cuba. On April 16, Tampans learned that 3,000 infantrymen were on their way to the city. Two days later Major J. W.
Pope came to arrange for their arrival. He found the railroad facilities adequate but everything beyond that had to be provided. He
selected relatively high and well drained lands in Tampa Heights
for a camp site. The city agreed to extend water, electricity and
streetcar service to the area. Pope also planned corrals for the large
number of horses and mules and purchased grain and forage for
them through local merchants. Five companies arrived on April 20.
A full fifty-car train from New Orleans brought twenty-three officers and 482 men with one car for horses, nine for mules, nine for
baggage, and fifteen for wagons. Troops continued to pour in far
beyond the 3,000 originally announced. On April 22 twenty-two
troop trains arrived. New camp sites at DeSoto Park, Palmetto
Beach, Fort Brooke, Port Tampa, Ybor City, and in a park directly
west of the Tampa Bay Hotel were soon filled with men. By May
19, there were 7,000 infantrymen at Tampa Heights, 3,000 cavalry-
men west of the hotel and 6,000 in other camps besides the troops
guarding the mounting store of supplies at the port. By May 25 the
total was 23,000 officers and men.

General Wade arrived on April 21 and made his headquarters
at the Tampa Bay Hotel, which had closed on April 9 but reopened
that day to be filled with civilians and soldiers. A large colony of
newspaper correspondents, some of them foreign, swelled the ranks.
By mid-June the weather was no longer cool and dry, and rains
flooded the whole area. The correspondents needed action if they
were to file publishable dispatches. They began to predict the invasion of Cuba even before any ships arrived to transport and convoy
men and supplies. Among the ten regiments of volunteers assembled
at Tampa was the First Florida with forty-eight officers and 956
men. Twenty companies of Florida volunteers were ready to serve,
but the War Department's quota for Florida was only twelve. Governor William D. Bloxham, unable to make the hard choice among
them, ordered all of the companies to Tampa. He hoped men in the
companies not selected might volunteer to fill the ranks of the more
fortunate. but the greater number refused the invitation and returned to their homes. The twelve companies selected were the

Tampa Bay Hotel, headquarters of Major Generals Shafter and Wade, commanding Cuban Expeditionary Forces, 1898.

Ocala Rifles, the Leesburg Rifles, the Orlando Shrine Guards, the Palatka Gem City Guards, the Jacksonville Light Infantry, the Jacksonville Rifles, the Saint Augustine Rifles, the Escambia Rifles, the Gadsden Guards, the Bradford Guards and the Suwannee Rifles from Live Oak. The governor made William F. Williams their colonel, and the men selected their own company officers. Their presence brought large numbers of weekend visitors to Tampa and spread the Tampa story throughout the state, as did a newspaper correspondent in each company.

Estrada Palma, speaking for the junta in New York, ordered all young and healthy unmarried Cubans disposed to go to Cuba to aid the rebel cause to make their way to Tampa. Forty Cubans from Jacksonville, 200 from New York, and 150 from Key West converged on the city. On May 21, Emilio Núñez, named a general of the army of the Cuban Republic in command of 600 of the Cuban volunteers, sailed with 7,000 rifles on the steamer *Florida* to join in the fighting.

The sudden multiplication of its population from 25,000 to 66,000 put a severe strain on the facilities and services of the port community, but Tampans protested the efforts of other Florida cities to divert troops to themselves. The vast amount of equipment and supplies added enormously to the congestion. Some items were in great over supply, some lacking altogether. At one time enough rations were on hand to feed 70,000 men for ninety days when there were not more than 30,000 men there and many of them due to embark for Cuba. Thousands of freight cars marked only "Military Supplies–Rush" came ahead of invoices, which if they had been sent were lost in the vast overloading of the small Tampa post office. The cars were opened to search for some needed items or in an effort to discover where they should be routed–to Commissary, Ordnance, Engineering or Medical Corps.

The probably temporary nature of the military projects produced difficulties. The Plant system hesitated to double the single track line to Port Tampa or to add storage and warehouse capacity. The Plant Company was in a strategic position to control the movement of men and equipment to the docks. Plant officials overplayed their hands several times. They urged that all supplies and equipment be stored at the port and be shipped via the Plant systems tracks. They delayed the transfer of cars that came over the Florida Southern and Peninsular, charged a two dollar switching fee and sixty dollars to move each car the nine miles to the dock area. Only a threat to seize the rail lines if Plant did not remove obstructions to free flow of traffic opened access of the cars to the port facilities.

One of the remarkable wonders of the wartime story was the

Camp scene in Tampa, 1898

way in which a small and undeveloped community could rise to the occasion. Planned originally to serve as a supply depot and to receive only 3,000 men, nearly ten times as many came almost without notice, creating serious problems of sanitation, policing, supply, housing and recreation. Baseball games, picnics, dances and socials sponsored by churches and ladies clubs, Red Cross and YMCA centers helped to provide recreation, and church people extended themselves to provide religious services. The cigar manufacturers distributed as many as 12,000 cigars a week. The ice factory set out barrels of ice water. Hillsborough County, over the protest of city officials, licensed saloons with scant regard for the consequences. Bawdy houses and all sorts of camp followers quickly found their way to the area. Soldiers complained about the heat, humidity, rain, mud, dust and sand. Regular troops who were the first comers endured the discomforts more stoically than the greater numbers of volunteers, who lacked army camp experience.

A consuming fear shared by civil and military authorities alike was the possibility of an outbreak of yellow fever. In spite of the precautions imposed by the State Health Department there was no assurance that this disease of unknown origin could be avoided. Dr. Joseph Y. Porter, the state health officer, had long required a strict quarantine of persons coming from Cuba. Wartime conditions made the ten-day waiting period all but impossible, but he refused to relax the rule. The War Department built a small hospital on Egmont Key and at times had as many as 150 patients there. To evacuate any wounded who might be brought from the battlefront, the authorities worked out a plan to place them in a hospital train at the dock and take them to hospitals farther north. Fate was kind to Florida that summer. In spite of several scares, no cases of yellow fever appeared.

Local businessmen prospered. Their only problem was keeping their shelves stocked with merchandise. The War Department, the railroads and local employers recruited men from far and wide. The Plant system in one instance brought 100 workers from Ocala. The first army payroll in early May was $325,000 and a month later it was close to a million. Correspondents gathered at the Tampa Bay Hotel boosted the prosperity the city was enjoying but found the action too slow for their purposes. General William Shafter arrived on May 11 and shortly thereafter received orders to take 12,000 men to Key West and then to Fort Jefferson for a move against Cuba. These orders were issued in the face of information that Key West was suffering a severe water shortage and Fort Jefferson had less. The orders also failed to take note of the time that might be required to get such an expedition under way. The Fourth Army Corps, 20,816 strong, received orders to proceed from Mobile to Tampa to replace it immediately. Shafter succeeded instead in having them enter a new camp at Jacksonville on May 23, and he finally got under way from Tampa three weeks later on June 14.

General Shafter moved ahead with plans to sail directly from Tampa to the war zone. Thirty-five ships were loaded with supplies and equipment including 2,300 horses and mules. At two o'clock in the afternoon on June 7 men began to embark. By nine the next evening, thirty-one hours later, the last unit was on board. This involved moving men by train from the camps to the docks at Port Tampa where spur tracks ran out on twin piers 3,200 feet into the bay, three lines on the south pier and one on the north. The docks were designed to handle twenty-four oceangoing ships at one time but in practice could accommodate only twelve to eighteen. Theodore Roosevelt and some of the correspondents pictured embarkation as an unplanned spectacle of confusion. Roosevelt went so far as to report later he had to commandeer a ship to get his men on board. Subsequent investigation showed that procedure had been rather orderly and only slightly behind schedule, the last a condition to which it was charged Teddy and his Rough Riders had contributed. Five more days passed before the invading force got under way. Departure was delayed while a rumor that Spanish cruisers were in wait nearby could be checked out and proved groundless. Finally at 3:30 A.M. on June 14, thirty-five transports carrying more than 16,000 soldiers, four tenders, one hospital ship and fourteen naval escorts began to move out to sea.

Shafter's departure left 12,000 men in the camps in Tampa, and the number grew to 18,000 by the end of the month, with more

Loading horses, Tampa, 1898

Loading U.S. Army transports, Port Tampa, 1898

to come. Nor did another expeditionary force to Cuba seem likely. All the newcomers were volunteers who, being untrained, were less disciplined and given to drunkenness, disorder and failure to observe even rudimentary rules of camp sanitation. Only another 6,000 men left Tampa and there were 25,000 men in the camps by July 20. By that time it was evident that some of the troops would be moved to other camps. The soldiers were ready to depart, even to be mustered out if they could not go to Cuba or some other battlefield. Most Tampans were ready to see them go. The city had been overwhelmed by them long enough.

On July 22 the First Florida Regiment entrained for Fernandina, and by August 20 the last military unit was gone, leaving behind mountains of stores and some 4,000 animals. By May 1899, one year after the first arrival at Tampa, one officer and a clerk in charge of some supplies in a single warehouse remained. Most of the supplies had been shipped to Cuba for the army of occupation and the remainder to other bases in the United States. Apparently the Plant system priced itself out of the market by high charges for handling, storage and docking. The war had come to Tampa and gone.

The search for new camp sites had begun in mid-May. The same problems existed to some degree everywhere. There was plenty of space, but water supply, food, recreation, transportation and sanitation were largely lacking. Though Lakeland, thirty miles east of Tampa, had only a thousand people and did not seek a camp, it proved to be a good location. The Seventy-First New York and the Second Massachusetts regiments of volunteers stopped there and pitched their tents on the shores of Lake Morton. Their two volunteer outfits had been out West and were much better trained than others. They were the only volunteers except Roosevelt's Rough Riders to go with Shafter to Cuba. The First and Tenth U.S. Cavalry also stopped at Lakeland. They knew the stay was only temporary and that they were on the way to Cuba. Other troops replaced them to keep the camp strength up to about 4,000 until mid-August, when all but the regimental hospital and a few tropical fever cases entrained for Huntsville, Alabama.

Jacksonville originally had little hope of getting a camp but did offer land, water, electricity and a scavenger service for any camps located there. On May 1, General Shafter had ordered the first troops sent there. They occupied three pleasant sites, two of them outside the city. Fitzhugh Lee, a nephew of Robert E. Lee, ex-consul at Havana, commanded the Seventh Army Corps at "Camp Cuba Libre." Beginning with the first arrivals on May 23, by June 8 eight regiments, just over 9,000 men, had arrived at the Jacksonville camps. Though planned for 20,000 men, the number reached 31,000 in September, when they began leaving; all were gone by December. The Jacksonville encampment had a better record than most others. Camp sites were better chosen, and the city was larger, better policed, and offered more recreation. Supplies and freight could be more easily handled. Only a high incidence of typhoid fever marred the camp's record. Saint Augustine got no camp, but the Florida East Coast Railroad ran excursion trains for a fifty-cent fare, and many soldiers visited the ancient city.

Because they had railroads and energetic railroad men to promote their claims, Fernandina and Miami got camps, but the experience was not good for either the army or the cities. The railroad had reached Miami only two years earlier. General Wade visited the small town on May 19 and 25 and turned it down as a camp site, but vice-president Parrott of the railroad company went ahead with plans for a camp. The Florida East Coast officials may have been encouraged by General Nelson W. Miles, who was planning an expedition to Puerto Rico and wanted more troops on hand, but the Miles expedition finally originated in Savannah. On June 20 General Theodore M. Schwan received orders to move his division of Alabama, Louisiana and Texas volunteers to Miami. The city was no place for 7,500 troops in the summer. The plan for the camp was well conceived but not adhered to. Four of the regiments found themselves beyond the sewer system provided by the city and resorted to a crude bucket system, which was blamed for the high incidence of typhoid fever. When the men used surface wells rather than the water piped in by the city, in violation of all health and sanitation rules, they paid a high price in disease. The men were unhappy from the first. The drill field was a mile away. The city offered little that was attractive. The men described it as a luxury hotel, the Royal Palm, and a wilderness. After a stay of only a little over a month they were ordered to Jacksonville.

Fernandina was an even less fortunate choice. The terminus of the Florida Central and Pacific Railroad boasted a good harbor and

3,500 inhabitants. The troops camped on the site of old Fort Clinch. Two officers from Tampa arrived on July 18 and one division of the Fourth Army Corps, some 7,200 men, had arrived by the end of the month. On August 22, the troops at Femandina departed for Huntsville, Alabama, headquarters for the corps. The *New York Times,* perhaps unable to find any other reason for locating a camp there, mistakenly charged that the land belonged to the family of Secretary of War Russell A. Alger.

Naval activity in Key West in 1898 was perhaps more important to the invasion of Cuba, but it touched the life of Floridians somewhat less than the presence of so many soldiers. Located less than a hundred miles from Havana, its sheltered harbor, the small naval yard for repairs, and its role as a coaling station for the steam-powered naval vessels and transports made for Key West a prominent role. Ships of the Atlantic squadron based there. The *Maine* had departed from there on its ill-fated journey, and the Plant Line steamer *Olivette* brought the survivors back to the island. On the eve of the conflict, it counted three battleships, seven cruisers, and nineteen other warcraft. The navy had been accumulating supplies there since March, bringing some of them from the nearest railheads at Miami and Tampa.

Key West, in spite of its long history as a naval base, proved ill prepared to meet the demands placed upon it for the invasion of Cuba. Storage space for reserve stocks of coal and ammunition were lacking. Improvements in harbor facilities were to take time. Coal bunkers were under construction, but the larger ships could not come in to them until the channels were deepened, and barges had to carry coal out to them. To do minor repairs the navy brought tools and mechanics from its Philadelphia yard. From May to August they did repairs on sixty-four vessels, thereby saving them the journey to a larger navy yard. Some ships also sailed to Pensacola to be repaired or fitted with guns at the yard there.

The harbor at Key West was busy. The regularly scheduled freight and passenger service continued. Newspaper dispatch boats and over 100 correspondents added their share of crowding and confusion. Construction activities of the army and the navy added further to the beehive activity. The navy added a bit of drama when it brought in thirty-four Spanish ships, twenty-nine of which were condemned and sold with their cargoes as prizes. In consequence 444 sailors and twenty-two passengers were held in prison.

Fort Taylor in early 1898 had only a caretaker garrison. Fort Jefferson, also obsolete, was abandoned for military purposes and was being used by the U.S. Health Service as a quarantine station. Both forts were reactivated. Taylor received new guns and a garrison, and two companies of infantry stood guard at Jefferson. Work on new batteries there began in March 1898 but was not completed until late 1899. Hospital service was available at the port hospital at Key West barracks and by a marine hospital service unit. The Mother Superior of the Convent of Mary Immaculate offered the convent and its school buildings for a hospital, and the twenty-three nuns who had served as nurses in yellow fever epidemics were ready to do so again if needed. This provided a 500-bed hospital, to which was added several small wooden buildings to serve as isolation wards.

The water supply at Key West, always a problem, was made more so in 1898 by a long drought that left not enough in the cisterns for normal uses. The navy had built a 7,000 gallons-per-day distilling plant in the Civil War. By May 25, the army was getting 50,000 gallons a day from newly installed condensers. Until that time, the navy had hauled water from Tampa at a cost of two cents a gallon. July rains brought further relief.

The war ended on August 12, but the army and the navy's expansion of facilities went on until the newly initiated projects were completed. On August 16 it looked as if all work were going to be abandoned. Warships took away all navy personnel, and the army followed six days later, taking along also many of the civilian employees. The navy, it turned out, had discovered three cases of fever that a young naval surgeon had reported to the Secretary of Navy as yellow fever. Dr. Joseph Y. Porter had called in two other physicians but had been unable to convince the navy doctor that it was not yellow fever. To everybody's relief it proved to be only den-

St. Mary's Convent in Key West was offered as a military hospital in the War for Cuban Independence in 1898.

gue fever, of which there were some 6,999 cases but no fatalities. After September 12 the army and navy contingents returned to finish their work.

When the war inspired work was done, Key West had a deeper channel, a more modern navy yard, improved coaling facilities and beefed up defenses. Pensacola had only a minor role in the war but secured considerable additions to its defenses and facilities. Forts Barrancas and Pickens received new long-range guns and garrisons. Fort McRee was in ruins, and it was replaced by batteries of sixteen-inch disappearing rifles. Expenditures for improvements at Pensacola were third after Tampa and Key West, and it became the best protected city on the Gulf coast, perhaps because of the growing interest in an isthmian canal.

Disease was the great killer in the Spanish American War. Most of the deaths occurred after the fighting had ceased, and mainly among volunteer soldiers who had never left the country. Only 379 men lost their lives in the fighting between June 22 and August 12. In July, 316 men died on the field and 439 from disease. In August there were only thirty-five casualties on the field but 1,349 from disease. In the succeeding months there were 1,511 in September, 799 in October, 359 in November, and 187 in December, for a grand total of 4,784. The First Florida Regiment enlisted all together 1,286 men and thirty-nine officers, none of whom left the country, but this regiment in camps at Tampa and Fernandina lost twenty-seven

Lighthouse and quarantine station, Fort Jefferson, Dry Tortugas, 1897

to typhoid fever. Another ninety-nine Floridians volunteered for the naval reserve and served from April 17, establishing signal stations at the mouth of the Saint Johns, on Egmont Key, Sanibel Island and the Dry Tortugas. Five officers and ninety-eight enlisted men formed Company C of the Third U.S. Volunteer Infantry Regiment, made up of men supposedly immune to tropical fevers. Mustered into the service on July 17, 1898, they served for a time at Guantanamo, Cuba, in the army of occupation and were discharged on May 2, 1899; they lost one man, the only Floridian to die while abroad. Other Florida volunteers joined non-Florida units and served with General Miles in Puerto Rico.

The War Department remained under fire throughout the war. There was little or no planning or coordination. The health record came in for the most severe condemnation. The fault lay with the national administration. The record of the Florida camps was no worse and no better than others. In September President McKinley ordered a commission to investigate health conditions and fix responsibility for any irregularities or dereliction of duty they found. Between September 24, 1898, and February 9, 1899, the commissioners visited camps and studied the health records of the personnel. They published a useful report, but it came too late to have any effect on camp conditions in that war. Surgeon General George Sternberg had become disturbed about the health situation early in July 1898, and Secretary of War Alger, who was receiving the brunt of the criticism, authorized him to employ a board of experts to study health problems in the camps. On August 1, Major Walter Reed became chairman of a board that began on August 18 to study all of the factors involved.

The Reed commission produced nine immediate and useful reports. Typhoid fever, they discovered, had struck every one of the regiments that entered the federal service. Forty-one, or thirty-eight percent of them, had brought cases of fever into the camps, where it spread rapidly. They found too many doctors who had no training or experience in military medicine or camp sanitation. In the volunteer units, state governors had appointed the doctors. Too frequently the little known fever was neither diagnosed nor treated correctly. The fact that regular units suffered less seems to bear out the charges that general lack of training and discipline was a major cause. The investigators found the camp sites suitably chosen, but some had been used too long and had been unnecessarily crowded, with latrines and garbage pits so close to the tents that they became sources of infection. The water was good until contaminated by poor camp sanitation of one kind or another. The War Department had been unprepared to expand from 26,000 to 273,000 men in four months and send expeditions on short notice to Cuba, Puerto Rico, and the Philippines.

The health record of the Florida camps damaged the state's reputation as a health resort. There was a strong disposition to blame diseases on the water supply and the warm humid climate. There was an especially strong tendency to blame the water supply for

Key West harbor about 1915. Note sponge and lumber sheds in fore-ground, fish docks and fishing fleet on shoreline, and P & O and FEC railroad docks in background. The large tanks were for storage of Cuban molasses, which was shipped north in tank cars.

typhoid fever, which caused eighty-seven percent of the deaths. Investigation proved water to be the source of infection in only one instance, and carelessness made it so there. Climate affected comfort rather than health, and Miami, which got the worst report, was not responsible except that it had a bad sewage disposal arrangement. The men took to the woods. The surface wells, which should not have been used in any case, became contaminated. One Jacksonville camp using the same arrangement experienced similar results. The Jacksonville camps were generally the best administered and had one of the best health records. For lack of illness the Fernandina site came out first. The only typhoid there arrived with the troops from Tampa. That city suffered most from overcrowding. The commissions of inquiry usually disproved if they did not overcome the bad publicity.

This was not Florida's first experience with epidemic disease. The state had prepared itself to cope with yellow fever as well as the limited knowledge of the day permitted. That there was no outbreak in 1898 is perhaps correctly attributed to the careful work of Dr. Joseph Porter. In spite of the criticisms of its water and weather, Florida became better known as a result of the attention focused on it during the war. Tampa, Key West and Pensacola came out of the conflict with greatly improved harbors and defenses. The communities that hosted camps had enjoyed a brief but frenzied economic prosperity. After the disastrous freeze in early 1895 had set them back so seriously, farmers and growers needed such a financial boost. The railroads were the greatest gainers, particularly the Plant system, whose facilities were used to capacity. The railroads also came out of the period of conflict with significant additions to their facilities paid for largely by the War Department. Had the short stay of the war correspondents and the armed services personnel and their families occurred in the winter months, the story might have been different. As it was, the whole inglorious episode took place between two winter tourist seasons.

21.

The Broward Era

The forces of popular discontent and demand for reform that had been growing in Florida life and politics for a generation reached a climax in the administration of Governor Napoleon Bonaparte Broward and continued with diminishing intensity in the next two administrations. The issues were not new, but they were more sharply defined and the contrast between the forces of conservatism and the demand for change was greater. In Broward the proponents of change had a champion who gave his name to an era of which he was as much heir as creator. The Progressive movement was in full swing all over the country. Theodore Roosevelt was giving it a shining national image, and Broward's predecessor in office had done much to prepare the way for his achievements.

In the early years of Broward's life there was much of the romantic and the tragic. Born in 1857 on a plantation in Duval County, he was descended from a French soldier in the American Revolution who settled shortly thereafter in Spanish Florida and received a substantial land grant in 1816. His grandfather had been a member of the first state senate. By standards of that day the family was reasonably well-to-do. Then the American Civil War brought tragedy. The slaves departed, the family fled to White Springs, their buildings were burned, and the fields grew up in weeds and pine saplings. Some of the land, greatly reduced in value, was sold for taxes. The father and the two sons, Napoleon and Montcalm, built a single-pen log cabin and recleared some of the land to plant garden and field crops, but with little success. The mother died in 1869 and the father a year later. The five children grew up in the homes of aunts and uncles and acquired along the way a rudimentary education. The future governor soon gravitated to work in several capacities on the Saint Johns River, with which he was always to be associated in some way. He held pilot's and master's licenses and became an owner of boats as well. In January 1883 he married Georgiana Carolina "Carrie" Kemp, daughter of his employer and later his partner in the operation of boats on the river. The young wife died in childbirth in less than a year and the infant six weeks later. On May 5, 1887, he married Annie Isabel Douglass and became the father of eight daughters and one son.

Napoleon Broward received his first public office in January 1888 when Governor Perry appointed him sheriff of Duval County. In that office he gained some reputation for courage and integrity by an attack on gambling interests in Jacksonville. In the fall of the same year he lost to a Republican when most of the white citizens had fled the city to escape the yellow fever epidemic. In March 1889, when the newly elected sheriff had been disqualified on a technicality, Broward again became sheriff by appointment. He then won the office in the election of 1892, only to be removed by Governor Mitchell because his excessive zeal in supervising an election in 1894 was called interference. Broward had placed special police and deputies in the polling places against the express instructions of Governor Mitchell. In some cases polls were closed in protest against the deputies. He won election for sheriff once more in 1896 after first refusing to run again and then being literally drafted to make the race.

A prizefight in Jacksonville in 1894 reflects something of the sense of public morality and sense of propriety of Broward and many other Floridians of the day. In November of the preceding year some Jacksonville sportsmen and businessmen organized the Duval Athletic Club to promote a heavyweight championship fight between James J. Corbett, the titleholder, and the Englishman Charles Mitchell. Governor Mitchell and Sheriff Broward were determined to prevent the fight, and the governor was ready to use the state militia if necessary. Only a court order forbidding their interference permitted the fight to go on at two in the afternoon on January 25, near the present site of the "Gator Bowl." Deputies arrested both fighters as soon as the fight was over. Released on $5,000 bond, a six-man jury acquitted Corbett, who had won in the third round, and the case against Mitchell was dropped.

The office of county sheriff is not commonly a path to political preferment, but it became so in Broward's case. In that office he became the leader of a faction of the local Democrats called "straightouts" who favored Populist-Progressive reforms directed principally against railroads and other corporate interests. His close associates were men of the same stamp across the state: John N. C. Stockton, William James Bryan, Nathan P. Bryan, Stephen R. Mallory, Jr., John M. Barrs, Frank Pope, William Sherman Jennings, and Wilkinson Call.

Broward's interest in boats and boating also led to his becoming well known up and down the Saint Johns. When he and his brother and George DeCottes joined forces in 1895 to build a powerful seagoing tug, which they named *Tfie Three Friends,* they were unwittingly pushing Broward closer to the governorship. *The Three Friends,* designed principally for towing, wrecking, and carrying passengers and freight from Jacksonville to and from Nassau, Bahamas, made her maiden voyage in January 1896. Fortunately for what proved to be a languishing business venture, the War for Cuban Independence had broken out again in February 1895, and the tug's owners soon found themselves in the lucrative if somewhat

The Three Friends *helped to make a Florida governor.*

risky business of trading with the Cuban rebels in violation of President Grover Cleveland's insistence upon strict neutrality. When the United States entered the war in April 1898, Broward and his associates were under indictment, but the case was dismissed for lack of evidence. Floridians, meanwhile, had watched with interest and applauded with gusto when Broward's filibustering exploits were reported and his illegal activities turned him into a public hero.

In 1900 Broward won a seat in the state legislature and in the session in 1901 further established himself as a liberal, anti-railroad, anti-corporation man when he defended the railroad commission and the primary system for nominating all candidates for elective office. He voted for the Flagler divorce bill and convinced his supporters that he did so on the merits of the bill rather than for Flagler money or political support. As governor, however, he signed a bill in 1905 repealing the law. After the legislative session he became active in the Jacksonville Towing and Wrecking Company. Between February 1902 and August 1903, he moved his family to South Florida where the company was operating. He later returned to Jacksonville and soon after decided to run for governor.

He was, then, as well known as any Floridian and not entirely without political experience. He had a firm political base with the "straight-outs" in Duval County. There existed no political organization of his own, however, except to the extent that he inherited the wholehearted support of outgoing Governor William Sherman Jennings who could supply the nucleus of an organization. Broward ran as the champion of farmers, cattlemen, small business, and labor against the growing power of urban corporate interests, especially railroads. The daily newspapers in the larger cities usually opposed him and his program. An exception had been the *Florida Times Union* until it was acquired by the Flagler interests on September 9, 1897, whereupon it joined the opposition. He could make a virtue of having no large and well-heeled organization to promote his cause, the cause of the people. He continued to support the railroad commission and the direct primary and to demand, in the Progressive language of the day, the regulation of trusts. He also championed Everglades drainage, picturing it as a crusade to rescue the public lands of the state from the railroads and the railroad-dominated trustees of the Internal Improvement Fund and save them for the people, the last a pledge he proved unable to keep. His support for statewide prohibition also became increasingly important.

His principal rival for the nomination was Robert W. Davis, a well-known Jacksonville attorney who had served one term in the state legislature and four in the national House of Representatives. Dannitte H. Mays of Monticello and C. M. Brown ran well enough to force the two leading contenders into a runoff, which Broward won by the narrow margin of 22,979 to 22,265. He then won easily in the general election in November, besting his Republican opponent, M. B. MacFarlane, by 28,357 to 6,357. W. R. Healy, running on the Socialist ticket, picked up 1,270 votes. The near even balance of interests is further indicated by James P. Taliaferro, probable successor to the William D. Chipley role as defender of the railroads and other interests, winning over John N. C. Stockton in the second primary for the United States Senate seat for which Wilkinson Call had been the third contender.

The Broward inaugural address was an expression of faith in democratic government and the belief that people should have more, not less, to do with it. He repeated his commitment to the primary election system, the railroad commission, the common school, Everglades drainage, economical government, and equal enforcement of the laws. In a bill of particulars he presented his program in more detail to the legislature on April 4, 1905. He urged a state board to equalize property assessments; wanted reorganization of schools of higher learning, better teachers with higher salaries, uniform textbooks, and increased appropriations for common schools; humane treatment of state convicts; making the railroad commission a constitutional part of state government; making primaries mandatory for choosing nominees for all public offices; requiring sworn statements of expenses by all candidates for nomination or election; state pensions for Confederate veterans to be paid by counties; a compulsory life insurance program with the state becoming involved in the life insurance business; better salaries for the state judiciary; and laws for the conservation of fish, oysters, game, and forests. Everglades drainage he reserved for a special message on May 3 in which he reviewed the long history of the subject.

Not all of these could be achieved, but the results were impressive. Men committed to Broward's program were in the majority in the house and senate. Drainage received approval in general, but adequate financing was denied, being limited to the proceeds of land sales and a tax on the lands to be drained. A uniform school textbook law died without action in the session. The Buckman Act accomplished a major reorganization of higher education by consolidating the seven state-supported schools into four—one for white men, one for white women, and one for blacks, and a school for the deaf, dumb, and blind-with a board of control to coordinate and supervise their activities. Out of this grew the modern University of Florida at Gainesville, all male until 1947; Florida State University, which was Florida State College for Women until 1947, at Tallahassee; and Florida A and M University at Tallahassee for blacks. The greatest opposition came from places that would lose state support, and the greatest problem proved to be making the decision to locate the university in east Florida at Gainesville.

The legislators showed little interest in the governor's proposal on life insurance. That body did appropriate $25,000 to build an executive mansion in Tallahassee and raised the governor's salary from $3,500 to $5,000 a year. The Browards became the first occupants of the mansion when they moved into it in late September 1907. The building was replaced in 1957 by the $350,000 Georgian colonial style mansion now occupied by Florida's governor. A joint resolution also acknowledged the return to Florida of Confederate battle flags captured from Florida units by Union forces in the War Between the States. Another appropriation provided for hospital buildings, salaries, and supplies for the hospital for the insane at Chattahoochee, where legislative investigation revealed inadequacies of all kinds.

In his lengthy address to the 1907 legislature, the governor pointed with pride to the growth revealed in the state census of 1905, which showed an increase in population from 1900 to 1905 of 86,303 or 16.4 percent and a 45.5 percent increase in the value of assessed property. His list of recommendations was longer as he repeated old and added new ones. Significant new features were an arsenal for state troops; a state tax on franchises or other privileges; codification of school laws, regulations, and rules; more equitable apportionment in the state legislature; compulsory schools and school attendance; good roads; state advertising for tourists and settlers; registration of lobbyists; restriction of child labor; punishment of public press for knowingly printing an untruth; and a proposal to buy up the property of all blacks in the United States and colonize them in a nation of their own where their territorial and political independence could be guaranteed. This strange last proposal he justified on the ground that he could see "no ultimate

The first governor's mansion housed governors from 1907 to 1957.

good results that can accrue from the education of a race, without planting in their being the hope of attaining the highest position in government affairs and society."

Again the laws enacted are as notable for the areas ignored as for those acted upon. Child labor was prohibited in factories, mines, and beer gardens. A pure food law reflecting the national interest in that subject was enacted. It also became illegal to sell or give cigarettes to minors. A state appropriation provided for a statue of General Edmund Kirby Smith in Statuary Hall, Washington, D.C. Also passed was a law to transport the remains of Ponce de León to Florida if permission could be secured. The legislature reaffirmed the commitment to drainage and the tax to support it. The first automobile speed law appeared on the statute books, requiring the operator of a motor vehicle to stop on request of a person riding, leading, or driving a restive horse and limiting speed to four miles an hour when approaching bridges or curves. Under a law of the previous administration owners of automobiles also had to register them with the secretary of state and pay a two-dollar fee. Almost 300 persons registered autos in 1906, and there were 733 in 1908. The historic St. Francis Barracks in Saint Augustine, leased from the federal government for a dollar a year, became the arsenal and headquarters for the state militia, with a campsite provided at Black

This handsome governor's mansion, occupied since 1957, reflects Florida's increasing wealth and sophistication.

Broward's place in the history of the state was secure. William T. Cash, historian of the Democratic party in Florida and a younger contemporary of Broward, concluded in 1936 that he was the most constructive governor the state ever had. It was Cash who gave the name Broward Era to his and the succeeding two administrations when his political philosophy and program remained dominant. In this regard it is worth observing that administration of Sidney J. Catts (1917-1921) had more Populist-Progressive character than is commonly noted.

Broward's career thereafter was brief. He entered the race for the United States Senate seat vacated by the death of Sephen R. Mallory, Jr. on December 23, 1907. Broward had appointed William James Bryan, who had been his campaign manager, to the post. He was the youngest man except Henry Clay ever to sit in the Senate. Bryan lived only until March 22, 1908, when he died of typhoid fever. Broward then appointed William Hill Milton of Marianna, a grandson of Florida's Civil War governor who did not choose to run for the full term, which left the way open for Broward. His platform for national office resembled his program for Florida. He came out for stronger regulation of the nation's railroads and urged that the Interstate Commerce Commission be given effective power to fix railroad rates. He supported a national drainage law, lower tariffs, prevention of price fixing on naval stores by trusts, the eight-hour day for labor, and extension of employer liability legislation.

In the first primary Broward received 10,078 votes, Duncan U. Fletcher 17,208, William B. Lamar 12,527, and John Beard 4,592. In the runoff Fletcher won by 29,152 votes to 25,563. The loss to another Progressive politician can be accounted for in a number of ways. Florida governors have been notoriously unable, with such notable exceptions as Park Trammell and Spessard L. Holland, to convert the governorship into anything but a political dead end. There is also another partial explanation. Broward had won with labor support in 1904, but he lost much of it in 1908 when he sent the state militia into Pensacola in a decidedly anti-union stand during a strike of electrical workers. Two years later when nominations for the Senate seat of James P. Taliaferro were open, Broward entered the race, as did Claude L'Engle. Broward led with 21,077 votes, but L'Engle's 4,677 votes forced a runoff, which Broward won by 25,780 to 23,193, only to die in October before taking the office that was to become vacant in March of the next year. In a special election in February 1911, Nathan P. Bryan, a Browardite, won the right to be sent to the Senate by the legislature; he was the last Floridian to reach the Senate by that route.

The Broward years were clearly transitional. The issues he championed were being achieved or giving way to new ones. Symbolic were the appearance of automobiles and the beginning of the good roads movement. Equally important were the growth of business and the concurrent rise of organized labor, which came prominently to public attention in the economic distress that followed the panic of 1907. Though not heavily industrialized, among Florida's numerous small businesses, many of them marginally financed in the first place, often went broke, and others took advantage of the opportunity, if not the necessity, to cut costs by reducing wages. Tampa, Jacksonville, and Pensacola suffered most. Pensacola with only 20,000 inhabitants had twenty-two identifiable unions. The workers lost the first strike when the Pensacola Street Railway Company threatened to import strikebreakers and the union failed to win public support. In April, Pensacola Electric Company workers struck again when the company refused to arbitrate differences. When a dozen strikebreakers brought in by the company were injured in a riot, the mayor of Pensacola wired the governor for aid, and Broward sent the militia, placed the city under martial law, and imposed a ten o'clock curfew. Broward also induced Mayor Goodman to revoke the permit for a labor rally, but Goodman later relented. This time the strikers had some support, but the company flatly refused to yield. After the troops were withdrawn, the company requested police protection for some strikebreakers brought in from West Virginia; twenty-five of the thirty-three men on the force resigned rather than help to break the strike. An injunction then forbade the union to interfere with the operation of the street railways system, but violence continued. When the public withdrew support, the strike collapsed.

The frustrated workers then turned to political action and added perhaps a thousand new registrants to the voter list. Since they could not hope to influence much less capture the major parties, they supported one or the other of the four minor parties. These were significant signs of the times. The *Jasper News,* an official Farmers Union newspaper, endorsed Broward but blasted his use of militia to protect "a foreign monopoly." Stone and Webster owned and operated the Pensacola Electric Company. Labor withdrew its support from Broward and gave some of it to John Beard, who supported Stockton when he was eliminated in the first primary. The Prohibition party picked up some votes by including in its platform government ownership of public lltilities, graduated income tax, and free textbooks. The Populists defended the right to organize, the eight-hour day, employer's liability, and government-sponsored public works during periods of unemployment, opposed the competition of convict labor with free labor, praised labor unions, and advised farmers to include urban workers in their organizations. The Independence party would prohibit blacklisting by employers, cease the arbitrary use of injunctions in labor disputes, and create a Department of Labor with cabinet status. The Socialist party with a mild platform in contrast to such radicals as the Industrial Workers of the World reached an all-time high in membership and drew the largest of the protest votes. Dividing the white labor vote raised the specter of black domination, but the frustration spent itself, wages and employment improved, and the workers returned to the major parties. They had, however, exhibited signs of a new day.

Albert Waller Gilchrist, who became governor of Florida in 1909, suffers by contrast with Broward, whose colorful personality and flair for publicity he lacked, and he has aptly been called "Florida's Middle-of-the-Road Governor." He may be charged with straddling and fence sitting. He had no wish to change the course of Florida politics and legislation and avoided controversy. But he might also be called one of the most creative salesmen and advertisers of Florida ever to sit in the governor's chair. His father had come to Quincy, Florida, in the 1840s and, as befitted a prominent landowner, sat in both houses of the legislature. The son attended Carolina Military Academy at Charlotte, North Carolina, where he studied engineering along with military training. He entered the United States Military Academy in 1878 but failed experimental philosophy three years later and was forced to withdraw. The civil engineering and military education, however, both materially affected his career.

Gilchrist became Inspector General of Militia in the administrations of Governors Perry and Fleming, and Governor Mitchell made him a brigadier general. At the outbreak of the Spanish American War, he enlisted as a private when he was denied an officer's commission. He was mustered out on May 2, 1899, with the rank of captain. President Grover Cleveland returned him to the military academy fifteen years after his dismissal as a member of the Board of Visitors. As a result of his education in civil engineering he became a well-known surveyor, real estate man, and promoter. His work took him into at least fifteen counties of the state but his major interests were around Punta Gorda. He repre-

The second U.S.S. Florida, *a 15-gun frigate, was built in 1864 and known originally as the U.S.S.* Wampanoag. *Its name was changed to* Florida *in 1869.*

sented DeSoto County for four terms in the state legislature, in 1905 was speaker of the house, and he knew well the workings of state government.

Gilchrist and John N. C. Stockton of Jacksonville were long-avowed candidates for the governorship. Also seeking the nomination were Jefferson B. Browne of Key West, who had been chairman of the State Railroad Commission, and R. Hudson Burr, then the chairman. Gilchrist urged that prohibitionists stay with the county option plan then in the constitution. He favored capital and labor and would grant labor the same right to organize that capital had. Stockton came out on a strong Broward type of platform only to find that those issues had lost some of their appeal, as did his charges that special interests supported Gilchrist. Burr withdrew from the race, and in the first count Gilchrist received 23,248 votes, Stockton 20,968, and Browne 8,986. Gilchrist won easily in the runoff by 32,465 to 23,291. In the November election he bested Republican John M. Cheney by 33,036 votes to 6,453, with 2,427 for A. J. Pettigrew, Socialist.

In his inaugural address Gilchrist expressed his pleasure at winning the offlce he had so long coveted. He noted growing interest in good roads, said that drainage was a business proposition to be continued if justifiable on that basis, and urged more humane treatment of female and infirm convicts. He was Florida's second bachelor governor, and his mother, Mrs. J. B. Gibbs, acted as his official hostess. At his request Miss Elizabeth Fleming, daughter of ex-govemor Francis P. Fleming, acted as sponsor to christen the battleship *Florida.* The citizens of Florida purchased a silver service for the wardroom of the ship; this silver was put on display in a small dining room of the executive mansion when the *Florida* was decommissioned in 1931.

The third U.S.S. Florida *on her trial run, May 4, 1912*

In his address to the legislature in April 1909, Gilchrist pointed to a 35.5 percent increase in population over the previous ten years, a decline in illiteracy, and a lower death rate. He observed that Florida had one-half of the phosphate deposits in the United States and one-third in the world and produced something like one-half of the naval stores in the country. He urged the legislature to make the Railroad Commission Act more specific, and to protect convicts and give the money received for their lease to counties on the basis of the assessed value of property. Thirty-six other states had a graduated inheritance tax; should Florida not have one? He stirred a minor tempest when he recommended that Lincoln's birthday become a legal holiday in the state, and one legislator threatened his impeachment if such a law was enacted. The governor proclaimed himself a southerner and defended the region.

Gilchrist traveled extensively to advertise the state. Speaking at Tammany Hall on July 4, 1909, he argued that the South treated the black as well as Pacific coast residents did the Chinese and Japanese. In August he spoke for drainage, good roads, and representation at a National Irrigation Congress in Spokane, Washington, where he also urged that the Mason and Dixon line be abolished. He traveled down the Mississippi River with President William Howard Taft, some cabinet members, twenty-three governors, and 117 members of Congress. He prepared a feature "Florida the Marvelous" for the *Chicago Examiner's* February 6, 1910, edition. He helped to promote a Panama Canal Celebration at Tampa from February 12 to 26, 1910, to which he invited the governors and people of other states. He secured for the occasion two companies each of cavalry, artillery, and infantry with bands as well as a visit by several U.S. battleships and cruisers.

The governor's address to the 1909 legislature offered few surprises. He recommended that state convicts be used for road building as was being done in Georgia and favored daylight saving time. The state had purchased 8,150.5 acres of land for a state prison farm, and he asked an appropriation to take up an option he had made to purchase an additional 7,445 acres at the same price of five dollars an acre. He also urged a general law to incorporate trust companies, the establishment of a state tuberculosis hospital, and an extension of time for the Florida East Coast Railroad to qualify for a land grant on the Key West Extension, which had been under construction since 1905 but whose completion was delayed by hurricanes in 1906, 1909, and 1910. The legislature was not overly generous in its response. The lawmakers did put telephone and telegraph rates under the supervision of the Railroad Commission, but this, it was charged, was to save them from piecemeal regulation by local government. The largest special appropriations were $100,000 for a supreme court building in Tallahassee and half that sum to finance an exposition at Saint Augustine. The same body refused to ratify the sixteenth or income tax amendment to the United States Constitution. The governor vetoed a bill to abolish the convict lease system and use the prisoners to work on roads because of serious defects in the title, and the veto was sustained.

In 1912 the Florida Democrats nominated Park Trammell of Lakeland to be governor. He had come up through the political ranks, having been a member of both houses of the legislature, president of the senate, and attorney general. Florida received a fourth member of the national House of Representatives as a result of the census of 1910, this member to be elected at large in 1912. In a runoff, Claude L'Engle won the Democratic nomination from a field of six candidates. L'Engle was no newcomer to the political wars. He had been editing and publishing controversial political newspapers since 1903 and has been called a muckraker. He was one of a galaxy of American journalists who wrote exposés of the corrupt alliance of business and politics early in this century. L'Engle was founder, publisher, and editor of the *Florida Sun,* which began as a weekly in January 1903 and became a daily in November 1903 but soon ceased publication because of financial difficulties. He started the *Sun* again in Tallahassee on June 23, 1906, modified to be less a newspaper and more a magazine; it continued to appear for some two years. His first exposé in December 1905 was an attack on the naval stores trust operating out of Savannah, Georgia, and the relations of a Jacksonville export company with it. He attacked legalized land-grabbing by buying up tax titles.

Included among his victims were trusts in beef, groceries, electricity, and ice. He favored a progressive income and inheritance tax; opposed child labor, patent medicine abuses, and excessive campaign contributions; and supported the direct primary, municipal ownership of public utilities, and conservation. He named those he considered unfit for public office and was credited with defeating the Democratic candidate for the legislature from Manatee County and electing A. J. Pettigrew, the only Socialist ever to sit in the Florida legislature.

He showed considerable independence in his views rather than following the national muckraker pattern. He supported organized labor and favored immigration, the latter reflecting the state's need for settlers. Unlike most muckrakers, he opposed Theodore Roosevelt. This may have been mere partisanship, but it may have sprung from his opposition to blacks to whom he felt Roosevelt was being too friendly. L'Engle won the state printing contract in the first year of the Broward administration. This usually meant high political favor, but L'Engle had not always been a Broward supporter nor did he remain so.

If the race for the governorship in Florida stirred less than usual interest in 1912, the national election aroused more than usual. Democratic aspirants for the nomination were Woodrow Wilson, governor of New Jersey; Oscar W. Underwood of Alabama, in the House of Representatives since 1890; Champ Clark of Missouri, Speaker of the House; and Judson Harmon, governor of Ohio. Underwood had the support of the Florida delegation to the Democratic National Convention until the forty-sixth ballot, when they split seven for Wilson and five for Clark. Only the *Miami Metropolis* of the Florida daily newspapers had supported Wilson, but when he was nominated, 70.18 percent of the voters supported him whereas Bryan had won only 63.02 percent four years earlier.

Republicans in Florida in 1912 were few in number and split into numerous factions. When the state convention convened in Palatka on February 6 and Taft men won control, almost half of the delegates, many of them blacks, walked out. When the seceders met in Jacksonville on May 18 to choose a Roosevelt delegation, C. H. Alston, a black lawyer from Tampa, led a bolt from that convention and chose a third set of delegates for the Republican National Convention, which was to meet in Chicago on June 18. When the credentials committee seated the Taft delegates by unanimous vote, the two dissenting factions joined the seceders, who formed the Progressive party. When the white Progressives in Florida who were to meet in Ocala set up a separate convention for blacks to meet in Saint Augustine, Alston repudiated both and called a third convention to choose a slate of delegates for Theodore Roosevelt. When the all-white Progressive slate of delegates won Roosevelt's approval, Alston and some of his associates withdrew from the party and voted for Woodrow Wilson, whose strong support for segregation did not become clear until after he was inaugurated. Blacks in Florida did not at the time have anywhere to go politically.

In spite of the apparent lack of issues in the election, the Trammell administration achieved a record of constructive legislation that rounded out the Populist-Progressive program for the state. He proposed to repeal the railroad land grant law, to abolish the convict lease system, to levy a graduated tax on inheritances and on corporate profits, to tighten election laws, to limit campaign expenditures, to strengthen the railroad commission, to provide for

Highway through Florida pine woods, 1922

absentee voting, and to introduce initiative, referendum, and recall in the law-making process, the ultimate in responsiveness of government to voters. Banks, he argued, should pay into a fund to insure deposits and pay interest on public money deposited with them for any time beyond current needs, counties should be authorized to employ agricultural agents, and there should be an experiment station in the Everglades to study the peculiar qualities of the soils, which had a high organic content but proved to lack certain minerals necessary to fruitful plant growing. He urged that the counties and the state should take steps to eradicate cattle ticks. He thought a five-hundred dollar tax exemption would encourage home building, that the state should give more financial support to schools at all levels, and that Florida must have a highway commission.

Proposal for a highway commission was not new, but the new incentive was the availability of matching funds from the federal government, which required such a state agency. This did not yet mean that the state should take over roadbuilding. Its function was largely to provide professional services and advice to county commissions. Its only source of funds for the state commission was the returns from the sale of automobile licenses. In 1913 the legislature did an extensive overhauling of the election laws. The state took over from the political parties the control of the nomination process in the primaries, a step which ultimately made the Democratic white primary illegal.

Because candidates were spending too much money to win nominations in primaries, the legislature set limits of $4,000 for governor and United States Senator, $2,500 for state cabinet posts, $2,000 for congressmen, and $600 for circuit judges and state attorneys. Fourteen years later the amounts in the respective categories were raised to $15,000, $5,000, $4,000, and $1,200, but such limits proved unrealistic in a short time. To the same end the law substituted second-choice voting for the second primary. The second choice counted only if first choice produced no candidate with a majority of the votes cast for that office. Voters either could not or would not avail themselves of the opportunity to name a second choice. The law was confusing and clumsy to administer, but it was the means of settling a number of contests and was used until 1931. Much of the governor's forward-looking program would later become law, but some of it, like the initiative, referendum, and recall, would lose popularity.

Florida was continuing to grow steadily but not spectacularly, in fact not much faster yet than the national average. Population was up in 1900 to 752,619, a forty-two percent increase in the decade. In 1910 Jacksonville became the largest city with 28,249 persons, Key West dropped to third place with 17,144, Pensacola rose to second with 17,747, and Tampa was a close fourth with 15,839. Jacksonville grew phenomenally in the next ten years-to 57,699 or more than 100 percent. Tampa was also growing rapidly as it reached 37,782. Key West, barely holding its own with 19,945, lost third place to Pensacola's 22,982. Three new counties, Saint Lucie in 1905, Palm Beach in 1909, and Pinellas in 1911, indicated areas of growth.

In 1912 Jacksonville moved ahead to meet the opportunity and the problems posed by the increase of river traffic. In response to a petition signed by twenty-two state senators and fifty-two house members, the Jacksonville Board of Trade, the Jacksonville Central Trades and Labor Council, and over 3,000 citizens, Governor Gilchrist called a special session of the legislature to authorize some harbor improvements. The city agreed to pay the cost of the session up to three days. The urgency arose from the fact that the

Passengers on the Overseas Railroad often saw only water on either side.

United States Army Engineers would recommend no more federal money for improvements on the Saint Johns River until the city undertook to construct and operate municipal docks, which at the time were in private hands. The special session authorized a $1,522,000 bond issue to be administered by a port commission made up of fifteen local citizens. The commission selected a site known as Old Soldiers' Home, purchased 144 acres, and began construction of docks and terminal which were ready for use by the fall of 1916. At the same time Miami was cutting a channel out to deep water in the hope of bringing that city a larger share of ocean-going traffic.

With the exception of the Key West Extension of the Florida East Coast Railroad, major railway construction had ended by 1900. After extensive surveys to select the most feasible route, construction following the line of the Florida Keys began in 1905. Causeways and bridges, one of which was seven miles long, were constructed to connect the keys. The Key West Extension appropriately became known as the "Overseas Railroad." The first train reached Key West on January 22, 1912.

Severe hurricanes in 1909 and 1910 interrupted the work and builders met unexpected construction problems, but Flagler had the means to complete the project and the conviction to see it through. The road never met the expectations of its builder. Key West re-

Captain Tony Jannus inaugurates the first regularly scheduled airline flight on January 11, 1914 at Saint Petersburg.

Louis Ross set a record mile at 38.05 in this Stanley Steamer on January 29, 1905.

mained simply the end of the line rather than becoming a terminal for transfer of freight and passengers to ocean-going craft for movement to points south and west. Nor did it affect very much the fortunes of Key West. Nevertheless, trains operated regularly until the 1935 hurricane disrupted service to such a degree that the extension was abandoned. It was converted to become the "Overseas Highway" for automobiles, utilizing the railroad right-of-way and bridges.

A new phase of transportation destined to become an index of Florida growth occurred in 1914 when Captain Tony Jannus operated two scheduled air flights daily between Tampa and Saint Petersburg. In the same year the first United States Naval Air Station was established at Pensacola, and World War I found Florida ready to participate in the coming air age that was destined to mean so much to the state's future. The automobile was attracting ever-increasing use and attention and was much advertised by races on the sand at Daytona Beach, inaugurated in 1903 when Alexander Winton drove his "Bullet" at the then-unbelievable speed of 68.198 miles per hour. Road building and cheaper autos were about to open up a new era in the entire country, but nowhere so much so as in Florida.

A long step toward the achievement of Florida's first national park occurred in 1916 when Royal Palm State Park was established on Paradise Key some fifteen miles southwest of Homestead and Florida City on the road to Flamingo. Interest in the biological treasures of this largest and richest in vegetation of the Everglades keys dated back to the last decade of the previous century when scientists began to observe and study them. The completion of a road from Florida City to the Key in 1915 opened up the possibility that the vegetation might be removed to clear the land for farming. The Florida Federation of Women's Clubs became interested as early as 1910. The Model Land Company, land agent for the Florida East Coast Railroad, and the state of Florida each contributed 960 acres. In 1929, upon the recommendation of Mrs. William Sherman Jennings, wife of the former governor, the Federation offered the park that the organization was maintaining to be part of an Everglades National Park if and when it should be established.

The wish for radical change in politics, in society, in economics, and in religion motivated the utopian groups which began settling in Florida after the depression year of 1893. Floridians were generally unsympathetic to the communal and socialistic ideals of the newcomers. The utopians, drawn south by Florida's reputation as last frontier and tropical Garden of Eden, met with only mixed success in demonstrating doctrines popular in other parts of the country. The Shakers installed a branch at Narcossee, Osceola County, in 1894, but abandoned it after seventeen years of effort with not a single convert. In 1899 the National Production Company, led by a Swedenborgian minister and composed of refugees from the failing Christian Commonwealth Colony in Georgia, was begun at East Point, near Apalachicola. The venture lasted no more than a year. Fruitcrest, a cooperative agricultural association founded by Thomas Elmer Will and dedicated to a "new order" was begun about 1916 in Everglades country south of Lake Okeechobee, and was a fiasco.

Two other attempts were more successful. Ruskin, a Christian-Socialist college town on Tampa Bay, was organized in 1908 by Dr. George McAnelly Miller. Ruskin College, dedicated to educating future labor-leaders, had previously been located in Missouri and Illinois. Classes began in 1910. Students worked in fields or shops for tuition and spending money. The College was also supported by the sale of land. Many students departed when the United States entered the Great War. Dr. Miller's death in 1919 doomed the college. The socialist beginnings of the town survive in a system of cooperative farming and marketing of vegetables which has made modern Ruskin prosperous. The cooperative was organized by Paul B. Dickman, a graduate of Ruskin College and a son of one of the founders of the town.

Estero, fifteen miles south of Fort Myers, was established as a colony of the Koreshan Unity of Chicago in 1894. The Unity's flamboyant leader, Dr. Cyrus R. Teed, transferred the headquarters of his movement to Estero in 1903 and was joined by nearly 200 pioneers. He promoted the town as a New Jerusalem, the site of a city which would combine earthly paradise, World's Fair, and atomic-powered Mediterranean metropolis. Unity leaders started a school, entered local politics, and opened several small businesses. Half a century of decline began in 1908 upon Dr. Teed's death. Few new members arrived, second and third-generation Koreshans departed, and the older members died or withdrew. The settlement, which passed to the State in 1961, was opened as Koreshan State Park in 1967, and the village has been restored as a historic site.[1]

22.

Management of
Natural Resources

Pioneers in any American community almost without exception have looked upon the resources that nature provides as something to be used without limit for their profit and pleasure. There once was such an apparently inexhaustible resource supply that talk about conservation or even careful use was likely to go unheeded. State governments correctly reflected the attitudes of most of their citizens when they insisted that the natural wealth must be used to attract settlers and capital to develop the state and get property on the tax rolls. Wildlife—fish, fowl, or animal—if on public land, was likely to be looked upon as common property with the right to use largely unrestricted. Florida is no exception to these generalizations. Only recently, when the natural endowment is gone or nearly so and countless thousands of new people are coming into the state to live, have Floridians become seriously concerned.

Because Florida had so large a proportion of its land area—more than one-fourth—overflowed or subject to overflow in times of heavy rainfall, the control of floods and the reclamation of these lands have been important concerns from earliest times. To those who surveyed the situation the problem seemed simple. There existed a surplus of water; get rid of the excess. Early efforts to apply this simple solution proved far more costly and complicated than was supposed and frequently created more problems than they solved. It became apparent that much of the area would suffer as much at times from water scarcity as from an excess in others. Concern about water surplus quickly became concern about water scarcity. Grazing cattle, growing crops, teeming city populations, new industries and conservation of wildlife increasingly demanded that water resources be guarded carefully. Hence, what was at first conceived as merely the removal of excess water has developed into a complex of water control and water use objectives that require extensive planning and the expenditure of tens of millions of dollars and involve participation of government at local, state and national levels.

Although commonly designated an Everglades phenomenon, the area involved is more than the Everglades. It is not a simple unit geographically. Much of it was and is still swampy and subject to overflow, and the water problems of the different parts are similar and sometimes interrelated. So flat and so related are the parts near the "divide" between the north-flowing Saint Johns and the south-flowing Kissimmee rivers that the direction of the wind or the distribution of rainfall may determine into which basin water standing on the ground will flow. The relationship of the parts added to the flatness of the whole terrain has made piecemeal attack on the problems of control inadequate and has proved that a comprehensive plan is essential to any degree of success. The region of greatest interest consists of four major parts. The upper Saint Johns and related areas extend north from near the Saint Lucie Canal to Lake Hamey and from the coastal ridge along the west side of Indian River westward to about the line of State Highway 15. A second part, the Kissimmee River basin, adjoins the first area on the west and includes Lake Istokpoga, Fisheating Creek, Taylor Creek, and the areas between. This area of some 4,400 square miles is generally flat with a gentle slope toward Lake Okeechobee. The third portion, the Everglades proper, lies south of Lake Okeechobee with arms extending around the eastern and western shores of the lake. The Everglades averages about forty miles in width and extends southward about one hundred miles, bending more and more to the southwest as it approaches the Gulf of Mexico. The ground surface elevation at Lake Okeechobee is about 15.0 feet (mean sea level), and at the latitude of Miami the surface is six to seven feet m.s.l., a fall of eight to nine feet in sixty-five miles. The Everglades is bounded on the west by a sandy region which rises to an elevation of as much as twenty-five feet in places and is overflowed only when rainfall is heaviest. On the east the Everglades is bounded by the coastal ridge which extends to a point south of Miami and deflects the water to the southwest except in times of highest water when the southern part of the ridge may be overflowed to the east through sloughs. This coastal ridge constitutes the fourth area. In it are the population centers from the Palm Beaches down through Fort Lauderdale, Hollywood, Miami, and Homestead where more than two million people resided by the 1970s. They look to the fresh water supplied by the Everglades to keep up the water table and insure their supplies of fresh water, and to the managers of the flood control district to prevent it from inundating them.

The desirability and the feasibility of draining the lake basin and the Everglades had been accepted from the beginning of the American occupation. The Buckingham Smith report in 1848, based in part on the observations of army and navy officers in the Seminole wars, agreed that the lands could and should be drained and suggested such uses as cattle raising and the growing of rice, sugarcane, vegetables and fruit. The military men added the opinion at that time that national defense would be well served if the entire peninsula were occupied by settlers.

The transfer of the swamp and overflowed lands to the state under an act of 1850, the creation of the Internal Improvement Fund to administer state lands and their use to subsidize canal and rail-road building were recounted earlier. Efforts to achieve drainage under private auspices by the Disston Drainage Contract in the Kissimmee River-Lake Okeechobee-Caloosahatchee complex indicated that the drained lands would grow crops, but also that drainage could not be accomplished piecemeal in the vast related areas and that the cost was beyond the possibility of private undertaking. In the absence of state or federal willingness to underwrite the cost, however, the trustees continued to seek private sponsors. In 1898, for example, they contracted with the Florida East Coast Drainage and Sugar Corporation to reclaim 800,000 acres near Miami, but nothing came of it. The twentieth century was to be another story. Although Governor Napoleon Bonaparte Broward gets most of the credit for initiating drainage under state auspices, his predecessor in office, William Sherman Jennings, actually prepared the way, first by establishing the state's claim to the lands for reclamation and thus shutting off railroad claims to them, and secondly by employing Fred G. Elliott, a drainage engineer for the United States Department of Agriculture, to survey the drainage and reclamation problem south of Lake Okeechobee. Elliott concluded after some ground surveys (the first ever made) that canals dredged to a grade of 0.3 to 0.4 feet per mile from the center of the area to either coast would accomplish the drainage. It was at this point that Broward assumed the leadership and pushed the program ahead.

In 1905 the state legislature passed the first comprehensive drainage law when it created a Board of Drainage Commissioners empowered to construct a system of canals to drain and reclaim swamp and overflowed lands. Governor Broward, as ex-officio chairman of the trustees of the Internal Improvement Fund, approved the employment of former Governor Jennings as general counsel for the new agency. In his first message to the legislature, Broward proposed that a canal be cut from Lake Okeechobee to the Saint Lucie River. He predicted that such a canal would lower the level of the lake for as much as four to six feet. He estimated that a canal two hundred feet wide and fifteen feet deep could be constructed in eighteen months at a cost of $250,000. He insisted that the drained area would produce all the sugar needs of the country. To finance the operation he recommended that the Board of Drainage Commissioners, the same ex-officio state officials as the trustees, have power to levy a yearly tax up to ten cents an acre, believing that the authority could tax the entire state. Voters in 1906 turned down the authority to make such a levy. The commissioners then created an Everglades Drainage District of 4,300,000 acres in the affected area and levied a tax of five cents an acre. They also ordered a survey of the proposed Saint Lucie Canal and contracted for two dredges. In November they made plans for a second canal route from the New River at Fort Lauderdale to Lake Okeechobee through lands wholly owned by the state.

Digging in the New River Canal began in the summer of 1906. The governor's critics maintained that years of research and study should have preceded such an undertaking, but he stuck to his guns, sure that his plan would work. In 1903, a Bureau of Drainage Investigation of the Office of Experiment Stations in the United States Department of Agriculture had begun to function. In February 1906 the bureau proffered its services to study feasibility of drainage in Florida. Surveys began in 1907 and continued in 1908. Broward was delighted that a national agency might support his claims, as he very much needed such support. Private landowners, principally railroad and timber companies with large tracts, were suing in the courts to invalidate the drainage tax on the ground that evidence of practicability had not been produced. They won their case, and the legislature in 1906 set specific boundaries for the district south and east of the lake, mostly on state-owned lands.

The prospect of drainage did sponsor a boom in land sales that provided enough funds for Broward to keep the project going. It also induced the private owners in the district to give up their opposition to the tax. In June 1908, R. P. Davie and Associates of Colorado contracted for 27,500 acres at two dollars an acre; in October, Walter R. Comfort of New York for 6,442 acres; in November, J. H. Tatum and Company of Miami, 12,000 acres; in December, the Davie Realty Company for 80,000 acres and Richard J. Bolles of New Mexico for 50,000 acres. The sale to Bolles extended payments to 1916 and provided for the construction of five main canals, on which at least fifty percent of the Bolles payments were to be used.

Broward had been unduly optimistic about the rate of progress and the cost of canal dredging. His successor in 1909 reported that the two dredges in the New River Canal had excavated fifteen miles at a cost of $377,642. The commissioners were also finding the scope of the operations too large for them to manage from Tallahassee, and late in 1909 they advertised for contractors to undertake the work of completing 235 miles of canals from Lake Okeechobee to the lower east coast.

When the report of the Department of Agriculture drainage engineers came to Governor Gilchrist in the winter of 1909, it failed to give all of the assurances that Broward had hoped. Supervising engineer James O. Wright prepared the report only to have his findings questioned by his associates and superiors. Governor Gilchrist was able, however, to publish an abstract of the full report that appeared to provide the hoped-for approval. Wright's report later proved to be almost as inadequately based as the opinions on which the board had proceeded, but in January 1910 Wright became the chief drainage engineer for the Everglades District and guided its destinies for the next ten years.

Senator Duncan U. Fletcher finally forced the publication of the controversial report as a Senate document along with other pertinent information on drainage. The Senate document contained a copy of every piece of legislation and every report that had been made on the subject of draining the Florida Everglades, including the Wright Report, which the Secretary of Agriculture meant to suppress because he considered it too favorable to the drainage program. When the first printing was exhausted, Senator Nathan P. Bryan secured the printing of an additional 4,800 copies.[1]

State and private agencies used extracts from the Wright report to promote land sales. On November 16, 1910, E. C. Chambers contracted for 50,000 acres at fifteen dollars an acre, a lucky break for it assured funds to continue the work and promoted other sales. By October 1911 the trustees were offering ten-acre tracts on the unfinished canals at thirty-five dollars an acre, the next tier of tracts at thirty dollars, and others at twenty-five. The Bolles Company sold ten thousand of its ten-acre farms at from twenty to twenty-four dollars an acre. The Everglades Land Company sold two thousand at about the same price. The Everglades Plantation Company did somewhat better, selling a thousand such tracts at thirty to fifty dollars an acre. Selling methods may have provided some lessons for promotion in the land boom in the next decade. The Everglades Land Sales Company, a Kansas City, Missouri, enterprise, sent out a letter from its Washington, D.C. office in 1910 and 1911 stating that six dredges were at work around the clock and others soon to begin. The advertising claimed that 224,000 acres had already been sold and only a limited acreage at fifty dollars an acre remained. Lantern slide lectures and a display of Florida products three nights a week were offered to prospective buyers. Dr. John C. Gifford of Miami, an enthusiastic believer in the value of Everglades drainage, estimated the cost at a dollar an acre. The application of lime and the cultivation of soil-building crops would maintain a high state of fertility, and five acres, he said, would support an ordinary family. At the end of World War II he reportedly suggested that all returning Florida servicemen be given five acres of Florida land and a jeep as endowment for a new life, possibly a parody on the "40 acres and a mule" plan for each former slave rumored at the end of the American Civil War.

The chorus of criticism mounted with the rising tide of sales promotion. A congressional investigation began with hearings early in February, 1912. Between February 3 and August 9 in forty-three hearings, the Moss Committee collected 1,759 pages of testimony and exhibits. The result was not favorable to the Department of Agriculture, but there were wide differences of opinion among members of Congress, state officials and engineers. Partly, no doubt because of the investigation, the flood of buyers dried up and no efforts on the part of trustees, drainage officials or private interests could keep it going. Unless new sources of financial support could be found, drainage efforts would have to cease. In 1913 the state legislature came to the rescue with authority for the commissioners to issue bonds up to a total of six million dollars. The commissioners, to defend their expenditures, employed (at a cost of $135,000) Isham Randolph, Marshall O. Leighton and Edmund T. Perkins to make a survey and evaluation of the project. The trio, after three months of study, recommended the Lake Okeechobee to Saint Lucie

River canal, which Governor Broward had proposed originally to control the water level in the big lake. The outbreak of the First World War placed a damper on such enterprises, and Everglades drainage was far from a reality. In 1915, in spite of failure to market the bonds authorized two years earlier, the commissioners let the contract for digging the twenty-five mile Saint Lucie Canal. The bond market then improved so that Governor Park Trammell could announce on January 1, 1917 the sale of $3,500,000 of the 1913 authorization. By 1925 the total authorized and sold reached $10,500,000, and drainage continued.

Reclamation of some lands was beginning to be a reality. In 1921 the United States Department of Agriculture established a sugarcane plant breeding station at Canal Point, and the Florida legislature located an agricultural experiment station at Belle Glade to study the special problems of growing crops on Everglades muck land, which proved to lack some of the basic minerals to grow crops and feed livestock on pastures. By that date there were sixteen settlements on or near the lake, with a total of about two thousand inhabitants doing reasonably well in dry years but likely to be drowned out in the more numerous wet years. Railroads, boats and highways provided more outlets for produce in the area. William J. 'Fingy" Conners, who had broken a finger in a dock fight with stevedores, came from Buffalo, New York, to West Palm Beach about 1917. The opening of the Palm Beach Canal to Lake Okeechobee opened his eyes to the possibility of speculation in Everglades land. He began with the purchase of 4,000 acres about six miles east of Canal Point but was not successful at farming. He next purchased the Southern States Land Company's experimental farm and named it Connersville. He planned to make a stock farm of it, but purebred cattle did not thrive and flooding ruined his hog raising plans. He continued to buy land, acquiring in order the townsite of Okeechobee and land around it and any available tracts between Okeechobee and Canal Point, in all about 12,000 acres. To provide access to his land he secured authority from the state to construct a toll road from the twenty-five mile bend west of West Palm Beach, nineteen miles along the canal to the lake and thirty-three miles around the lake to the town of Okeechobee. Building a road on the muck was something of a feat, but traffic began to flow over it on July 4, 1924. Conners collected tolls and sold land profitably. The year after he died in 1929 Palm Beach County acquired the road, abolished the tolls and turned it over to the State Road Department.

At much the same time, and with a more stimulating effect on development, the Florida East Coast Railroad extended its line to Okeechobee in 1915 and to Belle Glade in 1926. The Atlantic Coastline reached Moore Haven in 1918 and Clewiston in 1922, and the two joined at Lake Harbor shortly thereafter. Boats continued to operate regularly on the lake and the canals, but they had lost their monopoly and in time would lose out entirely to railroads and highways.

The collapse of the Florida land boom in 1926 brought to an end the effort to reclaim the Everglades under state auspices. The credit of the Everglades Drainage District had been used up, and the state was in no position to take up the financial burden. Much had been done, but much remained to be done, far more than was apparent at the time. There the whole matter might have ended somewhat as the efforts of Hamilton Disston in the eighties of the previous century. Yet, as it developed, too many persons had become residents and investors in the upper Everglades around the lake to be left to their fates unaided. A pair of natural disasters called attention to all of this in dramatic fashion. Rains flooded the Everglades in 1922, but 1924 and 1925 were dry years, and many glades fires burned over the area that was being drained, pointing up the fact that lowering the water table was not always desirable. Then the spring and summer of 1926 had unusually heavy rainfall followed by a rainy hurricane. The Labor Day Hurricane that signaled the end of the land boom in places like Miami blew the water out of the southwest end of the lake, overtopped and washed out a low earthen dike and flooded Moore Haven, killing some 300 people. Governor John W. Martin took the position that failure to finance and complete the drainage program was at fault and proposed a new $20,000,000 bond issue to go ahead with it. Demand for local control, which meant a unit attack on the problem, though somewhat naive, became amazingly strong. Three engineers employed by the commission in 1927 reviewed the work to that date and endorsed the unit approach to drainage. They proposed a revision of the overall plan to develop the Saint Lucie Canal and a system of east-west canals, pumping stations and a twenty-seven foot levee around the southern shores of the lake. The 1927 legislature approved the bond issue, but litigation prevented the sale. By June of that year all but maintenance operations on the uncompleted drainage system ceased. State auspices were not going to be enough to get the job done.

The second disaster came in a hurricane in September of 1928 that struck the coast at Palm Beach and moved inland to Lake Okeechobee. This time the winds drove the water against a weak eight-foot dike on the eastern and southeastern shores, overtopped it and swept away great parts of it, killing an estimated 2,000 people. There followed a new and perhaps final, if apparently never-ending, attack on the problem of controlling flood waters in Lake Okeechobee and the Everglades. The federal government, with token support from the state at first, took over the responsibility. The Rivers and Harbors Act in 1930 authorized the Secretary of War to provide deeper and wider channels to the Caloosahatchee and the Saint Lucie rivers and to construct a thirty-one foot dike in the affected lake area. The Congress provided ten million dollars with the proviso that other interests put up two million, but the federal government spent twice that amount on new works and maintenance, including a levee varying in height from thirty-four to thirty-eight feet, before water control entered into another phase after extensive flooding in 1947.

Meanwhile, the activities of the State Drainage Commission left a legacy of unpaid financial obligations that would plague the state for many years. In January 1929 the chief drainage engineer for the district reported that nearly $18,000,000 had been spent and that the bonded debt was $10,500,000. He placed the assessed value of property in the district at $106,000,000 and the population at 48,000. There were 586 miles of paved roads and 210 miles of railroad. He argued that property values had grown sixteen times for every dollar expended on water control. The depression beginning in 1929 killed any prospect of an early return to solvency. In July 1932 the commissioners released all employees and offered to cooperate with their creditors to work out a solution. The Reconstruction Finance Corporation seemed the most likely recourse, but the commissioners could reach no agreement with creditors until 1941 when Governor Spessard L. Holland led the legislature to action. In 1942 his office negotiated a Reconstruction Finance Corporation refunding bond issue of $5,600,000 to cover $9,400,000 of bonds, $3,640,000 of unpaid interest, $1,800,000 of unpaid canal construction bills and miscellaneous debts for another $1,200,000, or a total of $16,040,000 of indebtedness.

All of the effort and expenditure had failed to accomplish effective reclamation of the wet lands. More than that, they raised a

Flooding in Hialeah, October 18, 1922

host of no less important problems that led to a new attack on the complex of related problems. Fires in the peat-like soils burned down to rock bottom or to the underground water level the organic matter that had taken centuries to accumulate. The soil subsided as a result of the action of aerobic bacteria when the water was removed, more rapidly on the unused than on the cultivated lands, and posed the threat that the area might become a lake. Water was needed as desperately for irrigation in dry years as its removal was needed in wet ones. Freezes on the lower east coast in 1935 and 1939 raised the question of the relation of water level to air temperature. When the water table was lowered the growing municipalities on the coast became increasingly concerned about their sources of fresh water as salt water began to seep into areas formerly always fresh. Interest in the conservation of wildlife, sometimes in its introduction, produced concern about continuous water supply. The establishment of the Everglades National Park in 1947 was to add another area of concern. The pressure for immediate action came on the heels of new flood conditions in 1947 and 1948, which brought realization that flood control was by no means accomplished.

By August of 1947 extensive areas, including much farm and grazing land, were under water. Hurricanes in September and October brought added heavy rainfall. The average annual precipitation at Miami is about fifty-eight inches and somewhat less in the interior, but from January through October in 1947 it reached 102.43 inches at Dania and 96.11 at Fort Lauderdale. Vast sheets of water twenty to forty miles wide and six inches to ten feet deep formed and moved slowly southward over the land, covering perhaps as much as five million acres, spreading beyond the Everglades into low-lying coastal communities, some of which, in extreme instances, remained inundated for a month or more. Water covered eleven counties from five to eighty-five percent and parts of seven others had important areas affected.

The U.S. Army Corps of Engineers had already given considerable study and thought to a more comprehensive plan of water control and was able to submit a design to Congress on April 26, 1948, shortly after the floods had receded. If the lawmakers needed further impetus to action, new if somewhat less serious flooding occurred during the late summer of 1948. The proposal of the engineers was simple enough in concept, although far from it in execution. It aimed to provide drainage in appropriate areas, coupled with storage of the excess water for irrigation, and maintaining of a desirable water table; and to supply water for residential areas, hold back salt water intrusion, preserve wildlife, provide recreational areas and perhaps temper the winter climate. It involved the use of Lake Okeechobee as a reservoir and the creation of three reservoirs in Everglades areas deemed not suitable for farming and grazing.

Changes in administrative organization accompanied these changes in the program. In 1929 the Florida legislature created the Okeechobee Flood Control District to cooperate with the U.S.

Army Engineers in their efforts to control the flood waters in Lake Okeechobee. Up to that time the United States had spent $4,500,000 to improve navigation on the lake and its principal tributary streams. The Everglades Drainage District Commissioners had built a few levees along the lake, which, like those built by private interests, had proved completely inadequate in the 1926 and 1928 hurricanes. The engineers recommended floodway channels, control gates and major levees to control the water level on the lake. The state agency was to provide the land, maintain the works and contribute $2,000,000 of construction costs. In 1935 the Congress reduced the state's contribution by three-fourths and the Army Engineers took over maintenance. Between 1930 and 1937 they completed the project at a cost of $16,000,000. By 1952 maintenance and improvements had raised the total to $30,000,000.

To meet the demands of the new and expanded program, the state legislature in 1949 created the Central and Southern Florida Flood Control District, which first took over the functions of the Okeechobee Flood Control District and six years later assumed the operating responsibilities of the Everglades Drainage District, providing a single agency to administer the increasingly heavy state responsibility. The governing board of five men works with federal, state and local agencies in planning, construction and maintenance over an area involving all or a part of eighteen counties, in which nearly half of all Floridians live, nearly fifty percent of them in Dade County. Working with Army Engineers, they seek to remove flood waters rapidly, prevent overdrainage, protect developed areas, improve navigation, recharge groundwater, store surplus water, prevent salt water intrusion, permit additional urban and industrial development and conserve wildlife.

Since the days of Governor Broward, the emphasis has changed completely. The period of greatest concern in the future will likely be in times of water scarcity rather than excess. A by-product that seems not to have been recognized as being so important promises to make more friends for the Flood Control District than any other. The recreational possibilities are only beginning to be realized and developed, yet an estimated 750,000 people visited the area in 1969. This relieved some of the demand for parks and activities to take care of the needs of more and more residents and visitors.

Work on the project began with the construction of an east coast levee from Lake Okeechobee to a point north of Homestead in southern Dade County to prevent flood waters in the Everglades from moving eastward into the densely populated coastal areas and to form the eastern rim of the reservoir system. The next step was the construction of levees and canals in and around the 1,206 square miles south of the lake set aside for agricultural use to protect it from both flood and drought. West of the big dike and south of the agricultural area down to the Tamiami Trail, contained by a dike on the west side of the Everglades, lay the three reservoirs completed in 1962 into which excess water might be pumped and stored until needed.

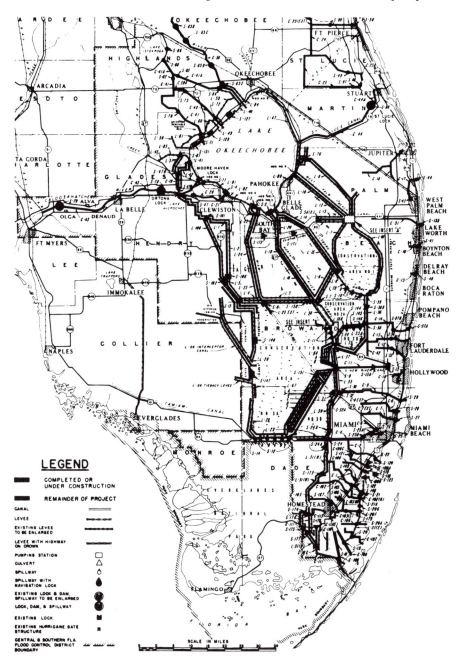

Central and Southern Florida Flood Control Project's design for water control in the southern Everglades in the late 1960s

Water control canals and reservoirs provide recreation areas.

The dimensions of the project and of Florida's water problems are indicated by the extent of the areas involved. Laked Okeechobee is about 730 square miles in area. The agricultural area of 1,206 miles square miles constitutes about half of the Everglades area. The conservation areas, 221 square miles, 210 square miles, and 914 square miles, cover another 44 percent. Some 196 square miles, about seven percent of the area, lies in the Everglades National Park south of the Tamiami Trail. In the entire eighteen-county flood control district are 15,673 square miles.

The plans for Lake Okeechobee measured the growing importance of water storage. The existing dikes were increased in height, and a new dike was extended completely around the lake to make it possible to raisehe water level in the lake as much as four feet. A series of hurricane gates and the two major outlets, the Caloosahatchee River and the Saint Lucie Canal, make it possible to control the level of water in the lake.

In the chain of lakes in the Orlando area and the Kissimmee River valley, the water historically drained southward through the Kissimmee River, leaving the lakes almost dry in the months of little rainfall. A series of interconnecting canals, dams, spillways and locks allows the rapid removal of flood water and the retention of needed water in the lakes. The main channel of the Kissimmee River has been widened and deepened to allow the rapid flow of water when necessary. The river is at the same time being held to a desirable level for fish, wildlife and sportsmen by a series of six spillways. Locks allow boaters full use of the river. The winding oxbows of the rambling old river are being preserved for fish breeding grounds and for use of other wildlife.

Construction got under way more slowly in the upper Saint Johns River valley. There was less appreciation of the value of the project to conserve and supply water for the coastal cities along the "missile coast," and land was not available at any price. A channel was constructed in the marshy headwaters area to aid the flow of water and allow access by small boats. A series of reservoirs to conserve water for agricultural, industrial and municipal uses also makes it possible to maintain a usable water level in the upper Saint Johns River. Fresh water in the region is of greater importance because the underground water is frequently contaminated by salt and mineral deposits from ancient seas. Floodwaters may be released to the ocean quickly through the Sebastian Canal in any emergency of excessively high water.

By 1970 the federal government had contributed over $170,000,000 and the state of Florida almost $60,000,000 to water control projects. The district operated fourteen large pumping stations, some 2,000 miles of canals and levees, more than sixty-five major spillways and dams, and several hundred lesser water control structures which were also part of the system. These included salinity control structures in all canals leading to the ocean to prevent salt water intrusion. Complete assurance of freedom from the intrusion of salt water required that the freshwater level of the interior be maintained at least two feet above that of the sea water.

Even as it was under construction, questions were raised about the long range feasibility of the Everglades project, which as we shall see later led to considerable changes in the 1990s. In the wet winter of 1969-70 threats to wildlife were serious as the deer were driven to high ground and much of the fawn crop lost. The high water also threatened the nesting birds.

The real issue is only temporarily that of excess water. Two years earlier questions of water scarcity received major attention. There was no agreement among the several interests competing for the use of the increasingly precious water. In the midst of the wet season early in 1970, Governor Claude Kirk warned of a water shortage in less than ten years, and a significant note in a conference in Miami in the same month was how to produce more water over the Everglades, even questioning that hurricanes should be prevented if it was to mean reduced rainfall. The recognition that water control was really part of a larger ecological system in 1972 led to a name change from "Flood Control," to the South Florida Water Management District

During a dry period in 1968 Congress came to the rescue with a plan that provided, beginning in 1976, for the release of 315,000 acre feet of water annually from the reservoirs into the Park. By the 1980s it was evident that the release of that amount of water might not be enough to simulate the seasonal water cycle, but, in any event, it appears certain that the "choice between alligators and people" has become a virtually perennnial problem.

Interior of pumping station S-5A, the world's largest low level pumping station located at Twenty Mile Bend in Palm Beach County

Aquatic plants also produced unforeseen maintenance problems and costs. The most familiar of these is the water hyacinth, but two others introduced into local waters from foreign countries by importers of tropical fish are increasingly important. Eurasian milfoil is found in the Homosassa, Crystal, and Chassahowitzka rivers and hydrilla (Florida elodea) in the lakes north of Lake Okeechobee and in the canals and conservation areas. Poisoning the plants kills desirable plants as well as fishes. An experiment with sea cows (manatees) was inconclusive. They eat the weeds but are susceptible to respiratory diseases when the weather chills, and their reproductive rate in this environment is uncertain. Marissa snails, which eat the underwater weeds voraciously and reproduce rapidly, are also being tried. Devices to cut the weeds under water and collect them with drag forks also leave something to be desired. Some form of biological control holds out hope of curtailing the growth if not actually eliminating the weeds.

Pollution was the new word added dramatically to the vocabulary of the conservation movement in the late nineteen sixties. The sudden and drastic impact is shown by the virtual stoppage of work on three major projects already well under construction. With approximately one-third of the work completed, new studies of economic feasibility and the possibility of damage to the ecology of the area through which it passes were ordered for the cross-state barge canal. In January 1971 President Nixon ordered that construction cease, pleasing those who worked to preserve the Oklawaha River.

The Dade County Port Authority without much initial protest acquired land in western Dade and eastern Collier counties in the Big Cypress about eight miles north of the Park boundaries to construct a jet training airport that would later become a base for the giant supersonic airplanes expected in the near future. When a two-mile landing strip for training purposes was about completed, the project was ordered stopped and the use limited to training. In April, 1970, guidelines for the location of a new commercial airport emphasized attention to the complex of service and satellite activities that would develop around such a facility. It was estimated that 1,500,000 people might eventually have settled near the Everglades jetport. Principal objection was the pollution of the air, soil and water of one of the principal sources of water for the western part of the Everglades National Park, outside of the conservation areas.

The Florida Power and Light Company got into hot water with anti-pollution authorities when it was charged that thermal pollution would destroy the ecological balance of the southern end of Biscayne Bay. The use of sea water to cool nuclear powered generators at the Turkey Point Plant southwest of Miami, it was charged, would raise the temperature of the water in the bay too much. The corrective effect of a six-mile cooling canal under construction was questioned and work stopped on it for a time, until the problem of cooling the generators was solved.

There was also growing concern that continued use of hard pesticides and chemical fertilizers in agricultural areas would poison the waters and load them with excess nutrients as they make their way slowly southward, not only to the Everglades National Park but also to the water table that is essential for domestic and commercial uses. Experiences with oil spills off the coasts of California and Louisiana focused attention upon the dangers of offshore drilling on the Gulf coast of Florida. Oil spills in waters around Florida brought demands for severe penalties for such damages.

Nor is this consciousness of pollution limited to any one area of the state. The phosphate industry has been criticized for polluting the air, water and soil where its processing plants are located; in some cases cattle and citrus growing become impossible in the immediate vicinity, and fish kills occur in streams into which incompletely treated wastes and by-products are accidentally released. At places like Fernandina where an entire community has been built up around new industries that dump wastes into the Amelia River, fear had been expressed that some of the industries might be closed down by the high cost of the corrective measures required to cut down or eliminate water pollution.

By the early 1970s it had become clear that no community in the state was entirely free of water and pollution problems. The

rapid growth of population, the increasing problems of sewage disposal and the dumping of chemical and industrial wastes, all occurring in a state committed to clean air, beaches and water for its
residents and tourists, made the issues doubly important in Florida.
Critics began to talk about correcting old abuses and preventing
new ones. There was a developing feeling that the answer lay in a
state-wide policy of "growth management." Such policies began to
emerge in the 1970s and after and will be dealt with in later chapters. It seems reasonable to say that dealing with the environment
and growth management will be major issues for Floridians well
into the 21st century.

23.

Florida During World War I

The Governor's race in 1916 and the administration of the winner, Sidney Johnson Catts, were remarkable and even unique in a number of respects. Catts was outside the mainstream of Florida politics. The campaign for the nomination revealed until then unsuspected religious and class prejudices. Although the point can easily be overemphasized, Catts demonstrated that the governorship could be won without the magic label of the Democratic party. In the same election Governor Park Trammell accomplished the rare feat of moving up to the United States Senate. Finally, the First World War, brief though it was, had measurably stimulating effects upon the economy of the state and set the stage for the booming twenties that followed.

Four of the five candidates for the Democratic party's nomination to the office of governor came to the contest by the conventional route of political experience in other offices in the state. The fifth, and finally the winner, was a newcomer to the state and a rank outsider in political circles. Ion L. Farris, a Jacksonville lawyer, had twice been speaker of the house and was at the time in the senate. Frederick M. Hudson, a Miami lawyer, had been president of the senate in 1908 and special counsel for the Florida Railroad Commission. William V. Knott of Tallahassee was the state comptroller and had also been the treasurer. Frank A. Wood, a Saint Petersburg banker, had served in the lower house. There was no significant difference in their platforms. A review of the issues they discussed reveals some Populist-Progressive survivals and some awareness of new problems to be faced. They all advocated more support for schools, liberal pensions for Confederate veterans, higher assessments on railroad property and a tax on franchises. Hudson and Wood advocated a state commission to supervise banks. Farris and Wood proposed to abolish the fee system in county offices and pay salaries to all public officials. Wood urged a special program to provide credit for farmers and liberal support for the state's penal and welfare institutions. Knott spoke in favor of good roads, the use of a budget system to plan and control state expenditures and libel laws to protect freedom of speech and press.

Catts injected new and controversial issues into the campaign for the Democratic nomination. He did not originate anti-Catholicism in the state, but he exploited what there was and heightened it in intensity. The Catholic population was only 24,658 in a state of 921,618—less than three percent. As late as 1897, Stephen R. Mallory II had been sent to the United States Senate by the Florida legislature and won renomination in 1902 in the first statewide primary without the issue of his Catholicism being raised. Nor had there been any anti-Semitism. The state had chosen David Levy Yulee for the United States Senate in 1845, the first Jew to sit in that body.

What then accounts for the emergence of the Catholic issue in 1916? The life and writings of Thomas E. Watson in Georgia were certainly a contributing factor in developing such a climate of opinion. Watson, a frustrated Populist who had been the party's nominee for vice president in 1896, soon thereafter turned to ranting demagoguery. His newspaper, *The Jeffersonian,* had preached anti-Catholic, anti-Jew, and anti-black doctrines for years. The rising tide of nationalism that was leading to the First World War and the possibility that the United States might be involved gave rise to the charge that Catholics gave their first loyalty to the church rather than the state. Some of the same sentiments found expression in secret societies. Watson helped to organize the Guardians of Liberty in 1911 to oppose foreign immigration and Roman Catholicism. In 1914, Billy Parker, a Pennsylvanian, organized a chapter of the Guardians in Jacksonville. The Patriotic Sons of America had been active as early as 1910. Though blacks were no longer a political threat, these same groups endorsed white supremacy. They also supported the prohibition movement, which was always closely associated with their fundamentalist religious views.

The State Democratic Executive Committee, aware of the possibility that religious and racist issues might be injected into state politics, sought to prevent it by a resolution on January 6, 1915, before the Catts candidacy was even suspected. The resolution, introduced by Chairman R. B. Sturkie of Pasco County, provided that voters in the primary should not be influenced by any religious consideration in casting ballots, nor should they be members of secret organizations that would influence political action or justify refusal to support any nominee of the party. The principal objection to the resolution was that it was unwise and unnecessary, but W. T. Cash, historian of the Democratic party in Florida, quotes one critic who called it a plot to "Romanize" Florida by refusing the ballot to all anti-Catholics. The committee on September 24 rescinded its action, but it provided Catts with an issue without which, Cash concluded, Catts might never have had any chance of success.

Sidney Johnson Catts was born into a moderately well-to-do Dallas County, Alabama, family on July 3, 1863. He enjoyed better than average educational opportunity and studied law at Cumberland University in Lebanon, Tennessee. His career as a lawyer was brief, and he became better known as a Baptist preacher. Converted in a revival in 1882, he entered the ministry and served as pastor in several Alabama churches until 1903 when he made his first try for political office. He ran against Congressman J. Tom Heflin, a demagogue of the Watson type, who soundly defeated him in the type of campaign that Catts was later to use in Florida. Catts then tried farming and mercantile pursuits until 1911 when he moved to DeFuniak Springs, Florida, as pastor of the First Baptist Church. In 1914 he resigned to become state representative of a fraternal life insurance company, but he continued to preach and speak widely as he traveled over the state for the company. He took shrewd stock of political conditions in the state and discovered neglected voters and issues that he believed he could use to become governor of the state. As his platform became clear, it included a surprisingly large number of issues, but three of them, prohibition, anti-Catholicism and an attack on recently enacted conservation laws, set him apart from the other candidates. He also favored economy in government, manual training schools for boys, higher taxes on corporations, larger pensions for Confederate veterans, lower freight rates, protection for depositors in banks and continued Everglades drainage.

He interpreted the Sturkie Resolution as a device to disfranchise anti-Catholics and defeat him. He visited every coastal village and appealed to commercial fishermen by attacking a 1913 law meant to protect fish and oysters and the allegedly high-handed methods of enforcement, which included an armed patrol boat. He thoroughly understood that the average Floridian, being accustomed to look upon the bounty of nature as his to use, was likely to ignore if not to resist any serious effort at conservation. What he might otherwise have done is not clear, but when the wartime demand for food raised the price of fish, Catts relaxed the restrictions on fishing, and much illegal netting and dynamiting occurred. Driving about in a Model T Ford, Catts followed every rude trail that served as a road and talked to people living in out-of-the-way places about the failure of politicians to pay any attention to their interests and problems.

Newspapers and the other candidates, only dimly aware of Catts and his campaign, largely ignored him. The people to whom Catts was appealing in villages and crossroads seldom saw an important newspaper. The *Miami Herald* reported as late as October 25, 1915, that, reminiscent of the tirades of Tom Watson, Catts was promising to open convents for inspection, make them pay taxes and make priests turn their collars right. Only ignorant people would believe that Catts could do such things, the newspaper concluded.

The writer evidently overlooked the number of "ignorant" people in the state. When the ballots in the primary were counted Catts had won over Knott by 30,092 first- and 3,891 second-choice votes to 24,765 first- and 8,674 second-choice ballots. The other three candidates ran far behind. In the same primary, retiring Governor Park Trammell won the senatorial contest over Nathan P. Bryan on a platform that included national prohibition, parcel post delivery, rural credits, preparedness, an adequate merchant marine, restricted immigration, federal aid for good roads and Everglades drainage.

Because of the closeness of the results and confusion concerning the counting of second-choice votes, it was clear almost immediately that Knott and his supporters would ask for a recount in many counties. When the courts ordered a recount and the case reached the Florida Supreme Court, the canvassing board was ordered to use the amended returns. In consequence, the board on October 7 reported that Knott had won the Democratic nomination by the narrow margin of 33,439 to 33,418.

Catts meanwhile had concluded that the final decision of the courts would go against him and in August started out on a political tour of the state, preceded by the Reverend Charles Winner, who was crusading against Catholicism. The Prohibition party, never an important factor in state politics, endorsed Catts and stated that he would be their candidate regardless of the outcome of the contested primary voting. Catts also petitioned boards of county commissions throughout the state to place his name on the ballot as an Independent, with the result that the Democratic Executive Committee read him out of the party when he lost the recount battle.

This was all grist for the Catts mill. Knott became the nominee of the court and Catts the people's choice. In November Catts received a whopping 39,546 votes in contrast to 30,343 for Knott, while George W. Allen, Republican, received 10,333, Socialist C. C. Allen 2,470, and another Independent, Noel A. Mitchell, garnered only 194 votes. What had happened in order to win so much support for Catts? Partly it was popular support for the underdog candidate, partly an acceptance by many of the likelihood that Catts had actually won the Democratic nomination. As a contributing factor certainly was the confusion about second-choice voting in the primary, particularly among the less sophisticated supporters of Catts. One newspaper warned at the beginning of the contest that if Knott contested the election and won, the election of Catts in 1920 would be assured. The historian Cash, who knew the campaign as a keen observer, stated that many newspapers that supported Knott in May neglected to support him in November although they did not always become Catts supporters. Knott was an able and well-known man who unfortunately earned a reputation as a bad loser. Had he accepted the first results of the primary gracefully, he might well have become governor four years later. As it was, he never sought the governorship again but had a long and honorable career as state treasurer. Catts had not deserted the Democratic party and later appeared three times in the party's primaries. The presidential election in 1916 was also a close one nationally, though Democrats won handily in all contests in Florida with 55,984 for Wilson and 14,611 for Hughes. Republican Charles Evans Hughes had gone to bed believing that he was elected to the presidency, only to awake to the fact that he had lost California to Wilson and with it the election.

The Catts campaign proved to be one of the most divisive in

Florida politics to that time. Some of the justices of the state supreme court did not feel disposed to attend the inaugural ceremonies, but they relented and Chief Justice Jefferson B. Browne administered the oath on January 2, 1917. The new governor, true to his religious principles, refused to attend the inaugural ball, where there was dancing, and withdrew his opposition to the serving of punch at the ball only when he was assured that inaugural ball punch was never "spiked."

Nor did Catts in his inaugural address show any disposition to forget the issues he had raised. Instead he made the most of his victory over what he called political rings, corporations, railroads, the press, organized black voters, the judiciary of the state and Roman Catholicism, all of which he interpreted as a victory for the people. He repeated the principal features of his platform and added proposals to abandon the Bryan primary law and return to the second primary system and a constitutional amendment to provide for initiative and referendum on legislation and recall of public officials. In spite of all the bitterness, controversy and dire predictions of the consequences of the Catts election, as is usual in such circumstances, one may accept as reasonable the judgment of Cash that Catts' administration was about as good as the average one, and that Catts was sincere when he said at the end of his term that his mistakes were of the mind and not the heart. Much of the image of "Cattsism" arises from the promises of the campaign rather than the acts of the chief executive. For example, he had promised to bring the institutions of higher learning and the state board of control under his control by new appointments, but the university system suffered nothing at his hands.

A major charge against Catts was extreme use of the spoils system and the appointment of his relatives to positions in state administration. He did dismiss many office holders and replace them with his relatives and friends. In 1920, during the contest for the Democratic senatorial nomination, Duncan U. Fletcher charged that no less than seven members of the Catts family had been on the state payroll at one time for a total of $32,000. Catts felt that his administration differed so sharply with any of his predecessors that more changes were necessary to insure loyalty to his leadership and program. He was by no means the last governor to demand personnel changes on the same grounds. Catts redeemed himself by making many good appointments and dismissing some of his own appointees who proved inept or corrupt.

One of the first acts of Governor Catts was to remove the state adjutant general who had held the office since 1901 and replace him first with a boyhood friend and later by his own son, Sidney, Jr. He at the same time moved the state military headquarters to Tallahassee; this was interpreted as a slap at Catholics in Saint Augustine where historic St. Francis Barracks had been the headquarters of the state militia since 1908. In 1867 the United States government had rebuilt the barracks, leaving the original coquina walls intact. Leased to the state of Florida in 1908, fire destroyed

Men of St. Francis Barracks hold a dress parade for President Chester A. Arthur in 1884.

much of the wooden parts of the structures in 1915, providing an occasion for the move in 1917. Not until 1921 did the legislature appropriate $40,000 to reconstruct the burned parts of the buildings, again using the coquina walls, which left the outward appearance much the same as the original. When the repairs were completed, the headquarters was returned to the St. Francis Barracks, where it still remains.

The legislative record of Catts' four years included many constructive features. The governor's message to the first session of the legislature proposed a general law to tax all property of churches except the parsonage and buildings used for purposes of worship. To nobody's surprise, he urged the repeal of second-choice voting in the primary. To meet the conditions for dollar matching of federal funds for public roads he urged that a fund of ninety to a hundred thousand dollars be set aside and that the labor of 300 convicts working on roads be counted at cash value as part of the state's contribution. He pointed out also that twenty-four counties with one-third of the population and twenty-one percent of the assessed value of property had half of the thirty-two senate seats and thirty-four of the seventy-five house seats, and he urged that representation be reapportioned. In an effort to redeem a promise to his less literate supporters, he proposed that the laws of the state be codified in simple language easier to understand. He also suggested that the law require the display of the flags of the United States and the state of Florida on all public buildings. He called a special session of the legislature on November 25, 1918, to consider the national prohibition amendment, the correction of unsatisfactory conditions at the Marianna School for Boys and other state institutions and the possibility of settling veterans of the recently concluded war on farms in Florida. In the second regular session in April 1919 the legislators ordered the governor's message printed without being read.

Prohibition of the manufacture, sale or use of alcoholic beverages in the state was approved by the legislature in 1917, ratified by the voters in 1918 and became effective in 1919. This was somewhat anticlimactic, as a majority of the counties were already dry by local option, and the legislature in 1918 approved the Eighteenth Amendment to the constitution, making prohibition a national law. Among important laws credited to the Catts term were compulsory school attendance, a state asylum for feeble-minded whites, assistance to women with dependent children, regulation of insurance companies, support for vocational education and a state marketing bureau. Another major step was the repeal of the convict lease system for the state's prisoners, though counties continued the practice until 1923. In 1917 the State Road Department received authority to construct roads and bridges and two years later to increase aid to the counties for the same purpose. The road board also assigned identifying numbers for a thousand miles of state roads. A special joint legislative committee reported after a survey that Florida had 4,767 miles of improved roads but needed another 3,600 miles to complete an integrated system. Flagler and Okeechobee counties were created. The legislature failed to act on the proposed bank guarantee fund and ignored two special messages on reapportionment. Nor were they ready to change the Bryan primary law or to pass any legislation that recognized organized labor.

The concern of Catts for the welfare of handicapped and underprivileged citizens led him to invite the Russell Sage Foundation to evaluate Florida's social welfare programs and resources. The investigators reported that the state had not begun to feel the great pressure of social needs, but that conditions growing out of the war would increase these needs and that planning should begin. Florida's public health services, thanks to the start made in the fight against yellow fever, were supported by per capita appropriations exceeded only in Pennsylvania. Teachers' salaries, on the other hand, were $387 per year below the national average. The investigators commended the use of the prisoners at the prison farm near Raiford to clear swamps, but found employment of prisoners in turpentine camps to be detrimental to their health. They called attention also to the lack of any effort at rehabilitation and reform aimed at making convicts useful citizens at the end of their prison terms.

The Nineteenth, or woman's suffrage, Amendment was added to the United States Constitution in 1920 but without the support of Florida. The movement originated in Florida at Tampa in 1892 under the leadership of Mrs. Ella C. Chamberlain, but it collapsed when she moved away in 1897 and remained dormant until 1912 when it was revived in Jacksonville. In that same year a small group of women attempted to register for a freeholders' election for sewer bonds but succeeded only in dramatizing their movement to secure the suffrage. The state legislature seriously considered the issue for the first time in 1913, and it came up regularly in the biennial sessions thereafter. In 1917 Mrs. William Jennings Bryan received a respectful hearing but won few votes for the cause. Though the lawmakers had approved several local bills to enfranchise women in municipal elections, they refused in 1919 to give the necessary three-fifths vote of approval to initiate an amendment to make it statewide. The amendment to the U.S. Constitution came too late for action in the 1919 session, and the governor refused to call a special session, believing as he did that it could not receive the necessary support. The amendment became the law of the land in August 1920, and the next Florida legislature saw no need to get on the bandwagon by ratifying it. Not until the 1969 session did the Florida legislature choose to go through the formality of approval. Women eventually made their way into the legislative halls. Orlando elected Mrs. Edna Giles Fuller the first house member in 1929. Orlando also provided the first woman member of the senate, when voters in that district chose Beth Johnson in 1962 to fill a vacancy. Earlier, Ruth Bryan Owen, the daughter of William Jennings Bryan, had represented the Fourth District in Congress for four years beginning March 1929.

This considerable legislative achievement should not be credited to the governor's leadership so much as to the coincidence that the two arrived separately at similar conclusions. Catts lost the support of the legislature, which passed many special acts to compensate public officials dismissed by the governor. Catts' intolerance and his ability to discover conspiracies all around him were more than political tricks. He alienated many of the friends who had helped to elect him and was never able to stage a comeback in state politics.

One month after Catts was inaugurated governor, the United States broke diplomatic relations with Germany. In March the Florida Naval Militia was brought up to full strength. Two days after the declaration of war against Germany on April 6,1917, the unit was ordered to duty at Charleston, South Carolina. On June 5, all men between the ages of twenty-one and thirty registered for the draft. They received their draft numbers on June 20 and began to be called to duty on July 25. Florida's first quota was 6,325 men. They trained at Camp Jackson at Columbia, South Carolina, and Camp Wheeler near Macon, Georgia. A total of 42,030 Floridians, 300 of them from the *Circulo Nacional Cubano* in Tampa, entered the armed services during the conflict. Three future governors of Florida went to war for their country's cause: David Sholtz in the navy, Spessard L. Holland in the coast artillery and in the 24th

Lieutenant Commander W.M. Corry, Jr., the first Floridian to enter flight training at Pensacola. Corry Field, at Pensacola, is named for him.

Flying Squadron in France, and Millard F. Caldwell in the army. Of the 176,000 men from the United States killed in action, 1,046 were Floridians. Eighteen men, including Spessard Holland, received the Distinguished Flying Cross.

The war was of too short duration for a full development of supporting services, but a foreshadowing of what was to happen twenty-four years later occurred in Florida. Aviation, then in its infancy, was important in Florida from the first. Five of the thirty-five flying schools in the country were in the state, at the Naval Air Station at Pensacola, Curtiss and Chapman fields at Miami and Carlstrom and Dorr fields at Arcadia. The Pensacola school began in 1914 with three instructors, twelve mechanics, and nine seaplanes. In 1915 Lieutenant Commander H. D. Martin made the first catapult launching from the deck of the U.S.S. *North Carolina.* Lighter-than-air training began a year later, and all navy dirigible pilots trained there until 1921. On July 1,1917, there were forty-five aviators, 200 student officers and 1,258 enlisted men in the naval air service, 1,000 of them at Pensacola. When the armistice was signed on November 11, 1918, there were 438 officers and 5,557 enlisted men at Pensacola. By the year 1919, a total of 921 seaplane, sixty-three dirigible and fifty-three balloon pilots had trained at Pensacola. Some 200 officers and 300 men trained at Curtiss

Field, the only Marine Corps school, using twenty-three flying Jennies. Chapman Field came into service very late in the war. Another naval air training base established briefly at Dinner Key on Biscayne Bay drew protests from the guests at the Royal Palm Hotel at the mouth of the Miami River and in downtown Miami. From the training fields at Arcadia the members of the famous Carlstrom Aerial Circus came after the war. Here also Charles Kettering and Lawrence Sperry conducted initial research in guided missiles, a project dropped at the conclusion of the war.

Key West again became the site of furious activity when a submarine station and a naval training station were set up. Patrol vessels, planes, dirigibles and observation balloons fanned out in all directions from the island bases to keep watch for any enemy operations on the nearby seas. Thomas A. Edison worked there on the development of depth bombs. A seaplane base and a wireless station at Fort Jefferson reactivated that isolated and largely abandoned base. Black Point on the Saint Johns River, now the site of the Jacksonville Air Station, was the scene of varied activity. The city acquired the 300 acres of land and turned it over to the state for a training camp. In 1916 Earl Dodge opened an aviation school, and the army used it to train pilots. In December 1917, now named Camp Joseph E. Johnston, it became Auxiliary Remount Depot 333. When the camp commander threatened to declare the city off-limits because of excessive drinking there by his men, Jacksonville became temporarily dry. In December 1918, the men departed and the camp was deactivated.

Protecting the long coastline became as always in war a matter of great concern. President Wilson established three Defensive Sea Areas in Florida, with bases at Key West, Tampa and Pensacola, and placed northeast Florida in the area centered at Savannah,

Camp Joseph E. Johnston, Jacksonville, November 22, 1918

Georgia. Ships had to wait outside to be checked and brought into port by the patrol. Other coastal patrols were operating at sea, in the air and on land. Home Guards replaced the National Guard, which entered the national service. The University of Florida added a Reserve Officer Military Training Program, and basic military training became for a time part of the high school curriculum for men. Florida contributed 228 of its 1,321 practicing physicians to military service, one of the highest ratios in the country. Since Florida was largely a food-producing state, wartime demands stimulated its normal development. Though there was no formal rationing and price fixing, Floridians responded to the urging of defense officials to observe meatless, wheatless and heatless days, lightless nights and gasless Sundays. Only users of sugar, beef and pork were actually limited as to amounts they could use or serve.

Other phases of the economy also felt the impact of war demands. At Jacksonville builders launched four 3,500-ton composite type steamers, fourteen 3,500-ton Ferris type steamers, five 6,000-ton all steam type ships and two 7,500-ton concrete tankers. Tampa shipyards contracted twenty-three steel ships and four wooden cargo vessels, only four of them for the government. One barge was built at the Millville shipyard in the panhandle, and a contract in July 1918 for eight three-masted schooners was cancelled in October. Lumber and allied products were in great demand at home, but exports dropped off sharply because of the uncertainties of shipping and the fact that they had been defined as contraband in 1914 at the beginning of the European war. The German-American Lumber Company, owned by a German syndicate since 1901 and employing some thirty-nine persons, was seized by the Alien Property Custodian and was operated as the American

Shipbuilding in Jacksonville, 1918

A million pounds of raw sugar is produced a day during full harvesting operation. A loader here picks up the cane stalks and loads them on the field wagon trains, which then go to railroad sidings.

Lumber Company until it was sold in 1919 to W. C. Sherman. Exports of phosphates, most of which like naval stores had gone to Germany, fell off sharply during the war but revived quickly after the close of hostilities. The development agent of the Seaboard Airline Railway contracted with the U.S. Signal Corps for the production of 10,000 acres of castor beans to be planted by farmers along the route of the railroad. The Mexican crop that was usually sold in the United States had been sold in Spain that year, probably to reach Germany eventually. When army worms threatened to destroy the plants that were to produce lubricating oil vital to the operation of airplane engines, entomologists of the Department of Agriculture came to the rescue with insecticides and saved much of the crop.

A Food Conservation Committee encouraged the production of beans, corn, pork and other foods rather than cotton and citrus. Fresh oranges and grapefruit had only limited use where wartime conditions prevailed, whereas the processing of citrus concentrates in World War II made it possible for the government to contract for the entire output. The governor dramatized the food-producing program by having the capital city set aside a local ordinance in order to allow him to feed table scraps to a pig he kept in a pen behind the state mansion. The wartime scarcity and high price of sugar revived interest in its production on a large scale in Florida, but its principal development came a few years after the war. Only the Southern States Land and Timber Company planted any considerable acreage during the conflict. In 1920 Judge John C. Gramling of Miami planted 200 acres of sugarcane east of Moore Haven. The Florida Sugar and Food Products Company acquired 4,000 acres in the Canal Point region and began mill operations in 1923. In 1921 the Pennsylvania Sugar Company planted 800 acres northwest of Miami and began grinding cane in 1924. The Moore Haven Sugar Corporation, buying a large part of the cane from small producers, in 1922 produced a low grade sugar, which was sent to Savannah for further refining. Whereas some 15,000 acres of cane was growing around Lake Okeechobee in 1922, high water and poor growing conditions reduced the acreage to less than 1,000 two years later. Prospects for sugar production began to improve when B. G. Dalberg, president of the Celotex Corporation, organized the Southern Sugar Company at Clewiston and purchased the equipment of the Florida Sugar and Products Company and the Pennsylvania Sugar Company. His primary interest was the waste product bagasse, the cane fibers after the juice was pressed out, which was used to manufacture Celotex. The enterprise survived the hurri-

On many Florida farms, sugarcane was grown to produce syrup, largely for local consumption.

canes in 1926 and 1928, was absorbed by the U.S. Sugar Corporation in 1931, and became the basis for successful commercial production of sugar in the state.

Scarcities and increased purchasing power made inevitable some
degree of inflation. William T. Cash reported in his *Story of Florida*
that farmers received $1.50 per gallon for cane syrup and $1.50 a
barrel for sweet potatoes. Consumers also paid as much as $2.25
for a twenty-four pound bag of flour, fifty cents a pound for pork
chops and a dollar for eight pounds of potatoes. Shoes doubled in
price, as did all clothing prices. Farmers paid highest prices for
fertilizers, farm machinery and labor, but good prices for crops made
operations possible. The great tragedy occurred when many farmers assumed that the inflated prices would continue and overex-
tended themselves financially to expand their production. People
with fixed income suffered losses in many instances. Teachers
sought higher pay and did make some gains but not enough to keep
pace with rising prices. Many teachers left the profession for better
pay and the greater personal freedom of private employment opened
up by the war. School officials in 1919 and 1921 found it necessary
to employ many instructors who could not meet certification requirements. Workers everywhere sought better jobs and higher pay. Railroad trainmen secured the Adamson Eight Hour a Day Law, passed
by Congress at the urging of President Wilson. Shipyard workers,
of which there were considerable numbers in Florida, won the eight-
hour day with time-and-a-half for overtime. Farm laborers became
scarce, and the Federal Bureau of Labor Office at the University of
Florida Experiment Station recommended sharecropping, which
meant profit sharing, to attract workers who would not accept the
wages being offered. Workers were brought in from the Bahamas
under a special treaty with Great Britain, a practice to have far
greater importance in the Second World War.

High school and college enrollments fell off slightly during the
war years as young men and some women left for military service
or employment. University of Florida enrollment, which still consisted solely of men, fell off less than might have been expected.
The figures for the war years beginning 1916-1919 were 539, 434,
434, and 612. In World War II the effect was far more drastic, with
enrollment dropping from 3,237 in 1941 to 691, 798, and 935 in the
next three years and returning to normalcy in 1945-1946 with 3,126.

Fear of espionage and sabotage, fed by rumors and reports of
incidents in Florida and elsewhere up the Atlantic coast, alarmed
Floridians from time to time. The German steamship *Frieda
Leonardt* was kept under surveillance at Jacksonville when a member of the crew threatened to blow up the municipal electric plant if
this country did go to war against Germany. The Tampa *Morning
Tribune* reported that on the last day of December in 1917 a note,
which was packed in an English walnut shell and picked up on the
street in Tallahassee, when read before a mirror declared: "Bombs
are Ready. don't fail me; Capital is unguarded; meet me tonight at
home." Though it had all the earmarks of a hoax, Governor Catts

could take no chances and stationed volunteer guards armed with shotguns loaded with buckshot shells to guard the state capital grounds. In April 1918 the food board warned of the possibility of ground glass in bread, but nothing happened.

Floridians oversubscribed four Liberty Loan drives and a Victory Bond drive early in 1919. To promote sales during the Victory Bond drive, the Carlstrom Flying Circus performed over Jacksonville, and army tanks destroyed the old abandoned wooden building of the "northern" Methodist Church at First Street and First Avenue. Jacksonville's bond purchases and contributions of funds added up to a total of $26,657,850. Many women joined the work force for the first time, and others did volunteer work for war relief agencies, rolling bandages and knitting socks and sweaters.

In the War for Cuban Independence, Florida had by some miracle escaped a yellow fever epidemic, but influenza hit Florida and the entire country with tragic consequences in 1918. Jacksonville bore the brunt of the epidemic. On September 18, a few prisoners at the city farm became ill, and by the end of the month the disease had reached epidemic proportions. Schools and motion picture theaters closed on October 7 and all amusement and soft drink places a day later. By the tenth a portable soup kitchen began to deliver food to persons unable to prepare meals. Two days later Camp Johnston authorities loaned four soup kitchens to the city. Thirty-nine persons died on October 13, the peak of the epidemic. Possibly as many as thirty thousand persons contracted the disease, and 464 died within four weeks. The "flu" returned in 1919 with 621 cases and sixty-four deaths and again in 1920 with 2,541 cases and seventy-nine deaths.

24.

Boom-Bust-Hurricane Twenties

The third decade of the twentieth century opened with some promise of accelerated growth but no premonition of its dimensions or of the succession of disasters, natural and man-made, that were to be a part of it. Growth was of boom proportions, but financial collapse and a tropical hurricane came together in 1926. Two years later came another devastating killer hurricane, followed by the stock market crash a year later and the onset of the Great Depression. In spite of these spectacular setbacks, the state came out at the end of the decade having made greater gains in population than in any comparable previous period.

From just under a million (968,470) Floridians in 1920, the count rose to 1,263,540 in 1925 and 1,468,211 in 1930. Something like the modern pattern of growth was also beginning to appear. Whereas all of Florida was growing, the most rapid increase was in the peninsula. Jacksonville remained the largest city with 129,549, but Miami had risen in ten years from fourth place with 29,571 residents to second place with 110,637. Though Tampa had doubled (from 51,608 to 101,161) it dropped to third place, and Saint Petersburg was fourth with 40,425. Thirteen new counties created in 1921, 1923, and 1925 brought the total to the present sixty-seven; only four, Dixie, Union, Gilchrist, and Gulf, none of which has grown rapidly, were in the northern part of the state. The addition of Charlotte, Glades, Hardee, Highlands, Sarasota, Collier, Hendry, Indian River, and Martin counties mark the growth of the lower part of the state.

Railroad construction, which had been at a virtual standstill between 1900 and 1920, reached new heights in the next decade and then began to decline as short lines and feeder lines were discontinued. Under the leadership of S. Davies Warfield, who banked heavily on the continued growth of Florida, the Seaboard Air Line extended its lines and services. The company built 238 miles of track from Coleman to Sebring, then across to Palm Beach and down the coast to Miami in 1927. In the process the line absorbed over 200 miles of other railroads, making a total increase of well over 500 miles. In the middle twenties the Atlantic Coast Line built the Perry cut-off to route trains from the Middle West to the Florida west coast without going by way of Jacksonville. The Atlantic Coast Line also reached Lake Okeechobee at Moore Haven in 1925, purchased the short line from Moore Haven to Clewiston, and extended it to Lake Harbor. The Florida East Coast extended its Okeechobee Branch to Canal Point and Belle Glade in 1924 and to Lake Harbor in 1928, connecting with the Atlantic Coast Line there. Meanwhile, the Coast Line double-tracked its line from Richmond to Jacksonville, and the Florida East Coast did the same from Jacksonville to Miami.

Probably the greatest overextension of railway mileage in the decade was on the lower west coast where the Seaboard and the Coast Line seemed to be racing each other to some unknown destination, possibly an extension to Key West by way of Cape Sable. The two lines lines reached Naples ten days apart, the Seaboard on December 27, 1926, and the Coast Line on January 7 of the next year. The Coast Line extended its line down to Marco Island in 1927. In 1942 the Seaboard pulled back to Fort Myers and sold its abandoned properties to the Coast Line, which took over the track and the better station location in Naples. Two years later the tracks to Marco were taken up. The Coast Line also extended service from Immokalee to Everglades in 1927 but abandoned the lower end of the line in the late fifties. When the flurry of building was done, the total mileage of Class I railroads in the state stood at just under 6,000, all but 500 miles of it in the three major systems. Two lines, the Louisville and Nashville, long the only road serving Pensacola, and the newcomer in the decade, the St. Louis and San Francisco, had little mileage in Florida but provided Pensacola with rail con-

New York Avenue, a 15-foot wide brick pavement built in 1911-1912, led from Jacksonville to Orange Park. Traffic was very light when this photo was taken May 15, 1917.

This floating dredge made its own waterway across the Everglades

nections to the interior that made it a great port city. Two of the big three, the Seaboard and the Coastline, merged into the Seaboard Coastline in 1968, with a total of almost 5,000 lines of rails.

The really revolutionary development of transportation in the twenties was the construction of a statewide system of public roads. Road building, particularly the financing of it, had been largely a function of local government, but before the election of 1924 the State Road Department had completed only 748 miles of hard surfaced road. Four years later, 1,588 miles had been paved by the state, fifty-nine were being paved, 214 were graded but not surfaced, and another seventy-eight were being graded. State and counties together counted 2,242 miles in 1928, and by 1930 the state was maintaining 3,254 miles of highway. Private enterprise accounted for one major and many lesser projects. George S. Gandy, a Philadelphia transportation expert, came to Saint Petersburg in 1903 and became obsessed with the idea of a bridge and a streetcar line to connect Tampa and Saint Petersburg and thereby reduce the travel distance from forty-three to nineteen miles. Financing became available in 1922 and continued until the Gandy Bridge was opened in November of 1924.

The story of the Tamiami Trail illustrates the handicaps under which underdeveloped areas operated in the construction of roads under local auspices over long distances. The route lay through areas least developed, least able to pay, and, as it turned out, involved some costly engineering problems. With little notion what the eventual cost would be, each community became a road and bridge district and bonded itself to finance the construction. But when districts south of Fort Myers had mortgaged themselves to the limit, a total of about half a million dollars, they barely had enough to start the work. Construction nevertheless began in 1915 and 1916. The Dade County portion of the grading was accomplished in 1918, but the contractor gave up in Lee County and the work stopped. The state legislature created Collier County in 1923 largely on the promise of Barron G. Collier, who owned some three-fourths of the land in the new county, that he would get construction of the Tamiami Trail under way. A $350,000 county bond issue provided funds to get construction going again. In August of 1926 the State Road Department took over the construction, and the Tamiami Trail officially opened on April 25,1928.

There was little in the experience or the political platforms of the candidates for the principal offices in the state in 1920 to prepare them for the momentous events that were soon to follow. One of the four gubernatorial candidates, Cary A. Hardee, a banker from Live Oak, had been born on a farm near Perry. As a young man he taught in rural schools and read law. Admitted to the bar, he served as state's attorney for the third judicial district from 1905 to 1913 and represented Suwannee County in the house, where he was speaker in 1915 and 1917. John W. Watson, a businessman and like Hardee a conservative, stayed in the race for only a short time. He advocated tax reduction, good roads, Everglades drainage, and restrictions on labor unions. He withdrew on May 5 and left the field to Hardee. Van Cicero Swearingen was more nearly heir to the Catts tradition. Catts had appointed him to the office of attorney general to fill out the term of Thomas F. West, who became a member of the state supreme court. Swearingen spoke about good roads and schools rather than the divisive issues raised by his political benefactor. He had been a farm boy and a blacksmith and had studied law at Mercer University at Macon, Georgia, before he went to Jacksonville to practice law and become city judge and mayor. Lincoln B. Hully, president of Stetson University since 1904 and senator from Volusia County, the twenty-eighth district, boasted of two bachelor of arts degrees, one master's and three doctor's, but won few votes. Hardee campaigned successfully against Swearingen as an extension of Cattsism and won easily with 52,591 first-choice votes to 30,240 for Swearingen and 5,591 for Hully.

The contest for the Democratic nomination for United States Senator between Governor Catts and the incumbent Duncan U. Fletcher outbid the governor's race for public interest. Catts announced on July 16, 1919, that he planned to run. Fletcher had won a law degree from Vanderbilt in 1880 and started his career as lawyer and politician. He started out a Browardite "straight-out" but gradually turned conservative. He became counsel for the Florida East Coast Railroad in 1905 and ran against Broward for the Senate seat in 1908. He had been author of the Merchant Marine Act, which resulted in the expenditure of some $50,000,000 in the shipyards of Jacksonville, Tampa, and Pensacola during and after the war. He could claim credit during his twelve years in the Senate for river and harbor improvements and for the part he played in securing military installations for the state. Fletcher attacked Catts' record as governor, particularly his having raised taxes after promising economy in expenditures, and his official favors to members of his family. Catts with justification pointed to improvements in the state's prisons, hospitals, and industrial schools and criticized Fletcher for his opposition to child labor legislation. Finding most of the newspapers against him, Catts resorted to a circular he addressed to the voters charging that his enemies—the railroads, the whiskey interests, and the Roman Catholics controlled the newspapers. He said he stood with the common people against the corporations and declared that the common man had only three friends, Jesus Christ, Sears Roebuck and Company, and Sidney J. Catts. Catts supported Prohibition but opposed the League of Nations, which Fletcher also opposed. The support of organized labor became important in 1920. Fletcher had lost some support when he helped defeat the labor-sponsored program to have the government continue to operate the railroads, but Catts received only lukewarm support of labor. In the governor's race Swearingen seemed to have the better of the labor support, and Hardee found it necessary to deny that he was an enemy of organized labor. A railroad strike beginning on April 8 caused the loss of enough fruit and vegetables to turn popular support against labor and its endorsement of Swearingen and Catts probably won votes for their rivals.

Fletcher and the conservatives had overestimated the strength of Catts and of organized labor. Fletcher bested Catts in the primary by 62,304 votes to 25,007. Fletcher and Hardee won handily over Republican rivals in the general election in November. At the end of his term, Governor Catts returned to his farm near DeFuniak Springs and opened a real estate office. He later turned to the patent medicine business. He showed enough political strength in 1924 to give concern to his rivals, and in 1928, when the presidential candidacy of Alfred E. Smith raised the Catholic issue again, Catts came near to winning the primary nomination for governor. In 1929 Cary A. Hardee defended him against a charge of counterfeiting. Catts died in 1936. Fletcher spent another sixteen years in the Senate and died in office in 1936.

More spectacular events in the twenties tend to overshadow the relatively constructive aspects of the Hardee administration. Florida in 1923 took a first long step toward improving the quality of its livestock by enacting a law to compel owners to dip their cattle in an insecticide solution to eradicate the cattle tick. The law was unpopular with many open range owners, who found it extremely difficult to round up scattered and semi-wild animals and drive them into the corrals and through the dipping vats. A decision to kill deer as the hosts of the ticks stirred a storm of protest—but not until 8,874 deer were killed was the tick quarantine lifted. The final solution of that problem came in 1949, after many counties had already taken the step, when the legislature passed a law to keep cattle behind fences, putting an end to the open-range cattle industry and making control of the animals and improvement of herds possible.

The long disputed convict lease system also came to an end in 1923 when a scandal in Leon County involving the death of a North Dakota youth focused attention on the abuses in this method of dealing with prisoners. The growing use of prison labor on public roads made the change easier. The promise of more support for public schools resulted in authority for school districts, previously limited to three mills, to levy up to ten mills for school purposes. In a continuing effort to attract people with capital to settle in Florida, the legislature passed and the voters approved a prohibition on state income and inheritance taxes. (The state now takes only the inheritance tax which the federal government would otherwise take from its citizens.) The office of state tax equalizer replaced that of the state tax commissioner (abandoned in 1918), and to meet the changes in population, the state senate was increased from thirty-two to thirty-eight members and the house to ninety-five, three house members for each of the five most populous counties, two each for the next eighteen, and one each for the remainder.

During and after World War I some 40,000 blacks had begun to migrate from Florida to the North. The post-war years also witnessed a continuation of racism by the Ku Klux Klan and the abuse of blacks who constituted 30% of the population. Florida led the nation in lynchings in the early 1920s at 4.5 per 10,000 blacks; a much greater rate than any of the other southern states. Four blacks were killed and an entire section of town destroyed in Ocoee, near Orlando, as blacks attempted to vote on election day in 1920. In January 1923, a race riot occurred in the small town of Rosewood, near Cedar Key, in which a number of buildings were destroyed with at least six blacks reported murdered. The total dead of both races may have been a large as seventeen.[1]

In 1924 the state's role in the building and maintenance of public roads became the major issue in the race for the Democratic nomination for governor. Five candidates offered themselves, among them former Governor Catts, who emphasized good roads along with better schools and enforcement of prohibition. John W. Martin, a native of Marion County who moved to Jacksonville where he studied law, practiced ten years, and served three terms as mayor, made a state road building program and businesslike administration of the state's offices his concern. He urged that convicts on the state prison farm stop losing money by raising boll weevil cotton and be employed in making automobile tags and other noncompetitive services to the state. Martin recognized Catts as the man to beat, and when the votes were counted he had 55,715 to Catts' 43,230. Frank E. Jennings had 37,962 votes, Worth W. Trammell, brother of Senator Park Trammell, 8,381, and Charles H. Spencer 1,408. Second-choice voting also favored Martin and gave him a 13,000 majority of the total vote count.

Martin became governor as the land sales boom was reaching its climax, and the legislature was affected by the inflationary spirit of the day. Appropriations were easier to secure, but the constitutional prohibition kept the state from going into debt by selling bonds. True to his campaign promises, Martin's administration took the lead in road building. Fish hatcheries and deer and quail restocking became part of a growing wildlife conservation program. Schools benefited by a greater than usual appropriation for state institutions and state financial assistance to public schools. Textbooks for the first six grades became free to pupils. Martin inherited some of the blame for heedless expansion of the public debt in local government but could have done little to prevent it. Other aspects of his administration are treated as part of the story of the land sales boom and its aftermath.

Students of the runaway inflation in land sales in the middle twenties are by no means in agreement as to the causes. Such phenomena are by no means unique in the United States, but explanations of why they occurred in Florida at that particular time should be noted. The increased use of the automobile and the roadbuilding program are given high place in the explanations. They made the boom possible if they did not cause it. A revolt against urbanization and industrialization, intensified by the strains of the war period, helped to drive people to new and less developed places. The material prosperity of the country provided new means for travel and speculative enterprise, and the confidence in Coolidge prosperity put a high premium upon business enterprise of a bold sort that promised sudden wealth.

None of these reasons explain really "why Florida?" and "why Miami?" Though the boom was statewide, its greatest activity was in Dade County. Roger Babson saw history repeating itself—just another boom. Kenneth Keyes saw the answer in building activities that gave solid assurance of substantial community growth. In fact, there was too much construction of streets, roads, and public buildings in many instances. Climate and accessibility to the populous Northeast account for some of the growing interest in Florida. The assurance that the state would levy no income and inheritance taxes attracted some. Examples of early successes and reports of first comers may have been most important. The storybook transformation of Miami Beach from a tropical jungle to a modern city in a dozen years was proof enough for George E. Merrick and his associates; they invested heavily in homes, public buildings, and streets for the well-planned city of Coral Gables. The announcement in 1925 that a university planned for greater Miami would be located in Coral Gables gave substance to the claims of that community that went beyond the speculative. Homer Vanderblue concluded that the only important new features in the Florida boom were extensive provisions to transport prospective customers by buses from great distances and the extensive advertising, which was extrava-

Developer's buses, Hialeah, Florida, in October 1921

gant both in quantity and content. The *Miami Herald* in 1925 had the largest advertising lineage of any newspaper in the United States, forty-two and a half million lines in contrast to thirty-three and a third by the nearest competitor. In the same year the *Miami News* could boast the largest single issue, celebrating the opening of the News Tower and the twenty-ninth birthday of the city. The twenty-two sections totaled 504 pages and required fifty carloads of newsprint.

In the winter of 1924-1925 the incipient boom that had been gathering force since 1921 became a reality. Instead of the usual slowing down of business at the end of the winter season, more and more people came. Speculation broke wide open in the late summer of 1925. Speculative projects ruined sound ones by pushing them too far in the growing competition for customers. Some measure of the expanding activity can be gathered from the City of Miami records, where the payroll grew 2,499 percent between 1921-1922 and 1925-1926, from $140,344 to $3,557,043. The assessed value of property increased 560 percent, from $63,800,000 to $421,101,367 in the same period. Mileage of paved streets grew from thirty-two to 420. Building permits climbed from a value of $4,478,044 to $58,647,656.

Tampa was rescued from serious business recession by increased real estate activity. Two war-born shipyards that had employed 5,000 men in 1918 had closed down. A crippling strike had idled 10,000 cigar workers in 1920, and a severe hurricane in October of 1921 added to the gloom. At the same time, almost unnoticed, an increasing number of tourists were coming in, mostly by automobiles, many of which were loaded down with tents, bedding, and canned goods. At DeSoto Park in the 1920-1921 winter, tourists organized themselves into the "Tin Can Tourists of the World." The construction of Gandy Bridge sparked real estate development. D. P. "Doc" Davis had seen the successful development of low-lying islands and bay-bottom land in Miami and Miami Beach and set

Before the rise of modern motels, Tin Can Tourist Camps appeared all over Florida just after World War I when traveling became popular and automobiles more plentiful. Gainesville had many such camps.

out to accomplish a similar miracle in Tampa. The first block of 300 lots sold on Saturday, October 4, 1924, within three hours, for a total of $1,638,582, and practically all of the lots were still under water. Before the end of 1925 the development had been sold out for a total of $18,138,000. Davis, unaware that the boom was coming to an end, moved to Saint Augustine to purchase a tract of land to repeat his Tampa success. By mid-1926 he faced disaster. Payments on contracts came in more slowly. All his cash reserves and the early payments had gone into developing Davis Island and the beginning of the Saint Augustine venture. On October 13, 1926, Davis died at sea, apparently falling overboard from the liner *Majestic* two days out on a voyage to Europe. Not every community had a dramatic figure to symbolize its boom like Davis, but Addison Mizner of Palm Beach, who designed and built great estates, was another such man who could hardly be outdone.

The decline of the boom began in 1925, and a host of problems began to plague the feverishly active communities. A shortage of housing for the rapidly growing population led to rent profiteering that produced resentment. Some developers tried setting up tents to accommodate customers that came their way. Transportation services broke down, and the movement of building supplies was slowed down so much that the building boom lost momentum that could never be regained. On August 18, 1925, the Florida East Coast Railroad announced an embargo and permit system on carload shipments except for fuel, petroleum, livestock, and perishable materials. The problem arose from long delays in unloading freight cars, which were being used by consignees as warehouses in the absence of storage facilities. At that time there were 851 carloads of freight on Miami sidetracks, another 150 outside of the usual waiting areas at Jacksonville, and 700 cars were en route or waiting. On October 29, the embargo became statewide and later included less than carload shipments. On February 26,1926, most of the restrictions were removed, but some lasted to May 15.

The story of steamship service was much the same. In Miami, the port was not yet fully developed, docking facilities were limited, labor was scarce, and there were wage disputes. In late December 1925 the *New York Times* reported that thirty-one ships lay off Miami Beach waiting their turns to come in and unload. Early in January the *Prinz Valdemar,* undergoing renovation to become a floating cabaret, slowly capsized and blocked the harbor, trapping eleven vessels in port from January 18 to February 29 before army engineers could cut a channel around the sunken vessel.

Florida began to get a bad press. However sound the real estate market may have been in earlier stages, the temptation to fraud proved too great to resist when trading became frenzied and buying purely speculative. Complaints multiplied, and the National Better Business Bureau, the Florida Real Estate Commission, and the Florida Association of Real Estate Boards made numerous investigations. Reports of these investigations and frauds did much to dampen the enthusiasm of land purchasers. Businessmen in communities all over the United States began to express concern over withdrawals of money and the migration of people to Florida. In a few major instances they started an active anti-Florida campaign in a serious effort to stop the flow of money and people to Florida. In August the *Miami Herald* reported that Savannah, Georgia, was alarmed that the post office there had received more than 6,000 requests for changes of address to Florida. The Massachusetts Savings Bank League reported that 100,000 of its 3,000,000 savings accounts had been drawn upon for a total of $20,000,000 and cautioned depositors against withdrawals for speculative purposes. The *New York Times* defended bankers in western, middlewestern, and northern states who protested the enormous volume of withdrawals. William A. Bartlett, writing in *Barron's,* pointed out opportunities as well as dangers but thought there must be enough lots laid out in Florida to house half the people of the United States.

The answer of Floridians was to circulate more and more attractive publicity to counteract any unfavorable impressions. The editor of the *Miami Herald* pointed out, truthfully enough, that the Miami boom involved investing the profits in public improvements, but this effort could not entirely overcome the effect of rising prices and the purely speculative character of some buying. Governor

Martin and a score of Floridians invited representatives of the country's newspapers and magazines to a "Truth About Florida" meeting at the Waldorf Astoria Hotel in New York, which led the *Times* to point out that Floridians must be bothered by the criticism. Florida communities also did some housecleaning. Miamians, for example, began by organizing a Better Business Bureau to answer complaints and expose unfair or illegal operations. The Miami Realty Board set up strict procedures for realtors. Down payments, or binders, had to be at least five percent of the sales price, and preferably ten percent. Dates of closing had to be within ten to fifteen days after delivery of abstracts of title, which had to be kept up-to-date, and property had to be delivered to purchasers, not to an assignee. Early in 1926 the anti-Florida propaganda slackened but so also did real estate activity.

Numerous other factors may have accounted for the slowing down of real estate sales. Concern over income taxes and the rumor of a tax cut in 1926 may have lessened efforts to complete transactions in 1925. A rumor as early as August 1925 that internal revenue agents and deputy collectors were coming to Florida to check on the reporting of speculative profits and a ruling (later rescinded) that tax must be paid on the profit of the entire transaction rather than the amount actually paid in the year, created a real scare. The *London Times* thought the decline might be due to a faltering of the stock market. Homer Vanderblue thought this might have been the final blow. Among the stocks that suffered from a sharp sell-off was the Seaboard Air Line Railway Company, which had extensive commitments in Florida. The same authority sets the "final ecstasy" of the boom in August and September of 1925.

Most communities remained optimistic, but measured by the sale of revenue stamps to be placed on deeds, February of 1926 was far below February of the previous year. Bank deposits fell off sharply in the summer of 1926, whereas they had risen sharply from $180 million in 1922 to $875 million in 1925. Combined resources of state and national banks rose more than one-third in 1924 and doubled in 1925, growing at the rate of $32 million a month in the season of 1924-1925 without any of the usual slackening of activity in the summer. By 1926 heavy withdrawals, coupled with the failure of buyers of property to make payments, began to produce failures among smaller and more recently organized banks.

The boom was definitely well over when a hurricane struck Miami on September 17-18 1926, and put an end to any lingering hope of revival. There had been no major hurricane in Florida since 1910. Much of the population of the lower east coast knew nothing of the tropical storms, and much of the construction had been done by persons innocent of any knowledge of the necessary safeguards against the force of wind and water in a heavy blow. Nor had local government reached the point of maturity and responsibility when adequate building codes and inspection to enforce them were provided. There was some disposition to blame meteorologist Richard W. Gray for not warning the community, but in reality his warnings went largely unheeded. Total casualties were 392 dead, 6,281 injured, and 17,784 families affected by losses, with the greatest loss at Moore Haven where some 300 persons died when a crumbling Okeechobee dike turned loose a tidal wave on the town.

Reactions to the disaster differed widely. Overzealous newsmen at first exaggerated the extent of the disaster, the *Miami Tribune* being a major instance. Other sources, moved by concern for the coming tourist season, tried to play it down. Peter O. Knight of Tampa saw the effort to raise money by appeals for help doing more harm to the Florida image than relief funds could do good. The mayor of Miami embarrassed Red Cross officials by minimizing reports of the damage, stopping many offers of assistance. Eventually, sanity returned to all concerned and more reliable reporting brought out the true state of affairs. Floridians have since become more sophisticated and can point out that hurricanes have done as much damage in other Gulf coast states as in Florida, but it is difficult to erase the image of southeast Florida as the special target of tropical storms. Improved hurricane warning service, stronger building codes, and greater public awareness now operate to reduce the toll in lives and property. The 1926 blow did not kill the boom, but it certainly buried it in devastating fashion.

It was Governor Martin's misfortune to hold the office through the collapse of the boom, the 1926 hurricane, and the even more damaging 1928 storm. In 1928 on the night of September 16, a hurricane with gusts up to 130 miles an hour struck at Palm Beach and moved inland, where it piled up water on the southeastern shore of Lake Okeechobee, overtopping a low earthen dike and pouring water on the settlements at Pelican Bay, Pahokee, Canal Point, Belle Glade, South Bay, and smaller intervening settlements. The final figure on loss of life provided by the National Red Cross was 1,770, but there were many others unaccounted for. The United States Department of Commerce estimate of 1,850 to 2,000 lives

The Land Boom–A sketch mapping out the Riviera section of Coral Gables, November 10, 1925.

lost may be more accurate. Three-fourths of the casualties were blacks, some from the Bahamas who were there for seasonal labor in the fields. Many bodies were carried far into the saw grass and their skeletons were discovered years later by workmen clearing land.

This time the governor made no effort to conceal the seriousness of the situation. He telegraphed all mayors in the state asking help, saying that the situation was worse than reported. Only the Johnstown and Galveston floods had drowned more people. Recovery was slow because the runoff of flood waters in the waterlogged area was so slow. The state provided machinery to restore the lakeshore levee, but 1,000 feet had been washed out in the Chosen-South Bay area alone. By October 12, five floating dredges were clearing ditches and repairing perimeter dikes. A freeze on December 30 killed a crop of beans nearing maturity. The Red Cross spent $2,702,463 for seed, livestock feed, and fertilizer as well as food, clothes, and shelter.

Political activity continued in the midst of flood and hurricanes. The Democratic senatorial primary in 1926 found veteran Senator Duncan U. Fletcher (1908, 1914, 1920) faced with new and active opposition when Jerry Carter emerged as what appeared to be a real contender. Governor Catts had named Carter as hotel commissioner, a position he held under the next two governors. Fletcher appealed to his long record of service to the people of the state and his seniority in the Senate, where he was the ranking Democrat on three major committees. Carter blamed Fletcher for increased railroad rates and ridiculed his votes for the World Court and against the woman suffrage amendment. Fletcher opportunely secured passage of legislation to provide $200,000 for a lighthouse at Key West. He also urged an addition to the Rivers and Harbors Bill that would provide for a canal to connect the upper Saint Johns River with Indian River. Carter ran a poor second with only 4,226 votes to 39,143 but continued a long career in public office in the state.

State elections in 1928 turned to a large degree on reaction to the collapse of the boom, the hurricanes in 1926 and 1928, Coolidge-Hoover prosperity, and the candidacy of Democrat Alfred E. Smith for the President. Doyle E. Carlton came from a pioneer family at Wauchula. He had lost his great-grandfather at Fort Meade in the Second Seminole War, and his grandfather was wounded in the same battle. He had attended three universities, Stetson, Chicago, and Columbia. His opponents were Fons A. Hathaway, who had been chairman of the State Road Department in the Martin administration when the state embarked on an extensive road program, and Sidney Catts. Catts, pointing to his record as governor, accused his successor of using the two million dollars he left in the treasury to discredit him. He proposed additional school funds from an added cent of gasoline tax and a tax on tobacco, he wanted to uphold and enforce prohibition laws and local option on legalized horse race betting, and he supported Herbert Hoover against Al Smith.

James M. Carson, member of another pioneer family, entered the race to campaign against Catts, fearing that Carlton and Hathaway might eliminate each other to the advantage of Catts. Catts apparently lost ground when he accepted the local option on horse betting. Hathaway ignored a charge of misuse of funds in highway construction and Carlton's challenge to debate the charge publicly, with some damage to his chances. Carlton won with 77,569 first-choice and 28,471 second-choice votes. Catts received 68,984 first- but only 9,066 second-choice votes. Hathaway received 67,849 votes. Governor Martin challenged Park Trammell for the Senate seat but Martin apparently had accumulated too many political liabilities in the collapse of the boom.

The presidential election of 1928 took on an unusual importance when the Democrats nominated Alfred E. Smith of New York. He won no delegates from Florida, but the opposition had no candidate with any chance for victory, and Smith won on the first ballot. The selection of Senator Joseph T. Robinson as a running mate helped to appease southerners. Robinson was a southerner, a Protestant, and a "dry" in contrast to Smith's big city-Tammany Hall political ties, his Catholicism, and his known opposition to prohibition. Militant prohibitionists and Protestants, largely without mentioning the religious issue, led an anti-Smith campaign that carried the state for Herbert Hoover. Floridians had not recovered from the collapse of their financial hopes in 1925 and 1926, but they hoped to share the prosperity associated with Calvin Coolidge that promised to continue under Hoover, who had a reputation as a business success.

Churchmen, some of them from outside the state, took the lead in the anti-Smith campaign. Early in August, Bishop James Cannon of the Methodist Church came to Jacksonville for a meeting sponsored by the Anti-Saloon League, the Women's Christian Temperance Union, and the Methodist ministers of the city. Sunday schools and youth organizations joined forces to support prohibition. Florida Democrats, unaccustomed to conducting a campaign in a one-party state, started too late to stop the "Hoovercrat" movement. Nor did all Democratic candidates for state and local office support the national ticket. In a vain effort to stem the tide of opposition, nationally-known Democrats came to Florida, among them Senators Robinson, Pat Harrison of Mississippi, James Reed of Missouri, Walter F. George of Georgia, and Tom Connally of Texas. Mrs. Franklin D. Roosevelt made an appeal in behalf of the New York governor. Republicans also had out-of-state visitors; in addition to Bishop Cannon there was the Reverend Doctor John Roach Stratton of New York. Alfred I. DuPont, a newcomer to the state and a Republican, gave strong support to the Hoover campaign. Hoover won by 144,168 votes to 101,764 for Smith. Democratic candidates for governor and United States Senator won by two to one, weakening somewhat the claim that Florida had become a two-party state. The Great Depression, however, destroyed Hoover's popularity, and four years later Franklin D. Roosevelt defeated Hoover

Moonshine whiskey still near Tampa, after a raid in 1920

by 206,000 to 69,000 votes.

The speculative extravagance of the land boom in the twenties helped to spawn and also fed upon an equally spectacular boom in rum running and the smuggling of aliens and narcotics. The beginning of national prohibition enforcement in January 1920, coupled with the long coastline with many inlets deep enough for small boats and the proximity to supplies in Cuba and the British West Indies, made the east coast of Florida one of the "leakiest spots" in the country. Local authorities proved indifferent if not outright hostile to enforcement, which was left to federal agents of whom there were never enough. Floridians resented federal interference with individual freedom and feared that enforcement would harm the tourist industry. Federal agents frequently found themselves hauled into court, and though never convicted, they often suffered considerable embarrassment.

Some of the liquor came from local moonshining operations, which flourished without undue interference, but most of it came from nearby offshore sources. The average annual import of liquor into the Bahamas rose from 50,000 gallons to 1,200,000 in 1922, and the greater part of it reached the United States through Florida. Most of the imports came into Florida directly by small boats; until 1924, when Great Britain permitted search of its ships, some of the cargo changed hands just outside the three-mile limit. The liquor was usually packed six quarts in straw in burlap bags known as "hams," which were convenient for handling and could be dropped overboard when a patrol boat came on the scene or could be deposited in shallow water for a later pickup. The only general use of airplanes was between Grand Bahama and Palm Beach, where twenty-one small planes reportedly operated at one time. Homestead was the distribution center for liquor and aliens from Cuba, but Key West frequently served as a way station. Moonshining flourished at Cape Sable, and at least one cargo of aliens was landed there. Bimini was the chief source of liquor supply for Miami.

Collusion between local officials and rum runners was not uncommon. In Nassau County prohibition agents once arrested the entire police force of Fernandina. A number of South Jacksonville officials suffered the same fate, as did others in Broward, Dade, and elsewhere. There was some hijacking of liquor supplies along all the routes followed, and cash receipts sometimes were lost to raiders. A serious effort to break up the illicit traffic occurred in 1928 when the United States Coast Guard sent thirty-one vessels to the Fort Lauderdale-Miami area and maintained a virtual blockade of the coast. But it was abandoned at the end of the season. Occasionally the coast guardsmen met violent opposition, but they often got their man. Convictions of law breakers and collaborators in local courts were difficult, however. One Miami rum runner and alien smuggler, Horace Alderman, was once considered the king of them all. He killed two coast guardsmen and wounded a third in an encounter on the high seas between Bimini and Miami in August of 1927 but paid the supreme penalty two years later when he was hanged. Like the land boom, it was an era of wild extravagance that soon passed.

In retrospect it is clear that much of what happened in Florida in the 1920s was a reflection of national policies. While this is obvious with respect to Prohibition and rum running, it is perhaps less so in the case of the land boom and the banking crash of 1926. The Federal Reserve System had, of course, been put in place just prior to World War I. As economists have noted, in 1924, and then again in 1927, the "Fed" greatly inflated the money supply. This was an important factor in the whole cultural attitude of the era, and, given the time it takes such actions to perculate through the economy, provided a boost to both land prices in the years 1925-26 and stock market prices which crashed in 1929.

This inflationary policy, as a recent study by Raymond B. Vickers demonstrates, led to less than sound speculation by some bankers. This resulted in the closing of 117 banks in Georgia and Florida during July, 1926, and was compounded when bank regulators denied that any such problems existed. Vickers suggests that such policies "involved massive insider abuses, a conscious conspiracy to defraud, or both," implicated developers such as Addison Mizner, who was also deeply involved in banking.[2] In the 1980s Florida would again find itself confronted with a similar banking crisis which is discussed in a later chapter.

25.

The Depression and the New Deal

The fourth decade of the twentieth century was at the same time an inseparable confusion of continuing depression in some areas of the economy and of recovery and new enterprise in others. At the governmental level there was a confusion of relief, recovery, and reform measures that transformed state and local goverment into units of a national program aimed at protecting the individual and promoting the general welfare. When a growing measure of economic recovery had been achieved at the end of the decade, there was no general agreement as to why it had happened–whether it was because of the New Deal or in spite of it. There was little doubt that the return to what was increasingly a war economy had much to do with it. There was no doubt that the role of government at all levels had been vastly increased.

The confusion in Florida history is further increased by the state depression that began in some sections of the economy in 1926, three years before the national crisis precipitated by the stock market crash in the fall of 1929. In another sense, depression during the era of Coolidge-Hoover industrial prosperity had been common in the South and to some degree in Florida. Agriculture, coal mining, and textile manufacturing had never shared the prosperity of the twenties. The land boom in Florida in the first half of the decade was merely an exception to the general rule of nonparticipation in the speculative affluence. Because values in Florida had already been deflated, Florida appeared statistically to suffer less in the national depression. On the other hand, because Florida's financial institutions and other businesses had been weakened by the earlier experience, they were less able to withstand the shock of the national crisis at the end of the decade.

The measure of the collapse in 1926 and the failure to recover are best seen in the decline of property values, the state of banking and other businesses, and the public debt, particularly of local governments. Between 1926 and 1930 the assessed value of real estate dropped from 623 to 441 million dollars; the operating revenues of railroads, two of which, the Florida East Coast and the Seaboard, went into receivership in 1931, from 91 to 46 million; and the reported net income of corporations, from 815 million in 1925 to 84 million in 1930. The most cautious banks could scarcely avoid being caught up in the inflationary spiraling of business. Nor could they withstand the strain of sustained deflation and depression that followed. By 1926, heavy withdrawals coupled with failures of buyers of land to make payments began to produce failures among the smaller and more recently organized institutions. In December 1925, sixty-two national and 274 state-chartered banks reported resources of $943 million. In 1926 resources fell by some $300 million, and more than forty banks closed their doors. More than half of these managed to reorganize and reopen, and enough new banks opened in the state to make a net gain in the number that year of four national and ten state banks.

The state government had been saved from bonded debt during the boom only by the constitutional provision against it. The debt of political subdivisions, counties, cities, and special tax districts had grown from $110 million in 1922 to $600 million in 1929. The first default on a bond payment had occurred in 1926, and three years later failures to meet payments were common throughout the state. The state government was behind in payments of current expenses, and capital expenditures ceased for the time being.

Bank failures in 1929 began before the stock market crash in October. On July 17 in Tampa the Citizens Bank and Trust Company, which had paid out to depositors $1,200,000 on the day before, did not open. Five affiliated banks in Tampa and four out of town, at Plant City, Bradenton, Sarasota, and Fort Meade, also closed. Heroic measures stopped runs on the First National, the Exchange National, and the First Savings and Trust Company. One million dollars came in by air and four million more by train the next day, but depositors suffered loss of confidence and harsher strains were to come. At the end of 1929 fifty-seven national and 178 state banks reported resources of $375,000,000. In that year forty-three state and ten national banks failed, and failures continued with thirty-four in 1930, fourteen in 1931, twelve in 1932, and twenty-five in 1933. In June of 1932, 135 state bank and trust companies were operating and 143 were in process of liquidation. In all, 157 state banks closed permanently between 1928 and 1940, of which only four paid depositors in full and another four paid nothing. National banks fared little better, one failing in 1926, two each in 1927 and 1928, seventeen in the next three years, three in 1932, and two in 1933. Between 1925 and 1934 forty-five national banks with deposits of some $31,000,000 failed, as did 171 state banks with $100,000,000 in deposits.

To make a generally bad economic picture worse in 1929, the Mediterranean fruit fly was discovered in a citrus grove near Orlando in April. It soon became evident that the infestation was widespread; 1,002 groves with seventy-two percent of all of the trees in the state proved to be playing host to the invader. In an all-out effort to rid the state of the pest that could ruin it for the production of many fruits and vegetables, state and federal embargoes prohibited shipment from the affected groves. All trees with evidence of the presence of the flies were systematically collected and burned. The state spent $281,474 and the federal government $6,471,161 before the quarantine was lifted on November 30, 1930. Production of citrus fell from 28,000,000 boxes in 1928-1929 to only 17,000,000 a year later. Some twenty thousand men had temporary employment in the destruction of the trees, but the citrus and related industries suffered a severe blow that helps to account for bank failures early in the national depression. Two more recent discoveries of the fruit fly have proved less destructive because of early detection and massive attacks by aerial spraying. Constant vigilance to guard against their return is maintained.

Economic problems growing out of depression completely dominated the administration of Doyle E. Carlton, who became governor in January 1929. He had campaigned in favor of a conservative approach to the problems of finance and taxation, demanding tax and debt relief. He observed that state expenditures had recently tripled, that the tax burden was as heavy as it could be made, and that the gap between expenditures and receipts should be closed by cutting the former, expressing the belief that a quarter of a million dollars could be cut from the state budget without impairing services. He proposed to increase experimental and extension work to improve agricultural output, to protect farmers from unfair and fraudulent competitors, and to improve conditions for marketing farm produce. He also urged that resources of the state to attract industry be studied. Anticipating the protective and regulatory legislation of the New Deal, he favored laws to provide more strict regulation of banking to protect depositors and stockholders. In his inaugural address he came back to the same proposals, identifying taxation and finances as the major problems of the state. He proposed to restrict the bonding powers of local government and to continue road building only on a pay-as-you-go basis. He would abolish useless offices and consolidate kindred functions. To retire the bonded debt of local governments, he urged that two cents of the gasoline tax be used, but counties less burdened with debt resisted this move. He repeated his objection to legalized betting on horse races. When the legislature proved slow to act in 1929, he addressed a joint session on May 23 to urge action. He called a special session in June to provide revenue for schools and the general fund appropriations. The revenue measure passed at the last minute without significant change, but not until a proposal by Senator Waybright for a gross sales tax and a bill to legalize parimutuel betting had been defeated, the latter losing by only five votes in the senate.

By the time Governor Carlton faced the 1931 legislature the conditions he had emphasized two years earlier had worsened, but he did not change his program. He condemned resorting to a sales tax but appeared willing to accept a very limited sales tax in place of realty taxes, which he preferred that the state drop. He recommended that money be saved by reducing the number of circuit

courts, using grand juries in fewer cases, reducing the number of
county offices and the salaries associated with them, consolidating
the offices for assessing and collecting taxes, and using central purchasing. The governor vetoed an inheritance tax bill, and the legislature could not muster the two-thirds vote to override the veto.
The senate offered a homestead exemption proposal on May 6, and
the house a few days later refused to consider a workmen's compensation measure.

The legalizing of parimutuel wagering at horse and dog tracks
coupled with a tax on the proceeds was finally achieved. On May 15
the senate approved the bill by twenty to fifteen, apparently believing it would yield a million dollars a year of much needed revenue.
When the house later approved the measure Carlton vetoed it, arguing that moral considerations outweighed all others. The governor at the same time declared himself opposed to a state income
tax, which would drive away wealthy people and deprive the state
of needed capital. On May 20, the session was drawing to a close,
the governor called a joint session to urge the lawmakers to act on
appropriations and taxes. Schools and other state services had to
be provided for. On June 3, the senate passed the racing bill over
the governor's veto by 26 to 12, but a special session was necessary
before final action on many bills could be taken. A revenue bill
providing $23,390,000 for the biennium, most of the increase com-
ing from a seventh cent of the gasoline tax, finally passed.

Horse racing was not new to Florida, for the sport had been
popular among the pre-Civil War gentry in Leon County. It had
been introduced into southern Florida when the first race was run
at Hialeah on January 15, 1925, and continued with some success
in 1926 and 1927. There was no racing in 1928, but it was renewed
in 1929 when the practice of selling fake options on horses was introduced. When the race was run, the track purchased the options
at the odds established by the purchasers. Joseph E. Widener became interested in the Hialeah track and helped to induce the legislature to legalize the operation in 1931. The racing tax, associated as it was with the legalizing of parimutuel wagering and the
creation of the State Racing Commission, was to prove of far-reach-

Horse breeding in Marion County. Ocala Stud Farm, 1957.

"Going to the dogs" at outdoor track in Hialeah, 1922

ing importance. The desperate need for a new source of state revenue, the possibility of attracting more tourists, and the introduction of a new industry finally outweighed doubts arising from the
possibility of attracting undesirable track followers and giving public approval to wagering. The clincher was no doubt the provision
that one-half of the proceeds of the tax should be distributed equally
among the counties. The result has been more than the proponents
could have dreamed. The tax produced $737,301 the first year, rose
steadily to two million in 1938-1939, and to $4,392,862 at the be-
ginning of World War II, after which it dropped off sharply. At the
end of the war tourists returned, and in 1945-1946 the racing tax
yielded $15,554,034 and continued to increase, reaching twenty
million in 1954 and twenty-five million in 1957. By that time four
horse tracks, fifteen dog tracks, and four jai-alai frontons were operating. In 1964 harness racing was inaugurated at Pompano Beach,
and horse racing began in the summer of 1970 in Dade County.
Another notable development has been the introduction of horse
breeding farms into the Ocala area. More than a hundred such
establishments now operate.

Recognition of the growing severity of the depression and the
extent of unemployment and the necessity to do something to alleviate the distress of the jobless began in 1931. On August 31, President Hoover, who had won an enviable reputation as the adminis-
trator of international relief for starving Europeans at the end of
World War I, created "The President's Organization on Unemployment Relief" with Walter S. Gifford, president of the American Telephone and Telegraph Company, as its chairman. Florida and other
states appointed similar committees to encourage projects that would
provide jobs for the unemployed. The Florida committee began con-

servatively by adopting a resolution stating unalterable opposition to the dole system of direct relief. The committee also requested Governor Carlton to notify President Hoover that Florida would take care of its own unemployment problems. The members of the committee did not yet appreciate the extent of the problem.

It thus fell to local government to make the first efforts at unemployment relief. In February 1931, seventeen of Florida's sixty-seven counties had public welfare programs administered by social workers, and fifteen employed full-time caseworkers. Their primary concern was with unemployables, but they grew increasingly concerned with the unemployed who could find no jobs. The cities had also responded in various ways to the worsening economic situation. Among the cities reported as having programs to provide relief for the distressed were Jacksonville, Tampa, Pensacola, West Palm Beach, Daytona Beach, Fort Myers, Lake Worth, Lakeland, Orlando, and Saint Petersburg. None of the communities had sufficient public or private funds to meet the growing emergencies. They could not have raised money by taxation if their charters had permitted it. The state administration was no more ready to consider relief measures in 1931. It should be said in their behalf that they were not alone in failure to realize that the depression would continue to worsen and that the entire economy was threatened if relief and recovery measures were not undertaken. The 1931 legislature earmarked one-half of the proceeds of the sixth cent of the gasoline tax to be returned to counties to assist them in debt retirement. At the same session, state aid to schools was more than doubled, but that brought the total to only fourteen million dollars and left Florida forty-first in the nation in per capita expenditure for schools.

The New Deal, to the extent that it meant concern of government for the welfare of the victims of depression, began in Florida and at the national level in 1932 in the administrations of a president and a governor who were reluctant to have the government play that role. The U.S. Congress on July 21, 1932, passed the Emergency Relief and Construction Act, which authorized the Reconstruction Finance Corporation (RFC) to lend 300 million dollars to the states to take care of relief needs beyond their own resources. The amounts were to be subtracted later from federal appropriations to state road departments. Governor Carlton asked the State Board of Public Welfare to make a survey and determine the needs of the state. Meanwhile, the governor requested $500,000 in four monthly installments to cover needs to the end of the year. He had underestimated the need for the funds. Florida received the first installment of RFC money on September 12, 1932, and a total of $1,841,125 by the end of the year, and by May 1933, when the program gave way to the Federal Emergency Relief Administration, or FERA, Florida had received a total of $3,886,512. In those first months of 1933 the number of Florida families on relief averaged about 90,000, a little more than one out of every five families in the state.

In 1932, state and national elections resulted in new leadership and new directions in the effort to cope with the problems growing out of the depression. Reaction to the worsening state of the economy was nowhere more apparent than in these elections. Generally speaking, it meant the repudiation of people and policies of administrations that had the misfortune to be in places of responsibility at the time. Floridians blamed Herbert Hoover for the depression as strongly as they had supported him for the promise of prosperity four years earlier. For governor they went outside the usual crop of political regulars. Of the eight Democrats who offered themselves for the nomination, two ex-governors, Cary A. Hardee and John W. Martin, were expected to have the advantage and wind up in a runoff (second choice voting had been abandoned in 1931). David Sholtz of Daytona Beach proved to be the best vote-getter. This Brooklyn-born Yale man who had a Stetson University law degree had practiced in Daytona Beach since 1915 with a term in the lower house of the legislature and time out for service in the Navy in the war. Very active in Chamber of Commerce work, he became president of the State Chamber of Commerce in 1927, an office which provided him with many contacts in the state.

Hardee and Martin ran on their previous records, which seemed hardly adequate to meet the demands of the crisis years. Sholtz promised a businesslike administration but made positive proposals for recovery. He urged a nine-month school term with full pay for teachers as a remedy for the shortened terms and reduced salaries, some of which were not being paid. More than half of the counties owed teachers some salary. The state superintendent's budget in 1933 included $312,408 to pay back salaries. Teachers in other places took reduced pay to keep the schools open a full term. Others cut out such "nonessentials" as home economics, physical education, art, music, and manual training. Saint Petersburg tried charging tuition and begging those without children to pay it for children whose parents were unable to pay. A final measure of the extent of the problem was revealed when the FERA granted $610,210 to school districts in fifty-five counties to pay back salaries to 4,461 teachers. Sholtz also supported free school textbooks, larger expenditures for public welfare, stronger regulation of banks, and workmen's compensation for accident laws. He campaigned in every county in the state and promised every effort to find jobs for the unemployed.

In the first primary he ran second to Martin with 55,406 to 66,940 and 50,427 for Hardee. In the hard-fought second primary, an attack on Sholtz's alleged Jewish ancestry apparently backfired. He ignored the controversy, continued to talk about the issues close to the hearts and minds of the voters, and won by the largest vote ever given to a gubernatorial candidate, 182,805 to 173,540. Republican W. J. Howey had a significantly high vote of 93,325 in November to Sholtz's 186,270.

The New Deal, which had begun in Florida before it did in the administration of Franklin D. Roosevelt, which began in March 1933, was limited in scope and philosophy. Supporters of Roosevelt were unaware that his administration would mean so much welfare legislation, for he campaigned on a platform to balance the budget, reduce salaries and expenditures, and to reduce rather than increase veterans' compensation. The New Deal had great economic importance in Florida throughout the thirties until the European war stimulated the economy late in the decade. Reactions to the New Deal measures as the programs for relief and recovery unfolded were mixed. The emergency bank legislation, the legalization of beer sales, and what at first looked like the lower costs of government met favor. On the other hand, the *Florida Times Union* called the president's request for $500,000,000 to put men to work at reforestation "the first questionable move," and the first proposals for public power development on the Tennessee River were denounced as government competition with citizens. The attitude had appeared earlier when Herbert Hoover proposed the Reconstruction Finance Corporation in June 1932, and the *Miami Herald* had commented. editorially: "The war was fought on credit. Now it is proposed to fight depression by the same means." The journal of the State Road Department and the Florida Engineering Society had dismissed the RFC as accomplishing little, but it conceded early in 1933 that government emergency financing for construction of roads might be an exception, an opinion strengthened materially when the chairman of the SRD became a member of the advisory committee to the Works Progress Administration, the WPA. Generally, Florida leadership approved relief and recovery measures when they did not interfere with local economic arrangements as to hours, wages, and working conditions.

By the time Governor Sholtz took over the reins of state government the worst effects of the Great Depression were being felt in Florida. The national banking holiday and the increasingly long lines of the unemployed waiting to be certified for relief measured the seriousness of the situation. Per capita accountable income dropped from $510 in 1929 by successive annual stages of $478 in 1930, $392 in 1931, $317 in 1932, to a low of $289 in 1933, after which it rose to $328 and $352 in the next two years. By the end of 1933 twenty-six percent of the state's people as counted in the 1930 census were receiving public assistance. The 226,868 whites constituted twenty-two percent of the total-number of whites, and the 155,239 blacks were thirty-six-percent of all blacks. The proportion of the population on relief varied from county to county. In nine of the sixty-seven counties, more than forty percent were receiving direct relief. In a dozen others more than one-third of the families were receiving assistance. In only three was the percentage less than ten.

In Florida, depression, unemployment, and need for public assistance were as common in rural as in urban areas. Almost one-third of the recipients of emergency relief lived in rural areas and towns under 500 people and only one-third lived in cities with more than 100,000 residents. Nor was unemployment limited to newcomers to the state. Twenty-nine percent of them had lived twenty-five or more years in the county where they received relief. Thirty-five percent had lived in the county from ten to twenty-five years and only one-fifth had come to Florida during the boom years, 1923 to 1928. Some of the unemployment was of long standing. Eight percent had lost their regular jobs five or more years before applying for direct relief. Sixty-one percent had been out of regular employment for from one to five years, and thirty-one percent one year or less.

The dependent aged fell into a somewhat different category. More than half of them had been receiving aid from city and county governments in the form of "pensions" paid only to the most destitute. In some counties the only relief being paid out was to the aged, and at the end of 1933 some of that responsibility was being transferred to federal emergency relief sources. In 1933 some 17,880 persons received $427,000 from city and county funds plus $84,000 administered by private agencies but deriving largely from public sources. Of the 13,100 persons sixty-five or older who received federal emergency relief in 1933, thirty-eight percent had been in Florida fifty or more years and twenty-three percent had entered the state between 1920 and 1929.

"Poor laws" in Florida dated back at least to a long-forgotten act of 1828, which authorized judges to bind out in apprenticeship orphans or children of fathers on the counties' pauper lists. The first step toward a more modern approach came in 1927 with the creation of the State Board of Public Welfare with protective and supervisory responsibilities. Funding and staffing had been inadequate for the board's work in normal times, and it was totally unprepared for the new emergency. Yet it did become the nucleus for the rapid development of state social service administration. It began in the midst of the depression with a series of studies designed to discover the nature and extent of needs that might have a claim upon public attention and ways to meet them. The concern was with the whole complex of social problems rather than with emergency relief, which was looked upon as temporary. Mentally and physically handicapped and neglected children, child dependency and delinquency, mothers' pensions, parole service, correctional training, and special protection had hitherto received little if any attention. For the aged the concept of self-respecting social security was to replace the keep-alive dole. The state board also took on as many administrative responsibilities connected with emergency relief. It certified people for Works Progress Administration and National Youth Administration employment, for selection as enrollees for the Civilian Conservation Corps, or CCC, and for the distribution of surplus commodoties, and it directed child welfare services. The present Department of Social Welfare was created in 1937.

However good the intentions of Governor Sholtz may have been, a major difficulty was the raising of funds necessary to pay the state's share of the cost of administering welfare and public works programs sponsored and financed largely by the federal government. When he tried in October of 1933 to pledge the state's credit on a loan, the state supreme court turned it down as beyond the powers of his office. Florida was one of the four debtless states in the Union, but the constitutional prohibition of borrowing and the unwilling-ness of the state legislature to levy the necessary taxes threw the burden of financing relief upon the already debt-ridden counties and municipalities. By January 1935, the state had contributed only $15,492, the cities $2,000,344, and the federal government $40,361,152.

The 1935 session of the state legislature made the first signifi-cant steps toward assuming state responsibility for a welfare pro-gram. One million dollars was made available for skilled labor and materials for public works, on which workers on relief did the greater part of the labor. New tax policy generated funds for support of rural schools, which had been kept open the previous year by a grant of $600,000 from federal relief funds. A constitutional amendment authorized the levying of taxes and the appropriating of money for relief payments. The Social Welfare Act of that year set aside $50,000 for the State Welfare Board, which was then eligible for federal grants in aid. The State Planning Board, formerly paid out of FERA funds, received $25,000 a year. In short, the state of Florida was putting up approximately two million dollars for the next two years, a major departure in policy if not an overwhelming amount of money.

The first New Deal agency to begin operations in Florida was the Civilian Conservation Corps in August 1933. The Olustee Na-tional Forest was selected as the site of the first camp, which was to employ 300 enrollees in a reforestation project. Florida's first quota of 3,000 enrollees was soon occupying twenty-six camps, principally in state, national, and private forests and state parks. The quota was later raised by 900, and some 2,200 young men came to camps in Florida from nearby states. Before the CCC was terminated in 1940 some 40,000 young men from 18 to 25 years of age from relief families had found temporary refuge in the work camps. Another 2,500 nonenrollees, administrators, and skilled workmen had also spent some time working with the corps. Enrollees received all of their living expenses, and twenty-five of the thirty dollars they earned went to their families, frequently to be returned to the en-rollees. They planted 13,605,000 trees, improved the forest stand in 218,013 acres, and cut 14,554 miles of firebreaks.

As the several New Deal relief administrations (the last the WPA in May 1935) succeeded each other, a number of problems, not all of them peculiar to Florida, developed. The Civil Works Administration, which lasted for only a little more than four months, to March 10, 1934, was a first step in the substitution of work relief for direct cash payments. It brought out sharply the distinction between employable and unemployable persons on relief when fed-eral officials insisted that the state take care of the unemployables. When workers on CWA projects received twelve dollars a week or thirty cents an hour for a forty-hour week, it brought protests from the citrus growers and turpentine operators who were paying about nine dollars a week or twenty to twenty-five cents an hour. Local employers finally obtained a ruling stating that persons who refused employment in private industry could not be certified for relief work.

Transients had long been a Florida problem. The lure of boom-time wages lived long after the collapse of the boom. The climate in Florida was attractive in the winter. The Federal Transient Bureau under the FERA reached a peak load in December of 1934 when it was caring for about 14,000 persons, eighty percent of them from outside Florida. Governor Sholtz wired governors in other southeastern states to warn that Florida had no jobs and to discourage migration. Efforts were made by agencies of the state and local government to turn back at the state line those without visible means of support.

Key West had a unique depression and New Deal experience. When the armed forces at the island city were reduced to a mere garrison after World War I, the city went into a decline. It had already lost two principal industries when the center of cigar making moved to Tampa and sponge fishing to Tarpon Springs. The boom left it relatively untouched, and its population declined in the twenties to 12,831 and by 1935 to 12,317. By 1933 the city debt was $5,000,000, interest of a quarter of a million was unpaid, and there were no funds for current expenses. In July of 1934 the city asked the governor of the state to declare a state of emergency so that the community could be turned over to the Federal Emergency Relief Administration of the New Deal. The FERA undertook to rehabilitate the city and make it the resort city of the tropics to rival Bermuda and Nassau. Citizens contributed nearly two million man hours of labor. Artists on relief from other areas came to decorate the walls of public buildings and cafes with murals. Classes in handicrafts taught residents to make novelties from local products to sell to tourists, for whom fetes and pageants were also to be provided. Wide advertising brought an estimated 40,000 visitors that winter, but what the ultimate result might have been was never to be known. The Labor Day hurricane of 1935 destroyed so much of the Overseas Railroad that had been the city's lifeline since 1912 that it was decided not to rebuild it. The Florida East Coast Railway Company sold the right-of-way and bridges to the state for $640,000, and the Monroe County Toll Bridge Commission, with WPA assistance, constructed a highway along the route from Florida City to Key West. The new roadway was opened in 1938. The coming of the Second World War revived the city and provided a water main from Florida City to supply fresh water, and the city looked hopefully for a desalinization plant to convert sea water for domestic uses, a hope not realized until nearly thirty years had passed. The Old Island Restoration Foundation now seeks to create in Key West a tourist attraction of genuine historical value. Population began to grow again, reaching 24,443 in 1950 and 35,956 in 1960.

Though it struck no centers of population, the Labor Day hurricane on September 2, 1935, was second only to that of 1928 in the number of lives it claimed. Possibly 500 residents lived in the path of the storm in the Florida Keys, but added to this were 684 veterans of the First World War in three Civilian Conservation Corps camps, one on Windley Key and two on Lower Matecumbe. An unfortunate combination of circumstances produced the tragedy. Until noon of the fateful day it was assumed that the blow would pass south of the Keys. Communication was made slow by the holiday absence of top army and railroad officials, and when a rescue train finally left Miami to evacuate them it was too late. Rushing wind and water at Islamorada overturned all of the cars and left only the engine standing on the tracks, with bridges and rights-of-way to the mainland washed out in places. The official report on the veterans was forty-four identified dead, 106 injured, and 238 missing or unidentified dead; 296 other veterans escaped mainly because they were away on holiday weekends. Conservative estimates placed the number of civilian casualties at ninety-six known dead and sixty-eight missing or unidentified.

The New Deal gave new life to a project as old as the white man's occupation of the Florida peninsula. Pedro Menéndez de Aviles, the founder of Saint Augustine, died hoping, if not believing, that there was an inland route from the Saint Johns River to Tampa Bay. When Franklin D. Roosevelt entered the White House, army engineers had already made twenty-eight surveys of possible canal routes across Florida. They had concluded that the best route was by way of the Saint Johns and Oklawaha rivers, and thence by way of a cut passing near Ocala to the Withlacoochee River and into the Gulf of Mexico at Port Inglis. Estimates of cost ranged from 146 to 200 million dollars. The National Gulf-Atlantic Ship Canal Association had unsuccessfully sought a Reconstruction Finance Corporation loan to initiate the project. When New Deal work relief funds became available, sponsors of the waterway took new hope.

On September 2, 1935, the fateful day of the Labor Day hurricane in the Florida Keys, the President announced that $5,000,000 of his emergency relief funds would be allocated to the ship canal project. This set off an incipient real estate boom along the route and elicited rather general approval in the area north of it. Central and South Florida reacted with doubts and outright opposition. Many people believed, rightly or wrongly, that the sea level canal would let salt water into and threaten their fresh water supply, nor were they appeased by new investigations and reports by geologists that there was no possibility of drying up underground sources of water or of salt intrusion. When the original appropriation had been expended in the summer of 1936, the work came to a halt. Secretary of Interior Harold Ickes refused to approve it as a WPA project, and the Congress denied F.D.R. the requested direct appropriation. Directors of the project had built Camp Roosevelt, cleared some 4,000 acres of right-of-way, and moved nearly thirteen million yards of earth. In January 1939, the president in a letter to the chairman of the Rivers and Harbors Committee urged an appropriation for the stalled project, but the Senate turned it down in May. Meanwhile, in 1937, some 3,000 students occupied the project's ninety barracks buildings three miles south of Ocala in a University of Florida Extension Division vocational rehabilitation school for the unemployed.

World War II intervened but did not kill the project. It failed in 1941 to win approval as a defense project, but reappeared in 1943 as a proposal for a barge canal to cost $44,000,000. The barge canal proposal removed the strongest objections, as the barge canal would follow roughly the contour of the land, the boats being raised by means of locks. Shortages of manpower, materials, and time outweighed the possibility of its use to move fuel from the Gulf to the northeastern part of the country. The canal project reappeared in 1956 with the added argument that it would lower freight costs, but sponsors could not get it going again. In February 1964 President Johnson came to Florida to participate in ceremonies in conjunction with the work on the barge canal. A major hitch in arrangements to purchase right-of-way for the 107 mile, 158 million dollar canal arose in 1965 when Governor Haydon Burns offered as an alternative to an appropriation from the general fund that the six counties involved float a bond issue to pay part of the cost. Work continued until January 1971 when President Nixon ordered it stopped, an order that has thus far remained intact.

To assess the contribution of the New Deal to recovery in Florida is difficult. The WPA certainly succeeded in switching from direct relief to the performance of useful labor. Business activity increased by 43.49 percent between March 1933 and March 1934. Employment was up 15.43 percent, payrolls up 22.51 percent, and wages per hour 21.65 percent, but unemployment continued at nearly the same levels. The withdrawal of relief funds helped to produce a recession in 1937-1938, and a large number of Floridians again found themselves out of work. On July 1, 1941, in spite of signs of recov-

Route of controversial Cross-Florida Barge Canal Project

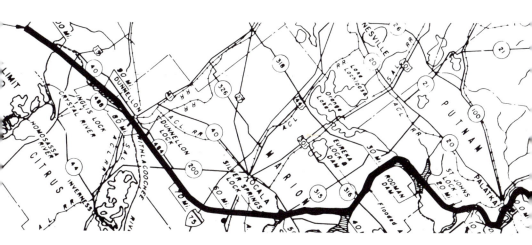

ery in many sectors of the economy, 72,464 persons were registered as eligible for relief work; and in midwinter 1942-1943, 43,000 families were still on the rolls. The welfare agency had become a preferred employer to some people rather than being a relief agency.

The importance of the New Deal in the economic and financial history of Florida can hardly be overestimated. One summary of federal expenditures in the decade points out that the amount rose from $12,772,000 in 1930 to $62,718,000 in 1934 and averaged over $54,000,000 for the next three years. In 1938 the total dropped to $48,657,000 but rose to $67,218,000 the next, when the cuts of the previous year produced a recession, and mounted to $64,920,000 in 1940. By June 1938 the WPA had completed 137 projects that included forty-two schools, twenty-seven water works, and six sewer systems. In 1940 relief employment was being provided for 1,185 persons per month. In another count through June 1940 the WPA had constructed 6,206 miles of highways and streets, built 245 new schools and improved 278 others, put up 601 public buildings and improved another 208, had constructed 1,237 bridges and viaducts, 6,272 culverts, 146 parks, 191 playgrounds and athletic fields, and 24,533 sanitary privies.

Banking institutions also reflected an improving economy. By the end of 1933, Florida banks, some with New Deal assistance, had weathered both the state and the national depressions. Resources at the end of the year totaled $226,400,000 and rose to $253,000,000 in six months. Within a few months after the creation of the Federal Deposit Insurance Corporation, all banks in the state but one had joined, and an air of confidence prevailed. Only Key West did not follow the normal route to recovery.

The Sholtz administration was a great beneficiary of the New Deal expenditures, without which he could scarcely have achieved many of the financial gains his administration could claim. He proposed to the legislature certain reasonable taxes, for instance, five dollars for automobile tags. To finance the school program for free textbooks and better teachers' salaries, he urged that money from auto license tags, the state's share of the parimutuel wagering tax, and the one-mill school levy provided for in the constitution be appropriated. State aid for public schools grew from $17,422,104 in the previous administration to $32,730,115 in his term. In a fireside radio chat broadcast at the end of his term he stated that his administration had started out with a deficit of $2,124,000 in state revenue, which by July 30, 1934, had become a surplus of $591,000, and that $400,000 in past due obligations had been paid off. By 1935 he saw recovery becoming clearly evident. He admitted that the government could not provide jobs for all who needed them but claimed he had followed the policies of national government, which had spent more than $50,000,000 a year in the state for relief. He pointed out that relief rolls had been reduced from 16,000 in 1933 to one-fourth that number in 1935.

The most significant legacy of the Sholtz administration was increased concern with welfare problems, reflected chiefly in cooperation with the national government. It also meant a long stride toward big government at the state as well as at the national level. No governor since Sholtz has been so "New Dealish," but the growth of state functions and the bureaucracy that administers it have increased steadily. In addition to the Welfare Board and its several functions there were a workmen's compensation act and an industrial commission to administer it, a mechanic's lien law, a state employment service, a planning board, a tuberculosis board, and pensions for the aged and the blind. A state park service and a conservation commission reflected growing interest in recreation and sports. A state beverage department grew out of the repeal of the prohibition amendment and the liquor tax as an important new source of state revenue. More attention was given to the marketing of citrus, and a tax on packaged citrus produced $400,000 in 1935-1936 to promote sales by an advertising program. Some much needed progress was made in the construction of institutional buildings made possible by matching federal funds at Orlando, Tallahassee, Chattahoochee, Gainesville, Ocala, Raiford, and Marianna.

The intervening election year 1934 is significant only in that it marked the appearance on the political horizon of Claude Pepper, who was soon to become one of the state's best known politicians. He and three others challenged Park Trammell for the Democratic nomination for Trammell's senate seat. Pepper received 79,000 votes to Trammell's 81,000, and in the runoff Trammell won by only 103,000 to 99,000.

In 1936 Florida experienced the highest degree of what V. O. Key, Jr., termed "political pulverization" when fourteen candidates sought the Democratic nomination for the governorship. The leading candidate received less than sixteen percent of the 329,132 votes cast and five of them a total of only 17,377. Four years later there were eleven candidates, after which the rising cost of political campaigns reduced the number sharply. Fred Cone, the eventual winner in 1936, was probably the best known of the lot. He had been active in Democratic politics for nearly fifty years, had served eight years in the state senate, where he was president in 1911, and had three times been a delegate to the party's national convention. Cone ran second to Raleigh W. Petteway, a Tampa lawyer and judge, but in the runoff Cone won by 184,540 to 129,150 and then won easily over Republican E. E. Callaway in November by 253,638 to 59,832. By reason of the deaths of Florida's two United States Senators, Park Trammell in May and Duncan U. Fletcher in June, a special primary to nominate successors was held on August 11, 1936. Neither of the appointees named by Governor Sholtz to serve until election time, Scott M. Loftin of Jacksonville for Trammell and Will J. Hill for Fletcher, chose to run in the general election. Claude Pepper was unopposed for Fletcher's seat, and Charles O. Andrews of Tampa won the other by 67,387 to 62,530 over former Governor Doyle E. Carlton.

Governor Cone was no New Dealer. His program assumed the possibility of reduced budgets and lower taxes. Some of his conser-

Use of Florida pine (and other woods to a lesser extent) for paper making produce modern scenes like this.

vatism has been called ill-advised since it led to refusal to match federal funds to improve old and add new facilities at state institutions that had not kept pace with growing needs. Cone recommended no increase to schools. He saw a need to relieve Floridians of hidden and indirect taxes that burdened industry as well as private persons. He urged that delinquent taxes on real estate, a legacy of the boom, be collected and suggested that when lands reverted to the state they might be homesteaded. The legislature responded with an increase in aid to schools and a general appropriations bill $800,000 higher than that of 1935. The Murphy Act provided for the sale of tax-delinquent property to get it back on the tax rolls. Other new revenue came from higher taxes on liquor and occupational licenses.

In 1939 the governor stuck to his guns, suggesting that an additional million dollars (over the 1935 sum) requested by the budget commission should not be granted. Some of his proposals did require new revenue, such as higher salaries for elected officials, more revenue for schools, and care for the aged and afflicted. The added revenue was to come from savings and an increase in the racing tax.

There were radical proposals in the legislature but they failed to become law. The house actually approved a law based on the Townsend Plan, but the senate rejected it. A house committee refused to consider a proposal for income and inheritance taxes. Racing and gambling continued to be the subjects of widely differing proposals ranging from the abolishing of dog racing to wide open gambling to be licensed and regulated by a state amusement commission. A proposal for a three percent retail sales tax received scant support. The livestock committee of the house failed to report

In the early 1920s in Dixie County, big wheel logging carts brought timber to loading points from virgin forests.

out a bill to put cattle behind fences and keep them off the open range. A tax on chain stores long sought by independent merchants also failed to reach the floor. A two-year experience with legalized slot machines killed all efforts to reenact that law.

The 1938 race for the Democratic nomination to the United States Senate demonstrates how risky it is to generalize about the degree of liberalism or conservatism in the state. If the election of Fred Cone as governor in 1936 showed a decided turn to the right, the nomination of Claude Pepper two years later seemed to ratify the New Deal. Running against Governor Sholtz and J. Mark Wilcox, Pepper came out strongly for wage and hour legislation, the Townsend Plan, and continued relief for the unemployed in the face of charges that 5,600 persons had been added to the relief rolls in March to "buy" votes for Pepper. Pepper's resounding victory was a boon to the New Dealers, who needed some reassurance in the midst of the recession following cutbacks in spending the previous year.

There were also some developments of new enterprise during the depression. For those who could provide the capital there were potentially valuable properties to be acquired at low prices. The most notable example was Alfred I. DuPont, who had moved his legal residence to Florida in 1926 after many years of visiting various parts of the state. In that year he began purchasing land, acquiring some 70,000 acres in Franklin, Bay, and Walton counties where, according to his biographer, Marquis James, he had idealistic plans to improve the lot of the "crackers" who inhabited the almost totally undeveloped northwest Florida region. DuPont also acquired control of the Florida National Bank in Jacksonville and made it the nucleus of what has become a group of thirty-one banks. In rapid succession DuPont banks opened at Bartow, Orlando, Daytona Beach, and Saint Petersburg. On December 30, 1930, when the banking structure of the state was tottering on the edge of ruin, the six banks named had deposits of some $21,000,000, and DuPont had the resources to protect them against runs of frightened depositors. In August 1931 he opened the Florida National in Miami, and by 1935 when the banking crisis had passed, the seven banks reported deposits of $50,000,000. It is not surprising that Governor Carlton saw in DuPont's entry into the banking field a sign of economic upturn if not a cause of it.

Unfortunately, DuPont died of a heart attack early in 1935. His wife, Jessie Ball DuPont, and her brother, Edward Ball, assumed control of the DuPont interests in Florida. Mrs. DuPont was a shrewd businesswoman and philanthropist, but "Ed" Ball was destined to be a moving force in both business and political matters in Florida for the next several decades as we shall see.

Equally significant for the future of the state, in 1931 the International Paper Company opened a pulp mill at Panama City, founding a market for pulpwood that made millions of acres of pineland more valuable and gave employment to large numbers of workers. Other mills soon followed at Port Saint Joe, Jacksonville, Fernandina, Pensacola, and Palatka. The legislature in 1935 created the Florida Forest Service principally to help provide fire protection, which it was estimated would increase production eight times, and to advise landowners on the planting and marketing of pine trees. The Forest Service, the paper mills, and the paper products industries supplied millions of trees to plant on unproductive and abandoned farm lands and on cut-over land that did not reseed naturally.

The depression years witnessed the birth of several significant educational institutions. One of them, the University of Miami, had been conceived in the real estate boom in 1925 when George E. Merrick, the creator of Coral Gables, induced the sponsors of a college for the Miami area to locate it in his city. In September 1926, before the first building was well under way, the severe hurricane had ended any hope that the boom might be revived and brought construction to a halt. The school opened instead in an abandoned apartment hotel building that was another victim of the collapse. The first years were largely a struggle for survival against the Florida depression, the threat of bankruptcy, and the national depression. Only during and since the war has its potential begun to be realized. Other boom-time structures suffered worse fates, one of them becoming a chicken farm.

The depths of a depression may seem an unusual time to start a university, but in the case of Tampa it brought together the factors to create an institution. In 1930 the city had no institution of higher education, but it did have young men and young women who needed an inexpensive way to attend college and a building that was a victim of the depression. There were also, as in Miami, teachers and administrators who were willing to invest their time and skills in an enterprise with which they might together overcome the depression. In 1931 a group of Tampa citizens inaugurated the Tampa Junior College, holding classes in the Hillsborough High School in the afternoons and evenings. In the fall of 1933 it became a four-year degree-granting institution and moved into the Tampa Bay Hotel, which the city had acquired for taxes in 1905 and had been leased out until the depression dried up the tourist business. The Palm Beach Junior College dates back to 1933. Another junior college had been operating privately at Saint Petersburg since 1927 but became public in 1947. Jacksonville University had its origin in the opening of Jacksonville Junior College in 1934. It moved to its own campus in the city ten years later, in 1947 moved to its present campus in Arlington, some eight miles east of Jacksonville, and in 1956 became a four-year college.

26.

World War II Opens a New Era

The fifth decade of the twentieth century opened in Florida on a note of recovery and optimism. The depression was apparently over. The relief and recovery spending and reforming activities of the New Deal had largely ceased. The New Deal left a legacy in greatly increased governmental activity, personnel, and expenditure that created administrative and financial problems with which political leadership had not yet come to grips. Almost unnoticed by Americans, a Second World War was already under way. The stimulus to the American economy reached into Florida. With a somewhat uneasy feeling of security behind their neutrality legislation, most Americans little dreamed that they would be totally involved in that conflict.

To guide them through what were to be war years, Floridians in 1940 chose Spessard L. Holland of Bartow, a veteran of the First World War, for governor. He was a graduate of the University of Florida Law School and had a well-established practice. He had been county judge and prosecuting attorney in Polk County and a state senator. Ten others, one of whom (Fuller Warren) was later to become governor, offered themselves in the Democratic primary. Second runner was Francis P. Whitehair, with 95,431 votes to Holland's 118,862. In the runoff Holland won 272,218 to 206,158 and in the general election Holland received 334,152 votes. The Republicans did not offer an opponent. Holland's was a notable administration, made so partly by the impact of the war but also by attention to some long-standing problems in public finance.

The full measure of prosperity had not yet returned to the state in 1941, and Holland's administration faced financial problems arising from the large bonded debt of local governments inherited from the booming twenties and the increased cost of expanded state administration and services. The new governor also found one and a half million dollars of unpaid bills. To ease the debt burden on local governments, Holland proposed a constitutional amendment setting aside two cents per gallon of the tax on gasoline for the next fifty years to finance payment of debts and the construction of roads in the counties, and a special board to supervise the payment of road bonds by the counties. Local governments with an assured income could refinance old obligations and make new ones. Almost equally important was a Reconstruction Finance Corporation loan of $5,600,000 to refinance some sixteen million dollars of Everglades Drainage District indebtedness to rescue drainage and reclamation activities from near bankruptcy.

By way of tax reform, new legislation eliminated the ad valorem tax on property for state purposes, leaving that source of revenue to local governments, and also repealed the gross receipts tax so long opposed by merchants. To make taxpayers of many who had escaped (by a combination of the $5,000 homestead exemption and low assessment value), and possibly to broaden the base for bond selling, a law required full value assessment of property by the counties. Full assessment was not immediately achieved; in fact, it is still a problem. In Dade County as late as 1964 a court order required the doubling of assessed values to more nearly meet the requirement. Dissatisfaction with the homestead exemption continued, mostly in favor of abolishing or graduating it, but one gubernatorial candidate in 1956 proposed to double it. More recently there has been an effort to increase it for senior citizens. Sarasota County in 1964 received constitutional authority to tax the first two thousand dollars of value and exempt the next five. To attract capital and strengthen the promise that there would be no state income tax, the legislature reduced the levy on intangible property from five to two mills and allotted one-fourth of the proceeds of the tax to the counties. To make up losses of state revenue and provide for growing needs, the state continued to rely upon use taxes, increasing the levy on alcoholic beverages, and adding packaged cigarettes to the list of taxed items. Wartime restrictions reduced the return from the gasoline and parimutuel betting taxes but also restricted state expenditures for building, so that Holland was able to leave a balance of some eight million dollars in the general fund and fourteen million in road building funding. But Florida's problems of public finance were postponed rather than solved.

State welfare programs continued to be an increasingly important segment of state government. Grants for old age assistance and for aid to the blind and to dependent children were increased substantially. Average payments for the nearly 40,000 aged grew from $12.01 to $28.40 per month, slightly above the national average; 2,274 blind persons received $29.40 per month, and 8,000 dependent children each received $14 per month. Because of near full employment during the war years, the pool of funds available for unemployment compensation grew from $12,000,000 to near $50,000,000. Teachers' salaries increased by nearly one-fourth in three years, and the teacher retirement system went into full effect in January 1941.

Road building continued at an increased rate, most of it associated with defense installations, for which the federal government provided the priorities for material and labor and paid part of the cost. The State Road Department in the four Holland years constructed 1,560 miles of highway at a cost of $44,535,729, of which

Storage facilities of Humble Oil and Refining Company at its Sunniland Field in Collier County, Florida's first commercial producer of oil

$15,394,851 were federal funds. By 1945 the state agency was maintaining about eight thousand miles of highway.

Not even the crowded events of the war years could obscure the bringing in of Florida's first oil well on September 26, 1943, in the Sunniland Field in northern Collier County. Exploration for oil had begun in the first year of the century near Pensacola. At least eighty-seven other explorations were made before another well near Pensacola reached a depth of near 10,000 feet without finding oil. Reports of geologists and the promise of a $50,000 prize for the first producing well spurred the search. The Humble Oil Company found oil in commercial quality and quantity in Gulf Coast Realties Corporation's Well Number 1 at a depth of 11,626 feet. By 1945 eleven wells in the field with an average depth of 11,575 feet were producing about a half million barrels of oil annually. In 1964 a new discovery by the Sun Oil Company at Felda in Hendry County again aroused the hopes of landowners and oil hunters. Humble Oil Company also added two wells in the Felda area, and Sunoco drilled twenty-seven wells in the area south of LaBelle just off State Road 29 and extended the Felda field into eastern Lee County. Faith in the continued productivity of the Sunniland and Felda fields was revealed in the construction of a seventy-four mile pipeline to Port Everglades on the east coast to deliver the crude oil for shipment to refineries. A 1970 discovery north of Jay in Santa Rosa County, some thirty miles from Pensacola, appeared promising as the well produced a little over 1,700 barrels a day of better grade oil. Since the new field lay just south of the Flomaton field in southern Alabama, the search for oil in the panhandle was stepped up. By the summer of 1970, seismologists were testing in Escambia Bay as well as on the mainland.

The war that broke upon the people of the United States late in 1941 ushered in a new era in Florida that was to set off a postwar boom that would transform the economy, push the state far up the list in population rank, and create vast problems arising from rapid growth in every direction. The Seminole, the Civil, the Spanish American, and the First World wars had all affected the state dramatically but not like the one ushered in by the attack on Pearl Harbor on December 7, 1941. The temporary disruption of the tourist business and all of its allied service industries was more than offset by the conversion of the state into a giant military training school and army and navy airfield. As a food producing state, the contribution of the agricultural regions was enormous, and the normal rate of growth was greatly accelerated.

Florida felt the increase in defense activities long before the country was directly involved in the war. Thousands of United States servicemen came to Florida to man new army and navy installations. There was a new naval air station at Jacksonville, an army training center at Camp Blanding near Starke, the reactivated naval base at Key West, Drew and McDill airfields at Tampa, Eglin at Valparaiso, and increased activity at long-established bases such as Pensacola. Royal Air Force Cadets studied navigation and meteorology in Miami. They were housed, fed, and given classroom

Barracks under construction at Camp Blanding near Starke, December, 1940.

instruction by the University of Miami, and Pan American World Airways gave them their in-flight training. Because of the great areas of flat and unoccupied land and the state's greater than average number of flying hours of good weather, pilot training bases and flying schools appeared in great numbers. With only six such installations at the beginning of the war, Florida had forty airfields in operation in 1945.

Almost unique to Florida was the conversion of tourist facilities to wartime needs. By April 1, 1942, the Army Air Force was using 70,000 hotel rooms on Miami Beach, where a replacement training center, an officer candidate school, and an officer training school were being operated. Restaurants frequently became mess halls. One-fourth of the Army Air Force officers and one-fifth of the enlisted men trained on Miami Beach. By October 1942 the Air Corps had graduated 8,425 officers and provided basic training to 75,000 others. Every major resort city in Florida turned its principal hotels over to some branch of the armed services. The Hollywood Beach Hotel housed a naval indoctrination school, the Ponce de Leon at Saint Augustine was a coast guard indoctrination center, and there was a WAAC training center at Daytona Beach. Training activity reached its peak in 1943, and as the war drew to a close, hotels became hospitals, convalescent homes, and redeployment centers. When male students deserted the college campuses, a variety of training units involving perhaps 10,000 men moved into their living quarters and classrooms.

Many families of servicemen made trips to Florida for the first time, crowding the buses and trains and the remaining hotel rooms, apartments, and eating places. They brought little money to spend, sought few of the recreational activities associated with tourism, and complained about the prices they paid in stores and eating places, but they kept fully operative segments of the economy that might otherwise have languished. Thus many people to whom it might otherwise have been totally unknown saw Florida. Their first response was not always favorable, as they saw it through eyes colored by wartime associations, but many of them discovered later that they had liked what they had seen and returned to help give the state a forty-six percent increase in population in the decade, 81.5 percent of it in the peninsula, from 1,897,414 to 2,271,305. In contrast, the country as a whole grew only fifteen percent and the southeast only fourteen.

Since it was not an industrial state, Florida's share of manufacturing contracts was small. Shipbuilding was the principal industry, and nonindustrial facilities such as airports, camps, bases, and housing accounted for more than half of the contracts awarded in Florida in the early years of the conflict. Three counties, Hillsborough, Duval, and Bay, accounted for almost half of the war contracts, chiefly industrial.

Citrus and vegetables dominated the agricultural scene. Citrus shipments increased in the 1945-1946 season by twenty-nine million boxes over the 1940-1941 season. From 1942 to 1945 the

Farm Labor Supply Centers like this one provided homes for wartime migrant workers.

government requisitioned all canned and processed fruits for military and lend-lease purposes. The development of a frozen concentrate process by Dr. L. G. McDowell of the Florida Citrus Commission and Dr. Arthur L. Stahl of the University of Florida Agricultural Experiment Station was a great boon to the citrus industry and to the food needs of the government. Users learned to eat the Florida range and pasture-grown beef, which was without benefit of being fed on grain. A wartime labor shortage became a threat to the food producing areas. Both local and migrant workers deserted seasonal employment for better paying and more stable jobs. The Federal-State Extension Service operated an emergency labor program from 1943 to 1947. It recruited women, youths, foreigners, prisoners of war, and men in the armed services to harvest perishable crops. In Lee County, 700 men from Buckingham Army Air Field volunteered to work on their three day monthly leaves to save a potato crop. Living in camps at Clewiston, Winter Haven, Leesburg, and Marianna, 971 prisoners of war stripped sugarcane and gathered peanuts, corn, and citrus. Services to migrant workers, foreign and domestic, included transportation, housing, food, and medical care. Foreign workers came in under contracts that protected their interests and provided for their future return to their homes. After 1947 major employers of migrant labor in sugar, vegetables, and fruit growing and processing continued to import labor from the Bahamas, Jamaica, and Barbados.

Research in insect control at the Bureau of Entomology and Plant Quarantine at Orlando produced results that found wide application during and after the war. Almost a dozen of some 10,000 experimental products found practical use, but by far the most important was DDT, a chemical combination discovered by a German chemist in 1874 and recognized for its value as an insecticide in 1939. Introduced into the United States in 1942, a year later it was being manufactured for use by the armed forces. Its residual qualities made it highly useful for impregnating clothing and other fabrics to kill lice, mosquitoes, or other disease-carrying insects. Possibly its use as a residual spray in heavy jungle areas was the greatest boon to the men who had to live and fight there. The possible ill effects of its use were not recognized until much later.

Many Floridians were involved directly in the war effort. In contrast to the 42,030 in the armed services in World War I, over a quarter of a million were in uniform in the Second World War. In 1940 when the National Guard was inducted into the national armed forces, 3,941 Floridians went on active duty, and between that time and 1947 a total of 254,358 other men and women entered the armed services. The Florida Defense Council created by Governor Catts in the First World War was reactivated in 1941 and, with 137 local and county councils, directed the efforts of more than a third of a million civilian volunteers. Their services ranged from their acting as air raid wardens, aircraft spotters, auxiliary firemen, and policemen to emergency medical assistants and nurses' aides. Enforcement of black-out and dim-out regulations were the special concern of others.

Coast defense soon became a serious matter in Florida. Early in 1942 when defenses in the North Atlantic became more effective, German submarines moved southward to the waters around Florida. On February 19 the *Pan Massachusetts* went down forty miles south of Cape Canaveral, and between that area and the Bahama beaches twenty-four ships, from which 504 persons were rescued, went down. In late May a Mexican tanker was sunk just off Miami and another off the Florida Keys. By the end of June the subs had moved around the tip of Florida into the Gulf of Mexico. Torpedoes sank a British tanker forty miles off Apalachicola on June 29, and in August they sank two ships traveling in a convoy from Key West to Cuba. In September the U-boats moved to waters near Trinidad.

The Civil Air Patrol, organized in March 1942, helped to guard Florida's coasts, flying from bases at Lantana, Flagler Beach, Miami, Sarasota, and Panama City. The Coastal Picket Patrol, composed of civilian small craft, yachts, fishing, and pleasure boats, also operated during the height of the submarine threat from July, 1942 to October of the following year. The closely related "Mosquito Fleet" also helped to patrol the coast, operating from bases at Jacksonville, Port Everglades, Key West, Saint Petersburg, and Pensacola. The Sub-Chaser Training School at Miami, dubbed the "Donald Duck Navy," trained some 10,000 officers and 37,000 enlisted men for the United States and 360 officers and 10,374 men for fourteen other countries in 1942 and 1943. As the war progressed, a combination of convoy protection and improved means of detection practically eliminated the submarine menace along the Florida coast.

Lighter-than-air craft that hovered over the area proved the most effective means of detecting submarines in the shallow off-shore waters of Florida. From blimps based at Key West, Richmond, and Banana River, they kept a close watch on the coastal area. Enemy submarine fire downed one blimp on July 18, 1942, off the lower east coast, but the crew was rescued by a destroyer. The most spectacular and costly damage to the blimp fleet occurred at the Richmond base twelve miles south of Miami on the night of September 15, 1945, when, fortunately, their service had been accomplished. At Richmond, three huge, sixteen-story hangars, 270 feet wide by 1,000 feet long and designed to withstand hurricane winds, burned. Stored there in the face of a hurricane threat were fourteen inflated and eleven deflated blimps, 366 airplanes, and 150 automobiles. The center of the hurricane with winds above 125 miles per hour passed over the base. Parts of the hangar roof began to blow away and probably fell inside, smashed some of the parked machines, and started the fire that completely destroyed the hangars and their contents.

Florida's long and largely uninhabited coastline was an invitation to spies and saboteurs seeking entry to the country. Coast Guard personnel patrolled many miles of the coast, often on foot accompanied by trained dogs, sometimes on horseback, or in cars or airplanes. On June 18, 1942, four German saboteurs from a submarine landed at Ponte Vedra Beach, dressed in American civilian clothes and carrying forged selective service and social security cards, $174,000 in cash and small bonds, and incendiary pens and pencils, which they buried in boxes in the sand. Another group of saboteurs landed at Long Island, and the leader of that group turned informer. He appeared at FBI headquarters and gave the information that led to the capture of the Florida group. The ones who had landed on the Florida beach apparently felt no fear of apprehension. They rode into Jacksonville by bus and stayed overnight in the city before two of them went to New York and the other two to Chicago, where they were taken into custody.

One of the longest air routes established during the war originated in Florida. Planes flew to the coast of Brazil, across the South Atlantic to the Gold Coast, crossed Africa to India, and through the Netherlands East Indies to the Philippines or Australia, or through Burma and across the "hump" to China. Though other routes to the South Pacific were opened up, all planes for the Near East, India, and China continued to fly from Florida. Military flights took off from Morrison Field at West Palm Beach, and civilian contract flights left from Miami. Pan American's Africa-Orient Division set up the "Cannon Ball Express" in 1942, flying from Miami to Karachi, India, with cargo for Burma and China, 11,500 miles in three and a half days. This division made 2,300 crossings of the Atlantic on military missions and logged more than fourteen and a half million miles in less than a year. In May 1942, Eastern Airlines planes began making daily flights to Trinidad for the Air Transport Command; these were later extended to Natal and Brazil and then to Accra on the Gold Coast of Africa. In three and a half years Eastern flew for the ATC 33,480,000 miles and carried 47,500,000 pounds of cargo and 130,000 passengers. National, Delta, and United Airlines also operated in Florida under military contracts.

In the midst of the war that was by that time turning more perceptibly in favor of the United States and her allies came the political campaigns and elections of 1944. On the national level it meant an unprecedented and much debated fourth term for Franklin D. Roosevelt. At the state level, Millard Fillmore Caldwell outran five other contenders for the Democratic nomination for governor. Caldwell had come from Tennessee in 1924 after serving in the First World War and studying law at the University of Virginia. He had represented Santa Rosa County in the legislature and won election to four terms as congressman from the Third District, but resigned in 1941 over policy differences with Roosevelt's New Deal policies to practice law in Tallahassee. The death of a son may have been a more important reason for his return to Florida. He had been an early advocate of military preparedness. His principal rival was Robert A. "Lex" Green, who had been in state politics since 1925 as a member of the national House of Representatives. Popular but with a relatively undistinguished record of achievement, he always had an eye for the governorship. He ran as the poor man's candidate, pictured Caldwell as an enemy of the New Deal and a servant of big business, and favored free land for returning veterans and substantial pay increases for teachers. Ernest R. Graham ran a strong third, particularly in Dade County.

The sectional character of Graham's candidacy is illustrated by published charges in west Florida that he favored a state university for south Florida, while at the same time he was challenging Dade Countians to stop playing Santa Claus to north Florida. Caldwell stayed out of any discussion of personalities, as did the other candidates. Voters were preoccupied with winning the war and had little time for political rallies. Caldwell led in the first primary with 116,000 votes to 113,000 for Green and 91,000 for Graham. In the runoff election, though Graham sought to throw the votes of his supporters to Green, Caldwell won by 215,000 to 174,000 votes. Republican Bert L. Acker defended the two-party system, questioned the fourth term for FDR, and called Caldwell an anti-New Dealer but lost by 96,321 to 361,007 in the general election. Incumbent Claude Pepper won renomination to the United States Senate over four rivals in the first primary and was unopposed in the general election. In 1946 Spessard L. Holland, appointed to complete the term of Charles O. Andrews who died September 14, 1946, entered the United States Senate, where he served until he declined to run again in 1970.

While Pepper won his election unopposed, he had made an important political enemy whose enmity would carry over into the next election. That man was Ed Ball, whose control of the DuPont interests after 1935, as noted in the previous chapter, had made him a formidable force in Florida politics. Ball had been quietly buying up bonds in the St. Joe Paper Company with vast acreage in north Florida as well as bonds in Florida East Coast Railway which went from receivership to bankrupcy in 1940. When he presented a reorganization plan, a lengthy battle for control ensued, while Ball continued to buy bonds so that by 1944 St. Joe held 53.5% of all outstanding bonds.

While Ball saw a chance to make a financial killing, his motives were also ideological. Since World War I liberal politicians in both parties argued that the government ought to takeover the financially strapped railroads. Ball felt such ideas were destroying the free enterprise system and that in developing the FEC he would demonstrate it was possible to operate a profitable railroad. At that point some monority bondholders appealed to the Interstate Commerce Commission to give operational control to the Atlantic Coast Line.

At the same time Senator Pepper made the issue a personal one by charging that such control would not be in the people's interest "when it is public knowledge that the estate is operated principally BY ONE MAN, Mr. Edward Ball." Thus began legal proceedings that would drag on for years. Ball had tried to influence Pepper in the 1930s, but while it was too late for him to do much about the election of 1944, he hoped to see Pepper defeated in 1950.

Meanwhile, in his inaugural address on January 2, 1945, the centennial year of Florida's statehood, Governor Caldwell reiterated his belief in local responsibility and self-government. He stressed a four-point program of education, public health, conservation, and advertising of the state's assets. Caldwell could be envied the treasury surplus he inherited but not the unfinished state business, which he warned required increased taxes. On order of war mobilizer Jarnes F. Byrnes, all racetracks were closed and the taxes on gasoline, alcoholic beverages, and cigarettes expired on June 30. The future of state revenue was uncertain enough to give advocates of legalized gambling a momentary hope that they might win legislative approval. Caldwell asked the legislature for an increase of $28,507,000 for the next biennium, but he recommended it be raised by increasing the excise taxes on cigarettes, beverages, and racing, and by adding a ten percent tax on private and public utilities, which proved so unpopular that he abandoned it. He also had to fight off resorting to a general sales tax. The legislators followed his lead on budget and finance and included a million dollars to advertise the state. The law also authorized a full time budget director and staff to carry on continuous study of needs and resources in that increasingly important area of state government. To make more manageable 270 separate state funds earmarked for special purposes, a law reduced them to six classifications.

Though the ban on racing was lifted on May 10, revenue for welfare payments had been reduced to the point where a $600,000 deficiency appropriation for 1945 was necessary. At the end of the war the number of claimants for benefits grew rapidly. The number requiring old age assistance increased from 40,651 in June 1945 to 61,198 in November 1948, and the cost rose from thirteen to twenty-five million dollars. In the same period the number of dependent children eligible for assistance rose from thirteen to forty-five thousand and the cost from under two million to eight million dollars. Caldwell made strong efforts to get full-time health units in every county. Starting with only thirty-six, all but two counties of the total of sixty-seven, Collier and Lee, had complied by the end of his term.

Educational problems received scant attention in the 1945 session. Proposals to introduce coeducation at the University of Florida and at Florida State College for Women were deferred until 1947 when education became a major concern of the lawmakers. Concern with race questions was apparent in Florida's participation in regional educational cooperation to provide graduate and professional education in separate but equal segregated schools, a path the state did not pursue very far. The legislature also refused to approve a proposal by Senator John Mathews, Sr., of Jacksonville to repeal all laws respecting party primaries and return the nominating process to the parties functioning as private clubs free to practice exclusion. This action was in response to the ruling by the United States Supreme Court that white primaries were unconstitutional. The same action in other states failed to pass the test of constitutionality. Governor Caldwell spoke out on two other questions of regional interest when he attacked protective tariffs and freight rate differentials as harmful to the South, and he was pleased that during his administration the Interstate Commerce Commission ruled out the differentials.

The 1947 legislature gave major attention to the lag in public buildings, inadequate in quantity and suffering from neglect. An appropriation of $41,000,000 included money for a Capitol wing, and buildings for the supreme court, the road department, and the industrial commission. It also provided for the rapidly growing state universities, thirteen million at the University of Florida, five at Florida State, and over four for Florida A & M. The remainder went for charitable and correctional institutions over the state.

Growing state functions, personnel, and expenditures had also outrun the administrative organization of state government, which had originated in less demanding days and had been expanded piecemeal without any overall planning. Many of the dozens of agencies and boards were made up in part if not wholly of ex-officio executive and administrative officers of the state. The governor and the cabinet officers made up all or part of the membership on thirty-two of thirty-eight ex-officio boards. By 1945 the governor was serving on twenty-four boards, the secretary of state on fifteen, the treasurer and the attorney general on twenty-one, and others somewhat smaller numbers.

The legislature in 1943 had by joint resolution created a special Joint Economy and Efficiency Committee to examine the possibility of administrative reorganization. Working with funds provided by Governor Holland, the three senators and four representatives on the committee submitted a report to the 1945 legislature. They proposed to reorganize the executive and administrative agencies into twenty-three divisions and sections, including nine ex-officio boards and commissions, ten appointive offices and boards, and thirteen appointive or ex-officio local statutory agencies. The report also urged that the governor be given full authority over matters of budget, civil service, central purchasing, revenue, public safety, and planning. The report became a point of departure for legislative action in succeeding sessions of the legislature and for additional studies.

Action on major items has been slow, and as state activity and functions grow the number of agencies tends to grow more rapidly than rationalization of administration. Some of this arises from decentralization imposed by an elective cabinet that often has more administrative power than the governor on ex-officio administrative boards. Unlike the governor, they were eligible for reelection. Under the new constitution, the governor may have successive terms, but there is no limit for cabinet posts. Governor Caldwell explained the weakness of the governor's position. The candidate rather than the party states the objectives on which he runs for office, and not until he is elected does the platform become even semi-official. The governor-elect lacks the experience to develop a well integrated plan of administration in time for the first session of the legislature, which is usually even less willing to take his proposals seriously in the second session. Hence the argument of those who feel that any real changes can be achieved only by constitutional revision that centralizes these activities in the governor's office.

Shifts in population from rural to urban and from north to south at an increasing rate in recent years have made the reapportionment of representation in the state legislature and the national Congress increasingly important. A constitutional amendment in 1924 was clear enough on the subject and made decennial reapportionment by the legislature mandatory, but the legislature had simply never acted to carry out the law. Governor Caldwell accepted the obligation as binding and called a special session on June 1, 1945, immediately after the regular session. In a fifty-three day session the lawmakers shifted two senatorial districts and three house seats from north to south Florida. Under no circumstances could the 1924 formula of three representatives each to the six largest counties, two each to the next sixteen, and one each to the remainder be made equal to population ratios. Nor was the situation in the senate much different. District 13, Dade County, had 315,000 residents while District 16, Nassau County, had only 11,000. In 1940 the seven most populous house and senate districts had one-half of the population but elected one-seventh of the senators and one-fifth of the representatives. Caldwell's attempt was only the first of a long series of failures to achieve meaningful reapportionment.

Florida emerged from World War II with its educational establishment in disrepair and disrepute at home and abroad. No adequate attention had been given to it since the collapse of the real estate boom in 1926. A study of the building needs of the counties in 1941-1942 produced an estimated need for $140 million to provide adequate buildings. The war years brought new life to the economy and new sources of public revenue but postponed action while the number of school children continued to grow. Late in 1944 Governor Holland appointed a Citizens Committee on Education to assess the needs and make recommendations to the state government. Governor Caldwell reappointed the committee, and the 1945 legislature gave its blessing in a concurrent resolution. The result was a 400 page report titled *Education and the Future of Florida,* with recommendations touching all phases of public education, most of which the 1947 legislature enacted into law.

The report rated the state third from the bottom among the forty-eight states in ratio of ability to pay to actual performance, called attention to the variations in educational opportunity from district to district within counties, and pointed out that the largest number of children of school age was often to be found in districts less able to pay for schools. The 1947 law provided a state fund to make up some of the economic differences. After assessing minimum educational needs in each area and the capability of the citizens to pay the costs, the state fund was used to make up the difference. In the counties, district boards and all special tax districts gave way to county boards and countywide taxation, with funds distributed among schools on the basis of the number of pupils. As the state assumed a larger share of the responsibility for financing public schools, it also did more to coordinate their activities to achieve certain minimum standards.

Tropical birds, Everglades National Park

After the disruption produced by the war, the state universities found themselves faced with vast numbers of students and new educational demands. In the last year of the conflict the enrollment at the University of Florida fell below one thousand, but in the summer of 1946 more than 8,000 students were seeking admission, at least a third more than its facilities could possibly accommodate. Many of them were ex-servicemen whose education had been disrupted and others to whom government financial assistance opened the way to higher education. In 1946 the university opened a branch in a deactivated army installation in Tallahassee to accommodate 500 men, and the legislature made the state university coeducational, as it did Florida State College for Women, renaming it Florida State University.

The citizens committee also recommended junior colleges in all population centers to be maintained jointly by the counties and the state. Sometimes called community colleges, their role in the total picture was not entirely clear. The committee apparently thought of them as extensions of high school to thirteenth and fourteenth grades. Others thought they should be more clearly articulated with four-year colleges, and yet others that they should be terminal and vocational. Officially they were to be and are multipurpose, though some are too small to have such a broad spectrum of objectives. The legislature adopted the program in 1947, but it got under way slowly. Only four areas were participating ten years later, but thereafter growth was rapid.

Another major step in 1947 was the appropriation of $2,000,000 to purchase private lands in the area set aside for the Everglades National Park. The first act of the legislature had been in 1929 when The Tropical Everglades National Park Commission was created. Spessard L. Holland supported the creation of the Park as governor and as United States Senator, and Governor Caldwell gave it political and financial support. The state had already contributed its acres of land and water within the Park boundaries, and the official dedication of the nation's third largest and only subtropical park occurred on December 6, 1947.

The 1948 race for the Democratic nomination for governor attracted nine candidates. The victory went to Fuller Warren, who had run a strong third in the 1940 primary. Runner-up was Daniel T. McCarty, a beef and citrus grower from Fort Pierce who was to become governor four years later. The presidential election aroused more than usual interest in the state in 1948. The more conservative of the Democrats liked neither the platform nor the candidate of the national organization. They joined other disaffected Democrats to support the Dixiecrats, who nominated Governor Strom Thurmond of South Carolina and Governor Fielding Wright of Mississippi on a strong states' rights platform. They had hoped for a more conservative Truman than he had proved to be when he succeeded to office upon the death of President Roosevelt. When the Truman-appointed Committee on Civil Rights, made up of two southerners and thirteen northerners, called for increased action to end segregation, to make lynching a federal offense, to abolish the poll tax as a voting requirement (accomplished in Florida in 1937), and to enact a federal Fair Employment Practices Act, they had had enough. The state legislature met in special session on September 14 and 15 to put the names of the state's rights electors on the ballot in November. Truman led the balloting with 281,988, and Thomas E. Dewey, Republican, was second with 194,780; Thurmond received 89,750 and Progressive Henry A. Wallace 11,620. In several later presidential elections many Florida Democrats expressed their dislike of the party's national leadership by voting Republican.

Fuller Warren was a native of Blountstown in Calhoun County and represented the county for one term in the legislature. He served as a naval gunner during the First World War, after which he moved to Jacksonville where he became a well-known criminal lawyer, served as a city councilman, and twice represented the county in the state legislature. During the war he had kept his name before the people of the state with letters to editors and a weekly column of news and comments. In sharp contrast to his predecessors, Holland and Caldwell, who represented a conservative businesslike approach to government, Warren had a strong populist strain in his political philosophy that ran counter to the way in which the state was growing away from its agrarian heritage. After his election, for example, he spoke in favor of a severance tax on phosphates.

He was in trouble almost before his administration began when he admitted that three of his personal friends, Louis Wolfson, Jacksonville industrialist, C. V. Griffin, a citrus grower, and William H. Johnston, who owned Chicago and Florida racetracks, had contributed almost all of his campaign funds. In vain, Warren argued that this freed him of the necessity to trade political favors for campaign funds and these friends expected nothing in return. The national as well as local concern with crime and political connections turned the Johnston connections into a political liability. The Florida legislature responded to the furor over campaign funds with the "who gave it, who got it" law which required candidates to report all receipts and expenditures and limited contributions by a single person to one thousand dollars.

Native American cowboys tending cattle on
Brighton Reservation, 1949

Florida's vast citrus crops are a major tourist attraction, besides adding many millions of dollars to the state's economy.

Warren inherited financial problems that Holland and Caldwell escaped only by the chance that war postponed building programs, and surplus left over from wartime allowed Caldwell to avoid crises. Caldwell did, however, warn the 1947 legislature that the existing tax structure would not continue to produce enough funds to meet the growing cost of state government. He also left a $500,000 deficit in the State Road Department and $9,000,000 worth of contracts waiting to be let. The gap between needs and income became more apparent when the budget commission received requests from operating agencies for $258,722,545 as against $166,797,000 for the previous biennium, when anticipated revenues for the two years

*The expansion of orange growing brought new wealth, new
problems, and beautiful scenery.*

would produce only $153,867,000. The budget commission reduced
the requests to $206,000,000. The legislature appropriated
$240,000,000 but adjourned without providing the necessary taxes
to produce the revenue. The lawmakers refused to consider any
alternative but the sales tax, which Warren was pledged to veto.
When the budget commission reduced allotments to all agencies by
twenty-five percent, it brought home the necessity for action to all
concerned. An eighteen-day special session in September produced
a three percent limited sales tax. It excluded food and clothing
purchases under ten dollars and Warren had little choice but to
accept it. The immediate financial crisis was passed, but costs of
state government continued to grow more rapidly than the tax base
being used.

The 1949 legislature did strengthen the citrus code to prevent
the shipment of fruit before it was ripe. Judge Amos Lewis of Tallahassee, Fuller Warren, and the State Chamber of Commerce had
been campaigning to get cattle and other livestock off the state's
highways, where in 1947 and 1948 they caused 933 accidents, in-

jured 257 people, and killed twenty-four. Florida cattle growers had accepted the value of the tick eradication program, but they continued to oppose any general law to require keeping cattle off the range. The "no fence" policy was for crops; cattle should be kept within fences. Actually, the end of the long struggle came in a round-about fashion. The legislature in 1949 barred cattle from all state roads effective July 1, 1950. Two years later when the state took over maintenance of county roads the cattle ban was extended to them also, and the open range cattle industry came to an end.

A falling off in racetrack revenue presumably caused by off-track betting resulted in an order from the governor to crack down on illegal gambling. The legislature passed the "anti-bookie wire service" bill to hamper the activities of bookmakers. Heavy rainfall and flooding in 1947 and only less so in 1948 induced the legislature also to support the now well-advanced water control program proposed by the United States Army Engineers.

Warren's real nemesis proved to be the revelation of wide open gambling in the state and the effort to link him with it. The Kefauver Crime Investigating Committee of the United States Senate held hearings in Miami in 1950 and exhibited open suspicion of the governor. The Miami Crime Commission and the *Miami Herald* attacked Warren and attempted to tie him to the Capone syndicate. When Warren refused to honor a subpoena to appear before the Senate committee in Washington, it counted heavily against him. At first he steadfastly refused to remove law enforcement officers who had not been indicted, but he did remove Sheriff Walter Clark of Broward County, who admitted part ownership of a gambling establishment. In October 1950 the Dade County grand jury indicted Sheriff James "Jimmy" Sullivan on the basis of the Kefauver Committee, Miami Crime Commission, and *Miami Herald* allegations. When the state supreme court threw out the indictment, Warren reinstated Sullivan, against whom the only thing ever proved was that he showed signs of considerable affluence on rather small pay. Anti-crime crusaders redoubled their attack on Warren, and two Dade County legislators, Dante Fascell and George Okell, asked the Kefauver Committee for evidence and introduced articles of impeachment in the 1951 session of the legislature. A house committee sifted the material, failed to find evidence of wrongdoing, and the house voted overwhelmingly to drop the charges.

The Warren years were turbulent in Florida and in the nation. The election in 1948 showed the Democratic party badly divided between extremes. Harry S. Truman was able to win but also remained controversial; Senator Joseph E. McCarthy was making wild charges of communism and disloyalty in high places; gambling and violence, which had been common since the war, suddenly became an alarming issue, and Florida found itself in an unfavorable national limelight, charged with gambling and official protection. Also, in late 1951 a wave of terrorist bombings across the state hit synagogues and the homes of blacks active in registering blacks to vote. Warren came out strongly against these atrocities and offered rewards for apprehension of those guilty, but his acknowledgment that he had once been a member of the Ku Klux Klan coupled with the record of his administration was not convincing. The 1951 legislature did pass a law forbidding the wearing of masks. Warren left the governorship very much a controversial figure, with his image sufficiently tarnished to make a political comeback impossible. Florida continued to grow rapidly in population. The 1950 census found the state growing so much faster than others that it received two new members in the national House of Representatives.

27.

Growth, Civil Rights and the Cuban Revolution

At mid-century it was apparent that, after a long and slow start, Florida was beginning to come into its own. Looking ahead, Floridians saw little reason to doubt that the state would continue to grow in population, resources and influence in the nation. Growth in the next two decades exceeded their wildest expectations. From a population at the turn of the century of about a half million and ranking thirty-second among the states, it had grown to 1,468,211 in 1930 and thirty-first place, and in 1940 to 1,897,414 and twenty-seventh place. Then growth really began to accelerate. In 1950 it was ranked twentieth with 2,771,305 persons, but by 1960 the population had exploded to 4,951,560, and if all those fleeing Cuba had been counted, might well have topped five million persons. This population increase of almost two and a quarter million people had pushed Florida into the top ten among the states.

Population growth was very unevenly distributed over the state. The steady movement from country to city characteristic of the nation was accompanied in Florida by an increasingly rapid shift in the center of population southward in the peninsula. Between 1940 and 1950 eighteen of the sixty-seven counties lying mostly in the northern part of the state lost population, ranging from fifteen persons in Hardee to 3,090 in Dixie. The range in population in the counties in 1950 was from 2,199 in Glades to 495,084 in Dade; and the combined populations of the twenty-seven smallest was less than 150,000. More than one-fourth of the gain in the forties was in Dade County with an increase of 227,453. Three other counties, Duval, Hillsborough, and Pinellas, accounted for another fourth. Six counties, Dade, Duval, Hillsborough, Pinellas, Polk, and Orange, accounted for fifty-two percent of the total. Others in the top ten were Palm Beach, Escambia, Broward, and Volusia. In the fifties, in spite of the phenomenal overall gains, a dozen counties lost population, ranging from one person in Wakulla to 3,104 in Holmes. Glades had grown to 2,950 and Dade to 935,047. All of them except

Lincoln Road looking west in 1915 (above). Miami Beach in 1933 (facing page, above) still showed little indication of what it would become in less than thirty years. Miami Beach in the 1960s (facing page, below) typified the urban growth that was occurring in many areas of Florida.

Union County had been in the losing column in the previous decade. In 1960 the seventeen counties each with less than 10,000 people totaled only slightly more than 100,000, whereas the eleven counties that each counted 100,000 reported a total of slightly more than three and one-half million. They were, in order of population, Dade, Duval, Hillsborough, Pinellas, Broward, Orange, Palm Beach, Polk, Escambia, Volusia, and Brevard. Population growth remained very unevenly distributed over the state.

Florida was also being more rapidly urbanized than the rest of the country. From just over one-third urban in 1920, almost three-fourths of the population lived in cities of over 2,500 in 1960, and farm population dropped in the fifties to 2.1 percent. The ten largest cities in 1960 were: Miami, 291,688; Tampa, 224,970; Jacksonville, 201,030; Saint Petersburg, 181,298; Orlando, 88,135; Fort Lauderdale, 83,648; Hialeah, 66,972; Miami Beach, 63,145; Pensacola, 56,572; and West Palm Beach, 56,208.

With five standard metropolitan areas in 1950—Miami, Jacksonville, Saint Petersburg-Tampa, Orlando and the Palm Beaches—three additional were notable by 1960: Fort Lauderdale-Hollywood; the fastest growing in the United States; Tallahassee

and Pensacola. Roughly three out of four persons in these population centers had been born outside the state. In 1960 only 36.1 percent of all Floridians had been born in the state. Significantly also, only 25.7 percent of the remainder were born in the South, while 27.3 percent came from the northeastern and north central states and 10.9 percent from elsewhere. Blacks made up nearly 29.3 percent of the total in 1950 but, though more numerous in 1960, were only 17.8 percent of the total.

The rapid urbanization of life in Florida might have been expected to have greater influence in politics than has been the case. The widely separated urban centers do not vote together in statewide elections that could bring to bear their numerical superiority. Nor do the legislators from the urban communities vote together. For example, legislators from Duval County, the Jacksonville area, have been inclined consistently to vote with the smaller counties against populous southeast Florida. This failure to reapportion representation in the legislature left control during the 1950s largely in the hands of northern counties, which were more rural and more southern in population and social attitudes. Of the membership of the legislature in 1957, sixty-nine of the ninety-five house members were born in Florida, sixteen in the neighboring states of Alabama and Georgia, and thirty of the thirty-eight senators were natives.

The political and legislative history of the years since 1950 reflects all of the major interests and problems of a rapidly growing and changing state now in the top ten in the nation. The race between incumbent United States Senator Claude Pepper and his challenger, Congressman George A. Smathers, for the senatorial nomination in the Democratic primary in 1950 brought into play most of the political forces in the state and aligned them more clearly than usual in two opposing camps. The result revealed the pattern for the years since that date, casting Florida politics definitely in the conservative mold. Because it pitted Pepper, well-established as a bellwether of the New Deal, against Smathers, with a somewhat anti-New Deal political philosophy, the contest had more than local significance.

Pepper, a native of Alabama, came to Perry, Florida, in 1925 and moved on to Tallahassee five years later, practicing law in both cities. In 1934 he challenged Senator Park Trammell for the Democratic nomination for the United States Senate and ran surprisingly well. Two years later he was nominated and elected without opposition to fill out the term of the late Duncan U. Fletcher. He became an ardent New Dealer and won nomination over four opponents and election to a full term in 1938. He supported Franklin D. Roosevelt, who had endorsed him, and his election was interpreted generally as indicating popularity of the New Deal. Six years later Pepper was running on the same New Deal platform and won, but conservative opposition was beginning to appear. The League for Constitutional Government placed five candidates in the field in an effort to force Pepper into a runoff and charged him with having supported federal bureaucracy, the Office of Price Administration, and organized labor. He was also accused of coddling blacks and was sometimes labeled a socialist. In 1948 Pepper supported the move to induce General Dwight D. Eisenhower to run for president on the Democratic ticket. Failing that, he offered himself as the heir to the Roosevelt political tradition. When Harry S. Truman won the nomination, Pepper gave him all-out support. Signs were not lacking that the Pepper platform was losing popularity at home, but the senator showed no disposition to change his stand. He succeeded Henry A. Wallace as leader of the liberal wing of the Democratic Party and challenged the conservatives as reactionaries at a time when liberalism was on the decline. Even his good record of getting federal money for the state could not outweigh the growing criticism of "Red Pepper."

Even before Smathers challenged Pepper for the Democratic nomination, Pepper's continued attacks on Ed Ball and the duPont business interests in the state since 1944 had motivated Ball to work behind the scenes to defeat the incumbent regardless of who ran against him. Conservative individuals and groups such as H.L. Hunt and the U.S. Chamber of Commerce contributed funds to the Smathers campaign.

George A. Smathers had come to Florida from New Jersey at the age of six when his family settled in Miami. He graduated from the University of Florida and its law school. He served thirty-nine months in the Marine Corps in World War II, returned to Miami, and went to the United States Congress from his district in 1946 and 1948, where he developed a somewhat more conservative voting record than that of Senator Pepper. Smathers came from an area that might normally be expected to give Pepper strong support. He enjoyed the support of business as represented by the Associated Industries of Florida and of thirty-eight of the state's major newspapers, whereas only two, the *Saint Petersburg Times* and *Daytona Beach News Journal,* favored Pepper. The medical profession opposed Pepper's advocacy of socialized medicine.

Smathers attacked Pepper as the spokesman of radicals and extremists and for his support of national health insurance, and accused him of straddling on the race issue and with promoting a welfare state on the basis of deficit financing. Pepper appealed to his record of services to the state, his seniority after fourteen years in the Senate, and the prosperity the state was enjoying, yielding nothing in his support of New Deal style policies and programs. The voters clearly had a choice in 1950. As the campaign developed, Smathers found the charge that Pepper supported a peacetime Fair Employment Practices Commission more damaging to the senator's chances than the earlier charge that he was soft on communism if not himself a socialist of some sort, and the challenger made the most of Pepper's support by organized labor. Some of Pepper's friends embarassed rather than helped him. Columnist Drew Pearson seemed to question the patriotism of Smathers, but after thirty-nine months of duty and the war all but over, the request of Smathers for a discharge did not seem unreasonable. Activity of the state's small number of Communists in his behalf could be used to confirm charges of friendliness to them. The drive to register more blacks to vote for Pepper undoubtedly aroused a greater number of whites to become politically active. The nominating primary took on the proportions of a minor national election when it received more than the usual national coverage. Fulton Lewis, Jr., press and radio commentator, supported Smathers, and Elmer Davis, an equally well-known reporter, spoke for Pepper.

Seventy percent of the registered Democrats, the highest turnout in the state's history, gave Smathers 387,215 votes to Pepper's 319,754; and in the general election Smathers defeated his Republican opponent John P. Booth by 283,987 to 74,228. Anthony F. Malafronte, in a study of the election, concluded that voting trends in the state should have forecast the outcome. From 1938 to 1944, Pepper had lost twenty counties, most of them in north Florida, and the eight counties he won were in the south. Pepper's 10,000 vote majority in Dade County six years earlier was reduced to 917 votes. Historically, liberalism had run its course for the time being, and the Smathers forces held the initiative most of the time and kept the incumbent on the defensive. Pepper's constituents had changed, but not he. Still sticking to his guns, Pepper challenged Spessard Holland's bid for renomination in 1958 and lost 321,370 to 408,048. He won election to the national House of Representatives from the Third District in south Florida in 1962. Smathers held the U.S. Senate seat until 1968 when he declined to run.

Further light on the issues that concerned Floridians was revealed in 1952 when five candidates sought the Democratic nomination for governor. Dan McCarty, who had run a close second to Fuller Warren in 1948, won the nomination on a platform promising to veto any proposal for more taxes, to reorganize state agencies to effect efficiency and economies, to dismiss from office any law enforcement officer who failed to do his duty, to build a four lane highway down the east coast, to create a state department of labor with cabinet rank, to obtain constitutional revision which would protect the existing distribution of revenues from taxes on racing and gasoline, to institute businesslike purchasing methods, to establish a tax commission but not necessarily a central agency to collect taxes, and to provide for study of the budget by experts. He bested his two chief rivals, Brailey Odham and Alto Adams, by 361,427 votes to 232,565 and 126,426, and outran Odham in the runoff by 384,200 to 336,716. Republican Harry D. Swain received 210,000 votes in November to 624,463 for McCarty. In the race for the presidency General Dwight D. Eisenhower defeated Adlai E. Stevenson in Florida by 544,036 to 444,958. Republicans were beginning to show strength in some parts of the state but were winning few offices. The much publicized reporting of campaign receipts and expenditures by candidates showed McCarty spending $156,054 in the first primary and $95,906 in the second but only $7,477 on the general election. Odham reported $72,755 and $84,617 and Adams $156,739.

Governor McCarty entered office with the state in good financial condition with $20 million in the general fund, and he hoped the state could always hold such a reserve. Early in his administration McCarty had occasion to declare himself on a question of continuing importance when he rejected proposals to explore for oil on state and private lands in the new Everglades National Park, and a majority of the cabinet supported him. As the governor prepared for the biennial session of the legislature, his dream of levying no new taxes and maintaining a treasury surplus began to fade. State agencies were asking for $334,745,000, and the budget commission recommended a $300 a year raise for all teachers. On February 27 the governor suffered a mild heart attack, first thought to be the flu, and he made his preparations for the session from a hospital bed through aides. His illness, though not considered serious at the time, raised again the question of succession should the office of governor become vacant. Subsequently the Democratic Executive Committee proposed an amendment to reinstate the office of lieutenant governor, which had been dropped from the constitution in 1885.

The attorney general Richard Ervin read to the legislature the governor's message, which proposed that insurance companies be relieved of the two percent tax on premiums collected in Florida if they established regional offices in the state, and it became the first bill to pass into law. It helped Jacksonville become the "insurance capital" of the southeast. McCarty added his contribution to the succession issue by proposing that the secretary of state succeed to the governorship so that someone elected at large should hold the office. The budget of the state advertising department was raised from $500,000 to $1,000,000, teachers' salaries were upped $350, the tax on dog tracks was raised only to have it declared discriminatory by the courts, a turnpike commission was created to build and operate the 110 miles of a toll highway from Miami to Fort Pierce, an act was passed to rotate horse racing dates on tracks in Dade County, which the governor vetoed, the Communist Party was outlawed in the state, and $352,229,935 was appropriated for the next biennium.

In early July the governor was reported taking over some of the duties of his office, but on September 23 he was back in the hospital with a bad cold. He died on the third day, the third Florida governor to die in office. Charley E. Johns, president of the senate, succeeded to the office, but the state supreme court ruled he would serve only as acting governor until an election could be held in November 1954 to complete McCarty's term. Johns was certainly no political novice. He had been elected to the lower house in 1934, to the senate two years later, reelected regularly since. Johns became its president in 1953. He stated that he would continue the State Road Department program, the policies on gambling set by McCarty, and practice economy in government expenditures, but he clearly did not intend for his tenure to be merely a holding operation. An opportunity arose to assert himself when it became known that the commissions of

Industrial plants like this Chemistrand distillation system near Pensacola came to be built in increasing numbers in the years after World War II.

thirty-one McCarty appointees had not been signed, and Johns assumed that he could appoint others to the posts.

He also announced that he expected the resignations of the "Little Cabinet," the appointed heads of the various boards and commissions, and suspended sixteen of them when they refused to resign. His defense was that only with an administration of his own choosing could he effectively discharge the duties of the executive office, a stand taken by other governors before and after him. He interested himself in the question of oil rights in the Everglades National Park and urged that no more lands be deeded for Park purposes until it was certain there was no oil there. When the trustees of the Internal Improvement Fund, of which he was the ex-officio chairman, leased some 30,000 acres of the mangrove coast for possible lumbering it aroused the apprehension of some supporters of the Park, but the lease was allowed to lapse. Not unlike other governors, he spurred highway construction and contracted for work beyond the time and resources available in his short term. He also removed tolls from the Overseas Highway to Key West when an investigation revealed that the tolls collected were more than paying for the roadway and bridges and that funds were being used loosely, if not fraudulently.

Johns announced his candidacy for the nomination for the governorship on October 23, 1953. He spoke for the completion of the Florida turnpike, four-laning U.S. 1, completing the Jacksonville expressway, improving mental health care facilities, cutting red tape from welfare programs, support for flood control, and the protection of oil rights in the Everglades. That he carried a card certifying membership in the Railway Conductors Union was scant comfort for most wage earners as his overall political position was essentially conservative.

Two months later state senator LeRoy Collins of Tallahassee entered the race on the McCarty platform, promising to reinstate the suspended state officials, a role apparently yielded to him by Daniel McCarty's brother John. Collins, who was the son of a neighborhood grocer in Tallahassee, earned his way through business and law schools, entered the legislature from Leon County in 1932 at the age of twenty-five, and continued in that office until 1940 when he entered the senate, where he served until 1954 with time out for service in the Navy during World War II. He won recognition several times as a most valuable member of the legislature, where he was generally identified with progressive forces in the state. He was married to a descendant of Territorial Governor Richard Keith Call and was well-endowed with personal assets.

The last candidate in the race was Brailey Odham. All candidates opposed new taxes and favored strict law enforcement, better pay for teachers, and adequate health and welfare services. They disagreed on constitutional revision, road building, a tax commission, the Florida Turnpike, and Everglades oil. They touched only lightly on the increasingly important question of racial segregation in public facilities. The three spent over a half million dollars in the first primary, in which Collins received 222,791 votes, Johns 255,767, and Odham 187,782. In the runoff Odham threw his support to Collins, who won by 380,323 to 314,198. In November, J. Tom Watson, former Democratic attorney general, the nominee of the Republicans, died prior to the election, and the party did not offer another candidate.

A more notable political item was the victory of William C. Cramer of Saint Petersburg, who won the Republican party's first Congressional seat since the decline of its fortunes at the end of Reconstruction. Republicans had begun to appear in the state legislature in 1928 and six won seats in 1954 with others running well. Cramer won reelection regularly until 1970 when he chose to run for the U.S. Senate seat being vacated by Spessard Holland and was defeated by Democrat Lawton Chiles.

During his two-year term Collins proved phenomenally successful in creating an image of progressive leadership, strong support for education at all levels, and great concern for the unfortunates in the population, while making a strong bid for capital and industry and avoiding the extremes of the segregation crisis

School busing was not a new innovation. This horse-drawn wagonette was used as a school bus in Duval County in 1898.

sweeping the country. He began by inducing the legislature to create the Florida Development Commission to consolidate all of the promotional work of the state government. To promote overseas trade an International Trade Department was added to the State Improvement Commission, the State Advertising Commission, and the new Industrial Services Division to offer some assistance to companies seeking locations. He urged the lawmakers to remove the "quickie" divorce reputation the state had acquired, but not until two years later was the law changed to double the residence requirement to six months to become a legal resident.

In the early 1950s the importance of space exploration was already apparent with the establishment of the missile and space complex at Cape Canaveral, later to be renamed Cape Kennedy in 1963, and then back to its original name a decade later. On July 24, 1950, the first missile was tested at the Cape. Although modest by later space efforts, this first missile was over 50 feet tall and consisted of two stages, or firings. The first stage was a modified German V-2 rocket which had been captured during World War II, and the second stage was a U.S. Army developed WAC Corporal rocket. During Collins' first term, the establishment of the Nuclear Development Commission measured the growing importance to the state of the space exploration activities at Cape Canaveral. In 1958 the National Aeronautics and Space Administration began operations at the Cape. It was largely a civilian agency involved in space operations related to launching communications, scientific and meterological satellites.

In two areas of growing concern, legislative reapportionment and constitutional revision, Collins was completely unsuccessful, but the effect on the Collins image was negligible. In spite of two extraordinary sessions in 1955, the legislators yielded nothing to changes in representation. They did create the Constitutional Advisory Commission to review the document and recommend changes. Probably the greatest obstacle to change was the threat to legislative control by a rural majority in north Florida and in counties with a small population all over the state who became known as "Pork Choppers," a term first applied to their leaders in the senate. The struggle undoubtedly cost Collins some votes in those counties in 1956.

Governor Collins accepted segregation as a part of Florida custom and law and promised to use the lawful processes of his office to maintain it. The Florida response to the 1954 United States Supreme Court decision outlawing school segregation was to appoint a group of social scientists in the state to study the effects of desegregating the schools. The attorney general then presented the report to the federal court as a protest and a request for a stay of execution. The 1955 legislature passed a law to authorize the assignment of pupils to schools on the basis of health, safety, order, and educational welfare but not race. Later in the same year the state supreme court ruled in the case of a black man, Virgil Hawkins, that he could not be denied admission to the University of Florida School of Law.

On March 21, 1956, at a high level conference, the governor, the cabinet and other high-ranking state officials agreed to recommend the establishment of a committee of jurists and lawyers to study legal means to retain segregation. The governor appointed L. L. Fabisinski, of Pensacola, a retired circuit court judge, to chair the committee. The committee later recommended to an extraordinary session of the legislature in July that the law give power to county school boards to assign pupils to schools, authorize the governor to regulate the use of public parks, buildings and the like, to preserve domestic order and to authorize the governor to use all of the law enforcement officers of the state including the state militia to suppress any disorder. Collins asked the 1957 legislature to approve a committee on race relations to help preserve domestic order, keep down inflammatory propaganda and help to improve the living standards of blacks. The lawmakers went further and passed, over the governor's opposition, an interposition resolution, alleging that the U.S. Supreme Court had enacted new legislation in *Brown v. Topeka Board of Education*, and that the governor should interpose the authority of the state between the citizens of the state and the effort of the national government to enforce the decision. In the same session a law was passed which provided that schools should be closed in the event the federal government used force to desegregate them. In spite of these actions it was Collins' moderation rather than the intransigence of the legislators that prevailed, and desegregation proceeded slowly but largely without violence.

*Former Governor Collins in 1965 with Selma, Alabama, march orga-
nizers (left to right): Andrew Young, Martin Luther King, Coretta Scott
King and Ralph Abernathy.*

The race for the Democratic nomination to the governorship in
1956 resulted in a campaign debate and an election that seemed to
say that the economic development of the state outweighed any local
opposition to desegregation. A Gallup poll in February 1956 showed
eight out of ten southern whites opposed to desegregation. In the
states with larger proportions of blacks than Florida the ratio was
nine to one. White Citizens Councils appeared in all of the states of
the southeast, and Senator Harry F. Byrd of Virginia led the
segregationists in Congress who called for massive resistance. On
March 12, 1956, Florida's two United States Senators, Holland and
Smathers, and six of the eight Congressmen, Bennett, Sikes,
Herlong, Rogers, Haley and Mathews, were among the nineteen
Senators and seventy-seven Representatives from the South who
issued what came to be called the Southern Manifesto, pledging
themselves to use all lawful means to reverse the United States
Supreme Court's desegregation decision. Only Democrat Dante
Fascell and Republican William Cramer did not sign in support of
the Manifesto. In spite of opposition proclaimed by officials from
the governor on down, acting under various pressures, principally
as applied by the federal government as well as the need to bid for
convention business and participate in intersectional athletics,
blacks found their way into most public facilities.

Governor Collins had already established a public image favoring a stable and progressive social climate that would attract industry to Florida. The Collins platform included constitutional revision, periodic automatic reapportionment, centralized purchasing, and an elected successor to the governor. Lieutenant General Sumter Lowry of Tampa, a national guard officer for thirty-five years who served overseas in both world wars and was a successful businessman, began his campaign on the single issue of keeping the public schools segregated. He had helped to organize the American Legion, opposed the United Nations and the movement for world federation, and supported General Eisenhower for president in 1952. Lowry at first refused to commit himself on any other question and offered a three-point program to defend segregation: cooperation with other states to combat federal interference, leadership by the governor as spokesman for the state, and interposition of state authority. He later began to mention better roads, schools, and tourist seeking.

C. Farris Bryant, who had established himself as one of Florida's ablest legislators, also offered himself as a candidate. He was a graduate of the Harvard Law School with a record of wartime service in the Navy. In 1952 as chairman of the Florida delegation to the Democratic National Convention he had supported Senator Richard Russell of Georgia for the presidency and generally supported the Collins administration except on reapportionment. Former Governor Fuller Warren also made a bid to return to state politics, and two unknowns, Peaslee Streets and W. B. "Bill" Price, rounded out the list of candidates. Warren ran on a forty-seven point platform that promised, among other things, to do everything in the governor's power to maintain segregation, to raise the homestead exemption to $10,000, to provide a factory for every county, and to have more strict law enforcement.

Collins benefited enormously by a combination of events that his rivals considered too good to be coincidental. There was a veritable flood of feature articles in national magazines, all of which spoke favorably of Florida's stable government, tax structure, and its governor. In the middle of the campaign, multimillionaire industrialist Howard Hughes announced that he was bringing a huge aircraft industry to Florida and a $100,000,000 medical center to Dade County. Only a small part of the Hughes projects, a medical research program, ever materialized, and the story embarrassed Collins even if it also helped him. In February 1956, accompanied by thirty businessmen, Collins went on his second annual tour of the Midwest in an attempt to lure industry to Florida. In the campaign, all but one of the daily newspapers which endorsed a candidate came out for Collins.

In the primary Collins received 434,274 votes, 51.7 percent of those cast. Lowry was second with 179,019; there were 110,469 votes for Bryant and 107,990 for Warren. The distribution of the votes was significant. Collins received over half of the votes cast in nineteen counties, all in south Florida except his home county Leon.

In Dade, Broward, and Palm Beach counties Collins had 155,306 votes to 53,895 for his three principal rivals. Lowry was top man in twenty-six counties, only four of them in south Florida, and he lost his home county Hillsborough to Collins. The Lowry strength was largely in the north and northwest counties where Warren had been strong in 1948. Black precincts in Jacksonville and Miami voted strongly enough for Collins to make a runoff unnecessary. In November Collins won over Republican nominee William A. Washburne, Jr., by almost three to one, while Eisenhower carried Florida over Adlai Stevenson by 643,849 votes to 480,317, a wider margin than in 1952. The 1956 campaign provided the first measure of the effect of television on statewide politics. In four weeks of campaigning the candidates spent $650,000–Collins, $291,183, Warren $194,682, Lowry, $115,216 and Bryant, $63,048. The cost has continued to rise at each election since that time.

Even as the election of 1956 was unfolding, events continued to escalate in the area of civil rights.[1] While other southern governors intensified their opposition to desegregation, Collins moved toward compromise. First, he alienated members of the legislature by adjourning it in August in order to prevent a debate that probably would have resulted in unconstitutional legislation with respect to segregation.

Then Collins was confronted with a bus boycott by blacks in Tallahassee not unlike what had occurred the previous year in Montgomery, Alabama. On New Year's Day, 1957, the tensions brought about by the boycott exploded into violence with windows broken at the home of a black minister and shotgun blasts into a grocery store. The Governor ordered the buses to cease operation and issued a proclamation blaming the extremists on both sides for what had happened.

It was in the context of this violence that Collins was sworn in for a second term. His speech to his fellow Floridians addressed the issues of race, segregation and civil rights. He asked that many whites recognize the realities of their position, concluding that ultimately the South must alter its traditions. To those who argued for a defiance of the law, he held that it would be "little short of rebellion and anarchy" for any state to oppose a decision of the Supreme Court through some "doctrine of nullification." While he still supported legal opposition to integration, the Governor pleaded for whites to understand the legitimacy of black demands, and acknowledged that "our attitude generally has been obstructive all along the line." Collins concluded his speech by noting, that "[t]his is a call to history–a history which grows impatient. Ours is a generation in which great decisions can no longer be passed to the next. We have a State to build–a South to save–a nation to convince– and a God to serve." While Collins' views won him praise from several newspapers for his courage in facing up to this controversial issue, it was clear his outlook was not shared by many spokesmen in other southern states nor by the leaders in the legislature of his own state.

Collins' disagreements with the legislature continued on into 1957. It was in Little Rock, Arkansas, however, that the major racial confrontation occurred as Governor Orval E. Faubus used armed state troops to defy the Supreme Court's order by ordering 270 National Guardsmen to block the entrance of nine black students into Central High School. At the end of September Faubus withdrew the troops and headed for the Southern Governors' Conference at Sea Island, Georgia, where, as luck would have it, Collins was scheduled to give the opening address for which he had selected the title, "Can a Southerner Be Elected President?"

With talk in the air of Collins as a possible vice-presidential candidate in 1960, there was speculation he would use the occasion of the address to answer Faubus' actions, although several advisors had warned him about advancing too far on the racial issue. In his speech Collins argued that a Southerner could be elected President but such a candidacy would require clearly defined goals. One of these was a realignment of federal-state relations. For Collins states rights also meant state responsibilites to protest the rights of all its citizens, something that had not always been done in the past. Interestingly, he suggested that foreign policy should consist of more than just anti-communism, that the U.S. needed to develop a moral component of foreign policy by helping the less developed parts of the world. Finally, he turned to the race issue, observing that the Supreme Court must be observed if we were to be a "land of the law" and concluding that southerners "must not forget that the first law of nature is change." As was to be expected, Collins' address was applauded by southern moderates and by liberals around the country, but gained him condemnation among many in the South and his own state.

As the tensions over integration continued, Collins consistently maintained that governmental reform and a new constitution were the most important problems facing Floridians. The situation, however, was little changed from two years earlier when the Pork Choppers had defied the Governor's efforts at reapportionment and refused to allow the legislature to call a constitutional convention which might take events beyond their control. Instead, they chose to amend the State's charter article by article. After an agreement with the Pork Choppers which would have added seven senators, four from south Florida, Collins called a special session on constitutional revision to meet at the end of September, 1957.

Some advocates of reapportionment criticized Collins' concessions to the Pork Choppers, but the Governor argued that "we can't get adequate reapportionment until we get better apportionment than we have now." Opposition to the plan forced its carry-over to the next legislative session. By 1959 Collins was losing the initiative. He had campaigned on the idea that "half a loaf was better than none," but the majority of Floridians voted against the amendment drafted by the rural forces in the legislature. There would be no fundamental governmental reform during Collins' term in office. The Pork Choppers had won.

The extent to which Florida had delayed dealing with the question of desegregation can perhaps best be observed in the fact that it was in February 1959, that the Dade County School Board finally assigned four black students to attend Miami's Orchard Villa Elementary School. Even as he neared the end of his term in 1960, Collins felt the need to veto a proposal to appropriate $500,000 for a statewide advertising campaign to suggest the positive effects of segregation. In the face of a riot resulting from a "sit-in" by blacks at a segregated department store lunch counter in Tallahassee, the Governor in a statewide radio and television address observed: "I don't mind saying that I think if a man has a department store and he invites the public generally to come into his department store and trade, I think then it is unfair and morally wrong for him to single out one department, though, and say he does not want or will not allow Negroes to patronize that one department. Now he has a legal right to do that, but I still don't think he can square that right with moral, simple justice."

During his six years in the governor's chair LeRoy Collins won several distinctions for himself and for the state. After serving as chairman of the Southern Governors' Conference and the National Governors' Conference in 1960, he became the first governor since the Civil War to serve as permanent chairman of the Democratic National Convention. After his term of office expired, he became president of the National Association of Broadcasters, a position he resigned in 1964 to join the staff of President Lyndon B. Johnson to work in an effort to secure compliance with the new civil rights legislation without resort to courts and force. In 1965 he became assistant secretary of commerce but resigned late in 1967 to return to Florida to prepare for a campaign to succeed to the seat given up by Senator George A. Smathers in 1968. His work on the Johnson civil rights staff probably cost him whatever chance he may have had to win the senatorship.

While the civil rights struggle of blacks drew considerable attention during the 1950s, a less publicized but perhaps no less intense, legal battle was being waged by the Seminole Indians. In the years after World War II many policymakers concerned with Indian affairs anticipated that the various clans comprising the Seminoles would eventually be integrated into American society. They also anticipated an end to the aid that the Indians had received from the Federal government. During the decade, however, a number of the Indian leaders moved to develop tribal status, which was opposed by almost a third of the members of the clans. By 1957, the Indians had achieved governmental recognition as the Seminole Tribe and an "assumption of sovereignty" that would give them enormous economic benefits in the future through gambling and other economic concessions. The group that failed to thwart Seminole recognition organized as the Miccosukee Tribe and received its own recognition in 1962.

There was one final problem facing Floridians in the late 1950s, the Cuban Revolution alluded to earlier and the subsequent waves of refugees fleeing the island. After almost forty years, this continues to be a multifaceted problem with repercussions in several areas. This was not, of course, the first time events in Cuba had had a serious impact on Florida, as was discussed in the chapter on "Florida and the War for Cuban Independence."

The Hispano-Cuban-American War of 1898 did not, from the Cuban standpoint, eventuate in real independence. Many Cubans believed that the United States had intervened at the last moment to prevent a Cuban victory over the Spanish. The Teller amendment disavowed annexation of the island, but the subsequent Platt Amendment, finally accepted by the Cubans, made Cuba a virtual protectorate of this country, under which the United States several times during the twentieth century had intervened in Cuban affairs.

During the Cuban Revolution of 1933, an American, Sumner Welles, directed affairs to the point that power eventually gravitated to a former army sergeant, Fulgencio Batista. In 1940 Batista brought together a broad coalition of interests, including the Communists, to write a constitution for the island. This was a radical document, probably the most radical in the Americas, and it gave the state vast powers to intervene in the economy and to nationalize property. Concerned American investors were told not to worry, that the document would never be fully implemented.

In 1944 Batista was defeated in the election for the presidency, retiring eventually to Daytona Beach, Florida. What followed under liberal politicians was a degree of corruption that shocked many of the Cuban people. In such circumstances Batista chose to run again in the elections of 1952, but was again defeated. This time, however, with the help of the army, he staged a *coup d'etat* and took control.

The next year a young militant, Fidel Castro, led a failed attack on the Moncado Barracks and was imprisoned on the Isle of Pines. He was freed in an amnesty several years later and subsequently launched an attack from Mexico into Cuba in 1956. Unable to effect a general uprising, Castro and his small band of followers retreated into the mountains, where they proceeded to carry on a guerrilla war.

Castro was certainly not the only organized opposition to Batista, but his activities, and the inability of the Cuban army to defeat his forces, made him a media celebrity increasingly well known to Americans, especially Floridians who had followed the events in Cuba closely.

Castro never made a secret of his intentions. Speaking from the Sierra Maestre mountains in 1957, he pronounced his commitment to the radical Constitution of 1940 and proclaimed that his Revolution, if successful, would be democratic and socialist. Over time it became clear that Castro would honor the latter commitment at the expense of the former. American policymakers were not unaware of the radical nature of Castro's program. As Batista's government lost support and Castro gained increasing sympathy among many Americans, the Eisenhower adminstration announced that it was cutting off military aid to the former. This policy, however, never went into effect. The military aid ostensibly denied Cuba was transshipped through Nicaragua where President Anastacio Somoza sent the supplies on to the Batista regime.

Despite this assistance, by late 1958 it was becoming clear that Batista's government was losing whatever legitimacy it had once held among the Cuban people. When, at the end of 1958, Batista at last fled Cuba, American policymakers had been unable to cobble together an army junta capable of retaining power. During those months of declining power many Batistianos, wealthy or otherwise, found it expedient to leave the island. Many came to Florida. In 1959 and after, as other revolutionary groups broke with Castro over the direction of the Cuban Revolution and left Cuba, they would often seek aid from American authorities in Florida, especially in Miami, only to find that the largesse was primarily dispensed by their old enemies, the Batistianos, who had arrived first and had ingratiated themselves with the Americans as staunch anti-Communists opposed to the leftist Revolution.

Castro's followers were only one part of the revolutionary coalition that had toppled Batista. But their organizational initiative and his leadership were crucial in the triumph of Castro over other elements in the coalition. As thousands of Cuban refugees sought asylum in Florida and dreamed of a return to the island, few realized the impact this immigration would have on the economic development and politics, not only of Florida, but of the whole United States and, especially, its foreign policy.

The 1960s would witness a continuing growth of the Sunshine State, fueled in large part by increasing waves of refugees from a now Communist Cuba deeply enmeshed in the Cold War confrontation between the United States and the Soviet Union. The Democrats would continue to battle over civil rights, reapportionment, and even a growing protest over American involvement in Vietnam. And, to top things off, Floridians would elect a Republican governor for the first time in almost a century.

28.

Protests, Exiles and Republican Revival

The major political issues in Florida did not change much in the 1960s. The most discussed questions in the 1960 campaign for the Democratic gubernatorial nomination were segregation, sit-down strikes, reapportionment, taxes and the economic development of the state. The basic decision not to allow a fight over desegregation to interfere with the economic expansion of the state had been made in 1956, but still to be decided were the questions of how much and when desegregation of schools and other public facilities and accommodations should be accomplished. All of the candidates supported segregation to some degree, but Harvie I. Belser and Bill Hendrix, who made it the key point in their platforms, ran poorly. Doyle E. Carlton, Jr. became known as the moderate on the issue somewhat in the Collins manner. Farris Bryant said less about the subject but earned a reputation as a strong segregationist. He joined Fred O. "Bud" Dickinson, Jr. and John McCarty in condemning sit-ins by demonstrators against segregation and demanded that the law be used to break up such disruptive activities. Thomas E. "Ted" David of Fort Lauderdale alone made reapportionment the central issue of his campaign.

Bryant and McCarty came out most strongly against new taxes, a pledge the winner could scarcely hope to keep. Haydon Burns, mayor of Jacksonville, ran amazingly well for a newcomer to the race. Jim McCovey was another also-ran candidate. Bryant received 193,507 votes in the first primary; Carlton, 186,228; Burns, 166,352; McCarty, 144,750; Dickinson, 115,520; and the others, lesser numbers. In the runoff, in spite of eleventh hour endorsement by Governor Collins, Carlton lost to Bryant by 416,052 to 512,751. Although it has been suggested that 50,000 to 100,000 votes came from disgruntled Carlton-Collins supporters, the growing interest of Republicans in the governorship was evident when George C. Petersen of Fort Lauderdale ran Bryant a closer than usual race: 569,936 to 848,407 votes.

In office Bryant remained true to his campaign promises to
provide a conservative administration. He expressed fear of federal
aid to education if strings were attached. He opposed any new taxes
but found the demands for extension of state services strong. He
committed himself to the need for new state universities at Boca
Raton and Pensacola but did not guarantee the necessary dollars.
At one time he expressed a choice for junior colleges over four-year
institutions since they cost less to the state and the students. He
proposed meeting the need for raises by transferring funds from
other state agencies with less need, and expressed the hope that big
business would help to employ big name professors at the
universities and help, thereby, to attract more big business. He
opposed racial integration but managed to avoid a showdown on
this thorny subject.

Governor Bryant was a strong supporter of tourism and business
expansion, which he hoped would produce enough new revenue to
make unnecessary a tax increase. He got off to a stormy start by
appointing Wendell H. Jarrard, a Tampa insurance man, to head
the development commission. Jarrard's tendency to ignore the rules
in hiring and firing as well as policy making and expenditures
created controversy. In December 1959, on the eve of his
inauguration, the governor-elect visited Panama, Colombia, and
Venezuela to discuss trade and tourism with heads of state. He sent
two traveling showcases to Europe for a year to appear finally at a
world travel congress at Cannes in France where 2,500 travel agents
and writers were gathered. At the same time he increased
advertising in the United States, especially in New York, where,
after a shaky start, Florida's pavilion at the World's Fair was
pronounced a success. He gave his support to the cross-state barge
canal, the 152-mile extension of the Florida Turnpike from Fort
Pierce to Wildwood, and the Everglades Turnpike from near Naples
in Collier County to Fort Lauderdale. Critics dubbed the latter road
"Alligator Alley" in derision, but supporters adopted the name and
made it official. To the delight of its backers, tolls provided more
than enough to pay for the road. The refinancing of the $66 million
in existing turnpike bonds in a new package at a higher rate
produced sharp criticism but made the package marketable at 4.75
percent. Significantly, Bryant showed no interest in such urban
problems as slum clearance and urban renewal.

On the racial front the principal issues in the Bryant
administration had to do mostly with the integration of public
accommodations and pending federal civil rights legislation. In May
1963 in Daytona and in Tallahassee, blacks demonstrated against
discrimination. The governor defended the right to demonstrate
but made it quite clear that he would not tolerate violence or
destruction of property. His official biographer, John E. Evans,
reports that he reorganized and strengthened the state militia and
called out units of the militia more than a dozen times, but almost
exclusively for use in civil disaster relief rather than for civil
disorders. Mayor Haydon Burns of Jacksonville, as part of his

campaign for the nomination to the governorship by the Democrats, declared that demonstrations should be stopped. As if to challenge him, a series of demonstrations began in that city. One black woman was killed and a number of others injured in an effort to desegregate bars, restaurants, and hotels. Other Democratic candidates, Fred O. Dickinson, Jr., John E. Mathews, Jr., and Frederick B. Karl, joined Burns in opposition to a national public accommodations law, and only Mayor Robert King High of Miami supported such legislation. In the same month some 1,500 blacks marched in support of civil rights legislation in Tallahassee without incident.

The spotlight then focused on Saint Augustine for a time. The historic city was in the midst of preparations for a quadracentennial celebration the following year. Federal funds, it was charged, were being used to support segregated activities. National interest guaranteed wide coverage. On March 30, 1964, thirty-seven persons, including the chaplain of Yale University and Mrs. Malcolm Peabody, age seventy-two, mother of the governor of Massachusetts, faced charges stemming from their efforts to desegregate motels and restaurants. Before calm was restored to the city on July 1, the Reverend Martin Luther King had been arrested. He paid his fine after a token stay in jail and called off the demonstrations later when an interracial council began work on an effort to reconcile differences.

During the early 1960s, the developing radicalization of the Cuban Revolution led by Fidel Castro also continued to have an impact on Florida. His program to nationalize properties owned by both Cubans and foreigners, especially American corporations, and his efforts at agrarian reform led to increasing tensions with the United States and a growing horde of refugees fleeing to Florida as a larger number of middle class Cubans found themselves in conflict with Castro's socialist oriented and increasingly dictatorial policies.

Castro needed capital to carry out his socialist vision for Cuba's economic development. He sought funds both from the United Nations and, especially, the United States. In an effort to force Cuba's economic development along lines satisfactory to the United States, American policymakers decided, as one of them put it, "to put Castro through the wringer." Foreign corporations were irritated that Castro had based their value on the assessments they had for years used for tax purposes in Cuba, and in nationalizing their properties, he offered to pay them off in relatively low interest rate Cuban bonds. Ironically, although the American government opposed Castro's proposals, his offer was not unlike what American policymakers had pressed on the defeated Japanese a decade or so earlier in an effort to break the hold of the large corporations known as the Zaibatsu and the large landholdings of some virtually feudal landlords. American policymakers expected a counter offer to their hard line, but Castro did not respond.

What American policymakers had not counted upon was that Castro might find other buyers for Cuban sugar, the favorable treatment of which on the United States' market had always been

Escapees from Cuba, April 11, 1961, only a few days before the Bay of Pigs invasion. The family of mechanic Oreste Ortega, seated, and an ex-Castro captain, Armando Rodriquez, wait in a Coast Guard boat in Key West after a night escape from Cuba in an open boat.

the basis for American influence on the island's economic development. Ultimately, Castro found buyers for Cuban sugar among members of the Soviet bloc, and especially in the Soviet Union itself. Thus, despite its economic pressures, the United States found itself unable to control events in Cuba as it had in the past.

As thousands of Cubans fled to Florida to escape Castro's increasingly radical policies, the Eisenhower administration ordered the Central Intelligence Agency (CIA) to recruit and organize Castro's opponents in Florida into a force capable of invading the island as the Cuban leader himself had done less than five years earlier. As the CIA ultimately continued training the refugee force in Nicaragua, it showed its preferences by placing control among the Batistiano exiles rather than more recent arrivals, who had played a role in the early phases of the Revolution before breaking with Castro.

All of this was taking place while the American presidential election of 1960 was contested between the Republican candidate, Richard M. Nixon, Eisenhower's Vice President, and the Democratic challenger, John F. Kennedy, the young Senator from Massachusetts. Kennedy's narrow victory in November 1960 meant that after his inauguration early in 1961 one of his first decisions would be what to do about the potential Cuban liberation invasion force encamped in Nicaragua.

In what would be viewed as the greatest failure of his presidency, Kennedy made the decision to move forward with the invasion. On April 17, 1961, Brigade 2506 launched the assault at the Bay of Pigs. The CIA's planning was such that the resistance within Cuba was not told until the day the operation began. The President's decision to withhold American air support doomed whatever chance the invasion might have had. By April 21, exactly sixty-three years since the United States had declared war on Spain over Cuba, Castro's forces had essentially captured the remnants of the invasion force. After paying a ransom of $62 million in medicine and food in December of 1962, President Kennedy faced the less than 1,200 survivors of the Brigade in the Orange Bowl in Miami, part of a Cuban crowd of 35,000 in the cavernous 75,000 seat stadium, and promised, "I can assure you that this flag will be returned to this Brigade in a free Havana."

Earlier, on October 22, 1962, Floridians had again been reminded of Cuba's proximity and the impact of events there on life in their state when Kennedy in a television address told the American people that the Russians had installed missiles on the island and that he was instituting a quarantine to force their removal. The Russian-Cuban missile crisis brought units of all the armed forces hurrying to southern Florida to set up anti-missile installations. In spite of a careful effort not to interfere with normal civilian activity, the prospect that it might become necessary to use the weapons raised fears of what might happen to the winter tourist business. Fortunately, the crisis passed without incident. In negotiating for the removal of the missiles the United States agreed to cease its effort to topple Castro through outright invasion as had been mounted in 1961.

The CIA's inept covert planning of the 1961 invasion, however, had a lasting effect on the thinking of one important Floridian, Congressman Dante Fascell of Miami, a relatively recent appointee to the House's Foreign Affairs Committee, who later would serve as its Chairman for more than a decade. As a result of the Cuban fiasco, even before the expanding American involvement in Vietnam in 1965, Fascell had begun to question the morality and effectiveness of this secrecy and military interventionism.

In a series of hearings and studies that extended on and off for more than a decade, Fascell's sub-committee explored various facets of America's response to the Cold War. What he ultimately concluded was that the United States had done a relatively poor job of explaining the American way of life to the people of other nations. Fascell began to develop the foundation of what has come to be called in recent years "public diplomacy." The fundamental idea is that involvement of Americans on a "people to people" basis is perhaps more significant in the long run than foreign aid, which may be misused and foster corruption, or military interventionism, which

Congressman Dante Fascell in 1959 with one of his young student interns in Washington, Bob Graham, future state legislator, governor and United States Senator.

seldom solves the basic problems facing underdeveloped nations. Senator J. William Fulbright of Arkansas has rightly received the credit for conceptualizing the program that has led to thousands of educational and cultural exchanges between Americans and the people of other nations, but it was Fascell who year after year pushed that funding through the House, a much more difficult task than was the case in the Senate.

Fascell saw early on that human rights issues were what really separated America from the other side in the Cold War. His efforts bore fruit in the 1980s when, through his work as a member of the American delegation to the Helsinki Accords, the Soviets ultimately agreed to accept the concept of human rights. In the winding down of the Cold War, it is relatively easy to measure the economic and military clout that played a role in events. The effect of public diplomacy, however, is very difficult to measure quantitatively, but

Fascell's stress on the importance of public diplomacy—of the voluntary interaction of people to people and business to business, in cultural, religious, educational and business affairs, as opposed to government to government relationships—has been a major factor in promoting international peace and understanding.

In the summer of 1965 discontent had reached such a point in Cuba that Castro allowed an exit of Cuban refugees by boat from the small fishing village of Camarioca. Within a few weeks regular "freedom flights" to Miami were instituted and would bring thousands of Cubans to Florida in the years to follow.

In a strange way these flights, viewed as an ideological weapon by the federal government in accepting political refugees, subsidizing their flight from Cuba and giving them aid upon arrival, were a vindication of Fascell's view that government actions might induce behaviors quite at odds with the intent of the policy. Thus individuals who were not necessarily ideologically anti-Cartro might seize upon an opportunity to better themselves economically. One family, interviewed in 1965 in the "Freedom Tower," as the old *Miami News* building came to be called, during the initial boatlift where one might have assumed the most ideologically anti-Castro would be found, was a perfect example of this behavior. The father explained he had been the "number two man" below Ché Guevara in the Ministry of Industries while his wife taught Communism in a high school and his daughter was a student there. Since he several times uttered the phrase, "Viva la Revolución Cubana," it was interesting to hear his reply to the question of why the family had left Cuba. It turned out his mother and two brothers were in Cleveland, Ohio, and not doing very well economically. Since he was the experienced businessman in the family, "Mother" had put enormous pressure on him to come and rescue the family fortunes. It was difficult to find much ideological anti-Castroism in an individual who kept repeating that he wished the Cuban Revolution well, while American taxpayers footed the bill for aid to these Cold War "political" refugees. It was, in fact, difficult to determine who was really a political refugee in contrast to someone simply seeking greater economic and political freedom in the United States.

At the same time the "freedom flights" were being initiated, President Lyndon Johnson was making the decision to commit American military forces in Vietnam. In the summer of 1965 several universities around the country held "teach-ins" very similar to the discussions after the Spanish-American War about the wisdom of the United States acquiring the Philippine Islands. A large "teach-in" was held at the University of Miami, where the featured speaker was Senator Ernest Gruening of Alaska, one of two senators who had voted against the Gulf of Tonkin Resolution, which had been the President's method of securing congressional approval for increased intervention in Asia. Interestingly, the Cuban exiles turned out in force for the "teach-in" at the University of Miami to support intervention in southeast Asia, for they fully understood that a Cold War interventionist policy there might lead to further an American policy of increased interventionism against the Castro government as well.

In the meantime, while these momentous foreign policy decisions were affecting Floridians in internal state political affairs, the 1963 legislative session was largely a repeat of that two years earlier, holding the line on taxes and expenditures and refusing to tackle the rising number of social problems. Further futile efforts at reapportionment in the state legislature and at constitutional reform, paradoxically, may have served to move those issues closer to ultimate solution. A significant political move was passage of an amendment to shift the principal state election away from the presidential election year by making the next term only two years and allowing incumbents to run again if they chose to do so.

Since the possibility that a victory in 1964 might mean, in effect, a six-year term, the Democrat candidates found themselves involved in an unusually strong rivalry for the nomination to the governorship. Mayor Burns of Jacksonville became the principal spokesman for the conservatives and Mayor Robert King High of Miami for the liberals. In the first primary Burns received 312,453 to 207,280 for High, but a substantial number of votes cast for other contenders forced a runoff. Scott Kelly of Lakeland received 205,078 votes; Fred O. Dickinson of West Palm Beach, 184,865; John E. "Jack" Mathews, Jr., of Jacksonville, 140,210; and Fred Karl of Daytona Beach, 85,953. In the run-off Burns bested High by 648,093 to 465,547. Burns won handily over Republican Charles R. Holley of Saint Petersburg in November.

The steadily climbing cost of running for governor finally reached the million dollar mark when the Democrats reported expenditures of $1,117,458.70, which were almost evenly distributed among the three candidates. Equally important were the sums spent by losers. High spent $204,727.27 in two primaries, while in the first primary Dickinson reported $651,898.16, Karl $282,637.97, Mathews $341,702.73, and Kelly $498,784.29. In short, the Democrats spent $1,979,750.42 to elect Burns to a two year term, a cost of nearly one dollar for each vote cast. Republicans reported expenditures of $99,986.00, ninety percent of it in the general election. The scent of victory in 1970 provided a stronger rivalry for the Republican nomination and election.

The short term was largely a waiting and preparation for the campaign for a full term in 1966. Burns continued the policy of fiscal conservatism, pronounced the state in good financial condition and saw no need for new taxes. He recognized the fnancial needs of education but offered no specific solutions. He did speak strongly for water conservation. His proposal for a $300 million bond issue for road building was turned down by the voters. It was becoming the fashion for voters in Florida more and more often also to reject county and municipal bonding proposals.

In the 1966 Democratic primary Burns ran first with 372,451 votes to 338,281 for High, 331,580 for Kelly, and 11,343 for Sam Foor of Tallahassee. Somewhat surprisingly, High defeated Burns in the runoff by 596,471 to 509,271. In the general election conservative Democrats threw enough votes to Claude R. Kirk, Jr., of Jacksonville, who had won the Republican nomination easily, to defeat High by the decisive vote of 821,190 to 668,233. If this trend to conservatism needed any further confirmation, it came in 1968 when Senator George A. Smathers chose not to run again. LeRoy Collins, who had been a highly successful governor, won the Democratic nomination over Earl Faircloth of Miami in a very close race but lost to Republican Edward J. Gurney, a newcomer to Florida politics, by 892,638 votes to 1,131,499.

This was another alarmingly costly election. Burns reported nearly a million and a half dollars spent on two primaries, High about a million on three contests, Kelly nearly a half million on the first primary, and Kirk $550,000, all but a little more than $41,000 on the general election. This, together with the disclosures that Tom Adams had won the race for secretary of state, incurring a campaign debt of $100,000, and that Collins owed an undisclosed sum on the losing senatorial campaign in 1968, turned the attention of the 1970 legislature to the problem of growing costs of political campaigns. Allegations that big donors were ignoring the existing laws regarding contributions to political campaigns added fuel to the flames of concern and controversy over campaigning.

The 1970 legislature sought again by law to limit the amount of campaign expenditures for nomination and election to statewide offices. Candidates for governor (including running mates) and for the United States Senate were allowed $350,000 for the primary and the same amount for the general election. Other statewide offices were limited to $250,000, congressmen to $75,000, and others to $25,000. That the law may sometimes fail in its purpose was shown in 1970 when Jack Eckerd reported spending $801,032, all but $27,500 of it his own money, in his campaign for the Republican gubernatorial nomination prior to July 1 when the new law became effective. All candidates for a higher office than the one they currently hold were also now required to resign from that office before they could qualify for election to the new office. Since the resignation need not become effective until the end of the year, however, it scarcely prevented the candidate from using his office as a base from which to run for higher office.

On the Republican side, Claude Kirk was a maverick even within his own party. Born in California in 1926, the year the Florida land boom collapsed, Kirk's family had moved around the country, starting from Illinois and then moving to Alabama when he was in his teens. After graduating from high school in Montgomery toward the end of World War II, he joined the Marine Corps. When the war ended, Kirk attended Duke University and then graduated with a law degree from the University of Alabama in 1949. He married in 1947, and before graduation became successful selling insurance. Kirk was called back to duty in the Korean War and afterward obtained a position with McCullough Industries, a large manufacturer of earth-moving and road-paving equipment.

Claude R. Kirk, Jr., first Republican Governor since Reconstruction.

Kirk also found time to rescue a struggling local insurance firm and arrange a merger, developing a friendship with Ashley Verlander, a Georgia insurance management consultant. In 1956, only a decade before his election as governor, he moved to Florida with, as he noted later, "four children, one wife and $4,000 in debt." With Verlander's help and the support of the Davis brothers, who owned the Winn-Dixie grocery store chain, he was able to establish what quickly became a successful business—the American Heritage Life Insurance Company.

His increasing wealth and travels around the state offered the opportunity to make numerous friends and contacts but was partly responsible for the ultimate break-up of his marriage, although he remained friendly with his ex-wife and her family, who supported him in his later political efforts. In 1962 Kirk left the insurance business to join the investment banking firm of Hayden, Stone, but within 18 months he was involved in investments in Brazil, where he met his future wife, Erika Mattfield, whom he married with great publicity after he assumed office in 1967.

Kirk's family had been politically active and he claimed later that he had headed a Democrats for Dewey-Warren chapter at the University of Alabama in 1948. In 1960 he directed a Democrats for Nixon effort in Florida, partly, perhaps, a reflection of his friendship for Robert Finch, a Nixon associate whom Kirk had met while in the Marines. Kirk's first effort for elective office occurred in 1964 when he became the Republican challenger to long-time Democratic Senator, Spessard Holland. Holland soundly defeated Kirk by a margin of 435,373 votes and carried all but one of the state's 67 counties. Nevertheless, the defeat was not a total one for Kirk. His total vote of 562,212 was a quarter of a million votes more than any previous Republican had garnered in any Florida race, and it gave Kirk a name recognition around the state that he had lacked prior to running for office.

The failure of Senator Barry Goldwater, the Republican presidential nominee, to carry Florida revealed a split between the Republican old-guard, which had controlled the Party, and a more militant group of Young Republicans who were determined to offer a greater opposition to the Democrats at both the state and local levels. Kirk was young, only forty in 1966, and had real appeal to the the Young Republicans. While William Cramer and other Party leaders seem to have written off Republican chances for the governorship in 1966, Kirk was the only one who anticipated the split which would fracture the Democratic Party.

The administration of Governor Kirk was a running political battle between the first Republican chief executive since Reconstruction, the elected cabinet (all Democrats), and a predominantly Democratic legislature. Kirk was unconventional in his tactics but managed to keep himself in the news and his opponents off balance. He was a master of what one of his biographers has called "the politics of confrontation." The legislature in 1969 provided him an issue by raising the salaries of its members to $12,000 a year. The constitution of 1968 left the fixing of salaries to the legislature, and the Eagleton Institute of Politics at Rutgers University, employed to evaluate its organization and procedures, recommended somewhat higher salaries. In the 1970 session, in defiance of a threat to veto any bill that called for new taxes, the lawmakers sent to the governor a budget that would produce a deficit unless there were a sharp upturn in the economy to produce more revenue from existing taxes. The governor accepted the challenge, vetoed the budget, and called the legislature back into session on Wednesday, June 10, only five days after the adjournment of the regular session. The $1,227,000,000 budget not only was out of balance, said the governor, it also provided additional sums to equalize educational opportunity in the less wealthy counties, which he called unconstitutional and nothing more than more money for a bad system which he insisted must first be reformed. The house responded by overriding the veto 77 to 37, and the senate by 32 to 14. Both houses also overrode, by 78 to 37 and 34 to 12, the governor's veto of the companion bill that continued the minimum foundation principle of school funding by beginning a four-year program of increased state aid to tax-poor, pupil-rich counties.

Several aspects of the Kirk administration are worth exploring beyond the fact that he was the first Republican governor since Reconstruction. Some political analysts have suggested that for many years the leadership for the small Republican party was not all that enthusiastic about building a larger organization. When the Republicans controlled the executive branch in Washington, for example, during the Eisenhower years, the small leadership in Florida had real control over the considerable federal patronage appointments. Some leaders might have perceived that a larger electoral base which was still not competitive with the Democrats, would simply give the existing leadership less control over federal patronage. Ironically, the Republican leadership was tied to the same economic interests, such as the Davis brothers of the Winn-Dixie food stores, as were the Democrats.[1]

That Kirk was not part of the inner party circle, was compounded by the party's leadership being a relatively small group with few people of experience ready to participate in helping run parts of the executive branch. Edmund Kallina suggests of Kirk that, rather than appointing political types, the governor brought a "measure of professionalism" to these areas. While that may be true to some extent, Kirk chose to bring in Charles Perry from Ohio to be his advisor in the important field of education which demonstrated the weakness of the Republicans when it came to personnel from the state. In some cases these men were not professionals in their fields at all.

For example, Kirk's selection of James Bax to head "the state agency that eventually became the Department of Health and Rehabilitative Services," certainly one of the growth areas of government for the next several decades, is illustrative of the way politics worked in Florida. Bax was certainly not a professional in anything related to that field. Coming from a middle class background in Clearwater, he graduated *summa cum laude* in engineering from the University of Florida and had married into a wealthy banking family in Delray Beach whose assets also included the Gulf Oil distributorship in the area. Bax began attending Florida Atlantic University which had opened in 1964 in order to obtain a master's degree and ended up very soon as chairman of the mathematics education area. When he enrolled in the doctoral program at the University of Miami, Bax was already considering a career in politics.

In a discussion before the Democratic run-off in which he made a small wager for Burns against High, Bax boasted that while Burns was his choice, he had given monies to both Democrats as well as to

Kirk. One way or the other, he anticipated going to Tallahassee. After Kirk's later defeat, Bax ended up with a similar adminstrative position in Idaho. By the 1980s he had mastered the technique of what would in the 1990s be referred to as "politipreneurship," that is, using government almost exclusively as a market for one's product rather than selling on the market to the public, Bax described his company as having a "lock" on producing the examinations for the various tests given by the Department of Business and Professional Regulation. After Hurricane Andrew in 1992, Bax would emerge as the head of the controversial Joint Underwriters Association created to deal with the crisis in insurance liability costs. If another definition of politipreneurship is getting government to assume the risk and liability usually borne by the entrepreneur or the private sector, Bax had become a master of the art.[2] The beginning of Bax's political career demonstrated the extent to which, despite the emergence of an opposition party, Florida politics remained every man for himself.

The governor, for his part, provided ammunition for the potshots of his political foes when he came into office by inaugurating a war against crime to be financed by private contributions and carried out by such organizations as the Wackenhut Corporation of Coral Gables, a private security agency, later based in Palm Beach Gardens. Doubts about the legality of the plan and the attendant publicity discouraged supporters, and some of the bills remained unpaid for several years. Less likely to be forgotten by the voters was the Governor's Club, whose membership was secret until publicity and threats of legal action induced the governor to reveal the members' names in the spring of 1970. Many persons employed by the state or holding state contracts paid $500 or more for membership. The money went largely to pay travel expenses of the governor on trips designed to improve the image of the state and, incidentally, of its chief executive. Such funds are by no means unique but may prove more of a liability than an asset. The governor also took a stand on one feature of the desegregation struggle when he took over the administration of the Manatee County schools in April 1969 in an effort, he said, to force the Supreme Court of the United States to rule on the legality of cross-busing to achieve racial balance in schools. He failed in that objective but staked out for himself a position on the most controversial issue in a year full of educational crises.

Three major developments of a nonpartisan character in the Kirk administration represented real achievement on long standing problems. Florida had had one of the most inequitably apportioned legislatures in the Union and was one of the most recalcitrant states about meeting the "one man-one vote" requirement of *Baker v. Carr* (1961), but the courts finally imposed a settlement of the question in 1967. According to the 1960 census figures, 12.3 percent of the voters elected a majority of the state senate and 14.7 percent, the lower house. The five most populous counties had over half of the population, but only 14 percent of the senators.

Efforts at reapportionment had begun with a special session called by Governor Collins in 1955. After that time, nine special sessions of the legislature were devoted primarily to reapportionment besides attempts in the regular sessions. The repeated efforts brought improvement and near success. By 1966 about 48 percent of the population could elect a majority of both houses, but it failed to satisfy the courts. On February 8, 1967, the three judge U.S. District Court in Miami rejected the latest effort and required that acceptable reapportionment be achieved before the regular session of the legislature scheduled for April could be convened. In view of the doubtful legality of the existing legislature, the court invited one and all to submit proposals. The plan adopted came in the form of an *amicus curiae* brief by Manning J. Dauer, a professor of political science at the University of Florida. In order for the districts not to be too large in the thinly populated areas, Dauer proposed and the court approved forty-eight senators and 119 representatives, somewhat the same numbers with which the legislature had been working. Gone was the old rule of one house member for each county, and at the other extreme, Dade, the most populous county, saw its delegation grow from one senator and three representatives to nine senators and twenty-two representatives.

In 1970, the federal census showed even greater concentration of population in the urban centers which would require further reapportionment in 1972. Under the new constitution of 1968 the senate could be made up of thirty to forty members, which meant dropping at least eight, and the house eighty to 120 members. The constitution provided that reapportionment take place after each decennial census, provided for automatic review by the state supreme court and required that the court file an apportionment plan if the legislature fails to produce an acceptable one.

The new constitution also required that the voters determine whether the members of the house shall have four-year terms. Performance in the 1970 session kept support alive for a smaller house or even a unicameral legislature. Bicameralism is strongly entrenched in American tradition and practice, but four-year terms for members of both houses could have strengthened the chances for a single house legislature. The voters in November 1970 turned down the four-year term for the lower house.

The rewriting of the much amended constitution of 1885 failed to please many people who accepted it as the best they could get at the time. Actually it was a monumental achievement at a time when voters were turning down efforts at revision in Kentucky, Maryland, and New York. Major changes allowed the governor to succeed himself if he had not served more than six years, and recreated the office of lieutenant governor, who would run on the ticket with the governor. In spite of the efforts of Governor Kirk and the recommendations of public administration experts to the contrary, Florida kept its often criticized elected cabinet, though the functions of the cabinet departments were somewhat redistributed by administrative reorganization.

Only the judicial section of the old document remained unchanged. The legislature would continue to meet annually. There was a ten mill limitation on levy of taxes for county purposes, for municipal purposes, or for school purposes. Additional millage could be voted for periods not to exceed two years, something the voters showed no disposition to do. An important new power was the ability to issue state bonds for financing of capital projects, subject to a vote of the electors, and the specific requirement of an appropriation of funds to pay debt service. There would henceforth be no distinction between married men and married women in property rights. A constitutional revision commission must be established ten years after the adoption of the constitution and every twenty years thereafter, and it made provisions for initiating amendments and calling a constitutional convention. An amendment initiated by the 1970 legislative session asked voters to determine if eighteen-year-olds should vote, and if all other privileges and rights of those twenty-one years of age should also be extended to them. It is doubtful that the legislators who voted for the amendment expected it to be approved by the voters, who failed to do so.

The legislative branch had thus taken some steps that won the approval of experts in government and public administration to modernize its structure and procedures. An organization session on the first Tuesday after the general election prepared the body ready to go to work for the session scheduled for the following April. In 1968, Senate Bill 135 abolished the Legislative Council and authorized both houses to establish as many permanent standing committees as was needed. One result was a further decline in the number of standing committees. The house in 1945 had fifty-nine, which decreased to thirty-two in 1967, and to twenty-eight in 1969 and the senate from thirty-seven in 1945 to twenty-five in 1967 and to twelve in 1969. Provision was made for prefiling bills, and the Department of Statutory Revision was transferred from the office of the attorney general to the legislature, where the revision actually takes place. Budget making became a function of the governor's office, which would then prepare the budget for presentation to the legislature.

There was one other area—the environment—where Kirk and his adminstration deserve considerable credit. When Kirk was elected, he was not especially keen on "conservation," as it was then called. The person most responsible for the governor's conversion to conservation was Nathaniel Reed, whom he had met during the course of the campaign. From the perspective of time, the environmental problems of the 1960s appear no less daunting. There was no effective land preservation policy, the state park system was just beginning and sewage disposal was a disaster waiting to happen. Except for Miami and Tampa, most cities disposed of their wastes by dumping them raw into streams, rivers, bays or the ocean. In Jacksonville, even the hospitals disposed of their operating room waste in this manner. Various dredge and fill projects were in operation around the state, especially in the south, and behind these developments were interests with powerfull connections which few political leaders had sought to challenge.

Reed produced a white paper in the campaign, which became the guidelines as he headed up environmental affairs. Reed was helped by his participation in what was by this time a growing environmental movement in Florida that included the Florida Audubon Society, the Izaak Walton League, the Florida Wildlife Federation as well as academic researchers as the University of Florida, Florida Atlantic University and the University of Miami. In 1967 two important environmental measures were passed. The first was the establishment of a Pollution Control Board empowered to issue permits for the discharge of waste and to enforce compliance with air and water standards. The bill allowed the state to begin compiling an inventory of where waste dumping was occurring, in what quantities and by whom.

The other measure was the Randall Act, named after a legislator from Fort Myers, which sought to correct the abuses resulting from dredging and filling. A biological impact study of the proposed dredging had to be made before a permit could be issued. As a result of the publicity generated by Kirk and Reed, permits for dredging and filling that had averaged 2,000 a year prior to 1967 dropped to about 200 a year during the next three years.

The Kirk adminstration also was involved in several other environmental disputes, including water management in the Everglades, the efforts to develop Biscayne Bay, the proposed jetport in the Everglades and the Cross-Florida Barge Canal. Reed's activities on environmentalism were extensive and non-partisan, and after Kirk's defeat he was retained in office by the newly elected Askew administration.

The decision of the veteran Democrat United States Senator Spessard L. Holland to retire from office in 1970 created a wide open race in both major parties for the position. For the Republicans, Congressman William C. Cramer, running at the invitation of President Nixon and national party leaders, seemed to have clear sailing until Judge G. Harrold Carswell failed to win approval of the United States Senate for appointment to the U.S. Supreme Court and decided to resign his U.S. Circuit Court seat and seek vindication at the polls in his home state by running for the Senate. Lieutenant Governor Ray Osborne, the only other announced candidate, withdrew and joined Governor Kirk and Senator Edward Gurney in support of the Carswell bid, all of which provided a donnybrook more characteristic of the Democrats in the past. Cramer won the Republican nomination handily, but the general election was to be a different matter.

Former Governor Farris Bryant returned to the political wars after an absence of six years to join four other Democrats in the contest for the party's favor in the senatorial race. His rivals were Joel T. Daves III of West Palm Beach, a former state representative, Lawton M. Chiles, Jr. of Lakeland, a state senator, Fred Schultz of Jacksonville, speaker of the house in 1970, and Alcee Hastings, a

Fort Lauderdale lawyer, the first black in modern times to offer himself for the United States Senate seat. Chiles wound up in a runoff with Bryant and won convincingly. He had come out of comparative political obscurity, but took his case to the voters in a 1,000 mile walk from Pensacola to Key West. All of the Democratic contenders gave unstinting support to Chiles, as did retiring Senator Holland. President Nixon gave strong support to Cramer, but Chiles came through with a good margin to spare.

The story of the 1970 race for the governorship was somewhat similar. Governor Kirk, running with Ray Osborne as lieutenant governor, had two rivals for the Republican nomination, L. A. "Skip" Bafalis, a state senator from Palm Beach, and Jack Eckerd, head of a chain of drugstores. Kirk won over Eckerd in a runoff. Democrats who offered themselves to become the party's candidate for governor in November were state senator Reubin Askew of Pensacola; John E. "Jack" Mathews, Jr., of Jacksonville, president of the senate; Attorney General Earl Faircloth of Miami, and Charles F. "Chuck" Hall, mayor of Metropolitan Dade County. Askew, running with Tom Adams, who had earlier abandoned his own ambition to become governor, won in a runoff with Earl Faircloth and his running mate, George Tapper. In the general election in November Askew defeated Kirk convincingly. Again, all Democratic contenders gave Askew their support.

After their 1966 and 1968 successes Republicans smelled further victories, and their primaries became hotly contested. The rivalries produced divisions as deep as those among the Democrats in the two previous elections. In 1970 the Democrats presented a greater measure of party unity than had been true for years. It was suggested that they had now become a party rather than a collection of individual contenders who often stand to lose rather than to gain by endorsing each other. In 1970 the number of registered Democrats was still three times that of the Republicans, and Democrats had less reason to cross party lines and vote Republican. Askew and Chiles were supported by liberals and conservatives, small counties and metropolitan areas. It appeared also as if fresh faces and new looks outweighed age and experience. Askew's "fair share" tax proposals and the walking senator somehow had greater appeal than ideas of some of the older politicians.

Growth is the only word to describe the economic developments of the almost half century before 1970. In fact, the rate of employment increase barely kept pace with the growing number of people to be employed. Such statistics of growth read almost like promotional literature unless one stops to recall the accompanying problems of providing roads, schools, housing, police and fire protection, water and waste disposal that bring pressure upon state and local governments for budgets and administration.

The pattern of Florida's economic development was pretty well set by 1950. This success story is best appreciated in the light of the fact that such a rate of growth was essential to provide employment for a population growing equally as fast. Though the growth in agriculture continued to be considerable, it was losing out in relative importance to a host of non-agricultural activities. The table of personal income by major sources, 1929 to 1969, reveals the absolute and relative importance of a dozen of the most important activities. Statistics of employment parallel those of source of income and reveal the same trends.

PERSONAL INCOME BY MAJOR SOURCES (In Millions of Dollars)

	1929	1939	1949	1959	1969
Personal	573	892	3,210	9,273	22,396
Wage and Salary	422	492	1,905	5,519	13,995
Farm	20	24	73	103	218
Contract Construction	16	22	148	578	1,231
Manufacturing	65	61	216	796	2,306
Wholesale & Retail Trade	87	111	463	1,276	2,778
Finance, Insurance, & Real Estate	30	22	85	338	828
Transportation	45	40	157	327	1,132
Railroad	33	28	71	93	111
Communications and Public Utilities	12	14	53	158	432
Services	77	77	278	767	2,222
Government	58	109	402	1,205	3,137
Federal Civil	12	46	110	263	683
Federal Military	8	11	114	362	678
State & Local	38	53	178	579	1,791
Proprietors	138	162	627	1,449	2,002
Farm	44	52	225	417	522
Non-Farm	94	110	402	1,032	1,480
Property	177	204	454	1,452	3,906

Other important indicators of the extent and direction of development in Florida since mid-century are to be found in two additional tables. The table of principal sources of state revenue shows by decades since 1949 the rapid growth of state government, the amount raised by state taxes (with only the principal sources indicated), and the growing importance of federal dollars in Florida government. The reliance upon sales, use, and excise taxes to produce revenue is also graphically illustrated.

FLORIDA'S PRINCIPAL SOURCES OF STATE REVENUE

	1949	1959	1969
Total Revenue	$229,644,366	$1,097,745,021	$3,131,238,249
Total State Taxes	147,741,595	521,944,571	1,371,088,116
U.S. Government	41,820,132	123,579,582	348,542,599

State Taxes

Sales and Use		148,148,363	573,779,401
Gasoline	46,272,040	112,549,471	196,615,184
Beverage	21,599,333	45,034,409	110,642,275
Cigarette	12,599,188	29,167,288	109,427,493
Racing	13,205,843	25,421,460	47,929,361
Motor Vehicle			
Licenses	18,500,823	47,888,659	77,360,136
Documentary			
Stamps	2,122,983	12,420,495	30,660,197
Unemployment	8,252,740	24,878,833	28,181,844

STATE OF FLORIDA PRINCIPAL DISBURSEMENTS

	1949	*1959*	*1969*
Total Disbursements	$250,762,772	$1,110,769,702	$3,181,141,557
Principal Disbursements			
Operating Expenses			
General Government	9,359,051	21,577,950	51,642,239
Protection to Person			
& Property	5,961,884	14,074,013	27,719,277
Hospital, Health,			
& Sanitation	13,710,390	41,504,960	96,746,322
Development &			
Conservation of			
Natural Resources	8,984,541	33,206,237	95,276,280
Highways	41,167,561	177,678,129	342,911,611
Old Age, Blind, & Aid			
Dependent Children	42,747,517	70,862,975	124,928,240
Unemployment			
Compensation	11,362,418	28,148,373	21,563,983
Higher Education	22,439,896	55,442,483	220,251,976
Other Education	4,214,620	11,083,657	44,115,637
Parks, Monuments,			
Memorials	148,647	1,154,279	4,978,310
Correctional			
Institutions	5,451,786	10,852,861	30,609,990
Aid to Cities	401,884	22,464,292	57,746,838
Aid to Counties	64,296,250	216,874,299	771,815,517
Education	(42,000,000)	(158,359,148)	(593,780,617)

Equally revealing concerning policy and the extent of government's increasing range of activities is the table of principal disbursements of state funds, with totals and principal purposes identified over these years. Here is the interesting revelation that the "welfare state" is as descriptive of the state of Florida as it is of the United States as a whole. Another measure of the same trend is to be found in the growing numbers of people employed by all levels of government in the state in the same years. In the federal service the numbers grew from 35,800 in 1949 to 53,200 in 1959 and 76,800 in 1969. During the same years state employees numbered 19,100, 36,400, and 72,200, while in local government the respective numbers of employees were 60,600, 118,600, and 245,300. Government at its various levels was among the fastest growing sectors in Fl;orida.

It should also be noted that the largest item in the aid to counties was for schools, specifically to maintain the equalization formula in the Minimum Foundation Program instituted in 1947 and increased in extent in 1970. The limit of the county tax for schools to ten mills without special authorization by voters implied that the state would take an even greater responsibility to maintain schools in the future.

From the perspective of the 1970s, politics promised to be far more lively in the future. Now that Florida had become the ninth largest state in the Union in population, the stakes were higher, and the partisan rivalry could be expected to produce a doubly exciting show. Four recent quadracentennials—commemorating the de Luna effort to settle Pensacola in 1559, the Ribault visit to the Saint Johns River in 1562, the establishment of Fort Caroline by the French near the mouth of the Saint Johns River in 1564, and the founding of Saint Augustine in 1565—reminded the country and the world of the antiquity of Florida's heritage. Floridians had announced their bid for a larger place in the world of the future.

29.

Stagflation, Education and Environmentalism

The 1970s might well be called the Askew Years, so indelibly was the stamp of Governor Reuben O'D. Askew's personality, character and leadership impressed upon the state and its government during his eight years in office. Two successive four-year terms were unprecedented. The constitution of 1968 strengthened the office of governor and also increased the importance of the legislature with annual sessions, permanent staffs for all major standing committees, its own budget, and salaries that were raised from $1,200 to $12,000 per year. The governor still did not have an appointed cabinet but shared executive and administrative functions and power with an elected cabinet. It was a decade of continued development marred by oil shortages that resulted in something new to Florida—inflation combined with recession, or what came to be known as "stagflation." At the same time the stream of Cuban refugees also continued.

Of the many topics of social and economic concern, several reflect developments in this decade and are worth exploring, especially when compared with the World War II era, when Florida had experienced a remarkable expansion in virtually every area. Money, banking, capital and credit considerations were closely related to the State's economic health and general growth. Cape Kennedy and the Florida Disney World enterprises represented the two principal economic aspirations of Florida in the 1970s. Cape Kennedy was an example of a sophisticated, highly skilled, and well-paid type of industrial development, while Disney World reflected the continuing search for a year-round tourist economy.

But nothing mirrored the related economic and cultural aspirations of Floridians better than the commitment, both public

and private, to education. The commitment, however, exceeded
the willingness to pay the price in 1970. Taxable wealth had not
increased as rapidly as had population and public needs, of which
education was a major one. Nor was Florida alone, in a time of
economic pessimism, in drawing back from financial commitments
implied in proclamations of interest in quality education and other
public activities.

A growing population and an expanding economy nearly always
require more money and credit for private business and public
improvements than its own financial institution and tax sources
can supply. Florida's government had at times come to the aid of
private enterprise in the effort to raise capital. Two early
experiences, the endorsement of "faith bonds" in the territorial period
and the mortgaging of the state's lands to underwrite railroad
building in the 1850s, did not turn out well. As a result, successive
state constitutions forbade the state to lend its credit to any
corporation or to sell state bonds, but this policy should not be
confused with the creation of state agencies such as a turnpike
authority that can sell bonds to be paid off from anticipated revenues.
The constitution of 1968 relaxed somewhat the authority of the state
to issue bonds, but previously Florida politicians had found other
ways to help railroad and canal transportation development by
granting subsidies of public land until nearly all of the land was
gone by early in the twentieth century. One consequence of the
limitation on bond issues was that the state came out of the booming
twenties without any bonded debt, but political subdivisions had
committed themselves for $600 million, on which they soon were
unable to pay either principal or interest. Long and painful refunding
finally cleared the record and resulted in the restoration of the credit
of county and municipal government.

As population and economic activities grew and per capita
income improved, savings increased more rapidly, but so did the
capital needs of private and public borrowers. Fortunately, the
reputation of Florida bonds in the markets of the country improved
in the 1950s at about the same time that adequate amounts of capital
became available.

The state's governmental and business leaders joined forces to
create the Industrial Development Corporation of Florida in 1961.
The Florida Development Commission organized a group of bankers,
savings and loan associations, and insurance companies for the
purpose of attracting new industries to the state and encouraging
expansion of existing businesses by providing venture type loans
not otherwise available. The 1970 legislature continued this policy
of encouraging new businesses by authorizing local governments to
sell bonds to construct buildings for lease to beginning enterprises,
reducing the original capital required for starting a business.

The state's expanding banking needs were met by a rapid
increase in the number of banks, both state and national, coupled
with new imaginative lending policies. From December 31, 1945, to
June 30, 1965, the total number of banking institutions increased

from 173 to 435. The number of national banks soared from 58 to 191. James J. Saxon, appointed by President John F. Kennedy to the position of Comptroller of Currency in 1960, favored branch banking to provide a higher ratio of banks to population, but when the small bankers had enough influence in the state legislature to prevent it, as they did in 1970, Saxon encouraged more single units, and twenty-four new charters were issued in 1964 alone.

The prohibition of branch banking hindered the concentration of bank ownership in Florida, but something of the same effect was achieved by the organization of bank holding companies. The practice began in Jacksonville with the Atlantic Bancorporation with six state and seven national banks, Barnett Banks of Florida with seven state and eleven national banks, and the Florida National Group of eight state and twenty national banks held by the Alfred I. DuPont estate. The movement grew phenomenally in the United States in 1969, and there was no sign at the end of the year that it was slackening in Florida. Of the state's 472 state and national banks, 164 or 34.7 percent were organized into thirteen bank holding companies that held 50.9 percent of all bank deposits and made 50.7 percent of all loans.

Savings and loan associations also played an important role in the development of business enterprise in Florida. While the number of commercial banks grew 150 percent and 90 percent over two decades from 1950 to 1970, the number of savings and loan associations increased 436 percent and 150 percent respectively.

This pattern of growth continued with little change. At the end of 1969 the number of national banks had grown to 209 with assets of $9,035,163,000 and loans totaling $4,319,151,000. The number of state banks had grown to 261 with assets of $2,352,504,000 and loans totaling $1,263,100,000. The number of federal savings and loan associations reached 136 with 177 branches, with total assets of $8,256,787,000 and loans of $7,209,015,000. Six state savings and loan associations at the same time reported assets of $143,671,174.

Three developments in banking and finance in the decade of the 1970s are worth noting. Branch banking within the limits of a county became legal in 1979, and combinations put together by means of holding companies were merged, thereby providing larger pools of capital to finance Florida's economic expansion. The State's "country bankers" successfully opposed any open, statewide entry into the banking field but the narrow defeat of such a measure in the closing hours of the 1979 legislative session indicated the potential for change. The second development was in the international field and directly affected Dade County. In June 1979, the fourteenth Edge Act bank opened its doors in Greater Miami. These were branches of national banks chartered in other states and set up solely to finance international trade. In addition, foreign investors, principally Latin Americans, were beginning to enter the Florida banking field by purchasing a controlling interest in existing institutions. As was expected foreign deposits became a more meaningful factor in the financial history of the community. The creation of a free trade zone at Port Everglades, where foreign goods could be landed duty-free for reshipment abroad, added to the commercial and financial attraction of the area. Finally, some foreign banks obtained permission to operate offices in Florida, as was the case in other financial centers of the country.

Closely related to the development of international banking was the growth of foreign investment in Florida. Private investors in the United Kingdom, West Germany, France and Japan made agriculture, industry and commerce as well as finance direct targets of their interest. The dollar's decline against their own currency in the rising inflation of the 1970s made these investments attractive. In other instances, they sought a safe place for their capital in the face of inflation at home. Purchase by foreigners, particularly of large tracts of farmland, was looked upon with mixed feelings in Florida and elsewhere, but an aggressive selling campaign abroad by Florida brokers helped to promote it.

If the banking industry was booming by the 1970s in Florida, the field of education was exploding—with students, with demands for new buildings and equipment and with the growing cost of administration. All this was complicated by controversy over desegregation. Education made seemingly impossible demands upon the planning and financial capabilities of the state and local governments. A strong commitment to education at all levels had been made but remained to be fully implemented. Floridians wanted a big share in the future, but they were late in preparing for it. Florida had emerged from World War II with its educational establishment in disrepair and facing accumulated demands for expansion and improvement. New building and maintenance had lagged even in the relatively slow growth of those years. An estimate of building needs in the sixty-seven counties in 1941-1942 placed the cost at $140 million. Little building could be done during the war, but school children began to register at an accelerated pace.

Aware of the pressing need, Governor Spessard L. Holland appointed a Citizens Committee on Education to study the needs and make recommendations to the legislature. Incoming Governor Millard F. Caldwell reappointed the committee, and the 1945 legislature gave its blessing in a joint resolution. A dozen subcommittees and fourteen consultants from federal agencies and some from other states participated. A 400-page report entitled *Education and the Future of Florida* guided the 1947 legislature in the enactment of what came to be known as the Minimum Foundation Program.

The report rated the state third from the bottom among the then forty-eight states in ratio of ability to pay to actual performance and called attention to great variations in educational opportunity from county to county and from district to district within counties. The larger number of children of school age was frequently found in communities less able to pay for schools. Under the new law the state assumed a large share of the cost of public schools and the coordination of their activities to achieve certain minimum standards. After assessing the minimal needs in each area and the capability of the citizens to pay, a state fund was used to bring the pupil-rich, tax-poor counties up to the minimum. District boards gave way to county boards, and all special tax districts were abolished, making the county a single tax district and giving all pupils in the county the same financial support.

Catching up was still a difficult process. In 1963-1964 the state ranked second in the southeast and thirty-fourth in the nation in educational expenditures, while it ranked first in the southeast in personal income and thirty-third in the nation. In the late sixties the state government seemed committed to taking over more and more and more of the cost of schools. The constitution of 1968 decreed that counties could not levy more than ten mills to support schools without a public referendum. At the same time, there appeared to be growing reluctance on the part of voters to approve bond issues to finance capital additions and improvements. Nor was the legislature in 1970 willing to raise the needed money by new taxes. Both the governor and a majority of the members of the legislature, reflecting the attitude of their constituents and the necessity in many cases to stand for election in November, were committed to no new taxes. School needs, aggravated by inflation, must again wait. How could the people of the state and their elected representatives reconcile the need for a quality school system to attract the kinds of people and businesses they sought with the promise to the same people that they would not be taxed too heavily?

Nowhere was the commitment to the future more evident than in plans for state-supported higher education, and here too the major developments came after mid-century as World War II had disrupted normal operations. In the last year of that conflict, 1945, enrollment at the University of Florida fell below one 1,000 but rose to 2,000 at Florida State College for Women. In the summer of 1946 the University of Florida received more than 8,000 applications for admission, at least a third more than its facilities could accommodate. The majority of them were ex-servicemen, some whose education had been interrupted and others to whom government assistance opened the way to college. The following year the legislature made the University of Florida and the Florida State College for Women coeducational and renamed the Tallahassee institution Florida State University. The Florida Agricultural and Mechanical College for Negroes became Florida A & M University in 1953. By the fall of 1965, the University of Florida was enrolling almost 16,000 students, Florida State more than 12,000 and A & M' 3,265.

The expansion of the state system of colleges and universities by adding new units was going on at the same time. The University of South Florida at Tampa began operating with only a freshman class in 1960, but by the fall of 1964 it counted almost 6,500 students in a four-year program of study. Florida Atlantic University opened its doors at Boca Raton in the fall of 1964 with 867 juniors and seniors, leaving the first two years to be provided by junior colleges in the populous communities along the southeast coast. In 1961 the legislature also created the Florida Institute for Continuing University Studies (FICUS) to administer entension courses throughout the state, and 6,633 students were enrolled in the fall of 1964. The plan to establish universities in all major population areas around the state resulted four years later in the abolition of FICUS and the turning over of its work to the universities. In the fall of 1967, The University of West Florida opened at Pensacola. In 1968 Florida Technological University opened at Orlando to specialize in space sciences and related research. Florida International University in Miami and the University of North Florida at Jacksonville opened in 1972.

To administer this increasingly complex system and to remove its control from politics, the legislature in 1963 provided for a Board of Regents appointed for staggered nine-year terms to replace the Board of Control, whose members had held four-year terms concurrent with that of the governor. When the legislature in 1965 created the office of chancellor of the state university system, the regents selected Dr. J. Broward Culpepper, who had been the executive secretary of the Board of Control and of the new Board of Regents.

The junior college movement in Florida, when it finally got going after a slow start, produced an even more dramatic story. The first publicly supported school, Palm Beach Junior College had opened in 1933. The expanded system was another outgrowth of the work of the Citizens Committee on Education in 1947. The committee proposed junior colleges in all population centers to be maintained jointly by the counties and the state, somewhat in the same manner as the elementary and secondary schools under the Minimum Foundation principle. The committee had assumed their association with high schools, and it was thought they might teach the thirteenth and fourteenth grades, with teachers required to have certification by the State Department of Education. They were sometimes called community colleges. Officially they were supposed to be multipurpose. They provided instruction for the first two college years for those with academic objectives. For others they offered technical and vocational training and for still others they performed a community service function through adult education programs.

In 1955 the legislature set up the Community College Council to develop long range plans and to establish priorities for the growth of the junior college system. The Council proposed that two years of college experience be provided within commuting distance of ninety-five percent of the state's inhabitants, a goal with which the legislature agreed. Meanwhile, although closely articulated with high school on one side and with senior colleges and universities on the other, junior colleges attained an identity of their own. In 1961 the Community College Council became the State Junior College Board, and Dr. James L. Wattenbarger became its first executive officer.

Thus, by the 1970s when Reuben Askew assumed the office of governor, education at various levels had become an issue in Florida politics. An area in which Governor Askew showed less interest and for which some of his critics condemned him was higher education. The issue was not quantity and availability, for, as was shown earlier, Florida had moved to increase educational opportunities, but quality. In 1972 virtually all of the units in the community college system and in the State University System (SUS) were in place. Expansion beyond this was by means of centers established in nearby populous areas and attached to the appropriate existing institution. What was still lacking was a clear sense of direction and a clear commitment to quality education.

Two basic problems were involved. First, political power was located in the populous urban areas where the newer upper level units of the SUS were located. All were ambitious to become full-blown universities and were unwilling to see only one or two become schools of exceptional quality. Nor were they willing to see any one institution receive the funding and the independence of politics requisite to a first-class regional university. This meant that practically all winners of merit scholarships and many of the best students went elsewhere for graduate and professional training. The 1979 legislature showed some awareness of these problems by appropriating $10 million for endowed professorships, $34 million for quality improvement programs and $18 million for laboratory and technological equipment independent of the student enrollment formula for making appropriations. The annual appropriation for the system had grown steadily, much of it accounted for by expansion and inflation. In 1972 the legislature provided $359,460,489 while for 1978-79 the sum was $638,745,418.

A brief survey of previous events is helpful to understanding the situation in the 1970s with respect to community colleges. The community colleges began as components of local school systems operated by county Boards of Public Instruction. In 1968 the legislature created local Boards of Trustees with corporate authority to operate the colleges within the framework of state law and regulations. In 1971 a law relieved the boards of financial responsibility. The cost was paid by the state with the help of limited federal grants and student fees, which increased over time.

State-level administration and coordination were provided by the Division of Community Colleges in the state Department of Education. These "junior colleges" provided general and academic courses of study parallel to the first and second years of study in the five units of the SUS that also accepted first and second-year students. They provided two-thirds of the first-time-in-college enrollment in state colleges. Since less than one-third of those entering went on to earn baccalaureate degrees, they tended to emphasize occupational programs, especially industrial technology, health occupations and services and service and distributive skills.

Junior colleges also served as centers for many kinds of community educational activity. By law, they were integral parts of the state system of higher education. They were directed to resist pressure to become four-year colleges. In short, they were to be neither mere extensions of the high school nor truncated versions of four year colleges. In 1969-70 they enrolled 69,069 students, and by 1976-77 the number had grown to 172,819. Appropriations grew from $93,130,185 in 1970-71 to $193,531,945 in 1978-79 and $222,400,000 for 1979-80. The ambitions of the four upper-division and graduate-school-only units to have their own freshman and sophomore classes threatened to reduce still further their purely academic programs.

In 1965, when there were five universities in operation and two more on the drawing board, a Board of Regents began to take over the planning and administration of the SUS. Up to that time each unit was relatively autonomous, dealing directly with the legislature and competing for programs and funding. The Regents were to preside over the orderly development of a coordinated system that was at least somewhat independent of politics. They faced numerous thorny questions. Should there be one or two showplaces of national eminence? Should there be a technological institution specializing in scientific study and research? Should there possibly be a tier of colleges between junior colleges and the SUS? Should each of the units somehow be free to reach its own natural limits as to programs and degrees? Should there be some alternative to funding on the basis of enrollment?

As events developed, policymakers recognized the early start and the lead established by the University of Florida, Florida State University and, to some extent, the University of South Florida, in graduate and professional study. No unit was to offer all programs in all disciplines at all levels. Rather, each was encouraged to develop excellence in areas peculiar to the region in which it was located and to its designated mission within the state. Originally, Florida Technological University was to emphasize science and technology related to activities at the Kennedy Space Center and the satellite industries in the region. It alone, of the five recently created university units, was to teach its own first and second-year students and to prepare them for the special subjects to be studied in the upper division. In 1978 it was renamed the University of Central Florida without the special emphasis, but it continued to offer a four-year undergraduate program. This also eliminated a name confusion with the Florida Institute of Technology, a private school at Melbourne.

Another principal objective was to control the proliferation of expensive programs that might result in duplication of effort and expenditure. There were four schools of engineering in the system but each had a different specialty. The shortage of medical education resulted in the creation of a medical school at the University of South Florida, the addition of the Florida Health Center at the University of Florida Medical School and preclinical medical studies at Florida State University and Florida A & M University, which led to admission to the University of Florida School of Medicine.

Continuing state support also encouraged the University of Miami School of Medicine to expand its program of study. Inter-university cooperation, at times involving several of the private universities, permitted a pooling of resources. By 1975, six of the nine SUS units plus one community college and two private universities were participating in the Florida Sea Grant Program. In that same year, the University of Florida, the University of Central Florida and the University of Miami began to operate the SUS Solar Center at an under-utilized university building complex near the Kennedy Space Center.

Private colleges and universities were given increased recognition for their contributions to the education of Florida students. The legislature authorized the Board of Regents to contract directly with private schools in certain instances. The state took over New College at Sarasota and operated it as an honors center attached to the University of South Florida. In 1979 the legislature authorized the payment of $750 a year on the tuition of *bona-fide* Florida students attending accredited private colleges in Florida.

The Association of Independent Colleges and Universities in Florida (ICUF) more or less replaced in importance the much older Florida Association of Colleges and Universities (FACU), which included both public and private members. In the fall of 1978 the seventeen colleges and universities in ICUF registered 29,684 undergraduates, of whom 9,177 were graduates of Florida high schools and 12,684 were legal residents of the state.

During these boom years in banking and education, Florida also became a major economic recipient of the efforts to launch rockets into outer space. The space exploration that resulted dramatically in moon landings in the late sixties began modestly with the establishment of a long range missile testing station that began to function in the summer of 1950. In 1958 a second major federal agency, the National Aeronautics and Space Administration (NASA), had begun operations at the Cape. This largely civilian agency was created for space operation of a peaceful nature, which included the launching of scientific, meteorological, and communications satellites. It took on vast new importance on August 25, 1961, when President John F. Kennedy announced an accelerated space exploration program for the decade aimed at landing a man on the moon and returning him to earth. Kennedy did not live to see this ambitious hope realized. He was the victim of an assassin's bullet on November 22, 1963. Six days later President Lyndon B. Johnson named the installation the John F. Kennedy Space Center and changed the name from Cape Canaveral to Cape Kennedy, which had been its name for a decade. In 1963 NASA acquired 88,000 acres on Merritt Island adjacent to the Cape to develop an industrial center for space exploration. More than fifty major buildings to accommodate manned lunar exploration went up as rapidly as adequate funding made them possible. Among them was the world's largest building, a fifty-two story vertical assembly building in which to ready rockets for blast-off.

The impact of national defense and space exploration activities at Cape Kennedy confronted a rapidly growing Florida with problems concentrated and multiplied many times over. Statistical data, some of them comparative, gives some indication of the magnitude of that impact. In 1940 Brevard County with a population of 16,142 people was primarily a rural area whose residents were engaged in the growing of cattle, citrus, and vegetables and in commercial fishing. Eau Gallie had 873 residents, Cocoa 3,098, Melbourne 2,622, and Titusville 2,220. The four grew by only a little less than four thousand to 1950, but by 1960 Eau Gallie had 12,300, Cocoa 12,244, Melbourne 11,982, and Titusville, the last to be affected, 6,410. Brevard County grew 371.1 percent from 1950 to 1960, while Florida grew 78.7 percent, the six-county area around the Cape 127.9 percent, and the United States 18.5 percent. The population of Brevard County almost doubled in the sixties, the greater part of it divided about equally among the four principal municipalities.

Development at the John F. Kennedy Space Center at Cape Canaveral (called Cape Kennedy from 1963 to 1973) reached its climax on July 16, 1969. Apollo 11 blasted off and two astronauts landed on the moon four days later. Thereafter, NASA activity at the Center declined, and the work force fell from a high of 23,500 to 16,235 in the mid-seventies. Space-oriented activity on a less dramatic scale continued. On May 14, 1973, the unmanned Skylab 1 was launched followed by the manned flight of Skylab 2 eleven days later. Development of the Space Shuttle project proceeded toward the goal of launching shuttles in the next decade. Much of the actual equipment used in the space voyages and facsimiles of other parts were gathered in a Space Museum and Visitors Center at the Cape. The whole complex continues to be a major tourist attraction.

This avalanche of new people required that new facilities and services be developed almost overnight. In 1950-1951 the county had 117 schoolrooms and an average daily attendance of 4,163 pupils. In 1963-1964, attendance had risen 851.8 percent to 39,873 in 1,473 rooms, and the school children of federally connected employees rose from a little over ten percent in 1950 to just under one-half of the total in 1963. In 1967-1968, the peak year of activity at the Cape, average daily attendance reached 57,090. Property assessments went up from $270 million in 1959 to $2.65 billion in 1969 but did not produce an adequate tax base for all of the long range capital improvements such as roads, buildings, water supply, and sewage disposal.

Brevard's population was unique in several respects. Although a large part of it was federally connected, it was civilian largely in the satellite and supporting industries and services. An estimate in 1962 stated that nearly 53 percent of all personal income in the region derived from civilian sources, the kinds of jobs that Florida liked to attract. The technicians, engineers, and scientists had special educational needs that resulted in the location of three educational institutions in the area.

Ironically, the Cape communities suffered from too many successes. Major construction activities had been completed. Immediate space probe aims had been achieved. Brevard County's population needed new worlds to conquer. NASA employment dropped from a peak of 24,292 in 1968 to about 18,500 by June 1970. The obvious weakness of Brevard County's development was its dependence upon a single source of employment as subject to fluctuations in financial support as space exploration. This also had always been one of the criticisms of the tourist industry—it was seasonal and it could dry up in the event of an economic recession. An amazingly successful conversion from space-oriented population and activity to more mundane life occurred in the cities of Brevard County that owed their mushrooming earlier growth to the needs of a burgeoning space industry. Whatever the final balance sheet may show, the Cape Kennedy development gave the Florida economy a tremendous boost. It brought innumerable people to visit the Cape and to witness launchings, and all of the world saw a little part of Florida when blasts-off to the moon were televised.

To put the proverbial frosting on the cake of Florida's economic success, there was the creation of Disney World near Orlando, which opened in 1971, an event not as dramatic as the moonshots from Cape Kennedy, but with equally far-reaching consequences. Located on a 27,000 acre site, with space for expansion, the attraction drew over eight million people the first year. Disney World was planned as a self-sufficient vacation community. Visitors found motel, hotel, and eating centers as well as entertainment. The proportions of the project and its long range plans were staggering. There was some opposition to the Disney World project by environmentalists, which was effective enough to yield assurance from Disney Enterprises that they would harmonize environmental values whenever possible.

Disney World was the great success story of the seventies. Its drawing power vastly exceeded expectations. Its continuing development of new features keeps people returning. It also spawned satellite amusement and recreational activities, not all of them successful. Disney World also stimulated activity in the so-called Great Eight in Florida's amusement park industry—companies that were large enough to expand their offerings and to advertise widely. These included, in addition to Disney World, Busch Gardens, Sea World, Cypress Gardens, Kennedy Space Center, Silver Springs, Miami Seaquarium and Marineland. There was some criticism and resentment of the autonomy enjoyed by the management of the huge Disney World enterprise and some protest from area residents over the crowded roads and the disturbed quiet of small communities, but, by and large, Disney World accomplished what was most hoped for—an amusement and educational center that would attract people year round and produce a stimulus to the tourist and entertainment industries throughout the state. The oil embargo in 1973 and the recession in 1974 and 1975 had emphasized again how important the Florida visitor was to the economy. The gasoline shortage and the economic slowdown in 1979 produced some concern, but Floridians were by nature optimistic about the future. Disney Enterprises continued to plan for the future with its Experimental Prototype Community of Tomorrow, EPCOT, which opened in the 1980s. EPCOT is a series of permanent exhibits by major industrial corporations and foreign countries unveiling the technology of the future.

Thus, when Askew was elected in 1970, he was the beneficiary of several decades of expansion in banking, education, population growth and state-wide overall economic development. The recently approved Constitution of 1968 provided a potential for effective leadership, but it was still necessary for the governor to exert it. It is a reasonable assumption that Reubin Askew would have been a more than ordinarily effective governor under the old constitution.

Blast off! Space exploration activities at Cape Canaveral

The most notable quality he demonstrated was the ability and readiness to take the issues to the voters when he could not otherwise achieve his objectives. This is a political quality reminiscent of the Populist-Progressive Era at the turn of the century, perhaps best illustrated by Napoleon Bonaparte Broward.

Askew was able to wield power as late as November 1978 in the general election when he was not a candidate and when an outgoing governor's influence ordinarily would have been negligible. He organized and led the opposition to a constitutional amendment to legalize casino gambling on the "Gold Coast," particularly Miami Beach, where the tourist industry was stagnating. He started his campaign of opposition at a time when there seemed an even chance that the proposal would be approved, and raised $830,000 in four weeks with which to finance the effort. The amendment was resoundingly defeated, losing in every county in Florida.

The direct appeal to voters began early in 1972 when Governor Askew faced the issue of a straw vote on busing school children to

Modern and modernistic designs like this monorail system characterize Walt Disney World

achieve racial balance in public school education. In February the legislature was in special session. It took up the busing issue and made provisions for putting it on the March 14 primary ballot. It asked the voters if they would support a constitutional amendment prohibiting forced busing. The governor prevailed upon the legislature to add another question asking the voters at the same time if they supported quality education for all. Askew raised some $32,000 to conduct a speaking tour, and he persuaded others to do likewise. He acknowledged his own opposition to busing but spoke of the overriding necessity to provide equality of opportunity in education. The antibusing question won three to one support and the governor's four to one.

Askew was the first governor since LeRoy Collins to do anything positive to improve race relations. Governors Farris Bryant, Haydon Burns, and Claude Kirk had allowed the desegregation of schools to

Governor Reuben O'D. Askew

be brought about, but they did little if anything to ease the process. When Askew took over he commissioned a survey which showed that blacks in state employment were in menial positions, for which 80% were earning wages below the poverty level. By an executive order Askew established an affirmative action plan, a step-by-step commitment to enact corrective measures pertaining to both the numbers and the status of black employees. The number of blacks in state employment doubled in the first year.

Governor Askew also used his appointing power to bring blacks into state government, thereby setting an example for all levels of government. He began by naming Athalie Range of Dade County as Secretary of the Department of Community Affairs, a post she later resigned to return to her Miami business. In 1978, by appointment of Governor Askew for an unexpired term, Jesse J. McCrary, Jr., became the first black Secretary of State in more than a century, but he declined to run for the full term. Askew appointed James J. Gardener of Fort Lauderdale to the Board of Regents of the State University System in 1972. His colleagues chose him as their chairman in 1978 and 1979. Askew appointed Joseph W. Hatchett to the state Supreme Court, the first black ever to sit on that bench, and Judge Hatchett was later appointed to the U.S. Fifth Circuit Court of Appeals. Another appointment was Dr. Johnny Jones by the Dade County (Miami) School Board to superintend the largest public school system in the state. Two other blacks from Dade County won election and reelection to the Florida House of Representatives, Joe Lang Kershaw in 1968 and Gwendolyn Sawyer Cherry from 1970 until her untimely death in 1979. Carrie P. Meek, another black, was elected to succeed Cherry. Others were elected to the House from Duval (Jacksonville) County.

There was, then, some measure of black participation in state and county government and administration. Professional and middle-class blacks made comparable progress in local government, education, and business, but they represented only the tip of the iceberg. The semiliterate or illiterate mass of blacks who were largely without skills were little better off, and young blacks had an unemployment rate double that of white youths. Blacks made up less than 15% of Florida's population, but the state ranked twelfth in the nation in the number of blacks. They did not exercise political influence equivalent to their numbers and had a generally poor voting record, in part because of their history. Too many of the middle-aged and older blacks lacked the formal requirements in education and experience for employment or political participation. Many had difficulty overcoming the psychological effects of generations of exclusion and non-participation, and their relatively small numbers made such efforts seem futile to some. Blacks growing up in this generation appeared to have a better chance in politics, but they faced such practices as gerrymandering to reduce their voting strength in some communities.

Another area of concern was the higher incarceration rate for blacks and their higher rate of execution for capital punishment.

Some of Askew's supporters found it hard to forgive him his part in the pardoning of Freddie Pitts and Wilbert Lee in 1972 when Askew sat as chairman of the Board for Executive Clemency, which is made up of the governor and his cabinet. Pitts and Lee had been found guilty in two trials for the murder of a service station operator in 1957; they were sentenced to death in 1963. The pardon was prompted by the confession of another convict to the killing. The 1979 legislature balked at the request to appropriate $100,000 for each man in compensation for twelve years spent in prison.

Florida was the first state to reestablish capital punishment. It did so by rewriting the law to meet the objections of the U.S. Supreme Court in 1971 that the statutes as then enacted and enforced constituted cruel and unjust punishment. The Court approved the new law in 1976, and the first convict in the nation to die against his will since 1967 occurred when John Spenkelink was executed in Florida on May 25, 1979. There were at the time, 131 convicts waiting on Florida's death row, the largest number in any state. Apparently a majority of Floridians felt that the death penalty was a justifiable punishment for and deterrent to such crimes as murder.

Askew's will prevailed in a referendum on a proposal to levy a tax on the income of corporations doing business in Florida—by 70% of the votes cast. The clinching argument probably was the fact that some national companies were doing business in Florida without paying any taxes at all. A somewhat unrealistic debate over who would really pay the tax, the manufacturer or the consumer, was an interesting part of the campaign. More persuasive was the argument that mail order houses charged the same for merchandise in neighboring Georgia, where they paid the tax, as in Florida where they did not.

The corporate income tax was the only major change in the tax structure in the decade. Rates changed relatively little. The combination of growing population, rising dollar volume of business, and increasing inflation provided steadily rising revenue for steadily rising state expenditures. Sales and use taxes, many paid by tourists and other visitors, continued to be the chief sources of state revenue. In 1977-78 sales and use taxes yielded $1,644,746,777, almost 27% of the total. The gasoline tax came next with $376,282,077, then the beverage tax and licenses of $258,497,238, the cigarette tax of $232,479,883, and motor vehicle taxes of $131,020,915. The corporate income tax yielded $256,189,174 or 4.2% of the total. Federal aid, some of it required to be matched wholly or in part by state appropriations, amounted to $1,335,494,575 or almost 22%.

The first use of the initiative process in the new constitution occurred in 1976 when, led by the governor, almost 220,000 voters signed petitions to put a full financial disclosure referendum on the ballot after the legislature failed to enact a meaningful law. Florida voters approved the "Sunshine Amendment."

Askew failed in 1978 to achieve constitutional revision that among other things, might have made the cabinet appointed rather than elected. The provision for revision that bypassed the state legislature as written into the constitution read: "Within thirty days after the adjournment of the regular session of the legislature convened in the tenth year following that in which this constitution is adopted, and each twentieth year thereafter there shall be established a Constitution Revision Commission. . . ." In 1977, jumping the gun as it were, Governor Askew appointed fifteen members of the commission, which was headed by a former member of the House of Representatives from Dade County, Talbot "Sandy" D'Alemberte, Senate President Lew Brantley named nine, House Speaker Donald Tucker another nine, and Chief Justice Ben Overton of the Florida Supreme Court three. Attorney General Robert Shevin was an ex-officio member.

The first of thirteen public hearings began in July. The commission submitted its report in May, 1978. Of the one hundred changes proposed, only Number 9, which provided for the legalization of casino gambling on the "Gold Coast," came by way of petition. Fifty of the proposed changes, which were largely administrative and procedural, were lumped together in Number 1. The others, more controversial, were put together in seven parts. Number 2, sometimes called "Little ERA," would have added sex to the anti-discrimination article. Number 3 provided for single member state legislative districts and an appointed commission to draw congressional and legislative districts each ten years. Number 4 provided for the appointment of cabinet members. Number 5 made the Public Service Commission seats appointed positions, but the legislature accomplished this by statute. Number 8 made the State Board of Education a body of appointed members and gave the Board of Regents constitutional independence to operate the State University System. In spite of a mighty effort to publicize the changes, every proposal was voted down. The stronger votes against the concept of an appointed cabinet, State School Board, and Public Service Commission showed clear preference for elected officials.

It has been suggested that Governor Askew gave up his effort to secure constitutional changes in order to campaign against the casino gambling proposal. This would be completely in character in light of his concept of what Florida should represent. In the "Watergate decade" some abuses in offices did appear, but the governor gave to state government a reputation for integrity that was refreshing.

The major political scandals at state level included the charge that Lieutenant Governor Tom Adams was using state equipment and employees on his farm. Three cabinet members were forced out of office; Education Commissioner Floyd Christian, Comptroller Fred O. Dickinson, and Treasurer Thomas O'Malley. Two Florida Supreme Court Justices, David L. McCain and Hal P. Dekle, resigned under threat of impeachment for improper conduct in office.

Askew won recognition for himself and Florida beyond the state level. He served as chairman of the Southern Governors Conference, the Democratic Governors Conference, the National Governors Conference, and the Education Commission of the States. In 1976 he delivered the Keynote Address at the Democratic National Convention and was mentioned prominently both in 1972 and 1976 as a vice-presidential possibility. At the end of his term of office as governor he appeared to have retired from public service when he became a member of a prominent law firm in Miami, where he established a home. That he was prepared to return to government service, however, became apparent in the summer of 1979 when he was named to head a special commission on the problem of illegal aliens in the United States. In early August President Carter named him to replace Robert Strauss as his special trade representative, a cabinet-level post for which his activity in that area as governor of Florida gave him some experience and insight.

Despite all these areas of controversy and political involvement, promoting Florida's development remained the major concern of Florida business and government. But voices were heard in increasing numbers in favor of limiting growth in the interest of a less crowded environment by those who already called Florida home.

To most Floridians, however, the search for new capital, new businesses, new jobs, a larger tax base, and more residents added up to growing property values and general well-being. Before the 1974-1975 recession there may have been some slackening of the pressure for new businesses, but the economic downturn led to a demand for an immediate renewal of effort. Governor Askew headed some trade missions. Incoming Governor Graham promised to push the search and announced that this would be a principal assignment of Lieutenant Governor Wayne Mixson, a respected farmer and businessman. The 1979 legislature added its input to the bid for new business by rewriting the state's Workers Compensation Law with an immediate 15% premium reduction and basing compensation on wages lost rather than on claims by doctors, lawyers, and juries as to the extent of loss. Another law established a one-stop permit system for all state-related permits required for an industry to locate in the state, thus preventing interminable delays. The lawmakers also provided a tax break of $107.4 million for industry as part of the one-year millage rollback of local school district ad valorem taxes.

This is not to suggest that other matters did not also have high priority. Significantly, when members of the State Chamber of Commerce were asked late in 1978 what issues the organization should emphasize, inflation and growing size and cost of state government ranked first and second. Economic development came in a close third, perhaps the first time it did not rank first. In June 1979, the Greater Miami Chamber of Commerce asked the same questions at a goals conference—305 members voted for improved quality of education and only 161 voted for more attention to promotion of economic growth. Without better education, it was argued, industry of the sort they sought could not be attracted nor could it be staffed.

This was but part of an increasing debate over what kind of growth should be promoted and what kinds of inducements could legitimately be offered. In his final message to the Florida Legislature in 1978, Governor Askew stated his position, a view held by an increasing number of Floridians. He urged that Florida be sold, not given away, that the tax base not be eroded, and that the natural environment not be sacrificed.

There was strong support for stable industry that paid high wages and employed many administrative and supervisory persons. These would be people concerned about community affairs, people who were willing and able to pay their share of the cost. The tax level in the state was relatively low and was not an issue. The state government had been urged from time to time to use the SUS to encourage industrial development as had been done in North Carolina and Georgia. In 1978 the legislature authorized the development throughout the state of Research and Development Parks in association with units of the SUS. Each locality was free to write its own charter to create a research center for the study of technology-based industry. As much activity as business and industry proved willing to support would be initiated.

Other inducements urged upon newcomers were climate, adequate water supply, international banking and trade zones, direct air routes to Europe, limited unionization of labor, and the "Right to Work" law. One of the strongest arguments against stringent environmental and pollution regulations was the possibility of discouraging industrial development. On the other hand, the Florida environment, its climate, water, air, recreational facilities, and wild life attracted many visitors and permanent residents. The commitment to protect and enhance the natural environment was clearly made. Tax breaks were likely to be given to existing industries to clean up their industrial processes and to eliminate pollution of water, air, and land. The tax on corporate profits was a clear indication that business was to pay its share of the cost of government but was not meant to suggest that Florida was becoming antibusiness.

The most dramatic turnaround in Florida government in the 1970s was the continuing extension of control over natural resources and the protection of the environment from misuse, pollution and destruction. It involved comprehensive water controls to insure supply and quality as well as to prevent flooding, purchase by the state of extensive acreage where the natural environment was endangered, and regulation of land use by planning. This was not intended as an effort to stop growth, but as a long-range measure to assure continuing orderly development for those already here and those to come.

The early history of drainage and water control was related earlier (see Chapter 22). What remained in the 1970s was to extend those principles to the entire state. The Water Resources Act made all waters of the state subject to regulation. It gave the Department of Natural Resources (DNR) the power and the responsibility to accomplish "the conservation, protection, management and control of the waters of the state." The state was now organized into six

Water Management Districts (WMDs) that became operational on January 1, 1977. The DNR was instructed to formulate an all-purpose state water-use plan. This was to be accomplished in consultation with concerned federal, state, and local agencies and the governing board of the WMDs. While the Act did not eliminate the use of the Army Corps of Engineers in the design and construction of water control projects for which Congress was the source of authority and funding, it did increase the role of the state in the initiation of projects and provided for a set of procedures that ultimately could amount to a virtual veto over a given project.

Before any project for which federal funding was sought or involved was approved, environmental impact studies had to be submitted that assessed the effect upon the environment measured against the projected benefits. All concerned state agencies then reviewed these reports while the Council on Environmental Quality made the final decision. Contrast this with the 1940s when the Corps of Engineers was given a free hand to achieve drainage at all costs and was allowed to do its own planning.

The most massive land purchases by the National Park Service were in the Big Cypress Swamp area, and the goal of the expenditure was to protect the watershed that supplies the water for the southeast coast and for the Everglades National Park. The state's share of the $156,000,000 to acquire 570,000 acres of the swamp was forty million dollars. Some 48,000 acres were publicly owned, and the remainder was acquired from thousands of private owners by negotiation and condemnation.

The acquisition of this area was accomplished with a minimum of controversy, but that was not true with respect to the expenditure of $200,000,000 by the DNR to acquire environmentally endangered land such as fragile marshes and beaches, nor with respect to the additional $40 million spent for other park and recreation areas. There were allegations of prices paid being too high, questionable appraisal practices and even of kickbacks. The Director of the DNR was suspended and later replaced. This might well have killed the program, but the 1970 legislature authorized the use of the six million dollars remaining in the fund, to be used over the next two years, and twenty million a year thereafter to be paid out of the severance tax on minerals. Also, a strict set of rules now governed the procedure of acquisition assigned to a new Division of Public Lands. As a result of the two types of land acquisition during the eight years of Askew's administration, the number of state parks grew from 63 with 87,751 acres to 87 with 132,000 acres, plus 23,580 acres added to 26 existing parks for a total state parks area of 155,585 acres. Also acquired were 22 tracts of environmentally endangered lands of 362,200 acres.

The case of the Florida Keys and Green Swamp is illustrative of this increase in government ownership of environmentally affected land. When the Supreme Court in 1978 threw out a law allowing the cabinet to designate environmentally endangered areas, specifically the Florida Keys and Green Swamp, as areas of critical state concern, stating that only the legislature had such power, a hastily called special session of the legislature placed them in a protected category until the 1979 session could act. Both areas were continued as areas of critical concern, but the Keys were left to management by Monroe County after its land-use policy was approved. Green Swamp was an area of 870 square miles of sandhills, forests, rivers, and lakes between Tampa and Orlando. It had the highest groundwater level in the Florida peninsula, and served as a recharge area for much of the state's water supply in the Florida Aquifer. Under the law, owners could alter sixty percent of the upland area, twenty-five percent of the pine flatwoods. and only ten percent of thc wetlands. Agricultural lands were excepted.

The best example of massive environmental pollution and what could be done to correct it was the phosphate industry. Worth two billion dollars a year, it was Florida's largest business, providing some 60,000 jobs. It was a business still largely centered in a small area in the middle of a resort state, only ten miles from Cypress Gardens and less than fifty miles from Disney World and all of its satellite developments. It had the usual problem of strip mining, which two decades before had been polluting water, soil, and air with gases and solids in solution that destroyed plant and animal life. The landscape was left scarred with pits and heaps of soil that were pushed aside in recovering the phosphate. But aftcr a sustained effort, by the mid-1970s the rivers in the area had been cleaned up, noxious gases recovered, topsoil replaced and some of the pits and hills leveled to be used for agriculture, grazing and even for homebuilding.

A final item of environmental concern was the Cross State Barge Canal, authorized in 1942 and partly constructed prior to 1971 when President Richard Nixon stopped work on it. The Canal was finally prepared for deauthorization in June 1979 as the state legislature voted to return $23 million to six counties along the route to compensate for the loss of tax revenues. They further elected to sell some of the land set aside for the canal zone to the national government, to use some of it for recreation and to re-sell some of it to the more than 300 previous owners. This all hinged upon the United States Congress deauthorizing the project, a move that was prevented in 1978 when two north Florida congressmen, William Chappell of Orlando and Charles E. Bennett of Jacksonville, objected, but, through the efforts of environmentalists, work on the Canal finally was stopped

Despite these efforts at conservation and environmentalism, the Arab oil embargo in 1973 reminded Floridians how vulnerable they were to fuel shortages. Travel and transportation are more than commonly essential to keep the economy moving. Florida has no coal, almost no waterpower, little oil, and no major refining facility for imported oil. Since 1970, when oil was first struck in the Jay Field, production averaged 100,000 barrels a day. In 1977, total yearly crude oil production was 46.6 million barrels, 89% of it in the northwest Florida fields. It was not surprising that nuclear energy became a favored source. In 1972 and 1973, the Florida Power and Light Company activated two nuclear generators at Turkey Point, eighteen miles below Miami on Biscayne Bay, and one in 1976 at Hutchinson Island, where a second generator also became operational in 1983. In 1977, the Florida Power Corporation put a unit into production at Crystal River. The accident at Three Mile Island Reactor near Harrisburg, Pennsylvania, in 1979 produced grave concern and redoubled safety precautions in Florida, but there was no serious disposition to abandon nuclear sources of power. The 1979 legislature gave tentative approval to the construction of a 1,500 mile coal slurry (a mixture of powdered coal and water) pipeline to Kentucky and Ohio coal fields to supply utility companies in Georgia and Florida. The large number of hours of sunshine throughout the year made Florida a likely place for the development of solar energy.

In the face of these increasing energy needs, population growth continued as a central theme in Florida's history. It increased 26.5%, from 6,791,000 in 1970 to an estimated 8,594,000 at the end of 1978. Only the thinly populated and relatively undeveloped states of Nevada, Alaska, and Wyoming were growing faster. Nearly 90% of the increase was from migration. A significant characteristic of the newcomers was the continuing increase in the proportion of older people among them. By 1980, those over sixty had reached one-fourth of the total, in contrast to one-tenth in the rest of the nation. New arrivals to Florida were moving into the gulf coast counties in greatest numbers. In Charlotte County, they had made up 10.8% in 1950, by the late 1970s they accounted for just over half the total, and in Sarasota, Manatee and Pasco counties they were just over 40%. The "senior citizens" were welcome residents, and although they required more emphasis on health care and recreation, they brought a large volume of social security and other retirement incomes. They tended to be political and social conservatives. Their political strength was considerable, and they have had a high level of voter turnout.

By all odds the most significant new group in the population was the more than one half million persons of Cuban origin who lived mostly in Dade County. Mostly refugees from the Castro regime in Cuba, they arrived in the last twenty-five years. In 1980 they made up a majority of the residents of the central city of Miami and of Hialeah. The newcomers moved rapidly into the economic life of the community, and they were credited with the revitalization of the inner city of Miami. They established numerous small businesses and professional associations, and together with others of Latin American origin began to move into such fields as banking and international trade. Many of the older Cubans did not attempt to qualify to vote. Some still dreamed of the possibility of returning to the Cuba they once knew. Many others seized upon the relaxation of travel restrictions to Cuba in the late 1970s to revisit their homeland and the relatives they left behind when they fled the country.

By 1979 less than 100,000 had qualified to vote. In 1976, in response to a special effort to induce them in the bicentennial year of the United States to become citizens eligible to vote, 26,245 took the oath of allegiance. Their children were growing up with bilingual education and were quickly entering into the political life of the community. In 1973 Dade County began to adopt bilingualism officially in a series of ordinances. By 1979, three of the five members of the Miami City Commission were Latin, one a Puerto Rican. Key West and Tampa absorbed large numbers of Cuban and other Spanish speaking people late in the last century, and although they gave a special flavor to the life of the communities they did not have the impact that the Cuban refugees have had upon Greater Miami.

This was a remarkable relocation of so many people in so short a time in so restricted an area. It was possible because the newcomers were largely from Cuba's professional and middle classes. These Cubans were better educated, more skilled and experienced, and more familiar with business methods and practices in this country than other immigrants. They had had more previous contact with Florida than had other Latin American nationals. The sharpest contrast in the late 1970s was with the Haitian refugees, who came mostly illegally and were almost completely unprepared to cope with the conditions they found in South Florida. The Cubans had some language and cultural barriers to overcome but no significant economic or political differences of an ideological nature and no racial bias to face. Although this transplanting was an overall success, it was not accomplished without stresses and strains. There were sharp differences and strong feelings among the refugees who came through such traumatic changes. They differ among themselves on such issues as the possibility of return to Cuba, of armed intervention, of United States recognition of Castro's government, of the possibility of ending the economic blockade, of the willingness of some of their numbers to negotiate with Castro for the release of family members and political prisoners and even over the lifting of some travel restrictions between Cuba and the United States. In 1974 there was a wave of violence among the exiles, with some bombings and deaths. Bombings, threats and intimidation, unfortunately, became a part of the Cuban political culture in south Florida.

Meanwhile, the saga of Florida's tiny Indian population continued. In the 1970 Census more than 6,000 Florida residents claimed descent from 34 American Indian tribes. The United States, however, recognized only the Miccosukee and Seminole tribes in Florida. They numbered less than 2,000, but like the Cuban population, American Indians were highly visible in the 1970s and showed little sign of losing their identity. They also showed clear indications of becoming self-governing and nearly self-sufficient economically. The Indians lived in approximately equal numbers on four reservations, with smaller groups in and west of Miami, near Immokalee, and in Fort Pierce. The largest reservations were the 70,000 acre Big Cypress Reservation mostly in Hendry County, and the 36,000-acre Brighton Reservation three miles northwest of Lake Okeechobee. They had substantial herds of cattle on improved pastures, and they rented some acreage to farmers and growers. The wealthiest was the Seminole's 480-acre Hollywood Reservation, across U.S. Highway 441 from the city of Hollywood in Broward County. All of the highway frontage was on long lease to businesses, and the rents provided funds for extensive tribal activities. The tribe had also begun to discover the possible profits from smoke shops and bingo games.

The Miccosukee lived on a small reservation on the northern rim of the Everglades National Park along the Tamiami Trail thirty-five miles west of Miami. Traditionally more independent and aggressive than their Seminole cousins with whom they were much intermixed, they led the opposition to removal from Florida in the last century. In 1962, they received recognition as a tribe. Tribal beliefs, religion and language were an integral part of their culture,

Seminole Indians in a dugout canoe on the undeveloped Miami River in 1912—a reminder of how quickly changes have occurred in the 20th century .

which was supplemented by education in Dade County public schools. In 1957, the United States Department of Interior issued a charter under which the Seminoles elected officers and set up a governing council to represent all of the Indians in the state. It may have been this move that led the Miccosukees to seek and to receive approval to secede and organize themselves as a separate tribe.

The 100,000-acre state reservation in western Broward County originally had no Indian residents. The upper 28,000 acres, including five sections in Palm Beach County, were placed under federal trust to become part of the adjoining Big Cypress Reservation. Another 16,000 acres were used by the South Florida Water Management District as a flowage easement. The remainder to the south was usable only for hunting and fishing, but since Alligator Alley bisected it, there was the possibility of future commercial development along the highway.

Under an act of Congress in 1950, which permitted Indian tribes to sue the U.S. government for treaty violations, the Seminoles of Florida and Oklahoma entered claims under the treaties made at Fort Moultrie in 1823 and Paynes Landing in 1832. A first award of $12.2 million was rejected as inadequate. The court ordered a rehearing of the basis of determining compensation, and the amount was raised to $16 million. Three-fourths of this compensation was allotted to the Seminoles in Oklahoma, who constitute about that proportion of the total number, but the Florida Seminoles argued that this was unfair because those in Oklahoma have received compensation in other ways that those in Florida did not share. Ultimately, in 1976 the two groups agreed to share a settlement of $16 million. Thus, by the late 1970s, the Indian tribes had moved very close to what the historian Harry Kersey has termed "the assumption of sovereignty."[1]

One final area of civil rights merits discussion. In the 1970s equal rights for women in Florida's population continued to be denied formal recognition in legislation. In May 1979 the Florida Senate again rejected ratification of the Equal Rights Amendment to the United States Constitution although the House of Representatives had approved it. This was done by the Senate in the face of active support by Governor Graham and President Jimmy Carter and in the face of allegations that national conventions, particularly in areas like education and labor, would not select sites for conventions in states that continued to so discriminate against women. Equal rights for the sexes might have become a reality in the state constitution but, like all other proposals of the Constitutional Revision Commission in 1978, it was rejected by the voters. It may safely be hazarded that enough Florida women voters were indifferent, if not opposed to ERA, to overcome the votes of men in the electorate who favored it. Meanwhile, women continued to move up the ladder in education, business, politics and the professions, but they remained far short of one-to-one equality with men in employment and compensation. As a consequence of new interest in the status of women, many communities "discovered" and gave somewhat belated recognition to women who had made substantial contributions in their own spheres of activity as well as to the community as a whole.

The ninth year of the decade opened with the inauguration of a new governor, D. Robert "Bob" Graham. His father, Ernest R. Graham, came to Miami in the early twenties to grow cane and to refine sugar for the Pennsylvania Sugar Company. The venture, as it turned out, was badly located. The Lake Okeechobee region proved more suitable for cane growing. Graham remained in Dade County to establish a dairy farm and to raise beef cattle on what were to have been cane fields. He was a state senator in the sessions of 1937-1943 and a member of the State Road Board from 1933 to 1935. In 1944 he ran a strong third in the race for the Democratic nomination for governor.

Born in 1936, Robert Graham began early to win distinction in school. He became president of his Miami Senior High School student body and as an undergraduate at the University of Florida was elected to Phi Beta Kappa and to the Blue Key honorary societies and was Chancellor of the Honor Court. In 1959, he married Adele Khoury of Miami Shores, also a student. He then matriculated in the Harvard Law School where he received his degree in 1962. The young Grahams returned to Dade County where Bob joined his brother, William, to develop the new town of Miami Lakes as well as to continue their interest in cattle. Bob was elected to the Florida House of Representatives in 1966 and 1968, and to the Florida Senate in 1970 and 1974.

In the Senate he became known for his concern with educational and environmental issues. In 1978, with ten years of political experience behind him, Graham became one of seven candidates for the Democratic nomination for governor. Robert L. Shevin, also of Dade County and eight years Florida's attorney general, was the most visible candidate and long an unannounced contender for the governorship. Graham lacked visibility and name recognition, but in a campaign reminiscent of U.S. Senate candidate Lawton Chiles, who in 1970 had walked from one end of the state to another, he took his cause directly to the voters. In what he called his 100 Workdays he spent one day at a job in selected places and occupations. The campaign attracted increasing media attention, and Graham published a small volume, *Workdays, Finding Florida on the Job*, that described part of the experience. He revealed a common touch that brought him the recognition he sought and demonstrated a sensitivity to the needs and aspirations of the average Floridian that no other politician in the gubernatorial race had exhibited.

In the first primary Graham ran second in a field of seven, with 261,972 votes to Shevin's 364,732. His running mate, Wayne Mixson of Marianna, described as "a rural expert on cities," the legislature's only full-time farmer and for seven years chairman of the House Agriculture Committee, proved very helpful with a large segment of the voters. In the second primary Graham and Mixson received 482,535 votes to 418,636 for Shevin and Jim Glisson. Democratic political campaigns at the statewide level were little changed. The party lacked structure, as the number of candidates indicated, and personalities, rather than issues, dominated the rival campaigns. In spite of bitter exchanges in the runoff, Shevin supported Graham in the general election in the contest with Republican Jack Eckerd and his running mate, Paula Hawkins, who had become well known as an outspoken member of the Public Service Commission.

The differences between the candidates were considerable. Eckerd, as he had done eight years earlier, urged support on the grounds that he would run the state like a business, such as the highly successful drug store chain he organized and operated. This might promise efficient administration, but it left some doubt where he stood on the issues. Graham spoke out more freely on the issues. He argued for a comprehensive review of taxes and spending, and for limiting the number of state employees; he promised active support for the search for new business to diversify the state's economy, and he urged that the state pay more of the cost of public schools and so relieve property owners of that burden. He promised to fund tax relief with a half-billion dollar surplus in the state treasury. Graham won over Eckerd by 1,406,580 to 1,123,888 votes. This demonstrated again how difficult it was for a Republican to win a statewide political conquest in Florida unless, as in 1966, the nominee of the Democrats was unacceptable to one wing of the party.

In 1978 the political struggle for the governorship was full of "firsts." There had never been an elected governor from south of Fort Pierce, but two Democrats from Dade County wound up in a runoff for the nomination. The winner and the loser in the general election each received more than a million votes. The cost of the campaigns was by far the largest ever—a total of more than ten million dollars. A state effort to limit campaign spending had been invalidated by the courts in 1976. Both finalists were millionaires, and the number of millionaires in both houses of the legislature also began to make headlines.

Graham supported the Workers Compensation law change and other aids to attract business to Florida. He asked for and received a moratorium on taxes and a commission to study the issue and prepare for action in 1980. Another major issue passed along to 1980 was the rewriting of the statutes governing higher education, also the subject for a commission study.

Florida approached the 1980s with a certain ambivalence. In spite of some effort to diversify the economy, continued reliance upon tourism made Florida vulnerable to recession and the growing cost and difficulty of travel. The experience with the petroleum shortage in 1973 and with recession in 1974 and 1975 were sobering events. Floridians, as well as the nation as a whole, were unhappy about the inflationary rise of prices during the decade. Concern remained about growth, the environment and education. The leftist Sandinista revolution in Nicaragua in 1979 threatened to bring a new wave of immigrants to the state. What was certain was that the next decade would offer a series of new challenges to Floridians.

30.

Rafters, Riots, Graham "Crackers" and Republicans

The 1980s opened with two traumatic events, both illustrative of the social tensions of the 1980s. The first was a large exodus of Cubans, over 125,000, from the port of Mariel, including some criminals, as Fidel Castro allowed a new immigration to Florida's shores, the second, race riots in Miami. The triumph of Ronald Reagan, who carried Florida in the presidential election, along with the election to the United States Senate of Paula Hawkins, was indicative of growing Republican Party strength in the state, culminating in the election of Republican Bob Martinez as Governor in 1986. That same year, 1986, saw the worst disaster of America's exploration of space when the spacecraft Challenger exploded shortly after liftoff from Cape Canaveral.

In the early years of the decade, Governor Bob Graham, re-elected in 1982, continued his quest to improve the educational system, expanded the state's environmental efforts and developed a statewide program of growth management. He also offered plans for Florida to become more involved in both international business and education.

The last part of the decade saw the failure of a number of savings and loan banks both nationally and in Florida, reminiscent of the bank failures of the 1920s. While Florida continued its spectacular population growth, from 9,746,342 at the beginning of the decade, to 12,937,926 in 1990, that growth was exceeded by increases in the size and cost of both local and state governments. There was a certain paradoxical irony to a decade in which politicians were elected with a promise to cut back on the size of government, while at all levels governments continued to increase taxes and pass legislation, such as the Growth Management Act of 1985, which greatly expanded governmental powers.

Ironically, what became known as the Mariel boatlift of 1980 developed out of a brief "opening" in the late 1970s between the Cuban government and that of the United States.[1] The administration of President Jimmy Carter, much to the chagrin of many Cuban exiles in Miami, sought to promote a détente with Fidel Castro.

In Miami, one of the Cubans seeking what came to be known as "the Dialogue," was a Cuban banker, Bernardo Benes, who traveled to Havana as a part of initiating intergovernmental contacts between the two countries. On the Cuban side, Castro spoke of a dialogue that would result in the release of 3,000 political dissidents.

For a short time, into early 1980, it was even possible for Cubans to return to their homeland to visit relatives. What ended these efforts for most of the rest of the decade was an apparently spontaneous demonstration at the Peruvian Embassy in the Miramar section of Havana. As early as May of 1979, when the initiatives of "the Dialogue" were underway, some Cubans had begun to smuggle themselves into the embassies of several Latin American nations in Havana, especially those of Venezuela and Peru. By March of 1980, over thirty Cubans had crashed vehicles through the gates of these embassies and taken refuge inside, much to the embarrassment of the Cuban government. At the same time, many younger Cubans were taking advantage of the black market opportunities of the renewed travel to protest the regime by wearing American designer clothes or "hippy" outfits.

On March 28, six dissidents stole a bus and crashed through one of the gates of the Peruvian embassy. In the ensuing crossfire by police stationed at the three entrances, a guard was killed. The new Peruvian ambassador refused to turn over the dissidents and Castro, in retaliation, removed the guards while ordering in steamrollers to flatten the gates and barricades.

As news of these events spread throughout Havana, thousands of Cubans began to gather at the embassy. Within two days, almost 11,000 Cubans had taken refuge there. The terrible sanitary conditions of such crowded humanity drew international attention and eventually the Cuban government consented to an airlift through which 7,500 people were airlifted to Costa Rica. Castro halted this approach, after four days, as the government began to organize a counter protest against the refugees calling them tools of American imperialism and physically attacking a group of 700 Cubans hoping for visas at the U.S. Interest Section office.

In the meantime, taking advantage of the chaotic conditions, some adventurous exiles in Miami had taken boats to Cuba in an attempt to rescue relatives, much like the effort at Camarioca in 1965. In the face of these developments, Castro on April 20, announced that all those who wished to leave Cuba would be allowed to do so. He urged these people to call their relatives to come pick them up, designating the port of Mariel, twenty miles west of Havana as the embarkation point for the exodus.

Thus began the boatlift of thousands of Cubans from Mariel to south Florida. As the émigrés gathered, food supplies were soon exhausted. The Cuban government sold ham sandwiches for ten dollars and a gallon of gasoline for fifteen dollars as a means of gaining American currency from those arriving from Miami. Those with boats were forced to take whichever émigrés the Cuban gov-

The Mariel Boatlift

ernment pressed upon them, relatives or not. Many boats were so
overloaded they encountered problems once at sea and had to be
rescued by the U.S. Coast Guard. By the end of May, the Coast
Guard had recorded 989 rescue operations, coming to the aid of thousands of refugees. Despite this heroic effort, twenty-five people died!

Meanwhile, Castro used the exodus to rid his regime not only of
political dissidents, but also of others ranging from psychotic mental patients to criminals released from jails and placed aboard the
boats bound for Florida. Eventually, more than 125,000 Cubans from
all walks of life would be among those making the voyage across
the Straits of Florida.

The arrival of this massive influx of refugees placed an enormous burden on the economy and existing refugee facilities and
services in south Florida. The first arrivals were processed in Key

West, and then in Tamiami Park and Opa-Locka, followed by two more centers on Krome Avenue in southwestern Dade County, where a growing number of Haitians were also being taken. Eventually, refugees were staying at the Orange Bowl, underneath a downtown Miami I-95 overpass, and even in some dog kennels.

By May 6, the federal government had declared a state of emergency and allocated ten million dollars in relief funds. Eglin Air Force Base in Florida; Fort Chaffee, Arkansas; Fort Indiantown Gap, Pennsylvania and Fort McCoy, Wisconsin, were opened as camps to house the refugees. Over 62,000, almost half the refugees, were sent to these camps to await sponsorship. While some were processed in days, others were still in the camps more than a year later.

The whole exodus was another triumph for Castro and left the Carter administration in no mood to continue developing a dialogue. The press played up the mentally ill and the criminals among them, yet these had been less than four percent of the total number of refugees. Enthusiasm for the boatlift waned over time as Floridians realized the enormous social and financial burden that had been placed upon the state. The 80,000 refugees, who had arrived in one month, were more than the total for any previous year since 1959.

In August of 1980 five airliners were hijacked to Cuba by refugees, one with the threat of a bomb which turned out to be a bar of soap. Three of the hijackings occurred immediately after the Federal Aviation Administration announced a plan to add "skymarshals," as well as increase screening and security at airports. In the meantime the various resettlement agencies in southern Florida dealing with Cubans, Haitians and Nicaraguans declared their inability to further process refugees unless funding was increased. The federal government responded by granting almost seventeen million dollars for health and educational services.

Even the Cuban exiles in Miami began to view the "Marielistos" as a distinctly different group. This attitude was partly the result of riots in the camps where many refugees had to endure the oppressive heat of the summer of 1980. In retrospect, however, what is amazing is the rapidity with which so many refugees were absorbed relatively quickly into Florida's society; another example of the powerful Americanization process which has characterized the state's as well as the nation's history.

As the boatlift saga was running its course, Miami was shaken by riots within its Liberty City section.[2] During the 1970s Dade County had experienced at least thirteen outbursts of race related violence, and the political downfall, due to accusations of corruption, of several leaders in the black community. There were also a number of incidents where actions by the police, the State Prosecutor's Office and the courts had raised doubts about any sense of equal treatment or justice for blacks.

What set off the riots on May 17, 1980, however, was the acquittal, by an all white jury in Tampa, of five Dade County police officers accused of having beaten to death the previous December 17, a thirty-three year old black insurance agent and Marine veteran, Arthur McDuffie. On December 16, McDuffie had borrowed a Kawasaki motorcycle from a cousin. Later, staying perhaps as late as one A.M. the next morning, he visited a female friend. According to the police, fifteen minutes later he was observed slowing down for a red light going north along North Miami Avenue. He "popped a wheelie," meaning he lifted the front wheel off the ground and gunned the cycle to lay some rubber, made a provocative gesture toward an officer parked near the intersection, and sped off into the night.

While it was never clear why McDuffie raced away, what ensued was a chase involving over a dozen police cars that lasted over eight minutes and at times exceeded speeds of over one-hundred miles an hour. He finally stopped as the police cars began to converge on him, including several from the City of Miami. All of the police officers were white.

While one officer held a gun on McDuffie, another grabbed him and pulled him off the cycle, claiming later that the black man had swung at him. Although he "was beaten by no fewer than six, and possibly as many as twelve Dade County officers," McDuffie managed to fight back in the beginning even though . . . held in a bear hug, but then he was pulled away . . . by other officers engaged in the mell." The uneven contest was over in three minutes. McDuffie lay unconscious, his head split open by a police flashlight, his brain swelling with blood. He died four days later.

The police attempted to cover-up what had happened, even running over McDuffie's cycle with one of the police cruisers. Several police officials, however, as well as the county medical examiner, were suspicious about inconsistencies in the police report of the incident, and an internal review was initiated. By the end of the week, the first newspaper article about the inconsistencies appeared in the *Miami Herald,* and one of the officers involved, Charles Veverka, came forward to tell his superiors what he knew about the incident. Nine officers were suspended as a result of the investigation; four of them were charged with manslaughter and tampering with evidence, and a fifth officer was charged with tampering as well.

When the manslaughter charge was announced, there were protests from the black media charging that State Attorney Janet Reno was a racist. When two of the officers agreed to turn state's evidence, Reno changed the charge against officer Alex Marrero to second-degree murder since the testimony was that he had delivered the fatal blow while McDuffie was handcuffed. By early January of 1980, the case had drawn national attention. The State also made the decision, which was later much criticized, to try all of the officers together, rather than individually.

Defense attorneys requested, because of the intense feelings about the case in Dade County, a change of venue. Despite misgivings in the black community, Judge Lenore Nesbitt on March 28 agreed to move the trial to Tampa, and observed: "This case is a time bomb. I don't want to see it go off in my courtroom or in this community."

When the trial opened in Tampa on March 31, the defense used all thirty-four of its peremptory challenges to eliminate blacks from the pool of potential jurors, and succeeded in obtaining an all-white jury. The trial testimony exposed the way in which McDuffie had been brutally beaten. Marrero claimed he had hit the black man because he thought the latter was trying to take his gun. The trial lasted six weeks, with the case going to the jury late in the morning on Saturday, May 17, exactly five months after McDuffie's death.

In less than three hours, the jury returned with a verdict of not guilty. It was a lengthy statement that took the clerk thirteen minutes to read, and which evoked several emotional outbursts in the

Liberty City Riots

courtroom. As psychologist and historian of the ensuing riots, Marvin Dunn, noted: "Thus began Miami's decade of fire."

By early afternoon, the news had reached Liberty City and many blacks began to voice their rage on the streets. By five o'clock, rocks and bottles were being thrown at autos driven by whites along Sixty-second street. As a crowd gathered, there were rumors of violence and the police set up road blocks to keep autos out of the area. Ultimately, the mob attacked three whites, beating and mutilating the two males.

Later, three more whites were savaged so badly one died at the hospital, a police officer of thirty years experience called it, "the most violent crime I've ever seen." The police could do little that night but keep score with nine people eventually dying from beatings, with the three days of rioting claiming over 400 victims, 417 of which were treated in local hospitals.

Meanwhile, the McDuffie verdict had also evoked an initially more moderate response as well. By Saturday evening, a crowd of perhaps a thousand people consisting mainly of younger blacks, but including some older blacks and even some whites, had gathered in front of the Metro Justice Building. As the group grew to as many as three thousand people, there were cries of "justice, justice, justice," and "Reno must go," mingled in with the singing of "We Shall Overcome," with the crowd swaying to the music. Tensions increased as those with radios learned of the violence in Liberty City.

With only fifteen officers allocated to keep order, the rally turned ugly, as the crowd, despite pleas for moderation by the leaders, moved toward acts of violence, first taunting the police inside and then kicking a hole in the glass front door. As one police car came near the crowd, some turned over an empty police car while others began to ignite rags stuffed into gas tanks. Despite the pleas of some blacks to stop the melee, it now became a full-scale riot. Fires were set inside the building and several other cars were overturned and set afire.

It was not until perhaps midnight before an effective perimeter was set up as, in the early morning, some National Guard units began to arrive. With orders from Governor Bob Graham not to use live ammunition, the one thousand troops were no match for the crowd. By that time, with thousands of people in the streets, incidents of burning and looting were occurring around black communities with the main actions again in Liberty City, where 213 fires were recorded with twenty-one in Opa-Locka and thirteen in Perrine. The numerous fires cast a glow over the city not unlike the fires that had in the past sometimes burned on the edge of the Everglades during a drought. Along a three-mile section of Seventh Avenue, virtually every business with goods that could be looted had been broken into and some torched. By three o'clock in the morning, there was a lull, often characteristic of such riots, as the looters returned home with their bounty.

Nine blacks were killed over Sunday and Monday as police and guardsmen moved in to recapture parts of the city. Some questioned whether some of the incidents were justified. By late Sunday night, with three thousand guardsmen now on hand, such incidents became less frequent into the morning. By Tuesday, police calls had declined, and by Wednesday, the riot was over. Schools opened, but with a curfew in effect until Friday.

In July, there was more violence in Liberty City as police chased a robber into a housing complex and an officer was shot in the back. In the ensuing rioting and car bombings, four other officers were shot and forty people arrested before order was restored.

The aftermath of the riots resulted in 135 defendants out of almost a thousand cases, receiving some kind of sentence. In the months that followed, there were a number of "emotionally charged race-related trials" held in Miami. The federal government, concerned that the riots might spread to other cities, sent Attorney General Benjamin Civiletti to Miami. A Task Force was established to develop an economic recovery plan for the city. President Jimmy Carter even came to the city, but his visit appeared less than satisfactory to the black community. While loans totaling forty million dollars were made available through the Small Business Administration, in the next several years only twenty-two million dollars were ever loaned out, with nearly 90 percent going to whites or Hispanics. Fewer than half of the looted businesses ever reopened. As Marvin Dunn has commented, "Indeed, the real impact of the loans seems to have been to help draw riot-damaged businesses away from the inner city rather than to keep them there."

The federal government also made funds available for job training, ultimately spending about six million dollars on that effort. The McDuffie family received $100,000 from the City of Miami and one million dollars from the Metro-Dade government. Probably the most important change after the riot was the Florida Supreme Court's 1984 decision "prohibiting the elimination of prospective jurors based upon their race alone."

Despite these efforts, Miami's racial incidents continued. Late in December, 1982, a young black, Nevel Johnson, was shot while playing a video game in a pool hall in Overtown, the historic black section of Miami. Two Hispanic police officers had initiated checking the establishment because it had a history as a meeting place for narcotics transactions. Officer Luis Alvarez shot Johnson when, he claimed, the latter made a sudden move as the officer searched him for a weapon. The police claimed Johnson carried a gun, but could not locate it when homicide investigators reached the scene. Three witnesses disputed this, saying that Johnson had been shot without provocation, however, his brother-in-law, who was standing nearby, acknowledged that Nevel carried a gun for self-protection, although later Johnson's family said he had never owned a gun.

Whatever the facts, Overtown experienced a minor version of what had occurred two and a half years earlier in Liberty City with several hundred blacks torching police cars, spraying them with bullets and looting several stores. In the ensuing riot, heroic actions by individual blacks in several incidents saved whites from violence.

A subsequent police investigation disclosed that Alvarez was outside his assigned patrol section and that he had modified his gun so that some believed it had, in effect, a "hair trigger." While a police panel recommended a two-week suspension for Alvarez, early in 1983, a Grand Jury charged that the officer had "acted recklessly and with culpable negligence," while many in Overtown insisted he be charged with murder.

The trial did not begin until early in 1984, with Alvarez represented by the well-known defense attorney, Roy Black. The jury of six was all white, including a Hispanic. With conflicting testimony from witnesses, the trial lasted nearly two months, while the jury deliberated two hours to find the officer not guilty. Again, there was rioting and looting in both Overtown and Liberty City, but less than in the previous riots. Later in the year, the City of Miami negotiated a settlement with Johnson's family which eventually brought them over a million dollars.

The third episode in this decade of racial violence in Miami took place in 1989. On January 16, Officer William Lozano, while calling in on his radio, heard of another policeman chasing a motorcyclist who was purportedly driving erratically. When he heard a cycle, driven by Clement Anthony Lloyd, coming in his direction "he stepped into the street with his weapon drawn and fired a single shot at the motorcycle," hitting Lloyd in the head and killing him. The cycle veered into a car, injuring the cycle's passenger, Allan Blanchard, who died the next day. The occupants of the car were not seriously injured and were quickly treated and released from the hospital.

Soon after the accident, several hundred Overtown residents took to the streets, throwing rocks and bottles and, within hours, another riot with burning and looting was in full swing spreading to Liberty City and Coconut Grove as well. By January 20, the riot was over, leaving one dead, eleven injured and 372 persons arrested. Eleven stores, several of them large supermarkets and a department store had been looted.

What became one of Florida's most sensational trials began October 23, 1989 as Lozano was charged with two counts of manslaughter. Choosing the jury again became a controversy in itself. The final jury consisted of three whites, two blacks and one Hispanic, with alternates including two whites and two Hispanics. During the trial, the testimony of the witnesses differed greatly with respect to what had occurred. It was found that Lloyd's system contained marijuana, alcohol and a trace of cocaine at the time of his death.

On December 7, the jury found Lozano guilty of manslaughter and early in 1990 he was sentenced to seven years in prison. In an appeal he was tried in Orlando in mid-1993 and found not guilty. In the interim the City of Miami agreed to a settlement that gave half a million dollars to each of the families of Lloyd and Blanchard.

In retrospect, what can be concluded about this decade of racial violence that had so drawn the whole nation's attention? While there would be more riots, for example, in St. Petersburg in the 1990s, as noted in the next chapter, it did appear that some headway had been made with respect to racial tensions, especially with regard to relations with the police. Both Miami and Metro-Dade added more blacks to their forces and more officers were disciplined as a result of complaints about excessive use of force and misconduct. In 1990, eight officers were fired for such behavior. Finally, the police developed "teams" to patrol in the large housing projects areas and mini-precinct police stations were opened in both Liberty City and Overtown.

While these developments were taking place, initiated by the 1980 boatlift from Cuba and the riots in Miami, other important events were also occurring around the state. In February 1980, the most serious nuclear accident since the problem at Three Mile Island in Pennsylvania, happened at the Crystal Springs plant when 40,000 gallons of radioactive water spilled after a power outage had disabled the reactor's emergency system. Another reminder of the fragile nature of the complex constructs of modern life took place on May 9, when a Liberian freighter rammed into Tampa Bay's Sunshine Skyway Bridge knocking out a 1,200-foot section of the edifice that fell 140 feet into the water. Thirty-five people died in the accident including those in a bus that fell into the bay. Governor Graham declared an area-wide state of emergency when the blockage closed the port of Tampa, then the nation's seventh busiest, causing losses of fifty million dollars a day.

In the area of state politics, voters in March 1980, passed an amendment to the Constitution that lowered property taxes for many by raising the homestead exemption to $25,000 thus attracting even more potential Floridians. The following month, Governor Graham delivered his state of the state speech calling for a surplus of over $400 million, tax incentives for businesses and thirty-two and a half million dollars for school maintenance, while at the same time asking for a limit on both state spending and government expansion.

Organized crime, especially the smuggling of drugs such as marijuana and cocaine as well as the "laundering" of drug generated funds through Florida banks continued to be of concern both to Florida law enforcement agencies and the federal government. For example, among many cases that might be cited, in February 1980, eight men arrested in 1979 were convicted of smuggling in $300 million of marijuana. One drug ring alone, the "Black Tuna" ring named after its Colombian supplier, was believed to have captured almost ten percent of the nation's trade in illegal drugs. The Federal Bureau of Investigation announced it had uncovered plots to kill both the judge and a witness in the case and also accused a juror in the case of accepting a bribe. This kind of violence, corruption and jury tampering were themes that would carry over into the next decade.

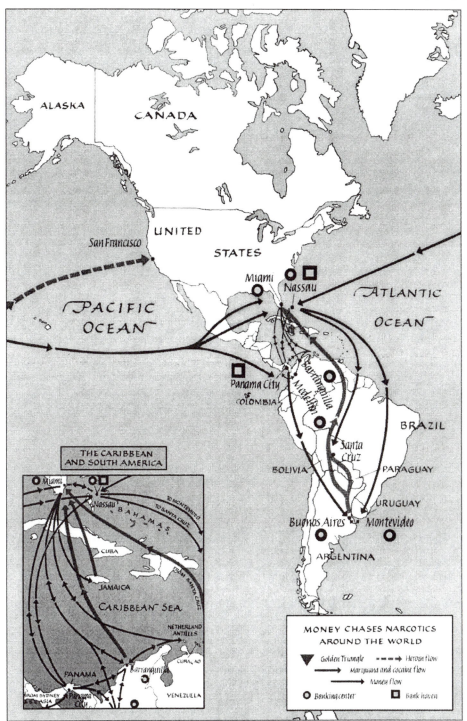

South Florida as a center of drug traffic and the "laundering" of drug monies.

In early June of 1980, the U.S. Senate's Banking and Urban
Affairs Committee held hearings in an effort to devise means to
deal with the enormous amount of drug-related funds being deposited in Florida's banks. Without any real hard data about the extent of such "informal economy," or "gray market" operations, as
these actrivities had now come to be euphemistically referred to,
Federal authorities speculated that the illegal narcotics trade was
perhaps South Florida's largest and most profitable industry. The
Committee discussed new rules that would require fuller disclosure of bank deposits. Several days later, the U.S. Supreme Court
overturned a State law that had kept out-of-state banks from doing
business in Florida indicating that the law had unduly protected
Florida banks from out-of-state competition. With the lifting of such
restrictions in 1985, there began an attrition of smaller banks and
an influx of larger, out of state banks into the state. Through a
series of mergers, within a decade these out-of-state banks would
be the dominant players in Florida's banking industry.

While the importation of drugs continued to grow, helped by
the development of "crack" cocaine, which greatly lowered the price
of that drug on the streets and thus increased its usage, American
farmers also turned to growing marijuana. That "informal economy"
product turned out to be perhaps the nation's third most important
agricultural. Farmers in the South battled drug enforcement agents
much as some moonshiners had fought "Revenuers" in the 1920s.
The advanced state of American agricultural technology meant that
farmers turned to producing high-quality marijuana seed for export abroad, a relatively greater profit producer per pound, to be
grown elsewhere with the final product finding its way back to U.S.
markets. Thus, South Florida found itself the center of a two-way
drug trade with lucrative profits funneled out through its banks.

Drug trafficking and the laundering of drug funds continued as
a problem throughout the decade. Early in 1985, for example, federal customs agents confiscated a shipment of cocaine weighing well
over a ton and valued at $600 million, stashed aboard a huge Co-
lombian Avianca Boeing 747 airliner. It was the thirty-fourth time
during the decade that airplanes from that airline had been found
to have drugs aboard. While stopping the drug traffic seemed an
endless task, there were some occasional victories. Two years later,
in early 1987, billionaire Colombian drug lord Carlos Lehder was
flown to Tampa under heavy guard after having been captured earlier in Colombia. He was reputed to be the head of the largest and
most powerful drug ring in the world controlling perhaps eighty
percent of the cocaine entering the country. The only problem with
such "successes" in the Drug War was that as one such drug lord
was captured, another soon moved in to take his place as the Colombian drug cartels battled each other for supremacy.

Meanwhile, in the political arena, in the November elections of
1980, Republican candidate Ronald Reagan was elected President
capturing Florida from the incumbent, Democrat Jimmy Carter, by
a vote of 2,046,957 to 1,419,475, while Independent candidate John

Anderson garnered 189,692 votes and Libertarian candidate Ed Clark had 30,524. Reagan's election not only indicated the continued growth of the Republican Party in Florida, it signified a growing conservative shift within that party away from the views of more moderate leaders such as Eisenhower and Nixon.

Also indicative of the continued Republican strength was former Public Service Commissioner Paula Hawkins' defeat of Democrat Bill Gunter for U.S. Senator by a vote of 1,829,460 to 1,705,409. Reagan's massive victory probably helped Hawkins win. Gaining her reputation by fighting against rate increases of electric power, Hawkins was viewed by the electorate as something of a populist. As a result of the elections, the State House was still controlled by the Democrats, eighty-one to thirty-nine, while in the Senate their advantage was twenty-seven to thirteen. In the Florida delegation in U.S. House of Representatives, the Democrats held a twelve to three edge over the Republicans. Women not only increased their role in politics, in the field of education, a significant event of late 1980 was the selection of a woman, Dr. Barbara Newell, as Chancellor of the growing State University System (SUS). In 1983, Dr. Helen Popovich was chosen as President of Florida Atlantic University, the first woman to hold that position in a university within the SUS.

In agriculture, the winter of 1981 was even worse for citrus growers than the previous year as the harshest freeze in twenty years destroyed a fifth of the State's two and a half billion dollar citrus harvest. This was followed in 1982 by a record freeze so severe that the Florida Citrus Commission ordered a ten day embargo on sales or shipment of citrus fruits. December of 1983 brought the third bad year of cold in a row and devastated a number of investors in the industry. The loss was estimated as great as $250 million and a quarter of the orange crop was lost. In January 1985, another severe cold spell damaged ninty percent of the citrus crop. Governor Graham declared a state of emergency in the face of what was estimated as the state's worst crop loss of the twentieth century. On top of these years of extraordinary freezes of the early 1980s, in August of 1984, citrus canker was discovered in a nursery in the south central part of the state. The spread of the bacteria, deadly to fruit trees, meant the ultimate loss or destruction of millions of trees. The following month the federal government ordered a stop to export of shipments of Florida citrus.

To top off the environmental and crop disasters of this decade, in May of 1985 wildfires caused by a long period without rain, broke out in over twenty of the state's sixty-seven counties. In one devastating week over 350 fires consumed more than 175,000 acres and destroyed some 200 homes including some expensive ones in exclusive sections of Palm Beach county. Again, Governor Graham was forced to declare a state of emergency with losses estimated at forty-four million dollars.

In the face of these "natural" disasters, there was an interesting "artificial" effort to "enhance" nature in May, 1983, in a very

Space shuttle piggy-backed over Tallahassee

extensive project to turn parts of Biscayne Bay a bright, shocking pink with huge swathes of plastic floating on the waters around a number of islands. As part of a beautification program that cost three million dollars, the Bulgarian concept artist, Varacheff Christo, created giant water lilies, using over 600,000 meters of material which lasted for two weeks.

Despite several on-site accidents, the early part of the decade witnessed a continued advance of the space program at Cape Canaveral. In April 1981, although three years behind schedule, the space shuttle Columbia was successfully launched. It was the first reusable spacecraft, designed to carry payloads into orbit. On Armistice Day the following year, the craft made its first operational flight with four astronauts on board for a five-day flight. A year later, in November of 1983, Columbia made a third space shuttle flight from Cape Canaveral. The mission was comprised of six astronauts, the largest crew thus far in space, along with the European built Skylab intended for a number of experiments in space.

By late 1985, a total of nine space shuttle flights had been undertaken. On December 19, Columbia's booster rocket experienced a malfunction of a hydraulic pump shortly before launch at the Cape and the mission had to be aborted. The next month, January 28, 1986, there occurred the worst disaster in the history of America's space program. As millions of people watched on television the one and a quarter billion dollar space shuttle Challenger burst into flames over the Atlantic ocean only seventy-three seconds after its launch from Cape Canaveral. The explosion killed six professional astronauts and thirty-seven year old Christa McAuliffe, the first civilian selected to journey out into space. The whole nation mourned the loss of the six astronauts and the courageous and popular teacher from Concord, New Hampshire. The cause of the accident was later diagnosed as "O" ring seals whose function was impaired by the cold weather that morning at the Cape. As a result, space shuttle missions were postponed for several years while solutions were sought to remedy these problems.

In the area of entertainment and tourism, Disney World's appeal to Americans and foreign visitors continued to grow. During April of 1982, Zaire's free-spending President, Mobuto Sese Seko, and an entourage visited the Kissimmee amusement park spending over two million dollars. In October, Walt Disney Productions opened an $800 million adult theme park originally conceived by Disney before his death in 1966. Located at nearby Lake Buena Vista, EPCOT as it was called, standing for Experimental Prototype Community of Tomorrow, immediately drew thousands of new visitors to the state. to view its futuristic exhibits.

On June 21, 1982 in a special session, the state Senate voted on ratification of the Equal Rights Amendment (ERA) intended to give the sexes equality before the law. The Senate voted twenty-two to sixteen against ratification. The vote came after a spirited campaign around the state by advocates of the ERA and an equally determined battle against it by opponents. Florida's vote was viewed as pivotal as the Amendment also failed nationally.

Two days later, reacting to an earlier boycott by surgeons who had refused to perform non-essential surgery as a protest against huge increases in medical malpractice insurance premiums, Governor Graham signed into law a bill intended to limit some of the rising rates of physicians' fees. While the bill denied the large surcharge planned by insurance companies, it left untouched the large annual premiums for malpractice insurance.

In the November election of 1982 Bob Graham was re-elected to a second term as Governor over his Republican opponent, L.A. "Skip" Bafalis, a State Senator from Palm Beach county, almost doubling the votes garnered by the latter in a landslide, 1,739,553 to 949,013. Democrat Lawton Chiles was also re-elected to the U.S. Senate over Republican Van B. Poole of Fort Lauderdale by a vote of 1,637,667 to 1,015,330. In the U.S. House of Representatives, the Florida ratio was still thirteen Democrats to six Republicans, and within the State Legislature, the Senate now held thirty-two Democrats and eight Republicans, while in the House the count was eighty-four to thirty-six, Democrats over Republicans.

It is worth summarizing the accomplishments of Graham's first term going back to early 1979. Polls late in 1982 showed Florida voters generally pleased with his performance as well as that of President Ronald Reagan after almost two years in office. In the face of all the crises with which he had had to deal, discussed above, including the inflation afflicting the whole country, Graham had sought to obtain new funds for education and to attempt to deal with reform of the tax structure. He was not the first, nor the last governor, to throw in the towel on tax reform with respect to the Legislature's unwilingness to follow his leadership.

The magnitude of the inflation and of the rising costs of government can be seen in his budget requests. His request for 1979-1981 had been fourteen billion dollars, while that for 1981-1983 was over twenty billion dollars to deal with crime, education and transportation. Graham was criticized for his failure to confront the Legislature over tax reform, and some critics, such as Broward's County Commission Chairman, Howard Foreman, pointed to continuing conflicts of interest with respect to government projects and the land holdings of some of the state's elite. When, for example, plans for the linking of I-75 in south Florida were announced late in 1980, several newspapers reported that the route ran along lands owned by such notables as the Jacksonville lawyer and owner of the Tampa Bay Buccaneers football team, Hugh Culverhouse, Attorney General Jim Smith, former State Representative Marshall Harris, the giant Arvida land corporation, as well as by the Sengra Corporation owned by the Graham family. Foreman was tempted to call it, he said, "one big happy family. When you look at the landowners, it's obvious your fighting with the power structure of the state."

This was not the first such accusation of conflict of interest against Graham. In the early 1970s, while still a State Senator, Graham had sponsored legislation to stop some of the dredging that was deemed harmful to the environment. When it was revealed that the Graham Companies had dredges operating twenty-four hours a day to complete dredging around a ten acre mangrove island near Naples before the legislation went into effect, Graham claimed that, as a vice president, he was not always aware of the operations of the firm. While some such businesses as the Deltona Corporation were fined $50,000, no fine was levied against the Graham Companies.

As Governor, however, Graham increasingly emphasized environmental issues. In the 1980 legislative session, he signed a three-bill package relating to disposal of hazardous waste and land use planning. One was an effort to prevent Florida from becoming a dumping ground of poisonous chemicals for the whole southeastern part of the nation. This had been a top priority of the Legislature that had been warned that the federal government might impose its own guidelines if the state did not act on this problem. With Florida's lax regulations, officials feared other states with tougher rules would choose to dump here. There was concern that much of the 600,000 metric tons of chemicals produced annually in Florida had already found its way into rivers and other waterways, was buried in the ground, or was stored at dump sites. Given the magnitude of the problem, the five million dollar trust fund created by the act to pay for the cleanup of any hazardous waste spills was literally a drop in the bucket. The two other bills dealt with restructuring the state's eleven regional planning councils to give the Governor more control over the decisions these councils made on building permits and land use.

One of the Governor's most significant acts in the first part of his second term with respect to what had come to be known as "growth management" was to bring to Tallahassee one of his former teachers at Gainesville, John DeGrove, a political scientist at Florida Atlantic University and a well-known scholar in the field of growth management, to serve as Secretary of the Department of Community Affairs (DCA) as well as to help develop an overall plan in that area. The final result was the Growth Management Act of 1985 discussed below.

In the November 1984 general elections, Republican President Ronald Reagan again captured the state's twenty-one electoral votes from the Democratic challenger Walter Mondale and his running mate, the first female vice presidential candidate, Geraldine Ferraro by an overwhelming vote of 2,728,775 to 1,445,344. In the Congress all incumbents were re-elected leaving the Democrats still dominant, thirteen to eight. Within the state the Democrats lost seven more seats in the House, but were still in control seventy-seven to forty-three, while the Senate remained the same with the Democrats in a majority thirty-two to eight.

A month later the state's voters repealed a unitary tax which had been pushed through by the Governor almost a year and a half earlier, and which had taxed a portion, if not all, world-wide profits earned by multinational corporations doing business within Florida. In July 1983, Graham had called the Legislature into a special session ostensibly to provide additional funds for school improvements. The U.S. Supreme Court, in a case involving the state of California and the Container Corporation of America, had recently upheld the unitary method of taxing multinational corporations. As it happened, estimates of what a unitary tax would bring into Florida's tax coffers was about what was sought to improve education.

Some experts on government taxation viewed such taxes as the "wave of the future," and in this situation as one student of state governments, Steven Gold, noted, "Florida struck like lightning." Within two days unitary taxation was proposed and passed by the legislature, "before the multinational business community could mobilize an effective lobbying effort to block it." The joke around

Tallahassee was that the Governor and the Legislature had moved so quickly, "that corporate lawyers were stranded in airports all over the country."[3]

The unitary tax idea enabled a state to tax the profits of a corporation's subsidiaries as well as the corporation itself. There were two versions of the tax. After Florida's lead on unitary taxation, in January 1984, a dozen states had adopted the first type, which was said to "stop at the water's edge," in the sense that it taxed only profits earned in the U.S. Florida, and eleven other states, had passed the second version, which attempted to extend the tax to corporate profits in foreign countries as well. It was this latter type which angered the business community, shook confidence in the future climate of business in the state and led to its repeal. Critics charged that this legislation had been a prime reason why the assessment of Florida's business climate by business organizations, once rated at the very top of the states, had been lowered.

On the other hand, Graham's realization of the increasing cost of Florida's international responsibilities caused him to write to President Reagan for help in paying off the unpaid bills of $150 million left from the boatlift five years earlier. At the same time, Graham had brought a new awareness to the state about the importance of international business, not just tourism, but international trade as well. As early as 1980, the Governor had noted that such trade had helped Florida to weather the worst aspects of the recession of 1980. Combining this idea with his long-held view about the importance of education, he had overseen the establishment of a growing number of international "linkage" institutes in 1986. These institutes joined community colleges and universities in eventually co-sponsoring the pursuit of business, educational and cultural exchanges between the state and nations such as Brazil, China, Costa Rica, Israel, Japan and the Caribbean in general.

While it may be too early to make an assessment about its long-range efficacy, the capstone of Graham's second term as Governer, and perhaps his legacy to Floridians, was the growth management legislation passed during his last two years in office. From former DCA director DeGrove's perspective, the down side of Florida's rapid growth during the previous decades was a legacy which had generated "a huge backlog of unmet infrastructure needs, inadequate public facilitiesand environmental degradation." Environmental planning, however, going back fifteen years to the early years of the Askew administration, had evolved as a system "designed to balance the competing interests of economic development and environmental preservation,"in which Florida had "become the bellwether state in growth management."[4]

What had happened over those years was an increasing role for the state as compared to local authorities, but also a combining of environmentalism with growth management; once thought of as two distinctly different concepts. In the 1970s environmentalism had grown enormously after the publication of Rachel Carson's *The Silent Spring*. But, cleaning up pollution, which might be accomplished with a number of market incentives rather than increased government intervention and regulation, was quite different from the kind of gloom and doom scenarios of *The Study of the Club of Rome,* or those of academics such as Paul Ehrlich, whose continued erroneous predictions seem never to have undercut his reputation for sagacity.

On the other hand, growth management, both in Florida and around the nation, had been, prior to the 1980s, largely unsuccessful due largely to the public's perception that it was an elitist, interest group issue. Those who had gotten their own land, now wanted to shut access off to others. This, for example, had been true among critics who saw the Graham family as, having developed their own properties, now became advocates of growth management. Curtailing the availability of land for development of some owners would, obviously, increase the value of those who held land that had been, or could be developed.

Adding environmentalism to the mix, by addressing "quality of life" issues was a stroke of brilliance as it had the effect of making the whole concept much more palatable to the public. Thus, the reform of the 1980s was more concerned with infrastructure, those "quality of life" issues that for DeGrove included "solid waste, water, sewer, parks, recreation" and "schools," but the "focus clearly" was "on transportation." The massive State Comprehensive Plan ultimately was built around "Concurrence," which he acknowledged would cost a great deal of money beyond the ten-year, forty billion has been determined to be consistent by the State Land Planning Agency, e.g., the Department of Community Affairs (DCA), no development permit may be approved by local government unless infrastructure needed to meet the impacts of that development will be available."[5]

Such a program, of course, was a boon to land use lawyers and public administration bureaucrats. Various local authorities among the 1,500 entities participating in the planning were always seeking exceptions to the plans that had been submitted. It was another layer of centralized bureaucracy beyond that already facing the Florida businessman. At a more theoretical level some critics likened growth mangement to a new kind of neo-feudalism; extensive government control over land utilization, which many believed had been eliminated in the triumph of the American Revolution. There was a certain irony in the fact that the election of Ronald Reagan to two terms in the presidency, seemingly signaling a return toward smaller government and market principles, in Florida would coincide with the adoption of legislation launching a vast set of land-use procedures and a bureaucracy to oversee them.

On the other hand, proponents of growth management and the expanded governmental services which it entailed, such as the political scientist, Lance DeHaven-Smith, noted that much of the program began to unravel shortly after Graham left office. After the Comprehensive Plan was passed in 1985, a committee was organized to calculate its cost and to recommend ways to pay for it. Com-

Governor Bob Martinez

posed of twenty-one leading legislators, civic and business leaders, the "Zwick Committee," as it came to be known, after its chairman, Charles J. Zwick, the head of Southeast Bank Corporation, did not issue its report until early 1987. It recommended the "sunsetting" in July of that year, of a number of sales tax exemptions on services, which would lead to a reconsideration of the state's whole tax structure if the Comprehensive Plan was to be adequately funded.[6] That issue would confront the legislature and the governor who came to office after Graham.

In the area of the environment, Graham had greatly expanded the efforts begun by governors Kirk and Askew. He used tax funds to preserve many of Florida's natural resources in programs such as Save Our Rivers, which in some ways, however, was contradicted by the ecological damage to the Kissimmee River as the Army Corps of Engineers continued efforts to "straighten" that waterway. In programs such as Save Our Coasts and Save Our Everglades, the state initiated a program of purchasing ecologically endangered lands, which would be given increased emphasis in the next decade.

One last facet of the Graham years is worth comment, his successful campaign to eliminate automobile inspections as distinct from auto emissions. Early in his first administration, he appointed a Task Force to examine the question. The Task Force concluded that while the three dollar inspection fee system paid for itself, it might be better to spend that money on driver education since more than half of all accidents were caused by speeding, inattention and improper evasive action.

As a result of the elimination of these inspections including those of front ends, brakes and other critical parts of the automobile, a number of dangerous clunkers were now found on Florida's roads. It would take several years before even auto emissions tests were introduced in the larger urban areas such as Dade, Broward, Duval and Hillsborough counties. Even then, while signs at the yearly emissions test centers proclaimed their effectiveness, by the late 1990s auto-makers had so improved the emissions of their autos that some emitted cleaner air than the polluted air around them. Several studies showed it was this improvement rather than the testing that was essentially responsible for the cleaner air. As for the type of auto inspections eliminated by Governor Graham, some suspected this had more to do with the liability question and that, with the erosion of the notion of "sovereign immunity," government was increasingly being held liable for some of its actions. One law suit with respect to a faulty brake or front end inspection could easily cancel out those small fees collected from millions of drivers. Ultimately, there was little liability problem with the emission test, and with a ten dollar fee, there was a nice cut in it for the state.

The senatorial election of 1986 proved very lively. Democrat Bob Graham concluded his two terms as Governor by choosing to run for Senator against incumbent Republican, Paula Hawkins, whom he had years before "fired" from the Public Service Commission. The two waged a spirited campaign for that office through the latter part of 1986; a popular, middle of the road, but increasingly conservative, Democrat against a Reaganite, conservative Republican. It was no surprise that in November the popular, soon to be ex-Governor, Bob Graham won by a vote of 1,877,543 to 1,552,376. In moving on to take the oath of office as a U.S. Senator, Graham stepped down from office three days before the end of his term, thus allowing Lieutenant Governor Wayne Mixson to add his name to those who had held the governorship of the state.

A much more contentious race was for the soon to be vacated governorship. The Democratic candidate who emerged from the primaries was State Senator Steve Pajcic, a liberal from Jacksonville. He was opposed by Republican Robert "Bob" Martinez, a former Mayor of Tampa. The race was in some ways reminiscent of one twenty years earlier between the conservative, former Democrat Claude Kirk and the liberal, Robert King High, except that there were then fewer Republican voters in the state.

Martinez had once been active in the teacher's union even as a lobbyist in Tallahassee, and had headed up Jimmy Carter's first presidential campaign in Florida. Now, as the Republican standard bearer, Martinez was a favorite of the business community for leading Tampa through a big spurt of growth and downtown development. As *Florida Trend* commented, "He cut the city bureaucracy, yet increased services, sometimes by farming out work to private contractors. He rebuilt roads and sewers. And best of all. . . the city was still able to cut its property taxes."

Martinez proposed getting rid of sales tax exemptions on some luxury items and opposed a sales tax on services which might cause some companies to switch their activities to other states. He said that newcomers should bear a burden of growth so that development would pay for itself and made implementing the Growth Management Act of 1985 a priority along with improving the operations of the Department of Transportation as well as the Department of Health and Rehabilitative Services. He indicated he would advocate two constitutional amendments, one requiring the Sunshine Law to apply to the Legislature and the other limiting Cabinet officials to two consecutive four-year terms.

Pajcic was regarded as one of the most able legislators in the Senate, and while his program did not differ that radically from Martinez', he couldn't shake his old image as a liberal and lost the election by a vote of 1,847,525 to 1,538,620. In the U.S. House of Representatives, the Democrats lost a seat to lead the Republicans nineteen to seven. In the Florida House, the Democrats lost only two seats to still lead by seventy-five to forty-five, but in the Senate the party lost seven seats so that its advantage over the Republicans was reduced to twenty-five to fifteen.

Apart from the governorship, perhaps the most interesting votes in 1986 pertained to several of the Amendments on the ballot concerning casino gambling and a state lottery. Despite considerable funds spent by those interested in introducing casino gambling as had been passed recently in other states, in Florida the measure overwhelmingly went down in defeat. That defeat meant the gambling facilities operated by the Seminole Tribe as part of the "assumption of sovereignty," were about to experience a number of years of extraordinary profitability. The lottery proved about as popular as gambling casinos had not. Scheduled to go into operation the next year, politicians talked about the estimated $300 million in potential profits that could be generated to ease the crisis in education. It appeared that voters were not worried about the moral aspects of gambling as long as it was controlled by government and generated profits to aid the burden of taxation, especially in a crucial area like education. While income from the lottery rose during its first decade of operation, proponents of education were disappointed in the amount which ultimately found its way to support that area.

One of the biggest events of 1987 was the visit of Pope John Paul II, whose arrival in Miami initiated a ten-day tour of the nation. He was greeted at Miami International Airport by President and Mrs. Reagan who took him on a tour of Vizcaya, the seventy-room mansion overlooking Biscayne Bay, now a public Museum and Gardens, where the two leaders had an opportunity to confer about global problems.

A violent thunderstorm the next day when the Pope celebrated a Mass did not lessen the enthusiasm of the thousands of Roman Catholics, especially Cubans and other Latin Americans, for his visit. Later he took the opportunity to meet with Jewish leaders about the problems facing relations between both religions from persecution of the Jews dating back thousands of years to more recent complaints about the handling of memorials at Auschwitz. That venture into foreign relations predated by over a decade the visit the same Pope would make to Fidel Castro's Cuba in 1998, and its repercussion in Florida, which is discussed in the next chapter.

During his first year in office, Martinez made a decision that would haunt his re-election campaign three years later. For some years a number of service industries had benefited from the sales tax exception which was about to expire, or sunset, shortly after he came into office. During the election, Martinez had favored the elimination of those exemptions. In office, and after a number of opinion polls showed a considerable opposition to the "services tax," the governor changed his views and called a special session of the legislature to, in effect, reinstitute the sales tax exemptions.

When the legislature adjourned without acting on his recommendation, the governor vowed to call it back into session in order to obtain his objective. The leadership in the still predominantly Democratic body counterattacked later in the year by holding a series of public hearings around the state in an effort to gain support for the tax. These were generally unsuccessful, and were countered by the protests of opponents of the tax, which received extensive media attention.

In another special session late in 1987, the legislature made an agreement with the governor to repeal the services tax–it was estimated this would cost the state at least $761 million in lost revenue– and to increase the sales tax from five to six cents. While this solved immediate revenue needs, it did not resolve Florida's fiscal problems, which were to carry over into the next decade. Many, however, applauded the governor's stand. For example, the Fort Lauderdale *Sun-Sentinel* noted his leadership "was a far cry from the early legislative encounters of". . . Bob Graham . . . who "was burdened by the moniker 'Gov. Jello' and was taunted as the weakest governor ever. . . ."

Among other successes of Martinez' adminstration were expanded indigent health care, sole control over the lottery, a speed-up of prison construction, a forty-eight hour cooling-off period for handgun purchases, a local option of a possible one cent sales tax increase and a commission to advise on transportation policy.

The governor's critics argued, however, that he had neglected implementation of the Growth Management Act, as promised, as well as the 1987 report of a State Comprehensive Plan Committee, which had also addressed the growth and environmental problems facing the State. That ten-year Plan, passed in the last year of Graham's final term had, as political scientists David Osborne and Ted Gaebler observed, "quickly degenerated into make[-]work. When this happens, strategic plans not only waste enormous time and money, they can become actual barriers to innovation."[7] While Martinez attempted to keep the budget under nineteen billion dollars, the services tax exemption ultimately meant he ended up signing a $770 million tax increase, the largest in state history.

Apart from the presidential vote, the elections of 1988 featured a hotly contested race for the Senate seat being vacated after eighteen years by Lawton Chiles, who chose not to run for re-election for a fourth term. He expressed a sense of disillusionment with politics in Washington, not the first politician to do so, as well as of "burnout," ultimately disclosing he was taking the drug Prozac to help ease the sense of depression.

In a very close battle for Chiles' Senate seat, Republican Connie Mack defeated Democrat Buddy MacKay 2,049,329 to 2,015,717 with the absentee ballots ultimately deciding the race. In the vote for President, the Republican nominee, George Bush, Vice President for eight years under Reagan, took the state from Michael Dukakis, the Democratic candidate and Governor of Massachusetts by a vote of 2,618,885 to 1,656,701. In the Florida delegation in the U.S. House of Representatives, the Democrats lost two more seats, their majority now a slight ten to nine, while in the State Senate another two seats were lost cutting the Democrat majority to twenty-three to seventeen, and in the State House another two Democratic seats were lost reducing the majority to seventy-three to forty-seven. Thus, with each election of the decade, Florida moved closer toward becoming a true, two-party state.

Florida's growing stature as a sports center, beyond its historic role as a location for major league baseball spring training, continued to expand. In the 1960s Miami had acquired a professional football team, the "Dolphins," which emerged with a perfect Super Bowl season in 1972 and repeated as world champions the next year. Tampa's Buccaneers, also in the National Football League, were less successful, but no less enthusiastically received. In 1987 Miami obtained a franchise for the "Heat" to become a team within the National Basketball Association while Orlando acquired the "Magic." These acquisitions were accompanied by the usual push to obtain public funds to build new stadiums and arenas. Some pointed to Joe Robbie Stadium, built by the original owner of the Dolphins, as a model for private financing of such multi-million dollar facilities. This was not, however, strictly speaking, correct. Almost seventy percent of the Stadium had been financed with Industrial Revenue Bonds (IRBs), referrred to by *Reason* magazine as "socialism for the rich," which carried low interest rates not obtainable to businesses having to borrow in the market, and with tax advantages for the wealthy. IRBs had been intended to build schools and other needed public buildings but were soon being used to finance shopping malls and other projects such as stadiums with corporate skyboxes, of dubious value to the general welfare. Joe Robbie Stadium was one of the last large IRB projects before the Congress moved to eliminate some of the worst abuses of such bonds.

At the college level, the University of Miami won national collegiate football championships in both 1983 and 1987, under first coach Howard Schnellenberger and then Jimmy Johnson, both of whom moved on to the professional ranks. At Florida State University, Coach Bobby Bowden began a streak of finishing year after year among the nation's top teams which would continue well into the next decade. The intense rivalries between Miami, Florida and Florida State led to the observation that, whichever team was State champion, would have a lock on the title as national champion. Unfortunately, at the end of the decade, the Florida "Gators" were placed on probation for various rule violations within the program.

Fortunately, the latter part of the decade did not have many severe hurricanes, but in 1989, the worst drought in twenty-seven years hit the state resulting in water restrictions, a portent of the water shortages of the next decade. In 1989, Claude Pepper, the "Grand Old Man" of Florida politics passed away. Going from the Legislature to the U.S. Senate during the New Deal, then defeated in 1950 in one of the most bitter fights in Florida's electoral history, Pepper had come back to serve with distinction for many years in the U.S. House of Representatives. Representing a district in south Florida, he had become nationally known as the champion of the rights of America's senior citizens, a large number of whom resided in his own state.

Pepper's over fifty years in Florida politics had borne witness to an enormous number of changes in his beloved state. During that half-century, dating back to those of the New Deal, no decade experienced changes greater than those of the 1980s: waves of immigrants, riots, inflation, crime, drugs, pollution, continued growth, bank failures; all of these came together during those ten years. Politically, the decade was dominated by Democrat Bob Graham, whose popularity among his Graham "Cracker" supporters had carried him first to the governor's mansion and then the U.S. Senate, while at the same time the state's Republican representation continued its growth. There was a fundamental contradiction, however, as John DeGrove had pointed out with respect to the specific area of growth management, between the seeming willingness of the people, legislature and governors to expand the role of government without accompanying this growing infrastructure with the fiscal means to pay for it. In the next chapter we explore how Floridians sought to resolve these issues in the 1990s.

31.

The "He-coon," the Hurricane and the Perils of Prosperity

The decade of the 1990s, culminating with the elections of 1998 and after, was dominated by Governor Lawton Chiles, the self-styled "He-coon," whose untimely death only a few weeks before completing his second term, ended an almost forty-year career in government. There were also devastating hurricanes, especially "Andrew," which cut a swath through southern Dade county in August 1992, but also "Georges," which hit both Key West and the Panhandle in 1998, coupled with another wave of severe forest fires.

Immigration continued from parts of the Caribbean and elsewhere, especially Cuba and Haiti, as refugees by boat and raft, sought to escape the wretched social, economic and political conditions there, with Florida caught within the tensions of American foreign policies in the Caribbean Basin. Due to such immigration and the continued movement of people from other states, it was estimated, early in 1999, that Florida's population had reached over fifteen million persons, up from the slightly over thirteen million at the beginning of the decade.

In 1996 another race riot erupted, this time in St. Petersburg. The Indian tribes began to make "gaming" a serious business, while demographic and economic growth also continued to play a major role in Florida's development. Term limit legislation was passed that would begin to affect state office holders at the turn of the century. The shift toward Republican party dominance at all levels continued in several elections including the victory of Jeb Bush for Governor in 1998, while a number of constitutional amendments were passed, placed on the ballot by the revision committee mandated with that task. Bush concluded a very successful first session with the Republican dominated Legislature. A school voucher plan was passed, the first at the state level in the nation and a record one billion dollars in taxes were cut to keep the budget at $48.9 billion. Tougher prison sentences were mandated for criminals using a gun to commit a crime and the multi-billion dollar "bullet train" from Miami to Orlando feasibility study was halted.

Perhaps the most important development, however, was the economic prosperity that began early in the decade and continued unabated into 1999. So great was the sense of prosperity that the specter of a presidential impeachment registered no more than a slight blip as the stock market continued upward. The sense of economic prosperity within Florida's government was such that warnings by Wall Street bond houses as late as 1996 about the state's taxation structure could, by 1999, be virtually ignored as Florida's politicians debated what to do with all the surplus revenues.

At the same time there was a sense of uneasy peril about the seemingly endless prosperity. Much of this derived from the increasing irrelevance of economic forecasting. Not only were such forecasts often wrong, orthodox economics did not explain the reasons for the prosperity very satisfactorily either, and a number of business organizations closed their formal forecasting units.[1] Such uneasiness might also serve as a warning to historians, who venture to explain this latest incredible decade in Florida's dynamic development.

The elections of 1990 featured a very spirited race for governor between the incumbent, Republican Governor Bob Martinez, and former U.S. Senator Lawton Chiles. Buddy MacKay, who had lost his race in 1988 to succeed Chiles as U.S. Senator to Connie Mack, coaxed Chiles back into politics and became his running-mate, joining him as the candidate for Lieutenant Governor on the Democratic ticket. Chiles defeated Martinez by a vote of 1,988,341 to 1,536,738, garnering 56.5% of the votes. The major decision in Chiles' campaign was to set a $100 limit on contributions; and, in contrast to Martinez's $1,500-a-plate fund-raising dinners, $1.50-a-guest hot-dog feasts.

Well attuned to the growing protests of the 1980s to big, inefficient government and influence politics led by President Ronald Reagan, Chiles made opposition to big money in Florida politics the cornerstone of his campaign. Some of his advisors questioned the contribution limits, but the wily politician once again demonstrated why he would come to be known as the old "He-coon." His expenditures for what *Time* magazine called a "corny but believable populist bid" for governor were astounding in the low cost per vote. Although Bill Nelson, his opponent in the Democratic primary, spent almost six and a half million dollars; Chiles, in the whole campaign spent only a bit over five million, while Martinez spent more than twice that in a losing effort.

The Democrats still retained a slight ten to nine lead in the U.S. House of Representatives, with 74 Democrats to 46 Republicans in the state House and 23 Democrats and 17 Republicans in the Senate. Gwen Margolis of North Miami Beach became the first woman chosen as President of the Senate. Voters also passed three amendments to the Constitution. The first began legislative sessions earlier, a second established a three-day waiting period for the final purchase of a hand-gun and the third made for more open government procedures.

Governor Lawton Chiles

The governor's rejuvenation from the "burn-out" and frustration with government bureaucracy, which had resulted in his stepping down from the U.S. Senate a mere fifteen-months earlier, was amazing. Aware of the public's own growing concern about inefficient government, the Governor early in his term began touting David Osburne and Ted Gaebler's ideas later published as *Reinventing Government: How the Entrepreneurial Spirit is Transforming the Public Sector* (1992), as a guide to what could be done to reform government in Florida.[2] Based on a number of their earlier articles, the authors were also active as consultants in Florida as well as a number of other states confronted with the problems of unresponsive government. Chiles' approach of bringing in experts and intellectuals was in some ways reminiscent of the Progressive movement of almost a century earlier. Then both Theodore Roosevelt and Woodrow Wilson pushed analyses of American politics by intellectuals such as Herbert Croly's *The Promise of American Life* and Walter Weyl's *The New Democracy*.

The chapter headings in *Reinventing Government* were a veritable catalogue of the terminology of those advocates of bringing entrepreneurial, market management into government and public administration: Introduction: An American *Perestroika;* 1. Catalytic Government: Steering Rather than Rowing; 2. Community-Owned Government: Empowering Rather than Serving; 3. Competitive Government: Injecting Competition into Service Delivery; 4. Mission-Driven Government: Transforming Rule-Driven Organizations; 5. Results-Oriented Government: Funding Outcomes, Not Inputs; 6. Customer-Driven Government: Meeting the Needs of the Customer, Not the Bureaucracy; 7. Enterprising Government: Earning Rather than Spending; 8. Anticipatory Government: Prevention Rather than Cure; 9. Decentralized Government: From Hierarchy to Participation and Teamwork; 10. Market-Oriented Government: Leveraging Change Through the Market. It utilized most of the buzz-words of modern business management theory, but applied them to government.

While the book was an admirable effort to deal with the "bankruptcy of bureaucratic government," its advocacy of "public entrepreneurs," critics suggested, was a confused mixing of the functions of government and the market. It is difficult to say to what extent Chiles was really committed to carrying out such a reform agenda. Be that as it may, however, the volume was a forerunner of the kinds of public-private efforts that became a goal of many of Florida's business and political leaders in the 1990s. But "reinventing government." apparently did not mean cutting back on its continued growth.

The Constitution of 1968 had provided for a redistricting after every Census. Those redistricting efforts, early in each of the two previous decades, had been "comparatively calm and agreeable affairs," as one legislative staff member observed. But 1992 proved to be quite different as the Legislature failed to adopt a plan for congressional redistricting, and came within a vote of not passing a resolution of legislative apportionment. A lawsuit by Hispanics and Republicans, reflected the growth of those two often over-lapping groups and their dissatisfaction with the existing apportionment, and resulted in the federal district court drawing up the map for the state's congressional districts.

The major event of 1992, perhaps of the entire decade in its ramifications, was initially unrelated to politics. In the early morning of August 24th hurricane "Andrew" cut across south Dade County leaving a swath of destruction in its wake. One observer later called it "the mother of all hurricanes, a tempest that would be remembered by an entire generation as Florida's Great Storm."[3] Most Floridians were unfamiliar with the events of the great hurricanes of 1926,

Destruction from Hurricane Andrew

1928 and 1935, and unprepared for the severity of Andrew. The winds of Andrew–with gusts of over 175 miles per hour–were exceeded only by the 1935 storm and "Camille" in 1969, among hurricanes which had hit the U.S. this century.

The damage from winds, tides and flooding made sections of south Dade appear as a war zone. Some of the shock was due to the realization that Andrew, only several days before, had appeared as a rather mild storm until it turned west, gained quickly in intensity, and slammed into Florida. Some compared the hurricane to something like a freak mini-tornado in the sense that it was not large–the winds extended thirty miles in all directions from the eye– but extremely severe near the center. The low pressure around the center was such that several survivors mentioned their ears popped and their teeth ached as they huddled in horror as parts of their homes blew away. Still others complained of sinus irritation. The low pressure of 27.23 inches was exceeded only by the measurements in the 1935 hurricane and Camille.

The severely hit area, about the size of the city of Chicago, was strewn with boats, cars and mobile homes and partially, or totally destroyed homes and businesses, with the city of Homestead virtually flattened. A particular tragedy was the damage done to the animals and natural habitat of the Miami-Dade Metro Zoo close to the center of the storm. Even offshore reefs were damaged. The overall estimated effects of Andrew in Florida were staggering:

43 deaths in Florida, 15 directly, 28 indirectly
$30 billion plus in damages
700,000 refugees evacuated
175,000 people homeless
80,000 housed in shelters
25,000 homes destroyed, 100,000 damaged
8,000 businesses damaged or destroyed
278 K-12 schools damaged, 23 heavily, 9 destroyed
2,300 street signal lights destroyed
50,000 street signs destroyed
29,300 troops deployed
100,000 persons forced to leave Dade County permanently
$70 million donated to the Red Cross for relief
35 million tons of debris, more than 30 years worth
6,382 construction fraud complaints, 1,125 charges filed

With another nine deaths in Louisiana and the Bahamas, and an additional $1.5 billion in damages, hurricane Andrew was ranked as the nation's worst-ever natural disaster. Even several weeks later National Guardsmen were still in the area helping to meet the basic needs of the homeless, and a "tent city" was erected that would house the homeless refugees for months to come.

Andrew raised three areas of serious concern. The first was how to prepare for such a severe storm in the future. The thousands of complaints were based upon the growing evidence of shoddy construction. Either city and county building inspectors were incredibly slipshod in their inspections of whether trusses had been strapped down properly, and other such crucial structural details, or they were willing to overlook such omissions for a price, or both. In the years that followed there were investigations which revealed examples of all three.

It is interesting that in this crisis, so little consideration was given to alternatives other than government inspections, although a few critics did point out that competent engineering firms were capable of providing the same services which would serve as a basis for securing both home mortgages and insurance. In promising to improve haphazard inspections and eliminate bribes, governments also sought to improve the construction codes with respect to hurricanes; one aspect of preparing for the next severe hurricane.

Some of the worst of the shoddy construction took place in the wake of the hurricane as unscrupulous builders and sub-contractors sought out those who had received insurance checks with promises of quickly rebuilding their homes. Getting them to deliver on those promises, after some payments had been made, was another matter. Roofers especially felt the force of public anger. Many homeowners came to feel that the frustration of this experience was ultimately worse than the hurricane itself.

The problem was that strict codes raised the cost of the average home by thousands of dollars. As with any such solution, while costs escalated in an effort to reduce risk and damages, there were diminishing returns for such expenditures as the risks came closer to zero. A concrete bunker might be a totally risk-free hurricane house but, of course, it would be costly and perhaps lack something in appearance and livability. Closely related to this problem was using such a severely focused storm as Andrew as a basis for establishing new building codes. It would cost billions of dollars to make every home in Florida capable of withstanding such a hurricane with minimum damage.

Finally, there was the insurance issue, also brought to a head by Andrew. State Farm Insurance, for example, paid out nearly $4 billion, over seven times as much as any previous pay-out by a company. Eleven insurance companies failed in the wake of Andrew and another forty companies withdrew from doing business in Florida, or cutback on their property underwriting business in the state.

As a result of these actions, the state was forced to examine the whole issue of hurricane damages and insurance. One worse-case scenario study concluded that if hurricane Andrew had come ashore a few miles to the north in the center of metropolitan Miami, the damages would have been two to three times worse; in the range of sixty to one hundred billion dollars. Such an amount would have wiped out many insurance companies and affected the whole infrastructure of international business in the city, including banking, exports and services. The scenario was even more grim had such a storm hit in the area of Tampa Bay.

The year after Andrew, the Legislature created the Florida Hurricane Catastrophe Fund which mandated that a small part of each homeowner's monthly premium be invested into a fund to help pay for residential damages. The purpose was to build up a fund that might help to pay for the cost of a future "Big One."

As a result of all of these lingering problems growing out of Andrew, the Legislature in 1995 requested leaders in the university community to put together what became known as the Florida Academic Task Force on Hurricane Catastrophe Insurance. The group was to explore this issue and make recommendations as to how to deal with it. One of the conclusions of the Task Force served as a warning for the future: as bad as it was, hurricane Andrew was not the "Big One." A "real 'Big One,' or worse—two 'Big Ones' hitting major metropolitan areas within a few years of each other—could bankrupt insurance companies, builders, Realtors, the State of Florida, hundreds of thousands of Florida's homeowners, and the banks which financed their homes. That's how big the potential of this problem is."

One aspect of the problem of insurance rates covering damages was that the frequency and intensity of hurricanes tend to run in long-term cycles. Despite the number of fierce storms we have had, a case can be made that the better part of this century, in which Florida has experienced its phenomenal growth, has been a relatively less intense cycle of hurricanes. This in turn resulted in insurance premiums that were much less than would have been the case had this century been characterized by even more frequent and intense hurricanes. If that is the case, Floridians have to also consider a scenario, in addition to the one or two "Big Ones," in which we experience a growing number of less intense storms which collectively cause an enormous cost in damages. And, in the meantime, as a result of Andrew, homeowners' insurance continued to rise. Understandably, Florida homeowners found it difficult to accept the reality that premiums had been calculated in a long cycle of relatively few hurricanes, which now appeared to be changing for the worst.

Since Andrew, the 1990s brought a few more nasty hurricanes, but a "Big One" did devastate parts of Central America. In July, 1994, tropical storm "Alberto" caused severe flooding and $40 million in losses in west Florida, and two months later "Beryl" flooded much of the same area, while in November "Gordon" caused considerable damage, and four deaths, in south Florida. For 1995 hurricane forecasters had predicted a dozen storms but then raised that estimate to sixteen, but nineteen were actually named. Of the eleven that reached hurricane force, seven actually threatened or hit the state. In early August, 1995, there was "Erin," which cut across central Florida, veered out into the Gulf of Mexico and then hit the Florida's Panhandle near Pensacola. In early October "Opal" also struck the Panhandle inflicting considerable damage. In 1998 Floridians were reminded that the "Big One" could still arrive when hurricane "Georges" swept across the Caribbean damaging homes and businesses in a number of islands including Puerto Rico, the Dominican Republic, Haiti, Jamaica and Cuba before hitting Key West, where it caused extensive damage. But the worst disaster in Caribbean Basin history was "Mitch," which also wandered across the Sea before smashing into Honduras, Nicaragua and Guatemala with seemingly unending rains that washed away whole villages in huge mud slides. The deaths, running into the thousands, may never be known with any degree of certainty. Floridians reached out to help these nations for humanitarian reasons, and in the knowledge that the unity of the political economy of the Basin was now such that a disaster in one part would eventually likely mean more refugees arriving in the state.

One final result of Andrew was the creation of joint underwriting associations (JUAs) by the legislature. As traditional insurance companies withdrew from writing policies, increasing numbers of people turned to these "thinly capitalized" entities, which quickly became the largest home insurers in the state. Any major hurricane would bankrupt them, or force them to issue public bonds to cover pay-outs.

In 1995 the damages from Erin and Opal caused a deficit among the JUAs. In a kind of "each according to his need" neo-socialist approach mandated by the legislature, each insurer doing business in the state was assessed an amount of money based upon its share of business to "bail out" the JUAs. The insurers were permitted to recoup these fees from their existing policyholders. Given that "Robinhood" approach, it was understandable that the JUAs became so popular so quickly. By 1996, the State found itself in the position of being the second largest insurer in Florida while even private companies asked for more support.

The 1992 elections saw Democrat Bob Graham re-elected as U.S. Senator over Republican Bill Grant by a margin of almost two to one. After 38 years of service in the U.S. House of Representatives, Dante Fascell retired while at the same time women and minorities continued to become more involved in politics. In losing to Democratic candidate William Jefferson "Bill" Clinton, the Governor of Arkansas, incumbent Republican President George Bush barely managed to capture Florida's electoral votes with 40.9 percent of the ballots, while his opponent had 39 percent. The big surprise, indicative of the deep dissatisfaction with government and the existing dominant two-party system which was manifest across the nation, was the showing of multi-billionaire businessman H. Ross Perot's Reform party. It garnered almost a fifth of the votes for president, thus barely depriving Bush of a clear majority in the state. In the Florida Senate both parties were now evenly split, but with the Democrats still holding a comfortable majority in the state's House. In the U.S. House of Representatives Republicans now outnumbered Democrats 12 to 11. Among minority newcomers was Cuban-American, Lincoln Diaz-Balart, who joined Ileano Ros-Lehtinen, elected in the previous decade, and blacks, Corrine Brown, Carrie Meek and Alcee Hastings.

Hastings' election was an interesting vindication by voters in a predominantly black district. In 1988, when sitting as a Federal District Judge in Fort Lauderdale, he was charged with perjury and conspiring to solicit a $150,000 bribe. Although acquitted of these charges in a criminal court, after a brief debate, the U.S. House of Representatives voted 413 to 3 to impeach Hastings, and the Senate voted to convict him. He had been a long-time political activist, who had run for Secretary of State and had been appointed to the bench in 1979 by President Jimmy Carter. In 1992 a Federal court voided his conviction, and, ironically, Hastings now found himself a member of the House in which many of his colleagues had earlier voted for the impeachment charges against him.

Perhaps the best example of the public's dissatisfaction with the existing political system early in the decade were the ten amendments proposed to the Constitution in 1992, nine of which appeared on the ballot, and eight of which were passed. The exception was a proposal to allow cities to add a penny sales tax, the vote on which was thus also indicative of a general feeling against more taxes. The amendment with the greatest potential long term impact was one proposed by citizen initiative which was passed by an over three to one ratio of voters. Often referred to as the "Eight is Enough" amendment, it limited legislators and elected office holders to that number of consecutive years in office. By the middle of the decade, the results were already evident as some powerful politicians took advantage of other political opportunities to leave before being forced to do so. The full effects of the amendment would not, of course, be felt until the elections in the year 2000.

At the federal level, however, the election of 1992 was the culmination of a gradual loss of senior Congressional leaders which had begun with Lawton Chiles stepping down as Senator in 1988. The Speaker of the U.S. House of Representatives, Thomas P. "Tip" O'Neill, had in the 1980s characterized the Florida delegation, especially those Democrats from the Miami area, as holding more power and using it more effectively than the representatives of any other state. Claude Pepper died in 1989, followed in 1992 by the retirement of several others who had held important committee positions such as Dante Fascell, William Lehman, Charles Bennett and Larry Smith.

If Florida's delegation had lost some clout, it remained one of the wealthiest in the nation's capitol. At a time when voter dissatisfaction and non-participation were at all-time highs, a report by *The Miami Herald* observed that the government was becoming something of a plutocracy, a "Millionaire's Club," as critics had once shouted in those long-gone eras of Populist and Progressive reform. One of every six congressmen was a millionaire, about thirty-five times as great as the population as a whole, as more candidates financed their own elections.

The Florida percentage was even higher, as eight of Florida's delegation of twenty-five members was in that elite "Club." Leading the group was Bob Graham with $6 million, ranking him twenty-fourth among all members of the Congress.

Upon becoming President in January 1993, one of Bill Clinton's first actions was to attempt to appoint a woman as Attorney General of the U.S. After several selections became mired in controversy as both drew criticism for having hired nannies illegally, on the recommendation of Senator Bob Graham, the President turned to Ms. Janet Reno of Miami. In 1978 Governor Reuben Askew had appointed Reno as the first woman State Attorney, serving in Dade County, where by 1993, she had compiled a distinguished record. She had the misfortune, however, to enter office as federal agents besieged a religious sect in Waco, Texas. In the ensuing fire a number of the members of the group perished. Reno assumed full responsibility for the decision to pursue a confrontation, based upon information, later questioned, that the sect was sexually abusing some of the younger members.

Reno's tenure as Attorney General has been a tumultuous one. She was caught in the crossfire of a number of special prosecutor and independent counsel investigations. These ranged from the death of presidential aide Vince Foster, to allegations of wrongdoing by Clinton and his wife, Hillary, on land deals such as Whitewater when he was governor, seeking election funds from Chinese sources, to allegations of sexual abuse and harassment, to perjury about an affair with White House intern Monica Lewinsky to name several. Based upon the investigation of Independent Counsel Kenneth Starr, the House of Representatives voted charges of impeachment, but the president was exonerated in the Senate. By 1999, despite criticisms of partisanship, and suffering from advancing Parkinson's disease, Reno had held office longer than any Attorney General this century, and appeared a safe bet to complete her term early in the year 2001.

Even before Reno's selection, another Florida woman, Carol Browner, chief of the state's Department of Environmental Regulation, had been named to head the U.S. Environmental Protection Agency. Lawton Chiles, in an effort to solve the environmental problem posed by the continued degradation of the Everglades, and the on-going battles between environmentalists on the one hand and ranchers and farmers on the other, appointed a Governor's Commission for a Sustainable South Florida composed of a number of distinguished government, business and environmental leaders headed by former House Speaker Richard Pettigrew. Tired of "trial by combat," where "we fight until everybody gets exhausted, and then fight in the courts," the Governor noted, "It's expensive, and much damage occurs when that happens." While this was a noble beginning effort, by 1999, as will be discussed later, plans for the Everglades were still being put forward, debated and modified with an eye to solving the problem at some point in the twenty-first century.

Nowhere was the contradiction of policies about the Everglades more evident than in the local and state politicians reactions to multi-millionaire Wayne Huizinga's proposal to build a giant amusement park–quickly dubbed "Wayne's World"–on the edge of the Everglades along the western border of Dade and Broward counties. Noted increasingly for his philanthropy, Huizinga had made his first fortune with the Waste Management Corporation. Bored with an early retirement, he had returned to become owner of Joe Robbie Stadium and the Miami Dolphins football team in addition to the Florida Marlins baseball team, which won the World Series in 1997, only to see itself dismantled to save on salaries and then sold in 1999, as well as the Florida Panthers hockey franchise. He had also made an even greater "splash" in the business world with the development of the highly successful, nationwide chain of Blockbuster video stores which he sold before going on to found yet another giant company, Republic Industries, doing business in automobile sales and rental as well as waste management, to name only a few of the conglomerate's interests.

In asking for a special taxing district and a land deal, Huizinga's lobbyists, joined interestingly by those of Disney World and Universal Studios in Orlando, made the usual pitch of jobs and economic development for the state. Environmentalists, however, not only pointed to the ecological damage such a massive project would inflict on the already fragile environment of the Everglades, but that at the state's present rate of purchase of environmentally endangered lands, Huizenga was seeking what amounted to almost a $27 million donation from the state. As a potential battle took shape, Huizenga sold his interest in Blockbuster to Viacom corporation, which decided it did not need a controversial amusement "world" on the edge of the Everglades, and by the following year the project died a quiet death in Tallahassee. Its interest lay in demonstrating the way in which businessmen sought subsidies.

During 1994 there also were successes and failures with respect to policies in both the Caribbean and Latin America. In December Miami was the host to an Inter-American conference led by President Bill Clinton, the Summit of the Americas, and attended by 34 nations in the hemisphere, with Cuba the conspicuous absentee. Among the twenty-three "action plans" and promises were: the goal of the creation of hemisphere-wide free trade by the year 2005, and other agreements to pursue others with respect to the environment, corruption, human rights, consolidation of democracy and the role of women in economic development. To remind the delegates of Cuba, during the conference some 50,000 Cuban-Americans staged an anti-Castro rally in Little Havana. While the Summit was a fitting year's end to hemispheric affairs, it was overshadowed by earlier tensions over refugees from both Cuba and Haiti.

Another confrontation with Cuba escalated quickly during August and September as Fidel Castro once again encouraged disaffected Cubans to take to the sea as an escape from the Island. This time, instead of a boatlift as in Mariel in 1980, people cobbled together rafts from whatever materials were available. In a little over a month over 30,000 people had fled, almost 25,000 of them to the U.S. Naval Base at Guantanamo Bay, where almost 15,000 Haitians refugees were also housed. While some observers felt Castro had gained what he desired as the U.S. increased its visa limit to 20,000 a year, others felt this was far short of what he would have preferred given those who wished to leave. Clinton's Cuba policy had been characterized by a series of shifts. Before his election, he had talked of achieving some kind of accommodation, but this changed when, in an early financial crisis in his campaign, conservative, hard-line Cubans in Miami came through with the cash to help keep him in the race.

It appeared in 1995 that the President might once again be considering a change in attitude toward Cuba. This possibility ended in February, 1996, when Cuban MIG fighters shot down an unarmed "Brothers-to-the-Rescue" airplane off the coast of Cuba, killing all four persons on board. The administration attempted to enforce the Helms-Burton act which, although called legally questionable by some experts in international law, sought to punish those foreign companies that had profited from lands or businesses nationalized by the Cuban government. It allowed them to be sued by foreign nationals who had claims against Cuba. While in 1999, the economic embargo against Cuba remained, backed by many—but not all—Cuban-Americans in Miami, it was estimated that perhaps $800 million was sent to Cuba each year by relatives in the U.S. These funds were probably larger than Cuba's profits from either sugar or tourism.

While the Castro regime talked of privatization and encouraging investments in an effort to secure dollars, its controls over the ragged Cuban economy remained extensive and its human rights record deplorable. Pope John Paul visited the Island early in 1998, hoping to influence the government's human rights policy, and there has been an increase not only in tourism, but also of travel by Americans to Cuba. Early in 1999, the regime arrested some well-known dissidents even as the Baltimore Orioles major league baseball team in late March traveled to Havana to play the Cuban National team, something no American team had done since 1959, and the Cubans reciprocated a month later.

The Haitian imbroglio developed out of two factors. The first was the military government earlier that had denied the presidency to Father Jean-Betrand Aristide, and whose record on human rights was less than satisfactory to the Clinton administration. The second was Haiti's deplorable economic condition. In such a situation, refugees from that nation continued to make their way through the Bahamas to Florida in whatever kind of boat was available, often unseaworthy and always loaded with human cargo. The U.S. first tried the economic pressure of an embargo, which cost the country dearly, given its $1 billion yearly trade with the U.S. Ultimately, the Clinton administration reverted to the old interventionist policy of sending 20,000 American troops to stabilize the situation there. By October 15, under pressure a compromise was worked out which returned Father Aristide to power.

Once again the U.S. re-learned a harsh truth; that nation building and stability tended to cease with the withdrawal of American troops and Aristide's backers were as intent on seeking vengeance as had been their opponents. Since the occupation, the situation in Haiti has improved only marginally. Conditions are not such as to attract badly needed foreign capital and the flow of refugees to Florida continues. Governor Chiles, especially, attempted to promote trade and exchanges of various kinds. A modest $500,000 of aid and a trade mission by 1998 were modest efforts to deal with the massive problems of poverty and political instability there.

In the face of these on-going problems over immigration, Governor Chiles initiated a lawsuit seeking a billion dollars in compensation for the schooling and medical costs, as well as other services, of the many undocumented immigrants arriving on Florida's shores.

The effort to improve race relations in Florida had one positive result during 1994. Earlier a study had been commissioned to belatedly examine the Rosewood massacre of 1923. Based on the report by several noted scholars, the Legislature voted slightly more than $2 million in compensation to survivors and relatives of that event.

The 1994 elections thus took place in the wake of the new wave of raft refugees from Cuba, and an increasing number of Haitian refugees due to the revolutionary situation there. In the state's Senate, Republicans now moved ahead of Democrats, 22 to 18, with

Republican Jim Scott of Fort Lauderdale as the new President of that body, while in the House, the Democrat's majority narrowed to 63-57. Republican incumbent U.S. Senator Connie Mack received over seventy percent of the vote in a smashing victory over Hugh Rodham, President Clinton's brother-in-law. The U.S. House of Representatives now contained a larger Republican majority; 14 to 9. Perhaps more important than the Republican majority in the state was the party's victory at the national level, so that it now held majorities in both houses of the Congress. U.S. House Speaker Newt Gingrich of Georgia had based a major part of the national election around a "Contract for America." The result was passage of "welfare to work-fare" legislation that would have an enormous impact at the state level as well, as the federal government began to shift responsibility for such programs back to the states.

The most interesting race, however, was for governor, between the clever, experienced, old "He-coon," Democrat Lawton Chiles, running in what clearly would be the last contest of his political career, and young Jeb Bush, the son of former President George Bush, who spoke fluent Spanish and was married to a Mexican-American. The election was extremely close, with Chiles' winning by some 65,000 votes. The final margin was due to the solid Democrat support of retirees in Broward County's large condominium organizations where the incumbent chalked up huge majorities. The campaign was the most costly to that date, with the candidates spending a combined total of over $17.5 million and laws that supposedly limited contributions to $3,000 per donor for each campaign.

As in the previous election, Chiles again developed some of his ideas around a book which reflected his concern about what had happened to government's effectiveness in Florida and America as well. This time the volume was *The Death of Common Sense: How Law is Suffocating America*, by a lawyer, Philip K. Howard which had been on the *New York Times'* best seller list.[4] The slim book was an essay about how the excessive codification of law often makes it more difficult to eliminate problems which the plethora of laws were intended to solve. It was loaded with stories of well-intentioned government bureaucrats, illustrating these efforts in futility. On the other hand, it is rather amazing that American readers, and especially an astute, observant politician like Chiles, who only a few years before had found himself a frustrated, burned-out Senator inside bureaucratic Washington, would find anything very original in the volume. Such legalism has plagued every civilization in history as it evolved into bureaucratic centralism, and over two thousand years ago the Chinese had a formal school of thought advocating such Legalism. These ideas were brought to Europe during the Enlightenment as means of opposing the divine right of kings. Voltaire, and Francophiles such as Thomas Jefferson, were apparently influenced by these views, and, as Alexis de Tocqueville saw bureaucracy developing in France, he once referred to it as "le system chinois." These views also carried over into the Progressive movement in America almost a century later, as reflected in the earlier mentioned work of intellectuals such as Croly, who advocated specialists, a cadre of trained mandarins in public administration, to oversee the new complexities of government.

If Chiles was serious about cutting back on the bureaucracies that had been growing for several decades in Tallahassee, and not just talking "intellectual politics," then "common sense" suggested he might well have started with the whole growth management empire in the capitol and throughout the state. Nonetheless, his annual address to the legislature focused on over regulation, as had his inaugural address, as the Governor pressed for improving schools as well as tax reform. He pointed to a stack of over 3,500 government rules, a pile of paper well over a foot high, and challenged the lawmakers to join him in their repeal.

A big event in Florida during 1995 was Sesquicentennial celebration of Florida's entry as a state into the union in 1845. That celebration, featuring meetings of all sorts around the state was intended, in part, to raise the citizens' level of awareness about the history of Florida. One area that benefited from this effort was the historic preservation movement dedicated to preserving many of the buildings that were an important part of the state's cultural and historic heritage.

One of the major issues of 1995 concerned prisons, and the extent to which the costs of building new prisons and housing the increased prison population, took funds away from education. While the nation and Florida had worried about rising crime rates in the 1980s and early 1990s, by mid-decade it was apparent that the crime rate was going down, especially with respect to violent crime. Law enforcement agencies were quick to take credit for the drop, but there was no shortage of theories advanced to account for the decline.

A large part of the prison building was to house inmates arrested on drug possession charges, what some critics of the system termed "victimless crimes." In some cases violent offenders were paroled from the crowded prisons in order to make room for such drug offenders. In 1985 the state's prison population was 28,000, but a decade later it had doubled to 56,000 and an anticipated 79,000 by 1998 with buildings under construction to hold 84,000 prisoners. Charles Reed, the Chancellor of the State University System, noted "What we are paying for 56,000 inmates is larger than what we are paying for 203,000 students [in the state's universities]." Construction costs per inmate averaged $22,000, plus $16,000 to house each prisoner per year, while the average cost per college student was only $5,500. Incarceration was, indeed, expensive.

At the same time, as crime rates began to drop in the 1990s, some social critics argued that it was not prisons or the criminal justice system that had experienced a growth within the state's government, but rather the welfare system. Thus, John R. Smith, the vice-president of the James Madison Institute for Public Policy in Tallahassee, countered Reed. He noted that while education's share of the budget had indeed dropped between 1990 and 1995,

from 38.6% of the budget to 28.6%, this was not due to any increase
in the percentage given to the criminal justice system. That also
had declined in the same period from 5.2% of the budget to 4.8%,
while the budget itself had escalated from $23.2 billion to $38.8
billion; a 60% overall increase in only half a decade.

Smith pointed out two areas which had been "the most successful
rivals for state tax dollars;" the Department of Community Affairs
(DCA) was one, but "the most insatiable competitor by far" was "the
state's welfare entitlement programs, especially Medicaid." Thus,
the DCA, which enforced the growth-management laws, for the past
several years had "been the state's fastest growing department;" a
case of managing growth other than its own.

But the growth of Medicaid was an even greater problem, or as
Senator Bob Graham noted, it was "the great white shark that
threatens to gobble up Florida's budget for schools and everything
else." In that five year period welfare had grown form 24.3% of the
budget to 31.6%. In terms of actual dollars, the $12.3 billion spent
on welfare was $1.4 billion more than was spent on education.

In discussing the shortage of funds for schools, educators pointed
out that when the lottery was begun in 1988, a rationale had been
that its profits would go to help education. Instead, the $800 million
produced by the lottery had enabled the Legislature to take tax
revenues away from education, while replacing them with only a
portion of the profits from gambling, so that educational funding
had dropped by almost half.

That the budget crisis, predicted by bond houses and other
investors, did not occur after 1996, was due to several factors. The
rapidly increasing Medicaid rolls leveled off and the state reformed
its welfare policies, shifting toward the work-fare legislation passed
by the federal government, while huge cuts once projected in federal
spending never materialized.

Indeed, by mid-decade, Florida presented an interesting
contrast. On the one hand, when a Harris Poll asked Americans
where they would choose to live if they could be in any state except
their present home, Florida was the number one choice, followed by
Arizona, California, Colorado, Tennessee, North Carolina and
Hawaii, in that order. At the sane time another study showed that
for children and young people, Florida ranked 46th in the overall
quality of life. Given this situation, it is understandable that concern
for the welfare of Florida's children would become a central focus of
Governor Lawton Chiles during his final term in office, and perhaps
his greatest legacy.

The 1996 Legislature addressed a number of welfare reforms
including education and job-training provisions for welfare mothers
to help them secure jobs, but with some cut in benefits. In August
1996, however, the U.S. Congress passed, and President Bill Clinton
signed into law, the Personal Responsibility and Work Opportunity
Act of 1996 (P.L. 104-193), which represented sweeping changes in
the nation's welfare system replacing Aid to Families with
Dependent Children (AFDC), with a new program called Temporary

Assistance to Needy Families (TANF). This legislation passed the House by a margin of 256 to 170, and the Senate by a margin of 94 to 24.

The bill included strict time limits, effective October 1, 1996, when eligibility for Temporary Cash Assistance became limited to no more than 24 cumulative months in any consecutive 60 month period. The time limit began with the first month for which the family received benefits. There is a lifetime cumulative total of 48 months as an adult, with a federal lifetime limit of 60 months. These time limits are not tied to any economic indicators. While great strides have been made in reducing the size of the welfare rolls in Florida, what will happen to those who have exhausted their eligibility, when the economy takes a downturn?

An effort was also made to cut down on fraud, which appeared widespread among Health Maintenance Organizations (HMOs), while at the same time encouraging more Medicaid recipients to obtain their health care needs from HMOs. In the area of education, graduation standards were raised somewhat, and experimental charter schools free of many of the regulations of public schools, yet financed with some public funds, were also approved.

One of the most astounding stories of the late 1990s was the emerging tale of election fraud, bribery and simple fiscal mismanagement in the City of Miami. It would take a chapter to detail all of the events of that saga. Given the essential bankruptcy of the City, the Governor was forced to appoint a committee to oversee its operation and approve a plan to restore its fiscal integrity. There was an enormous contrast between the economic success of the cruise ship industry based in the City's port and the striking revitalization and popularity of South Beach of the one hand and the ineffectiveness and corruption of its government on the other. The good news was that by 1999, the City might be said to be able to see the light at the end of the fiscal and budgetary tunnel.

While south Florida experienced problems of corruption and budgetary mismanagement, a racial riot exploded in St. Petersburg reminiscent of the Miami riots of the early 1980s. The violence erupted on October 24, 1996 when a white policeman shot a black motorist, and then later in November, after a grand jury ruled that the killing was justified, with property damages of over $6 million. It was the seventh police shooting of the year in that city, six of which had involved police shooting at an automobile. The protest was exacerbated when police appeared at the headquarters of the National People's Democratic Uhuru Movement, a black socialist organization and long time critic of the police department. U.S. Housing Secretary Henry Cisneros spoke of the city as one of the most racially troubled in the country, and a local historian, Raymond Arsenault called the city's mood "potentially explosive." What appeared to be a major problem was the disparity of incomes between those at the top of the city's income pyramid and those at the bottom. On the one hand 25% of the households earned over $50,000, while according to *Florida Trend* magazine, the metropolitan area led the state in retail sales and effective buying income. At the other extreme, 30% of blacks lived below the poverty level, while the median income for whites of almost $16,000 was more than twice the $7,500 of the black community. These statistics and the riots served to remind Floridians how far the state still had to go to create a greater sense of equity among its diverse citizenry.

The election of 1996 featured neither a gubernatorial race nor one for U.S. Senator; it was a presidential election year. The incumbent, Democrat Bill Clinton carried the state against the Republican challenger, Bob Dole, the first time that party had won in Florida since 1976. Only 67.4% of the voters turned out, however, the worst showing of the century. Clinton's 48% was not even a majority of the over five million votes cast as third parties took almost 10% of the vote, another reminder of the dissatisfaction with the existing system. In the U.S. House of Representatives, however, the Republicans picked up another seat, giving the party a 15 to 8 advantage. At the state level, that party increased its Senate majority by two, 23 to 17 and in the House by four, giving it for the first time a majority, 61 to 59. Clearly, the trend toward Republican dominance continued among Florida's voters.

Perhaps the most interesting part of the voting was with respect to the constitutional amendments that now appeared with regularity on the ballot. Amendment One, proposed by initiative, passed overwhelmingly. It prohibited the imposition of new State taxes or fees after November 8, 1994 by constitutional amendment unless approved by two-thirds of the voters voting in the election. Amendments Two and Three, proposed by the Legislature, also passed with large majorities. The former convened the Constitutional Revision Commission a year early in preparation for 1998 and added taxation issues which might otherwise be reviewed by the Taxation and Budget Reform Commission, while the latter restructured the area of judicial qualifications and appointments. The Fourth Amendment, proposed by initiative, was defeated by 250,000 votes of the over 5 million votes cast. It had proposed a one cent per pound tax on sugar grown in the Everglades area for a 25 year period to help pay the costs of cleaning up the pollution in that area. Somewhat related to the Fourth, a Fifth Amendment, introduced by initiative, passed overwhelmingly. It provided that those who caused pollution in the Everglades be responsible for paying for its abatement. The Sixth, and final Amendment, also by initiative, passed by a large majority, and provided for the establishment of an Everglades Trust Fund to be administered by the South Florida Water Management District for purposes of conservation and protection of natural resources in that area. The Fund can receive funding from a variety of sources, including gifts as well as state and federal funds. One of the first contributions to the Fund was the $199,000 paid by the City of Cocoa to the General Accounting Office in order to acquire the old federal post office building in that city as a home for a new facility—the Tebeau-Field Library—and headquarters of the Florida Historical Society.

The Dedication of the Florida Historical Society Tebeau-Field Library of Florida History, the old Cocoa post office, prior to its renovation.

In 1997, through a generous donation from Alma Clyde Field, the Historical Society then purchased the building from the city. After undergoing over $450,000 in renovation costs, the Library will again be open to the public late in 1999. Named after historian Charlton W. Tebeau and philanthropist, Field, for their contributions to, and support of, the study of the history of Florida, the archives, exhibits and bookstore of the new Library will be focal points for those wishing to learn more about the state's history.

Chiles' last two years in office were highlighted by his successful effort, along with several other states, to sue tobacco companies for the medical costs incurred in the attempt to help alleviate the pain and suffering of chronic smokers. While critics, including the Governor, complained of the huge amounts claimed by the lawyers in the lawsuit, and the federal government also sought to join the litigation, by 1999 the state appeared to have a windfall of some $13 billion. At the same time, Chiles sought a 10 cent increase in the cigarette tax. On their part, the tobacco companies ceased fighting the lawsuits, not unaware that a settlement did define their liability, and secure in the fact that the cost could be passed on to the purchasers of tobacco products. While the state used some of these funds to warn young people of the health dangers of smoking, it would at the same time also reap taxes from those smokers who paid the increased taxes built into the rising costs of tobacco products. In short, it was a nice arrangement, if somewhat ethically contradictory to potential young smokers, for most of the parties concerned.

The year 1997 was perhaps the least dramatic of the decade, although not without important developments. The previous year as part of an effort to cut back bureaucracy and to promote public-private organizations, the Department of Commerce was abolished in favor of a new entity; Enterprise Florida (EF). It was not only to function as an organization to promote tourism, but also to develop into other areas, especially venture capital, as part of an effort to attract more high technology businesses to the state. After one year in existence, the new organization drew a mixed response. As *The Miami Herald* described the new approach: "Take almost $100 million in state funds, add the tasks of the [former] Commerce Department, fold in support from the captains of industry and finance, sprinkle with a dash of free rein and out comes Enterprise Florida–the state's biggest experiment in reinventing government."

Within EF, Capital Development is the umbrella group for a network of state loan programs aimed at financing expanding companies–from small export firms and minority businesses to upstart technology companies. Capital Equity Fund, into which some of the state's major banks put in funds in the hundreds of thousands of dollars, was created not to invest directly in Florida but, managed by Capital Management in Boston, to invest in national venture capital firms known for lucrative returns. Florida, it appears, which ranks very low in venture capital investment, has a long way to go before setting up its own fund for investment in the state.

Some legislators had already begun to complain that the organization still had no strategic plan and was not keeping them informed. The state's Comptroller raised questions about EF's compliance with certain guidelines and briefly withheld funds. Others were outraged that some officials in EF who had moved over from the Department of Commerce, had received raises in the range of $25,000 to $30,000 a year. As a result, in 1997 the Legislature laid down rather stringent rules and guidelines to be met in two years. In 1999, as a result of EF's problems in meeting earlier target dates, at the urging of Governor Bush, the Legislature agreed to "streamline" the organization by combining its multiple boards into one main decision-making panel. It also relieved the public-private agency from some of its responsibilities for raising private-sector cash contributions.

Perhaps EF's most successful activity was interacting with the economic development that was occurring as a part of the shift from welfare to work-fare. By 1998 more than 116,000 families had made the transition toward self-sufficiency. This represented over 47% of those who had previously been on the welfare rolls. It was estimated the state was saving $25 million a month–$300 million a year–over earlier costs.

Governor Chiles was in the last years of his final term, facing a Republican dominated Legislature. Both the Governor and the Legislature sought to focus on educational reforms of various kinds. After almost thirteen years as Chancellor of the State University System (SUS), Charles Reed resigned in October 1997 to take a somewhat similar position with the much larger California State University System. Adam Herbert, the President of the University of North Florida, succeeded him as Chancellor. Herbert was the first black to serve as both a university president within the SUS and then as the head of the System. During Reed's term in office the SUS had continued to grow, adding a new university in Fort Myers, Florida Gulf Coast University, which opened in 1997. On the other hand, he had carried the centralization of the system to a point that resulted in a growing series of clashes with several of the presidents of universities within it, especially John Lombardi, the President of the University of Florida. At times it had appeared the state was not large enough to house the ambitions of both men.

One of the most significant events of 1997 was the selection of the Constitution Revision Committee (CRC)–mandated every twenty years by the Constitution–to formulate proposed amendments to be voted upon in 1998. There was concern that the process would not essentially end in failure as had occurred twenty years before. That first Committee had met 25 times and conducted 14 public hearings over a 10-month period, listened to 600 witnesses and considered 257 changes. Finally, eight amendments had reached the ballot, but all went down to defeat at the hands of the voters. The new Committee, that began 11 months of hearings in June 1997, drew immediate criticism. The Fort Lauderdale *Sun-Sentinel* observed that "unfortunately, the CRC's independence, impartiality and credibility are in doubt. Gov. Lawton Chiles, House Speaker Daniel Webster, Senate President Toni Jennings and Supreme Court Chief Justice Gerald Kogen loaded the panel with a number of politicians, ex-politicians, lawyers, lobbyists and political cronies. Jennings and Kogen even named themselves." The editorial concluded, that "so many political insiders make it more urgent for 'we the people' to participate." To its credit, not only did the Committee hold public hearings all over the state before making its report in May 1998, it also prepared a 16-page citizen's guide, a video, an educational lesson plan for students, a monthly newsletter and a comprehensive Internet web site. The amendments it placed on the ballot, which did not suffer the same massive defeat as the earlier ones, are discussed below.

The year 1998 opened with Pope John Paul's visit to Cuba, noted earlier, that created an anticipatory excitement in the Cuban community in Miami. During the dry months there were forest fires along I-95 in central, northeast Florida which rivaled those of the 1980s. Another reminder of the power of Mother Nature came when hurricane "Georges," after smashing through the Caribbean, hit Key West causing considerable damage, but nothing on the scale of Andrew. Finally, the winds and rains of "Mitch" created in terms of damages and loss of life, what was perhaps the worst disaster in the history of the hemisphere. Sending aid to the victims in Honduras, Nicaragua and Guatemala, helped to remind Floridians of the cultural and economic interdependency of the region.

In the elections of 1998, Bob Graham was easily re-elected to the U.S. Senate and remained the most important of the state's Democrats. The Republicans maintained their dominance in the U.S. House of Representatives. In the Legislature the Republican Senate majority was a striking 24 to 16 and in the House 65 to 55.

The big race, of course, was for governor, where Jeb Bush opposed Buddy MacKay, who had served for eight years as Chiles' Lieutenant Governor. Given the growing Republican strength in the state, MacKay was never able to cut into the lead early on predicted for Bush. Since his defeat in 1994, Bush had spent the four years preparing for 1998. Like his brother, George W. Bush, the Governor of Texas, he sought to develop a "compassionate" conservatism that sought to moderate some of the harsher social measures often associated with traditional conservatives. As a result, Bush won the election without any great challenge from MacKay. His running mate was James Brogan, who had served earlier as Commissioner of Education.

Perhaps of more long-term significance was the voting on the 13 amendments that had been placed on the ballot, all but one of which passed. Dexter Douglas, a Tallahassee lawyer and chairman of the Constitutional Revision Committee, that wrote nine of the amendments, observed that "in four or five years people will see great changes. They will notice every one of these."

One of the amendments eliminates, in four years, three of the Cabinet positions; the commissioners of insurance and education

The Inauguration of Governor John Ellis "Jeb" Bush, with his father, George Bush, the former President, at his left, his wife, Columba, in hat, in the foreground and his brother, George W. Bush, the Governor of Texas, at his right.

and the secretary of state. The only elected offices remaining are now the attorney general, a chief financial officer who combines the jobs of insurance commissioner and comptroller, and the commissioner of agriculture. As Dexter noted, "under the present system, we had six little governors." Of the 25 departments, the governor had control of only 12. "The governor's responsibility will be much more binding. The governor will have to belly up to the bar on what the people want."

Another amendment offers additional homestead exemption to senior, lower income Floridians, while yet another shifts many court costs from the counties to the state. Amendment #11 makes it easier for third party candidates to get on the ballot. This was an area where Florida's restrictive laws were rather undemocratic, when compared with similar ballot access laws in other states, a legacy of the fear of populist candidates such as George Wallace.

In his inaugural address early in 1999, Bush again stressed the three issues he had consistently noted during the previous campaign: education, public safety and the environment. In terms of costs, one of his first actions was to withdraw the exploration of a proposed multi-billion dollar "bullet train" to run between south Florida and Orlando, the planning funds of which had already exceeded $10 million, although advocates of the project vowed to continue their efforts.

With respect to education, after his defeat in 1994, Bush had increasingly become involved with charter schools and vouchers as an alternative answer to Florida's continued crisis in public education. Specifically, he was part of an effort, with blacks, to operate a charter school in Liberty City, site of the worst race rioting in 1980.

The 1999 session of the Legislature passed a voucher plan for schools that is certain to be a battle ground in the years ahead as it moves toward implementation. A billion dollars in tax relief was approved while keeping the budget under $49 billion, and in the field of public safety, longer sentences were mandated for those using guns to commit crimes of violence. The "Florida Forever" land preservation program was extended for another 10 years with $300 million a year allocated for the purchase of environmentally sensitive land to be added to the more than one million acres purchased during the decade. Finally, the Lawton Chiles Endowment for Health and Human Services was established. Its earnings are to be derived from the $13 billion settlement, which the state expects to receive from the major cigarette and tobacco companies, long pursued by Chiles, $1.3 billion of which has already been banked. The proceeds will go to help fund social services and cancer research.

At the end of this brief, essentially yearly, chronology of the decade of the 1990s, there are a few additional areas worth comment where events evolved over those years and beyond. One of these concerns the growing gambling, or "gaming," restaurants and even boxing promotion businesses of the Indian tribes that now have extensive advertising in the media and their own web pages on the Internet. All of this has become rather big business. While the state's voters have rejected casino gambling, legal challenges have erupted between the State and the tribes as to what, ultimately is meant by the assumption of sovereignty. What are the limits of such tribal sovereignty? Perhaps the widest possible interpretation has emerged in Oklahoma, where some argue that the Indians should be allowed to go into off-shore banking. One can imagine such a tribal bank in Florida very soon becoming the transaction place of choice for laundering drug money. Why bother going to the Bahamas! While it is unlikely the federal government will accept such examples of sovereignty, these are important issues that will have to be addressed in the next century.

At the end of 1998 the Army Corps of Engineers presented and held hearings on its much anticipated plan to restore the water flow and viability of the Everglades. In the works since 1993, the

*No more Chickees! The Headquarters of the Seminole
Tribe, Inc., just off the Florida Turnpike in Hollywood.*

$7.8 billion plan would take several decades to complete, at probably
much greater expenditure than estimated. In June of that year
Governor Chiles had vetoed a proposal in the Legislature backed by
the sugar interests because he feared any such action might stall
the federal effort. Concerned environmentalists immediately began
to raise questions about the Corps of Engineers' plan soon after it
was presented. Given the history of such efforts, about the most
that can be offered to interested observers is "stay tuned into the
next century." Finally, the extensive forest fires of 1998 and the
Everglades fires of 1999, which erupted during long dry spells, served
to remind Floridians that the water issues of the years ahead involve
not only quality but quantity.

The population growth of two million people in this decade has
been accompanied by expansion in sports franchises in professional
football, baseball, basketball and hockey, and a mania for football
at the college level as well. To add to the University of Miami's two

national collegiate football championships of the 1980s, each of the three major football powers in the state–Miami, Florida State University and the University of Florida–were selected as national champions during the 1990s. The University of Central Florida fielded a team during the decade, and with Board of Regents approval for the University of South Florida, Florida International University and Florida Atlantic University to do likewise. At times it appeared a national championship football team was the indispensable criterion for defining academic excellence at major universities in the Sunshine state.

Such concern with football was not pressed by faculty, or even most alumni. Faculty unions were chiefly occupied with salary issues, tenure and the possible threat to the medieval lecture system posed by new technologies of learning. It was chiefly university presidents who seemed intent on developing such programs, sometimes coupled with dreams of expensive, domed stadiums. Many presidents also felt it necessary to push for expensive new professional programs in areas such as medicine and law, despite studies which indicate there is a plentitude of lawyers in Florida at this time and for the anticipated future. Florida Atlantic University's agreement with the University of Miami in medicine offered a model for saving funds without starting an entire new medical school.

For some years, as the pay gap between administrators and faculty widened under the centralizing efforts of Chancellor Reed, university presidents came to be compared to Chief Executive Officers (CEOs). Often such comparison was by members of the Board of Regents, who voted the presidents large pay increases, exceeded only by those of the football coaches of the championship teams. But a university president is ultimately not like the CEO of a business, chiefly involved in the private sector. They are salesmen seeking grants and also lobbyists pursuing more state funding. On the other hand, they have virtually ignored the entrepreneurial opportunities in, for example, that part of the university most in need of restructuring, curriculum reform. To do so would bring them into conflict with the vested interests of the faculty as it is now structured, a matter to be avoided at all costs. Real CEOs, in the market, have had to face such tough choices in the economic turmoil of the last several decades, or see their business fail.

Florida is far from alone in this problem. Probably the saddest educational story of 1998 was the rejection by the Massachusetts Institute of Technology (MIT), perhaps the finest engineering school in the world, of a $200 million grant from the Olin Foundation to start an innovative, interdisciplinary undergraduate program in that field.

The universities have also been drawn into the public-private sector initiatives begun with Enterprise Florida, with university, and even community college, presidents again leading the charge. The incentive is for the president to do something spectacular on his/her watch rather than engaging in long term planning. All but forgotten are warnings by leaders from the past such as President

Dwight Eisenhower or J. William Fulbright, both of whom had also served as university presidents before moving on to politics, about the dangers of an alliance between government, industry and universities. To imagine this warning applies only to the military and its contractors is to ignore all that is known about bureaucracy, cartel behavior, academic freedom and the integrity of research.

The question of liability also lurks in the background of such partnerships. It was certainly predictable that some businesses would agree to share liability costs with the states, as did the tobacco industry in obtaining limits of liability, albeit at a high, but fixed, price. It is worth considering what will happen as the universities become partners with companies involved in, for example, biogenetic research. Such an endeavor, from a liability standpoint, may not be as safe as was the patent on Gatorade. Would not the State also be held liable in lawsuits which could run into the billions?

Florida has charter schools and now the nation's first statewide school voucher plan. If, in the near future, these are successful, how long will it be before some enterprising faculty ask, if that model is good enough for K-12, why not offer such choices to older students, and extend these to universities as well? Given new technologies, need a university be a huge organization with a football team to educate effectively?

As the economic good times rolled on into 1999, some found it difficult to recall the overall fiscal situation in the state that major bond houses in New York City had warned about as late as 1996. In both 1994 and 1998, the Cato Institute in Washington issued "A Fiscal Policy Report Card on America's Governor's." The value of the 1998 Report, granted that Institute's libertarian, low tax bias, was that it compared 46 of the states, with the grades ranging from A to F. The governors of only three states received an F; five a D; 17 a C; 17 a B and two an A. Governor Lawton Chiles received an F, and the increasingly Republican dominated Legislature appeared almost as addicted to spending and pet project "turkeys" as did the Democrats.

In the decade 1989-1999, the state's budget more than doubled, from $23.2 billion to $48.9 billion, a far greater increase than warranted by the inflation rate or the growth of the economy in either size or productivity. This budget increase contradicts the notion that Florida is a low tax state. In the short run, the budget increases have been sustained, and any crisis postponed, by the overall prosperity of the economy.[2] One can only wonder how large the budget might have been if advocates of growth management had had their way in asking for even larger expenditures with which to administer Florida's growth, and how such increasingly large government related to the ideas of "reinventing government" and the "death of common sense."

At the base of the prosperity was the surge in technology and the stocks associated with it. If Andrew was Florida's single most traumatic event of the decade, the emergence and spectacular growth of the Internet and the World Wide Web (www) may prove to be the most significant for the state as well as the nation and beyond. Hardly a blip on the economy five years ago, their growth has been phenomenal. The future implications for Florida's history, as the Internet continues to develop, are beyond prediction.

The growth of government, and its increasing interaction with the economy, has meant that virtually every issue of public policy involves both government and the economy; an acknowledged interaction that in the past caused the two areas to be combined as "political economy." The technology inherent in the Internet has demonstrated how a new technology can quickly threaten the existing political-economic arrangements.

For example, along with other states, Florida raised the tax on cigarettes and California recently passed a massive tax increase on tobacco products including expensive cigars. As a result the sales of roll-your-own cigarette machines skyrocketed across the country since there is no tax on bulk tobacco, while sales of cigars on the Internet, and many other items for that matter, have increased enormously, partly to avoid the sales tax. Such technology offers a challenge to those who believe that the answer to every problem is more government spending, and that increasing taxation is a relatively simple matter.

Recently, the U.S. Senate discussed legislating control of gambling on the Internet, but the response of the press was that the international aspects of the Internet made it beyond the senators' control. If Internet gambling keeps increasing, it may pose a greater threat to the income for education and other items which Florida has derived from that source, than does the growing number of states establishing such Lotto type games.

The concluding chapter examines the emergence of several of these public policy issues as Florida approaches the twenty-first century, as well as the importance of the study of history to the citizens of the state as a way of helping them to better understand such issues. It also explores a model of historical development which might help the reader to analyze such issues.

32.

History as a Way of Learning: Public Policy in the 21st Century

In 2013 Florida will celebrate its Quincentennial–five hundred years since Juan Ponce de León "officially" encountered the Indians, then the sole inhabitants of the peninsula, and named it La Florida. The hostile reaction of the natives suggests he was not the first Spaniard to have visited the area. Slavers, wishing to keep secret their source of supply, were most likely the initial Europeans to land.

These almost five centuries have witnessed an escalating rate of growth and development, especially as we approach the 21st century. At the conclusion of this survey of these events, it seems appropriate to look backward over this panorama, not only because of the richness of that story, but also as a guide into the next century. As the historian William Appleman Willliams noted, history can be a valuable "way of learning." In order to do that, we need to place some of the multitude of facts in the previous chapters into some kind of perspective.

Perhaps the first observation to be made is Florida's increase to more than fifteen million people, its growing economy and its interactions with a number of countries, especially in the Caribbean and to the south, which suggests that it is conceptually useful to begin to think of it as a nation-state. South Florida alone is a rather large metropolitan city-state that rivals several of the great city-states of world history. Our economy, even without its "informal" component, ranks among the top thirty or so nations of the world, and that of Miami-Dade county alone, is greater than twenty-six of the states within the United States.

It seems useful to point this out, if for no other reason than the need to transcend some of the constraints that have tended to circumscribe the study of state and local history within the United States. It is no secret that, within academia, the study of state and local history does not carry much "prestige" among those concerned with the evolutionary development of nations, civilizations and the philosophy of history. To put it bluntly, it is unlikely that a historian of state and local history will ever be elected president of the American Historical Association.

Assuming, however, that there have been some discernable patterns of development among cultures, societies, nations and civilizations, the question arises are states somehow exempt from these tendencies? If not, then competent state historians require the same kind of training to understand such patterns at that level as those who choose to study them at some "higher" level. Was, for example, General Andrew Jackson any less of an historical figure when he was fighting Indians in Florida than when he was serving as President of the United States? Of course not! Florida's history is part of a seamless web that is at the same time a part of American history just as the latter is a part of Western Civilization, which in turn is a part of World history. Given that assumption, then the same kind of conceptual tools, right up to an awareness of the relevance of a philosophy of history, are as necessary for the study of state history as for any other kind of history.

A comparative example is perhaps instructive. At over fifteen million people, Florida has about the same population, as does The Netherlands. That nation, however, is so much smaller than Florida that our "growth management" problem fades into insignificance when compared with that faced by the Dutch. Both countries have had great concerns about water with The Netherlands for centuries using canals, dikes and levees to claim land from the North Sea much as Florida increasingly attempted to do in the last century or more in wresting land from the Everglades. Yet, in the last few years, and especially significant given the relatively small land area of that nation, The Netherlands has returned over three percent of its land to the North Sea, while in Florida politicians, scientists and environmentalists continue to wrangle about how to "save" the Everglades with "solutions" projected well into the twenty-first century.

A second observation, in addition to Florida's growth beyond that of many nation-states, is that this growth has been accompanied by an even greater expansion of the role of government, not only in the economy but into other aspects of the lives of its citizens as well. The destruction of the ecology of the Everglades, for example, was massively advanced by "reformist," "progressive," "well-intentioned" governors such as Napoleon Bonaparte Broward at the turn of the century. The worldview of political leaders such as Broward, or his "intellectual" mentor Theodore Roosevelt, often called neo-mercantilist, was that government, utilizing experts, ought to have the power to transform not only nature, but society and the economy as well; all for the benefit of the people.

This growth in the role of government has meant that virtually every issue or problem becomes one of public policy. A "governmental" alternative is advanced as the preferred solution to any emerging problem. Certainly, as we move into the new century, Floridians need to have the opportunity to explore as many alternative solutions as possible with respect to any given problem. To talk about freedom, liberty, independence or autonomy in the face of an absence of fundamental alternatives is to make a mockery of the meaning of these words. Given the growth in the role of government in this century, it is especially important to make certain that other, non-governmental alternatives are explored as well as those seeking to use government to solve environmental and social problems.

Sources of Value and Worldviews

Without getting heavily into the whole methodology of exploring such worldviews as a basis for defining alternatives, suffice it to say that two components of one's worldview are of fundamental importance. The first of these is with respect to what might be called one's basic source of values, a second is what one conceives as the "proper" relationship between government and the economy.

With respect to the first, in American society, and certainly in Florida, "equality," however defined–and there is considerable disagreement over the meaning of that word–remains a fundamental value of our society. That was the case long before Alexis de Tocqueville called attention to its importance. But the idea of equality, despite its significance in history, is a secondary, or derived value, rather than an ultimate source of value, in and of itself.

This becomes evident when the question is raised, "upon what basis does one believe in equality?" It appears there are only three ultimate sources upon which to derive values, although these have often been combined. One is what might be called "supernatural" value or law. A secondary value such as equality is so because God so ordained it. Of course, some kings and emperors, along with their priests and other intellectual advisors, have more often argued that God ordained some hierarchy and inequality, including the King's authority to rule by "divine right." Christianity offers a whole spectrum of sects across the equality question in this life, although all presumably offer equality in the hereafter. In those religions that believe in reincarnation, if one behaves in this life (accepts the existing order) there is hope for upward mobility in the next life of an eternal cycle.

A second source of value might be called "natural" law or the laws of nature. This can be combined with supernatural law as a basis for equalitarian values as Thomas Jefferson did in the Declaration of Independence, but can also stand alone, and also be used as a justification for inequalities of various kinds, often with a heavy overlay of "science."

Finally, there is what has been called the positivist, state basis of values or law. Something is so, because the state, whether authoritarian or democratic, says so. With respect to changes in secondary values, supernatural law is rather absolute, although it does change slowly in some cases over time. Natural law tends to reflect what a given society understands about nature/science at any given point in time. It might be thought of as relatively absolute. Positivist, state values can change much more quickly, such as a nation's view about the consumption of alcohol, and are, therefore, rather relative. While supernatural law and natural law remain viable concepts, what seems inescapable, as compared to the era of the American Revolution, is that positivist, state law has experienced a massive increase, especially during the twentieth century.

A Continuum of Political Economy Worldviews

Within the parameters of a worldview and its value assumptions, no two institutional mechanisms are of greater consequence than that of the state (government) on the one hand and the economy (the market) on the other. At the conceptual level, historically, there appear to be four fundamental worldviews about the proper relationship of the political and the economic, of what many have called the political economy. Across a continuum these can be labeled for the sake of convenience, socialism, interest group corporatism, mercantilism and the free market:

|—————————————————————————————————————|

Socialism   Interest Group Corporatism   Mercantilism   Free Market

Most people, including many scholars, tend to discuss these "isms" as if they were neat, discrete entities, allowing at times that there are also some kinds of "mixed" economies. In many cases, these concepts tend to become reified into virtually a dichotomy of socialism on the one hand and capitalism on the other.

One of the major points made by the historian Carroll Quigley, who earlier studied mathematics, is that we need to learn to conceptualize as does science, in terms of continua rather than discrete entities. In *The Evolution of Civilizations: An Introduction to Historical Analysis* (1961, 1979), he discusses, for example, the color spectrum in which it becomes evident there is no such entity as "the" color orange, but rather a continuous series of gradations across that spectrum. While there is something in the middle of what we might call orange that has the essence of orangeness, at some points, on either side of it, those points themselves become very difficult to pinpoint, the spectrum no longer emits a color that we might characterize as having any degree of orangeness to it.

Another way to explore these four political economies, as did the historian William Appleman Williams in *The Tragedy of American Diplomacy* (1962), is to think of them in terms of the possible relationships between a black billiard ball representing the market and a white one representing the state, as shown below.

In socialism, government attempts to remove private property and totally control the market. As we know, there are major problems with incentives, and the system lacks a way to assess the real cost of the production of a commodity due to the lack of a pricing mechanism. The market cannot, however, be totally eliminated, and

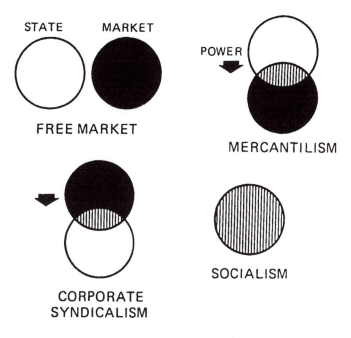

STATE   MARKET

FREE MARKET

POWER

MERCANTILISM

CORPORATE
SYNDICALISM

SOCIALISM

Four Models of Political Economies[1]

what has always remained has been a "black" market, sometimes today also called "informal" or "gray," which takes into account the risks and payoffs necessary for the system to function. Within that context, lacking any outside impetus, aspects of a socialist economy can function in a stagnant state for a considerable length of time. It is ironic that while claiming to promote equality, socialism historically developed a ruling bureaucracy to administer the system, which inevitably places itself above the rest of the society, or as the writer George Orwell put it, "All animals are equal, but some animals are more equal than others."

Mercantilism was an almost natural outgrowth of the development of the centralized, national state in the early modern era, including Spain's efforts to develop Florida. So were later American Whigs such as Henry Clay with his mercantilist "American System," and his devoted follower, Abraham Lincoln. While the mercantilist worldview accepts the idea of the private ownership of property, those "fee simple," as opposed to "allodial," property rights emanate from the state rather than from some other base such as natural rights or even a labor theory of value. Since there is never enough economic "pie" to satisfy all governments, economic nationalism accepts the idea that a zero sum game exists in which one nation may find it necessary to take from others. In order to fulfill the public good, or general welfare, it is necessary for the political leadership to regulate, subsidize and otherwise tinker with the economy. Mercantilism, by definition, means government interventionism in the economy.

The basic problem with mercantilism is that it is a very unstable kind of institutional structure. If government becomes too powerful, it tends to evolve into bureaucratic socialism, while if the economic groups within it acquire more power, it tends to develop into an interest group, corporatist structure. From a market perspective, that problem is inherent in mercantilism because the leadership will always define the general welfare and public good from its own point of view.

At the other end of the spectrum/continuum is the market, or free market, as it is often referred to. In this model government's role is to create a set of "rules of the game" so as to make opportunities as equal and equitable as possible for everyone, rather than regulating or subsidizing one group over another. Fundamental to this outlook is the notion that the size of the economic pie is not fixed, and can grow, so that everyone can have a larger piece without having to take from someone else. A market-oriented political economy tends to generate considerable differences in wealth. Critics will invariably refer to these as "inequalties" of income because of the loaded moral connotation of that term, but that accusation must be examined closely. One person can have a million dollars of income while another may have "only" $200,000, a considerable "difference," yet both can have been obtained without fraud, or some kind of governmental preference.

Which brings us to the final form of political economy, what can be referred to as the corporate syndicalist, or one might say, "interest group" model. The important point to understand about this model is that just as mercantilism creates a part of the economy in which the government becomes involved in a variety of ways, in the interest group model, government itself becomes a kind of pseudo-market for what was in earlier chapters termed "politipreneurs," rather than entrepreneurs. Politicians and government bureaucrats soon become aware that they control a rather lucrative franchising mechanism, while the powerful interest groups and their lobbyists understand what is up for sale. The party system is also an integral part of this process as can be seen today in the enormous amounts of "soft" money being contributed to them, in some cases by foreign governments interested in influencing governmental policies. Any reader who believes this to be a new phenomenon may find Walter Karp's classic exploration of almost two centuries of institutionalized party corruption, *Indispensable Enemies: The Politics of Misrule in America* (1973), worth examination.

Given these four kinds of political economies, it is understandable that those interested in power and wealth do not always reveal their true positions. With the decline of socialism, for example, many socialists emerged, predictably, as neo-mercantilists. With the recent popularity of so-called "free market" ideas, even a few neo-mercantilists have taken to using market rhetoric, and, of course, politipreneurial, interest group types have always talked of themselves as either neo-mercantilists or, more likely, "free market capitalists" to the core.

Public Policy Political Economy Alternatives

A public policy "problem" emerges when there is a clash among proponents of these four political economy worldviews as to how to deal with a given issue. That conflict can be shown by the following chart below:

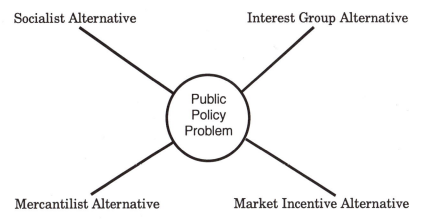

Socialist Alternative   Interest Group Alternative

Public Policy Problem

Mercantilist Alternative   Market Incentive Alternative

It is possible to insert any problem into the middle of the circle, for example, the scarcity, or shortage of water, and then explore how each of the four approaches to political economy would propose to deal with that particular issue. As we approach the new century, Florida faces a number of such issues of public policy, ranging from problems of growth, including a number of "quality of life" issues such as water, pollution, transportation, education, taxation, political reform, immigration, liability and relations with neighboring nations, to name only a choice few. This last is not often thought of as a part of disccussions of public policy, but an argument can be made that it ought to be included.

Diplomacy as an Aspect of Public Policy

With trade missions on a global scale and involvement especially in the Caribbean and to the south, it is clear that Florida already has an emerging foreign policy. Closely related to domestic public policy, the question emerges, what sort of policies ought Florida to pursue abroad?

Relations between nations can be thought of as closely related to domestic public policy choices since all four of the political economies worldviews discussed above also concern trade among nations. The mercantilist worldview, especially, conceives of international trade in a rather nationalistic fashion, but such trade is an essential component of all four systems.

In terms of trade or exchanges between two nations, there are three groups that participate in such relationships, in various combinations. The first is a people to people, or individual to individual, kind of exchange. This would include various organized, volunteer groups or organizations in Florida helping similar individuals, groups or organizations in another country such as help to Central America after hurricane Mitch in 1998. The funds sent south of the border to relatives by Mexican-Americans is also an example of this kind of exchange. While difficult to measure, these have been estimated at more than several billion dollars a year, a considerable savings perhaps of foreign aid funds. Despite the Embargo, Cuban-Americans sent funds estimated at $ 800 million or more to relatives in Cuba during the last year. These funds provide more exchange to the Cuban economy than either tourism or sugar.

A second kind of foreign trade exchange or investment is business to business, that is, between a company in Florida and one abroad. Finally, there are exchanges at the level of government to government such as U.S. foreign aid, or Florida's aid to Haiti, which was more than half a million dollars in 1998.

We can chart these three kinds of exchange relationships and their combinations thus:

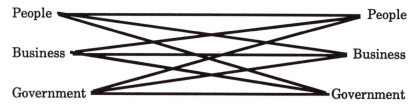

People   People

Business   Business

Government   Government

Before concluding with an analysis of the policy options both in domestic and foreign policies, it may be useful to explore the interactions of these political economic worldviews both in the American experience and Florida in particular as described through the centuries of history covered by this volume.

The Political Economy Debate in Florida's History

European exploration and settlement took place during the articulation of mercantilism as the political economy of the emerging national state. Florida was never much more than a strategic base from which to protect the larger parameters of Spanish mercantilism. Control of the peninsula was necessary as the Spanish galleons sailed north to catch the trade winds that would carry them across to Spain. Thus, the double-edged sword of Spanish colonization was the soldier on the one hand and the priest on the other. The ideal success story, which few settlers would realize, was to obtain great wealth in the New World, in order to return to Spain as a rich hidalgo.

As is usually the case with empires, the erosion of Spanish power in Florida had its source in the problems of Spanish mercantilism at home. First, the enormous wealth obtained by the Crown, broke the back of the once-emergent power of the Cortes, which at one point in the late fifteenth century perhaps surpassed the rights which the English Parliament to that point had been able to obtain from the Monarchy. The influx of gold and silver fueled an inflation which eroded the position of the middle classes, in addition to the drain of currency required for the dynastic struggles fought around Europe by the Spanish Hapsburgs. There is a certain irony in the fact we are now aware that Spanish Scholastics in the late Middle Ages and during this period were among the first in Western Civilization to understand some of the workings of the market mechanism.

The unstable nature of mercantilism, and its propensity to devolve toward the interest group model is clearly evident in Spain. At its best, mercantilism attempts to pursue a program to protect the welfare of all of society. Thus, Spanish priests and some governmental officials waged an unrelenting battle to protect the Indians and later slaves from those seeking to use governmental power to abuse them. Certainly, the Spanish record is no worse than that of the English in this regard. One is reminded of satirist H.L. Mencken's observation that the Puritans "fell first upon their knees, and then upon the aborigines."

A perfect example of the devolution of mercantilism was the way in which Seville obtained a monopoly over Spain's trade with the New World. The government's granting of monopoly privileges is, of course, one of the key aspects of mercantilism as was evident in the favorable terms to sell tea given to the British East India Company, and which led to the American Revolution, as well as in later efforts to offer monopoly rights for such things as the telephone service or electricity a hundred or so years later.

That trade monopoly enriched Seville, but impoverished the rest of Spain, while the Spanish in Florida had to settle for high priced, poorer quality goods that seldom arrived on time. Such circumstances offered a marvelous opportunity for British "informal" market operations. What prospective Spanish Florida bride would risk the chance of losing a husband while waiting for a bolt of lace for a wedding dress to make its way from Seville, when she could obtain a better quality one at a lower price much more readily from an English trader?

Finally, there was the mesta, a guild of sheep and cattle owners in Spain dating back into the late Middle Ages. As England and Flanders moved toward the weaving of cloth, the income from a tax on raw wool exports led the Spanish kings to favor that guild whose foraging animals crossed the country as Spain fell behind in an industrial development that might have accompanied the production of wool. Thus, we see repeated examples of the supposed "public welfare" of the mercantilist worldview falling prey to influential interest groups and devolving into the interest group model.

While French mercantilism never made any serious inroads on Spain in Florida, as Spanish power declined, a much more efficient British mercantilism, often inadvertently functioned as an "informal" market system. This included smuggling, as the unofficial policy of "Salutary Neglect," as Edmund Burke called it, began to expand toward Florida, especially after the settlement of Georgia in 1733. Acquisition of Florida in 1763 was an acknowledgement of the triumph of British power over Spain in the Caribbean, as well as part of an effort to make the former's mercantilist system more coherent.

Only partially hidden in the events of the American Revolution was a mercantilist-empire versus market-republic debate that involved Florida, and which would ultimately end in its acquisition by the United States. Suffice it to observe here that a number of the American leaders, nabobs such as George Washington, and especially Benjamin Franklin, envisaged a mercantilist "rising empire" which they hoped would include Florida. That leadership rejected peace overtures in 1778 because they still hoped to acquire both Florida and Canada as a result of the success of the American Revolution.

From the standpoint of the political economy debate between mercantilism and the market, perhaps the most significant event was the publication in 1776, on the same day as the formal signing of the Declaration of Independence, of Adam Smith's *The Wealth of Nations*, which some have called the most important book of the eighteenth century. His attack on mercantilism resonated among those Americans such as Thomas Jefferson, who feared the kind of powerful, centralized government associated with mercantilist policies. As we shall see, that debate became one of the most enduring themes, not only of American politics, but of Florida's as well.

The worldview of many of the leaders who wanted an active government with a "Standing Army" involved in an expansionist effort to supercede British mercantilism was very different from the militia-oriented Americans who wanted a weak, market oriented government that would essentially leave them alone. This fundamental difference was evident in 1781 when Washington sent General Lafayette north with the idea of launching another expedition to take Canada, by which time it was already clear the Canadians did not wish to be absorbed by the Americans. The Green Mountain Boys understood the situation all too well, and demanded "double pay, double rations and plunder" to participate in such an imperial venture, which Lafayette explained he was not authorized to offer. The Americans eventually made a peace that did not include these areas, and the acquisition of Florida had to wait until American power had grown accordingly

Banking, or the money question, is one of those fundamental fault lines that cuts across the political economy continuum. Hard versus soft money advocates had played a major role in colonial

American politics, as well as during and after the Revolution. Many had distrusted the Bank of England and felt likewise about the Bank of the United States. Florida's first constitution reflected this fear held by many in the debtor agrarian South. Bankers were not allowed to run for either the governorship, or the legislature, for up to a year after concluding their relationship with a bank

Florida's territorial and early statehood years before the Civil War coincided with one of America's great debates about which political economy worldview would dominate the nation's development. On the one hand were Jeffersonians and then Jacksonians, who articulated a *laissez faire*, market rhetoric, but often did not honor it in practice, opting for interest group opportunities, while on the other, were those mercantilists from Alexander Hamilton to John Quincy Adams and Henry Clay and the Whigs, who also often had difficulties honoring their rhetoric. ,

This debate can be seen in Florida over issues such as banking, land policy, railroad and canal construction, and Indian policy as well as attitudes toward blacks and slavery, the specifics of which were covered in detail earlier. What is often evident is that, rhetoric aside, both mercantilist and at times some so-called market advocates were intent on using government as a means to advance their own interests, a wonderful example of the political economy of the "interest group" state in action.

Thus, some so-called *laissez-faire* Jacksonians talked about limiting the role of government, but worked to get "pet" banks for themselves, rip off the Indians with respect to treaty obligations, increase government rules about slavery and use government to allocate and fund railroad and canal projects with about the same energy as did the supposedly mercantilist Whigs. It was not until the virtually socialist experiments with railroads during World War One that government financing and involvement exceeded what had been done by government at several levels during this supposedly *laissez-faire* era before the Civil War.

In recent years it has been popular to equate "Capitalism and Slavery," as in the title of Sir Eric Williams' well-known study, but the two are really opposites on a continuum. An important aspect of the market worldview is the freedom to exchange one's property, but at the core of that outlook is fundamental assumption that we own ourselves, and that certainly was not true of a slave. Likewise, in recent years, there has been a heated debate among historians about the "profitability" of slavery, without taking into account the enormous governmental indirect subsidies contributed to maintain the interests of the slave owners. Without these indirect subsidies slavery would have been less profitable. Given these problems, there was an inherent market tendency toward manumission, but this was undercut by an increasing number of restrictions on allowing owners to pursue that option. Taken together this suggests that slavery had begun as an integral part of mercantilist policy and was protected and expanded by an increasing number of governmental statutes. Thus, to suggest that slavery and "market capitalism" are compatable only adds confusion to any effort to arrive at a coherent definition.

Part of the reason for acquiring Florida was to deprive runaway slaves of a sanctuary. Slave patrols, required by law, were in a very real sense a tax on the non-slaveholder in favor of the slaveholder. Absent such governmentally mandated subsidies, the labor costs in a market-oriented society would tend toward manumission of slaves. The best evidence that such economic tendencies were operative is that laws were increasingly passed over the years to make manumission of slaves more difficult. Why would such laws have been necessary unless manumission was an option that undercut the slave system imposed by government? In any event, such massive governmental political-economic interventionism on behalf of the slave owning interest group is hardly descriptive of a *laissez faire*, small government, market-oriented society. That was the monumental contradiction in political economy theory and practice in Florida and the Ante-Bellum South.

Clay and his followers were consistent in working to colonize former slaves back to Africa through the American Colonization Society on the one hand, and removing the Indians to the West in a move many army veterans called the sorriest activity of their life, but the former was a voluntary group, while the latter represented an example of government sanctioned violence. As several historians and writers such as W. A. Williams and Gore Vidal have pointed out, perhaps John Quincy Adams was the most consistent mercantilist of this period in terms of attempting to develop equitable policies that encompassed different groups and interests within America. With respect to the Civil War, what else need be said beyond Lincoln's observation that he never had an opinion on slavery beyond what he got from Clay, and even late in the Civil War he was still contemplating sending blacks to Cow Island in the Caribbean.

The aftermath of the Civil War to the end of the 19th century, usually characterized as a great period of *laissez-faire*, market capitalism was, in many ways, nothing of the sort. How else to describe the virtual giveaway of public land, both state and federal, to various railroad interests and individuals such as Hamilton Disston but as perfect examples of the political economy of the "interest group" state. The Bourbons, to be sure, wanted a small government in terms of expenditures, but that did not preclude dealing away vast amounts of land and other assets, nor cracking down hard on blacks who dared challenge the emerging Jim Crow segregation laws. Not only was government sanctioned violence used against blacks, but vagrancy laws were passed to force them into participation in the restructured plantation, share cropper system, and laws were also passed to deprive them of political participation. Again, such massive governmental intervention in behalf of a majority interest group to establish "white supremacy" cannot be characterized as either a balanced, public welfare mercantilism on the one hand, or any kind of free market oriented society on the other. All such actions are governmental interventions into the area of social relations. That segregationists found them necessary so early after the Civil War suggests that blacks were making more progress economically than is often assumed.

The choices made with respect to the political economy of public policy by the reform movement at the end of the nineteenth and early twentieth centuries have influenced events up to the present. There were, of course, three alternatives open to reformers who wished to move away from the essentially interest group state which had characterized much of American history, and through which possibly develop a form of government in which the citizenry as a whole would have greater choices in public policy, rather than having choices narrowly defined by interest groups and their political friends.

A first alternative would have been to attempt to develop a socialist political economy as advocated by some workers and intellectuals, but even the vestiges of that movement were spent before World War Two. The neo-mercantilist policies of the successful reformers in many areas led to somewhat Socialist institutions as some New Dealers frankly admired the Fascism of Mussolini's Italy or Stalin's Communist Soviet Union. The publication of the writings of John Maynard Keynes came to provide a rationalization of government intervention in the economy that was already well underway.

A second alternative would have been to attempt to develop a really equitable market-oriented political economy as advocated by 19th century Classical Liberals such as Samuel J. Tilden (perhaps the best potential President we never had in terms of market ideas) or his disciple Grover Cleveland, rather than the interest group state model, whose primary beneficiaries often proclaimed themselves Capitalists. But that alternative also fell by the wayside, viewed by many as outdated, if not impossible.

What triumphed instead was a kind of neo-mercantilism laced with a heavy dose of imperialism and racism by "reformers" such as Theodore Roosevelt and Woodrow Wilson. What both had in common, drawn from intellectuals such as Herbert Croly and Walter Weyl, was a belief that this neo-mercantilism could be equitably administered at the local, state and national levels by a professionally trained bureaucracy of managers since the corrupt party politicians could not be trusted to keep from colluding (franchising out favors) with the powerful economic interests which dominated the interest group state.

Florida, of course, had its bevy of politicians who represented these various worldviews at the state level including such notables as Napoleon Bonaparte Broward and Sidney J. Catts, but on the whole conservative, neo-Bourbons kept control of the machinery of local and state government in the Sunshine State.

The 1920s Land Boom that initiated Florida's economic take-off, offers a wonderful example of the continuing interest group state in action. An important "reform" of the progressives was to institute a central banking system on the European model known as the Federal Reserve System which enabled the national government to inflate the currency as a new means to promote the general welfare of the people. There were several such "injections" of money, in 1924, and again in 1927. Since such inflations cause people to look around for speculative investments, land promoters in Florida were happy to oblige, as was the stock market. Since it takes a year or so for the effects of the inflation to work its way down through the economy, the land crash of 1926 ought not to have been unexpected and occurred before the devastating hurricane of that year helped the process along. The final push toward depression was the Smoot-Hawley Tariff of 1929 which severely restricted the country's ability to trade with other nations.

Among the primary beneficiaries of this inflation were the bankers, who took the opportunity of creating money like a duck takes to water. Of all the books on Florida's 20th century history, none is more important than Raymond Vickers' perceptive *Panic in Paradise*, mentioned in an earlier chapter, in revealing the actual financial workings of the political economy of the interest group state in the 1920s. Florida's banking laws and controls lent themselves to collusion between the bankers and those supposedly regulating them. Some bankers, such as Addison Mizner, who was also a noted land developer, were deeply involved in these activities. A variant of these events took place in the savings and loan debacle of the 1980s, with government again coming to the aid of that banking interest group to protect its losses and liabilities.

Early in the 1920s some opponents of an unrestrained market society such as Herbert Hoover attempted to steer a middle course between that alternative and the kind of increasingly popular interest group corporatism emerging in Mussolini's Italy, or a radical American socialism which had been partly manifested in the agrarian, Populist Revolt at the turn of the century, let alone the Russian Soviet type Communism advocated by some American communists. The perceived socialist threat in the 1920s was the initial reason for the passage of Florida's notorious ballot access laws, later because of the potential populist appeal of George Wallace in the late 1960s and after.

It is important to understand the meaning of the triumph of the New Deal in terms of political economies as well as its effect on Florida politics. Since the Civil War and the end of the century protests, Florida had become an increasingly Democrat, one-party state. Gaining the nomination of that party for office was considered in the "Solid South" as "tantamount to election". The Democrat alliance of labor, northern urban political bosses and the South, meant that Florida's United States senators and congressional representatives would play a significant role in the distribution of the increased government spending which was a major part of the New Deal.

The Cold War, which touched Florida in the several crises of the 1960s, was another reason given for the need to expand the expenditures in areas such as the space race, Florida certainly benefited economically from these vast expenditures.

World War Two thus ushered in a long period of growth in Florida that at the end of the century has not yet abated to any great degree. But government involvement in various areas of the lives of Floridians increased even more rapidly, with the commensurate expenditures as discussed in several earlier chapters in areas such as welfare, health, child care, growth management and liability to mention several.

The collapse of Communism in Europe, and the modest "market" reforms in China, have muted the accusations of socialist-oriented intellectuals in the United States, Florida and elsewhere, that the market system is an inefficient method of production. At the same time advocates of socialism and neo-mercantilism have shifted the argument to what have come to be called "quality of life" issues, suggesting that government's size and scope must be expanded to deal with these problems. It is these "quality of life" issues that require examination, for many of them will comprise the majority of the public policy issues of the twenty-first century.

"Quality of Life" Issues and Public Policy

There is not space here to discuss the specifics of all of the public policy issues which various polls show to be of continuing concern to Floridians such as education, crime, economic development, etc., all of which are related to the political economy alternatives discussed earlier. Like death and taxes, they are apt to remain with us in one form or another for a long time to come.

Fortunately, for Floridians, the debate between neo-mercantilists and market advocates initiated by Adam Smith over two centuries ago, is alive and well as we move into the twenty-first century, not only among political parties, but among the State's intellectuals as well.

Since the New Deal, the Democratic Party has been primarily identified with advancing a neo-mercantile agenda, both nationally and in Florida, while in the last several decades, certainly since the early 1980s, the Republicans have been more likely to favor quasi-market solutions. To some extent, this can be seen in Republican Governor Jeb Bush's recent push for school vouchers.

It would be an error, however, to imagine that either party is irrevocably tied to any particular political economy worldview. For much of the nineteenth and early twentieth century, it was the Democrats, from Jackson through Tilden and Cleveland, who tended to advocate market solutions, while the Whigs and their successor, the Republican party, were noted for a mercantilist worldview and sympathy toward big business. Such a *volte face* could well occur again.

The most recent intellectual statement of an increasing governmental role in a rather neo-mercantilist framework is found in David R. Colburn and Lance deHaven-Smith's *Government in the Sunshine State: Florida Since Statehood* (1999). The authors, respectively professor of history at the University of Florida and professor of public administration at Florida State University, write candidly of the need for more funding and a necessary increase in governmental power in such areas as growth management. Thus they note:

> And yet *unregulated* growth represents the major threat to the state's future. No state, even one as large as Florida, can continue to accommodate 2 million or more new residents every decade without experiencing a profound impact on its *quality of life*. Moreover, Florida's fragile environment and its water supply, especially in south Florida, are threatened by *uncontrolled growth*. ...[M]ore and more Floridians are seeking ways to *regulate growth*.To do so, state and local governments must be able and willing to *regulate growth*.... [p. 149, all italics added].

These observations, the repeated use of terms such as "regulate," or "unregulated," and "uncontrolled," in a negative sense, offer an almost perfect insight into the neo-mercantilist mind set, as the proponents of that worldview now turn their attention toward "quality of life" issues.

In the typical mandarin, bureaucratic outlook of the neo-mercantilist advocate of greater governmental regulation, their book repeatedly criticizes the electorate for having "such a negative attitude toward political leadership that they do not trust their politicians to provide suitable direction for the state." Both former governors Reubin Askew and Bob Graham (now U.S. Senator), the governors most associated with expanding growth management and regulation in general, have endorsed the book. Clearly, some politicians and their intellectual allies, are unhappy that the voters have such a "negative attitude" and lack of "trust" of the nostrums of the neo-mercantilist, regulatory state.

Nowhere in this slim volume is there any indication that the authors are aware of the market solutions to growth and quality of life problems that are being discussed elsewhere around the world and within the U.S. Their arguments are essentially those of the 1970s, with demands for even more money and control to implement this regulatory solution that somehow has not yet accomplished its goal. If Florida's voters display the "negative attitude" and lack of "trust," described by Colburn and deHaven-Smith, it may simply be that they want some more imaginative solutions to quality of life issues than have been offered by the existing political and intellectual elite. Some of the critics have even suggested that such regulatory neo-mercantilism, far from solving these issues, has actually exacerbated them.

If one believes that the role of the intellectual is to inform both the public and the political elite about public policy alternatives, then Florida has one of the most significant such intellectuals with respect to offering market solutions to quality of life issues as the state approaches the twenty-first century. In *Public Policy and the*

Quality of Life: Market Incentives versus Government Planning (1995), Randall G. Holcombe, the DeVoe Moore Professor of Economics at Florida State University, develops a contrasting analysis of Florida's quality of life issues to that of Colburn and deHaven-Smith.

Holcombe begins with a discussion of the differences between government planning (regulation) on the one hand and markets and market incentives on the other. "[I]n the real world," he observes, "government plans are likely to work less well than can be foreseen, while markets are likely to work better than anticipated." Often, when people suggest that government get involved in solving a problem, "they view the government as a benevolent dictator who thinks the same as they do." People do not, however, agree readily on how government ought to solve a given problem, and that opens the door to what was discussed earlier in this chapter as the various interest groups and their lobbyists. And, as Holcombe observes, "Trying to solve problems through the political process invites conflict."

> The problems only begin here, because, while people have an ideal view of what those in government ought to be doing, the people working in the government may not be doing what those outside the government think they ought to do. With markets, businesses have an incentive to satisfy the desires of their customers because only by doing so will they earn the profits to keep the business afloat.... Incentives are different in the government because the government is going to collect taxes to pay for its programs regardless of how well the customers are served.
>
> Often, the incentives are perverse, so that the less well an agency does its job, the more money will flow into it. If environmental problems grow, for example, more money is likely to be appropriated to the Environmental Protection Agency (EPA).... Rather than just viewing governmental bureaucracies as agencies that unwaveringly do the best thing, it is worthwhile to examine the incentives more closely to see if they really can be counted upon to serve the public interest. [pp. 17-18].

Holcombe follows with an analysis of the incentives for a bureaucracy as well as the role of special interests and other political influences in the system. In this respect, it is worth noting that the "Eight is Enough" term limits on political office recently upheld by the courts, is apt to increase the power of bureaucracies and the special interests relative to that of elected officials in the state, thereby decreasing the real powers of the electorate.

There is not space here to explore Holcombe's chapters on "Protecting Future Resources," "Protecting the Environment," "Growth Management and Land Use," "Housing and Homelessness," "The Regulation of Quality Standards," "The Regulation of Health Care," "Health Insurance and Public Health," and "The Drug Problem," but the reader interested in exploring the specifics of market solutions to these various problems will find his book illuminating with respect to the range of possible market alternatives in these areas.

Water Issues and Government Liability

Two specific domestic public policy issues facing Floridians as we approach the twenty-first century deserve further comment. The first of these is the water problem, noted above by Colburn and deHaven-Smith, the other is the more general question of liablity, not only in the case of individuals and businesses as in the recent lawsuits over tobacco pushed especially by Governor Lawton Chiles, but with respect to government as well.

In recent years there has been a growing concern about the depletion of Florida's water reserves as well as of the quality of the water that is consumed. Advocates of market incentives would argue that, despite its growth, Florida has an enormous reserve of water; that it is not a matter of scarcity, but rather shortages caused by existing policies.

In *The Wealth of Nations*, Adam Smith noted the paradox that while water was essential to human existence, it cost only a pittance. Little has changed in America in the last more than two centuries. As a recent article, "How to Stop Squandering Water? Raise its Price," in the *New York Times* noted, one "can fill an eight-ounce glass of water with tap water 2,500 hundred times for less than the cost of a can of soda."

The reason Floridians do not conserve water, but on the contrary have one of the highest per person usages on earth, is because it has been exceedingly plentiful and there has been no real cost mechanism associated with it as the demand has risen and the quality declined. Given no cost factors, agriculture uses, and also wastes, by far the greater portion of Florida's water supply.

When water meters are added to those communities that formerly had none, water usage drops by 40 percent. Studies by the American Water Works Association indicate that 39 percent of the nation's 60,000 public water systems have uniform pricing, no matter how much water is used, and that a third actually encourage waste by offering volume discounts. That is essentially the situation in Florida as well.

A complaint to establishing a real cost/price for water is that this will hurt the poor, but we can follow the lead of electric utilities that subsidize a base kilowatt-hour electricity use with very low "life-line rates." As the price of water goes up for those with increased usage, other means of increasing supply, such as desalinization which has dropped dramatically due to new technologies, increasingly come into play. Increased cost to real price levels not only helps conserve, but generates funds to deal with the quality of water as well. If we continue present policies, the ecology will be permanently damaged by lowered water tables as on the southwest coast of the state and the subsequent salt water intrusion.

coast of the state and the subsequent salt water intrusion.

But the amount of water available is also related to the ways in which we have chosen to dispose of waste water and sewage. Quite apart from introducing real cost into the water equation, the amount of waste water and sewage that can be recycled without great expense, places a totally different perspective on the water problem, always one of the issues stressed by proponents of greater growth management regulation.

Septic tanks, for example, have been seen as great sources of potential pollution. Thus, new suburban communities must have centralized sewage systems, an elaborate and expensive series of lines leading to a processing station, where the effluent, often not fully processed is then pumped off to pollute such waters as the Gulfstream, the Gulf of Mexico, or into the acquifer. This process also means that a great portion of water, as with that released in the ocean by the dams in the water control system is not allowed to return into the ground where it can recycle into the acquifer.

But it is government restrictions, not the technology itself, which have created the notion of the inefficient, polluting septic tank. This has suited government planners because it made the regulation of the number of septic tank permits an easy way to control growth. The septic tank is not, however, inherently inefficient, only the anaerobic type which, because of a lack of circulating air, prevents bacteria from efficiently converting sewage.

During the late 1970s, some experiments were made with aerobic units. Had these been continued, costs would have dropped and the rational for using septic tank permits to control growth would have come into question. It is possible to obtain potable water with such a system, should that be desired. The growth of suburbs with ample size lots offers efficient filtration to recycle such waste into the ground on a vast, but decentralized, scale that also avoids the pumping of less than processed wastes into deep wells as is practiced in many areas.

But improving the toilet technology of the septic tank runs contrary to the desires of the many special interests that have become institutionalized around this area of the environment. Centralized sewage systems mean a vast expenditure of governmental funds as well as establishing an organization to operate them, often the selling of huge bond offerings and nice profits for those who obtain the contracts to build the projects. This has been one of the prime areas of corruption in Florida and elsewhere, but even without corruption the system is quite profitable for a number of the groups involved in the process. Finally, the city or county has a monopoly over the system. It can raise fees, and obtain a nice income from the users of the system long after the bonds have been retired.

In observing this system in action, the historian is reminded of the decline of other societies and civilizations where those in control refused to allow the introduction of new technologies because they understood that would threaten the structure of the existing order. Roman engineers, for example, understood the technology of the steam engine that later fueled the Industrial Revolution in the West, and used it to power childrens' merry-go-rounds, but it was never allowed to replace the system of slave labor.

One of the problems of allowing government to define the parameters within which a problem can be solved is that those interest groups with access to government will seek to keep potential solutions within existing paradigms under their control rather than allow market incentive solutions which might lead to the conceptualization and exploration of new paradigms.

This brings us to the final domestic public policy issue to be explored here, that of liability. For politicians real liability seems to be reserved for those entities with deep pockets, notably these days the big tobacco companies which Governor Lawton Chiles took such pride at having taken to the woodshed, so to speak. Quarrels over lawyers' fees apart, these questions are far from settled, and in the meantime the 1997 federal tax law seems to have "accidentally" given the tobacco industry a $50 billion tax break which over the years should help to pay those damages. The interest group state is alive and well!

At the same time, although much less noticed, government is also beginning to be held liable for some of its actions. It is our view that this will, indeed, become the great public policy issue early in the next century.

For centuries states cultivated the idea of "sovereign immunity" with the same dedication which White House lawyers of both parties have, over the last 25 years, argued for expanded notions of the idea of "executive privilege." Both are concepts well suited for the Leviathan state based on political economies of either socialism or mercantilism. The view that government is "immune" from the liabilities and responsibilities to which individuals and businesses are regularly held is fundamentally inconsistent with a belief in a free society based on a rule of law.

Interestingly, as shown by legal scholars such as Peter H. Schuck of the Yale Law School, in his book, *Suing Government: Citizen Remedies for Official Wrongs* (1983), the civil rights laws of the 1960s have been instrumental in undercutting government's claim to sovereign immunity. In short, it can be held liable and sued just like the rest of us. These events form a backdrop to the modest compensation given by the State of Florida to surviving families of the Rosedale massacre of blacks in the 1920s.

But something like that massacre is but the tip of the iceberg when it comes to the question of government's potential liability. As we learn more about government's role in environmental damage during the past century, including to the property rights of numerous individuals, the costs could be enormous.

Lawsuits aside, government's financial liabilities are rather large in and of themselves. This has been muted of late by the economic prosperity and modest surpluses of the 1990s, but these obligations remain, and in some cases, are rather open-ended. Only three years ago, before the euphoria developed about the economic the State's monetary and fiscal affairs were in less than ideal shape. The boom economy, however, has quieted any calls for structural reform.

At a national level some economists have talked about the more than $4 trillion debt, while others have pointed out that total governmental debt in the US, including state off-budget expenditures, exceeds $20 trillion. The problem in our State, however, is compounded beyond such items as pensions, etc., by the question of liability with respect to hurricanes and now, increasingly, from tornado and flooding damage. While the State has tried to reduce its liability in the Joint Underwriters Association (JUA) formed after hurricane Andrew, it is impossible to predict how many billions of dollars in liability might be involved if several severe hurricanes should hit Florida in the years ahead.

In over a century, the greatest damage to Florida's ecology such as dredging canals, building levees, creating breakwaters and then restoring beach sand, has been the result of government policies. It is good that government has conceded that "straightening" out the bends in the Kissimmee river was not a very good idea ecologically, after all, but is no one accountable for the ensuing monetary damages to property owners over the years?

Public Diplomacy in the 21st Century

Florida's expanding role in foreign affairs was noted earlier in terms of several kinds of possible interactions; people, private, voluntary organizations, businesses and government. From numerous studies it is clear that government to government aid has not been all that effective, quite apart from the corruption, especially in less developed countries as in the Caribbean Basin and to the south.

Increasing business contacts and trade offer enormous opportunities both for Floridians and those nations with which we trade. In the case of Cuba, it may be time to try such an alternative rather than continuing the Embargo that appears to hurt the Cuban people more than it does the government of Fidel Castro. There has been much talk about free trade, as if the North American Free Trade Association (NAFTA), passed in the early 1990s, represented such a movement. But the hundreds of pages of regulations and schedules are almost a contradiction to the idea of free trade. NAFTA is more accurately described as a regional trade organization in the neo-mercantilist tradition, designed to compete with other such units such as the European Union.

The best thing that government in Florida could do is push to remove the empediments to travel and other restrictions which hinder individuals and private organizations from increasing contacts of all kinds between the state and other nations. In this regard, it is interesting how government seeks to define the very terminology we employ to describe reality. The successes of individuals and the private sector in aiding other peoples and nations has given rise to the idea of the Non-Governmental Organization (NGO), which government has already sought to direct toward its own goals. Why should a private organization be defined by its relationship to government? The key characteristic of such organizations, often religious groups, is that they are voluntary and in the private sector. Is it really necessary to add the negative case, that they are "non" governmental?

These developments shed an interesting light on several of the observations of Alexis de Tocqueville, that great interpreter of American democracy and equality. While praising the numerous voluntary associations as the real source of America's strength, he noted that foreign policy was the one area where the will of the people was less effectively reflected. If that is so, then perhaps we need a people's diplomacy, or rather a people to people diplomacy, instead of a government to government foreign policy, to rectify that situation.

As noted in an earlier chapter, a Floridian, Congressman Dante Fascell, was perhaps the greatest, enduring proponent of people to people diplomacy in this century. It was fitting that before his recent death he received a presidential medal in honor of his work for peace and that the North-South Center at the University of Miami is named in his honor.

Dynamism at "the Edge"

In a number of areas such as geography, biology, the environment and systems theory in general, there is a concept known by various terms such as "the edge," "the periphery," "the frontier" or "the interstices." What this means, simply, is that in any system, it is at that point of interaction that one finds the greatest energy, synergy and creativity.

Geography placed Florida at just such a point on the edge of North America. Now cultural interactions have placed her at the interstices between a North American culture and a Hispanic culture to the south. It is clear from the writings of José Martí more than a century ago that he viewed Cuba as having a similar destiny. In living in the United States and raising funds for the Cuban Revolution, he had the opportunity to observe American society much as had Tocqueville a half century before. In 1887 he noted that while retaining the appearance of a republic, the United States was becoming more "imperialistic" and "plutocratic." America's continued global interventionism and the on-going debate about "soft" money contributions to political parties, as well as the increasing role of lobbyists and interest groups, suggests his assessment is still relevant.

To the extent that Martí was correct, a people to people diplomacy will allow Floridians to find creative opportunities in which to channel the enormous energy that is generated "at the edge." It is ironic that a great deal of that energy is a product of the diverse cultural heritage that characterizes our State. In the final analysis, it is always the human capital that determines the success of market entrepreneurship, and Florida has that in abundance. Florida's diversity in human capital is not a weakness, but rather a strength.

With respect to a people to people and business to business Public Diplomacy with our neighbors to the south, a new generation of Floridians is emerging. Usually bilingual, often born here of Hispanic or Hispanic-American parents, this generation is ideally suited to develop an increasing business and Public Diplomacy with the nations to the south. Whether as a traditional American state or functioning almost as a nation-state, the new century offers Florida the chance to assume the leadership in developing the trade and economic development of the Caribbean Basin and Latin America.

This potential carries over into domestic policy issues as well. There is great ground for optimism as we approach the twenty-first century. The electorate has grown tired of the neo-mercantilist promise that more government and more taxes will solve any problem,, both foreign and domestic. Even some politicians have begun to explore the use of market solutions and market incentives to quality of life issues and beyond.

In this situation, the role of intellectuals and the media is clear: to develop new ideas about how to deal with these problems and to disseminate these ideas to the public at large for its consideration. Any solutions that involve an increased governmental role in the solution to a given problem, beyond setting up rules within which market incentives can be used to solve such it, need to be constantly monitored because of the propensity to attract special interests, and their symbiotic relationship to political parties and politicians, as well as the bureaucracies established to "regulate" the problem. This truly represents "The End of Liberalism," as described by the political scientist Theodore Lowi several decades ago in a book of that title.

Perhaps the greatest tragedy would be if the present emphasis on public-private relationships, which has already witnessed problems with Enterprise Florida, were to continue to expand into businesses and the universities. Structurally, this concept is very close to the corporatist ideas pushed early in the New Deal, and later declared unconstitutional by the courts. Critics and defenders at the time, drew the analogy with the emerging fascism in Italy, while other nations, such as Germany and Japan, carried the concept even further as detailed in Robert Brady's book, *Business as a System of Power* (1943). The continued development of such interlocking interest groups and government in Florida will make social change and political reform much more difficult.

Dealing with these problems will require a renewed emphasis on the study of market economics, especially in the areas where this intersects with law. Providing the historical context of such debates and developments is the task of the historian. It is, in fact, a "beautiful" congruence of events, that as we enter the twenty-first century, the Florida Historical Society, the essential private, volunteer, institutional organization to support such study, finally has a permanent home in the newly restored Tebeau-Field Historical Library in Cocoa. As Florida moves toward its second half-millenium of historical development, the Society and the Library are poised to play a significant supporting role in advancing the study of Florida's past; the indispensable foundation for any in-depth historical analysis of public policy issues of concern to the citizens of the Sunshine State.

One thing is fairly certain. If the past is any indication, Florida will be one of the most dynamic global centers of growth and development as the world enters the 21st century.

Notes

Chapter 7:
(1), p. 91. This chapter is based largely on Helen H. Tanner's, *Zespedes in East Florida*. See the *Selected Bibliography* for more citation information for this note and several of the others below.

Chapter 11:
(1), p. 145. A double issue of the *Florida Historical Quarterly* (Vol. XXXIII, Nos. # and 4, January-April 1955) presents and examines all of the conflicting evidence with respect to Osceola.

Chapter 21:
(1), p. 328. The final three paragraphs of this Chapter were contributed by Dr. Elliot J. Mackle, Jr., whose dissertation at Emory University was "The Eden of the south: Florida's Image. . ."

Chapter 22:
(1), p. 333. Senate Document No. 89, 62nd Congress, 1 Session (Washington, D.C., Government Printing Office, 1911), edited by Thomas Elmer Will of Belle Glade, Florida.

Chapter 24:
(1), p. 366. After an investigative Report, the Legislature in 1996 finally offered some compensation to survivors and their families.
(2), p. 376. Raymond B. Vickers, *Panic in Paradise: Florida's Banking Crash of 1926* (1994). For the role of the central banking system in the coming of the Crash of 1929 and after, see Murray N. Rothbard, *America's Great Depression* (1962).

Chapter 27:
(1), p. 430. For Collins' role in civil rights, see Tom R. Wagy, *Governor LeRoy Collins of Florida: Spokesman of the New South* (1985).

Chapter 28:
(1), p. 446. Edmund F. Kallina, Jr., *Claude Kirk, and the Politics of Confrontation* (1993). For a critique of the two-party oligopoly functioning essentially as an economic cartel, see Walter Karp, *Indispensable Enemies: The Politics of Misrule in America* (1973)
(2), p. 447. William Marina, discussions with James Bax in the Fall of 1966 and the Spring of 1990.

Chapter 29:
(1), p. 479. Harry A. Kersey, Jr., *An Assumption of Sovereignty: Social and Political Transformation among the Florida Seminoles, 1953-1979* (1996).

Chapter 30:
(1), p. 483. The discussion of the Mariel boatlift is based upon María Cristina García, *Havana USA: Cuban Exiles and Cuban-Americans*

in South Florida, 1959-1994 (1996).

(2), p. 486. The description of the Miami riots relies upon Marvin Dunn, *Black Miami in the Twentieth Century* (1997).

(3), p. 500. Steven Gold, "Unitary Tax: Wave of the Future?" Thad L. Beyle, ed., *State Government: CQ's Guide to Current Issues and Activities, 1985-86* (1985), pp. 169-171.

(4), p. 500. John M. DeGrove, in Westi Jo deHaven-Smith, ed., *Growth Management Innovations in Florida* (1988).

(5), p. 501. *Ibid.*

(6), p. 502. Lance deHaven-Smith, in *Ibid.*

(7), p. 506. David Osborne and Ted Gaebler, *Reinventing Government* (1992).

Chapter 31:
(1), p. 510. Jonathan Fuerbringer, "A Science Truly Dismal at Prediction," *New York Times*, Feb 23, 1999, discussing much of contemporary academic Economics.
(2), p. 535. As this volume goes to print in November, 1999, several recent developments deserve comment:

In October hurricane Irene demonstrated that heavy rains, flooding and the backup of sewage in centralized systems, could pose a danger to persons and huge property losses even without the severe winds associated with hurricanes such as Andrew.

Second, despite the continued economic prosperity, the State's long-run financial soundness began to be questioned. A draft Report on bonds indicated that in the last decade, while the budget had more that doubled to over $48 billion, the State's bonded indebtedness had almost tripled in the same period to almost $17 billion. The State's politicians had discovered a clever way to avoid raising taxes even higher. The draft Report warned that any economic downturn might find Florida's bond rating such that further bonds might prove difficult to float even at higher interest rates. Each Floridian was an astonishing $787 in debt on bonds alone. Quite a legacy to foist on its youth.

Finally, the sense of governmental corruption reached such levels of public awareness that Governor Jeb Bush appointed a blue-ribbon committee to examine the issue. It will be interesting to see what recommendations the group will make, short of cutting both the size and cost of government.

Chapter 32:
(1), p. 541. The graphic is from William Marina, *Egalitarianism and Empire*, (1975, 1979, 1989), p. 12.

Selected Bibliography

This is not a complete listing of authors and titles of articles and books on Florida subjects. The aim is to indicate the principal sources of the contents of this volume and to provide a useful guide to further reading. Many of the items listed contain extensive references in footnotes and bibliographies.

Articles are rarely listed. The one indispensable source for articles, book reviews and references for further study is the *Florida Historical Quarterly*. There is an index for the first fifty-three volumes and out-of-print numbers are available on microfilm. Other useful periodicals are *Tequesta,* published annually since 1941 by the Historical Association of Southern Florida: the Jacksonville Historical Society *Papers,* published occasionally, *Tampa Bay History*, and the *Florida Anthropologist,* published quarterly by the Florida Anthropological Society. Articles and book reviews of interest to students of Florida history also appear with some regularity in the *Journal of Southern History*. Titles that are useful in more than one period are included only in the one in which they are first important.

An enormous number of books and articles have been published in the almost three decades since the initial publication of this volume. An exhaustive bibliographical listing would today comprise a volume of its own. In this Third Edition we have added a few important new sources consulted in the revisions and additions of the book to the expanded Selected Bibliography.

The explosive development of the Internet and World Wide Web in the last several years has added a new component to traditional publishing and scholarship. Within a very short time, for example, all of the back issues of the *Florida Historical Quarterly* will be available on the Web. In the Preface to this Third Edition, we listed two Web Home Pages with information about the history of Florida:

http://www.wmarina.com
http://www.floridareport.com

The first of these lists materials relevant to teaching Florida history as well as other areas taught by Professor Marina. The second serves as a source of all kinds of materials and bibliographical information for the study of the history of the Florida as well as various public policy issues. We hope readers will consult these for the latest in reviews and bibliographical information. Finally, we recommend the Home Page of the Florida Historical Society for all sorts of information relevant to the study of Florida:

http://florida-historical-soc.org

General Works

Barnes, Jay. *Florida's Hurricane History*. Chapel Hill: University of North Carolina Press, 1998.

Bloodworth, Bertha E. and Morris, Alton C. *Places in the Sun: The History and Romance of Florida Place Names*. Gainesville: University of Florida Press, 1978.

Brevard, Caroline. *A History of Florida*. Edited by James A. Robertson. 2 vols. Deland, FL: Florida State Historical Society, 1924-1925.

Carson, Ruby Leach and Tebeau, Charlton W. *Florida: From Indian Trail to Space Age*. 3 vols. Delray Beach, FL: Southern Publishing Co., 1966.

Cash, William T. *The Story of Florida*. 4 vols. New York: The American Historical Society, Inc., 1938.

Colburn, David and DeHaven-Smith, Lance. *Government in the Sunshine State*. Gainesville: University Press of Florida, 1999.

Colburn, David, and Landers, Jane L., eds. *The African-American Heritage of Florida*. Gainesville: University Press of Florida, 1995.

Covington, James W. *The Seminoles of Florida*. Gainesville: University Press of Florida, 1993.

Covington, James W. *The Story of Southwestern Florida*. New York: Lewis Publishing Co., 1957.

Douglas, Marjorie Stoneman. *Florida: The Long Frontier*. New York: Harper and Row, 1967.

Dovell, Junius E. *Florida: Historic, Dramatic, Contemporary*. 4 vols. New York: Lewis Publishing Co., 1952.

Federal Writer's Project. *Florida: A Guide to the Southernmost State*. New York: Oxford University Press, 1939.

Flynn, Stephen J. *Florida, Land of Fortune*. Washington, D.C.: Luce, 1962.

Fuller, Walter P. *St. Petersburg and Its People*. St. Petersburg, FL: Great Outdoors Publishing Co., 1972.

Gannon, Michael, ed. *The New History of Florida*. Gainesville: University Press of Florida, 1994.

Gannon, Michael. *Florida: A Short History*. Gainesville: University Press of Florida, 1993.

George, Paul S., ed. *A Guide to the History of Florida*. New York: Greenwood Press, 1989.

Hanna, Alfred J. and Hanna, Kathryn A. *Florida's Golden Sands*. Indianapolis: Bobbs Merrill Co., 1950.

Hanna, Kathryn A. *Florida Land of Change*. Chapel Hill: University of North Carolina Press, 1941, 1948.

Horgan, James J., and Wynne, Lewis N., eds. *Florida Decades: A Sesquincentennial History, 1845-1995*. St. Leo, FL: St. Leo College Press, 1995.

Jahoda, Gloria. *Florida: A Bicentennial History*. New York: W.W. Norton Co., 1976.

McKay, D.B., ed. *Pioneer Florida*. 3 vols. Tampa, Fl.: Southern Publishing Co., 1959.

Milanich, Jerald T. *Florida's Indians: From Ancient Times to the Present.* Gainesville: University Press of Florida, 1998.

Miller, Randall M., and Pozzetta, George E., eds. *Shades of the Sunbelt: Essays on Ethnicity, Race and the Urban South.* Boca Raton: Florida Atlantic University Press, 1989.

Morris, Allen. The Florida Handbook. Published biennially since 1947. The indispensable source of factual and statistical data. Tallahassee: Peninsula Publishing Co.

Morris, Allen. *Florida Place Names.* Coral Gables, FL: University of Miami Press, 1974.

Nance, Elwood C., ed. *The East Coast of Florida: A History.* Delray Beach, FL: The Southern Publishing Co., 1962.

Patrick, Rembert W. and Morris, Allen. *Florida Under Five Flags.* 4th edition. Gainesville: University of Florida Press, 1967.

Raisz, Erwin, et al; text by Dunkle, John R. *Atlas of Florida.* Gainesville: University of Florida Press, 1964.

Rerick, Rowland H. *Memoirs of Florida.* 2 vols. Atlanta: The Southern Historical Association, 1902.

Shofner, Jerrell H. *History of Jefferson County.*Tallahassee, FL: Sentry Press, 1976.

Natural History and Indians

Austin, Elizabeth, comp. and ed. *Frank M. Chapman in Florida: His Journals and Letters.* Gainesville: University of Florida Press, 1967.

Bartram, John. *Diary of a Journey Through the Carolinas, Georgia and Florida from July 1, 1965 to April 10, 1942.* Philadelphia: American Philosophical Society, 1952.

Bartram, William. *Travels.* Edited, with commentary and annotated index by Francis Harper. Naturalist ed. New Haven: Yale University Press, 1958.

Bartram, William. *Travels.* Edited by Mark Van Doren. New York: Dover Publications, 1951.

Bickel, Karl A. *The Mangrove Coast.*New York: Coward-McCann, Inc. 1942

Cabell, James Branch and Hanna, Alfred J. *The St. Johns: A Parade of Diversities.* New York: Farrar & Rinehart, 1943.

Calver, James. "Mining and Mineral Resources." Florida Geological Survey *Bulletin* 39(1957).

Capron, Louis. "The Medicine Bundles of the Florida Seminoles and the Green Corn Dance." Smithsonian Institution, Bureau of American Ethnology, *Bulletin* 51(1953):155-210.

Chapin, Henry and Smith, F.G. Walton. *The Ocean River, the Story of the Gulf Stream.* New York: Scribner, 1952.

Cooke, C. Wythe. "Geology of Florida." Florida Geological Survey *Bulletin* 29(1945).

Cushing, Frank H. *A Preliminary Report on the Explorations of Ancient Key-dweller Remains on the Gulf Coast of Florida Com-*

municated to the American Philosophical Society, Nov. 6, 1897. Philadelphia: McCalla and Co., 1897.

Douglas, Marjory S. *Everglades: River of Grass.* New York: Rinehart and Co., 1947. Rev. ed.

Douglas, Marjory S. *Hurricane.* New York: Rinehart and Co., 1958.

Dunn, Gordon E. and Miller, Banner I. *Atlantic Hurricanes.* Baton Rouge: Louisiana State University Press, 1964.

Ferguson, G.E., Lingham, C.W., Love, S.K. and Vernon, R.O. "Springs of Florida." Florida Geological Society *Bulletin* 31(1947).

Gifford, John C. *The Everglades and Other Essays Relating to Southern Florida.* Kansas City: Everglades Land Sales Co., 1911.

Gilliland, Marion Spjut. *The Material Culture of Key Marco, Florida.* Gainesville: University of Florida Press, 1975.

Gonzalez, Thomas A. *The Caloosahatchee.* Estero, FL: Koreshan Unity Press, 1932.

Hanna, Alfred J. and Hanna, Kathryn A. *Lake Okeechobee, Wellspring of the Everglades.* Indianapolis: Bobbs-Merrill, 1948.

Howard, Philip K. *The Death of Common Sense. How Law is Suffocating America.* New York: Warner Books, 1994.

Karp, Walter. *Indespensable Enemies: The Politics of Misrule in America.* New York: Saturday Review Press, 1973.

Kennedy, Stetson. *Palmetto Country.* New York: Duell, Sloan and Pearce, 1942.

MacCauley, Clay. *The Seminole Indians of Florida.* Smithsonian Institution, Bureau of American Ethnology, Fifth Annual Report, 1883,1884. Washington, D.C., 1887.

Mahon. John K. *The Second Seminole War.* Gainesville: University of Florida Press, 1968.

Matschat, Cecile. *Suwannee River: Strange Green Land.* New York: Farrar and Rinehart, 1938.

Matson, George and Sanford, Samuel. *Geology and Ground Waters of Florida.* Washington, D.C.: Government Printing Office, 1913.

McDuffee, Lillie B. *Lures of the Manatee.* 2nd ed. Bradenton, FL: B. McDuffee Fletcher, 1961.

Milanich, Jerald R., and Sturtevant, William C., with Emilio F. Norman, Translator. *Francisco Pareja's 1613 Confessionario: A Documentary Survey of Timucuan Ethnography.* Tallahassee: Division of Archives, History and Records Management, Florida Department of State, 1972.

Nash, Roy A. *A Survey of the Seminole Indians of Florida.* U.S. Senate, Doc. 314, 71st Cong., 3rd sess. 1931.

Neill, Wilfred T. *The Story of Florida's Seminole Indians.* St. Petersburg, FL: Great Outdoors Publishing Co., 1964.

Olson, Stanley J. "Fossil Mammals of Florida." Florida Geological Survey, *Special Bulletin* No. 6. Tallahassee, FL, 1957.

Osborne, David, and Gaebler, Ted. *Reinventing Government: How the Entrepreneurial Spirit is Transforming the Public Sector.*

Selected Bibliography [567]

Reading, MA: Addison-Wesley Publishing Co., 1992.

Romans, Bernard. *A Concise and Natural History of East and West Florida 1775.* Edited by Rembert W. Patrick. Floridiana Facsimile and Reprint Series. Gainesville: University of Florida Press, 1962.

Simpson, George S. "Extinct Land Mammals of Florida." Florida Geological Survey, *20th Annual Report.* Tallahassee, Fl, 1929.

Stork, William. *An Account of East Florida, with a Journal kept by John Bartram of Philadelphia, Botanist to his Majesty for the Floridas, upon a Journey from St. Augustine up the River St. Johns.* London: W. Nicoll and G. Woodfall, 1766.

Swanton, John R. *The Early History of the Creek Indians and Their Neighbors.* Bulletin 73, Bureau of Ethnology, Smithsonian Institution, Washington, D.C.: Government Printing Office, 1964.

Tacachale: Essays on the Indians of Florida and Southeastern Georgia During the Historic Period. Edited by Jerald Milanich and Samuel Proctor. Gainesville: University of Florida Press, 1975.

Wright, Albert H. *Okefenokee Swamp: Its History and Its Cartography.* Ithaca, N.Y.: Cornell University Press, 1945.

Spanish Florida, 1513-1763, 1784-1821

Andrews, Evangeline W. and Andrews, Charles McLean, eds. *Jonathan Dickinson's Journal; or God's Protecting Providence.* New Haven: Yale University Press, 1945.

Arnade, Charles W. *The Siege of St. Augustine in 1702.* Gainesville: University of Florida Press, 1959.

Arnade, Charles W. *Florida on Trial, 1593-1602.* Coral Gables: University of Miami Press, 1959.

Barcia, Carvallido y Zuñiga, André G. de. *Chronological History of the Continent of Florida, 1512-1722* Translated by Anthony Kerrigan. Gainesville: University of Florida Press, 1951.

Barrientos, Bartolomé. *Pedro Menéndez de Avilés, Founder of Florida.* Translated by Anthony Kerrigan, Floridiana Facsimile and Reprint Series. Gainesville: University of Florida Press, 1965.

Bennett, Charles E. *Laudonnière and Fort Caroline: History and Documents.* Gainesville: University of Florida Press, 1964.

Bennett, Charles E. *Settlement of Florida.* Gainesville: University of Florida Press, 1968.

Bennett, Charles E. *Three Voyages by Rene Laudonnière.* Translated with an introduction and notes. Gainesville: University of Florida Press, 1975.

Brooks, Philip C. *Diplomacy and the Borderlands: The Adams-Onis Treaty of 1819.* Berkeley: University of California Press, 1939.

Bourne, Edward G. *Narratives of the Career of Hernando de Soto.* 2 vols. London: David Nutt, 1905.

Boyd, Mark F. Smith, Hale G. and Griffin, John W. *Here They Once Stood: The Tragic End of the Apalachee Missions.* Gainesville: University of Florida Press, 1951.

Cabeza de Vaca, Alvar Núñez. *The Journey of Alvar Núñez Cabeza de Vaca and His Companions from Florida to the Pacific, 1528-1536.* Translated by Fanny Bandelier from original narrative first published in 1542. New York, 1905.

Caruso, John A. *The Southern Frontier.* Indianapolis: Bobbs-Merrill, 1963.

Caughey, John W. *Bernardo de Gálvez in Louisiana, 1776-1783.* Berkeley: University of California Press, 1934.

Chatelain, Vern E. *The Defenses of Spanish Florida. 1565-1763.* Washington, D.C.: Carnegie Institution, 1941.

Connor, Jeannette Thurber, trans. and ed. *Colonial Records of Spanish Florida.* 2 vols. DeLand, FL: Florida State Historical Society, 1925, 1930.

Corse, Carita Doggett. *Key to the Golden Islands.* Chapel Hill: University of North Carolina Press, 1931.

Covington, James W., ed. Translated by A.F. Falcones. *Pirates, Indians and Spaniards: Father Escobedo's "La Florida."* St. Petersburg, FL: Great Outdoors Publishing Co.,1963.

Cox, Isaac J. *The West Florida Controversy, 1778-1813.* Baltimore: Johns Hopkins University Press, 1918.

Crane, Verner W. *The Southern Frontier, 1670-1732.* Ann Arbor: University of Michigan Press, 1929.

Curley, Michael J. *Church and State in the Spanish Floridas, 1783-1822.* Washington, D.C.: Catholic University Press, 1940.

Dunn, W.E. *Spanish and French Rivalry in the Gulf Region of the United States, 1678-1702* Austin: University of Texas Press, 1917.

Fairbanks, George R. *The History and Antiqiuities of the City of St. Augustine, Florida, Founded A.D. 1565.* New York: C.B. Norton, 1858.

Federal Writers' Project. *The Spanish Missions of Florida.* St. Augustine,FL, 1858.

Ford, Lawrence C. *The Triangular Struggle for Spanish Pensacola, 1689-1739.* Washington, D.C.: Catholic University Press, 1939.

Gannon,Michael W. *The Cross in the Sand: The Early Catholic Church in Florida, 1513-1870.* Gainesville: University of Florida Press, 1965.

Geiger, Maynard J., Trans. *The Martyrs of Florida, 1513-1616.* By Luis Gerónimo de Oré, New York: J.F.Wagner, Inc. 1936.

Goggin, John M. Edited by Charles H. Fairbanks, Irving Rouse and William C. Sturtevant. *Indian and Spanish Selected Writings.* Coral Gables, FL: University of Miami Press, 1964.

Hamilton, Peter J. *Colonial Mobile.* Boston: Houghton Mifflin and Co., 1897.

Irving, Theodore. *The Conquest of Florida by Hernando De Soto.* London: G. Bell and Sons, 1881.

Jackson, W.R. *Early Florida Through Spanish Eyes.* Coral Gables, FL: University of Miami Press, 1954.

James, Marquis. *Andrew Jackson: The Border Captain.* Indianapolis: Bobbs-Merrill, 1933.

Kelly, William E. *The Franciscans in Florida.* Ithaca, N.Y.: Cornell University Press, 1946.

Lanning, John Tate. *The Spanish Missions of Georgia.* Chapel Hill: University of North Carolina Press, 1935.

Lanning, John Tate. *The St. Augustine Expedition of 1740.* Columbia: South Carolina Archives Department, 1954.

Leonard, Irving A. *The Spanish Approach to Pensacola, 1689-1693.* Albuquerque: The Quivira Society, 1936.

Lorant, Stefan. *The New World: The First Pictures of America Made by John White and Jacques Lemoyne and Engraved by Theodore de Bry with Contemporary Narratives of the French Settlement in Florida, 1562-1565, and English Colonies in Virginia, 1585-1590.* New and revised edition, New York: Duell, Sloan and Pearce, 1965.

Lowery, Woodbury. *The Spanish Settlements Within the Present Limits of the United States.* 2 vols. New York: Russell and Russell, 1901, 1905.

Lyon, Eugene. *The Enterprise of Florida: Pedro Menéndez de Avilés and the Spanish Conquest of 1565-1568.* Gainesville: University of Florida Press, 1976.

Manucy, Albert. *Florida's Menéndez: Captain of the Ocean Sea.* St. Augustine: St. Augustine Historical Society, 1965.

Manucy, Albert. *The Houses of St. Augustine, 1565-1821.* St. Augustine: St. Augustine Historical Society, 1962.

Maynard, Theodore. *De Soto and the Conquistidores.* New York: Longmans, Green and Co., 1930.

McGann, Thomas F. "Ordeal of Cabeza de Vaca," *American Heritage* X(December 1960): 32-37, 78-82.

Merás, Gonzalo Solis de. *Pedro Menéndez de Avilés, Adelantado, Governor and Captain General of Florida.* Translated by Jeanette Thurber Connor. DeLand, FL: Florida State Historical Society, 1923.

Murdock, Richard K. *The Georgia-Florida Frontier, 1793-1796.* Berkeley and Los Angeles: University of California Press, 1951.

O'Daniel, V.F. *The Dominicans in Early Florida.* New York: The United States Catholic Historical Society, 1928.

Patrick, Rembert W. *Florida Fiasco: Rampant Rebels on the Georgia-Florida Frontier, 1810-1815.* Athens: University of Georgia Press, 1954.

Priestley, Herbert I., trans. and ed. *The Luna Paper.* 2 vols. DeLand, FL: Florida State Historical Society, 1928.

Priestley, Herbert I. *Tristan de Luna.* Glendale, CA: Arthur H. Clark Co., 1936.

Proctor, Samuel, ed. *Eighteenth-Century Florida and the Caribbean.* Gainesville: University of Florida Press, 1976.

Ribault, Jean. *The Whole and True Discouerye of Terra Florida. (1563).* Edited by David L. Dowd. Florida State Historical Society edition of 1927, including a biography of Ribault by Jeanette Thurber Connor. Floridiana Facsimile and Reprint Series. Gainesville: University of Florida Press, 1964.

Robertson, James A., trans. and ed. *Narrative of a Gentleman of Elvas.* DeLand, FL: Florida State Historical Society, 1933.

Smith, Buckingham, trans. *Relation of Alvar Núñez Cabeza de Vaca.* New York: Printed by J. Munsell for H.C. Murphy, 1871.

Tanner, Helen H. *Zéspedes in East Florida, 1784-1790.* Coral Gables: University of Miami Press, 1963.

TePaske, John Jay. *The Governorship of Spanish Florida, 1700-1763.* Durham, N.C.: Duke University Press, 1964.

True, David O., ed. and trans. *Memoir of D. d'Escalente Fontaneda Respecting Florida.* Spain, ca. 1474. Tr. by Buckingham Smith, Washington D.C., 1854. Reprinted with revisions, David O. True, ed. Miami: University of Miami and Historical Association of Southern Florida, 1944.

Varner, John Grier and Varner, Jeanette J., trans. and eds. *The Florida of the Inca* by Garcilaso de la Vega. Austin: University of Texas Press, 1951.

Whitaker, Arthur P., ed. and trans. *Documents Relating to the Commercial Policy of Spain in the Floridas.* DeLand, FL: Florida State Historical Society, 1931.

Whitaker, Arthur P. *The Spanish-America Frontier.* Boston: Houghton Mifflin Co., 1927.

The British Era, 1763-1784

Alden, John R. *John Stuart and the Southern Colonial Frontier.* Ann Arbor: University of Michigan Press, 1944.

Barrs, Burton. *East Florida in the American Revolution.* Jacksonville, FL: Cooper Press, 1949.

Coker, William S. and Rea, Robert S., eds. *Anglo-Spanish Confrontation on the Gulf Coast During the American Revolution.* Pensacola: University of West Florida Press, 1982.

Coker, William S. *The Military Presence on the Gulf Coast.* Pensacola: University of West Florida Press, 1978.

Corse, Carita D. *Dr. Andrew Turnbull and the New Smyrna Colony of Florida.* Jacksonville, FL: The Drew Press, 1919.

Cruickshank, Helen G., ed. *John and William Bartram's America.* New York: The Devin Adair Co., 1957.

Gold, Robert L. *Borderlands in Transition: The Triple Nation Transfer of Florida.* Carbondale: Southern Illinois University Press, 1969.

The next five items are the papers of as many symposia sponsored by the Florida Bicentennial Commission in 1972-1976 at units of the State University System. They are all edited by Samuel Proctor and published by the University of Florida Press, Gainesville.

Eighteenth Century Florida and Its Borderlands, 1975.
Eighteenth Century Florida and the Caribbean, 1976.
Eighteenth Century Florida Life on the Frontier, 1976.
Eighteenth Century Florida and the Revolutionary South, 1978.
Eighteenth Century Florida : The Impact of the American Revolu-

tion, 1978.

Howard, Clinton N. *The British Development of West Florida, 1763-1769.* Berkeley: University of California Press, 1947.

Johnson, Cecil. *British West Florida, 1763-1783.* New Haven,CT: Yale University Press, 1943.

Lockey, Joseph Bryne, ed. and trans. *East Florida, 1783-1785.* Berkeley: University of California Press, 1949.

Mowatt, Charles L. *East Florida as a British Province, 1763-1784.* Berkeley: University of California Press, 1943.

Panagopoulos, E.P. *New Smyrna: An Eighteenth Century Greek Odyssey.* Gainesville: University of Florida Press, 1966.

Proctor, Samuel, ed. *Eighteenth-Century Florida and the Revolutionary South.* Gainesville: University of Florida Press, 1976.

Quinn, Jane. *Minorcans in Florida: Their History and Heritage.* St. Augustine: Mission Press, 1975.

Searcy, Martha Condray. *The Georgia-Florida Contest in the American Revolution, 1776-1778.* Tuscaloosa: University of Alabama Press, 1985.

Shaw, Helen L. *British Administration of the Southern Indians, 1756-1783.* Lancaster, PA: Lancaster Press, Inc., 1929.

Siebert, Wilbur H. *Loyalists in East Florida, 1774-1785.* Deland, FL: Florida Historical Society, 1929.

Starr, J. Barton. *Tories, Dons, and Rebels: The American Revolution in West Florida.* Gainesville: University of Florida Press, 1976.

Stork, William. *An Account of East Florida with Remarks on its Future Importance to Trade and Commerce.* London: W. Nicoll and G. Woodfall, 1766.

Tingley, Helen E. "Florida Under the British Flag, 1763-1783." Master's thesis, Stetson University, 1914.

Wright, J. Leitch, Jr. *Britain and the American Frontier, 1813-1815.* Athens: University of Georgia Press, 1976.

Wright, J. Leitch, Jr. *Florida in the American Revolution.* Gainesville: University of Florida Press, 1976.

Antebellum Florida, 1821-1860

Audubon, Lucy S. *The Life of John James Audubon.* New York: Putnam, 1868.

Anderson, Edward C. *Florida Territory in 1844.* Edited by W. Stanley Hoole. Tuscaloosa: University of Alabama Press, 1977.

Biddle, Margaret S.F. *Hibernia: The Unreturning Tide.* New York: Privately printed, 1947.

Boggess, F.C. *A Veteran of Four Wars.* Arcadia, FL: Champion Job Rooms, 1900.

Brinton, Daniel G. *Notes on the Florida Peninsula.* Phildelphia: J. Sabin, 1859.

Buker, George E. *Swamp Sailors: Riverine Warfare in the Everglades,1835-1842.* Gainesville: University of Florida Press, 1975.

Bushnell, David I., Jr. *Tribal Migrations East of the Mississippi.* Smithsonian Institution, Miscellaneous Collections, Vol 80, No. 12. Washiington, D.C.: Government Printing Office, 1934.

Canova, Andrew P. *Life and Adventures in South Florida.* Tampa, FL: The Southern Sun Publishing House, 1934.

Carter, Clarence E., ed. *Territorial Papers of the United States.* Vols. XXII-XXVI, *Florida.* Washington, D.C.: Government Printing Office, 1956-1965.

Caughey, John W. *McGillivray of the Creeks.* Norman: University of Oklahoma Press, 1938.

Coe, Charles H. *Red Patriots: The Story of the Seminoles.* Cincinnati: The Editor Publishing Co., 1868

Cohen, M.M. *Notice of Florida and the Campaigns, 1836.* Edited by O.Z. Tyler, Jr. Floridiana Facsimile and Reprint Series. Gainesville: University of Florida Press, 1954.

Cushman, Joseph D., Jr. *A Goodly Heritage: The Episcopal Church in Florida, 1821-1892.* Gainesville: University of Florida Press, 1965.

Dodd, Dorothy. *Florida Becomes a State.* Tallahassee, FL: Florida Centennial Commission, 1945.

Doherty, Herbert J., Jr. *Richard Keith Call: Southern Unionist.* Gainesville: University of Florida Press, 1959.

Doherty, Herbert J., Jr. *The Whigs of Florida, 1845-1854.* Gainesville: University of Florida Press, 1959.

Dovell, Junius E. *History of Banking in Florida, 1828-1954.* Orlando: Florida Bankers Association, 1955.

Dovell, Junius E. *First Supplement 1954-1963.* Orlando: Florida Bankers Association, 1963.

Dyer, Brainerd. *Zachary Taylor.* Baton Rouge: Louisiana State University Press, 1964.

Eooes, Susan Bradford. *Through Some Eventful Years, 1926.* Edited by Joseph D. Cushman, Jr., Floridiana Facsimile and Reprint Series. Gainesville: University of Florida Press, 1967.

Forbes, James Grant. *Sketches, Historical and Topographical, of the Floridas: More Particularly of East Florida, 1821.* Edited by James W. Covington. Floridiana Facsimile and Reprint Series. Gainesville: University of Florida Press, 1964.

Foremamn, Grant. *Indian Removal: The Emigration of the Five Civilized Tribes.* Norman: University of Oklahoma Press, 1934.

Fourake, Warren G. "The Administration of Robert Raymond Reid." Master's thesis, Florida State University, 1949.

Fuller, Hubert B. *The Purchase of Florida: Its History and Diplomacy, 1906.* Edited by Weymouth T. Jordan. Floridiana Facsimile and Reprint Series. Gainesville: University of Florida Press, 1964.

Giddings, Joshua R. *The Exiles of Florida.* Edited by Arthur W. Thompson. Floridiana Facsimile and Reprint Series. Gainesville: University of Florida Press, 1964.

Gold, Daniel P. *History of Duval County, Including Early History of East Florida.* St. Augustine, FL, 1929.

Goene, Bertram H. *Anter-Bellum Tallahassee.* Tallahassee: The Heritage Foundation, 1971.

Hanna, Alfred J. *A Prince in Their Midst: The Adventurous Life of Achille Murat on the American Frontier.* Norman: University of Oklahoma Press, 1946.

Huhner, Leon. "David L. Yulee, Florida's First Senator." American Jewish Historical Society *Publication* s XXV(1917).

Knauss, James O. *Territorial Florida Journalism.* DeLand, FL: Florida State Historical Society, 1926.

Krogman, Wilton M. "The Racial Compostion of the Seminole Indians of Florida and Oklahoma." *Journal of Negro History* XIX (October, 1934): 412-430.

Laumer, Frank. *Massacre!* Gainesville: University of Florida Press, 1968.

Long, Ellen Call. *Florida Breezes, or Florida, New and Old.* 1883. Edited by Margaret Chapman. Floridiana Facsimile and Reprint Series. Gainesville: University of Florida Press, 1962.

Lord, Mille M., Jr. "David Levy Yulee, Statesman and Railroad Builder." Master Thesis, University of Florida, 1940.

Mahon, John K. *History of the Second Seminole War, 1835-1842.* Gainesville: University of Florida Press, 1967.

Martin, Sidney Walter. *Florida During Territorial Days.* Athens: University of Georgia Press, 1944.

McCall, George A. *Letters from the Frontiers.* Philadelphia: Lippincott and Co., 1868.

McReynols, Edwin C. *The Seminoles.* Norman: University of Oklahoma Press, 1957.

Merritt, Webster. *A Century of Medicine in Jacksonville and Duval Counties.* Gainesville: University of Florida Press, 1949.

Mool, James Bulger. "Florida in Federal Politics: Statehood to Secession." Master's thesis, Duke University, 1940.

Niles Weekly Register (Baltimore), 1811-1849.

Ott. Eloise R., and Chazal, Louis Hickman. *Ocali County, Kingdom of the Sun: A History of Marion County, Florida 1559-1965.* Ocala, FL: Marion Publishers, Inc. 1966.

Patrick, Rembert W. *Aristocrat in Uniform: General Duncan Lamont Clinch.* Gainesville: University of Florida Press, 1963.

Phillips, U.B. and Glunt, James David, eds. *Florida Plantation Records.* St. Louis: Missouri Historical Society, 1927.

Pizzo, Anthony P. *Tampa Town 1824-1886: Cracker Village with a Latin Accent.* Miami: Hurricane House, 1968.

Rosser, John Leonidas, *A History of Florida Baptists.* Nashville: Broadman Press, 1949.

Shepard, Birse. *The Lore of the Wreckers.* Boston: Beacon Press, 1961.

Shippee, Lester B. *Bishop Whipple's Southern Diary 1843-1844.* Minneapolis, Plenum, 1937.

Silver, James W. *Edmund Pendleton Gaines, Frontier General.* Baton Rouge: Louisiana State University Press, 1949.

Smith, Julia Floyd. *Slavery and Plantation Growth in Ante-Bellum Florida, 1821-1860*. Gainesville: University of Florida Press, 1973.

Sprague, John T. *The Origin, Progress, and Conclusion of the Florida War, 1848*. Edited by John K. Mahon. Floridiana Facsimile and Reprint Series. Gainesville: University of Florida Press, 1964.

Strickland, Alice. *The Valiant Pioneers: A History of Ormond Beach, Volusia County, Florida*. Coral Gables: University of Miami Press, 1963.

Thompson, Arthur W. "David Yulee: A Study of Nineteenth Century Thought and Enterprise." Ph.D dissertation, Columbia University, 1954.

Thompson, Arthur W. *Jacksonian Democracy on the Florida Frontier*. Gainesville: University of Florida Press, 1961.

Thrift, Charles T. *The Trail of the Florida Circuit Rider: An Introduction to the Rise of Methodism in Middle and East Florida*. Lakeland, FL: Florida Southern College Press, 1944.

Vignoles, Charles B. *Observations Upon Florida*. New York: E. Bliss and E. White, 1823.

Weinberg, Sidney J. "Slavery and Secession in Florida." Master's thesis, University of Florida, 1948.

Wells, E. Alva. "Osceola and the Second Seminole War." Master's thesis, University of Oklahoma, 1936.

Williams, Edwin L., Jr. "Florida in the Union 1845-1861." Ph.D. dissertation, University of North Carolina, 1951.

Williams, John Lee. *Territory of Florida, 1837*. Edited by Herbert J. Doherty, Jr. Floridiana Facsimile and Reprint Series. Gainesville: University of Florida Press, 1962.

Williams, John Lee. *A View of West Florida*. Philadelphia: Printed for H.S. Tanner and the author, 1827.

The Civil War and Reconstruction, 1861-77

Barnard, Church E. "The Federal Blockade of Florida During the Civil War." Master's thesis, University of Miami, 1966.

Bentley, George R. *A History of the Freedman's Bureau*. Philadelphia: University of Pennsylvania Press. 1955.

Bill, Ledyard. *A Winter in Florida*. New York: Wood and Holbrook, 1870.

Brinton, Daniel G. *A Guide-Book of Florida and the South for Tourists, Invalids and Emigrants*. Philadelphia: G. Maclean, 1869.

Davis, William Watson. *The Civil War and Reconstruction in Florida*. New York: Columbia University Press, 1913.

Deland, Margaret. *Florida Days*. Boston: Little Brown and Co., 1889.

Dickison, Mary Elizabeth. *Dickison and His Men: Reminiscences of the War in Florida, 1890*. Edited by Samuel Proctor. Floridiana Facsimile and Reprint Series. Gainesville: University of Florida Press, 1962.

Durkin, Josoeph T. *Stephen R. Mallory: Confederate Navy Chief.* Chapel Hill: University of North Carolina Press, 1954.

Field, Henry M. *Bright Skies and Dark Shadows.* New York: Scribner's, 1890.

Futch, Ovid L. "Salmon P. Chase and Radical Politics in Florida, 1862-1865." Master's thesis, University of Florida, 1952.

Gannon, Michael V. *Rebel Bishop: The Life and Era of Augustus Verot.* New York: Bruce Publishing Co., 1964.

Hadd, Donald R. "The Secession Movement in Florida, 1850-1861." Master's thesis, Florida State University, 1960.

Hanna, Alfred J. *Flight into Oblivion.* Richmond, VA: Johnson Publishing Co., 1938.

Haworth, Paul Leland. *The Hayes-Tilden Election.* Indianapolis: Bobbs Merrill, 1927.

Hopley, Catherine Cooper. *Life in the South From the Commencement of the War.* London: Chapman and Hall, 1863.

Johns, John E. *Florida During the Civil War.* Gainesville: University of Florida Press, 1963.

Klingman, Peter D. *Josiah Walls: Florida's Black Congressman of Reconstruction.* Gainesville: University of Florida Press, 1976.

L'Engle, Susan Fatio. *Notes on my Family and Recollections of My Early Age.* Jacksonville, FL, 1887.

Lonn, Ella. *Salt as a Factor in the Confedreacy.* New York: Walter Neale, 1933.

Meredith, Evelyn T. "The Secession Movement in Florida." Master's thesis, Duke University, 1940.

Motte, Jacob Rhett. *Journey Into Wilderness: An Army Surgeon's Account of Life in Camp and Field During the Creek and Seminole Wars, 1836-1838.* Edited by James F. Sunderman. Gainesville: University of Florida Press, 1953.

Parks, Joseph H. *General Edmond Kirby Smith, C.S.A.* Baton Rouge: Louisiana State University Press, 1944.

Official Records of the Union and Confederate Navies in the War of the Rebellion. 30 vols. Washington, D.C.: Government Printing Office, 1894-1927.

Patrick, Rembert W. *Jefferson Davis and His Cabinet.* Baton Rouge: Louisiana State University Press, 1944.

Proctor, Samuel, ed. *Florida 100 Years Ago.* Monthly, Dec. 1960-Sept. 1963 by Civil War Centennial Committee; October 1963 to June 1965 by Florida Library and Historical Commission.

Reid, Whitelaw. *After the War: A Southern Tour.* Cincinnati, New York: Moore Wilstach and Baldwin, 1866.

Richardson, Joseph M. *The Negro in the Reconstruction of Florida.* Tallahassee: Florida State University Press, 1965.

Richardson, Joseph M. "The Freedmen's Bureau." Master's thesis, Florida State University, 1959.

Robertson, Fred L. *Soldiers of Florida in the Seminole Indian, Civil and Spanish America Wars.* Live Oak, FL: Democrat Book and Job Print Co., 1903.

Shofner, Jerrell H. *Nor Is It Over Yet: Florida in the Era of Recon-*

struction, 1863-1877. Gainesville: University of Florida Press, 1974.

Stowe, Harriet Beecher. *Palmetto Leaves. 1873.* Edited by Mary B. Graff, Introduction by Edith Cowles. Floridiana Facsimile and Reprint Series. Gainesville: University of Florida Press, 1968.

Taylor, Robert A. *Rebel Storehouse: Florida in theConfederate Economy.* Tuscaloosa: University of Alabama Press, 1995.

Townshend, F. Trench. *Wild Life in Florida, With A Visit to Cuba.* London: Hurst and Blackett, 1875.

U.S., *The War of the Rebellion: Compilation of the Official Records of the Union and Confederate Armies.* 128 vols. Washington, D.C.: Government Printing Office, 1880-1901.

Wallace, John. *Carpetbag Rule in Florida: The Inside Workings of Civil Government in Florida After the Close of the Civil War. 1888.* Edited by Allan Nevins. Floridiana Facsmile and Reprint Series. Gainesville: University of Florida Press, 1964.

Warner, Ezra J. *Generals in Gray: Lives of the Confederate Commanders.* Baton Rouge: Louisiana State University Press, 1959.

Williamson, Edward C. *Florida Politics in the Gilded Age, 1877-1893.* Gainesville: University of Florida Press, 1976.

Woodward, C. Vann. *Reunion and Reaction; The Compromise of 1877 and the End of Reconstruction.* Boston: Little Brown, 1951.

The Bourbon-Populist Era, 1877-1900

Abel, Ruth E. *One Hundred Years in Palmetto: History of Palmetto, Florida, 1868-1968.* Palmetto, FL: Palmetto Centennial Association, 1967.

Alger, Russell A. *The Spanish American War.* New York: Harper and Row, 1901.

Atkins, Emily Howard. "A History of Jacksonville, Florida 1867-1902." Master's thesis, Duke University, 1941.

Belknap, Reginald. "The Naval Base at Key West in 1898." U.S. Naval Institute, *Proceedings* XLI (1915): 1443-1473.

Browne, Jefferson B. *Key West, The Old and the New.* St. Augustine: The Record Co., 1912.

Bush, George G. *History of Education in Florida.* Washington, D.C.: Government Printing Office, 1889.

Campbell, A. Stuart. *The Cigar Industry of Tampa.* Gainesville: University of Florida Press, 1939.

Cantreel, Elizabeth. *When Kissimmee was Young.* Kissimmee, FL: Philathea Class, 1948.

Carper, N. Gordon. "The Convict Lease System in Florida." Ph.D. dissertation, Florida State University. 1964.

Carson, Ruby Leach. "William Dunnington Bloxham: Florida's Two Term Governor." Master's thesis, University of Florida, 1945.

Cash, W.T. *History of the Democratic Party in Florida.* Live Oak, FL: Democratic Historical Foundation, 1936.

Cory, Lloyd Walter. "The Florida Farmer's Alliance, 1887-1892."

Master's thesis, Florida State University, 1963.

Davidson, James Wood. *The Florida of Today*. New York: Appleton and Co., 1889.

Davis, Richard Harding. *The Cuban and Puerto Rican Campaigns*. New York: Scribner's, 1898.

Davis, T. Frederick. *A History of Jacksonville, Florida and Vicinity, 1513-1924*. St. Augustine, FL, 1925.

Dewhurst, William W. *History of St. Augustine*. New York: The Knickerbocker Press, 1886.

Fritz, Florence. *Unknown Florida*. Coral Gables: University of Miami Press, 1963.

Grismer, Karl A. *Tampa: A History*. St. Petersburg, FL: St. Petersburg Publishing Co., 1950.

Hanna, Alfred J. *Fort Maitland: Its Origin and History*. Maitland, FL: The Fort Maitland Committee, 1936.

Hardy, Iza Duffus. *Oranges and Alligators*. London: Ward and Downey, 1887.

Hebel, Ianthe Bond. *Centennial History of Volusia County, Florida, 1854-1954*. Daytona Beach, FL: Volusia County Hisitorical Commission, 1955.

Jacques, D.H. *Florida as a Permanent Home*. Jacksonville, FL: C.W. Blew, 1877.

Kelley, W.D. *The Old South and the New*. New York: G.P. Putnam's, 1888.

Lanier, Sidney. *Florida Its Scenery, Climate and History*. Philadelphia: J.P. Lippincott and Co., 1876.

Ley, John C. *Fifty-two Years in Florida*. Nashville: Publishing House of the M.E. Church South, 1899.

Maloney, Walter C. *A Sketch of the History of Key West, Florida, 1876*. Edited by Thelma Peters, Floridiana Facsimile and Reprint Series. Gainesville: University of Florida Press, 1968.

Martin, Sidney Walter. *Florida's Flagler*. Athens: University of Georgia Press, 1949.

Miley, John D. *In Cuba With Shafter*. New York: Scribner's, 1899.

Ober, Frederick A. *The Knockabout Club in the Everglades*. Boston: Estes and Lauriat, 1887.

Ober, Frederick A. *"Rambler," Guide to Florida, 1875*. Edited by Rembert W. Patrick. Floridiana Facsimile and Reprint Series. Gainesville: University of Florida Press, 1964.

Paisley, Clifton. *From Cotton to Quail; An Agricultural Chronicle of Leon County, Florida, 1860-1967*. Gainesville: University of Florida Press, 1968.

Parks, Arva Moore. *The Forgotten Frontier: Florida Through the Lens of Ralph Middleton Monroe*. Coral Gables, FL: Banyan Books, 1977.

Pierce, Charles W. *Pioneer Life in Southeast Florida*. Edited by Donald W. Curl. Coral Gables, FL: University of Miami Press, 1970.

Proctor, Samuel. "Filibustering Aboard the Three Friends." *Mid-America* XXXVIII(1956): 84-100.

Proctor, Samuel. *Napoleon Bonaparte Broward: Florida's Fighting Democrat*. Gainesville: University of Florida Press, 1950.
Pyburn, Nita K. *Docoumentary History of Education in Florida, 1822-1860*. Tallahassee: Florida State University Press, 1951.
Pyburn, Nita K. *The History of the Development of a Single System of Education in Florida, 1822-1903*. Tallahassee: Florida State University Press, 1951.
Rickenbach, Richard Vernon. "History of Filibustering, Florida to Cuba, 1895-1898." Master's thesis, University of Florida, 1948.
Robbins, Sarah Stuart. *One Happy Winter or, A Visit to Florida*. Boston: Buller Bros., 1878.
Rose, Rufus E. *The Swamp and Overflowed Lands of Florida: The Disston Contract and Sale*. Tallahassee, FL, 1916.
Schellings, William J. "Tampa, Florida: Its Role in the Spanish American War, 1898." Master's thesis, University of Miami, 1953.
Schellings, William J. "The Role of Florida in the Spanish American War, 1898." Ph.D. dissertation, University of Florida, 1958.
Smyth, G. Hutchinson. *The Life of Henry Bradley Plant*. New York, 1898.
Stockbridge, Frank Parker and Perry, John Holliday. *Florida in the Making*. New York: The deBower Publishing Co., 1926.
U,S., Florida, Trustees of the Internal Improvement Fund. *Minutes and Annual Reports*.

The Twentieth Century

Adams, Judge Alto Lee. *The Fourth Quarter: As Told to Tom Dunkin*. Privately Published. Fort Pierce, FL, 1975.
Akerman, Joe A., Jr. *Florida Cowman: A History of Florida Cattle Raising*. Kissimmee: Florida Cattlemen's Association, 1976.
Akin, Edward. *Flagler: Rockefeller Partner and Florida Baron*. Kent, Ohio: Kent State University Press, 1988.
Allman, T.D. *Miami: City of the Future*. New York: The Atlantic Monthly Press, 1987.
American National Red Cross. *The Florida Hurricane: September 18, 1926*. Washington, D.C.: National Red Cross, 1927.
American National Red Cross. *The West Indies Hurricane Disaster, September, 1928*. Washington, D.C.: National Red Cross, 1929.
Ammidown, Margot, and Rodriquez. Wilderness to Metropolis. Miami: Metropolitan Dade County, 1982.
Anderson, Marie. *Julia's Daughters: Women in Dade History*. Miami: Herstory of Florida, 1980.
Andrews, Allen H. *A Yank Pioneer in Florida*. Jacksonville: Douglas Printing Co., 1950
Arend, Geoffrey. *Great Airports: Miami.*. New York: Air Cargo News, 1986.
Armbrister, Ann. *The Life and Times of Miami Beach*. New York: Alfred A. Knopf, 1995.

Armstrong, Orlando Kay. *The Life and Work of Dr. A. Murphree.* St. Augustine, FL: Murphree Memorial Fund, 1928.

Bald, Ralph D. *A History of Jacksonville University: The First Twenty-Five Years, 1934-1959.* Jacksonville, FL: Jacksonville University Press, 1959.

Barbour, Ralph Henry. *Let's Go to Florida.* New York: Dodd, Mead and Company, 1926.

Bell, Harold W. *Glimpses of the Panhandle.* Chicago: Adams Press, 1961.

Bellman, Samuel I. *Marjorie Kinnan Rawlings.* New York: Twayne Publishers, Inc., 1974.

Benson, Charles D., and Faherty, William Barnaby. *Moonport: A History of Apollo Launch Facilities and Operations.* NASA History Series, Washington, D.C.: 1978.

Bigelow, Gordon E. *Frontier Eden: The Literary Career of Marjory Kinnan Rawlings.* Gainesville: University of Florida Press, 1966.

Blake, Nelson. *Land into Water–Water into Land.* Gainesville: University Presses of Florida, 1980.

Blakey, Arch Frederic. *The Florida Phosphate Industry: A History of the Development and Use of a Vital Mineral.* Cambridge, Mass. Wertheim Committee, Harvard University, 1973.

Budina, John W., Jr. *History of Banking in Florida, 1964-1975.* Orlando: Florida Bankers Association, 1976.

Caldwell, Millard F. *The Administration of Millard F. Caldwell as Governor of Florida, 1945-1949.* Tallahassee, FL: Rose Printing Co., 1949.

Campbell, Doak S. *A University in Transition.* Tallahassee: Florida State University Press, 1964.

Carter, Luther J. *The Florida Experience: Land and Water Policy in a Growth State.* Baltimore: Johns Hopkins University Press, 1976.

Cason, N.H. "The New Florida." *Munsey's Magazine* XL(February, 1909), 587-604.

Cave, Hugh Barnett. *Wings Across the World: The Story of the Air Transport Command.* New York, 1945.

Church, George B., Jr. "Henry Laurens Mitchell." Master's thesis, University of Florida, 1969.

Conradi, Edward. *Memoirs of Edward Conradi: President of Florida State College for Women, 1909-1941.* Tallahassee: Florida State College for Women, 1945.

Croucher, Sheila L. *Imagining Miami: Ethnic Politics in a Postmodern World.* Charlottesville: University Press of Virginia, 1997.

Cushman, Josoeph D., Jr. *The Sound of Bells: The Episcopal Church in South Florida, 1892-1969.* Gainesville: University of Florida Press, 1976.

Deal, John R., Jr. "Sidney Johnson Catts, Stormy Rebel of Florida Politics." Master's thesis, University of Florida, 1949.

DeBerard, Phillip E., Jr. "Promoting Florida: Some Aspects of the

Uses of Advertising and Publicity in the Development of the Sunshine State." Master's thesis, University of Florida, 1951.

deHaven-Smith, Westi Jo, ed. *Growth Management Innovations in Florida*. Fort Lauderdale: Florida Atlantic University & Florida International University Joint Center for Environmental and Urban Problems, 1988.

Derr, Mark. *Some Kind of Paradise*. New York: William Morrow, 1989.

Dovell, Junius E. "A History of the Everglades of Florida." Ph.D. dissertation, University of North Carolina, 1947.

Dovell, Junius E. "The Everglades-Florida Frontier." *Economic Leaflets* VI (April-May), 1947.

Dunn, Marvin. *Black Miami in the Twentieth Century*. Gainesville: University Press of Florida, 1997.

Duvall, Grayce M. *"The Florida Development Commission and Its Antecedents."* Master's thesis, University of Miami, 1968.

Ellsworth, Lucius and Linda. *The Deep Water City: A Pictorial and Entertaining Commentary on the Growth and Development of Pensacola, Florida*. Tulsa, OK: 1982.

Evans, John E. *Time for Florida: Report on the Administration of Farris Bryant, Governor, 1961-1965*. Tallahassee, Fl, 1965.

Federal Writers' Project. Works Progress Administration. American Guide Series. This series, compiled and written for the Federal Writers' Project of the WPA, produced numerous state and local guidebooks whose information is now dated but which contain a fund of data about the regions involved. Some of these have been reprinted and are still being sold; others are available only in libraries. Besides the titles referred to elsewhere in this bibliography, the following are of interest:

> *A Guide to Key West*. Revised 2nd ed. New York: Hastings House, 1949.
>
> *Planning for a Vacation in Florida: Miami and Dade County*, 1941.
>
> *Seeing Fernandina in Florida*, 1940.
>
> *Seeing St. Augustine*, 1937.

Florida Across the Threshold: An Account of the Collins Administration, Jan. 4, 1955-Jan. 3, 1961: Report. Tallahassee, FL, 1961.

Flynt, Wayne. *Duncan Upshaw Fletcher: Dixie's Reluctant Progressive*. Tallahassee: Florida State University Press, 1971.

Flynt, Wayne. *Cracker Messiah. Governor Sidney J. Catts of Florida*. Baton Rouge: Louisiana State University Press, 1977.

Ford, Robert N. "A Resource Use Analysis and Evaluation of the Everglades Agricultural Area." Departmentof Geography, Research paper No. 4102. Ph.D. dissertation, University of Chicago, 1956.

"Four Fruitful Years: The Administration of Spessard L. Holland as Governor of Florida." *Florida Highways* XIII(December 1944).

Fox, Charles D. *The Truth About Florida*. New York: Charles

Rinard Corp., 1925.

García, María Cristina. *Havana USA: Cuban Exiles and Cuban Americans in South Florida, 1959-1994*. Berkeley: University of California Press, 1996.

Garrett, George. *The Finished Man*. New York: Scribner's, 1959

Graff, Mary B. *Mandarin on the St. Johns*. Gainesville: University of Florida Press, 1953.

Graham, Bob. *Workdays: Finding Florida on the Job*. Miami, FL: Banyan Books, 1978.

Gray, Robert A. *The Power and the Glory: Some Tinsel Also*. Tallahassee, FL: Rose Printing Co., Inc., 1965.

Gray, Robert A. *My Story: Fifty Years in the Shadow of the Near Great*. Tallahassee, FL: Rose Printing Co., Inc.,1958.

Green, George N. "Florida Politics and Socialism at the Crossroads of the Progressive Era, 1912." Master's thesis, Florida State University, 1962.

Grenier, Guillermo J., and Stepick, Alex, III, eds. *Miami Now! Immigration, Ethnicity and Social Change*. Gainesville: University Press of Florida, 1992.

Griffin, Leon Odell. *John Holiday Perry: Florida Press Lord*. Tampa: Trend House, 1975.

Grismer, Karl H. *The Story of Ft. Meyers*. St. Petersburg, FL: St. Petersburg Printing Co., 1949.

Grismer, Karl H. *The Story of St. Petersburg*. St. Petersburg, FL: St. Petersburg Printing Co., 1950.

Grismer, Karl H. *Tampa: History of the City of Tampa Region of Florida*. Edited by D.B. McKay. St. Petersburg, FL: St. Petersburg Printing Co., 1950.

Hartley, Ellen R. and Hartley, William B. *A Woman Set Apart* [Biography of Deaconess Harriet M. Bedell.] New York: Dodd, Mead & Co., 1963.

Hartsfield, Mary Alice and Grigg, Charles M. *Summary Report: NASA Impact on Brevard County*. Tallahassee, FL: Institute for Social Research, Florida State University, 1966.

Havard, William C. and Beth, Loren P. *The Politics of Misrepresentation*. Baton Rouge: Louisiana Stat University Press, 1966.

Hemenway, Robert E. *Zora Neale Hurston: A Literary Biography*. Urbana: University of Illinois Press, 1967.

Henshall, James A. *Camping and Cruising in Florida*. Cincinnati: R. Clarke and Co., 1884.

Holt, Rackham. *Mary McLeod Bethune*. Garden City, N.Y.: Doubleday, 1964.

Hopkins, James. *Fifty Years of Citrus: The Florida Citrus Exchange, 1909-1959*. Gainesville: University of Florida Press, 1960.

Hurston, Zora Neale. *Dust Tracks on a Road*. Philadelphia: J.B. Lippincott, 1942.

Jacobstein, Helen L. "The Segregation Factor in the Florida Democratic Gubernatorial Primary of 1956." Master's thesis, University of Miami, 1964.

Jahoda, Gloria. *The Other Florida*. New York: Scribner's. 1967.

Jahoda, Gloria. *The Road to Samarkand: Frederick Delius and His Music.* New York: Charles Scribner's Sons, 1967.
James, Marquis. *Alfred I. DuPont, the Family Rebel.* Indianapolis: Bobbs-Merrill, 1941.
Jennings, William S. "Florida's Public Lands." *Legislative Bluebook.* Tallahassee, 1917.
Johnson, Evans C. "Oscar W. Underwood: The Development of a National Statesman." Ph.D. dissertation. University of North Carolina. 1953.
Johnson, James Weldon. *Along This Way.* New York: Viking, 1933.
Johnson, Lamar. *Beyond the Fourth Generation.* Gainesville: University of Florida Press, 1974.
Johnston, Alva. *The Legendary Mizners.* New York: Strauss & Young, 1953.
Joiner, Edward Earl. *A History of Florida Baptists.* Jacksonville: Convention Press, Inc., 1972.
Joubert, William H. "A History of the Seaboard Air Line Railway Company." Master's thesis, University of Florida, 1935.
Kallina, Edmund F., Jr. *Claude Kirk and the Politics of Confrontation.* Gainesville: University Press of Florida, 1993.
Kendrick, Baynard. *Florida Trails to Turnpikes, 1914-1964.* Gainesville: University of Florida Press, 1964.
Kersey, Harry A., Jr. *An Assumption of Sovereignty: Social and Political Transformation among the Florida Seminoles, 1953-1979.* Lincoln: University of Nebraska Press, 1996.
Kersey, Harry A., Jr. *Pelts, Plumes and Hides: White Traders Among the Seminole Indians, 1870-1930.* Gainesville: University of Florida Press, 1975.
Key, V.O., Jr. *Southern Politics in State and Nation.* New York: Random House, 1949.
Kilpatrick, Wylie, coordinator. *Florida's Economy: Past Trends and Prospects for 1970.* Gainesville: University of Florida Press, 1956.
Knipling, E.F. "Insect Control Investigation of the Orlando, Florida Laboratory During World War II." Smithsonian Institution, *Annual Report.* Washington, D.C., 1948.
Lazarus, William C. *Wings in the Sun: the Annals of Aviation in Florida.* Orlando, FL: Tyn Cobb's Florida Press, 1951.
Levy, Eugene. *James Weldon Johnson: Black Leader, Black Voice.* Chicago: University of Chicago Press, 1975.
Lummus, John N. *The Miracle of Miami Beach.* Miami: The Teacher Publishing Co., 1940.
Lundberg, Emma O. *Social Welfare in Florida.* State Board of Public Welfare Publication No. 4, Tallahassee, FL, 1934.
Malafronte, Anthony F. "Claude Pepper, Florida Maverick: The 1950 Florida Senatorial Primary." Master's thesis, University of Miami, 1963.
Marina, William. "Black Education in Florida," in Justin, Neal E., and Kersey, Harry A., Jr., eds. *Florida Education in the 70's.* Dubuque, Iowa: Kendall/Hunt Publishing Co., 1973.

Mason, Raymond K. and Virginia Harrison. *Confusion to the Enemy: A Biography of Ed Ball.* New York: Dodd Mead, 1976.

May, E.C. *Gators, Skeeters and Malary: Recollections of a Pioneer Florida Judge.* New York: Vantage Press, 1953.

Mayo, Nathan. *Florida: An Advancing State.* St. Petersburg FL: Lassing Publishing Co., 1928.

McDonnell, Victoria H. "The Businessman's Politician: A Study of the Administration of John Welborn Martin, 1925-1929." Master's thesis, University of Florida, 1968.

McGovern, James R. "Helen Hunt West: Florida's Pioneer for ERA." *Florida Historical Quarterly,* LVII, No. 1 (July, 1978): 39-53. Footnote 1 is an extensive bibliographical note on women in Florida.

McGovern, James R. *The Emergence of a City in the Modern South: Pensacola, 1900-1945.* DeLeon Springs, FL: E.O. Painter Printing Co., 1977.

Moss, Ralph W. "Report of the Committee of the House of Representatives on Expenditures in the Department of Agriculture." *House Reports,* No. 1027. 62nd Cong., 2nd sess. 1912.

Muir, Helen. *Miami USA.* New York: Holt, 1953.

Munroe, Ralph Middleton. *The Commodore's Story.* New York: Ives Washburn, 1930. Reprinted, Miami: Historical Association of Southern Florida, 1967.

Nash, Charles E. *The Magic of Miami Beach..* Philadelphia: David McKay Co., 1938.

Neyland, Leedell W. and Riley, John W. *The History of Florida Agricultural and Mechanical University.* Gainesville: University of Florida Press, 1963.

Parks, Arva Moore. *Miami: The Magic City.* Miami: Florida Centennial Press, 1990.

Plowden, Gene. *Those Amazing Ringlings and Their Circus.* Caldwell, Idaho: Caxton Press, 1967.

Price, Hugh Douglas. *The Negro and Southern Politics: A Chapter of Florida History.* New York: New York University Press, 1957.

Proctor, Samuel. "History of the University of Florida." Ph.D. dissertation, University of Florida, 1956.

Rackleff, Robert B. *Close to Crisis: Florida's Environmental Problems.* Tallahassee, Fl: New Issues Press, 1972.

Rasmussen, Wayne D. *A History of the Emergency Farm Labor Supply Program, 1943-1949.* Agriculture Monograph No. 13, U.S. Department of Agriculture. Bureau of Agricultural Economics. Washington, D.C., 1951.

Redford, Polly. *Billion Dollar Sandbar: A Biograpy of Miami Beach.* New York: Dutton, 1970.

Roberts, Kenneth L. *Florida.* New York: Harper and Brothers, 1926.

Roberts, Kenneth L. *Sun Hunting.* Indianapolis: Bobbs-Merrill, 1922.

Scott, J. Irving E. *The Education of Black People in Florida.* Philadelphia: Dorrance & Co., 1974.

Sessa, Frank B. "Real Estate Expansion and Boom in Miami Beach and Its Environs During the 1920's." Ph.D. dissertation, University of Pittsburgh, 1950.

Shofner, Jerrell H. *David Ladd: Merchant Prince of Florida.* Gainesville: University of Florida Press, 1978.

Sitterson, J. Carlyle. *Sugar Country: The Cane Industry in the South, 1753-1950.* Lexington: University of Kentucky Press, 1953.

Small, John K. *From Eden to Sahara: Florida's Tragedy.* Lancaster, Pa: The Science Press Printing Co., 1929.

Smiley, Nixon. *Knights of the Fourth Estate. The Story of the Miami Herald.* Miami: E.A. Seemann, 1975.

Staid, Sister Mary Elizabeth. "Albert Walker Gilchrist, Florida's Middle of the Road Governor." Master's thesis, University of Florida, 1950.

Stephens, Gertrude H. "Senator Duncan U. Fletcher, Legislator." Master's thesis, University of Florida, 1951.

Talbert, Samuel S. "Treatment of the Presidential Campaign of 1928 by the Florida Press." Master's thesis, University of Florida, 1947.

Tebeau, Charlton W. *Florida's Last Frontier: The History of Collier County.* Rev. ed. Coral Gables, FL: University of Miami Press, 1966.

Tebeau, Charlton W. *Man in the Everglades: 2000 Years of Human History in the Everglades National Park.* Revised ed. (Originally published under the title *They Lived in the Park,* 1964.) Coral Gables, FL: University of Miami Press, 1968.

Tebeau, Charlton W. *Synagogue in the Central City: Temple Israel of Greater Miami, 1922-1972.* Coral Gables, FL: University of Miami Press, 1972.

Tebeau Charleton W. *The University of Miami: A Golden Anniversary History, 1926-1976.* Coral Gable, FL: University of Miami Press, 1976.

Thulesius, Olav. *Edison in Florida: The Green Laboratory.* Gainesville: University Press of Florida, 1997.

Tindall, George B. "The Bubble in the Sun." *American Heritage* XVI(August, 1965): 76-83, 109-111.

Triay, Victor Andres. *FleeingCastro: Operation Pedro Pan and the Cuban Children's Program.* Gainesville: University Press of Florida, 1998.

U.S., Florida, Central and Southern Florida Flood Control District, *Annual Reports, 1949-1969.* West Palm Beach, Florida.

Vanderblue, Homer B. "The Florida Land Boom." *Journal of Land and Public Utility Economics* III(May 1927):113-131.

Vickers, Raymond B. *Panic in Paradise: Florida's Banking Crash of 1926.* Tuscaloosa: University of Alabama Press, 1994.

Wagy, Tom. *Governor LeRoy Collins of Florida: Spokesman of the New South.* Tuscaloosa: University of Alabama Press, 1985.

Warren, Fuller and Morris, Allen. *How to Win in Politics.* Tallahassee, FL: Peninsular Publishing Co., 1949.

Wattenbarger, James L. *A State Plan for Public Junior Colleges:*

With Special Reference to Florida. Gainesville: University of Florida Press, 1953.

Weidling, Philip and Burghard, August. *Checkered Sunshine: The Story of Fort Lauderdale, 1793-1955.* Gainesville: University of Florida Press, 1966.

Weigall, Theyre Hamilton. *Boom in Paradise.* New York: A.H. King, 1932.

Wells, William James. "Duncan Upshaw Fletcher, Florida's Grand Old Man." Master's thesis, Stetson University, 1942.

Wilkinson, Alex. *Big Sugar: Seasons in the Cane Fields of Florida.* New York: Alfred AS. Knopf, 1989.

Will, Lawrence E. *A Cracker History of Lake Okeechobee.* St. Petersburg, FL: Great Outdoors Publishing Co., 1964.

Will, Lawrence E. *A Dredgeman of Cape Sable.* St. Petersburg, FL: Great Outdoors Publishing Co., 1967.

Will, Lawrence E. *Okeechobee Boats and Skippers.* St. Petersburg, FL: Great Outdoors Publishing Co., 1965.

Will, Lawrence E. *Okeechobee Catfishing.* St. Petersburg, FL: Great Outdoors Publishing Co., 1965.

Will, Lawrence E. *Okeechobee Hurricane and the Hoover Dike.* St. Petersburg, FL: Great Outdoors Publishing Co., 1961.

Will, Lawrence E. *Swamp to Sugar Bowl: Pioneer Days in Belle Glade.* St. Petersburg, FL: Great Outdoors Publishing Co., 1968.

Willoughby, Malcolm F. *The U.S. Coast Guard in World War II.* Annapolis, MD: U.S. Naval Institute, 1957.

Wynne, Lewis N., ed. *Florida at War.* St. Leo, FL: St. Leo College Press, 1993.

Zehnder, Leonard E. *Florida's Disney World: Promises and Problems.* Tallahassee, FL: Peninsular Publishing Co., 1975.

Ziegler, Louis W. and Wolfe, Herbert S. *Citrus Growing in Florida.* Gainesville: University of Florida Press, 1961.

Index

sugarcane 158, 330, 334
Summerlin, Jacob 170, 242
Sunniland Field 399
Sunshine Amendment 470
Sunshine Skyway Bridge 492
Supreme Court 469
Swain, Harry D. 422
swamp and overflowed lands 164, 178
Swepson, George 251

T

Tallahassee 110, 112-
      113, 118, 183, 200-201
Tallahassee Railroad Company 130
Tamiami Trail 363 -364, 478
Tampa 132-133, 158, 165, 167,
      170, 266, 268-269, 273,
      297-298, 361, 363, 365,
      368-369, 372, 492, 494
Tampa Bay 129
Tapper, George 451
Tatum, J. H. and Company 332
tax reform 498
taxes 509, 517, 526, 528
Taylor, Zachary 176
"teach-ins" 441
Teed, Cyrus R. 328
Teller Amendment 297
Teller amendment 433
Tequesta 13-15
Term limit 509
territorial government 129, 131
Thayer, Eli 248
Thompson, Col. George T. 242
Thompson, Gen. Wiley 143
Three Friends 296, 312
timber 132-133, 136, 249
Timucua 10, 12-14, 39, 42-44, 137
Tonyn, Patrick 81
tools 8, 10, 12, 14, 15
tourism 253, 400-401, 436
Townsend Plan 392-393
Trammell, Gov. Park 318,
      322, 345, 347
Trammell, Senator Park 420
Trapier, General James H. 195
Trejada, Francisco de San
      Buenaventura y 46
Truman, Harry S. 414, 421
Tucker, Donald 471
Turkey Point 476
turnpike commission 423

typhoid fever 304, 308, 309

U

U.S. Army Corps of Engineers 337
U.S. Sugar Corporation 358
Union Bank of Florida 131
Union Bank of Tallahassee 174
Unionists 196-198
unitary tax 499, 500
United States Department of Agricul-
      ture 331
universities 436
University of Central Florida 462
University of Florida 459,
      462, 463, 480
University of Miami 463
University of North Florida 460
University of South Florida 459,
      462, 463
University of West Florida 460
Upper Creeks 138, 145
urbanization 418, 420
utopian groups 328

V

Vaca, Alvar Nunez Cabeza de 20
Vanderblue, Homer 367, 371
Velasco, Luís de 23
Verlander, Ashley 444
Verot, Augustin 171
Veverka, Charles 487
Villafane 25
Virginius 293
Vogdes, Israel 188, 242
Vose, Francis 262
vouchers 532, 535

W

Wackenhut Corporation 447
Walker, David S. 178, 180
Wallace, Henry A. 421
Wallace, John 236, 246
Walls, Josiah T. 235
Walt Disney Productions 497
War for Cuban Independence 269
War of 1812 93, 95, 97, 100
Ward, George T. 168, 178, 180-182
Warren, Fuller 397, 410-
      411, 413, 422, 429
Washburne, William A. Jr 430
Waste Management Corporation 519